Nissan Frontier & Xterra Automotive Repair Manual

by Jay Storer
and John H Haynes

Member of the Guild of Motoring Writers

Models covered:

Frontier pick-ups - 2005 through 2012
Xterra - 2005 through 2012
Two- and four-wheel drive models

(72032 - 1S4)

ABCDE
FGHIJ
KLMN

Haynes Publishing Group
Sparkford Nr Yeovil
Somerset BA22 7JJ England

Haynes North America, Inc
861 Lawrence Drive
Newbury Park
California 91320 USA

Acknowledgements

Wiring diagrams originated exclusively for Haynes North America, Inc. by Valley Forge Technical Information Services.

© **Haynes North America, Inc. 2008, 2011, 2014**

With permission from J.H. Haynes & Co. Ltd.

A book in the Haynes Automotive Repair Manual Series

Printed in the U.S.A.

ISBN-13: 978-1-62092-086-2
ISBN-10: 1-62092-086-7

Library of Congress Control Number 2013957928

Contents

Haynes photographer and mechanic with 2007 Nissan Xterra

About this manual

Its purpose

The purpose of this manual is to help you get the best value from your vehicle. It can do so in several ways. It can help you decide what work must be done, even if you choose to have it done by a dealer service department or a repair shop; it provides information and procedures for routine maintenance and servicing; and it offers diagnostic and repair procedures to follow when trouble occurs.

We hope you use the manual to tackle the work yourself. For many simpler jobs, doing it yourself may be quicker than arranging an appointment to get the vehicle into a shop and making the trips to leave it and pick it up. More importantly, a lot of money can be saved by avoiding the expense the shop must pass on to you to cover its labor and overhead

costs. An added benefit is the sense of satisfaction and accomplishment that you feel after doing the job yourself.

Using the manual

The manual is divided into Chapters. Each Chapter is divided into numbered Sections, which are headed in bold type between horizontal lines. Each Section consists of consecutively numbered paragraphs.

At the beginning of each numbered Section you will be referred to any illustrations which apply to the procedures in that Section. The reference numbers used in illustration captions pinpoint the pertinent Section and the Step within that Section. That is, illustration 3.2 means the illustration refers to Section 3 and Step (or paragraph) 2 within that Section.

Procedures, once described in the text, are not normally repeated. When it's necessary to refer to another Chapter, the reference will be given as Chapter and Section number. Cross references given without use of the word "Chapter" apply to Sections and/or paragraphs in the same Chapter. For example, "see Section 8" means in the same Chapter.

References to the left or right side of the vehicle assume you are sitting in the driver's seat, facing forward.

Even though we have prepared this manual with extreme care, neither the publisher nor the author can accept responsibility for any errors in, or omissions from, the information given.

NOTE

A **Note** provides information necessary to properly complete a procedure or information which will make the procedure easier to understand.

CAUTION

A **Caution** provides a special procedure or special steps which must be taken while completing the procedure where the Caution is found. Not heeding a Caution can result in damage to the assembly being worked on.

WARNING

A **Warning** provides a special procedure or special steps which must be taken while completing the procedure where the Warning is found. Not heeding a Warning can result in personal injury.

Introduction to the Nissan Frontier and Xterra

Nissan Frontier pick-ups are available in either king cab (extended cab) or crew-cab (four-door) models. The Nissan Xterra SUV is available only in a four-door "wagon" style body.

The Frontier pickups are equipped with either a 2.5L OHC four-cylinder engine, or a 4.0L OHC V6, while the Xterra is available only with the V6. All engines used in these vehicles are equipped with electronic fuel injection.

The chassis layout is conventional, with the engine mounted at the front and the power being transmitted from either a five-speed or six-speed manual transmission or a five-speed automatic transmission through a driveshaft to the rear axle. On 4WD models, a transfer case directs the power through a driveshaft to the front differential and independent driveaxles to the front wheels.

Both models have the same independent front suspensions design, with upper

and lower control arms and struts/coil spring assemblies. All models have a solid rear axle (not independent) suspended from the vehicle with leaf springs and shock absorbers. Steering on all models is via power-assisted rack-and-pinion steering gear.

Frontier and Xterra models all have four-wheel disc brakes and four-wheel ABS (antilock brakes), with power assist standard. The parking brake system utilizes small drum brake shoes inside the rear brake discs.

Vehicle identification numbers

Modifications are a continuing and unpublicized process in vehicle manufacturing. Since spare parts manuals and lists are compiled on a numerical basis, the individual vehicle numbers are essential to correctly identify the component required.

Vehicle Identification Number (VIN)

The Vehicle Identification Number (VIN), which appears on the Vehicle Certificate of Title and Registration, is also embossed on a plate located in the left (driver's side) corner of the dashboard, near the windshield (see illustration). The VIN tells you when and where a vehicle was manufactured, its country of origin, make, type, passenger safety system, line, series, body style, engine and assembly plant.

VIN engine and model year codes

Two particularly important pieces of information found in the VIN are the engine code and the model year code. Counting from the left, the engine code letter designation is the 4th character and the model year code is the 10th character.

On the models covered by this manual the engine codes are:

    A 4.0L V6 (VQ40DE)
    B 2.5L 4-cylinder (QR25DE)

On the models covered by this manual the model year codes are:

    5 2005
    6 2006
    7 2007
    8 2008
    9 2009
    A 2010
    B 2011
    C...............2012

Vehicle Safety Certification label

The Vehicle Safety Certification label is attached to the rear edge of the driver's door or on the door post (see illustration). The label contains the name of the manufacturer, the month and year of production, the Gross Vehicle Weight Rating (GVWR), the Gross Axle Weight Rating (GAWR) and the certification statement. On most models, the label also includes the OEM tire sizes and pressures.

Engine Identification Number (EIN)

The Engine Identification Number (EIN) on V6 engines is stamped into the engine block on a machined surface just behind the right (passenger's side) cylinder head. On four-cylinder engines the EIN is located on the left rear side of the engine block, just below the cylinder head and rearward of the exhaust manifold.

Transmission Identification Number (TIN)

The manual Transmission Identification Number (TIN) is stamped into the top of the transmission bellhousing. On automatic transmissions, the number is stamped into a tag and fastened to the transmission with a bolt (see illustrations).

Transfer case identification label

The transfer case identification information is stamped into the top of the case.

The VIN plate is visible from the outside of the vehicle, through the driver's side of the windshield

The Vehicle Safety Certification label is affixed to the driver's side door end or post

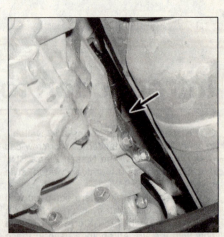

Automatic transmission identification tag - 2WD four-cylinder Frontier

Automatic transmission identification tag - 4WD Xterra

Recall information

Vehicle recalls are carried out by the manufacturer in the rare event of a possible safety-related defect. The vehicle's registered owner is contacted at the address on file at the Department of Motor Vehicles and given the details of the recall. Remedial work is carried out free of charge at a dealer service department.

If you are the new owner of a used vehicle which was subject to a recall and you want to be sure that the work has been carried out, it's best to contact a dealer service department and ask about your individual vehicle - you'll need to furnish them your Vehicle Identification Number (VIN).

The table below is based on information provided by the National Highway Traffic Safety Administration (NHTSA), the body which oversees vehicle recalls in the United States. The recall database is updated constantly. For the latest information on vehicle recalls, check the NHTSA website at www.nhtsa.gov, or call the NHTSA hotline at 1-888-327-4236.

Recall date	Recall campaign number	Model(s) affected	Concern
Mar 28, 2006	06V092000	2005/2006 Frontier	On certain king cab trucks, in a severe side impact crash, there is a possibility that deformation of the vehicle's body could cause the fuel filler cap tether to be stretched to the point of unscrewing the fuel filler cap. This may result in a fuel spill which in the presence of an ignition source could result in a fire.
Jul 10, 2006	06E064000	2005/2006 Frontier	Certain Tradesonic combination lamps sold as replacement lamps for use on certain models are not equipped with amber side reflectors, and fail to conform with the requirements of Federal Motor Vehicle Safety Standard no. 108, lamps, reflective devices, and associated equipment. Lack of amber side reflectors in the lamps will decrease lighting visibility to other drivers and may possibly result in a vehicle crash.
Jun 25, 2007	07E046000	2005/2006 Frontier 2005/2006 Xterra	Certain Hopkins aftermarket trailer brake control connection harnesses sold for use on certain models of Nissan vehicles. The internal part numbers within Hopkins are: 1010476025, 1040376025, 1110476025, 1170376025, 1290376025, 1010476035, 1040376035, 1110476035, 1170376035, and 1290376035. A wire may have been placed in an incorrect position in the electrical connector housing. This results in an incorrect routing of wires between the trailer brake controller and the towing vehicle wiring system. This harness would result in power from the trailer brake controller going to the towing vehicle dash light circuit rather than the trailer brakes. This result would be the lack of trailer braking when the towing vehicle brakes were applied. It would also result in the towing vehicles dash lights being activated when the vehicle brakes were applied. The failure of the application of the trailer brake could result in reduced ability to stop and contribute to a possible crash.
Nov 16, 2007	07V528000	2008 Xterra	On certain sport utility vehicles, the Antilock Brake System/ Vehicle Dynamic Control (ABS/VDC) actuator is designed with one ball in the valve section. Some ABS/VDC actuators were manufactured with more than one ball in the valve. In ABS/VDC actuators with more than one ball, it is possible that fluid flow could be blocked and cause a reduction in brake force in one or both front wheels or affect operation of the ABS and/or VDC. This could result in a reduction in brake effectiveness without warning increasing the risk of a crash.
Dec 04, 2007	07E105000	2008 Xterra	On certain Continental Automotive ABS and ESC control modules, some of the hydraulic valves in the ESC module were built with extra check balls. The extra check balls can restrict the flow of brake fluid through the valve and cause reduction of brake force.

Recall date	Recall campaign number	Model(s) affected	Concern
Jan 23, 2008	08V045000	2008 Frontier and Xterra	Some vehicles fail to comply with the requirements of Federal Motor Vehicle Safety Standard No. 110, "Tire Selection and Rims for Motor Vehicles," because the tire placard lists an incorrect vehicle capacity weight. This standard specifies requirements for tire selection to prevent overloading.
Dec 18, 2008	08V690000	2005 through 2009 Frontier and Xterra	On some vehicles in areas that use heavy concentrations of road salt in winter, a mixture of snow (or water) and salt can enter the front crash zone sensor housing, which might rust internally, resulting in a signal interruption (which should illuminate the red air bag warning light). This could result in the non-deployment of the driver and passenger airbags in a crash, increasing the risk of personal injury.
Feb 26, 2010	10V075000	2006 and 2008 Frontier and Xterra	On some vehicles, the molded fuel tank shells can deform, causing the fuel sender float arm to contact an embossment molded into the tank shell, causing the instrument panel fuel level gauge to indicate that the vehicle has about one-quarter tank of fuel when the tank is actually empty. This could cause the vehicle to run out of gas and stall in traffic, increasing the risk of a crash.
May 12, 2010 May 14, 2010	10E019000 10V208000	2005 through 2010 Frontier and Xterra	The lower control arms have welded cylindrical collars that form the inboard attachment points to the chassis. On some vehicles, these collars were incorrectly welded and do not meet strength specifications. If a collar weld separates, vehicle handling will deteriorate, possibly resulting in a crash.
Aug 9, 2010	10V372000	2010 Frontier	Some King Cab vehicles fail to comply with requirements of Federal Motor Vehicle Safety Standard No. 225, "Child Restraint Anchorage Systems." The weld between the tether anchor and the seat gusset bracket is out of specification. As a result, the tether anchor could separate from the seat in the event of a crash, increasing the risk of injury to an occupant in a child seat that uses the tether anchor.
Sep 2, 2010	10E043000	2009 and 2010 Frontier and Xterra	Some Marathon seat covers (brand name: Superhides) sold for use as aftermarket equipment, are made of heavier thread and are not compatible with seats containing side-impact airbags. The heavier seat cover could interfere with full deployment of the airbag in a crash, which could result in serious injury.
Sep 3, 2010	10V401000	2008 through 2010 Frontier and Xterra	Some vehicles were equipped with a Garmin Nuvi Model 750 navigation system. The GPS unit is equipped with batteries that can overheat. The overheated batteries could result in a fire.
Dec 19, 2011	11V592000	2011 and 2012 Frontier and Xterra	On some models, some of the bolts that connect the engine oil cooler and the engine oil filter to the engine may have been manufactured to below specification strength. As a result, the bolt may break at the oil filter attachment point and can cause an engine oil leak. If there is an engine oil leak, the engine oil pressure would drop and the engine could seize, increasing the risk of a crash.
Sep 20, 2012	12V462000	2012 Frontier and Xterra	Some two-wheel drive models may have been equipped with front wheel hubs that may not meet the design hardness specifications. A wheel hub that was manufactured below hardness specification may wear prematurely and eventually crack. If the vehicle is driven in this condition, the wheel hub may break, possibly resulting in a crash.

Jacking and towing

Jacking

The jack supplied with the vehicle should only be used for raising the vehicle when changing a tire or placing jackstands under the frame. NEVER work under the vehicle or start the engine when the vehicle supported only by a jack.

The vehicle should be parked on level ground with the wheels blocked, the parking brake applied and the transmission in Park (automatic) or Reverse (manual). If the vehicle is parked alongside the roadway, or in any other hazardous situation, turn on the emergency hazard flashers. If a tire is to be changed, loosen the lug nuts one-half turn before raising off the ground.

Place the jack under the vehicle in the indicated positions **(see illustrations)**. Operate the jack with a slow, smooth motion until the wheel is raised off the ground. Remove the lug nuts, pull off the wheel, install the spare and thread the lug nuts back on with the beveled side facing in. Tighten the lug nuts snugly, lower the vehicle until some weight is on the wheel, then tighten them completely in a criss-cross pattern and remove the jack.

Towing

Equipment specifically designed for towing should be used and attached to the main structural members of the vehicle. Optional tow hooks may be attached to the frame at both ends of the vehicle; they are intended for emergency use only, for rescuing a stranded vehicle. Do not use the tow hooks for highway towing. Stand clear when using tow straps or chains; they may break, causing serious injury.

The manufacturer recommends that these vehicles be towed only by wheel-lift equipment or a flatbed car-carrier.

Safety is a major consideration when towing and all applicable state and local laws must be obeyed. In addition to a tow bar, a safety chain must be used for all towing.

Two-wheel drive vehicles with automatic transmission may be towed with the rear wheels on a towing dolly with no mileage restriction (at posted highway speeds). If the vehicle is being towed with four wheels on the ground, speed should be no more than 35 mph (56 km/h) for no more than 50 miles (80 km), or damage may be done to the automatic transmission.

Two-wheel drive vehicles with a manual transmission can be towed up to 500 miles with the ignition lock in the Off (not lock) position and the transmission in Neutral.

The manufacturer states that four-wheel drive vehicles cannot be towed with any wheels on the ground, or severe damage will occur.

Front jacking location - place the jack directly under the arrow (A) stamped in the frame rail

Rear jacking location

Booster battery (jump) starting

Observe these precautions when using a booster battery to start a vehicle:

a) *Before connecting the booster battery, make sure the ignition switch is in the Off position.*
b) *Turn off the lights, heater and other electrical loads.*
c) *Your eyes should be shielded. Safety goggles are a good idea.*
d) *Make sure the booster battery is the same voltage as the dead one in the vehicle.*
e) *The two vehicles MUST NOT TOUCH each other!*
f) *Make sure the transaxle is in Neutral (manual) or Park (automatic).*
g) *If the booster battery is not a maintenance-free type, remove the vent caps and lay a cloth over the vent holes.*

Connect the red-colored jumper cable to the positive (+) terminal of the booster battery and the other end to the positive (+) terminal of the dead battery. Then connect one end of the black jumper cable to the negative (-) terminal of the booster battery, and the other end of the cable to a good ground, such as a bolt or bracket.

Start the engine using the booster battery, then run the booster vehicle at a fast idle for a few minutes to instill some charge in the dead battery. Let the engine idle, then disconnect the jumper cables in the reverse order of connection. The vehicle with the dead battery may have to be driven for 20 minutes or more to sufficiently recharge the battery for independent starting.

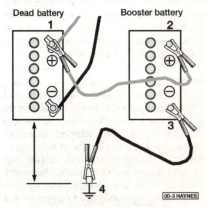

Make the booster battery cable connections in the numerical order shown (note that the negative cable of the booster battery is NOT attached to the negative terminal of the dead battery)

Buying parts

Replacement parts are available from many sources, which generally fall into one of two categories - authorized dealer parts departments and independent retail auto parts stores. Our advice concerning these parts is as follows:

Retail auto parts stores: Good auto parts stores will stock frequently needed components which wear out relatively fast, such as clutch components, exhaust systems, brake parts, tune-up parts, etc. These stores often supply new or reconditioned parts on

an exchange basis, which can save a considerable amount of money. Discount auto parts stores are often very good places to buy materials and parts needed for general vehicle maintenance such as oil, grease, filters, spark plugs, belts, touch-up paint, bulbs, etc. They also usually sell tools and general accessories, have convenient hours, charge lower prices and can often be found not far from home.

Authorized dealer parts department: This is the best source for parts which are

unique to the vehicle and not generally available elsewhere (such as major engine parts, transmission parts, trim pieces, etc.).

Warranty information: If the vehicle is still covered under warranty, be sure that any replacement parts purchased - regardless of the source - do not invalidate the warranty!

To be sure of obtaining the correct parts, have engine and chassis numbers available and, if possible, take the old parts along for positive identification.

Maintenance techniques, tools and working facilities

Maintenance techniques

There are a number of techniques involved in maintenance and repair that will be referred to throughout this manual. Application of these techniques will enable the home mechanic to be more efficient, better organized and capable of performing the various tasks properly, which will ensure that the repair job is thorough and complete.

Fasteners

Fasteners are nuts, bolts, studs and screws used to hold two or more parts together. There are a few things to keep in mind when working with fasteners. Almost all of them use a locking device of some type, either a lockwasher, locknut, locking tab or thread adhesive. All threaded fasteners should be clean and straight, with undamaged threads and undamaged corners on the hex head where the wrench fits. Develop the habit of replacing all damaged nuts and bolts with new ones. Special locknuts with nylon or fiber inserts can only be used once. If they are removed, they lose their locking ability and

must be replaced with new ones.

Rusted nuts and bolts should be treated with a penetrating fluid to ease removal and prevent breakage. Some mechanics use turpentine in a spout-type oil can, which works quite well. After applying the rust penetrant, let it work for a few minutes before trying to loosen the nut or bolt. Badly rusted fasteners may have to be chiseled or sawed off or removed with a special nut breaker, available at tool stores.

If a bolt or stud breaks off in an assembly, it can be drilled and removed with a special tool commonly available for this purpose. Most automotive machine shops can perform this task, as well as other repair procedures, such as the repair of threaded holes that have been stripped out.

Flat washers and lockwashers, when removed from an assembly, should always be replaced exactly as removed. Replace any damaged washers with new ones. Never use a lockwasher on any soft metal surface (such as aluminum), thin sheet metal or plastic.

Fastener sizes

For a number of reasons, automobile manufacturers are making wider and wider use of metric fasteners. Therefore, it is important to be able to tell the difference between standard (sometimes called U.S. or SAE) and metric hardware, since they cannot be interchanged.

All bolts, whether standard or metric, are sized according to diameter, thread pitch and length. For example, a standard 1/2 - 13 x 1 bolt is 1/2 inch in diameter, has 13 threads per inch and is 1 inch long. An M12 - 1.75 x 25 metric bolt is 12 mm in diameter, has a thread pitch of 1.75 mm (the distance between threads) and is 25 mm long. The two bolts are nearly identical, and easily confused, but they are not interchangeable.

In addition to the differences in diameter, thread pitch and length, metric and standard bolts can also be distinguished by examining the bolt heads. To begin with, the distance across the flats on a standard bolt head is measured in inches, while the same dimension on a metric bolt is sized in millimeters (the same is true for nuts). As a result, a standard wrench should not be used on a metric bolt and a metric wrench should not be used on a standard bolt. Also, most standard bolts have slashes radiating out from the center of the head to denote the grade or strength of the bolt, which is an indication of the amount of torque that can be applied to it. The greater the number of slashes, the greater the strength of the bolt. Grades 0 through 5 are commonly used on automobiles. Metric bolts have a property class (grade) number, rather than a slash, molded into their heads to indicate bolt strength. In this case, the higher the number, the stronger the bolt. Property class numbers 8.8, 9.8 and 10.9 are commonly used on automobiles.

Strength markings can also be used to distinguish standard hex nuts from metric hex nuts. Many standard nuts have dots stamped into one side, while metric nuts are marked with a number. The greater the number of

dots, or the higher the number, the greater the strength of the nut.

Metric studs are also marked on their ends according to property class (grade). Larger studs are numbered (the same as metric bolts), while smaller studs carry a geometric code to denote grade.

It should be noted that many fasteners, especially Grades 0 through 2, have no distinguishing marks on them. When such is the case, the only way to determine whether it is standard or metric is to measure the thread pitch or compare it to a known fastener of the same size.

Standard fasteners are often referred to as SAE, as opposed to metric. However, it should be noted that SAE technically refers to a non-metric fine thread fastener only. Coarse thread non-metric fasteners are referred to as USS sizes.

Since fasteners of the same size (both standard and metric) may have different

strength ratings, be sure to reinstall any bolts, studs or nuts removed from your vehicle in their original locations. Also, when replacing a fastener with a new one, make sure that the new one has a strength rating equal to or greater than the original.

Tightening sequences and procedures

Most threaded fasteners should be tightened to a specific torque value (torque is the twisting force applied to a threaded component such as a nut or bolt). Overtightening the fastener can weaken it and cause it to break, while undertightening can cause it to eventually come loose. Bolts, screws and studs, depending on the material they are made of and their thread diameters, have specific torque values, many of which are noted in the Specifications at the beginning of each Chapter. Be sure to follow the torque recommendations closely. For fasteners not assigned a

Grade 1 or 2   Grade 5   Grade 8

Bolt strength marking (standard/SAE/USS; bottom - metric)

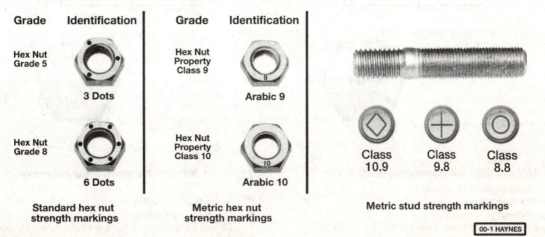

Grade	Identification
Hex Nut Grade 5	3 Dots
Hex Nut Grade 8	6 Dots

Standard hex nut strength markings

Grade	Identification
Hex Nut Property Class 9	Arabic 9
Hex Nut Property Class 10	Arabic 10

Metric hex nut strength markings

Class 10.9   Class 9.8   Class 8.8

Metric stud strength markings

00-1 HAYNES

specific torque, a general torque value chart is presented here as a guide. These torque values are for dry (unlubricated) fasteners threaded into steel or cast iron (not aluminum). As was previously mentioned, the size and grade of a fastener determine the amount of torque that can safely be applied to it. The figures listed here are approximate for Grade 2 and Grade 3 fasteners. Higher grades can tolerate higher torque values.

Fasteners laid out in a pattern, such as cylinder head bolts, oil pan bolts, differential cover bolts, etc., must be loosened or tightened in sequence to avoid warping the component. This sequence will normally be shown in the appropriate Chapter. If a specific pattern is not given, the following procedures can be used to prevent warping.

Initially, the bolts or nuts should be assembled finger-tight only. Next, they should be tightened one full turn each, in a criss-cross or diagonal pattern. After each one has been tightened one full turn, return to the first one and tighten them all one-half turn, following the same pattern. Finally, tighten each of them one-quarter turn at a time until each fastener has been tightened to the proper torque. To loosen and remove the fasteners, the procedure would be reversed.

Component disassembly

Component disassembly should be done with care and purpose to help ensure that

Metric thread sizes	Ft-lbs	Nm
M-6	6 to 9	9 to 12
M-8	14 to 21	19 to 28
M-10	28 to 40	38 to 54
M-12	50 to 71	68 to 96
M-14	80 to 140	109 to 154
Pipe thread sizes		
1/8	5 to 8	7 to 10
1/4	12 to 18	17 to 24
3/8	22 to 33	30 to 44
1/2	25 to 35	34 to 47
U.S. thread sizes		
1/4 - 20	6 to 9	9 to 12
5/16 - 18	12 to 18	17 to 24
5/16 - 24	14 to 20	19 to 27
3/8 - 16	22 to 32	30 to 43
3/8 - 24	27 to 38	37 to 51
7/16 - 14	40 to 55	55 to 74
7/16 - 20	40 to 60	55 to 81
1/2 - 13	55 to 80	75 to 108

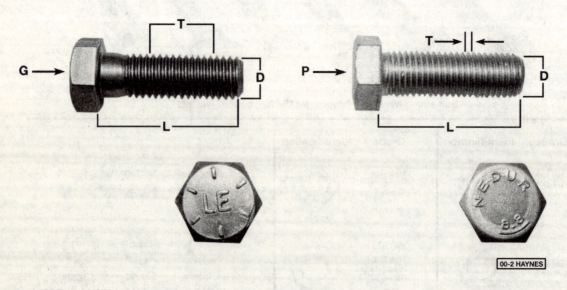

Standard (SAE and USS) bolt dimensions/grade marks

G   Grade marks (bolt strength)
L   Length (in inches)
T   Thread pitch (number of threads per inch)
D   Nominal diameter (in inches)

Metric bolt dimensions/grade marks

P   Property class (bolt strength)
L   Length (in millimeters)
T   Thread pitch (distance between threads in millimeters)
D   Diameter

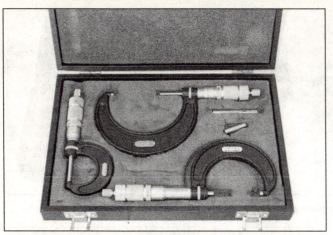

Micrometer set

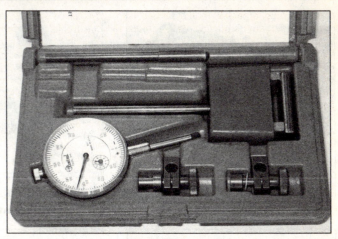
Dial indicator set

the parts go back together properly. Always keep track of the sequence in which parts are removed. Make note of special characteristics or marks on parts that can be installed more than one way, such as a grooved thrust washer on a shaft. It is a good idea to lay the disassembled parts out on a clean surface in the order that they were removed. It may also be helpful to make sketches or take instant photos of components before removal.

When removing fasteners from a component, keep track of their locations. Sometimes threading a bolt back in a part, or putting the washers and nut back on a stud, can prevent mix-ups later. If nuts and bolts cannot be returned to their original locations, they should be kept in a compartmented box or a series of small boxes. A cupcake or muffin tin is ideal for this purpose, since each cavity can hold the bolts and nuts from a particular area (i.e. oil pan bolts, valve cover bolts, engine mount bolts, etc.). A pan of this type is especially helpful when working on assemblies with very small parts, such as the carburetor, alternator, valve train or interior dash and trim pieces. The cavities can be marked with paint or tape to identify the contents.

Whenever wiring looms, harnesses or connectors are separated, it is a good idea to identify the two halves with numbered pieces of masking tape so they can be easily reconnected.

Gasket sealing surfaces

Throughout any vehicle, gaskets are used to seal the mating surfaces between two parts and keep lubricants, fluids, vacuum or pressure contained in an assembly.

Many times these gaskets are coated with a liquid or paste-type gasket sealing compound before assembly. Age, heat and pressure can sometimes cause the two parts to stick together so tightly that they are very difficult to separate. Often, the assembly can be loosened by striking it with a soft-face hammer near the mating surfaces. A regular hammer can be used if a block of wood is placed between the hammer and the part. Do

not hammer on cast parts or parts that could be easily damaged. With any particularly stubborn part, always recheck to make sure that every fastener has been removed.

Avoid using a screwdriver or bar to pry apart an assembly, as they can easily mar the gasket sealing surfaces of the parts, which must remain smooth. If prying is absolutely necessary, use an old broom handle, but keep in mind that extra clean up will be necessary if the wood splinters.

After the parts are separated, the old gasket must be carefully scraped off and the gasket surfaces cleaned. Stubborn gasket material can be soaked with rust penetrant or treated with a special chemical to soften it so it can be easily scraped off. **Caution:** *Never use gasket removal solutions or caustic chemicals on plastic or other composite components.* A scraper can be fashioned from a piece of copper tubing by flattening and sharpening one end. Copper is recommended because it is usually softer than the surfaces to be scraped, which reduces the chance of gouging the part. Some gaskets can be removed with a wire brush, but regardless of the method used, the mating surfaces must be left clean and smooth. If for some reason the gasket surface is gouged, then a gasket sealer thick enough to fill scratches will have to be used during reassembly of the components. For most applications, a non-drying (or semi-drying) gasket sealer should be used.

Hose removal tips

Warning: *If the vehicle is equipped with air conditioning, do not disconnect any of the A/C hoses without first having the system depressurized by a dealer service department or a service station.*

Hose removal precautions closely parallel gasket removal precautions. Avoid scratching or gouging the surface that the hose mates against or the connection may leak. This is especially true for radiator hoses. Because of various chemical reactions, the rubber in hoses can bond itself to the metal spigot that the hose fits over. To remove

a hose, first loosen the hose clamps that secure it to the spigot. Then, with slip-joint pliers, grab the hose at the clamp and rotate it around the spigot. Work it back and forth until it is completely free, then pull it off. Silicone or other lubricants will ease removal if they can be applied between the hose and the outside of the spigot. Apply the same lubricant to the inside of the hose and the outside of the spigot to simplify installation.

As a last resort (and if the hose is to be replaced with a new one anyway), the rubber can be slit with a knife and the hose peeled from the spigot. If this must be done, be careful that the metal connection is not damaged.

If a hose clamp is broken or damaged, do not reuse it. Wire-type clamps usually weaken with age, so it is a good idea to replace them with screw-type clamps whenever a hose is removed.

Tools

A selection of good tools is a basic requirement for anyone who plans to maintain and repair his or her own vehicle. For the owner who has few tools, the initial investment might seem high, but when compared to the spiraling costs of professional auto maintenance and repair, it is a wise one.

To help the owner decide which tools are needed to perform the tasks detailed in this manual, the following tool lists are offered: *Maintenance and minor repair, Repair/overhaul* and *Special.*

The newcomer to practical mechanics should start off with the *maintenance and minor repair* tool kit, which is adequate for the simpler jobs performed on a vehicle. Then, as confidence and experience grow, the owner can tackle more difficult tasks, buying additional tools as they are needed. Eventually the basic kit will be expanded into the *repair and overhaul* tool set. Over a period of time, the experienced do-it-yourselfer will assemble a tool set complete enough for most repair and overhaul procedures and will add tools from the special category when it is felt that the expense is justified by the frequency of use.

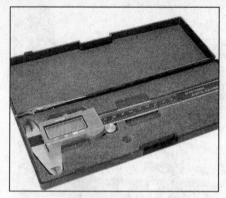

Dial caliper

Hand-operated vacuum pump

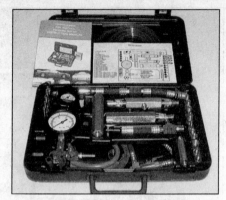

Fuel pressure gauge set

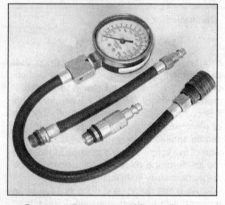

Compression gauge with spark plug hole adapter

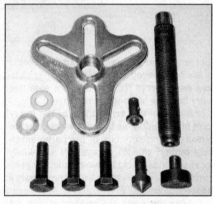

Damper/steering wheel puller

General purpose puller

Hydraulic lifter removal tool

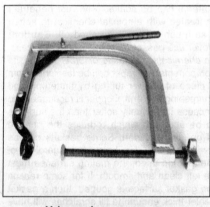

Valve spring compressor

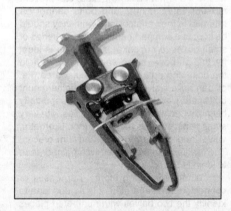

Valve spring compressor

Ridge reamer

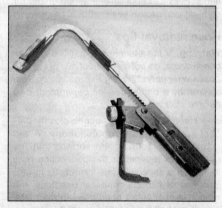

Piston ring groove cleaning tool

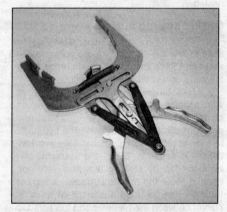

Ring removal/installation tool

Ring compressor

Cylinder hone

Brake hold-down spring tool

Torque angle gauge

Clutch plate alignment tool

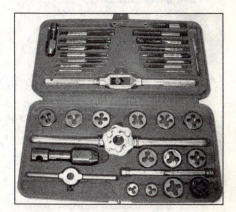

Tap and die set

Maintenance and minor repair tool kit

The tools in this list should be considered the minimum required for performance of routine maintenance, servicing and minor repair work. We recommend the purchase of combination wrenches (box-end and open-end combined in one wrench). While more expensive than open end wrenches, they offer the advantages of both types of wrench.

Combination wrench set (1/4-inch to 1 inch or 6 mm to 19 mm)
Adjustable wrench, 8 inch
Spark plug wrench with rubber insert
Spark plug gap adjusting tool
Feeler gauge set
Brake bleeder wrench
Standard screwdriver (5/16-inch x 6 inch)
Phillips screwdriver (No. 2 x 6 inch)
Combination pliers - 6 inch
Hacksaw and assortment of blades
Tire pressure gauge
Grease gun
Oil can
Fine emery cloth
Wire brush
Battery post and cable cleaning tool
Oil filter wrench
Funnel (medium size)
Safety goggles
Jackstands (2)
Drain pan

Note: *If basic tune-ups are going to be part of routine maintenance, it will be necessary to purchase a good quality stroboscopic timing light and combination tachometer/dwell meter. Although they are included in the list of special tools, it is mentioned here because they are absolutely necessary for tuning most vehicles properly.*

Repair and overhaul tool set

These tools are essential for anyone who plans to perform major repairs and are in addition to those in the maintenance and minor repair tool kit. Included is a comprehensive set of sockets which, though expensive, are invaluable because of their versatility, especially when various extensions and drives are available. We recommend the 1/2-inch drive over the 3/8-inch drive. Although the larger drive is bulky and more expensive, it has the capacity of accepting a very wide range of large sockets. Ideally, however, the mechanic should have a 3/8-inch drive set and a 1/2-inch drive set.

Socket set(s)
Reversible ratchet
Extension - 10 inch
Universal joint
Torque wrench (same size drive as sockets)
Ball peen hammer - 8 ounce
Soft-face hammer (plastic/rubber)
Standard screwdriver (1/4-inch x 6 inch)

Standard screwdriver (stubby - 5/16-inch)
Phillips screwdriver (No. 3 x 8 inch)
Phillips screwdriver (stubby - No. 2)
Pliers - vise grip
Pliers - lineman's
Pliers - needle nose
Pliers - snap-ring (internal and external)
Cold chisel - 1/2-inch
Scribe
Scraper (made from flattened copper tubing)
Centerpunch
Pin punches (1/16, 1/8, 3/16-inch)
Steel rule/straightedge - 12 inch
Allen wrench set (1/8 to 3/8-inch or 4 mm to 10 mm)
A selection of files
Wire brush (large)
Jackstands (second set)
Jack (scissor or hydraulic type)

Note: *Another tool which is often useful is an electric drill with a chuck capacity of 3/8-inch and a set of good quality drill bits.*

Special tools

The tools in this list include those which are not used regularly, are expensive to buy, or which need to be used in accordance with their manufacturer's instructions. Unless these tools will be used frequently, it is not very economical to purchase many of them. A consideration would be to split the cost and use between yourself and a friend or friends. In addition, most of these tools can be obtained from a tool rental shop on a temporary basis.

This list primarily contains only those tools and instruments widely available to the public, and not those special tools produced by the vehicle manufacturer for distribution to dealer service departments. Occasionally, references to the manufacturer's special tools are included in the text of this manual. Generally, an alternative method of doing the job without the special tool is offered. However, sometimes there is no alternative to their use. Where this is the case, and the tool cannot be purchased or borrowed, the work should be turned over to the dealer service department or an automotive repair shop.

> *Valve spring compressor*
> *Piston ring groove cleaning tool*
> *Piston ring compressor*
> *Piston ring installation tool*
> *Cylinder compression gauge*
> *Cylinder ridge reamer*
> *Cylinder surfacing hone*
> *Cylinder bore gauge*
> *Micrometers and/or dial calipers*
> *Hydraulic lifter removal tool*
> *Balljoint separator*
> *Universal-type puller*
> *Impact screwdriver*
> *Dial indicator set*
> *Stroboscopic timing light (inductive*
>   *pick-up)*
> *Hand operated vacuum/pressure pump*
> *Tachometer/dwell meter*
> *Universal electrical multimeter*
> *Cable hoist*
> *Brake spring removal and installation*
>   *tools*
> *Floor jack*

Buying tools

For the do-it-yourselfer who is just starting to get involved in vehicle maintenance and repair, there are a number of options available when purchasing tools. If maintenance and minor repair is the extent of the work to be done, the purchase of individual tools is satisfactory. If, on the other hand, extensive work is planned, it would be a good idea to purchase a modest tool set from one of the large retail chain stores. A set can usually be bought at a substantial savings over the individual tool prices, and they often come with a tool box. As additional tools are needed, add-on sets, individual tools and a larger tool box can be purchased to expand the tool selection. Building a tool set gradually allows the cost of the tools to be spread over a longer period of time and gives the mechanic the freedom to choose only those tools that will actually be used.

Tool stores will often be the only source of some of the special tools that are needed,

but regardless of where tools are bought, try to avoid cheap ones, especially when buying screwdrivers and sockets, because they won't last very long. The expense involved in replacing cheap tools will eventually be greater than the initial cost of quality tools.

Care and maintenance of tools

Good tools are expensive, so it makes sense to treat them with respect. Keep them clean and in usable condition and store them properly when not in use. Always wipe off any dirt, grease or metal chips before putting them away. Never leave tools lying around in the work area. Upon completion of a job, always check closely under the hood for tools that may have been left there so they won't get lost during a test drive.

Some tools, such as screwdrivers, pliers, wrenches and sockets, can be hung on a panel mounted on the garage or workshop wall, while others should be kept in a tool box or tray. Measuring instruments, gauges, meters, etc. must be carefully stored where they cannot be damaged by weather or impact from other tools.

When tools are used with care and stored properly, they will last a very long time. Even with the best of care, though, tools will wear out if used frequently. When a tool is damaged or worn out, replace it. Subsequent jobs will be safer and more enjoyable if you do.

How to repair damaged threads

Sometimes, the internal threads of a nut or bolt hole can become stripped, usually from overtightening. Stripping threads is an all-too-common occurrence, especially when working with aluminum parts, because aluminum is so soft that it easily strips out.

Usually, external or internal threads are only partially stripped. After they've been cleaned up with a tap or die, they'll still work. Sometimes, however, threads are badly damaged. When this happens, you've got three choices:

1) *Drill and tap the hole to the next suitable oversize and install a larger diameter bolt, screw or stud.*
2) *Drill and tap the hole to accept a threaded plug, then drill and tap the plug to the original screw size. You can also buy a plug already threaded to the original size. Then you simply drill a hole to the specified size, then run the threaded plug into the hole with a bolt and jam nut. Once the plug is fully seated, remove the jam nut and bolt.*
3) *The third method uses a patented thread repair kit like Heli-Coil or Slimsert. These*

easy-to-use kits are designed to repair damaged threads in straight-through holes and blind holes. Both are available as kits which can handle a variety of sizes and thread patterns. Drill the hole, then tap it with the special included tap. Install the Heli-Coil and the hole is back to its original diameter and thread pitch.

Regardless of which method you use, be sure to proceed calmly and carefully. A little impatience or carelessness during one of these relatively simple procedures can ruin your whole day's work and cost you a bundle if you wreck an expensive part.

Working facilities

Not to be overlooked when discussing tools is the workshop. If anything more than routine maintenance is to be carried out, some sort of suitable work area is essential.

It is understood, and appreciated, that many home mechanics do not have a good workshop or garage available, and end up removing an engine or doing major repairs outside. It is recommended, however, that the overhaul or repair be completed under the cover of a roof.

A clean, flat workbench or table of comfortable working height is an absolute necessity. The workbench should be equipped with a vise that has a jaw opening of at least four inches.

As mentioned previously, some clean, dry storage space is also required for tools, as well as the lubricants, fluids, cleaning solvents, etc. which soon become necessary.

Sometimes waste oil and fluids, drained from the engine or cooling system during normal maintenance or repairs, present a disposal problem. To avoid pouring them on the ground or into a sewage system, pour the used fluids into large containers, seal them with caps and take them to an authorized disposal site or recycling center. Plastic jugs, such as old antifreeze containers, are ideal for this purpose.

Always keep a supply of old newspapers and clean rags available. Old towels are excellent for mopping up spills. Many mechanics use rolls of paper towels for most work because they are readily available and disposable. To help keep the area under the vehicle clean, a large cardboard box can be cut open and flattened to protect the garage or shop floor.

Whenever working over a painted surface, such as when leaning over a fender to service something under the hood, always cover it with an old blanket or bedspread to protect the finish. Vinyl covered pads, made especially for this purpose, are available at auto parts stores.

Automotive chemicals and lubricants

A number of automotive chemicals and lubricants are available for use during vehicle maintenance and repair. They include a wide variety of products ranging from cleaning solvents and degreasers to lubricants and protective sprays for rubber, plastic and vinyl.

Cleaners

Carburetor cleaner and choke cleaner is a strong solvent for gum, varnish and carbon. Most carburetor cleaners leave a dry-type lubricant film which will not harden or gum up. Because of this film it is not recommended for use on electrical components.

Brake system cleaner is used to remove brake dust, grease and brake fluid from the brake system, where clean surfaces are absolutely necessary. It leaves no residue and often eliminates brake squeal caused by contaminants.

Electrical cleaner removes oxidation, corrosion and carbon deposits from electrical contacts, restoring full current flow. It can also be used to clean spark plugs, carburetor jets, voltage regulators and other parts where an oil-free surface is desired.

Demoisturants remove water and moisture from electrical components such as alternators, voltage regulators, electrical connectors and fuse blocks. They are non-conductive and non-corrosive.

Degreasers are heavy-duty solvents used to remove grease from the outside of the engine and from chassis components. They can be sprayed or brushed on and, depending on the type, are rinsed off either with water or solvent.

Lubricants

Motor oil is the lubricant formulated for use in engines. It normally contains a wide variety of additives to prevent corrosion and reduce foaming and wear. Motor oil comes in various weights (viscosity ratings) from 0 to 50. The recommended weight of the oil depends on the season, temperature and the demands on the engine. Light oil is used in cold climates and under light load conditions. Heavy oil is used in hot climates and where high loads are encountered. Multi-viscosity oils are designed to have characteristics of both light and heavy oils and are available in a number of weights from 0W-20 to 20W-50.

Gear oil is designed to be used in differentials, manual transmissions and other areas where high-temperature lubrication is required.

Chassis and wheel bearing grease is a heavy grease used where increased loads and friction are encountered, such as for wheel bearings, balljoints, tie-rod ends and universal joints.

High-temperature wheel bearing grease is designed to withstand the extreme temperatures encountered by wheel bearings in disc brake equipped vehicles. It usually contains molybdenum disulfide (moly), which is a dry-type lubricant.

White grease is a heavy grease for metal-to-metal applications where water is a problem. White grease stays soft under both low and high temperatures (usually from -100 to +190-degrees F), and will not wash off or dilute in the presence of water.

Assembly lube is a special extreme pressure lubricant, usually containing moly, used to lubricate high-load parts (such as main and rod bearings and cam lobes) for initial start-up of a new engine. The assembly lube lubricates the parts without being squeezed out or washed away until the engine oiling system begins to function.

Silicone lubricants are used to protect rubber, plastic, vinyl and nylon parts.

Graphite lubricants are used where oils cannot be used due to contamination problems, such as in locks. The dry graphite will lubricate metal parts while remaining uncontaminated by dirt, water, oil or acids. It is electrically conductive and will not foul electrical contacts in locks such as the ignition switch.

Moly penetrants loosen and lubricate frozen, rusted and corroded fasteners and prevent future rusting or freezing.

Heat-sink grease is a special electrically non-conductive grease that is used for mounting electronic ignition modules where it is essential that heat is transferred away from the module.

Sealants

RTV sealant is one of the most widely used gasket compounds. Made from silicone, RTV is air curing, it seals, bonds, waterproofs, fills surface irregularities, remains flexible, doesn't shrink, is relatively easy to remove, and is used as a supplementary sealer with almost all low and medium temperature gaskets.

Anaerobic sealant is much like RTV in that it can be used either to seal gaskets or to form gaskets by itself. It remains flexible, is solvent resistant and fills surface imperfections. The difference between an anaerobic sealant and an RTV-type sealant is in the curing. RTV cures when exposed to air, while an anaerobic sealant cures only in the absence of air. This means that an anaerobic sealant cures only after the assembly of parts, sealing them together.

Thread and pipe sealant is used for sealing hydraulic and pneumatic fittings and vacuum lines. It is usually made from a Teflon compound, and comes in a spray, a paint-on liquid and as a wrap-around tape.

Chemicals

Anti-seize compound prevents seizing, galling, cold welding, rust and corrosion in fasteners. High-temperature ant-seize, usually made with copper and graphite lubricants, is used for exhaust system and exhaust manifold bolts.

Anaerobic locking compounds are used to keep fasteners from vibrating or working loose and cure only after installation, in the absence of air. Medium strength locking compound is used for small nuts, bolts and screws that may be removed later. High-strength locking compound is for large nuts, bolts and studs which aren't removed on a regular basis.

Oil additives range from viscosity index improvers to chemical treatments that claim to reduce internal engine friction. It should be noted that most oil manufacturers caution against using additives with their oils.

Gas additives perform several functions, depending on their chemical makeup. They usually contain solvents that help dissolve gum and varnish that build up on carburetor, fuel injection and intake parts. They also serve to break down carbon deposits that form on the inside surfaces of the combustion chambers. Some additives contain upper cylinder lubricants for valves and piston rings, and others contain chemicals to remove condensation from the gas tank.

Miscellaneous

Brake fluid is specially formulated hydraulic fluid that can withstand the heat and pressure encountered in brake systems. Care must be taken so this fluid does not come in contact with painted surfaces or plastics. An opened container should always be resealed to prevent contamination by water or dirt.

Weatherstrip adhesive is used to bond weatherstripping around doors, windows and trunk lids. It is sometimes used to attach trim pieces.

Undercoating is a petroleum-based, tar-like substance that is designed to protect metal surfaces on the underside of the vehicle from corrosion. It also acts as a sound-deadening agent by insulating the bottom of the vehicle.

Waxes and polishes are used to help protect painted and plated surfaces from the weather. Different types of paint may require the use of different types of wax and polish. Some polishes utilize a chemical or abrasive cleaner to help remove the top layer of oxidized (dull) paint on older vehicles. In recent years many non-wax polishes that contain a wide variety of chemicals such as polymers and silicones have been introduced. These non-wax polishes are usually easier to apply and last longer than conventional waxes and polishes.

Conversion factors

Length (distance)
Inches (in)	X 25.4	= Millimeters (mm)	X 0.0394	= Inches (in)	
Feet (ft)	X 0.305	= Meters (m)	X 3.281	= Feet (ft)	
Miles	X 1.609	= Kilometers (km)	X 0.621	= Miles	

Volume (capacity)
Cubic inches (cu in; in³)	X 16.387	= Cubic centimeters (cc; cm³)	X 0.061	= Cubic inches (cu in; in³)
Imperial pints (Imp pt)	X 0.568	= Liters (l)	X 1.76	= Imperial pints (Imp pt)
Imperial quarts (Imp qt)	X 1.137	= Liters (l)	X 0.88	= Imperial quarts (Imp qt)
Imperial quarts (Imp qt)	X 1.201	= US quarts (US qt)	X 0.833	= Imperial quarts (Imp qt)
US quarts (US qt)	X 0.946	= Liters (l)	X 1.057	= US quarts (US qt)
Imperial gallons (Imp gal)	X 4.546	= Liters (l)	X 0.22	= Imperial gallons (Imp gal)
Imperial gallons (Imp gal)	X 1.201	= US gallons (US gal)	X 0.833	= Imperial gallons (Imp gal)
US gallons (US gal)	X 3.785	= Liters (l)	X 0.264	= US gallons (US gal)

Mass (weight)
Ounces (oz)	X 28.35	= Grams (g)	X 0.035	= Ounces (oz)
Pounds (lb)	X 0.454	= Kilograms (kg)	X 2.205	= Pounds (lb)

Force
Ounces-force (ozf; oz)	X 0.278	= Newtons (N)	X 3.6	= Ounces-force (ozf; oz)
Pounds-force (lbf; lb)	X 4.448	= Newtons (N)	X 0.225	= Pounds-force (lbf; lb)
Newtons (N)	X 0.1	= Kilograms-force (kgf; kg)	X 9.81	= Newtons (N)

Pressure
Pounds-force per square inch (psi; lbf/in²; lb/in²)	X 0.070	= Kilograms-force per square centimeter (kgf/cm²; kg/cm²)	X 14.223	= Pounds-force per square inch (psi; lbf/in²; lb/in²)
Pounds-force per square inch (psi; lbf/in²; lb/in²)	X 0.068	= Atmospheres (atm)	X 14.696	= Pounds-force per square inch (psi; lbf/in²; lb/in²)
Pounds-force per square inch (psi; lbf/in²; lb/in²)	X 0.069	= Bars	X 14.5	= Pounds-force per square inch (psi; lbf/in²; lb/in²)
Pounds-force per square inch (psi; lbf/in²; lb/in²)	X 6.895	= Kilopascals (kPa)	X 0.145	= Pounds-force per square inch (psi; lbf/in²; lb/in²)
Kilopascals (kPa)	X 0.01	= Kilograms-force per square centimeter (kgf/cm²; kg/cm²)	X 98.1	= Kilopascals (kPa)

Torque (moment of force)
Pounds-force inches (lbf in; lb in)	X 1.152	= Kilograms-force centimeter (kgf cm; kg cm)	X 0.868	= Pounds-force inches (lbf in; lb in)
Pounds-force inches (lbf in; lb in)	X 0.113	= Newton meters (Nm)	X 8.85	= Pounds-force inches (lbf in; lb in)
Pounds-force inches (lbf in; lb in)	X 0.083	= Pounds-force feet (lbf ft; lb ft)	X 12	= Pounds-force inches (lbf in; lb in)
Pounds-force feet (lbf ft; lb ft)	X 0.138	= Kilograms-force meters (kgf m; kg m)	X 7.233	= Pounds-force feet (lbf ft; lb ft)
Pounds-force feet (lbf ft; lb ft)	X 1.356	= Newton meters (Nm)	X 0.738	= Pounds-force feet (lbf ft; lb ft)
Newton meters (Nm)	X 0.102	= Kilograms-force meters (kgf m; kg m)	X 9.804	= Newton meters (Nm)

Vacuum
Inches mercury (in. Hg)	X 3.377	= Kilopascals (kPa)	X 0.2961	= Inches mercury
Inches mercury (in. Hg)	X 25.4	= Millimeters mercury (mm Hg)	X 0.0394	= Inches mercury

Power
Horsepower (hp)	X 745.7	= Watts (W)	X 0.0013	= Horsepower (hp)

Velocity (speed)
Miles per hour (miles/hr; mph)	X 1.609	= Kilometers per hour (km/hr; kph)	X 0.621	= Miles per hour (miles/hr; mph)

Fuel consumption*
Miles per gallon, Imperial (mpg)	X 0.354	= Kilometers per liter (km/l)	X 2.825	= Miles per gallon, Imperial (mpg)
Miles per gallon, US (mpg)	X 0.425	= Kilometers per liter (km/l)	X 2.352	= Miles per gallon, US (mpg)

Temperature
Degrees Fahrenheit = (°C x 1.8) + 32

Degrees Celsius (Degrees Centigrade; °C) = (°F - 32) x 0.56

*It is common practice to convert from miles per gallon (mpg) to liters/100 kilometers (l/100km), where mpg (Imperial) x l/100 km = 282 and mpg (US) x l/100 km = 235

DECIMALS to MILLIMETERS

Decimal	mm	Decimal	mm
0.001	0.0254	0.500	12.7000
0.002	0.0508	0.510	12.9540
0.003	0.0762	0.520	13.2080
0.004	0.1016	0.530	13.4620
0.005	0.1270	0.540	13.7160
0.006	0.1524	0.550	13.9700
0.007	0.1778	0.560	14.2240
0.008	0.2032	0.570	14.4780
0.009	0.2286	0.580	14.7320
0.010	0.2540	0.590	14.9860
0.020	0.5080	0.600	15.2400
0.030	0.7620	0.610	15.4940
0.040	1.0160	0.620	15.7480
0.050	1.2700	0.630	16.0020
0.060	1.5240	0.640	16.2560
0.070	1.7780	0.650	16.5100
0.080	2.0320	0.660	16.7640
0.090	2.2860	0.670	17.0180
0.100	2.5400	0.680	17.2720
0.110	2.7940	0.690	17.5260
0.120	3.0480	0.700	17.7800
0.130	3.3020	0.710	18.0340
0.140	3.5560	0.720	18.2880
0.150	3.8100	0.730	18.5420
0.160	4.0640	0.740	18.7960
0.170	4.3180	0.750	19.0500
0.180	4.5720	0.760	19.3040
0.190	4.8260	0.770	19.5580
0.200	5.0800	0.780	19.8120
0.210	5.3340	0.790	20.0660
0.220	5.5880	0.800	20.3200
0.230	5.8420	0.810	20.5740
0.240	6.0960	0.820	21.8280
0.250	6.3500	0.830	21.0820
0.260	6.6040	0.840	21.3360
0.270	6.8580	0.850	21.5900
0.280	7.1120	0.860	21.8440
0.290	7.3660	0.870	22.0980
0.300	7.6200	0.880	22.3520
0.310	7.8740	0.890	22.6060
0.320	8.1280	0.900	22.8600
0.330	8.3820	0.910	23.1140
0.340	8.6360	0.920	23.3680
0.350	8.8900	0.930	23.6220
0.360	9.1440	0.940	23.8760
0.370	9.3980	0.950	24.1300
0.380	9.6520	0.960	24.3840
0.390	9.9060	0.970	24.6380
0.400	10.1600	0.980	24.8920
0.410	10.4140	0.990	25.1460
0.420	10.6680	1.000	25.4000
0.430	10.9220		
0.440	11.1760		
0.450	11.4300		
0.460	11.6840		
0.470	11.9380		
0.480	12.1920		
0.490	12.4460		

FRACTIONS to DECIMALS to MILLIMETERS

Fraction	Decimal	mm	Fraction	Decimal	mm
1/64	0.0156	0.3969	33/64	0.5156	13.0969
1/32	0.0312	0.7938	17/32	0.5312	13.4938
3/64	0.0469	1.1906	35/64	0.5469	13.8906
1/16	0.0625	1.5875	9/16	0.5625	14.2875
5/64	0.0781	1.9844	37/64	0.5781	14.6844
3/32	0.0938	2.3812	19/32	0.5938	15.0812
7/64	0.1094	2.7781	39/64	0.6094	15.4781
1/8	0.1250	3.1750	5/8	0.6250	15.8750
9/64	0.1406	3.5719	41/64	0.6406	16.2719
5/32	0.1562	3.9688	21/32	0.6562	16.6688
11/64	0.1719	4.3656	43/64	0.6719	17.0656
3/16	0.1875	4.7625	11/16	0.6875	17.4625
13/64	0.2031	5.1594	45/64	0.7031	17.8594
7/32	0.2188	5.5562	23/32	0.7188	18.2562
15/64	0.2344	5.9531	47/64	0.7344	18.6531
1/4	0.2500	6.3500	3/4	0.7500	19.0500
17/64	0.2656	6.7469	49/64	0.7656	19.4469
9/32	0.2812	7.1438	25/32	0.7812	19.8438
19/64	0.2969	7.5406	51/64	0.7969	20.2406
5/16	0.3125	7.9375	13/16	0.8125	20.6375
21/64	0.3281	8.3344	53/64	0.8281	21.0344
11/32	0.3438	8.7312	27/32	0.8438	21.4312
23/64	0.3594	9.1281	55/64	0.8594	21.8281
3/8	0.3750	9.5250	7/8	0.8750	22.2250
25/64	0.3906	9.9219	57/64	0.8906	22.6219
13/32	0.4062	10.3188	29/32	0.9062	23.0188
27/64	0.4219	10.7156	59/64	0.9219	23.4156
7/16	0.4375	11.1125	15/16	0.9375	23.8125
29/64	0.4531	11.5094	61/64	0.9531	24.2094
15/32	0.4688	11.9062	31/32	0.9688	24.6062
31/64	0.4844	12.3031	63/64	0.9844	25.0031
1/2	0.5000	12.7000	1	1.0000	25.4000

Safety first!

Regardless of how enthusiastic you may be about getting on with the job at hand, take the time to ensure that your safety is not jeopardized. A moment's lack of attention can result in an accident, as can failure to observe certain simple safety precautions. The possibility of an accident will always exist, and the following points should not be considered a comprehensive list of all dangers. Rather, they are intended to make you aware of the risks and to encourage a safety conscious approach to all work you carry out on your vehicle.

Essential DOs and DON'Ts

DON'T rely on a jack when working under the vehicle. Always use approved jackstands to support the weight of the vehicle and place them under the recommended lift or support points.

DON'T attempt to loosen extremely tight fasteners (i.e. wheel lug nuts) while the vehicle is on a jack - it may fall.

DON'T start the engine without first making sure that the transmission is in Neutral (or Park where applicable) and the parking brake is set.

DON'T remove the radiator cap from a hot cooling system - let it cool or cover it with a cloth and release the pressure gradually.

DON'T attempt to drain the engine oil until you are sure it has cooled to the point that it will not burn you.

DON'T touch any part of the engine or exhaust system until it has cooled sufficiently to avoid burns.

DON'T siphon toxic liquids such as gasoline, antifreeze and brake fluid by mouth, or allow them to remain on your skin.

DON'T inhale brake lining dust - it is potentially hazardous (see *Asbestos* below).

DON'T allow spilled oil or grease to remain on the floor - wipe it up before someone slips on it.

DON'T use loose fitting wrenches or other tools which may slip and cause injury.

DON'T push on wrenches when loosening or tightening nuts or bolts. Always try to pull the wrench toward you. If the situation calls for pushing the wrench away, push with an open hand to avoid scraped knuckles if the wrench should slip.

DON'T attempt to lift a heavy component alone - get someone to help you.

DON'T *rush or take unsafe shortcuts to finish a job.*

DON'T allow children or animals in or around the vehicle while you are working on it.

DO wear eye protection when using power tools such as a drill, sander, bench grinder, etc. and when working under a vehicle.

DO keep loose clothing and long hair well out of the way of moving parts.

DO make sure that any hoist used has a safe working load rating adequate for the job.

DO get someone to check on you periodically when working alone on a vehicle.

DO carry out work in a logical sequence and make sure that everything is correctly assembled and tightened.

DO keep chemicals and fluids tightly capped and out of the reach of children and pets.

DO remember that your vehicle's safety affects that of yourself and others. If in doubt on any point, get professional advice.

Steering, suspension and brakes

These systems are essential to driving safety, so make sure you have a qualified shop or individual check your work. Also, compressed suspension springs can cause injury if released suddenly - be sure to use a spring compressor.

Airbags

Airbags are explosive devices that can **CAUSE** injury if they deploy while you're working on the vehicle. Follow the manufacturer's instructions to disable the airbag whenever you're working in the vicinity of airbag components.

Asbestos

Certain friction, insulating, sealing, and other products - such as brake linings, brake bands, clutch linings, torque converters, gaskets, etc. - may contain asbestos or other hazardous friction material. Extreme care must be taken to avoid inhalation of dust from such products, since it is hazardous to health. If in doubt, assume that they do contain asbestos.

Fire

Remember at all times that gasoline is highly flammable. Never smoke or have any kind of open flame around when working on a vehicle. But the risk does not end there. A spark caused by an electrical short circuit, by two metal surfaces contacting each other, or even by static electricity built up in your body under certain conditions, can ignite gasoline vapors, which in a confined space are highly explosive. Do not, under any circumstances, use gasoline for cleaning parts. Use an approved safety solvent.

Always disconnect the battery ground (-) cable at the battery before working on any part of the fuel system or electrical system. Never risk spilling fuel on a hot engine or exhaust component. It is strongly recommended that a fire extinguisher suitable for use on fuel and electrical fires be kept handy in the garage or workshop at all times. Never try to extinguish a fuel or electrical fire with water.

Fumes

Certain fumes are highly toxic and can quickly cause unconsciousness and even death if inhaled to any extent. Gasoline vapor falls into this category, as do the vapors from some cleaning solvents. Any draining or pouring of such volatile fluids should be done in a well ventilated area.

When using cleaning fluids and solvents, read the instructions on the container carefully. Never use materials from unmarked containers.

Never run the engine in an enclosed space, such as a garage. Exhaust fumes contain carbon monoxide, which is extremely poisonous. If you need to run the engine, always do so in the open air, or at least have the rear of the vehicle outside the work area.

The battery

Never create a spark or allow a bare light bulb near a battery. They normally give off a certain amount of hydrogen gas, which is highly explosive.

Always disconnect the battery ground (-) cable at the battery before working on the fuel or electrical systems.

If possible, loosen the filler caps or cover when charging the battery from an external source (this does not apply to sealed or maintenance-free batteries). Do not charge at an excessive rate or the battery may burst.

Take care when adding water to a non maintenance-free battery and when carrying a battery. The electrolyte, even when diluted, is very corrosive and should not be allowed to contact clothing or skin.

Always wear eye protection when cleaning the battery to prevent the caustic deposits from entering your eyes.

Household current

When using an electric power tool, inspection light, etc., which operates on household current, always make sure that the tool is correctly connected to its plug and that, where necessary, it is properly grounded. Do not use such items in damp conditions and, again, do not create a spark or apply excessive heat in the vicinity of fuel or fuel vapor.

Secondary ignition system voltage

A severe electric shock can result from touching certain parts of the ignition system (such as the spark plug wires) when the engine is running or being cranked, particularly if components are damp or the insulation is defective. In the case of an electronic ignition system, the secondary system voltage is much higher and could prove fatal.

Hydrofluoric acid

This extremely corrosive acid is formed when certain types of synthetic rubber, found in some O-rings, oil seals, fuel hoses, etc. are exposed to temperatures above 750-degrees F (400-degrees C). The rubber changes into a charred or sticky substance containing the acid. *Once formed, the acid remains dangerous for years. If it gets onto the skin, it may be necessary to amputate the limb concerned.*

When dealing with a vehicle which has suffered a fire, or with components salvaged from such a vehicle, wear protective gloves and discard them after use.

Troubleshooting

Contents

This section provides an easy reference guide to the more common problems that may occur during the operation of your vehicle. These problems and possible causes are grouped under various components or systems; i.e. Engine, Cooling System, etc., and also refer to the Chapter and/or Section that deals with the problem.

Remember that successful troubleshooting is not a mysterious black art practiced only by professional mechanics. It's simply the result of a bit of knowledge combined with an intelligent, systematic approach to the problem. Always work by a process of elimination, starting with the simplest solution and working through to the most complex - and never overlook the obvious. Anyone can forget to fill the gas tank or leave the lights on overnight, so don't assume that you are above such oversights.

Finally, always get clear in your mind why a problem has occurred and take steps to ensure that it doesn't happen again. If the electrical system fails because of a poor connection, check all other connections in the system to make sure that they don't fail as well. If a particular fuse continues to blow, find out why - don't just go on replacing fuses. Remember, failure of a small component can often be indicative of potential failure or incorrect functioning of a more important component or system.

Engine

1   Engine will not rotate when attempting to start

1   Battery terminal connections loose or corroded. Check the cable terminals at the battery. Tighten the cable or remove corrosion as necessary.
2   Battery discharged or faulty. If the cable connections are clean and tight on the battery posts, turn the key to the On position and switch on the headlights and/or windshield wipers. If they fail to function, the battery is discharged.
3   Automatic transmission not completely engaged in Park or Neutral or clutch pedal not completely depressed.
4   Broken, loose or disconnected wiring in the starting circuit. Inspect all wiring and connectors at the battery, starter solenoid and ignition switch.
5   Starter motor pinion jammed in flywheel ring gear. If manual transmission, place transmission in gear and rock the vehicle to manually turn the engine. Remove starter and inspect pinion and flywheel at earliest convenience (Chapter 5).
6   Starter solenoid faulty (Chapter 5).
7   Starter motor faulty (Chapter 5).
8   Ignition switch faulty (Chapter 12).

2   Engine rotates but will not start

1   Fuel tank empty, fuel filter plugged or fuel line restricted.
2   Fault in the fuel injection system (Chapter 4).
3   Battery discharged (engine rotates slowly). Check the operation of electrical components as described in the previous Section.
4   Battery terminal connections loose or corroded (see previous Section).
5   Fuel pump faulty (Chapter 4).
6   Excessive moisture on, or damage to, ignition components (see Chapter 5).
7   Worn, faulty or incorrectly gapped spark plugs (Chapter 1).
8   Broken, loose or disconnected wiring in the starting circuit (see previous Section).
9   Broken, loose or disconnected wires at the ignition coils (Chapter 5).

3   Starter motor operates without rotating engine

1   Starter pinion sticking. Remove the starter (Chapter 5) and inspect.
2   Starter pinion or flywheel teeth worn or broken. Remove the flywheel/driveplate access cover and inspect.

4   Engine hard to start when cold

1   Discharged or low battery. Check as described in Section 1.
2   Fault in the fuel or ignition systems (Chapters 4 and 5).
3   Injector(s) leaking (Chapter 4).

5   Engine hard to start when hot

1   Air filter clogged (Chapter 1).
2   Fault in the fuel or ignition systems (Chapters 4 and 5).
3   Fuel not reaching the injectors (see Chapter 4).
4   Low cylinder compression (Chapter 2D).
5   Malfunctioning EVAP system (Chapter 6).

6   Starter motor noisy or excessively rough in engagement

1   Pinion or flywheel gear teeth worn or broken. Remove the cover at the rear of the engine (if equipped) and inspect.
2   Starter motor mounting bolts loose or missing.

7   Engine starts but stops immediately

1   Loose or faulty electrical connections at the coils or alternator.
2   Fault in the fuel or ignition systems (Chapters 4 and 5).
3   Vacuum leak at the gasket surfaces of the intake manifold. Make sure all mounting bolts/nuts are tightened securely and all vacuum hoses connected to the manifold are positioned properly and in good condition.
4   Restricted intake or exhaust systems (Chapter 4).

8   Engine lopes while idling or idles erratically

1   Vacuum leakage. Check the mounting bolts/nuts at the throttle body and intake manifold for tightness. Make sure all vacuum hoses are connected and in good condition. Use a stethoscope or a length of fuel hose held against your ear to listen for vacuum leaks while the engine is running. A hissing sound will be heard. A soapy water solution will also detect leaks.
2   Fault in the fuel or ignition systems (Chapters 4 and 5).
3   Plugged PCV valve or hose (see Chapters 1 and 6).
4   Air filter clogged (Chapter 1).
5   Fuel pump not delivering sufficient fuel to the fuel injectors (see Chapter 4).
6   Leaking head gasket. Perform a compression check (Chapter 2C).
7   Camshaft lobes worn (Chapter 2).

9   Engine misses at idle speed

1   Spark plugs worn, fouled or not gapped properly (Chapter 1).
2   Fault in the fuel or ignition systems (Chapters 4 and 5).
3   Faulty ignition coil(s) (Chapter 1).
4   Vacuum leaks at intake or hose connections. Check as described in Section 8.
5   Uneven or low cylinder compression. Check compression as described in Chapter 2D.

10   Engine misses throughout driving speed range

1   Fuel filter clogged and/or impurities in the fuel system (Chapter 1).
2   Faulty or incorrectly gapped spark plugs (Chapter 1).
3   Fault in the fuel or ignition systems (Chapters 4 and 5).
4   Defective spark plug boots or coils (Chapter 1).

5   Faulty emissions system components (Chapter 6).
6   Low or uneven cylinder compression pressures. Check compression as described in Chapter 2D
8   Vacuum leaks at the throttle body, intake manifold or vacuum hoses (see Section 8).

11   Engine stalls

1   Fuel filter clogged and/or water and impurities in the fuel system (Chapter 1).
2   Fault in the fuel system or sensors (Chapters 4 and 6).
3   Faulty emissions system components (Chapter 6).
4   Faulty or incorrectly gapped spark plugs (Chapter 1). Also check the ignition coils (Chapter 1).
5   Vacuum leak at the throttle body, intake manifold or vacuum hoses. Check as described in Section 8.

12   Engine lacks power

1   Fault in the fuel or ignition systems (Chapters 4 and 5).
2   Faulty or incorrectly gapped spark plugs (Chapter 1).
3   Faulty coils (Chapter 5).
4   Brakes binding (Chapter 1).
5   Automatic transmission fluid level incorrect (Chapter 1).
6   Clutch slipping (Chapter 8).
7   Fuel filter clogged and/or impurities in the fuel system (Chapter 1).
8   Emissions control system not functioning properly (Chapter 6).
9   Use of substandard fuel. Fill the tank with the proper fuel.
10   Low or uneven cylinder compression pressures (Chapter 2C).
11   Restriction in the intake or exhaust system (Chapter 4).

13   Engine backfires

1   Emissions system not functioning properly (Chapter 6).
2   Fault in the fuel or ignition systems (Chapters 4 and 5).
3   Faulty ignition system (Chapters 1 and 5).
4   Fuel injection system not functioning properly (Chapter 4).
5   Vacuum leak at the throttle body, intake manifold or vacuum hoses. Check as described in Section 8.
6   Valves sticking (Chapter 2).
7   Crossed plug wires (Chapter 1).

14   Pinging or knocking engine sounds during acceleration or uphill

1   Incorrect grade of fuel. Fill the tank with fuel of the proper octane rating.
2   Fault in the fuel or ignition systems (Chapters 4 and 5).
3   Improper spark plugs. Check the plug type against the VECI label located in the engine compartment. Also check the plugs and coils for damage (Chapter 1).
4   Faulty emissions system or knock sensor (Chapter 6).
5   Vacuum leak. Check as described in Section 9.

15   Engine continues to run after switching off

1   Idle speed too high (Chapter 4).
2   Fault in the fuel or ignition systems (Chapters 4 and 5).
3   Excessive engine operating temperature. Probable causes of this are a low coolant level (see Chapter 1), malfunctioning thermostat, clogged radiator or faulty water pump (see Chapter 3).

Engine electrical system

16   Battery will not hold a charge

1   Alternator drivebelt defective or not adjusted properly (Chapter 1).
2   Electrolyte level low or battery discharged (Chapter 1).
3   Battery terminals loose or corroded (Chapter 1).
4   Alternator not charging properly (Chapter 5).
5   Loose, broken or faulty wiring in the charging circuit (Chapter 5).
6   Short in the vehicle wiring causing a continuous drain on the battery (refer to Chapter 12 and the Wiring Diagrams).
7   Battery defective internally.

17   Alternator light fails to go out

1   Fault in the alternator or charging circuit (Chapter 5).
2   Alternator drivebelt defective or not properly adjusted (Chapter 1).

18   Alternator light fails to come on when key is turned on

1   Instrument cluster warning light bulb defective (Chapter 12).
2   Alternator faulty (Chapter 5).
3   Fault in the instrument cluster printed circuit, dashboard wiring or bulb holder (Chapter 12).

Fuel system

19   Excessive fuel consumption

1   Dirty or clogged air filter element (Chapter 1).
2   Emissions system not functioning properly (Chapter 6).
3   Fault in the fuel or ignition systems (Chapters 4 and 5).
4   Low tire pressure or incorrect tire size (Chapter 1).
5   Restricted exhaust system (Chapter 4).

20   Fuel leakage and/or fuel odor

1   Leak in a fuel feed or vent line (Chapter 4).
2   Tank overfilled. Fill only to automatic shut-off.
3   Evaporative emissions system canister clogged (Chapter 6).
4   Vapor leaks from system lines or injectors (Chapter 4).

Cooling system

21   Overheating

1   Insufficient coolant in the system (Chapter 1).
2   Water pump drivebelt defective or not adjusted properly (Chapter 1).
3   Radiator core blocked or radiator grille dirty and restricted (see Chapter 3).
4   Thermostat faulty (Chapter 3).
5   Fan blades broken or cracked (Chapter 3).
6   Radiator cap not maintaining proper pressure. Have the cap pressure tested by a gas station or repair shop.
7   Problem in the electric cooling fan circuit (see Chapter 3).

22   Overcooling

1   Thermostat faulty (Chapter 3).
2   Inaccurate temperature gauge (Chapter 12).
3   Defective fan clutch (see Chapter 3).

23   External coolant leakage

1   Deteriorated or damaged hoses or loose clamps. Replace hoses and/or tighten the clamps at the hose connections (Chapter 1).
2   Water pump seals defective (Chapter 3).
3   Leakage from the radiator core or tank(s). This will require the radiator to be professionally repaired (see Chapter 3 for removal procedures).

4   Engine drain plug(s) leaking (Chapter 1) or water jacket core plugs leaking (see Chapter 2).
5   Leakage at the heater core. Signs of leakage should show up on interior carpeting (Chapter 3).

24   Internal coolant leakage

Note: *Internal coolant leaks can usually be detected by examining the oil. Check the dipstick and inside of the valve cover for water deposits and an oil consistency like that of a milkshake.*
1   Leaking cylinder head gasket. Have the cooling system pressure tested.
2   Cracked cylinder bore or cylinder head. Remove the head(s) and inspect (Chapter 2).
3   Leaking intake manifold gasket (Chapter 2).

25   Coolant loss

1   Too much coolant in the system (Chapter 1).
2   Coolant boiling away due to overheating (see Section 15).
3   External or internal leakage (see Sections 23 and 24).
4   Faulty radiator cap. Have the cap pressure tested.

26   Poor coolant circulation

1   Inoperative water pump. A quick test is to pinch the top radiator hose closed with your hand while the engine is idling, then let it loose. You should feel the surge of coolant if the pump is working properly (see Chapter 1).
2   Restriction in the cooling system. Drain, flush and refill the system (Chapter 1). If necessary, remove the radiator (Chapter 3) and have it reverse flushed.
3   Water pump drivebelt defective or not adjusted properly (Chapter 1).
4   Thermostat sticking (Chapter 3).

Clutch

27   Fails to release (pedal pressed to the floor - shift lever does not move freely in and out of Reverse)

1   Leak in the clutch hydraulic system. Check the master cylinder, slave cylinder and lines (Chapters 1 and 8).
2   Clutch plate warped or damaged (Chapter 8).
3   Broken release bearing (Chapter 8).

28   Clutch slips (engine speed increases with no increase in vehicle speed)

1   Clutch plate oil-soaked or lining worn. Remove clutch (Chapter 8) and inspect.
2   Clutch plate not seated. It may take 30 or 40 normal starts for a new one to seat.
3   Pressure plate worn (Chapter 8).

29   Grabbing (chattering) as clutch is engaged

1   Oil on clutch plate lining. Remove (Chapter 8) and inspect. Correct any leakage source.
2   Worn or loose engine or transmission mounts. Inspect the mounts and bolts (Chapter 2).
3   Worn splines on clutch plate hub. Remove the clutch components (Chapter 8) and inspect.
4   Warped pressure plate or flywheel. Remove the clutch components and inspect.

30   Squeal or rumble with clutch fully engaged (pedal released)

Release bearing binding on transmission bearing retainer. Remove clutch components (Chapter 8) and check slave cylinder and release bearing assembly. Remove any burrs or nicks; clean and relubricate before installing.

31   Squeal or rumble with clutch fully disengaged (pedal depressed)

1   Worn, defective or broken release bearing (Chapter 8).
2   Worn or broken pressure plate springs (or diaphragm fingers) (Chapter 8).

32   Clutch pedal stays on floor when disengaged

1   Release bearing binding, or a fault in the hydraulic system (Chapter 8).
2   Clutch master cylinder faulty (Chapter 8).

Manual transmission
Note: *All the following references are in Chapter 7A, unless noted.*

33   Noisy in Neutral with engine running

1   Input shaft bearing worn.
2   Damaged main drive gear bearing.

3   Worn countershaft bearings.
4   Worn or damaged countershaft endplay shims.

34   Noisy in all gears

1   Any of the above causes, and/or:
2   Insufficient lubricant (see the checking procedures in Chapter 1).

35   Noisy in one particular gear

1   Worn, damaged or chipped gear teeth for that particular gear.
2   Worn or damaged synchronizer for that particular gear.

36   Slips out of high gear

1   Transmission loose on clutch housing.
2   Dirt between the transmission case and engine or misalignment of the transmission.

37   Difficulty in engaging gears

1   Clutch not releasing completely (see clutch adjustment in Chapter 1).
2   Loose or damaged shifter. Make a thorough inspection, replacing parts as necessary.

38   Oil leakage

1   Excessive amount of lubricant in the transmission (see Chapter 1 for correct checking procedures). Drain lubricant as required.
2   Transmission oil seal in need of replacement.

Automatic transmission
Note: *Due to the complexity of the automatic transmission, it's difficult for the home mechanic to properly diagnose and service this component. For problems other than the following, the vehicle should be taken to a dealer service department or a transmission shop.*

39   General shift mechanism problems

1   Chapter 7B deals with checking and adjusting the shift cable on automatic transmissions. Common problems that may be attributed to poorly adjusted cable are:

a) *Engine starting in gears other than Park or Neutral.*

b) *Indicator on shifter pointing to a gear other than the one actually being selected.*

c) *Vehicle moves when in Park.*

2 Refer to Chapter 7B to adjust the cable.

40 Transmission will not downshift with accelerator pedal pressed to the floor

1 Transmission pressure control solenoid valve faulty. Check for Diagnostic Trouble Codes (Chapter 6).

41 Transmission slips, shifts rough, is noisy or has no drive in forward or reverse gears

1 Of the many probable causes for the above problems, the home mechanic should be concerned with only one possibility - fluid level.

2 Before taking the vehicle to a repair shop, check the level and condition of the fluid as described in Chapter 1. Correct fluid level as necessary or change the fluid and filter if needed. If the problem persists, have a professional diagnose the probable cause.

3 If the transmission shifts late and the shifts are harsh, suspect a faulty transmission pressure control solenoid valve. Check for Diagnostic Trouble Codes (Chapter 6).

42 Fluid leakage

1 Automatic transmission fluid is a deep red color. Fluid leaks should not be confused with engine oil, which can easily be blown by airflow to the transmission.

2 To pinpoint a leak, first remove all built-up dirt and grime from around the transmission. Degreasing agents and/or steam cleaning will achieve this. With the underside clean, drive the vehicle at low speeds so airflow will not blow the leak far from its source. Raise the vehicle and determine where the leak is coming from. Common areas of leakage are:

a) *Pan: Tighten the mounting bolts and/or replace the pan gasket as necessary (see Chapter 1).*

b) *Filler pipe: Replace the rubber seal where the pipe enters the transmission case.*

c) *Transmission oil lines: Tighten the connectors where the lines enter the transmission case and/or replace the lines.*

d) *Vent pipe: Transmission overfilled and/or water in fluid (see checking procedures, Chapter 1).*

e) *Speed sensor connector: Replace the O-ring where the vehicle speed sensor enters the transmission case (Chapter 6).*

Transfer case

43 Transfer case is difficult to shift into the desired range

1 Speed may be too great to permit engagement. Stop the vehicle and shift into the desired range.

2 If the vehicle has been driven on a paved surface for some time, the driveline torque can make shifting difficult. Stop and shift into two-wheel drive on paved or hard surfaces.

3 Insufficient or incorrect grade of lubricant. Drain and refill the transfer case with the specified lubricant. (Chapter 1).

4 Worn or damaged internal components. Disassembly and overhaul of the transfer case, by a qualified shop, may be necessary.

44 Transfer case noisy in all gears

Insufficient or incorrect grade of lubricant. Drain and refill (Chapter 1).

45 Noisy or jumps out of four-wheel drive Low range

1 Transfer case not fully engaged. Stop the vehicle, shift into Neutral and then engage 4L.

2 Shift linkage loose, worn or binding. Tighten, repair or lubricate linkage as necessary.

3 Shift fork cracked, inserts worn or fork binding on the rail.

46 Lubricant leaks from the vent or output shaft seals

1 Transfer case is overfilled. Drain to the proper level (Chapter 1).

2 Vent is clogged or jammed closed. Clear or replace the vent.

3 Output shaft seal incorrectly installed or damaged. Replace the seal and check contact surfaces for nicks and scoring.

Driveshaft

47 Oil leak at seal end of driveshaft

Defective transmission or transfer case oil seal. See Chapter 7 for replacement pro-

cedures. While this is done, check the splined yoke for burrs or a rough condition that may be damaging the seal. Burrs can be removed with crocus cloth or a fine whetstone.

48 Knock or clunk when the transmission is under initial load (just after transmission is put into gear)

1 Loose or disconnected rear suspension components. Check all mounting bolts, nuts and bushings (see Chapter 10).

2 Loose driveshaft bolts. Inspect all bolts and nuts and tighten them to the specified torque.

3 Worn or damaged universal joint bearings. Check for wear (see Chapter 8).

49 Metallic grinding sound consistent with vehicle speed

Pronounced wear in the universal joint bearings. Check as described in Chapter 8.

50 Vibration

Note: *Before assuming that the driveshaft is at fault, make sure the tires are perfectly balanced and perform the following test.*

1 Install a tachometer inside the vehicle to monitor engine speed as the vehicle is driven. Drive the vehicle and note the engine speed at which the vibration (roughness) is most pronounced. Now shift the transmission to a different gear and bring the engine speed to the same point.

2 If the vibration occurs at the same engine speed (rpm) regardless of which gear the transmission is in, the driveshaft is NOT at fault since the driveshaft speed varies.

3 If the vibration decreases or is eliminated when the transmission is in a different gear at the same engine speed, refer to the following probable causes.

4 Bent or dented driveshaft. Inspect and replace as necessary (see Chapter 8).

5 Undercoating or built-up dirt, etc. on the driveshaft. Clean the shaft thoroughly and recheck.

6 Worn universal joint bearings. Remove and inspect (see Chapter 8).

7 Driveshaft and/or companion flange out of balance. Check for missing weights on the shaft. Remove the driveshaft (see Chapter 8) and reinstall 180-degrees from original position, then retest. Have the driveshaft professionally balanced if the problem persists.

8 Center support bearing worn out (two-piece driveshafts) (Chapter 8).

Axles

51 Noise

1   Road noise. No corrective procedures available.
2   Tire noise. Inspect tires and check tire pressures (Chapter 1).
3   Rear axle bearings worn or damaged (Chapter 8).

52 Vibration

See probable causes under *Driveshaft*. Proceed under the guidelines listed for the driveshaft. If the problem persists, check the rear wheel bearings by raising the rear of the vehicle and spinning the rear wheels by hand. Listen for evidence of rough (noisy) bearings. Remove and inspect (see Chapter 8).

53 Oil leakage

1   Pinion seal damaged (see Chapter 8).
2   Axleshaft oil seals damaged (see Chapter 8).
3   Differential inspection cover leaking. Tighten the bolts, or replace the gasket as required (see Chapter 8).

Driveaxles (4WD)

54 Clicking noise on turns

Worn or damaged outboard CV joints (Chapter 8).

55 Shudder or vibration during acceleration

1   Excessive toe-in. Have alignment checked.
2   Incorrect spring heights (Chapter 10).
3   Worn or damaged inboard or outboard CV joints (Chapter 8).
4   Sticking inboard CV joint assembly (Chapter 8).

56 Vibration at highway speeds

1   Out-of-balance front wheels and/or tires (Chapters 1 and 10).
2   Out-of-round front tires (Chapters 1 and 10).
3   Worn CV joints (Chapter 8).

Brakes

Note: *Before assuming that a brake problem exists, make sure that the tires are in good condition and inflated properly (see Chapter 1), that the front-end alignment is correct and that the vehicle is not loaded with weight in an unequal manner.*

57 Vehicle pulls to one side during braking

1   Defective, damaged or oil contaminated disc brake pads on one side. Inspect as described in Chapter 9.
2   Excessive wear of brake pad material or drum/disc on one side. Inspect and correct as necessary.
3   Loose or disconnected front suspension components. Inspect and tighten all bolts to the specified torque (Chapter 10).
4   Defective brake caliper assembly. Remove the caliper and inspect for a stuck piston or other damage (Chapter 9).
5   Inadequate lubrication of front brake caliper slide pins. Remove caliper and lubricate slide pins (Chapter 9).

58 Noise (high-pitched squeal with the brakes applied)

1   Disc brake pads worn out. The noise comes from the wear sensor rubbing against the disc (does not apply to all vehicles) or the actual pad backing plate itself if the material is completely worn away. Replace the pads with new ones immediately (Chapter 9). If the pad material has worn completely away, the brake discs should be inspected for damage as described in Chapter 9.
2   Missing or damaged brake pad insulators. Replace pad insulators (see Chapter 9).
3   Linings contaminated with dirt or grease. Replace pads.
4   Incorrect linings. Replace with correct linings.

59 Excessive brake pedal travel

1   Partial brake system failure. Inspect the entire system (Chapter 9) and correct as required.
2   Insufficient fluid in the master cylinder. Check (Chapter 1), add fluid and bleed the system if necessary (Chapter 9).

60 Brake pedal feels spongy when depressed

1   Air in the hydraulic lines. Bleed the brake system (Chapter 9).
2   Faulty flexible hoses. Inspect all system hoses and lines. Replace parts as necessary.
3   Master cylinder mounting bolts/nuts loose.
4   Master cylinder defective (Chapter 9).

61 Excessive effort required to stop vehicle

1   Power brake booster not operating properly (see check in Chapter 1, repairs in Chapter 9).
2   Excessively worn pads or shoes. Inspect and replace if necessary (Chapter 9).
3   One or more caliper pistons seized or sticking. Inspect and replace as required (Chapter 9).
4   One or more wheel cylinder pistons seized or sticking. Inspect and replace as required (Chapter 9).
5   Brake pads or shoes contaminated with oil or grease. Inspect and replace as required (Chapter 9).
6   New pads or shoes installed and not yet seated. It will take a while for the new material to seat against the disc or drum.

62 Pedal travels to the floor with little resistance

1   Little or no fluid in the master cylinder reservoir caused by leaking caliper piston(s), loose, damaged or disconnected brake lines. Inspect the entire system and correct as necessary.
2   Worn master cylinder seals (Chapter 9).

63 Brake pedal pulsates during brake application

1   Caliper improperly installed. Remove and inspect (Chapter 9).
2   Disc(s) defective. Remove (Chapter 9) and check for excessive lateral runout and parallelism. Have the disc(s) resurfaced or replace it with a new one.

Suspension and steering systems

64 Vehicle pulls to one side

1   Tire pressures uneven or tires mismatched (Chapter 1).
2   Defective tire (Chapter 1).
3   Excessive wear in suspension or steering components (Chapter 10).
4   Front end in need of alignment.
5   Front brakes dragging. Inspect the brakes as described in Chapter 9.

65 Shimmy, shake or vibration

1   Tire or wheel out-of-balance or out-of-round. Have professionally balanced.
2   Loose, worn or out-of-adjustment front wheel bearings (Chapter 1).
3   Shock absorbers and/or suspension components worn or damaged (Chapter 10).

66 Excessive pitching and/or rolling around corners or during braking

1   Defective shock absorbers. Replace as a set (Chapter 10).
2   Broken or weak springs and/or suspension components. Inspect as described in Chapters 1 and 10.

67 Excessively stiff steering

1   Lack of fluid in power steering fluid reservoir (Chapter 1).
2   Incorrect tire pressures (Chapter 1).
3   Lack of lubrication at steering joints (see Chapter 1).
4   Front end out of alignment.
5   Lack of power assistance (see Section 69).

68 Excessive play in steering

1   Loose front wheel bearings (Chapters 1 and 10).
2   Excessive wear in suspension or steering components (Chapter 10).
3   Steering gear damaged or out of adjustment (Chapter 10).

69 Lack of power assistance

1   Steering pump drivebelt faulty or not adjusted properly (Chapter 1).
2   Fluid level low (Chapter 1).
3   Hoses or lines restricted. Inspect and replace parts as necessary.
4   Air in power steering system. Bleed the system (Chapter 10).

70 Excessive tire wear (not specific to one area)

1   Incorrect tire pressures (Chapter 1).
2   Tires out-of-balance. Have professionally balanced.
3   Wheels damaged. Inspect and replace as necessary.
4   Suspension or steering components excessively worn (Chapter 10).

71 Excessive tire wear on outside edge

1   Inflation pressures incorrect (Chapter 1).
2   Excessive speed in turns.
3   Front-end alignment incorrect. Have the front end professionally aligned.
4   Suspension arm bent or twisted (Chapter 10).

72 Excessive tire wear on inside edge

1   Inflation pressures incorrect (Chapter 1).
2   Front-end alignment incorrect. Have the front end professionally aligned.
3   Loose or damaged steering components (Chapter 10).

73 Tire tread worn in one place

1   Tires out-of-balance.
2   Damaged or buckled wheel. Inspect and replace if necessary.
3   Defective tire (Chapter 1).

Notes

Chapter 1
Tune-up and routine maintenance

Contents

Specifications

Recommended lubricants and fluids

Note: *Listed here are manufacturer recommendations at the time this manual was written. Manufacturers occasionally upgrade their fluid and lubricant specifications, so check with your local auto parts store for current recommendations.*

Engine oil
    Type .... API "certified for gasoline engines"
    Viscosity .... See accompanying chart
Fuel.. 87 octane minimum

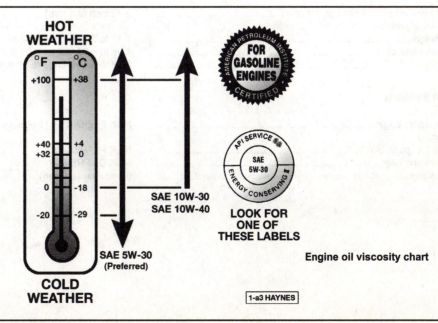

Engine oil viscosity chart

1-a3 HAYNES

Recommended lubricants and fluids (continued)

Manual transmission lubricant... 75W-85 GL 4 gear oil
Automatic transmission fluid.. Nissan Matic J or Nissan Matic S automatic transmission fluid
Power steering fluid
   U.S. models.. Nissan PSF or equivalent
   Canadian models .... Nissan PSF, Nissan ATF, DEXRON III or
                      MERCON automatic transmission fluid

Transfer case lubricant
   U.S. models.. Nissan Matic D automatic transmission fluid or equivalent
   Canadian models .... Nissan Matic D automatic transmission fluid, Nissan ATF,
                      DEXRON III or MERCON automatic transmission fluid

Differential lubricant
   Front (4WD models)... SAE GL-5 80W-90 gear oil
   Rear
      Except models with a 6-speed manual transmission or 4WD....... API GL-5 synthetic 75W-90 gear oil
      Models with a 6-speed manual transmission or 4WD.................. API GL-5 synthetic 75W-140 gear oil
Brake fluid... DOT 3 brake fluid
Engine coolant... 50/50 mixture of ethylene glycol-based
                      antifreeze and distilled or demineralized
                      water
Chassis lubrication grease .... NLGI No. 2 moly-based chassis grease
Key lock cylinder lubricant... Graphite spray

Cylinder numbering diagram - four-cylinder engine

Capacities*

Engine oil (including filter)
   Four-cylinder engine
      2005 through 2008.. 5-1/8 quarts (4.9 liters)
      2009 and later.. 4-7/8 quarts (4.6 liters)
   V6 engine .... 5-3/8 quarts (5.1 liters)
Manual transmission
   Four-cylinder engine (five-speed) .... Up to 3-7/8 quarts (2.9 liters)
   V6 engine (six-speed)
      2WD... Up to 4-1/4 quarts (4.0 liters)
      4WD... Up to 4-3/8 quarts (4.2 liters)
Automatic transmission (fluid and filter change), all models................... Up to 10-7/8 quarts (the best way to determine the amount of fluid to add during a routine fluid change is to measure the amount drained; this way you won't overfill the transmission)
Transfer case.. 2-1/8 quarts (2.0 liters)
Cooling system
   Four-cylinder engine .... 2-1/2 gallons (9.4 liters)
   V6 engine .... 2-3/4 gallons (10.2 liters)

* All capacities approximate. Add as necessary to bring to the appropriate level.

Cylinder numbering diagram - V6 engine

Brakes

Disc brake pad lining thickness (minimum)... 3/32 inch (2.4 mm)
Brake pedal adjustments
   Free height.. 7.17 to 7.58 inches (182 to 192 mm)
   Reserve distance .... 4.06 to 4.84 inches (103 to 123 mm)
   Freeplay .... 0.12 to 0.43 inch (3 to 11 mm)

Ignition system

Spark plug type
   Four-cylinder engine .... NGK PLZKAR6A-11 or equivalent
   V6 engine
      2005 through 2007.. NGK PLFR5A-11
      2008 and later.. NGK DILFR5A-11
Spark plug gap .... 0.043 inch (1.1 mm)

Torque specifications

	Ft-lbs (unless otherwise indicated)	Nm

Note: One foot-pound (ft-lb) of torque is equivalent to 12 inch-pounds (in-lbs) of torque. Torque values below approximately 15 ft-lbs are expressed in inch-pounds, since most foot-pound torque wrenches are not accurate at these smaller values.

	Ft-lbs	Nm
Engine oil drain plug	25	34
Drivebelt tensioner bolt(s)		
Four-cylinder engine	16	22
V6 engine	41	55
Automatic transmission		
Pan bolts	70 in-lbs	8
Drain plug	25	34
Manual transmission drain/fill plugs	25	35
Transfer case drain/fill plugs	26	35
Differential drain/fill plugs		
2005 through 2008	25	34
2009 and later	32	43
Spark plugs		
Four-cylinder engine	168 in-lbs	20
V6 engine	18	25
Wheel lug nuts	98	133

Engine compartment components - Frontier with a 2.5L four-cylinder engine

1	Brake fluid reservoir	5	Fuse/relay box
2	Spark plugs (not visible)	6	Windshield washer fluid reservoir
3	Engine oil filler cap	7	Radiator cap
4	Engine oil dipstick	8	Coolant reservoir/expansion tank

9	Battery
10	Power steering fluid reservoir
11	Air filter housing

Engine compartment components - 2007 Pathfinder with a 4.0L V6 engine

1	Engine oil dipstick	6	Radiator cap	9	Battery
2	Brake fluid reservoir	7	Radiator hose	10	Power steering fluid reservoir
3	Engine oil filler cap	8	Windshield/rear window washer fluid	11	Automatic transmission fluid dipstick
4	Air filter housing		reservoir		
5	Coolant reservoir/expansion tank				

Engine compartment underside components - 2WD Xterra (4WD Frontier and Xterra similar)

1   Radiator drain plug (behind cover)
2   Engine oil filter (behind cover)
3   Stabilizer bar
4   Tie-rod end
5   Lower control arm bushings
6   Lower control arm balljoint
7   Engine oil drain plug
8   Automatic transmission drain plug

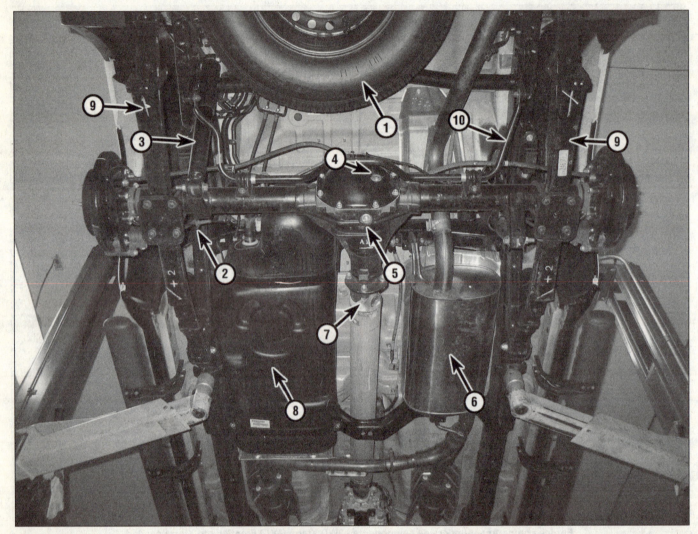

Rear underside components - Xterra (Frontier similar)

1   Spare tire
2   Brake hose
3   Shock absorber
4   Differential lubricant check/fill plug
5   Differential lubricant drain plug
6   Muffler
7   Universal joint
8   Fuel tank
9   Leaf springs
10 Stabilizer bar

Maintenance schedule

The following maintenance intervals are based on the assumption that the vehicle owner will be doing the maintenance or service work, as opposed to having a dealer service department do the work. These are the minimum maintenance intervals recommended by the factory for vehicles that are driven daily. If you wish to keep your vehicle in peak condition at all times, you may wish to perform some of these procedures even more often. Because frequent maintenance enhances the efficiency, performance and resale value of your car, we encourage you to do so. If you drive in dusty areas, tow a trailer, idle or drive at low speeds for extended periods or drive for short distances (less than four miles) in below freezing temperatures, shorter intervals are also recommended.

When the vehicle is new, follow the maintenance schedule to the letter, record the maintenance performed in your owner's manual and keep all receipts to protect the new vehicle warranty. In many cases the initial maintenance check is done at no cost to the owner (check with your dealer service department for more information).

Every 250 miles or weekly, whichever comes first

Check the engine oil level (Section 4)
Check the coolant level (Section 4)
Check the windshield washer fluid level (Section 4)
Check the brake and clutch fluid levels (Section 4)
Check the tires and tire pressures (Section 5)

Every 3000 miles or 3 months, whichever comes first

All items listed above, plus . . .
Check the power steering fluid level (Section 6)
Check the automatic transmission fluid level (Section 7)
Change the engine oil and filter (Section 8)

Every 6000 miles or 6 months, whichever comes first

All items listed above, plus . . .
Check the seat belts (Section 9)
Inspect the windshield wiper blades (Section 10)
Check and service the battery (Section 11)
Check the engine drivebelt (Section 12)
Inspect underhood hoses (Section 13)
Check the cooling system (Section 14)
Rotate the tires (Section 15)
Check the exhaust system (Section 16)

Every 15,000 miles or 12 months, whichever comes first

All items listed above, plus . . .
Check the lubricant level in the front (4x4) and rear axles (Section 17)
Check the manual transmission lubricant level (Section 18)
Check the transfer case lubricant level - 4WD (Section 19)
Lubricate the chassis (Section 20)
Check the fuel system (Section 21)
Check the suspension, steering, and driveaxle boots (Section 22)
Check the brake system (Section 23)*
Replace the cabin air filters (Section 24)

Every 30,000 miles or 24 months, whichever comes first

All items listed above, plus . . .
Change the brake fluid (Section 25)
Replace the air filter (Section 26)*
Inspect the front and rear wheel bearings (Section 27)
Check the evaporative emissions control system (Section 28)
Replace the spark plugs (conventional, non-platinum) (Section 29)
Service the cooling system (drain, flush and refill) (green-colored ethylene glycol anti-freeze only) (Section 30)
Change the automatic transmission fluid and filter (Section 31)**
Replace the Positive Crankcase Ventilation (PCV) valve (Section 32)
If noisy, check and, if necessary, adjust the valve clearances (Chapter 2A or 2B).

Every 60,000 miles or 48 months, whichever comes first

Inspect the spark plug boots and ignition coils (Section 33)
Change the manual transmission lubricant (Section 34)
Change the transfer case lubricant (Section 35)
Change the differential lubricant (Section 36)**

Every 100,000 miles or 60 months, whichever comes first

Replace the spark plugs (platinum type) (Section 29)
Replace the timing belt (V6 engine) (Chapter 2, Part B)
* *This item is affected by "severe" operating conditions, as described below. If the vehicle is operated under severe conditions, perform all maintenance indicated with an asterisk (*) at half the indicated intervals. Severe conditions exist if you mainly operate the vehicle . . .*
in dusty areas
towing a trailer
idling for extended periods
driving at low speeds when outside temperatures remain below freezing and most trips are less than four miles long
** *Perform this procedure at half the recommended interval if operated under one or more of the following conditions:*
in heavy city traffic where the outside temperature regularly reaches 90-degrees F or higher in hilly or mountainous terrain
frequent trailer towing
if the vehicle has been driven through deep water

4.2a Location of the engine oil dipstick - four-cylinder engine

4.2b Location of the engine oil dipstick - V6 engine

2   Introduction

This Chapter is designed to help the home mechanic maintain the Nissan Frontier and Xterra with the goals of maximum performance, economy, safety and reliability in mind.

Included is a master maintenance schedule, followed by procedures dealing specifically with each item on the schedule. Visual checks, adjustments, component replacement and other helpful items are included. Refer to the accompanying illustrations of the engine compartment and the underside of the vehicle for the locations of various components.

Servicing your vehicle in accordance with the mileage/time maintenance schedule and the step-by-step procedures will result in a planned maintenance program that should produce a long and reliable service life. Keep in mind that it's a comprehensive plan, so maintaining some items but not others at the specified intervals will not produce the same results.

As you service your vehicle, you will discover that many of the procedures can - and should - be grouped together because of the nature of the particular procedure you're performing or because of the close proximity of two otherwise unrelated components to one another.

For example, if the vehicle is raised for chassis lubrication, you should inspect the exhaust, suspension, steering and fuel systems while you're under the vehicle. When you're rotating the tires, it makes good sense to check the brakes since the wheels are already removed. Finally, let's suppose you have to borrow or rent a torque wrench. Even if you only need it to tighten the spark plugs, you might as well check the torque of as many critical fasteners as time allows.

The first step in this maintenance program is to prepare yourself before the actual work begins. Read through all the procedures you're planning to do, then gather up all the parts and tools needed. If it looks like you might run into problems during a particular job, seek advice from a mechanic or an experienced do-it-yourselfer.

3   Tune-up general information

The term tune-up is used in this manual to represent a combination of individual operations rather than one specific procedure that will maintain a gasoline engine in proper tune.

If, from the time the vehicle is new, the routine maintenance schedule is followed closely and frequent checks are made of fluid levels and high wear items, as suggested throughout this manual, the engine will be kept in relatively good running condition and the need for additional work will be minimized.

More likely than not, however, there may be times when the engine is running poorly due to lack of regular maintenance. This is even more likely if a used vehicle, which has not received regular and frequent maintenance checks, is purchased. In such cases, an engine tune-up will be needed outside of the regular routine maintenance intervals.

The first step in any tune-up or diagnostic procedure to help correct a poor running engine is a cylinder compression check. A compression check (see Chapter 2C) will help determine the condition of internal engine components and should be used as a guide for tune-up and repair procedures. If, for instance, the compression check indicates serious internal engine wear, a conventional tune-up won't improve the performance of the engine and would be a waste of time and money. Because of its importance, the compression check should be done by someone with the right equipment and the knowledge to use it properly.

The following procedures are those most often needed to bring a generally poor running engine back into a proper state of tune.

Minor tune-up

Check all engine related fluids (Section 4)
Clean, inspect and test the battery (Section 11)
Check the drivebelt (Section 12)
Check all underhood hoses (Section 13)
Check the cooling system (Section 14)

Check the air filter (Section 26)
Replace the spark plugs (Section 29)

Major tune-up

All items listed under Minor tune-up, plus . . .
Replace the air filter (Section 26)
Check the ignition system (Chapter 5)
Check the charging system (Chapter 5)

4   Fluid level checks (every 250 miles or weekly)

Note: *The following are fluid level checks to be done on a 250 mile or weekly basis. Additional fluid level checks can be found in specific maintenance procedures that follow. Regardless of intervals, be alert to fluid leaks under the vehicle, which would indicate a fault to be corrected immediately.*

1   Fluids are an essential part of the lubrication, cooling, brake, clutch and windshield washer systems. Because the fluids gradually become depleted and/or contaminated during normal operation of the vehicle, they must be periodically replenished. See *Recommended lubricants and fluids* at the beginning of this Chapter before adding fluid to any of the following components. **Note:** *The vehicle must be on level ground when fluid levels are checked.*

Engine oil

Refer to illustrations 4.2a, 4.2b, 4.4 and 4.6

2   The engine oil level is checked with a dipstick that extends through a tube and into the oil pan at the bottom of the engine **(see illustrations)**.

3   The oil level should be checked before the vehicle has been driven, or about 5 minutes after the engine has been shut off. If the oil is checked immediately after driving the vehicle, some of the oil will remain in the upper engine components, resulting in an inaccurate reading on the dipstick.

4   Pull the dipstick out of the tube and wipe all the oil from the end with a clean rag or paper towel. Insert the clean dipstick all the

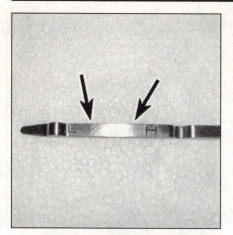

4.4 The oil level must be maintained between the marks at all times - it takes one quart of oil to raise the level from the L to the H mark

4.6 Oil is added to the engine after unscrewing the oil filler cap from the valve cover - always make sure the area around the opening is clean before removing the cap to prevent dirt from contaminating the engine (V6 engine shown)

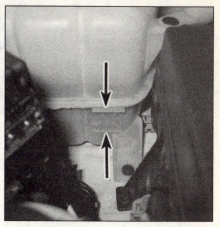

4.8 Keep the coolant level near the MAX mark or MIN mark on the side of the reservoir, depending on engine temperature

way back into the tube, then pull it out again. Note the oil at the end of the dipstick. Add oil as necessary to keep the level between the L and H marks or within the cross-hatched zone on the dipstick (**see illustration**).

5   Do not overfill the engine by adding too much oil since this may result in oil-fouled spark plugs, oil leaks or oil seal failures.

6   Oil is added to the engine after unscrewing a cap from the valve cover (**see illustration**). A funnel may help to reduce spills.

7   Checking the oil level is an important preventive maintenance step. A consistently low oil level indicates oil leakage through damaged seals, defective gaskets or past worn rings or valve guides. If the oil looks milky or has water droplets in it, the cylinder head gasket(s) may be blown or the head(s) or block may be cracked. The engine should be checked immediately. The condition of the oil should also be checked. Whenever you check the oil level, slide your thumb and index finger up the dipstick before wiping off the oil. If you see small dirt or metal particles clinging to the dipstick, the oil should be changed (see Section 8).

Engine coolant

Refer to illustration 4.8

Warning: *Do not allow antifreeze to come in contact with your skin or painted surfaces of the vehicle. Rinse off spills immediately with plenty of water. Antifreeze is highly toxic if ingested. Never leave antifreeze lying around in an open container or in puddles on the floor; children and pets are attracted by its sweet smell and may drink it. Check with local authorities on disposing of used antifreeze. Many communities have collection centers that will see that antifreeze is disposed of safely.*

Note: *Non-toxic antifreeze is now manufactured and available at local auto parts stores, but even this type should be disposed of properly.*

8   All vehicles covered by this manual are equipped with a pressurized coolant recov-

ery system. A white plastic coolant reservoir/expansion tank located in the engine compartment is connected by a hose to the radiator filler neck (**see illustration**).

9   The coolant level in the reservoir should be checked regularly. **Warning:** *Do not remove the pressure cap on the radiator or the reservoir/expansion tank to check the coolant level when the engine is warm.* The level of coolant in the reservoir varies with the temperature of the engine. When the engine is cold, the coolant level should be at or slightly above the MIN mark on the reservoir. Once the engine has warmed up, the level should be at or near the MAX mark. If it isn't, add coolant to the reservoir. To add coolant, simply twist open the cap and add a 50/50 mixture of ethylene glycol based antifreeze and water.

10   Drive the vehicle and recheck the coolant level. If only a small amount of coolant is required to bring the system up to the proper level, water can be used. However, repeated additions of water will dilute the antifreeze and water solution. In order to maintain the proper ratio of antifreeze and water, always top up the coolant level with the correct mixture. An empty plastic milk jug or bleach bottle makes an excellent container for mixing coolant. Do not use rust inhibitors or additives.

11   If the coolant level drops consistently, there may be a leak in the system. Inspect the radiator, hoses, filler cap, drain plugs and water pump (see Section 14). If no leaks are noted, have the radiator cap tested by a service station.

12   If you have to remove the radiator cap or the reservoir/expansion tank cap, wait until the engine has cooled completely, then wrap a thick cloth around the cap and turn it to the first stop. If coolant or steam escapes, let the engine cool down longer, then remove the cap.

13   Check the condition of the coolant as well. It should be relatively clear. If it is brown

or rust colored, the system should be drained, flushed and refilled. Even if the coolant appears to be normal, the corrosion inhibitors wear out, so it must be replaced at the specified intervals.

Windshield washer fluid

Refer to illustration 4.14

14   Fluid for the windshield washer system is located in a plastic reservoir on the right side of the engine compartment (**see illustration**).

15   In milder climates, plain water can be used in the reservoir, but it should be kept no more than 2/3 full to allow for expansion if the water freezes. In colder climates, use windshield washer system antifreeze, available at any auto parts store, to lower the freezing point of the fluid. Mix the antifreeze with water in accordance with the manufacturer's directions on the container. **Caution:** *Don't use cooling system antifreeze - it will damage the vehicle's paint.* **Note:** *To help prevent icing in cold weather, warm the windshield with the defroster before using the washer.*

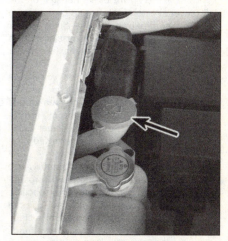

4.14 The windshield washer fluid reservoir is located on the right side of the engine compartment

4.16 The electrolyte level can be checked on original equipment batteries; some have individual cell plugs that can be unscrewed, while others have caps which must be pried off

4.18a Never let the brake fluid level drop below the MIN mark

4.18b Clutch fluid reservoir level marks

Battery electrolyte

Refer to illustration 4.16

16   On models not equipped with a sealed battery, check the electrolyte level of all six battery cells. On models with a translucent battery case, minimum and maximum level marks are present on the side of the case; keep the electrolyte level at the MAX mark. On models with an opaque case, carefully remove the cell caps to check the level or add water. Some batteries have six individual cell plugs that can be unscrewed, but others have two cell caps that must be carefully pried off **(see illustration)**.

17   If the level is low, add *distilled* water until the level is up to the MAX mark (translucent batteries) or up to the bottom of the split-ring indicators (opaque batteries).

Brake and clutch fluid

Refer to illustrations 4.18a and 4.18b

18   The brake master cylinder is mounted on the front of the power brake booster, on the left (driver's) side of the engine compartment firewall **(see illustration)**. The clutch master cylinder used on manual transmission models is mounted next to the brake master cylinder **(see illustration)**.

19   The translucent plastic reservoir allows the fluid inside to be checked without removing the cap. Be sure to wipe the area around either reservoir cap with a clean rag to prevent contamination of the brake and/or clutch system before removing the cap. Keep the fluid level at or near the MAX mark.

20   When adding fluid, pour it carefully into the reservoir to avoid spilling it on surrounding painted surfaces. Be sure the specified fluid is used, since mixing different types of brake fluid can cause damage to the system. See *Recommended lubricants and fluids* at the front of this Chapter or your owner's manual. **Warning:** *Brake fluid can harm your eyes and damage painted surfaces, so use extreme caution when handling or pouring it.*

Do not use brake fluid that has been standing open or is more than one year old. Brake fluid absorbs moisture from the air. Moisture in the system can cause a dangerous loss of brake performance.

21   At this time, the fluid and master cylinder can be inspected for contamination. The system should be drained and refilled if deposits, dirt particles or water droplets are seen in the fluid.

22   After filling the reservoir to the proper level, make sure the cap is on tight to prevent fluid leakage.

23   The brake fluid level in the master cylinder will drop slightly as the pads at the front wheels wear down during normal operation. If the master cylinder requires repeated additions to keep it at the proper level, it's an indication of leakage in the brake system, which should be corrected immediately. Check all brake lines and connections (see Section 23 for more information).

24   If, upon checking the master cylinder fluid level, you discover the reservoir empty or nearly empty, the brake system should be bled and thoroughly inspected (see Chapter 9).

5   Tire and tire pressure checks (every 250 miles or weekly)

Refer to illustrations 5.2, 5.3, 5.4a, 5.4b and 5.8

1   Periodic inspection of the tires may spare you the inconvenience of being stranded with a flat tire. It can also provide you with vital information regarding possible problems in the steering and suspension systems before major damage occurs.

2   The original tires on this vehicle are equipped with 1/2-inch wide wear bands that will appear when tread depth reaches 1/16-inch, at which point the tires can be considered worn out. Tread wear can be monitored with a simple, inexpensive device known as a tread depth indicator **(see illustration)**.

3   Note any abnormal tread wear **(see illustration)**. Tread pattern irregularities such

as cupping, flat spots and more wear on one side than the other are indications of front end alignment and/or balance problems. If any of these conditions are noted, take the vehicle to a tire shop or service station to correct the problem.

4   Look closely for cuts, punctures and embedded nails or tacks. Sometimes a tire will hold air pressure for a short time or leak down very slowly after a nail has embedded itself in the tread. If a slow leak persists, check the valve stem core to make sure it's tight **(see illustration)**. Examine the tread for an object that may have embedded itself in the tire or for a "plug" that may have begun to leak (radial tire punctures are repaired with a plug that's installed in a puncture). If a puncture is suspected, it can be easily verified by spraying a solution of soapy water onto the puncture area **(see illustration)**. The soapy solution will bubble if there's a leak. Unless the puncture is unusually large, a tire shop or service station can usually repair the tire.

5   Carefully inspect the inner sidewall of each tire for evidence of brake fluid leakage. If you see any, inspect the brakes immediately.

6   Correct air pressure adds miles to the lifespan of the tires, improves mileage and

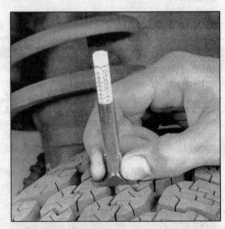

5.2 Use a tire tread depth indicator to monitor tire wear - they are available at auto parts stores and service stations and cost very little

UNDERINFLATION

CUPPING

Cupping may be caused by:
- **Underinflation and/or mechanical irregularities such as out-of-balance condition of wheel and/or tire, and bent or damaged wheel.**
- **Loose or worn steering tie-rod or steering idler arm.**
- **Loose, damaged or worn front suspension parts.**

OVERINFLATION

INCORRECT TOE-IN OR EXTREME CAMBER

FEATHERING DUE TO MISALIGNMENT

5.3 This chart will help you determine the condition of the tires and the probable cause(s) of abnormal wear

enhances overall ride quality. Tire pressure cannot be accurately estimated by looking at a tire, especially if it's a radial. A tire pressure gauge is essential. Keep an accurate gauge in the vehicle. The pressure gauges attached to the nozzles of air hoses at gas stations are often inaccurate.

7   Always check tire pressure when the tires are cold. Cold, in this case, means the vehicle has not been driven over a mile in the three hours preceding a tire pressure check. A pressure rise of four to eight pounds is not uncommon once the tires are warm.

8   Unscrew the valve cap protruding from the wheel or hubcap and push the gauge firmly onto the valve stem **(see illustration)**. Note the reading on the gauge and compare the figure to the recommended tire pressure shown on the placard on the driver's side door pillar. Be sure to reinstall the valve cap to keep dirt and moisture out of the valve stem mechanism. Check all four tires and, if necessary, add enough air to bring them up to the recommended pressure.

9   Don't forget to keep the spare tire inflated to the specified pressure (refer to your owner's manual or the tire sidewall).

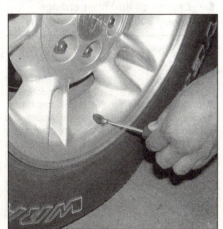

5.4a If a tire loses air on a steady basis, check the valve stem core first to make sure it's snug (special inexpensive wrenches are commonly available at auto parts stores)

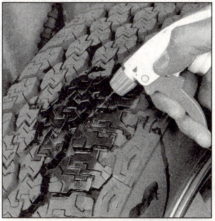

5.4b If the valve stem core is tight, raise the corner of the vehicle with the low tire and spray a soapy water solution onto the tread as the tire is turned slowly - leaks will cause small bubbles to appear

5.8 To extend the life of the tires, check the air pressure at least once a week with an accurate gauge (don't forget the spare!)

6.5 On models with a translucent reservoir, the power steering fluid level can be checked without removing the cap

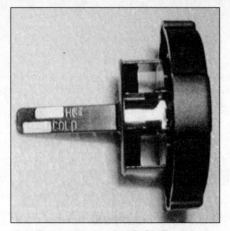

6.6 The power steering fluid dipstick, on models without a translucent reservoir, has marks on it so the fluid can be checked hot or cold

7.3 Remove the bolt securing the automatic transmission dipstick to its bracket, then pull up the dipstick

6 Power steering fluid level check (every 3000 miles or 3 months)

Refer to illustrations 6.5 and 6.6

1   Unlike manual steering, the power steering system relies on fluid which may, over a period of time, require replenishing.
2   All models have remote power steering fluid reservoirs mounted on the right (passenger's) side of the engine compartment. Some models have translucent reservoirs which allow the fluid to be checked without removing the cap; models without translucent reservoirs incorporate a dipstick on the underside of the cap.
3   For the check, the front wheels should be pointed straight ahead and the engine should be off.
4   Use a clean rag to wipe off the reservoir cap and the area around the cap. This will help prevent any foreign matter from entering the reservoir during the check.
5   Feel the reservoir to check the temperature of the fluid. On models with a translucent reservoir, check the level of the fluid on the side of the reservoir **(see illustration)**. The level should be at the HOT or MAX mark if the reservoir was hot to the touch. If the reservoir felt cool, the level should be at the COLD mark (but not below the MIN level).
6   On models with a dipstick, unscrew the cap, wipe off the fluid with a clean rag, reinsert the dipstick, then withdraw it and read the fluid level. The fluid should be at the proper level, depending on whether it was checked hot or cold **(see illustration)**. Never allow the fluid level to drop below the lower mark on the dipstick.
7   If additional fluid is required, pour the specified type directly into the reservoir, using a funnel to prevent spills.
8   If the reservoir requires frequent fluid additions, all power steering hoses, hose connections, steering gear and the power steering pump should be carefully checked for leaks.

7 Automatic transmission fluid level check (every 3000 miles or 3 months)

Refer to illustrations 7.3 and 7.6

1   The automatic transmission fluid level should be carefully maintained. Low fluid level can lead to slipping or loss of drive, while overfilling can cause foaming and loss of fluid.
2   With the parking brake set, start the engine, then move the shift lever through all the gear ranges, ending in Park. The fluid level must be checked with the vehicle level and the engine running at idle. **Note:** *Incorrect fluid level readings will result if the vehicle has just been driven at high speeds for an extended period, in hot weather in city traffic, or if it has been pulling a trailer. If any of these conditions apply, wait until the fluid has cooled (about 30 minutes).*
3   With the transmission at normal operating temperature, remove the dipstick from the filler tube. The dipstick is located at the rear of the engine on the passenger's side **(see illustration)**.
4   Wipe the fluid from the dipstick with a clean rag and push it back into the filler tube until the cap seats.
5   Pull the dipstick out again and note the fluid level.
6   If the fluid is cool to warm, the level should be in the crosshatched area on the COLD side of the dipstick **(see illustration)**. If it's hot, the level should be in the cross-hatched area on the HOT side of the dipstick. If additional fluid is required, add it directly into the tube using a funnel. It takes about one pint to raise the level from the bottom of the crosshatched area to the top with a hot transmission, so add the fluid a little at a time and keep checking the level until it's correct.
7   The condition of the fluid should also be checked along with the level. If the fluid at the end of the dipstick is a dark reddish-brown color, or if it smells burned, it should be changed. If you are in doubt about the condi-

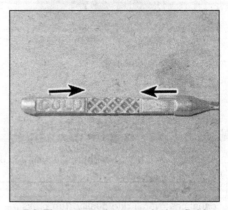

7.6 The automatic transmission fluid must be kept in the cross-hatched area, depending on the fluid temperature

tion of the fluid, purchase some new fluid and compare the two for color and smell.

8 Engine oil and filter change (every 3000 miles or 3 months)

Refer to illustrations 8.3, 8.9, 8.14a, 8.14b, 8.14c and 8.18

1   Frequent oil changes are the most important preventive maintenance procedures that can be done by the home mechanic. As engine oil ages, it becomes diluted and contaminated, which leads to premature engine wear.
2   Although some sources recommend oil filter changes every other oil change, we feel that the minimal cost of an oil filter and the relative ease with which it is installed dictate that a new filter be installed every time the oil is changed.
3   Gather together all necessary tools and materials before beginning this procedure **(see illustration)**.
4   You should have plenty of clean rags and newspapers handy to mop up any spills. Access to the under side of the vehicle may

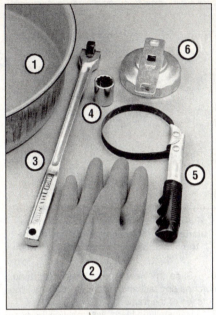

8.3 These tools are required when changing the engine oil and filter

1   ***Drain pan*** - *It should be fairly shallow in depth, but wide to prevent spills*
2   ***Rubber gloves*** - *When removing the drain plug and filter, you will get oil on your hands (the gloves will prevent burns)*
3   ***Breaker bar*** - *Sometimes the oil drain plug is tight, and a long breaker bar is needed to loosen it*
4   ***Socket*** - *To be used with the breaker bar or a ratchet (must be the correct size to fit the drain plug - six-point preferred)*
5   ***Filter wrench*** - *This is a metal band-type wrench, which requires clearance around the filter to be effective*
6   ***Filter wrench*** - *This type fits on the bottom of the filter and can be turned with a ratchet or breaker bar (different-size wrenches are available for different types of filters)*

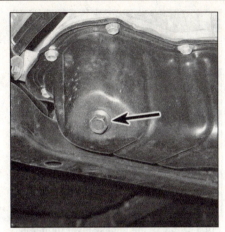

8.9 Use a proper size box-end wrench or socket to remove the oil drain plug and avoid rounding it off

8.14a The oil filter on four-cylinder models is on the right side of the engine block

be improved if the vehicle can be lifted on a hoist, driven onto ramps or supported by jackstands. **Warning:** *Do not work under a vehicle which is supported only by a jack.*

5   If this is your first oil change, familiarize yourself with the locations of the oil drain plug and the oil filter.

6   Warm the engine to normal operating temperature. If the new oil or any tools are needed, use this warm-up time to gather everything necessary for the job. The correct type of oil for your application can be found in *Recommended lubricants and fluids* at the beginning of this Chapter.

7   With the engine oil warm (warm engine oil will drain better and more built-up sludge will be removed with it), raise and support the vehicle. Make sure it's safely supported!

8   Move all necessary tools, rags and newspapers under the vehicle. Set the drain pan under the drain plug. Keep in mind that the oil will initially flow from the pan with some force; position the pan accordingly.

9   Being careful not to touch any of the hot exhaust components, use a box-end wrench or a socket to remove the drain plug near the bottom of the oil pan **(see illustration).**

Depending on how hot the oil is, you may want to wear gloves while unscrewing the plug the final few turns.

10   Allow the oil to drain into the pan. It may be necessary to move the pan as the oil flow slows to a trickle.

11   After all the oil has drained, wipe off the drain plug with a clean rag. Small metal particles may cling to the plug and would immediately contaminate the new oil.

12   Clean the area around the drain plug opening and reinstall the plug. Tighten the plug securely with the wrench. If a torque wrench is available, use it to tighten the plug to the torque listed in this Chapter's Specifications.

13   Move the drain pan into position under the oil filter. If you're working on a model with a four-cylinder engine, remove the right (passenger's) side inner fender panel. It isn't necessary to remove the wheel, but doing so makes removing the oil filter easier.

14   Use the oil filter wrench to loosen the oil filter **(see illustrations)**.

15   Completely unscrew the old filter. Be careful: it's full of oil. Empty the oil inside the filter into the drain pan, then lower the filter.

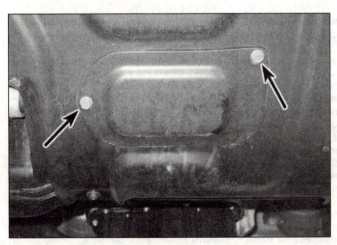

8.14b On V6 models, remove this cover from the engine undercover to access the oil filter

8.14c Oil filter location on V6 models

8.18 Lubricate the oil filter gasket with clean engine oil before installing the filter on the engine

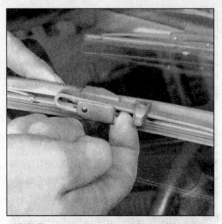

10.3 Depress the release lever (finger is on it here) and slide the wiper assembly down the wiper arm and out of the hook in the end of the arm

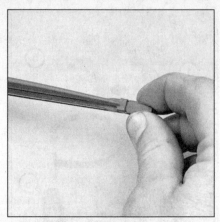

10.4 Squeeze the metal prongs on the blade element to allow it to slide out of the assembly - you may need pliers

16   Compare the old filter with the new one to make sure they're the same type.

17   Use a clean rag to remove all oil, dirt and sludge from the area where the oil filter mounts to the engine. Check the old filter to make sure the rubber gasket isn't stuck to the engine. If the gasket is stuck to the engine (use a flashlight if necessary), remove it.

18   Apply a light coat of clean oil to the rubber gasket on the new oil filter **(see illustration)**.

19   Attach the new filter to the engine, following the tightening directions printed on the filter canister or packing box. Most filter manufacturers recommend against using a filter wrench due to the possibility of overtightening and damage to the seal.

20   If you're working on a four-cylinder model, install the right side inner fender panel. Remove all tools, rags, etc. from under the vehicle, being careful not to spill the oil in the drain pan, then lower the vehicle.

21   Move to the engine compartment and locate the oil filler cap.

22   Pour the fresh oil through the filler opening. A funnel may be helpful.

23   Refer to the engine oil capacity in this Chapter's Specifications and add the proper amount of fresh oil into the engine. Wait a few minutes to allow the oil to drain into the pan, then check the level on the oil dipstick (see Section 4 if necessary). If the oil level is above the hatched area, start the engine and allow the new oil to circulate.

24   Run the engine for only about a minute and then shut it off. Immediately look under the vehicle and check for leaks at the oil pan drain plug and around the oil filter.

25   With the new oil circulated and the filter now completely full, recheck the level on the dipstick and add more oil as necessary.

26   During the first few trips after an oil change, make it a point to check frequently for leaks and proper oil level.

27   The old oil drained from the engine cannot be reused in its present state and should be disposed of. Check with your local auto parts store, disposal facility or environmental agency to see if they will accept the oil for

recycling. After the oil has cooled it can be drained into a container (capped plastic jugs, topped bottles, milk cartons, etc.) for transport to one of these disposal sites. Don't dispose of the oil by pouring it on the ground or down a drain!

9   Seat belt check (every 6000 miles or 6 months)

1   Check the seat belts, buckles, latch plates and guide loops for obvious damage and signs of wear.

2   Where the seat belt receptacle bolts to the floor of the vehicle, check that the bolts are secure.

3   See if the seat belt reminder light comes on when the key is turned to the Run or Start position. A chime should also sound.

10   Wiper blade inspection and replacement (every 6000 miles or 6 months)

Refer to illustrations 10.3 and 10.4

1   The windshield wiper blade elements should be checked periodically for cracks and deterioration.

2   Lift the wiper blade assembly away from the glass.

3   Press the release lever and slide the blade assembly out of the hook in the end of the wiper arm **(see illustration)**.

4   Squeeze the two rubber prongs at the end of the blade element, then slide the element out of the frame **(see illustration)**.

5   Compare the new element with the old for length, design, etc. Some replacement elements come in a three-piece design (two metal strips, one on either side of the rubber) that is held together by several small plastic sleeves. Keep the sleeves in place on this design until you start sliding the element into the frame. Remove each of the plastic sleeves as needed when they reach the frame.

6   Slide the new element into the frame, notched end last and secure the clips into the notches of the frame.

7   Reinstall the blade assembly on the arm, wet the windshield and test for proper operation.

11   Battery check, maintenance and charging (every 6000 miles or 6 months)

Refer to illustrations 11.1, 11.5, 11.6a, 11.6b, 11.7a and 11.7b

Warning: *Certain precautions must be followed when checking and servicing the battery. Hydrogen gas, which is highly flammable, is always present in the battery cells, so keep lighted tobacco and all other open flames and sparks away from the battery. The electrolyte inside the battery is actually dilute sulfuric acid, which will cause injury if splashed on your skin or in your eyes. It will also ruin clothes and painted surfaces. When removing the battery cables, always detach the negative cable first and hook it up last!*

1   A routine preventive maintenance program for the battery in your vehicle is the only way to ensure quick and reliable starts. But before performing any battery maintenance, make sure that you have the proper equipment necessary to work safely around the battery **(see illustration)**.

2   There are also several precautions that should be taken whenever battery maintenance is performed. Before servicing the battery, always turn the engine and all accessories off and disconnect the cable from the negative terminal of the battery.

3   The battery produces hydrogen gas, which is both flammable and explosive. Never create a spark, smoke or light a match around the battery. Always charge the battery in a ventilated area.

4   Electrolyte contains poisonous and corrosive sulfuric acid. Do not allow it to get in your eyes, on your skin or on your clothes. Never ingest it. Wear protective safety glasses

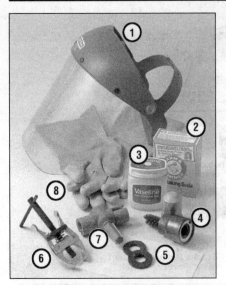

11.1 Tools and materials required for battery maintenance

1 **Face shield/safety goggles** - *When removing corrosion with a brush, the acidic particles can easily fly up into your eyes*

2 **Baking soda** - *A solution of baking soda and water can be used to neutralize corrosion*

3 **Petroleum jelly** - *A layer of this on the battery posts will help prevent corrosion*

4 **Battery post/cable cleaner** - *This wire brush cleaning tool will remove all traces of corrosion from the battery posts and cable clamps*

5 **Treated felt washers** - *Placing one of these on each post, directly under the cable clamps, will help prevent corrosion*

6 **Puller** - *Sometimes the cable clamps are very difficult to pull off the posts, even after the nut/bolt has been completely loosened. This tool pulls the clamp straight up and off the post without damage*

7 **Battery post/cable cleaner** - *Here is another cleaning tool that is a slightly different version of Number 4 above, but it does the same thing*

8 **Rubber gloves** - *Another safety item to consider when servicing the battery; remember that's acid inside the battery!*

when working near the battery. Keep children away from the battery.

5   Note the external condition of the battery. If the positive terminal and cable clamp on your vehicle's battery is equipped with a rubber protector, make sure that it's not torn or damaged. It should completely cover the terminal. Look for any corroded or loose connections, cracks in the case or cover or loose hold-down clamps. Also check the entire length of each cable for cracks and frayed conductors **(see illustration)**.

6   If corrosion, which looks like white, fluffy

Terminal end corrosion or damage.

Insulation cracks.

Chafed insulation or exposed wires.

Burned or melted insulation.

11.5 Typical battery cable problems

deposits is evident, particularly around the terminals, the battery should be removed for cleaning **(see illustration)**. Loosen the cable nuts with a wrench or battery pliers, being careful to remove the ground cable first, and slide them off the terminals **(see illustration)**. Then disconnect the hold-down clamp bolt and nut, remove the clamp and lift the battery from the engine compartment.

7   Clean the cable ends thoroughly with a battery brush or a terminal cleaner and a solution of warm water and baking soda. Wash the terminals and the battery case with the same solution but make sure that the solution doesn't get into the battery. When cleaning the cables, terminals and battery case, wear safety goggles and rubber gloves to prevent any solution from coming in contact with your eyes or hands. Wear old clothes too - even diluted, sulfuric acid splashed onto clothes will burn holes in them. If the terminals have been corroded, clean them up with a terminal cleaner **(see illustrations)**. Thoroughly wash all cleaned areas with plain water.

8   Make sure that the battery tray is in good condition and the hold-down clamp bolts are tight. If the battery is removed from the tray, make sure no parts remain in the bottom of the tray when the battery is reinstalled. When reinstalling the hold-down clamp bolts, do not overtighten them.

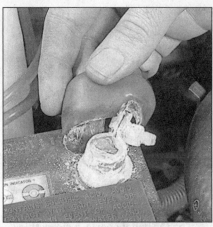

11.6a Battery terminal corrosion usually appears as light, fluffy powder

11.6b If the battery cable terminal is in good shape and not corroded, it can usually be loosened with a wrench - sometimes special battery pliers are required if corrosion has caused deterioration of the nut hex (always remove the ground cable first and hook it up last!)

11.7a When cleaning the cable clamps, all corrosion must be removed (the inside of the clamp is tapered to match the taper on the post, so don't remove too much material)

11.7b Regardless of the type of tool used on the battery posts, a clean, shiny surface should be the result

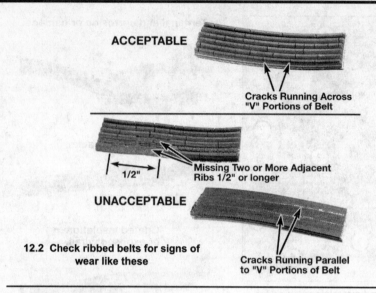

12.2 Check ribbed belts for signs of wear like these

9   Any metal parts of the vehicle damaged by corrosion should be covered with a zinc-based primer, then painted.

10   Information on removing and installing the battery can be found in Chapter 5. Information on jump starting can be found at the front of this manual. For more detailed battery checking procedures, refer to the *Haynes Automotive Electrical Manual*.

Charging

Warning: *When batteries are being charged, hydrogen gas, which is very explosive and flammable, is produced. Do not smoke or allow open flames near a charging or a recently charged battery. Wear eye protection when near the battery during charging. Also, make sure the charger is unplugged before connecting or disconnecting the battery from the charger.*

Note: *It is recommended that the battery be removed from the vehicle for charging because the gas that escapes during this procedure can damage the paint. Fast charging with the battery cables connected can result in damage to the electrical system.*

11   Slow-rate charging is the best way to restore a battery that's discharged to the point where it will not start the engine. It's also a good way to maintain the battery charge in a vehicle that's only driven a few miles between starts. Maintaining the battery charge is particularly important in the winter when the battery must work harder to start the engine and electrical accessories that drain the battery are in greater use.

12   It's best to use a one or two-amp battery charger (sometimes called a "trickle" charger). They are the safest and put the least strain on the battery. They are also the least expensive. For a faster charge, you can use a higher amperage charger, but don't use one rated more than 1/10th the amp/hour rating of the battery. Rapid boost charges that claim to restore the power of the battery in one to two hours are hardest on the battery and can damage batteries not in good condition. This type of charging should only be used in emergency situations.

13   The average time necessary to charge a battery should be listed in the instructions that come with the charger. As a general rule, a trickle charger will charge a battery in 12 to 16 hours.

14   Remove all the cell caps (if equipped - see Section 4) and cover the holes with a clean cloth to prevent spattering electrolyte. Disconnect the negative battery cable and hook the battery charger cable clamps up to the battery posts (positive-to-positive, negative-to-negative), then plug in the charger. Make sure it is set at 12-volts if it has a selector switch.

15   If you're using a charger with a rate higher than two amps, check the battery regularly during charging to make sure it doesn't overheat. If you're using a trickle charger, you can safely let the battery charge overnight after you've checked it regularly for the first couple of hours.

16   If the battery has removable cell caps, measure the specific gravity with a hydrometer every hour during the last few hours of the charging cycle. Hydrometers are available inexpensively from auto parts stores - follow the instructions that come with the hydrometer. Consider the battery charged when there's no change in the specific gravity reading for two hours and the electrolyte in the cells is gassing (bubbling) freely. The specific gravity reading from each cell should be very close to the others. If not, the battery probably has a bad cell(s).

17   Some batteries with sealed tops have built-in hydrometers on the top that indicate the state of charge by the color displayed in the hydrometer window. Normally, a bright-colored hydrometer indicates a full charge and a dark hydrometer indicates the battery still needs charging.

18   If the battery has a sealed top and no built-in hydrometer, you can hook up a digital voltmeter across the battery terminals to check the charge. A fully charged battery should read 12.5 volts or higher.

19   Further information on the battery and

jump-starting can be found in Chapter 5 and at the front of this manual.

12 Drivebelt check and replacement (every 6000 miles or 6 months)

Refer to illustrations 12.2 and 12.4

1   A drivebelt is located at the front of the engine and plays an important role in the overall operation of the engine and its components. Due to its function and material make up, the belt is prone to wear and should be periodically inspected. All models have a single, ribbed serpentine belt to drive all the engine accessories.

Check

Refer to illustrations 12.5a, 12.5b and 12.5c

2   With the engine off, open the hood and use your fingers (and a flashlight, if necessary) to move along the belt, checking for cracks and separation of the belt plies. Also check for fraying and glazing, which gives the belt a shiny appearance **(see illustration)**. Both sides of the belt should be inspected, which means you will have to twist the belt to

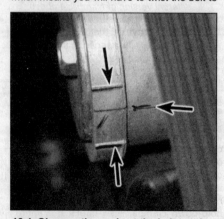

12.4 Observe the scale at the belt tension automatic adjuster; if the fixed mark is at the outer range, replace the belt

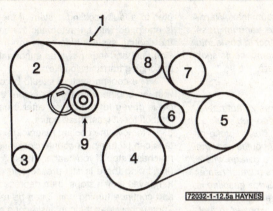

12.5a Drivebelt routing diagram - four-cylinder engine

1	Drivebelt	6	Idler pulley
2	Power steering pump	7	Water pump
3	Alternator	8	Idler pulley
4	Crankshaft pulley	9	Tensioner
5	Air conditioning compressor (if equipped) or idler pulley		

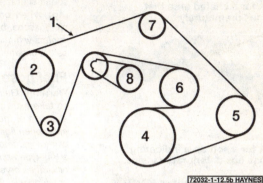

12.5b Drivebelt routing diagram - V6 engine (Frontier/Xterra)

1	Drivebelt	5	Air conditioning compressor
2	Power steering pump	6	Cooling fan pulley
3	Alternator	7	Idler pulley
4	Crankshaft pulley	8	Tensioner

check the underside.

3   Check the ribs on the underside of the belt. They should all be the same depth, with none of the surface uneven.

4   Inspect the indicator marks next to the automatic belt tensioner. If the stationary mark is aligned with the outer limit of the tensioner's travel, the belt has become too loose and must be replaced **(see illustration)**.

Replacement

Refer to illustrations 12.5a, 12.5b and 12.7

5   Refer to the accompanying illustrations for the belt routing diagram for your vehicle **(see illustrations)**.

6   Disconnect the cable from the negative terminal of the battery. Remove the intake air duct and air filter housing (see Chapter 4).

7   To replace the belt, rotate the tensioner to relieve the tension on the belt **(see illustration)**. All models have a square hole in the tensioner arm that will accept a breaker bar or ratchet.

12.7 Use a breaker bar or other square-drive tool in this square opening to rotate the tensioner long enough to remove the drivebelt, then slowly release the tensioner

8   Remove the belt from the auxiliary components and carefully release the tensioner.

9   Route the new belt over the various pulleys, again rotating the tensioner to allow the belt to be installed, then release the belt tensioner. Make sure the belt fits properly into the pulley grooves - it must be completely engaged.

10   Reconnect the battery.

Tensioner replacement

11   Remove the drivebelt.

Four-cylinder engine

12   Unbolt the power steering pump and set it aside without disconnecting the hoses (see Chapter 10).

13   Remove the alternator (see Chapter 5).

14   Remove the three bolts and remove the tensioner assembly.

15   Installation is the reverse of removal. Tighten the bolts to the torque listed in this Chapter's Specifications.

V6 engine

16   Remove the electric engine cooling fan assembly (see Chapter 3).

17   Remove the bolt that secures the drivebelt tensioner to the engine, then remove the tensioner. The idler pulley is also secured by a single bolt.

18   Installation is the reverse of removal. Tighten the mounting bolt to the torque listed in this Chapter's Specifications.

13   Underhood hose check and replacement (every 6000 miles or 6 months)

General

Caution: *Replacement of air conditioning hoses must be left to a dealer service department or air conditioning shop that has the*

equipment to depressurize the system safely and recover the refrigerant. Never remove air conditioning components or hoses until the system has been depressurized.

1   High temperatures in the engine compartment can cause the deterioration of the rubber and plastic hoses used for engine, accessory and emission systems operation. Periodic inspection should be made for cracks, loose clamps, material hardening and leaks. Information specific to the cooling system hoses can be found in Section 14.

2   Some, but not all, hoses are secured to their fittings with clamps. Where clamps are used, check to be sure they haven't lost their tension, allowing the hose to leak. If clamps aren't used, make sure the hose has not expanded and/or hardened where it slips over the fitting, allowing it to leak.

Vacuum hoses

3   It's quite common for vacuum hoses, especially those in the emissions system, to be color-coded or identified by colored stripes molded into them. Various systems require hoses with different wall thickness, collapse resistance and temperature resistance. When replacing hoses, be sure the new ones are made of the same material.

4   Often the only effective way to check a hose is to remove it completely from the vehicle. If more than one hose is removed, be sure to label the hoses and fittings to ensure correct installation.

5   When checking vacuum hoses, be sure to include any plastic T-fittings in the check. Inspect the fittings for cracks and the hose where it fits over the fitting for distortion, which could cause leakage.

6   A small piece of vacuum hose (1/4-inch inside diameter) can be used as a stethoscope to detect vacuum leaks. Hold one end of the hose to your ear and probe around vacuum hoses and fittings, listening for the "hissing"

Check for a chafed area that could fail prematurely.

Check for a soft area indicating the hose has deteriorated inside.

Overtightening the clamp on a hardened hose will damage the hose and cause a leak.

Check each hose for swelling and oil-soaked ends. Cracks and breaks can be located by squeezing the hose.

14.4 Hoses, like drivebelts, have a habit of failing at the worst possible time - to prevent the inconvenience of a blown radiator or heater hose, inspect them carefully as shown here

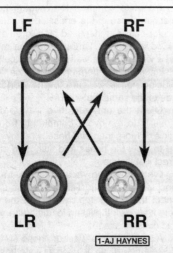

15.2 The recommended four-tire rotation pattern for non-directional radial tires

sound characteristic of a vacuum leak. **Warning:** *When probing with the vacuum hose stethoscope, be very careful not to come into contact with moving engine components such as the drivebelt, cooling fan, etc.*

Fuel hose

Warning: *Gasoline is extremely flammable, so take extra precautions when you work on any part of the fuel system. Don't smoke or allow open flames or bare light bulbs near the work area, and don't work in a garage where a gas-type appliance (such as a water heater or clothes dryer) is present. Since gasoline is carcinogenic, wear fuel-resistant gloves when there's a possibility of being exposed to fuel, and, if you spill any fuel on your skin, rinse it off immediately with soap and water. Mop up any spills immediately and do not store fuel-soaked rags where they could ignite. When you perform any kind of work on the fuel system, wear safety glasses and have a Class B type fire extinguisher on hand. The fuel system is under pressure, so if any lines must be disconnected, the pressure in the system must be relieved first (see Chapter 4 for more information).*

7   Check all rubber fuel lines for deterioration and chafing. Check especially for cracks in areas where the hose bends and just before fittings, such as where a hose attaches to the fuel filter and fuel injection unit.

8   High quality fuel line, specifically designed for high-pressure fuel injection applications, must be used for fuel line replacement. Never, under any circumstances, use regular fuel line, unreinforced vacuum line, clear plastic tubing or water hose for fuel lines.

9   Spring-type (pinch) clamps are commonly used on fuel lines. These clamps often lose their tension over a period of time, and can be "sprung" during removal. Replace all spring-type clamps with screw clamps whenever a hose is replaced.

Metal lines

10   Sections of metal line are routed along the frame, between the fuel tank and the engine. Check carefully to be sure the line has not been bent or crimped and no cracks have started in the line.

11   If a section of metal fuel line must be replaced, only seamless steel tubing should be used, since copper and aluminum tubing don't have the strength necessary to withstand normal engine vibration.

12   Check the metal brake lines where they enter the master cylinder and brake proportioning unit for cracks in the lines or loose fittings. Any sign of brake fluid leakage calls for an immediate and thorough inspection of the brake system.

---

14   Cooling system check (every 6000 miles or 6 months)

Refer to illustration 14.4

1   Many major engine failures can be attrib-

uted to a faulty cooling system. If the vehicle is equipped with an automatic transmission, the cooling system also cools the transmission fluid and thus plays an important role in prolonging transmission life.

2   The cooling system should be checked with the engine cold. Do this before the vehicle is driven for the day or after it has been shut off for at least three hours.

3   Remove the coolant reservoir/expansion tank cap by turning it counterclockwise until it reaches a stop. If you hear any hissing sounds (indicating there is still pressure in the system), wait until it stops, then depress the cap and continue turning until it can be removed. Thoroughly clean the cap, inside and out, with clean water. Also remove the radiator cap and clean the filler neck on the radiator. All traces of corrosion should be removed. The coolant inside the radiator (and coolant reservoir) should be relatively transparent. If it is rust colored, the system should be drained and refilled (see Section 30). If the coolant level is low, add additional antifreeze/coolant mixture (see Section 4).

4   Carefully check the large upper and lower radiator hoses along with any smaller diameter heater hoses that run from the engine to the firewall. Inspect each hose along its entire length, replacing any hose that is cracked, swollen or shows signs of deterioration. Cracks may become more apparent if the hose is squeezed **(see illustration)**.

5   Make sure all hose connections are tight. A leak in the cooling system will usually show up as white or rust-colored deposits on the areas adjoining the leak. If spring-type clamps are used at the ends of the hoses, it may be wise to replace them with more secure, screw-type clamps.

6   Use compressed air or a soft brush to remove bugs, leaves, etc. from the front of the radiator or air conditioning condenser. Be careful not to damage the delicate cooling fins or cut yourself on them.

7   Every other inspection, or at the first indication of cooling system problems, have the cap and system pressure tested. If you don't have a pressure tester, most gas stations and repair shops will do this for a minimal charge.

---

15   Tire rotation (every 6000 miles or 6 months)

Refer to illustration 15.2

1   The tires should be rotated at the specified intervals and whenever uneven wear is noticed.

2   Tires must be rotated in the recommended pattern **(see illustration)**.

3   Refer to the information in *Jacking and towing* at the front of this manual for the proper procedures to follow when raising the vehicle and changing a tire. If the brakes are to be checked, don't apply the parking brake as stated. Make sure the tires are blocked to prevent the vehicle from rolling as it's raised. Before raising the vehicle, loosen the wheel

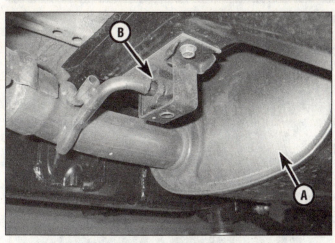

16.2a Inspect the muffler (A) for signs of deterioration, and all hangers (B)

16.2b Inspect all flanged joints for signs of exhaust gas leakage

lug nuts slightly.

4   Preferably, the entire vehicle should be raised at the same time. This can be done on a hoist or by jacking up each corner and then lowering the vehicle onto jackstands placed under the frame rails. Always use four jackstands and make sure the vehicle is safely supported.

5   After rotation, check and adjust the tire pressures as necessary. Tighten the lug nuts to the torque listed in this Chapter's Specifications.

16 Exhaust system check (every 6,000 miles or 6 months)

Refer to illustrations 16.2a and 16.2b

1   With the engine cold (at least three hours after the vehicle has been driven), check the complete exhaust system from the manifold to the end of the tailpipe. Be careful around the catalytic converter, which may be hot even after three hours. The inspection should be done with the vehicle on a hoist to permit unrestricted access. If a hoist isn't available,

raise the vehicle and support it securely on jackstands.

2   Check the exhaust pipes and connections for signs of leakage and/or corrosion indicating a potential failure. Make sure that all brackets and hangers are in good condition and tight **(see illustrations)**.

3   Inspect the underside of the body for holes, corrosion, open seams, etc. which may allow exhaust gasses to enter the passenger compartment. Seal all body openings with silicone sealant or body putty.

4   Rattles and other noises can often be traced to the exhaust system, especially the hangers, mounts and heat shields. Try to move the pipes, mufflers and catalytic converter. If the components can come in contact with the body or suspension parts, secure the exhaust system with new brackets and hangers.

17 Differential lubricant level check (every 15,000 miles or 12 months)

Refer to illustrations 17.2a and 17.2b
Note: *4WD vehicles have two differentials -*

one in the center of each axle. 2WD vehicles have one differential - in the center of the rear axle. On 4WD vehicles, be sure to check the lubricant level in both differentials.

1   The check/filler plug on the differential(s) is a threaded metal type and can be loosened with a 1/2-inch drive ratchet or breaker bar (rear) or a large hex bit (front). If the vehicle is raised to gain access to the plug, be sure to support it safely on jackstands - DO NOT crawl under the vehicle when it's supported only by the jack. Be sure the vehicle is level or the check may not be accurate.

2   Remove the plug from the filler hole in the differential housing or cover **(see illustrations)**.

3   The lubricant level should be up to the bottom of the filler hole. If not, use a pump or squeeze bottle to add the recommended lubricant until it just starts to run out of the opening.

4   Install the plug in the filler hole and tighten it to the torque listed in this Chapter's Specifications.

17.2a Remove the rear axle filler plug to check the differential lubricant level

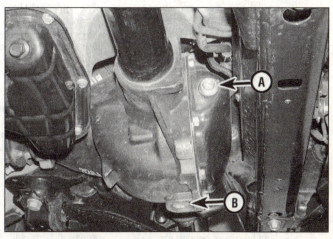

17.2b Front differential filler plug (A) and drain plug (B) - 4WD models

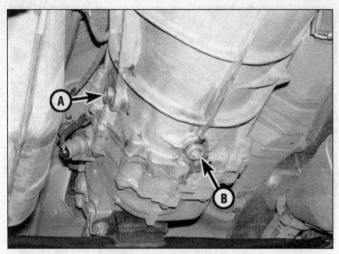

18.2 Manual transmission filler plug (A) and drain plug (B)

19.1 Transfer case filler plug (A) (the drain plug is on the other side)

18 Manual transmission lubricant level check (every 15,000 miles or 12 months)

Refer to illustration 18.2

1   The manual transmission has a filler plug which must be removed to check the lubricant level. If the vehicle is raised to gain access to the plug, be sure to support it safely on jackstands - DO NOT crawl under a vehicle that is supported only by a jack! Be sure the vehicle

20.1 Materials required for chassis and body lubrication

1   *Engine oil* - Light engine oil in a can like this can be used for door and hood hinges
2   *Graphite spray* - Used to lubricate lock cylinders
3   *Grease* - Grease, in a variety of types and weights, is available for use in a grease gun. Check the Specifications for your requirements
4   *Grease gun* - A common grease gun, shown here with a detachable hose and nozzle, is needed for chassis lubrication. After use, clean it thoroughly!

is level or the check may be inaccurate.
2   Using the appropriate wrench, unscrew the plug from the transmission **(see illustration)**.
3   Use your little finger to reach inside the housing to feel the lubricant level. The level should be at or near the bottom of the plug hole. If it isn't, add the recommended lubricant through the plug hole with a syringe or squeeze bottle.
4   Install and tighten the plug. Check for leaks after the first few miles of driving.

19 Transfer case lubricant level check (4WD models) (every 15,000 miles or 12 months)

Refer to illustration 19.1

1   The transfer case lubricant level is checked by removing the upper plug located at the rear of the case **(see illustration)**.
2   After removing the plug, reach inside the hole. The lubricant level should be just at the bottom of the hole. If not, add the appropriate lubricant through the opening.

20 Chassis lubrication (every 15,000 miles or 12 months)

Refer to illustration 20.1

1   Refer to *Recommended lubricants and fluids* at the front of this Chapter to obtain the necessary grease, etc. You'll also need a grease gun **(see illustration)**. If a suspension component has no grease fitting in place, this indicates the part is sealed and doesn't require periodic lubrication.
2   Look under the vehicle and locate the grease fittings. Occasionally, plugs may be installed rather than grease fittings. If so, grease fittings will have to be purchased and installed (they're available at auto parts stores).

3   For easier access under the vehicle, raise it with a jack and place jackstands under the frame. Make sure it's safely supported by the stands. If the wheels are to be removed at this interval for tire rotation or brake inspection, loosen the lug nuts slightly while the vehicle is still on the ground.
4   Before beginning, force a little grease out of the nozzle to remove any dirt from the end of the gun. Wipe the nozzle clean with a rag.
5   With the grease gun and plenty of clean rags, crawl under the vehicle and begin lubricating the components.
6   Wipe one of the grease fittings clean and push the nozzle firmly over it. Pump the gun until the component is completely lubricated. On balljoints, stop pumping when the rubber seal is firm to the touch. Do not pump too much grease into the fitting as it could rupture the seal. For all other suspension and steering components, continue pumping grease into the fitting until it oozes out of the joint between the two components. If it escapes around the grease gun nozzle, the fitting is clogged or the nozzle is not completely seated on the fitting. Resecure the gun nozzle to the fitting and try again. If necessary, replace the fitting with a new one.
7   Wipe the excess grease from the components and the grease fitting. Repeat the procedure for the remaining fittings.
8   Clean the fitting and pump grease into the driveline universal joints until the grease can be seen coming out of the contact points. The other U-joints are sealed and do not require lubrication. **Note:** *Most replacement driveshaft U-joints aren't permanently sealed, and are sold with grease fittings. If your U-joints have been replaced, make sure you include them in your routine chassis lubrication.*
9   Also clean and lubricate the parking brake cable guides and levers. **Caution:** *Do not use chassis lubrication on the brake cables themselves. The grease will cause the cable housings to deteriorate.*

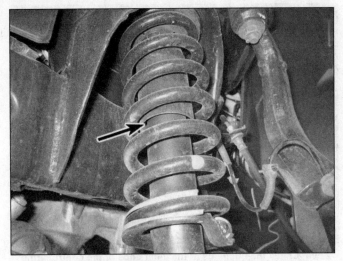

22.6a Check for signs of fluid leakage at this point on shock absorbers (rear shock shown)

22.6b Check the front shock absorbers for fluid leakage where the piston rod enters the shock body

21 Fuel system check (every 15,000 miles or 12 months)

Warning: *Gasoline is extremely flammable, so take extra precautions when you work on any part of the fuel system. Don't smoke or allow open flames or bare light bulbs near the work area, and don't work in a garage where a gas-type appliance (such as a water heater or clothes dryer) is present. Since gasoline is carcinogenic, wear fuel-resistant gloves when there's a possibility of being exposed to fuel, and, if you spill any fuel on your skin, rinse it off immediately with soap and water. Mop up any spills immediately and do not store fuel-soaked rags where they could ignite. When you perform any kind of work on the fuel system, wear safety glasses and have a Class B type fire extinguisher on hand. The fuel system is under constant pressure, so, before any lines are disconnected, the fuel system pressure must be relieved (see Chapter 4).*

1   If you smell gasoline while driving or after the vehicle has been sitting in the sun, inspect the fuel system immediately.

2   Remove the fuel filler cap and inspect it for damage and corrosion. The gasket should have an unbroken sealing imprint. If the gasket is damaged or corroded, install a new cap.

3   Inspect the fuel feed and return lines for cracks. Make sure that the connections between the fuel lines and the fuel injection system are tight. **Warning:** *Your vehicle is fuel injected, so you must relieve the fuel system pressure before servicing fuel system components. The fuel system pressure relief procedure is described in Chapter 4.*

4   If the fuel injectors are visible, look for signs of fuel leakage (wet spots) around any of the injectors - they may need new O-rings (see Chapter 4).

5   Since some components of the fuel system - the fuel tank and part of the fuel feed

and return lines, for example - are underneath the vehicle, they can be inspected more easily with the vehicle raised on a hoist. If that's not possible, raise the vehicle and support it securely on jackstands.

6   With the vehicle raised and safely supported, inspect the fuel tank and filler neck for punctures, cracks and other damage. The connection between the filler neck and the tank is particularly critical. Sometimes a rubber filler neck will leak because of loose clamps or deteriorated rubber. Inspect all fuel tank mounting brackets and straps to be sure that the tank is securely attached to the vehicle. **Warning:** *Do not, under any circumstances, try to repair a fuel tank (except rubber components). A welding torch or any open flame can easily cause fuel vapors inside the tank to explode.*

7   Carefully check all rubber hoses and metal lines leading away from the fuel tank. Check for loose connections, deteriorated hoses, crimped lines and other damage. Repair or replace damaged sections as necessary (see Chapter 4).

8   The evaporative emissions control system can also be a source of fuel odors. The function of the system is to store fuel vapors from the fuel tank in a charcoal canister until they can be routed to the intake manifold, where they mix with incoming air before being burned in the combustion chambers.

9   The most common symptom of a faulty evaporative emissions system is a strong odor of fuel near the charcoal canister, which is mounted under the rear of the vehicle on all models. If a fuel odor has been detected, and you have already checked the areas described above, check the charcoal canister and the hoses connected to it (see Section 28).

22 Suspension, steering and driveaxle boot check (every 15,000 miles or 12 months)

Note: *The steering linkage and suspension components should be checked periodically. Worn or damaged suspension and steering linkage components can result in excessive and abnormal tire wear, poor ride quality and vehicle handling and reduced fuel economy. For detailed illustrations of the steering and suspension components, refer to Chapter 10.*

Shock absorber check

Refer to illustrations 22.6a and 22.6b

1   Park the vehicle on level ground, turn the engine off and set the parking brake. Check the tire pressures.

2   Push down at one corner of the vehicle, then release it while noting the movement of the body. It should stop moving and come to rest in a level position within one or two bounces.

3   If the vehicle continues to move up-and-down or if it fails to return to its original position, a worn or weak shock absorber is probably the reason.

4   Repeat the above check at each of the three remaining corners of the vehicle.

5   Raise the vehicle and support it securely on jackstands.

6   Check the shock absorbers for evidence of fluid leakage **(see illustrations)**. A light film of fluid is no cause for concern. Make sure that any fluid noted is from the shocks and not from some other source. If leakage is noted, replace the shocks as a set (front or rear).

7   Check the shocks to be sure they are securely mounted and undamaged. Check the upper mounts for damage and wear. If damage or wear is noted, replace the shocks as a set (front or rear).

8   If the shocks must be replaced, refer to Chapter 10 for the procedure.

22.9a Check the bushings at the inner ends of the control arms for deterioration

22.9b Inspect the tie-rod ends (A) and the balljoints (B, lower balljoint)

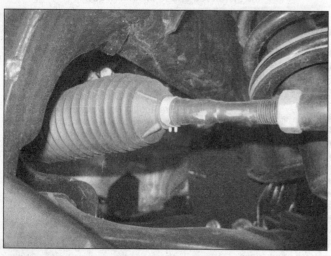

22.9c Inspect the steering gear boots for signs of cracking or fluid leakage (if fluid leakage is noted, the rack seals are faulty)

22.11 With the steering wheel in the locked position and the vehicle raised, grasp the front tire as shown and try to move it back-and-forth - if any play is noted, check the steering gear mounts and tie-rod ends for looseness

Steering and suspension check

Refer to illustrations 22.9a, 22.9b, 22.9c and 22.11

9   Visually inspect the steering and suspension components (front and rear) for damage and distortion. Look for damaged seals, boots and bushings and leaks of any kind. Examine the bushings where the control arms meet the chassis **(see illustrations)**.

10   Clean the lower end of the steering knuckle. Have an assistant grasp the lower edge of the tire and move the wheel in-and-out while you look for movement at the steering knuckle-to-control arm balljoint. If there is any movement, the suspension balljoint(s) must be replaced.

11   Grasp each front tire at the front and rear edges, push in at the front, pull out at the rear and feel for play in the steering system components. If any freeplay is noted, check the idler arm and the tie-rod ends for looseness **(see illustration)**.

12   Additional steering and suspension system information and illustrations can be found in Chapter 10.

Driveaxle boot check (4WD models)

Refer to illustration 22.14

13   The driveaxle boots are very important because they prevent dirt, water and foreign material from entering and damaging the constant velocity (CV) joints. Oil and grease can cause the boot material to deteriorate prematurely, so it's a good idea to wash the boots with soap and water. Because it constantly pivots back and forth following the steering action of the front hub, the outer CV boot wears out sooner and should be inspected regularly.

14   Inspect the boots for tears and cracks as well as loose clamps **(see illustration)**. If there is any evidence of cracks or leaking lubricant, they must be replaced as described in Chapter 8.

22.14 Inspect the inner and outer driveaxle boots on 4WD models for loose clamps, cracks or signs of leaking lubricant

23.7 With the wheel off, check the thickness of the inner brake pads through the inspection hole

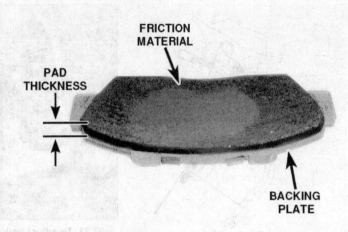

23.9 If a more precise measurement of pad thickness is necessary, remove the pads and measure the remaining friction material

23 Brake system check (every 15,000 miles or 12 months)

Warning: *The dust created by the brake system is harmful to your health. Never blow it out with compressed air and don't inhale any of it. An approved filtering mask should be worn when working on the brakes. Do not, under any circumstances, use petroleum-based solvents to clean brake parts. Use brake system cleaner only! Try to use non-asbestos replacement parts whenever possible.*

Note: *For detailed photographs of the brake system, refer to Chapter 9.*

1   In addition to the specified intervals, the brakes should be inspected every time the wheels are removed or whenever a defect is suspected.

2   Any of the following symptoms could indicate a potential brake system defect: The vehicle pulls to one side when the brake pedal is depressed; the brakes make squealing or dragging noises when applied; brake pedal travel is excessive; the pedal pulsates; or brake fluid leaks, usually onto the inside of the tire or wheel.

3   Loosen the wheel lug nuts.

4   Raise the vehicle and place it securely on jackstands.

5   Remove the wheels (see *Jacking and towing* at the front of this book, or your owner's manual, if necessary).

Disc brakes

Refer to illustrations 23.7, 23.9 and 23.11

6   There are two pads (an outer and an inner) in each caliper. The pads are visible with the wheels removed.

7   Check the pad thickness by looking at each end of the caliper and through the inspection window in the caliper body **(see illustration)**. If the lining material is less than the thickness listed in this Chapter's Specifications, replace the pads. **Note:** *Keep in mind that the lining material is riveted or bonded to*

a metal backing plate and the metal portion is not included in this measurement.

8   If it is difficult to determine the exact thickness of the remaining pad material by the above method, or if you are at all concerned about the condition of the pads, remove the pads for further inspection (see Chapter 9).

9   Once the pads are removed from the calipers, clean them with brake cleaner and re-measure them with a ruler or a vernier caliper **(see illustration)**.

10   Measure the disc thickness with a micrometer to make sure that it still has service life remaining. If any disc is thinner than the specified minimum thickness, replace it (see Chapter 9). Even if the disc has service life remaining, check its condition. Look for scoring, gouging and burned spots. If these conditions exist, remove the disc and have it resurfaced (see Chapter 9).

11   Before installing the wheels, check all brake lines and hoses for damage, wear, deformation, cracks, corrosion, leakage, bends and twists, particularly in the vicinity of the rubber hoses at the calipers **(see illustration)**. Check the clamps for tightness and

the connections for leakage. Make sure that all hoses and lines are clear of sharp edges, moving parts and the exhaust system. If any of the above conditions are noted, repair, reroute or replace the lines and/or fittings as necessary (see Chapter 9).

Brake booster check

12   Sit in the driver's seat and perform the following sequence of tests.

13   With the brake fully depressed, start the engine - the pedal should move down a little when the engine starts.

14   With the engine running, depress the brake pedal several times - the travel distance should not change.

15   Depress the brake, stop the engine and hold the pedal in for about 30 seconds - the pedal should neither sink nor rise.

16   Restart the engine, run it for about a minute and turn it off. Then firmly depress the brake several times - the pedal travel should decrease with each application.

17   If your brakes do not operate as described, the brake booster has failed. Refer to Chapter 9 for the replacement procedure.

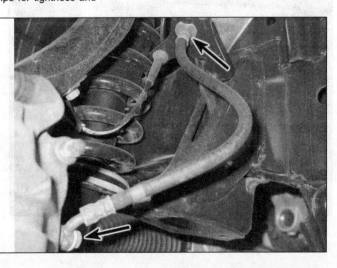

23.11 Check along the brake hoses and at each fitting for seepage, deterioration and cracks

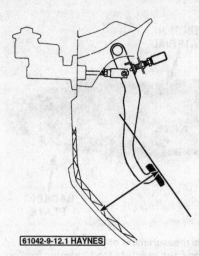

23.19 With the brake pedal fully released, measure the distance from the top of the pad to the floor

23.21 To adjust brake pedal released height, loosen the locknut in front of the brake booster clevis and turn the input rod until free height is correct (this procedure is also used to adjust brake pedal freeplay)

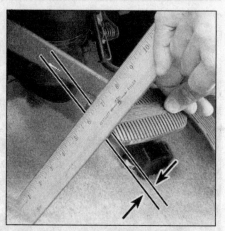

23.25 To measure brake pedal freeplay, press down lightly on the brake pedal and measure the distance that it moves freely before resistance is felt

Parking brake

18   One method of checking the parking brake is to park the vehicle on a steep hill with the parking brake set and the transmission in Neutral (be sure to stay in the vehicle during this check!). If the parking brake cannot prevent the vehicle from rolling, it's in need of adjustment (see Chapter 9).

Brake pedal

Brake pedal released height

Refer to illustrations 23.19 and 23.21

19   Peel back the carpet and insulator pad. With the brake pedal fully released, measure the distance from the top of the pad to the floor **(see illustration)**.
20   If the height is not as listed in the Specifications Section at the beginning of this Chapter, it must be adjusted.
21   Loosen the locknut just in front of the power brake booster clevis **(see illustration)**.
22   Turn the booster input rod until the pedal height is correct.

23   Tighten the locknut.
24   After adjusting the pedal height, check the freeplay. It may also be necessary to adjust the brake light switch (see Chapter 9).

Brake pedal freeplay

Refer to illustration 23.25

25   Press down lightly on the brake pedal and measure the distance that it moves freely before resistance is felt **(see illustration)**. The freeplay should be within the specified limits. If it isn't, it must be adjusted.
26   Loosen the locknut for the brake booster clevis **(see illustration 23.21)**.
27   Turn the booster input rod until the pedal freeplay is correct.
28   Tighten the locknut.

Brake pedal depressed height

29   After checking and, if necessary, adjusting the pedal released height and freeplay, the pedal depressed height must be checked.
30   With the engine running, press the brake

pedal fully and measure the pedal pad-to-floor distance.
31   If the minimum depressed height is below that listed in the Specifications Section at the beginning of this Chapter, check the brake system for leaks or other damage.

24   Cabin air filters - replacement (every 15,000 miles or 12 months)

Refer to illustrations 24.2, 24.3, and 24.5

1   The manufacturer recommends replacing the cabin air filters at the specified interval, to maintain the performance of the HVAC system.
2   Open the glove box and squeeze in the two sides, then allow the glove box door to drop all the way down **(see illustration)**.
3   Remove the bolt securing the cover of the filter drawer in the heating/air conditioning unit, then remove the cover **(see illustration)**. Note: *The first time the filter cover is removed, the factory plastic retaining tab will break off. When reinstalling the cover, install*

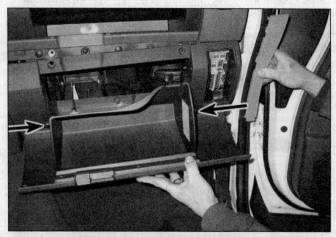

24.2 Squeeze in the sides of the glove box to allow it to drop down

24.3 Remove the filter cover; when reinstalling the cover, bolt it to the tab provided

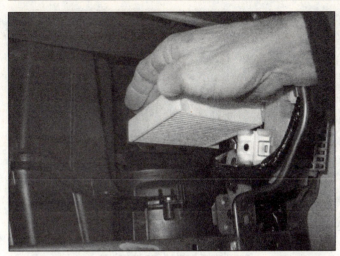

24.5 When the two new filters are inserted properly, the airflow indicator arrows should point down

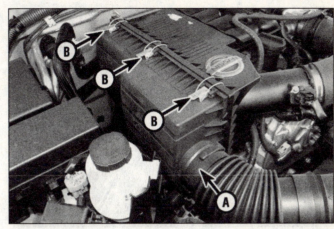

26.1a To replace the four-cylinder air filter, twist the air inlet hose (A) counterclockwise to remove, then release the three clamps (B) and move the housing away from the intake manifold to access the filter

a wire-tie or a small bolt and nut to secure the cover to the tab provided.

4   Withdraw the two filters.

5   Install the new filters, which are marked with arrows to indicate which side faces down. The ends marked with the arrow should be visible when the new filters are installed **(see illustration)**. **Note:** *Install one filter first and nudge it to the right as far as it will go before installing the second filter.*

6   The remainder of installation is the reverse of the removal procedure.

25 Brake fluid change (every 30,000 miles or 24 months)

Warning: *Brake fluid can harm your eyes and damage painted surfaces, so use extreme caution when handling or pouring it. Do not use brake fluid that has been standing open or is more than one year old. Brake fluid absorbs moisture from the air. Excess moisture can cause a dangerous loss of braking effectiveness.*

1   At the specified intervals, the brake fluid

should be drained and replaced. Since the brake fluid may drip or splash when pouring it, place plenty of rags around the master cylinder to protect any surrounding painted surfaces.

2   Before beginning work, purchase the specified brake fluid (see *Recommended lubricants and fluids* at the beginning of this Chapter).

3   Remove the cap from the master cylinder reservoir.

4   Using a hand suction pump or similar device, withdraw the fluid from the master cylinder reservoir.

5   Add new fluid to the master cylinder until it rises to the line indicated on the reservoir.

6   Bleed the brake system as described in Chapter 9 at all four brakes until new and uncontaminated fluid is expelled from the bleeder screw. Be sure to maintain the fluid level in the master cylinder as you perform the bleeding process. If you allow the master cylinder to run dry, air will enter the system.

7   Refill the master cylinder with fluid and check the operation of the brakes. The pedal should feel solid when depressed, with no

sponginess. **Warning:** *Do not operate the vehicle if you are in doubt about the effectiveness of the brake system.*

26 Air filter replacement (every 30,000 miles or 24 months)

Refer to illustrations 26.1a, 26.1b and 26.1c

1   The air filter on four-cylinder models is contained within a housing attached to the side of the intake manifold assembly. To change the filter, unlatch the clips at the intake manifold and pull the outer cover away, then pull out the old filter element **(see illustration)**. On V6 engines, the filter housing is near the left-front of the engine compartment. Release the two clips securing the housing halves and pull the upper half away enough to remove the filter element **(see illustrations)**.

2   Inspect the outer surface of the filter element. If it is dirty, replace it. If it is only moderately dusty, it can be reused by blowing it clean from the back to the front surface with compressed air. Because it is a pleated paper type filter, it cannot be washed or oiled. If it

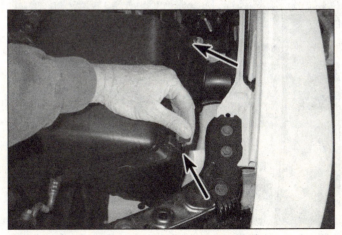

26.1b On V6 models, release the clips on the filter housing . . .

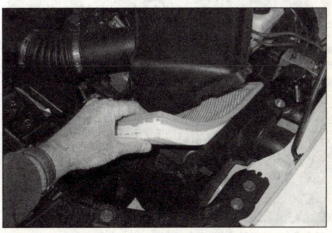

26.1c . . . then lift the cover, slide the old filter out and insert a new filter

27.2 Check the front wheel bearing assembly for play or noise when spinning it

27.3 Front wheel bearing assembly-to-knuckle mounting bolts (seen from behind the knuckle)

cannot be cleaned satisfactorily with compressed air, discard and replace it. While the cover is off, be careful not to drop anything down into the housing. **Caution:** *Never drive the vehicle with the air cleaner removed. Excessive engine wear could result and backfiring could even cause a fire under the hood.*

3   Wipe out the inside of the air cleaner housing.

4   Place the new filter into the air cleaner housing, making sure it seats properly.

5   Installation of the cover is the reverse of removal.

27   Wheel bearings - inspection and replacement (every 30,000 miles or 24 months)

Refer to illustrations 27.2, 27.3, 27.5 and 27.6

Front

1   Loosen the wheel lug nuts. Raise the front of the vehicle and support it on jackstands, then chock the wheels at the rear of the vehicle.

2   Remove the wheel and inspect the wheel bearing for signs of damage or excessive rust. The front wheel bearings are inside a sealed housing with permanent lubrication and require no adjustment. Spin the wheel bearing assembly, listening for unusual noise and feeling for any roughness **(see illustration)**. Try to move the bearing assembly in or out, and try to tilt it relative to the knuckle. If there is any noise or play in the assembly, it must be replaced.

3   The sealed bearing assembly is bolted to the steering knuckle. If the bearing assembly must be replaced, remove the driveaxle (4WD models, see Chapter 8), remove the four bolts at the rear of the steering knuckle and remove the bearing assembly **(see illustration)**. Install the new assembly to the knuckle and torque the bolts to the Specification in Chapter 10. **Note:** *Always replace wheel bearings in pairs - both fronts or both rears at the same time.*

Rear

4   The rear wheel bearings are mounted at the outboard ends of the axle housing. Check the axle bearings with both rear wheels

removed and the transmission in Neutral. Make sure the vehicle is properly supported and the front wheels are chocked to prevent movement. Listen and feel for noise or roughness in the rear axle bearings. There should be no axial play when trying to move the axle.

5   The axle bearings are secured to the axle and must be pressed off and new ones pressed on. Refer to Chapter 9 and remove the brake calipers and discs, then remove the parking brake assembly. At the inboard side of the axle housing ends, remove the four nuts and lockwashers on each end of the axle housing, and remove the bolt and disconnect the parking brake cable from each side **(see illustration)**.

6   Use a slide-hammer (these can be rented at equipment rental yards and some auto parts stores) attached to the rear axle's wheel studs to pull the axle out **(see illustration)**.

7   Bring both axles to a machine shop to have the bearings replaced.

8   Before reinstalling the axles, use a seal-remover tool to pry the old axle housing seals out and drive new ones in with a properly-sized socket and hammer.

27.5 Rear wheel bearing retainer-to-rear axle housing mounting nuts (A) and parking brake cable bolt (B)

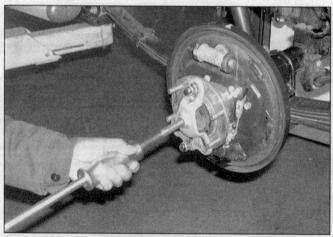

27.6 Use a slide-hammer to pull the axle and bearing from the axle housing (typical)

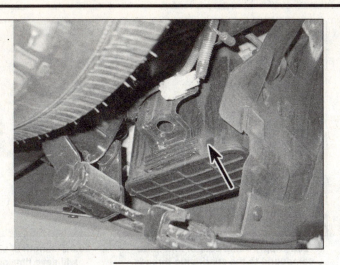

28.2 Check the charcoal canister for damage and the hose connections for cracks and deterioration

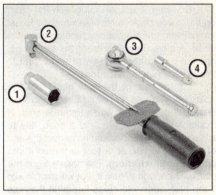

29.1 Tools required for changing spark plugs

1 **Spark plug socket** - *This will have special padding inside to protect the spark plug's porcelain insulator*
2 **Torque wrench** - *Although not mandatory, using this tool is the best way to ensure the plugs are tightened properly*
3 **Ratchet** - *Standard hand tool to fit the spark plug socket*
4 **Extension** - *Depending on model and accessories, you may need special extensions and universal joints to reach one or more of the plugs*

9   Axle installation is the reverse of the removal procedure. Be sure to use a new gasket on the bearing retainer flange, and tighten the bearing retainer nuts to the torque listed in the Chapter 8 Specifications.

28 Evaporative emissions control system check (every 30,000 miles or 24 months)

Refer to illustration 28.2

1   The function of the evaporative emissions control system is to draw fuel vapors from the gas tank and fuel system, store them in a charcoal canister and route them to the intake manifold during normal engine operation.
2   The most common symptom of a fault in the evaporative emissions system is a strong fuel odor. If a fuel odor is detected, inspect the charcoal canister, located inboard of the left rear wheel, close to the fuel tank. Check the canister and hoses for damage, leaks or deterioration **(see illustration)**.
3   The evaporative emissions control system is explained in more detail in Chapter 6.

29 Spark plug replacement (see maintenance schedule for replacement interval)

Refer to illustrations 29.1, 29.4, 29.6, 29.7 and 29.8

Note: *The manufacturer recommends against checking the spark plug gap, as the platinum or iridium coating could be scraped off, thereby greatly reducing the life of the spark plugs.*

1   In most cases, the tools necessary for spark plug replacement include a spark plug socket which fits onto a ratchet (spark plug sockets are padded inside to prevent damage to the porcelain insulators on the new plugs), and various extensions **(see illustration)**.
2   When buying the new spark plugs, be sure to obtain the correct plug type for your particular engine. This information can be found in the vehicle owner's manual and the Specifications at the front of this Chapter.
3   Allow the engine to cool completely before attempting to remove any of the plugs. While you're waiting for the engine to cool, check the new plugs for defects.
4   Remove the intake manifold (four-cyl-

inder engine, see Chapter 2A) or the upper intake manifold (plenum) (V6 engine, see Chapter 2B). Disconnect the electrical connector at the ignition coil for one cylinder, then remove the bolt and pull up on the coil/plug boot assembly **(see illustration)**. Replace one plug at a time.
5   If compressed air is available, use it to blow any dirt or foreign material away from the spark plug hole. The idea here is to eliminate the possibility of debris falling into the cylinder as the spark plug is removed.
6   Place the spark plug socket over the plug and remove it from the engine by turning it in a counterclockwise direction **(see illustration)**.

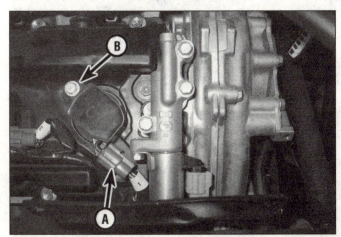

29.4 Disconnect the electrical connector (A) at an ignition coil, then remove the mounting bolt (B) and pull up on the coil/boot assembly to access the spark plug below

29.6 Use a socket and extension to unscrew the spark plugs

7   Compare the spark plug with the chart on the inside back cover of this manual to get an indication of the general running condition of the engine. Before installing the new plugs, apply a thin coat of anti-seize compound to the threads (see illustration).

8   Thread one of the new plugs into the hole until you can no longer turn it with your fingers, then tighten it with a torque wrench (if available) or the ratchet. It is a good idea to slip a short length of rubber hose over the end of the plug to use as a tool to thread it into place (see illustration). The hose will grip the plug well enough to turn it, but will start to slip if the plug begins to cross-thread in the hole - this will prevent damaged threads and the accompanying repair costs.

9   Attach the ignition coil to the new spark plug, again using a twisting motion on the boot until it's seated on the spark plug.

10   Repeat the procedure for the remaining spark plugs.

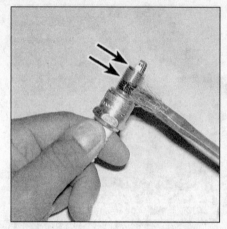

29.7 Apply a thin coat of anti-seize compound to the spark plug threads, being careful not to get any near the lower threads

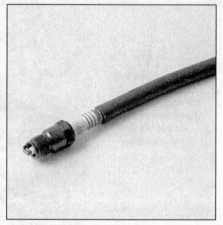

29.8 A length of snug-fitting rubber hose will save time and prevent damaged threads when installing the spark plugs

30   Cooling system servicing (draining, flushing and refilling) (every 30000 miles or 24 months)

Warning: *Do not allow antifreeze to come in contact with your skin or painted surfaces of the vehicle. Flush contacted areas immediately with plenty of water. Do not store new coolant or leave old coolant lying around where it is easily accessible to children and pets, because they are attracted by its sweet smell. Ingestion of even a small amount can be fatal. Wipe up the garage floor and drip pan coolant spills immediately. Keep antifreeze containers covered and repair leaks in your cooling system immediately. Antifreeze is flammable - be sure to read the precautions on the container.*

Note: *Non-toxic coolant is available at local auto parts stores. Although the coolant is non-toxic when fresh, proper disposal is still required.*

Draining

Refer to illustrations 30.3a, 30.3b and 30.4

1   Periodically, the cooling system should be drained, flushed and refilled to replenish the antifreeze mixture and prevent formation of rust and corrosion, which can impair the performance of the cooling system and cause engine damage. When the cooling system is serviced, all hoses and the radiator cap should be checked and replaced if necessary.

2   Apply the parking brake and block the wheels. **Warning:** *If the vehicle has just been driven, wait several hours to allow the engine to cool down before beginning this procedure.* Turn the ignition key to the On position, then set the heater control to the maximum heat position. Wait at least ten seconds, then turn the ignition Off.

3   Move a large container under the radiator drain to catch the coolant. Remove the plastic fasteners from the cover under the radiator (if equipped), then tuck the cover back over the frame for access to the drain plug, which is located in the radiator's lower tank (see illustrations). Unscrew the drain fitting with a Phillips screwdriver, then remove the radiator cap.

4   After coolant stops flowing out of the radiator, move the container under the engine block drain plug(s) - on four-cylinder engines the plug is on the right side of the block (see illustration); on the V6 there's one on each side of the engine block. Remove the plugs and allow the coolant in the block to drain. **Note:** *Frequently, the coolant will not drain from the block after the plug is removed. This is due to a rust layer that has built up behind the plug. Insert a Phillips screwdriver into the hole to break the rust barrier.*

5   While the coolant is draining, check the condition of the radiator hoses, heater hoses and clamps (refer to Section 14 if necessary). Remove the coolant reservoir (see Chapter 3) and pour the coolant into the drain pan. Rinse out the reservoir with clean water.

6   Once the coolant has drained completely, replace any damaged clamps or hoses. Apply thread sealant to the drain plugs, reinstall them and tighten them securely.

30.3a Pry out these plastic fasteners that secure this cover under the radiator, then fold the cover back for access to the radiator drain plug

30.3b Loosen the radiator drain plug with a Phillips screwdriver

30.4 The engine block drain plug on four-cylinder engines is on the right side of the block, near the front of the engine

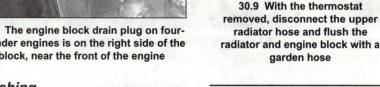
30.9 With the thermostat removed, disconnect the upper radiator hose and flush the radiator and engine block with a garden hose

Flushing

Refer to illustration 30.9

Note 1: *In severe cases of contamination or clogging of the radiator, remove the radiator (see Chapter 3) and have a radiator repair facility clean and repair it if necessary.*

Note 2: *Many deposits can be removed by the chemical action of a cleaner available at auto parts stores. Follow the procedure outlined in the manufacturer's instructions. However, when the coolant is regularly drained and the system refilled with the correct antifreeze/water mixture, there should be no need to use chemical cleaners or descalers.*

7   Make sure your heating system controls are still set to Hot, so that the heater core will be flushed at the same time as the rest of the cooling system.

8   Once the system is completely drained, remove the thermostat from the engine (see Chapter 3). Then reinstall the thermostat housing without the thermostat. This will allow the system to be thoroughly flushed.

9   Disconnect the upper radiator hose, then place a garden hose in the upper radiator inlet and flush the system until the water runs clear at the upper radiator hose **(see illustration)**.

Refilling

10   To refill the system, install the thermostat (if removed), reconnect any radiator hoses and install the reservoir and the overflow hose.

11   Place the heater temperature control in the maximum heat position.

12   Make sure to use the proper coolant listed in this Chapter's Specifications. Slowly fill the radiator with the recommended mixture of antifreeze and water until coolant reaches the base of the radiator filler neck. Then add coolant to the reservoir until it reaches the FULL COLD mark. Wait five minutes and recheck the coolant level in the radiator, adding if necessary.

13   Leave the radiator cap off and run the engine in a well-ventilated area until the thermostat opens (coolant will begin flowing through the radiator and the upper radiator hose will become hot).

14   Rev the engine to approximately 2500 rpm for ten seconds then let it idle; do this a few times.

15   Turn the engine off and let it cool. Add more coolant mixture to bring the level back

up to the base of the filler neck.

16   Squeeze the upper radiator hose to expel air, then add more coolant mixture if necessary. Reinstall the radiator cap. Add coolant to the reservoir, if necessary.

17   Start the engine, allow it to reach normal operating temperature and check for leaks.

31 Automatic transmission fluid and filter change (every 30,000 miles or 24 months)

Refer to illustrations 31.5, 31.8, 31.9, 31.11 and 31.12

1   At the specified intervals, the transmission fluid should be drained and replaced. Since the fluid will remain hot long after driving, perform this procedure only after the engine has cooled down completely.

2   Before beginning work, purchase the specified transmission fluid (see *Recommended lubricants and fluids* at the front of this Chapter) and a new filter and pan gasket.

3   Other tools necessary for this job include a floor jack, jackstands to support the vehicle in a raised position, a drain pan capable of holding at least eight quarts, newspapers and clean rags.

4   Raise the vehicle and support it securely on jackstands.

5   Place the drain pan underneath the transmission pan. Remove the drain plug and allow the fluid to drain, then reinsert the plug and tighten it securely **(see illustration)**. Measure the amount of fluid drained (the same amount will be added to the transmission later).

6   Remove the transmission pan bolts **(see illustration 31.5)**, then remove the pan, prying gently if necessary. **Warning:** *There is still some transmission fluid in the pan.*

7   Carefully clean the gasket surface of the

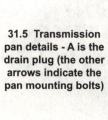
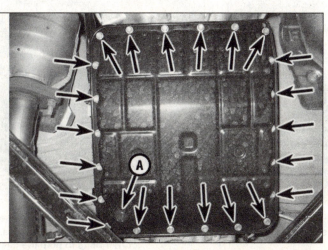
31.5 Transmission pan details - A is the drain plug (the other arrows indicate the pan mounting bolts)

31.8 After cleaning the pan and magnet, reinstall the magnet in its proper position

31.9 Remove these bolts and detach the strainer from the valve body

transmission and pan to remove all traces of the old gasket and sealant.

8   Clean the pan with solvent and dry it. **Note:** *Some models are equipped with magnets in the transmission pan to catch metal debris* (**see illustration**). *Clean the magnet thoroughly. A small amount of metal material is normal at the magnet. If there is considerable debris, consult a dealer or transmission specialist.*

9   Remove the strainer from the valve body inside the transmission (**see illustration**).

10   Clean the strainer with solvent and dry it with compressed air, if available. If compressed air isn't available, pour some clean automatic transmission fluid through it.

11   Install a new O-ring on the strainer (**see illustration**).

12   Make sure the gasket surface on the transmission pan is clean, then install a new gasket on the pan (**see illustration**). Put the pan in place against the transmission and install the bolts. Tighten each bolt a little at a time to the torque listed in this Chapter's Specifications.

13   Lower the vehicle and add the specified type of automatic transmission fluid (the same amount that was drained in Step 5), through the filler tube (see Section 7).

14   With the transmission in Park and the parking brake set, run the engine at a fast idle, but don't race it.

15   Move the gear selector through each range and back to Park, then let the engine idle for a few minutes. Check the fluid level. It may be low. Add enough fluid to bring the level to the proper mark on the dipstick. Be careful not to overfill.

16   Check under the vehicle for leaks during the first few trips. Check the fluid level again when the transmission is hot (see Section 7).

32 Positive Crankcase Ventilation (PCV) valve and hose check and replacement (30,000 miles or 24 months)

Refer to illustration 32.1

1   On both four-cylinder and V6 engines, the PCV valve is located in the valve cover

(**see illustration**). Detach the hose from the valve, then pull the valve from the grommet in the valve cover.

2   Shake the PCV valve, listening for a rattle. If the valve doesn't rattle, replace it with a new one.

3   When purchasing a replacement PCV valve, make sure it's for your particular vehicle and engine size. Compare the old valve with the new one to make sure they're the same.

33 Spark plug boots and ignition coils - cleaning and inspection (every 60,000 miles or 48 months)

Refer to illustration 33.2

1   All engines in the models covered by this manual have individual ignition coils for each cylinder. These models do not have a traditional distributor or spark plug wires. Each coil has a boot on the bottom that connects directly to the top of its spark plug.

2   Whenever spark plugs are replaced (see Section 29), the coils/boots are removed to

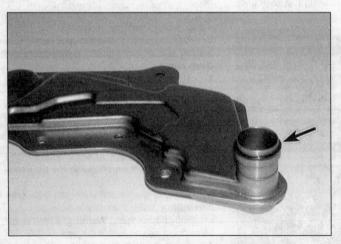

31.11 Install a new O-ring on the strainer

31.12 Place the gasket on the transmission pan and install the corner bolts to hold the gasket in place

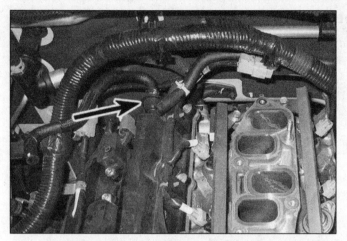

32.1 The PCV valve on V6 engines is located at the rear of the right valve cover (intake plenum removed for clarity)

33.2 Examine the spark plug boots and the individual ignition coils for signs of damage

access the plugs. Examine both the boots and the coils for any signs of carbon tracking, cracks or other damage **(see illustration)**. Clean them with a dampened cloth and dry them thoroughly before installation.

34 Manual transmission lubricant change (every 60,000 miles or 48 months)

1   This procedure should be performed after the vehicle has been driven so the lubricant will be warm and therefore will flow out of the transmission more easily. Raise the vehicle and support it securely on jackstands.
2   Move a drain pan, rags, newspapers and wrenches under the transmission.
3   Remove the fill plug from the side of the transmission case, then remove the transmission drain plug at the bottom of the case and allow the lubricant to drain into the pan (see Section 18).
4   After the lubricant has drained completely, reinstall the drain plug and tighten it to the torque listed in this Chapter's Specifications.
5   Using a hand pump, syringe or squeeze bottle, fill the transmission with the specified lubricant until it just reaches the bottom edge

of the hole. Reinstall the fill plug and tighten it to the torque listed in this Chapter's Specifications.
6   Lower the vehicle.
7   Drive the vehicle for a short distance, then check the drain and fill plugs for leakage.

35 Transfer case lubricant change (4WD models) (every 60,000 miles or 48 months)

1   This procedure should be performed after the vehicle has been driven so the lubricant will be warm and therefore will flow out of the transfer case more easily.
2   Raise the vehicle and support it securely on jackstands.
3   Remove the filler plug from the case (see Section 19).
4   Remove the drain plug from the lower part of the case and allow the lubricant to drain completely.
5   After the case is completely drained, carefully clean and install the drain plug. Tighten the plug to the torque listed in this Chapter's Specifications.
6   Fill the case with the specified lubricant until it is level with the lower edge of the filler hole.

7   Install the filler plug and tighten it to the torque listed in this Chapter's Specifications.
8   Drive the vehicle for a short distance and recheck the lubricant level. In some instances a small amount of additional lubricant will have to be added.

36 Differential lubricant change (every 60,000 miles or 48 months)

1   This procedure should be performed after the vehicle has been driven, so the lubricant will be warm and therefore will flow out of the differential more easily.
2   Raise the vehicle and support it securely on jackstands. You'll be draining the lubricant by removing the drain plug, so move a drain pan, rags, newspapers and wrenches under the vehicle.
3   Remove the fill plug, then remove the drain plug (see Section 17) and allow the lubricant to drain into the pan, then clean and reinstall the drain plug. Tighten the plug to the torque listed in this Chapter's Specifications.
4   Using a hand pump, syringe or squeeze bottle, fill the differential housing with the specified lubricant until it's level with the bottom of the fill-plug hole. Install the plug and tighten it to the torque listed in this Chapter's Specifications.

Notes

Chapter 2 Part A
2.5L four-cylinder engine

Contents

Specifications

General
Engine designation	QR25DE
Displacement	151.8 cubic inches (2.5 liters)
Bore	3.50 inches (89.0 mm)
Stroke	3.93 inches (100 mm)
Cylinder numbers (front to rear)	1-2-3-4
Firing order	1-3-4-2

FRONT OF VEHICLE
④③②①
72031-1-SPECS HAYNES
Cylinder locations

Cylinder head warpage limit
0.004 inch (0.1 mm)

Camshaft
Thrust clearance (end play)	0.0045 to 0.0074 inch (0.115 to 0.188 mm)
Camshaft journal diameter	1.0998 to 1.1006 inches (27.935 to 27.955 mm)
Camshaft bearing inside diameter	1.1024 to 1.1033 inches (28.000 to 28.025 mm)
Bearing oil clearance (standard)	0.0018 to 0.0035 inch (0.045 to 0.090 mm)
Runout limit	0.0008 inch (0.02 mm)
Intake lobe height	1.772 to 1.780 inches (45.015 to 45.202 mm)
Exhaust lobe height	1.731 to 1.739 inches (43.975 to 44.165 mm)

Valve clearance (cold)
Intake.. 0.009 to 0.013 inch (0.24 to 0.32 mm)
Exhaust... 0.010 to 0.013 inch (0.26 to 0.34 mm)

Oil pump
Body-to-outer rotor clearance.. 0.0047 to 0.0077 inch (0.120 to 0.195 mm)
Inner rotor-to-outer rotor tip clearance... 0.0024 to 0.0063 inch (0.06 to 0.16 mm)
Inner rotor-to-body clearance... 0.0012 to 0.0028 inch (0.030 to 0.070 mm)
Outer rotor-to-body clearance .... 0.0020 to 0.0035 inch (0.05 to 0.09 mm)

Torque specifications

	Ft-lbs (unless otherwise indicated)	Nm

Note: *One foot-pound (ft-lb) of torque is equivalent to 12 inch-pounds (in-lbs) of torque. Torque values below approximately 15 ft-lbs are expressed in inch-pounds, since most foot-pound torque wrenches are not accurate at these smaller values.*

	Ft-lbs	Nm
Camshaft bearing caps (see illustration 8.12b)		
Step 1 (bolts 9-11)...	17 in-lbs	2
Step 2 (bolts 1-8)...	17 in-lbs	2
Step 3 (bolts 1-11)...	52 in-lbs	6
Step 4 (bolts 1-11)...	92 in-lbs	10
Balancer assembly mounting bolts (see illustration 7.30)		
Step 1 (bolts 1 through 4)...	35	47
Step 2 (bolts 1 through 4)...	Tighten an additional 100 degrees	
Step 3 (bolts 1 through 4)...	Loosen fully	
Step 4 (bolts 1 through 4)...	35	47
Step 5 (bolts 1 through 4)...	Tighten an additional 100 degrees	
Step 6 (bolts 5 and 6)..	22	30
Camshaft sprocket bolts..	105	142
Crankshaft pulley-to-crankshaft bolt.....................................	31	42
Cylinder head bolts (see illustration 11.20)		
2005, 2006 and 2010		
Step 1	72	98
Step 2	Loosen all bolts in reverse order of tightening	
Step 3	29	39
Step 4	Tighten an additional 75-degrees	
Step 5	Tighten an additional 75-degrees	
2007 through 2009		
Step 1	37	50
Step 2	Tighten an additional 60-degrees	
Step 3	Loosen all bolts in reverse order of tightening	
Step 4	29	39
Step 5	Tighten an additional 75-degrees	
Step 6	Tighten an additional 75-degrees	
2011 and later		
Step 1	41	55
Step 2	Loosen all bolts in reverse order of tightening	
Step 3	29	39
Step 4	Tighten an additional 75-degrees	
Step 5	Tighten an additional 75-degrees	
Driveplate/flywheel bolts...	80	108
Exhaust manifold bolts (see illustration 10.13)......................	132 in-lbs	15
Engine mount-to-mount bracket nut.......................................	36	49
Engine mount-to-frame bolts..	65	88
Engine mount bracket-to-block bolts......................................	36	49
Intake manifold bolts/nuts (see illustration 9.9).....................	83 in-lbs	9
Oil pump-to-block mounting bolt and screw	61 in-lbs	7
Oil pump body screws	61 in-lbs	7
Oil pump regulator valve plug..	36	49
Oil strainer mounting bolts...	16	22
Oil pan bolts (see illustration 14.14)......................................	16	22
Oil pan drain plug	80 in-lbs	9
Timing chain tensioner bolts	62 in-lbs	7
Timing chain cover bolts (see illustration 7.36)	108 in-lbs	12
Valve cover bolts (see illustration 4.4)		
Step 1...	18 in-lbs	2
Step 2...	73 in-lbs	8

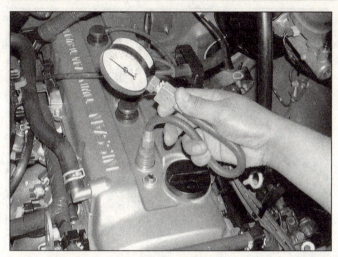

3.5 A compression gauge can be used in the number one plug hole to assist in finding TDC

3.8 Align the TDC mark on the crankshaft pulley with the pointer on the front timing cover - note that the TDC mark is the second mark from the left

1   General information

This Part of Chapter 2 is devoted to in-vehicle repair procedures for the QR25DE 2.5L Dual Overhead Camshaft (DOHC) four cylinder engine. Information concerning engine removal, installation and overhaul can be found in Chapter 2, Part C.

The following repair procedures are based on the assumption that the engine is installed in the vehicle. If the engine has been removed from the vehicle and mounted on a stand, many of the steps outlined in this Part of Chapter 2 will not apply.

2   Repair operations possible with the engine in the vehicle

Many major repair operations can be accomplished without removing the engine from the vehicle.

Clean the engine compartment and the exterior of the engine with some type of degreaser before any work is done. It will make the job easier and help keep dirt out of the internal areas of the engine.

Depending on the components involved, it may be helpful to remove the hood to improve access to the engine as repairs are performed (refer to Chapter 11 if necessary). Cover the fenders to prevent damage to the paint. Special pads are available, but an old bedspread or blanket will also work.

If vacuum, exhaust, oil or coolant leaks develop, indicating a need for gasket or seal replacement, the repairs can generally be made with the engine in the vehicle. The intake and exhaust manifold gaskets, oil pan gasket, crankshaft oil seals and cylinder head gasket are all accessible with the engine in place.

Exterior engine components, such as the intake and exhaust manifolds, the oil pan, the oil pump, the water pump, the starter motor, the alternator, the distributor and the fuel sys-tem components can be removed for repair with the engine in place.

Since the cylinder head can be removed without pulling the engine, camshaft and valve component servicing can also be accomplished with the engine in the vehicle. Replacement of the timing chain and sprock-ets is also possible with the engine in the vehicle.

In extreme cases caused by a lack of necessary equipment, repair or replacement of piston rings, pistons, connecting rods and rod bearings is possible with the engine in the vehicle. However, this practice is not recom-mended because of the cleaning and prepa-ration work that must be done to the compo-nents involved.

3   Top Dead Center (TDC) for number one piston - locating

Refer to illustrations 3.5 and 3.8

1   Top Dead Center (TDC) is the highest point in the cylinder that each piston reaches as it travels up the cylinder bore. Each piston reaches TDC on the compression stroke and again on the exhaust stroke, but TDC gener-ally refers to piston position on the compres-sion stroke.

2   Positioning the piston(s) at TDC is an essential part of many procedures such as valve timing, camshaft and timing chain/ sprocket removal.

3   Before beginning this procedure, be sure to place the transmission in Neutral and apply the parking brake or block the rear wheels. Disable the ignition system by disconnecting the primary electrical connectors at the igni-tion coil packs and remove the spark plugs (see Chapter 1). Disable the fuel system (see Chapter 4, Section 2).

4   In order to bring any piston to TDC, the crankshaft must be turned using one of the methods outlined below. When looking at the front of the engine, normal crankshaft rotation is clockwise.

a) *The preferred method is to turn the crankshaft with a socket and ratchet attached to the bolt threaded into the front of the crankshaft. Turn the bolt in a clockwise direction.*

b) *A remote starter switch, which may save some time, can also be used. Follow the instructions included with the switch. Once the piston is close to TDC, use a socket and ratchet as described in the previous paragraph.*

c) *If an assistant is available to turn the ignition switch to the Start position in short bursts, you can get the piston close to TDC without a remote starter switch. Make sure your assistant is out of the vehicle, away from the ignition switch, then use a socket and ratchet as described in Paragraph (a) to complete the procedure.*

5   Install a compression pressure gauge in the number one spark plug hole **(see illustra-tion)**. It should be a gauge with a screw-in fit-ting and a hose at least six inches long.

6   Rotate the crankshaft using one of the methods described above while observing for pressure on the compression gauge. The moment the gauge shows pressure indicates that the number one cylinder has begun the compression stroke.

7   Once the compression stroke has begun, TDC for the compression stroke is reached by bringing the piston to the top of the cylinder.

8   Continue turning the crankshaft until the TDC notch in the crankshaft damper is aligned with the pointer on the front cover **(see illus-tration)**. At this point, the number one cylinder is at TDC on the compression stroke. If the marks are aligned but there was no compres-sion, the piston was on the exhaust stroke. Continue rotating the crankshaft 360-degrees (1-turn). **Note:** *If a compression gauge is not available, you can simply place a blunt object*

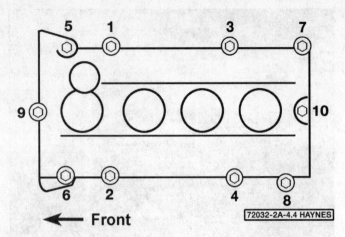

4.4 Valve cover retaining fastener *tightening* sequence

4.5 The spark plug tubes are sealed by a rubber strip (arrows) -
replace if cracked or leaking

(such as the end of a screwdriver handle) over the spark plug hole and listen for compression as the engine is rotated. Once compression at the No.1 spark plug hole is noted, the remainder of the Step is the same.

9   After the number one piston has been positioned at TDC on the compression stroke, TDC for any of the remaining cylinders can be located by turning the crankshaft clockwise 180-degrees and following the firing order (refer to the Specifications). Rotating the engine 180-degrees past TDC #1 will put the engine at TDC compression for cylinder #3.

4   Valve cover - removal and installation

Removal

Refer to illustrations 4.4 and 4.5

1   Disconnect the cable from the negative terminal of the battery.
2   Remove the intake manifold (see Section 9).
3   Disconnect the PCV hoses at the valve cover and remove the ignition coils (see Chapter 1).
4   Remove the valve cover retaining bolts/nuts (see illustration). If the cover is stuck to the cylinder head, bump the end with a wood block and a hammer to jar it loose. If that doesn't work, try to slip a flexible putty knife between the cylinder head and cover to break the seal. **Caution:** *Don't pry at the cover or housing-to-cylinder head joint or damage to the sealing surfaces may occur, leading to oil leaks after the cover is reinstalled.*
5   Remove the gasket from the valve cover. Check the condition of the spark plug tube seal (see illustration), and replace it if necessary.

Installation

6   The mating surfaces of the valve cover and cylinder head must be clean when the

cover is installed. Remove all traces of sealant from the front corners of the valve cover gasket, then clean the mating surfaces with lacquer thinner or acetone. If there's residue or oil on the mating surfaces when the cover is installed, oil leaks may develop. **Caution:** *Use care when scraping the soft aluminum of the cylinder head or valve cover. It is soft, and deep scratches may lead to oil leaks.*
7   Press the new gasket into the groove on the valve cover. Apply RTV sealant to the front corners of the valve cover gasket and install the valve cover onto the engine.
8   Tighten the bolts/nuts, a little at a time and in the recommended sequence (see illustration 4.4), to the torque listed in this Chapter's Specifications.

5   Valve clearance - check and adjustment

Refer to illustrations 5.6a, 5.6b, 5.7 and 5.9
Note 1: *The manufacturer recommends adjusting the valve clearance at the specified interval only if the valve train is making excessive noise.*

Note 2: *Wait until the engine is completely cool before checking the valve clearances.*
1   Disconnect the cable from the negative terminal of the battery.
2   Remove the valve cover (see Section 4).
3   On manual transmission vehicles set the parking brake and place the transmission in the neutral position.
4   Remove the spark plugs (see Chapter 1).
5   Position the number 1 piston at TDC on the compression stroke and align the TDC mark with the pointer on the front cover (see Section 3).
6   Measure the clearance of the indicated valves with a feeler gauge (see illustrations). Record each measurement and compare your measurements with the desired valve clearance found in this Chapter's Specifications. Note which are out of specification, this data will be used later to determine the required replacement shims.
7   Turn the crankshaft one complete revolution and realign the TDC mark. Measure and record the clearances of the remaining valves (see illustration).
8   After all of the clearances have been measured and written down, if there are lifters

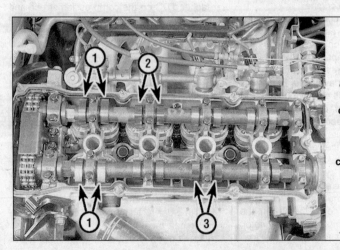

5.6a When the no. 1 piston is at TDC on the compression stroke, the valve clearance for the no. 1 and no. 3 cylinder exhaust valves and the no. 1 and no. 2 cylinder intake valves can be measured

5.6b Measure the clearance for each valve with a feeler gauge of the specified thickness - if the clearance is correct, you should feel a slight drag on the gauge as you pull it out

5.7 When the no. 4 piston is at TDC on the compression stroke, the valve clearances for the no. 2 and no. 4 cylinder exhaust valves and the no. 3 and no. 4 cylinder intake valves can be measured

whose specs are out of range, these lifters will need to be replaced. There are no lifter shims on this engine for adjustment of valve clearance.

9   Refer to Section 8 and remove the camshafts. Carefully mark on the lifters that are removed the cylinder they came from and whether they were on the Intake or Exhaust side. Measure the thickness of the lifter head with a micrometer (see illustration).

10   New lifters are available in 26 thicknesses from 6.96 mm to 7.46 mm. To determine which new lifters to order, subtract the standard lifter clearance (0.011 inch for intake, 0.012 for exhaust) from the clearance you measured on a lifter. The replacement lifter thickness should be that amount thicker than the one you are replacing. Select a lifter as close as possible to the desired measurement. Lifters are marked on the underside with their measurement.

11   The remainder of the installation is the reverse of the removal procedure.

6   Valve springs, retainers and seals - replacement

Refer to illustrations 6.5, 6.7a, 6.7b, 6.13a, 6.13b, 6.14 and 6.15

Note: *Broken valve springs and defective valve stem seals can be replaced without removing the cylinder heads. Two special tools and a compressed air source are normally required to perform this operation, so read through this Section carefully. The universal shaft-type valve spring compressor required for the tight valve spring pockets of this vehicle may not be available at all tool rental yards, so check on the availability before beginning the job.*

1   Remove the valve cover (see Section 4).

2   Refer to Section 7 and remove the upper timing chain, then refer to Section 8 and remove the camshafts and lifters from the cylinder head.

3   Remove the spark plug from the cylinder that has the defective component. If all of the valve stem seals are being replaced, all of the

spark plugs should be removed.

4   Turn the crankshaft until the piston in the affected cylinder is at Top Dead Center on the compression stroke (see Section 3). If you're replacing all of the valve stem seals, begin with cylinder number one and work on the valves for one cylinder at a time. Move from cylinder-to-cylinder following the firing order sequence (see this Chapter's Specifications).

5   Thread a long adapter into the spark plug hole and connect an air hose from a compressed air source to it (see illustration). Most auto parts stores can supply the air hose adapter. **Note:** *Because of the length of the spark plug tubes, it will be necessary to use a long spark plug adapter with a length of hose attached (as used on many cylinder compression gauges) utilizing a quick-disconnect fitting to hook to your air source.*

6   Apply compressed air to the cylinder. **Warning:** *The piston may be forced down by the compressed air, causing the crankshaft to turn suddenly. If the wrench used when positioning the number one piston at TDC is still*

5.9 Measure the lifter thickness with a micrometer

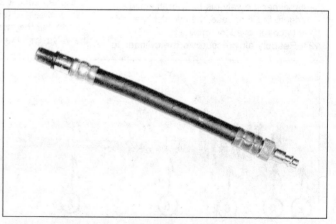

6.5 The air hose adapter threads into the spark plug hole - they're commonly available from auto parts stores

6.7a Compress the valve spring enough to release the
valve stem keepers . . .

6.7b . . . and lift them out with a magnet or needle-nose pliers

attached to the bolt in the crankshaft nose, it
could cause damage or injury when the crankshaft moves.

7   Stuff shop rags into the cylinder head
holes around the valves to prevent parts and
tools from falling into the engine, then use a
valve spring compressor to compress the
spring (see illustrations). Remove the valve
stem keepers with small needle-nose pliers or
a magnet. Note: The valves should be held
in place by the air pressure. If the valve faces
or seats are in poor condition, leaks may prevent air pressure from retaining the valves.
If the valves cannot hold air, the cylinder
head should be removed for a valve job at a
machine shop.

8   Remove the spring retainer and valve
spring, then remove the valve stem seal.

9   Wrap a rubber band or tape around the
top of the valve stem so the valve won't fall
into the combustion chamber, then release
the air pressure.

10   Inspect the valve stem for damage.
Rotate the valve in the guide and check the
end for eccentric movement, which would
indicate that the valve is bent.

11   Move the valve up-and-down in the guide
and make sure it doesn't bind. If the valve stem
binds, either the valve is bent or the guide is
damaged. In either case, the cylinder head will
have to be removed for repair.

12   Reapply air pressure to the cylinder to

6.13a Lubricate the new seal and slip it
over the valve stem, past the
valve keeper groove

6.13b Using a deep socket and hammer,
gently tap the new seals onto the valve
guide only until seated

retain the valve in the closed position, then
remove the tape or rubber band from the
valve stem.

13   Lubricate the valve stems with engine
oil and install a new valve stem seals. Valve
stem seals can be installed with a special tool,
or a deep socket and hammer - tap the seal
only until seated (see illustrations).

14   Install the valve spring in position over
the valve, with the more closely-wound spring

coils and/or the paint mark toward the cylinder
head (see illustration).

15   Install the valve spring retainer. Compress the valve springs and carefully position
the keepers in the groove. Apply a small dab
of grease to the inside of each keeper to hold
it in place (see illustration).

6.15 Apply a small dab of grease to each
keeper as shown here before installation -
it will hold them in place on the valve stem
as the spring is released

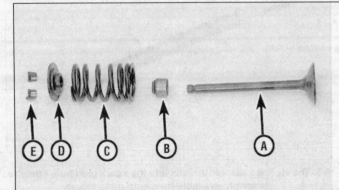

6.14 Arrangement of
the valve components

A   Valve
B   Valve stem seal
C   Valve spring
D   Retainer
E   Keepers

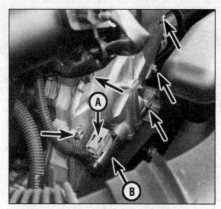

7.14 Disconnect the IVT connector (A), unbolt the IVT solenoid (B), then remove the IVT cover mounting bolts (not all bolts are visible here)

16   Remove the pressure from the spring tool and make sure the keepers are seated.
17   Disconnect the air hose and remove the adapter from the spark plug hole.
18   Refer to Section 8 and install the camshaft and lifters, then refer to Section 7 and install the timing chain.
19   Refer to Section 4 and install the valve covers.
20   Install the spark plugs and the spark plug wires.
21   Start and run the engine, then check for oil leaks and unusual sounds coming from the valve cover area.

7   Timing chain and sprockets- removal, inspection and installation

Removal

Refer to illustrations 7.14 and 7.16

Caution: *The timing system is complex. Severe engine damage will occur if you make any mistakes. Do not attempt this procedure unless you are highly experienced with this type of repair. If you are at all unsure of your abilities, consult an expert. Double-check all your work and be sure everything is correct before you attempt to start the engine.*
1   Position the engine at TDC for number one cylinder (see Section 3). Relieve the fuel system pressure (see Chapter 4).
2   Drain the cooling system (see Chapter 1).
3   Remove the intake air duct connected to the intake manifold (see Chapter 4).
4   Remove the valve cover (see Section 4).
5   Remove the alternator and bracket (see Chapter 5).
6   Remove the upper radiator hose (see Chapter 3).
7   Remove the drivebelt and drivebelt tensioner (see Chapter 1).
8   Drain the engine oil and remove the oil pan and oil pump pick-up (see Sections 14 and 15).

9   Lower the vehicle and install an engine support fixture. **Note:** *After the oil pan is removed, the crossmember and front and rear mounts can be temporarily installed again for support.*
10   Without disconnecting the refrigerant lines, unbolt and set aside the air conditioning compressor (see Chapter 3).
11   Remove the coolant reservoir (see Chapter 3).
12   Unbolt and set aside the power steering pump, without disconnecting the hoses (see Chapter 10).
13   Disconnect the electrical connector for the Intake Variable Valve Timing (IVT) Control solenoid.
14   Remove the bolts retaining the IVT (Intake Variable Valve timing) timing chain cover to the timing chain main cover **(see illustration)**. Remove the IVT cover. **Note:** *You may have to use a sharp utility knife to cut the RTV around the IVT cover, then use a thin putty knife to separate the IVT cover from the timing cover.*
15   Remove the upper chain guide from between the two camshaft sprockets.
16   Check the position of the camshaft sprockets. They should be aligned at TDC

number 1 **(see illustration)**.
17   Remove the crankshaft pulley (see Section 12).
18   Remove the front engine cover. Follow the reverse of the tightening sequence to remove the bolts **(see illustration 7.36)**.
19   Remove the timing chain tensioner. Using the tip of a screwdriver, push down on the tensioner plunger and insert a stopper pin of the correct diameter into the hole on the tensioner **(see illustration 7.16)**. Once the tensioner is locked in the retracted position, remove the bolts and the tensioner from the front of the engine.
20   Use a large open end-wrench on the hex to hold the camshaft as you unbolt the camshaft sprocket bolts.
21   Remove the timing chain tensioner, the tensioner guide, the timing chain and the oil pump drive spacer.
22   Remove the balance shaft chain. Lift the tensioner lever up to release the ratchet claw mechanism on the balance shaft chain tensioner **(see illustration 7.16)**.
23   Pull the tensioner sleeve in and hold the sleeve stationary.
24   Install a staking pin into the lever to lock the lever with the tensioner sleeve.

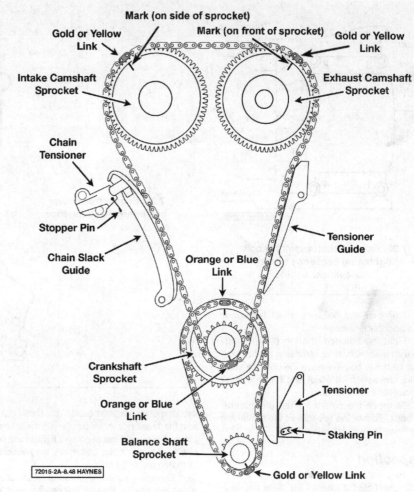

7.16 Check the position of the camshaft sprocket marks at TDC number 1

2A-8 Chapter 2 Part A 2.5L four-cylinder engine

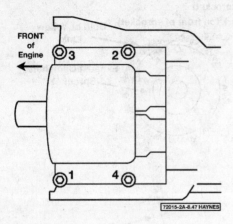

7.30 Balance shaft assembly bolt tightening sequence on the four-cylinder engine

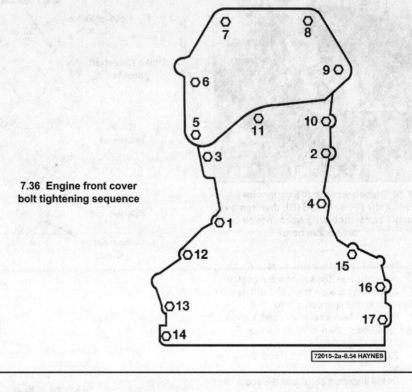

7.36 Engine front cover bolt tightening sequence

25   Remove the balance shaft tensioner bolts and the tensioner.
26   Hold the balance shaft in the hex portion with a wrench while removing the balance shaft sprocket bolt. Remove the balance shaft chain, crankshaft sprocket and balance shaft sprocket at the same time.
27   Remove the balance shaft unit mounting bolts. Follow the reverse of the tightening sequence **(see illustration 7.30)**.

Inspection

28   Inspect the camshaft, idler and crankshaft sprockets for wear of the teeth and keyways. Inspect the chains for cracks or excessive wear of the rollers. Inspect the facing of the chain guides for excessive wear.

Installation

Refer to illustrations 7.30 and 7.36
Caution: *Before starting the engine, carefully rotate the crankshaft by hand through at least two full revolutions (use a socket and breaker bar on the crankshaft pulley center bolt). If you feel any resistance, STOP! There is something wrong - most likely, valves are contacting the pistons. You must find the problem before proceeding. Check your work and see if any updated repair information is available.*
29   Install the crankshaft sprocket and the balance shaft chain and sprocket. Make sure the painted links on the balance shaft chain align with the mating marks on the crankshaft sprocket and the balance shaft sprocket.
30   Connect the chain to the balance shaft unit, then mount the unit using new bolts. Follow the correct torque sequence when tightening the bolts **(see illustration)**. Tighten the bolts to the torque listed in this Chapter's Specifications.
31   Install the balance shaft tensioner bolts and the tensioner **(see illustration 7.16)**. The bolt hole positions may have changed since

the tensioner was removed. The chain guide and the tensioner move freely with the staking pin as the pivot. First align and tighten the two chain tensioner bolts and move the tensioner to match the bolt holes.
32   Double check the balance shaft chain alignment marks. Repeat the procedure if the alignment marks are incorrect. Release the staking pin from the tensioner to apply tension to the balance shaft chain.
33   Install the timing chain. Align the painted links with the mating marks on the camshaft and crankshaft sprockets.
34   Install the timing chain guide and slack chain guide. Tighten the bolts to the torque listed in this Chapter's Specifications.
35   Install the timing chain tensioner and release the stopper pin. Double check the timing chain alignment marks and if they are incorrect, repeat the procedure. Tighten the sprocket bolts to the torque listed in this Chapter's Specifications. Replace the O-rings between the block and the timing cover.
36   Install the engine front cover. Tighten the cover bolts in the correct sequence **(see illustration)** and to the torque listed in this Chapter's Specifications.
37   The remainder of the installation is the reverse of the disassembly sequence.

8   Camshafts and lifters - removal, inspection and installation

Note: *The camshafts and lifters should always be thoroughly inspected before instal-*

lation and camshaft endplay should always be checked prior to camshaft removal.

Removal

Refer to illustrations 8.7, 8.9a and 8.9b
1   Detach the cable from the negative terminal of the battery.
2   Remove the valve cover (see Section 4) and the air intake duct (see Chapter 4).
3   Refer to Section 7 for removal of the IVT timing cover, then align/mark the TDC marks on the chain and camshaft sprockets. At the rear of the cylinder head, disconnect the electrical connector from the Camshaft Position Sensor, then remove the mounting bolt and the sensor.
4   With the TDC marks aligned, apply a dab of paint to the timing chain links and the sprockets to aid in the installation process. Also mark the sprockets "I" for intake or "E" for exhaust. The sprockets must be reinstalled in their original location.
5   Using a wrench to hold the camshaft sprockets from turning (on the hexagonal portion of the camshaft only), loosen the camshaft sprocket bolts several turns. If the camshaft sprockets have rotated during the bolt loosening process, rotate the engine clockwise until the "TDC" marks on the crankshaft pulley are once again aligned.
6   Push back the plunger on the upper timing chain tensioner and insert a stopper pin to hold it in the retracted position **(see illustration 7.16)**. Remove the camshaft sprocket bolts and the camshaft sprockets. **Note:** *As long as the main timing chain cover is in*

8.7 The camshaft bearing caps are numbered and have an arrow that should face the timing chain end of the engine

8.9a Mark the lifters (I for intake, E for exhaust and number their location) and pull them straight up to remove them or use a magnetic retrieval tool

place on the block, the timing chain will not fall below enough to become inaccessible for reassembly.

7   Loosen the camshaft bearing caps in two or three steps, in the reverse of the tightening sequence **(see illustration 8.12b)**. They are numbered from 1 to 5, are stamped with an

"I" or an "E" to indicate intake or exhaust, and have arrows to indicate which way faces the timing-chain end of the engine **(see illustration)**. **Caution:** *Keep the caps in order. They must go back in the same location they were removed from.*

8   Remove the bearing caps and lift the camshafts straight up and out. Also mark the camshafts "I" for intake or "E" for exhaust. If the camshafts are to be reused, they must be reinstalled in their original location.

9   Pull the lifters straight up, and store them in numbered plastic bags or a marked box **(see illustrations)**.

Installation

Refer to illustrations 8.10, 8.12a and 8.12b

10   Lubricate the lifters with clean engine oil and install them in their original locations. Apply moly-based engine assembly lubricant to the camshaft lobes and journals and install the camshafts into the cylinder head with the dowel pin on the exhaust camshaft in the 12 o'clock position and the dowel pin on the intake camshaft in the 9 o'clock position **(see illustration)**. If the old camshafts are being used, make sure they're installed in the exact location from which they came.

11   Install the bearing caps and bolts and tighten them hand tight.

12   Tighten the bearing cap bolts in several equal steps, to the torque listed in this Chapter's Specifications, using the proper tightening sequence **(see illustrations)**.

8.9b The lifters can be stored in individually-marked plastic bags, or in a divided, marked box like this one

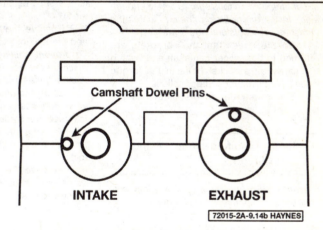

8.10 Position of the camshaft dowel pins before installing the sprockets

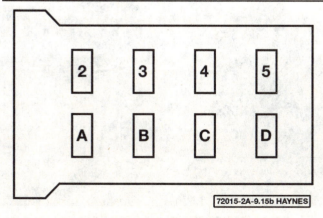

8.12a Camshaft bearing cap designations

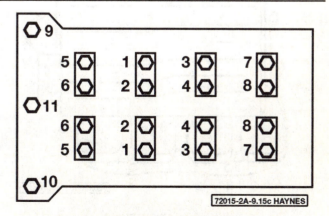

8.12b Camshaft bearing cap bolt tightening sequence

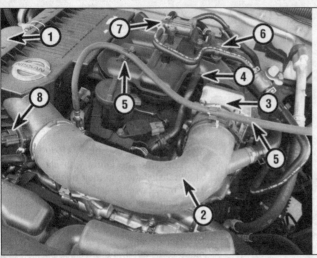

1   Air filter cover, remove
2   Air tube to throttle body, remove
3   Throttle body, disconnect hoses and electrical connector
4   PCV hose, disconnect
5   Fuel line, release from clips
6   EVAP hose, release from clips
7   EVAP solenoid, unbolt and set aside
8   MAF sensor, disconnect

9.4 Intake manifold removal details

13   Engage the camshaft sprocket teeth with the timing chain links so that the match marks made during removal align with the marks on the sprockets, then position the sprockets over the dowels on the camshaft hubs and install the camshaft sprocket bolts finger tight. **Note:** *It will be necessary to depress the upper timing chain tensioner to create enough slack in the upper timing chain to install the camshaft sprockets onto the dowel pins.*
14   Double check that the sprockets are returned to the proper camshaft and tighten the camshaft sprocket bolts to the torque listed in this Chapter's Specifications.
15   The remainder of installation is the reverse of removal.

9   Intake manifold - removal and installation

Warning: *Wait until the engine is completely cool before beginning this procedure.*

Removal

Refer to illustration 9.4

1   Relieve the fuel system pressure (see Chapter 4). Disconnect the cable from the negative terminal of the battery.
2   Remove the air filter housing and air filter from the intake manifold (see Chapter 1).
3   Remove the throttle body, the fuel rail and the fuel injectors (see Chapter 4). **Note:** *To prevent spilling coolant, use clamps to pinch-off the hoses before disconnecting the coolant hoses from the throttle body.*
4   Label and detach all wire harnesses and vacuum hoses connected to the intake manifold **(see illustration)**.
5   Working underneath the vehicle, unbolt the lower brace from the intake manifold.
6   Remove the mounting nuts/bolts, then detach the manifold from the engine **(see illustration 9.9)**.

Installation

Refer to illustration 9.9

7   Remove all traces of old gasket material and sealant from the manifold and cylinder head.
8   Install a new gasket, then position the manifold on the cylinder head and install the nuts/bolts.
9   Tighten the nuts/bolts in three or four equal steps to the torque listed in this Chapter's Specifications. Follow the recommended tightening sequence **(see illustration)**.
10   Install the remaining parts in the reverse order of removal. Refill the cooling system (see Chapter 1).
11   Run the engine and check for coolant and vacuum leaks. Road test the vehicle and check for proper operation of all accessories.

10   Exhaust manifold - removal and installation

Warning: *The engine must be completely cool before beginning this procedure.*

Removal

Refer to illustrations 10.4 and 10.7

1   Disconnect the cable from the negative terminal of the battery.
2   Block the rear wheels and set the parking brake. Raise the front of the vehicle and support it securely on jackstands.
3   Remove the engine splash shields (if equipped).
4   Working underneath the vehicle, disconnect the exhaust pipe from the exhaust manifold **(see illustration)**. Also remove the brace from the catalytic converter to the transmission. **Note:** *Applying penetrating oil to the exhaust manifold fasteners may make removing the nuts/bolts easier.*
5   Working in the engine compartment, remove the lower heat shield from the exhaust manifold.

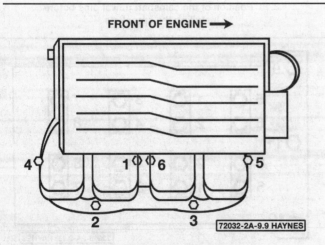

FRONT OF ENGINE →

72032-2A-9.9 HAYNES

9.9 Intake manifold TIGHTENING sequence

10.4 Remove the nuts (arrows) retaining the exhaust pipe to the exhaust manifold

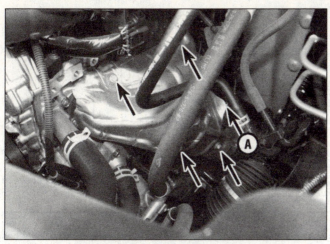

10.7 Heat shield mounting bolts - (A) is the oxygen sensor connector

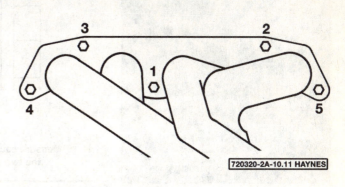

720320-2A-10.11 HAYNES

10.13 Exhaust manifold TIGHTENING sequence

6   Disconnect the electrical connector from the oxygen sensor.

7   Remove the heat shield from the exhaust manifold **(see illustration)**.

8   Disconnect the EGR pipe from the exhaust manifold.

9   Remove the exhaust manifold-to-cylinder head nuts, working from the outside toward the middle, and detach the manifold and gaskets **(see illustration 10.13)**.

Installation

Refer to illustration 10.13

10   Use a scraper to remove all traces of old gasket material and carbon deposits from the exhaust manifold and cylinder head mating surfaces.

11   Position the new exhaust manifold gaskets over the cylinder head studs.

12   Install the manifold and thread the mounting nuts into place.

13   Tighten the nuts in the recommended sequence to the torque listed in this Chapter's Specifications **(see illustration)**.

14   Reinstall the remaining parts in the reverse order of removal. Use anti-seize lubricant on the exhaust pipe studs and the EGR pipe nut.

15   Run the engine and check for exhaust leaks.

---

11   Cylinder head - removal and installation

Warning: *The engine must be completely cool before beginning this procedure.*

Removal

Refer to illustrations 11.7 and 11.8

1   Disconnect the cable from the negative battery terminal.

2   Drain the cooling system (see Chapter 1).

3   Refer to Section 7 and remove the timing chain.

4   Remove the camshafts and lifters (see

Section 8). **Note:** *It is only necessary to follow Steps 7 through 9 in the camshaft removal procedure, since the camshaft sprockets and the primary timing chain are already removed.*

5   Remove the exhaust manifold (see Section 10).

6   Label and remove any remaining items attached to the cylinder head, such as coolant fittings, oil dipstick tube, cables, hoses or wiring harness.

7   Using a breaker bar and the appropriate-sized hex bit, loosen the cylinder head bolts in 1/4-turn increments until they can be removed by hand **(see illustration)**. Loosen the bolts in the reverse of the tightening sequence **(see illustration 11.20)** to avoid warping or cracking the cylinder head.

8   Lift the cylinder head off the engine block. If it's stuck, very carefully pry up at a casting protrusion, beyond the gasket surface **(see illustration)**.

9   Remove all external components from the cylinder head to allow for thorough cleaning and inspection.

11.7 Use a hex bit and a long extension to loosen the cylinder head bolts

11.8 Pry the cylinder head off at a casting protrusion - do not pry under the gasket surface

11.11 Remove all traces of old gasket material - the cylinder head and block mating surfaces must be perfectly clean to ensure a good gasket seal

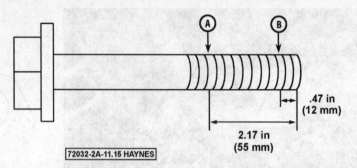

72032-2A-11.15 HAYNES

11.15 Measure each cylinder head bolt at point A and point B - If the difference between the two exceeds the specification, the bolt will have to be replaced

Installation

Refer to illustrations 11.11, 11.15 and 11.20

10   The mating surfaces of the cylinder head and block must be perfectly clean when the cylinder head is installed.

11   Use a gasket scraper to remove all traces of carbon and old gasket material from the block and the cylinder head, being careful not to gouge the aluminum **(see illustration)**. Then clean the mating surfaces with brake system cleaner. If there's oil on the mating surfaces when the cylinder head is installed, the gasket may not seal correctly and leaks could develop.

12   When working on the block, stuff the cylinders with clean shop rags to keep out debris. Use a vacuum cleaner to remove material that falls into the cylinders.

13   Check the block and cylinder head mating surfaces for nicks, deep scratches and other damage. If damage is slight, it can be removed with a fine file; if it's excessive, machining may be the only alternative.

14   Use a tap of the correct size to chase the threads in the cylinder head bolt holes, then clean the holes with compressed air - make sure that nothing remains in the holes. **Warning:** *Wear eye protection when using compressed air!*

15   Use a wire wheel or brush to remove cor-

rosion and dirt from the bolt threads. Dirt, corrosion and sealant will affect torque readings. Measure each cylinder head bolt for stretching **(see illustration)**. If the diameter of the bolt threads at point A and the diameter of the bolt threads at point B differ more than 0.0043 inch (0.11 mm), the bolts have exceeded the maximum amount of stretch and will need to be replaced.

16   Once the cylinder head's gasket surface is clean, check the cylinder head for warpage (see Chapter 2B, **illustration 11.15**). Also check the intake and exhaust manifolds for warpage.

17   Install the components that were removed from the cylinder head, including the intake manifold (see Section 9).

18   Position the new cylinder head gasket over the dowel pins in the block and carefully set the cylinder head on the block without disturbing the gasket.

19   Before installing the cylinder head bolts, apply a small amount of clean engine oil to the threads and hardened washers. The chamfered side of the washers must face the bolt heads, and the flat side of the washers must face the cylinder head. **Caution:** *The manufacturer suggests that the head bolts be replaced with new ones when reinstalling the head.*

20   Install the cylinder head bolts in their original locations and tighten them in the recommended sequence to the torque listed in this Chapter's Specifications **(see illustration)**.

21   Refer to Section 8 and install the lifters and the camshafts on the cylinder head. If any

machine work was done to the cylinder head (a valve job), it will be necessary to check and adjust the valve clearances (see Section 5).

22   Follow the timing chain installation procedure in Section 7.

23   The remaining installation steps are the reverse of removal.

24   Change the engine oil and filter (see Chapter 1).

25   Refill the cooling system (see Chapter 1), then run the engine and check for leaks.

12   Crankshaft pulley - removal and installation

Refer to illustrations 12.4 and 12.5

1   Disconnect the negative cable from the battery. Raise the front of the vehicle and secure it on jackstands.

2   Remove the engine under cover. Remove the lower radiator shroud and remove the engine cooling fan (see Chapter 3).

3   Remove the drivebelts (see Chapter 1).

4   Use a strap wrench around the crankshaft pulley to hold it while using a breaker bar and socket to remove the crankshaft pulley center bolt **(see illustration)**.

5   Wedge a prybar or two screwdrivers behind the crankshaft pulley and carefully pry it off the crankshaft **(see illustration)**. If the pulley is difficult to remove, use a jaw-type puller and pull it off.

6   Installation is the reverse of removal. Tighten the pulley bolt to the torque listed in this Chapter's Specifications.

7   Adjust the drivebelts (see Chapter 1).

13   Crankshaft front oil seal - replacement

Crankshaft front oil seal replacement for the four cylinder engine is identical to the crankshaft front oil seal replacement procedure for the V6 engine. Refer to Section 12 for the crankshaft pulley removal procedure, then refer to Chapter 2B for the front oil seal removal procedure. Be sure to use the torque figures in this Chapter's Specifications.

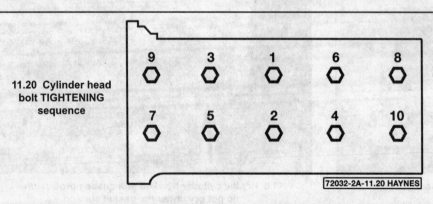

11.20 Cylinder head bolt TIGHTENING sequence

72032-2A-11.20 HAYNES

12.4 Use a strap wrench to hold the crankshaft pulley while removing the center bolt (a chain-type wrench may be used if you wrap a section of old drivebelt around the crankshaft pulley first)

12.5 If the pulley is difficult to remove, place a three-jaw puller around the center hub and pull it off

14 Oil pan - removal and installation

Removal

1   Disconnect the cable from the negative terminal of the battery.
2   Raise the vehicle and securely support it on jackstands.
3   Remove the engine undercover.
4   Drain the engine oil and remove the oil filter (see Chapter 1).
5   On automatic transmission models, unclip the transmission fluid lines from the brackets on the oil pan mounting flange.
6   Remove the engine oil dipstick.
7   Remove the oil pan mounting bolts, following the reverse of the tightening sequence **(see illustration 14.14)**.
8   The oil pan may be stuck to the block, since it utilizes RTV sealant rather than a gasket. Use a utility knife or razor to slice between the block and oil pan to separate most of the RTV at the seam.
9   Detach the oil pan. Do not pry between the pan and block, as a tool could distort the

oil pan mounting flange.
10   If necessary, use a rubber hammer against the pan to dislodge it from the block.
11   Use a gasket scraper to remove all traces of old gasket material and sealant from the engine block and pan. Clean the mating surfaces with brake system cleaner.

Installation

Refer to illustrations 14.13 and 14.14

12   Ensure that the threaded holes in the engine block are clean (use a tap to remove any sealant or corrosion from the threads).
13   Apply a continuous 5/32-inch (3.5 mm) bead of RTV sealant to the inner sealing surface of the oil pan **(see illustration)**. **Note:** *Install the oil pan within five minutes of sealant application.*
14   Install the oil pan and tighten the bolts in three or four steps following the sequence shown **(see illustration)** to the torque listed in this Chapter's Specifications.
15   The remaining installation steps are the reverse of removal.

16   Allow at least 30 minutes for the sealant to dry, add oil and a new oil filter, start the engine and check for oil pressure and leaks.

15 Oil pump and pick-up tube - removal, inspection and installation

Removal

Refer to illustration 15.6

1   Disconnect the cable from the negative terminal of the battery.
2   Position the engine at TDC for cylinder number 1 (see Section 3).
3   Remove the engine front cover and the timing chain (see Section 7).
4   The oil pump assembly is bolted to the lower portion of the front of the block, centered on the crankshaft snout.
5   Remove the bolt(s) securing the oil strainer and tube to the block and separate the tube from the oil pump.

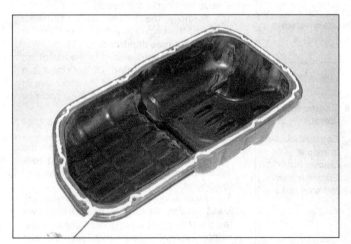

14.13 Apply a bead of RTV sealant around the perimeter of the oil pan

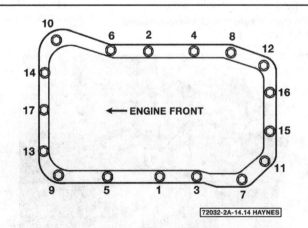

`72032-2A-14.14 HAYNES`

14.14 Oil pan bolt TIGHTENING sequence

6   Remove the one bolt and one screw securing the oil pump to the block (**see illustration**). Slide the oil pump off the crankshaft.

Inspection

7   Remove the screws securing both halves of the pump body. Remove, clean and examine the condition of the inner rotors. **Note:** *Make note of which way they are facing within the oil pump body.*
8   Using feeler gauges and a micrometer or vernier calipers, check the clearances of the oil pump components against the measurements in this Chapter's Specifications.
9   If any of the clearances are not within specifications, replace the entire oil pump as a unit.

Installation

10   Reassemble the pump components, using petroleum jelly to lubricate the rotors.
11   Install the pump body screws, tightening them to this Chapter's Specifications.
12   The remainder of installation is the reverse of the removal procedure. Make sure the flats inside the oil pump align with the flats on the crankshaft snout when installing the oil pump.
13   Reinstall the oil pump pickup tube, using a new O-ring or gasket. Install a new oil filter and add engine oil to the crankcase.
14   Start the engine and check for oil pressure and leaks.
15   Recheck the oil level.

---

16   Flywheel/driveplate - removal and installation

The flywheel/driveplate replacement for the four cylinder engine is identical to the flywheel/driveplate replacement procedure for the V6 engine. Refer to Chapter 2 Part B for the procedure and use the torque figures in this Chapter's Specifications.

---

17   Rear main oil seal - replacement

---

1   Remove the transmission (see Chapter 7A or 7B).
2   On manual transmission models, remove the clutch (see Chapter 8)

15.6 Oil pump assembly details

A   Main oil pump body
B   Outer rotor
C   Inner rotor
D   Oil pump cover
E   Regulator plug
F   Regulator valve springs
G   Regulator valve

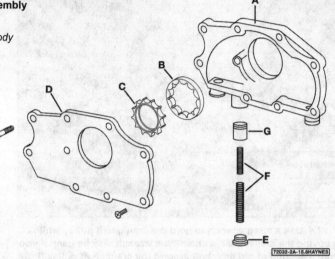

3   Remove the flywheel/driveplate, noting any spacers that may be used.
4   Use a screwdriver or seal removal tool to pry out the rear seal, being careful not to scratch the crankshaft's seal surface. Note which way the lip on the old seal faced.
5   Clean the seal bore and apply fresh engine oil to the lip and edge of the new seal.
6   Slide the seal over the crankshaft, then drive it in squarely with a seal driver.
7   The remainder of installation is the reverse of the removal procedure.

---

18   Engine mounts - check and replacement

---

1   Engine mounts seldom require attention, but broken or deteriorated mounts should be replaced immediately or the added strain placed on the driveline components may cause damage or wear.

Check

2   During the check, the engine must be raised slightly to remove the weight from the mounts.
3   Raise the vehicle and support it securely on jackstands. Remove the splash shields.
4   Position a jack under the engine oil pan.

Place a large wood block between the jack head and the oil pan, then carefully raise the engine *just enough* to take the weight off the mounts. Do not place the wood block under the oil pan drain plug. **Warning:** *DO NOT place any part of your body under the engine when it's supported only by a jack!*
5   Check the mounts to see if the rubber is cracked, hardened or separated from the metal plates. Sometimes the rubber will split right down the center.
6   Check for relative movement between the mount plates and the engine or frame using a large screwdriver or prybar to attempt to move the mounts. If movement is noted, lower the engine and tighten the mount fasteners.
7   Rubber preservative should be applied to the mounts to slow deterioration.

Replacement

Refer to illustration 18.10

8   Disconnect the cable from the negative terminal of the battery, set the parking brake and block the rear wheels.
9   Raise the front of the vehicle and support it securely on jackstands. Remove the splash shields from under the vehicle.
10   Remove the engine mount-to-frame bolts and the engine mount-to-mount bracket retaining nut (**see illustration**).
11   Attach an engine hoist to the top of the engine for lifting. **Caution:** *Do not use a jack under the oil pan to support the entire weight of the engine or the oil pump pick-up could be damaged.*
12   Raise the engine slightly until the engine mount can be removed from the vehicle.
13   To remove the mount brackets from the engine, simply detach the four retaining bolts securing the mount bracket to each side of the engine.
14   Installation is the reverse of removal. Make sure to reinstall the heat shields over the top of each mount and use thread locking compound on the mount nuts before tightening them to the torque listed in this Chapter's Specifications.

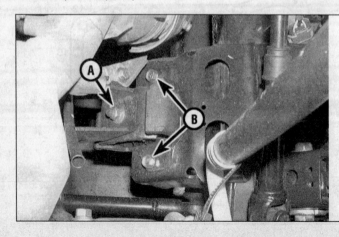

18.10 Engine mount details

A   Engine mount-to-mount bracket nut
B   Engine mount-to-frame bolts

Chapter 2 Part B
4.0L V6 engine

Contents

Specifications

General

Engine designation	VQ40DE
Displacement	241 cubic inches (4.0 liters)
Bore	3.76 inches (95.5 mm)
Stroke	3.622 inches (92 mm)
Cylinder numbers (front to rear)	
Right (passenger side)	1-3-5
Left (driver's side)	2-4-6
Firing order	1-2-3-4-5-6

FRONT OF VEHICLE

⑤ ⑥
③ ④
❶ ②

72031-1-SPECS HAYNES

Cylinder location diagram

Cylinder head warpage limit ... 0.004 inch (0.1 mm)

Camshaft

Endplay	
Standard	0.0045 to 0.0074 inch (0.115 to 0.188 mm)
Limit	Not available
Journal diameter	
No. 1	1.0211 to 1.0218 inches (25.935 to 25.955 mm)
No. 2 through 4	0.9230 to 0.9238 inch (23.445 to 23.465 mm)
Bearing inside diameter	
No. 1	1.0236 to 1.0244 inches (26.000 to 26.021 mm)
No. 2 through 4	0.9252 to 0.9260 inch (23.500 to 23.521 mm)
Bearing oil clearance	
No. 1	0.0018 to 0.0034 inch (0.045 to 0.086 mm)
No. 2 through 4	0.0014 to 0.0030 inch (0.035 to 0.076 mm)
Service limit	Not available
Runout limit	0.0020 inch maximum (0.05 mm)
Lobe height	
Intake	1.7900 to 1.7974 inches (45.465 to 45.655 mm)
Exhaust	1.7746 to 1.7821 inches (45.075 to 45.265 mm)

Valve clearance (cold)

Intake	0.010 to 0.013 inch (0.26 to 0.34 mm)
Exhaust	0.011 to 0.015 inch (0.29 to 0.37 mm)

Oil pump

Body-to-outer rotor clearance	0.0047 to 0.0077 inch (0.120 to 0.195 mm)
Inner rotor-to-outer rotor tip clearance	0.0024 to 0.0063 inch (0.06 to 0.16 mm)
Inner rotor-to-body clearance	0.0012 to 0.0028 inch (0.030 to 0.070 mm)
Outer rotor-to-body clearance	0.0020 to 0.0035 inch (0.05 to 0.09 mm)

Torque specifications

Note: *One foot-pound (ft-lb) of torque is equivalent to 12 inch-pounds (in-lbs) of torque. Torque values below approximately 15 ft-lbs are expressed in inch-pounds, since most foot-pound torque wrenches are not accurate at these smaller values.*

	Ft-lbs (unless otherwise indicated)	Nm
Camshaft bearing caps (see illustration 8.13a)		
Step 1 (bolts 7-10)	17 in-lbs	2
Step 2 (bolts 1-6)	17 in-lbs	2
Step 3 (bolts 7-10)	52 in-lbs	6
Camshaft sprocket bolts	76	103
Crankshaft pulley-to-crankshaft bolt		
Step 1	33	44
Step 2	Tighten an additional 84 to 90 degrees	
Cylinder head bolts (see illustration 11.20)		
Step 1	72	98
Step 2	Loosen all bolts in reverse order of tightening	
Step 3	29	39
Step 4	Tighten an additional 90 degrees	
Step 5	Tighten an additional 90 degrees	
Driveplate/flywheel bolts	65	88
Exhaust manifold bolts	22	30
Exhaust manifold heat-shield bolts	51 in-lbs	5.5
Engine mount nuts	65	88
Engine mount-to-frame bolts	65	88
Engine mount bracket-to-block bolts	36	49
Intake plenum bolts/nuts (see illustration 9.7)	96 in-lbs	11
Intake manifold-to-head bolts/nuts (see illustration 9.16)		
Step 1	60 in-lbs	7
Step 2	21	29
Oil cooler-to-engine block bolt	36	49
Oil pressure switch	132 in-lbs	15
Oil pump-to-front cover bolts	61 in-lbs	7
Oil pump-to-front cover screws	61 in-lbs	7
Oil strainer mounting bolts	16	22
Oil pan bolts (steel lower pan) (see illustration 14.22)	80 in-lbs	9
Oil pan bolts (aluminum upper pan) (see illustration 14.19)	16	22
Oil pan drain plug	25	34
Timing chain tensioner bolts		
Primary chain	72 in-lbs	8
Secondary chain	75 in-lbs	8.5
Primary guide pivot bolt	144 in-lbs	16
Timing chain cover bolts		
Front cover		
10mm bolts	41	55
6mm bolts	108 in-lbs	12
Rear cover bolts	108 in-lbs	12
Valve cover bolts (see illustration 4.13)		
Step 1	17 in-lbs	2
Step 2	74 in-lbs	8
Variable valve timing cover bolts	96 in-lbs	11

1 General information

This Part of Chapter 2 is devoted to in-vehicle repair procedures for the VQ40DE 4.0L Dual Overhead Camshaft (DOHC) V6 engine. Information concerning engine removal, installation and overhaul can be found in Part C of this Chapter.

The following repair procedures are based on the assumption that the engine is installed in the vehicle. If the engine has been removed from the vehicle and mounted on a stand, many of the steps outlined in this Part of Chapter 2 will not apply.

2 Repair operations possible with the engine in the vehicle

Many major repair operations can be accomplished without removing the engine from the vehicle.

Clean the engine compartment and the exterior of the engine with some type of degreaser before any work is done. It will make the job easier and help keep dirt out of the internal areas of the engine.

Depending on the components involved, it may be helpful to remove the hood to improve access to the engine as repairs are performed (refer to Chapter 11 if necessary). Cover the fenders to prevent damage to the paint. Special pads are available, but an old bedspread or blanket will also work.

If vacuum, exhaust, oil or coolant leaks develop, indicating a need for gasket or seal replacement, the repairs can generally be made with the engine in the vehicle. The intake and exhaust manifold gaskets, oil pan gasket, crankshaft oil seals and cylinder head gaskets are all accessible with the engine in place.

Exterior engine components, such as the intake and exhaust manifolds, the oil pan, the oil pump, the water pump (see Chapter 3), the starter motor, the alternator and the fuel system components (see Chapter 4) can be removed for repair with the engine in place.

Since the cylinder heads can be removed without pulling the engine, valve component servicing can also be accomplished with the engine in the vehicle. Replacement of the camshafts, timing chains and sprockets are also possible with the engine in the vehicle.

In extreme cases caused by a lack of necessary equipment, repair or replacement of piston rings, pistons, connecting rods and rod bearings is possible with the engine in the vehicle. However, this practice is not recommended because of the cleaning and preparation work that must be done to the components involved.

3 Top Dead Center (TDC) for number one piston - locating

Refer to illustration 3.8

1 Top Dead Center (TDC) is the highest point in the cylinder that each piston reaches as it travels up the cylinder bore. Each piston reaches TDC on the compression stroke and again on the exhaust stroke, but TDC generally refers to piston position on the compression stroke.

2 Positioning the piston(s) at TDC is an essential part of many procedures such as valve timing, camshaft and timing chain/sprocket removal.

3 Before beginning this procedure, be sure to place the transmission in Park (automatic) or Neutral (manual) and apply the parking brake or block the rear wheels. Disable the ignition system by disconnecting the primary electrical connectors at the ignition coil packs, then remove the coil packs and spark plugs (see Chapter 1). Disable the fuel system (see Chapter 4, Section 2).

4 In order to bring any piston to TDC, the crankshaft must be turned using one of the methods outlined below. When looking at the front of the engine, normal crankshaft rotation is clockwise.

a) The preferred method is to turn the crankshaft with a socket and ratchet attached to the bolt threaded into the front of the crankshaft. Turn the bolt in a clockwise direction.
b) A remote starter switch, which may save some time, can also be used. Follow the instructions included with the switch. Once the piston is close to TDC, use a socket and ratchet as described in the previous paragraph.
c) If an assistant is available to turn the ignition switch to the Start position in short bursts, you can get the piston close to TDC without a remote starter switch. Make sure your assistant is out of the vehicle, away from the ignition switch, then use a socket and ratchet as described in Paragraph (a) to complete the procedure.

5 Install a compression pressure gauge in the number one spark plug hole (refer to Chapter 2C). It should be a gauge with a screw-in fitting and a hose at least six inches long.

6 Rotate the crankshaft using one of the methods described above while observing for pressure on the compression gauge. The moment the gauge shows pressure indicates that the number one cylinder has begun the compression stroke.

7 Once the compression stroke has begun, TDC for the compression stroke is reached by bringing the piston to the top of the cylinder.

8 Continue turning the crankshaft until the TDC notch in the crankshaft damper is aligned with the pointer on the front cover **(see illustration)**. At this point, the number one cylinder is at TDC on the compression stroke. If the marks are aligned but there was no compression, the piston was on the exhaust stroke. Continue rotating the crankshaft 360-degrees (1-turn). **Note:** *If a compression gauge is not available, you can simply place a blunt object (such as the end of a screwdriver handle) over the spark plug hole and listen for compression as the engine is rotated. Once compression at the No.1 spark plug hole is noted the remainder of the Step is the same.*

9 After the number one piston has been positioned at TDC on the compression stroke, TDC for any of the remaining cylinders can be located by turning the crankshaft 120 degrees and following the firing order (refer to the Specifications). Rotating the engine 120 degrees past TDC #1 will put the engine at TDC compression for cylinder #2.

4 Valve covers - removal and installation

Removal

Refer to illustrations 4.2, 4.5a and 4.5b

1 Disconnect the cable from the negative terminal of the battery.

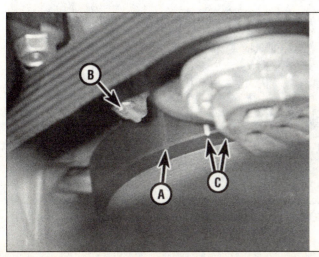

3.8 Align the TDC notch on the crankshaft pulley (A) with the pointer on the timing chain cover (B) - the TDC notch is the one farthest to the left when facing the front of the engine. (C) are the timing advance marks (one not visible in this photo)

4.2 Remove the fasteners (arrows) and detach the engine cover

4.5a Left valve cover details: A, remove the ignition coils and their harness; B, disconnect the PCV hose; and C, remove the valve cover bolts (three visible here)

2   Remove the engine cover **(see illustration)**. If removing the right valve cover, refer to Section 9 and remove the intake manifold plenum.

3   Remove the ignition coils from the valve cover (see Chapter 5). If both valve covers are being removed, remove all six of the ignition coils.

4   Remove the breather hose by sliding the hose clamp back and pulling the hose off the fitting on the valve cover.

5   Detach the PCV hose and any wiring which would interfere with valve cover removal **(see illustrations)**.

6   Remove the valve cover bolts and washers in the reverse order of the tightening sequence **(see illustration 4.13)**.

7   Detach the valve cover. **Note:** *If the cover is stuck to the cylinder head, bump one end with a block of wood and a hammer to jar it loose. If that doesn't work, try to slip a flexible putty knife between the cylinder head and cover to break the gasket seal. Don't pry at*

the cover-to-cylinder head joint or damage to the sealing surfaces may occur (leading to oil leaks in the future).

Installation

Refer to illustrations 4.10 and 4.13

8   The mating surfaces of each cylinder head and valve cover must be perfectly clean when the covers are installed. Use a gasket scraper to remove all traces of sealant and old gasket material, then clean the mating surfaces with brake system cleaner. If there's sealant or oil on the mating surfaces when the cover is installed, oil leaks may develop.

9   If necessary, clean the mounting bolt threads with a wire wheel to remove any corrosion. Make sure the threaded holes in the cylinder head are clean - run a tap into them to remove corrosion and restore damaged threads.

10   Inspect and replace, if necessary, the

spark plug tube sealing washers **(see illustration)**.

11   The valve cover gaskets should be mated to the covers before the covers are installed. Apply a thin coat of RTV sealant to the cover groove and to the corners on the front camshaft journal cap, then position the gasket inside the cover and allow the sealant to set up so the gasket adheres to the cover. If the sealant isn't allowed to set, the gasket may fall out of the cover as it's installed on the engine.

12   Carefully position the cover on the cylinder head and install the bolts.

13   Following the recommended tightening sequence, tighten the bolts, in two equal steps, to the torque listed in this Chapter's Specifications **(see illustration)**.

14   The remaining installation steps are the reverse of removal.

15   Start the engine and check carefully for oil leaks.

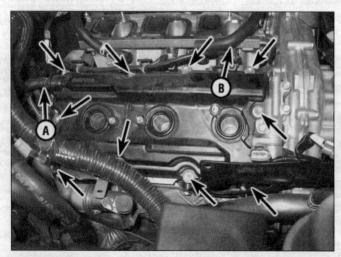

4.5b Remove the breather hose (A) and the PCV hose (B, already disconnected) and position aside any wiring harness that would interfere with the removal of the valve cover, then remove the bolts

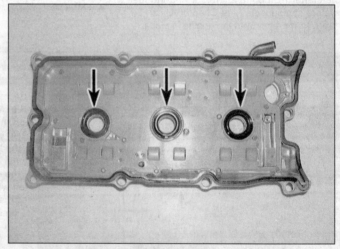

4.10 Make sure to install new spark plug tube seals (arrows) into the valve cover

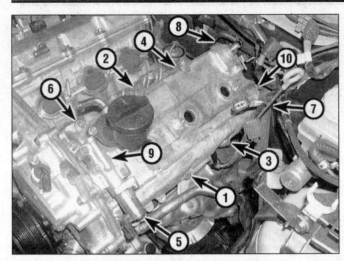

4.13 Valve cover TIGHTENING sequence

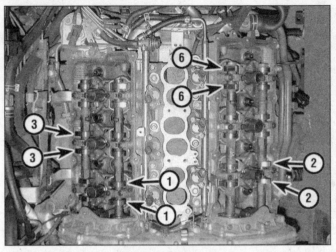

5.6a When the no. 1 piston is at TDC on the compression stroke, the valve clearance for the no. 1 and no. 6 cylinder intake valves and the no. 2 and no. 3 cylinder exhaust valves can be measured

5 Valve clearance - check and adjustment

Refer to illustrations 5.6a, 5.6b, 5.7, 5.8 and 5.10

Note 1: *The manufacturer recommends adjusting the valve clearance at the specified interval only if the valve train is making excessive noise.*

Note 2: *Wait until the engine is completely cool before checking the valve clearances.*

1 Disconnect the cable from the negative terminal of the battery.

2 Remove the valve cover (see Section 4).

3 On manual transmission vehicles, set the parking brake and place the transmission in the neutral position.

4 Remove the spark plugs (see Chapter 1).

5 Position the number 1 piston at TDC on the compression stroke and align the timing marks (see Section 3).

6 Measure the clearance of the indicated valves with a feeler gauge **(see illustrations)**. Record each measurement and compare your measurements with the desired valve clearance found in this Chapter's Specifications. Note which are out of specification, as this data will be used later to determine the required replacement lifters.

7 Turn the crankshaft 240 degrees clockwise. Measure and record the clearances of the indicated valves **(see illustration)**.

8 Turn the crankshaft an additional 240 degrees clockwise. Measure and record the clearances of the indicated valves **(see illustration)**.

9 The V6 engine does not use valve adjusting shims. If a lifter is out of specification for clearance, the lifter must be replaced with a new lifter that has a different thickness

5.6b Measure the clearance for each valve with a feeler gauge of the specified thickness - if the clearance is correct, you should feel a slight drag on the gauge as you pull it out

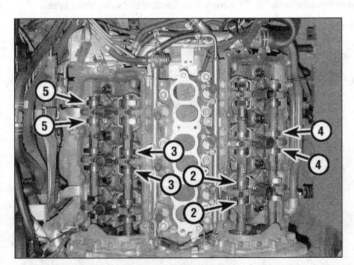

5.7 After checking the valves indicated in illustration 5.6a, turn the crankshaft 240 degrees (1/3-turn) clockwise and check the valve clearances for the no. 2 and no. 3 cylinder intake valves and the no. 4 and no. 5 cylinder exhaust valves

5.8 After checking the valves indicated in illustration 5.7, turn the crankshaft 240 degrees (1/3-turn) clockwise and check the valve clearances for the no. 4 and no. 5 cylinder intake valves and the no. 1 and no. 6 cylinder exhaust valves

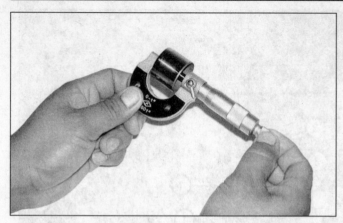

5.10 Measure the lifter thickness with a micrometer

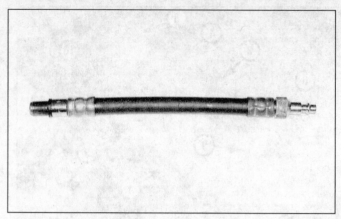

6.5 The air hose adapter threads into the spark plug hole -
they're commonly available from auto parts stores

head to correct the clearance. Refer to Section 8 and remove the camshafts to access the lifters.

10   Mark the lifters that are to be replaced, and record which valve they came from. Use a micrometer to measure the thickness of the lifter in the center, making sure the measurement is precise and on the center projection on the underside of the lifter **(see illustration)**.

11   To calculate the correct thickness for a replacement lifter that will place the valve clearance within the specified value, use the following formula:

Intake side: $N = R + (M - 0.012$ inch $[0.30$ mm])

Exhaust side: $N = R + (M - 0.013$ inch $[0.33$ mm])

R = thickness of old lifter
M = measured valve clearance
N = thickness of new lifter

12   New lifters are available in 27 standard thicknesses, from 0.3102 inch to 0.3291 inch (7.88 to 8.36 mm). Lifters are marked on the underside as to their size.

13   Mark the new lifters as to their destination, lubricate them with engine assembly lube and install them. After replacing the lifters, refer to Section 8 and reinstall the camshafts.

14   The remainder of installation is the reverse of removal.

6   Valve springs, retainers and seals - replacement

Refer to illustrations 6.5, 6.7a, 6.7b, 6.13 and 6.15

Note: *Broken valve springs and defective valve stem seals can be replaced without removing the cylinder heads. Two special tools and a compressed air source are normally required to perform this operation, so read through this Section carefully. The universal shaft-type valve spring compressor required for the tight valve spring pockets of this vehicle may not be available at all tool*

rental yards, so check on the availability before beginning the job.

1   Remove the intake plenum (see Section 9) and the valve covers (see Section 4).

2   Refer to Section 7 and remove the timing chain, then refer to Section 8 and remove the camshafts and lifters from both cylinder heads.

3   Remove the spark plugs (see Chapter 1).

4   Turn the crankshaft until the piston in the affected cylinder is at Top Dead Center on the compression stroke (see Section 3). If you're replacing all of the valve stem seals, begin with cylinder number one and work on the valves for one cylinder at a time. Move from cylinder-to-cylinder following the firing order sequence (see this Chapter's Specifications), turning the crankshaft 120-degrees to bring the next cylinder to TDC.

5   Thread a long adapter into the spark plug hole and connect an air hose from a compressed air source to it **(see illustration)**. Most auto parts stores can supply the air hose adapter. **Note:** *Because of the length of the spark plug tubes, it will be necessary to use a*

long spark plug adapter with a length of hose attached (as used on many cylinder compression gauges) utilizing a quick-disconnect fitting to hook to your air source.

6   Apply compressed air to the cylinder. **Warning:** *The piston may be forced down by the compressed air, causing the crankshaft to turn suddenly. If the wrench used when positioning the number one piston at TDC is still attached to the bolt in the crankshaft nose, it could cause damage or injury when the crankshaft moves.*

7   Stuff shop rags into the cylinder head holes around the valves to prevent parts and tools from falling into the engine, then use a valve spring compressor to compress the spring **(see illustrations)**. Remove the keepers with small needle-nose pliers or a magnet. **Note:** *The valves should be held in place by the air pressure. If the valve faces or seats are in poor condition, leaks may prevent air pressure from retaining the valves. If the valves cannot hold air, the cylinder head should be removed for a valve job at a machine shop.*

8   Remove the spring retainer and valve spring, then remove the valve stem seal.

6.7a Compress the valve spring enough to release the valve stem keepers . . .

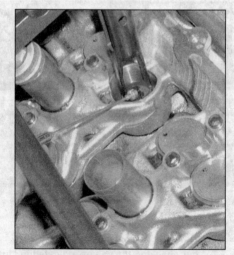

6.7b . . . and lift them out with a magnet or needle-nose pliers

9   Wrap a rubber band or tape around the top of the valve stem so the valve won't fall into the combustion chamber, then release the air pressure.

10   Inspect the valve stem for damage. Rotate the valve in the guide and check the end for eccentric movement, which would indicate that the valve is bent.

11   Move the valve up-and-down in the guide and make sure it doesn't bind. If the valve stem binds, either the valve is bent or the guide is damaged. In either case, the cylinder head will have to be removed for repair.

12   Reapply air pressure to the cylinder to retain the valve in the closed position, then remove the tape or rubber band from the valve stem.

13   Lubricate the valve stems with engine oil and install a new valve stem seals. Valve stem seals can be installed with a special tool, or a deep socket and hammer - tap the seal only until seated **(see illustration)**.

14   Install the valve spring in position over the valve, with the more closely-wound spring coils and the paint mark toward the cylinder head.

15   Install the valve spring retainer. Compress the valve springs and carefully position the keepers in the groove. Apply a small dab of grease to the inside of each keeper to hold it in place **(see illustration)**.

16   Remove the pressure from the spring tool and make sure the keepers are seated.

17   Disconnect the air hose and remove the adapter from the spark plug hole.

18   Refer to Section 8 and install the camshafts and lifters, then refer to Section 7 and install the timing chain.

19   Refer to Section 4 and install the valve covers.

20   Install the spark plugs, ignition coils and the upper and lower intake plenum referring to the appropriate Sections as necessary.

21   Start and run the engine, then check for oil leaks and unusual sounds coming from the valve cover area.

---

7   Timing chains and sprockets - removal, inspection and installation

Warning: *The engine must be completely cool before beginning this procedure.*

Removal

Refer to illustrations 7.14, 7.16, 7.19, 7.20, 7.21, 7.22, 7.23a, 7.23b, 7.24, 7.26 and 7.27

Caution: *The timing system is complex. Severe engine damage will occur if you make any mistakes. Do not attempt this procedure unless you are highly experienced with this type of repair. If you are at all unsure of your abilities, consult an expert. Double-check all your work and be sure everything is correct before you attempt to start the engine.*

1   Relieve the system fuel pressure (see Chapter 4).

6.13 Using a deep socket and hammer, gently tap the new seals onto the valve guide only until seated

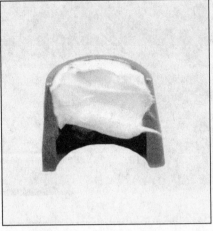

6.15 Apply a small dab of grease to each keeper as shown here before installation - it will hold them in place on the valve stem as the spring is released

2   Disconnect the cable from the negative terminal of the battery.

3   Remove the engine cover **(see illustration 4.2)**.

4   Remove the drivebelts (see Chapter 1) and the idler pulley brackets.

5   Remove the spark plugs (see Chapter 1).

6   Position the number one piston at TDC on the compression stroke (see Section 3).

7   Block the rear wheels and set the parking brake. Raise the front of the vehicle and support it securely on jackstands.

8   Drain the cooling system and the engine oil (see Chapter 1).

9   Remove the crankshaft pulley (see Section 12). **Note:** *Don't allow the crankshaft to rotate during removal of the pulley. If the crankshaft moves, the number one piston will no longer be at TDC.*

10   Remove the air conditioning compressor (see Chapter 3) and position it aside without disconnecting the refrigerant lines. Also remove the air conditioning compressor bracket from the engine.

11   Remove the upper and lower oil pans

(see Section 14), then lower the vehicle.

12   Remove the upper and lower intake manifold plenums (see Section 9). **Note:** *If only the primary timing chain is to be removed, the valve covers do not have to be removed.*

13   Remove the valve covers (see Section 4). **Note:** *If only the primary timing chain is to be removed, the valve covers do not have to be removed.*

14   Remove the power steering pump (see Chapter 10) and position it aside without disconnecting the fluid lines. Also remove the fan pulley bracket and the power steering pump bracket **(see illustration)**.

15   Remove the alternator (see Chapter 5).

16   Remove the water by-pass pipe from the front of the engine. Using masking tape and a pen, mark the location of the coolant and vacuum hoses at the front of the engine, then remove any hoses that would interfere with the removal of the water by-pass pipe **(see illustration)**.

17   Remove the camshaft sensors from the rear of the cylinder heads (see Chapter 6) and the variable valve timing (VVT) sensors from the front timing chain cover (see Chap-

7.14 Front timing chain cover details: A, remove the power steering pump and its mounting bracket; B, remove the bolts (4 of 5 seen here) for the fan mounting bracket and idler pulley . . .

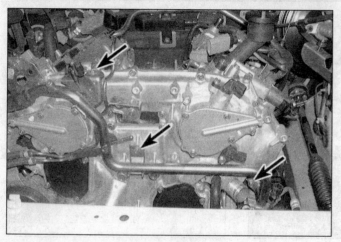

7.16 . . . and the water by-pass pipe

7.19 Insert a screwdriver into the notch at the top of the timing cover and pry the front timing cover off the engine

7.20 Verify the engine is at TDC by confirming that the intake and exhaust camshaft lobes on the number one cylinder are pointing upward

ter 6). Remove the variable valve timing actuator covers. Loosen the bolts in the reverse order of the tightening sequence (see illustration 7.41c) and pull the covers straight out to disengage them from the intake camshaft sprocket actuator assemblies.

18 Detach the wiring harness from the brackets at the top of the timing chain cover. Starting with the two bolts at the front of the oil pan, remove the bolts securing the front timing chain cover in the reverse order of the tightening sequence (see illustration 7.40b). Note that various types and sizes of bolts are used. They must be reinstalled in their original locations. Mark each bolt or make a sketch to help remember where they go.

19 Remove the front timing chain cover (see illustration).

20 Confirm that the number one piston is still at TDC on the compression stroke by verifying that the intake and exhaust camshaft lobes on the number one cylinder are pointing upward (see illustration).

21 Relieve tension on the primary timing

chain by releasing the spring clip. Depress the primary tensioner inward and lock it into place by inserting a suitable stopper pin into the hole on the front of the tensioner (see illustration). Note: *The 4.0L DOHC engine utilizes three timing chains to produce proper valve timing. The primary timing chain runs around the crankshaft sprocket, the water pump and around two intake camshaft sprockets. This chain synchronizes the valve timing with the crankshaft and pistons, while two secondary timing chains run around the rear of the intake sprockets and separate exhaust camshaft sprockets to synchronize the intake and exhaust camshaft events.*

22 Remove the primary timing chain tensioner, the tensioner pivot arm/chain guide and the upper timing chain guides from the primary timing chain (see illustration).

23 Depress the secondary timing chain tensioners and lock the tensioners in place by inserting a suitable stopper pin into the hole on the front of each tensioner (see illustrations).

7.21 An ordinary paper clip can be straightened and used to lock the timing chain tensioner(s) in place

7.22 Remove the primary timing chain tensioner mounting bolts (A), the tensioner arm/chain guide pivot bolt (B) and the upper chain guides (C)

7.23a Bend two paper clips so that they're long enough to protrude out past the camshaft sprocket once they're installed . . .

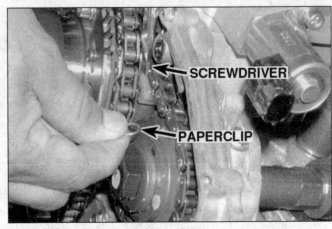

7.23b . . . then depress the secondary tensioners with a screwdriver and lock them in place by inserting a paper clip into the hole on the side of each tensioner - note that the secondary tensioner on the right bank points downward, while the secondary tensioner on the left bank points upward

24   Remove the camshaft sprocket bolts **(see illustration)**.

25   Disengage the primary timing chain from the teeth on the chain sprockets and remove it from the engine.

26   Mark the camshaft sprockets with either an R or L to indicate the right or left side, then remove the camshaft sprockets and the secondary timing chains from the engine. Don't mix the sprockets up. They must be installed on the same camshaft from which they were removed **(see illustration)**. **Caution:** *The intake camshaft sprockets are identified by the variable valve timing actuator and sensor ring which is fastened to the front of the sprocket. Be extremely careful not to damage or place a magnetic object of any kind near the sensor ring or a no start condition may occur after installation. Do Not disassemble the variable valve timing actuator assembly from the intake camshaft sprocket for any reason.*

27   Remove the crankshaft sprocket and the lower timing chain guide **(see illustration)**.

7.24 Hold the hexagonal lug on the camshaft with a wrench to keep it from rotating as the sprocket bolts are loosened (arrows indicate two of four bolts)

7.26 Note that the left intake camshaft sprocket has a sensor ring (arrow) which is fastened to the front of the sprocket - be extremely careful not to damage or place a magnetic object of any kind near the sensor ring or a no start condition may occur

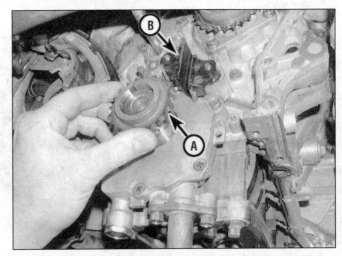

7.27 Remove the crankshaft sprocket (A) and the lower chain guide; make a note that the mark (B) on the chain guide must face up when reinstalling

7.28a Examine the chain guides for deep grooves and excessive wear - replace them if necessary

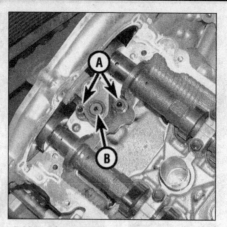

7.28b Secondary timing chain tensioner mounting bolts (A) - be sure to replace the O-ring (B) before reinstalling the front camshaft bearing cap

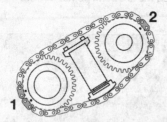

Rear cylinder bank

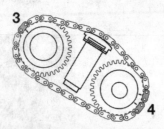

Front cylinder bank

72016-2B-6.34 HAYNES

7.32 Secondary timing chain alignment details

1   Rear cylinder bank exhaust camshaft sprocket: Align the two colored links with the two round marks
2   Rear cylinder bank intake camshaft sprocket: Align the single colored link with the single round mark (mark is on the backside of sprocket)
3   Front cylinder bank intake camshaft sprocket: Align the single colored link with the single oval mark (mark is on the backside of sprocket)
4   Front cylinder bank exhaust camshaft sprocket: Align the two colored links with the two oval marks

7.33 Note that the alignment of the exhaust camshaft sprocket mark (B) to the copper colored link (A) of the secondary chain can only be viewed from the front

7.34a The yellow colored or gold link on the timing chain (arrow) aligns with the mark on the crankshaft sprocket

Inspection

Refer to illustrations 7.28a and 7.28b

28   Inspect the camshaft, water pump and crankshaft sprockets for wear on the teeth and keyways. Inspect the chains for cracks or excessive wear of the rollers. Inspect the facing of the chain guides and the secondary timing chain tensioners for excessive wear **(see illustration)**. **Note:** *If the secondary timing chain tensioners need to be replaced, the front camshaft bearing cap will have to be removed from the affected cylinder head to allow access to the secondary tensioner bolts* **(see illustration)**.

Installation

Refer to illustrations 7.32, 7.33, 7.34a, 7.34b, 7.39, 7.40a, 7.40b, 7.41a, 7.41b and 7.41c

Caution: *Before starting the engine, carefully rotate the crankshaft by hand through at least two full revolutions (use a socket and breaker bar on the crankshaft pulley center bolt). If you feel any resistance, STOP! There is something wrong - most likely, valves are contacting the pistons. You must find the problem before proceeding. Check your work and see if any updated repair information is available.*

29   Install the crankshaft sprocket and the lower timing chain guide with mark facing up **(see illustration 7.27)**.

30   Verify that you have the correct timing chains for your vehicle by counting the number of links each chain has and comparing the new chains with the old chains. Also compare the position of the colored links in the new chains with the position of the colored links in the old chains.

31   If the secondary tensioners were removed, reinstall them and make sure the tensioner spring is locked in place.

32   Make sure the camshafts are positioned with the dowels on the exhaust camshafts in the 12 o'clock position in relation to the top of the cylinder head mating surface; the intake camshafts must be positioned with the small diameter dowel pin hole in the 12 o'clock position in relation to the top of the cylinder head mating surface. Install the secondary timing chains and sprocket assemblies on the camshafts with the timing marks aligned as shown **(see illustration)**. Install the camshaft sprocket bolts hand tight.

33   Reconfirm that the secondary camshaft sprocket timing marks are aligned correctly with the copper colored links on the secondary timing chains and remove the stopper pins from the secondary chain tensioners **(see illustration)**.

34   Install the primary timing chain onto the engine by looping the chain around the crankshaft sprocket and aligning the yellow or gold colored chain link with the mark on the crankshaft sprocket. Then place the chain around the water pump sprocket and finally around the primary camshaft sprockets making sure the yellow colored links align with their respective marks on the sprockets **(see illustrations)**. **Note:** *It may be necessary to rotate the camshafts slightly in order to align the yellow colored chain links with the marks*

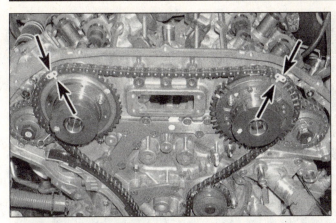

7.34b Make sure the copper colored links (upper arrows) on the primary timing chain align with the marks (lower arrows) on the intake camshaft sprockets

7.39 Install new O-rings at the indicated area on the right and left side of the rear timing cover case

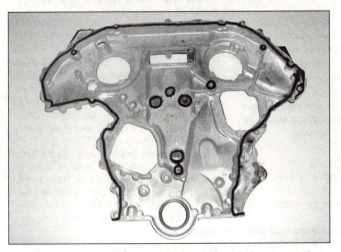

7.40a Apply RTV sealant to the front timing chain cover at the areas shown - be sure to wipe off any excess sealant

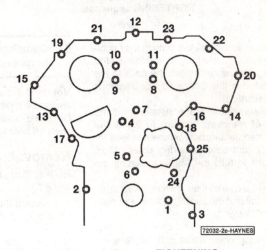

7.40b Front timing chain cover TIGHTENING sequence

on the primary timing chain sprockets.

35   Install the upper timing chain guides.

36   Install the primary tensioner arm/chain guide and the timing chain tensioner assembly **(see illustration 7.22)**. Reconfirm that the number one piston is still at TDC on the compression stroke and that the timing marks on the camshaft and crankshaft sprockets are aligned with the colored links on the chain, then remove the stopper pin from the primary timing chain tensioner.

37   Tighten the camshaft sprocket bolts to the torque listed in this Chapter's Specifications.

38   Remove all traces of old sealant from the front timing chain cover, the cover bolts and the rear cover bolt holes.

39   Install new O-rings in the variable valve timing oil control orifice of the rear timing cover **(see illustration)**.

40   Apply an 1/8-inch (3 mm) diameter bead of RTV sealant to the timing cover sealing surfaces **(see illustration)**. Place the front timing cover in position on the engine and install the bolts in their original locations. Following the recommended tightening sequence, tighten the bolts to the torque listed in this Chapter's Specifications **(see illustration)**. **Note:** *It will also be*

necessary to install the power steering pump bracket and the fan pulley bracket in order to tighten the bolts in the proper sequence.

41   Install new O-rings in the VVT orifices of the front timing chain cover and on the VVT

actuator covers. Then apply a 1/8-inch (3 mm) diameter bead of RTV sealant to the sealing surface of the variable valve timing actuator covers **(see illustrations)**. Place the VVT covers in position over the dowels on the front

7.41a Install new O-rings in both of the VVT orifices on the front timing chain cover

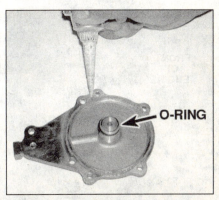

7.41b Apply a light film of engine oil to the new O-rings and install them in the groove on the VVT actuator covers, then apply an 1/8-inch (3 mm) diameter bead of RTV sealant to the mating surface

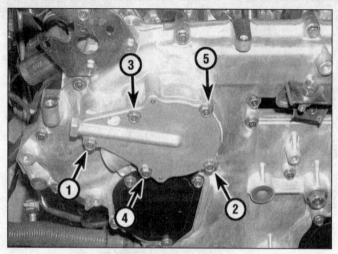

7.41c Variable Valve Timing actuator cover TIGHTENING sequence

8.4 Remove the variable valve timing valve(s) from the No.1 camshaft bearing cap(s)

timing cover and install the bolts in their original locations. Following the recommended tightening sequence, tighten the bolts to the torque listed in this Chapter's Specifications **(see illustration)**.

42   The remainder of the installation is the reverse of removal. Be sure to follow the sealant manufacturers recommendations for assembly and sealant curing times. Allow all sealant to fully cure before starting the engine.

43   Install a new oil filter, then refill the crankcase with oil and the cooling system with coolant (see Chapter 1).

44   Start the engine and check for leaks. **Note:** *Timing chain noise may be apparent after performing this procedure. This noise is normal and should only last until the air has bled out of the high pressure chamber of the primary timing chain tensioner. If after several minutes the noise is still apparent, simply run the engine at 3,000 rpm with the transmission in neutral or park until the noise subsides.*

8   Camshafts and lifters - removal, inspection and installation

Note: *The camshafts and lifters should always be thoroughly inspected before installation and camshaft endplay should always be checked prior to camshaft removal.*

Removal

Refer to illustrations 8.4, 8.5, 8.6, 8.7a and 8.7b

1   Detach the cable from the negative terminal of the battery.

2   Remove the intake plenum (see Section 9) and the valve covers (see Section 4).

3   Remove the timing chains and the camshaft sprockets (see Section 7).

4   Remove the variable valve timing valve(s) from the top of the number one camshaft journal(s) **(see illustration)**.

5   Mark the camshaft bearing caps from 1 to 4, and with an "I" or an "E," to indi-

cate intake or exhaust. Also mark arrows indicating the front of the engine **(see illustration)**. Loosen the camshaft bearing caps in two or three steps, in the reverse order of the tightening sequence **(see illustration 8.13a and 8.13b)**. **Caution:** *Keep the caps in order. They must go back in the same location they were removed from.*

6   Remove the bearing caps and the camshafts. Make a note of the camshaft markings to ensure correct installation **(see illustration)**.

7   Remove the lifters **(see illustrations)**. **Caution:** *Keep the lifters in order. They must go back in the same location they were removed from.*

Inspection

Refer to illustrations 8.9a, 8.9b, 8.13a and 8.13b

8   Visually examine the camshaft lobes, journals, bearing caps and lifters. Check for score marks, pitting and evidence of overheating (blue, discolored areas). If wear is exces-

8.5 The camshaft bearing caps should be marked with a number and letter stamp or a marker to ensure correct reinstallation

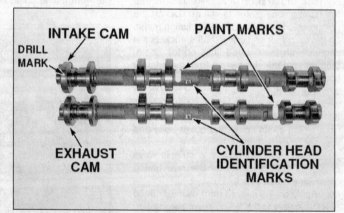

8.6 The ID mark in the center of each camshaft identifies which cylinder head the camshaft belongs to; "L" for left (front) and "R" for right (rear) - paint marks between the No. 2 and No. 3 journals indicate that it is an intake camshaft, while paint marks between the No. 3 and No. 4 journals indicate that it is an exhaust camshaft

8.7a Pull straight up to remove each lifter

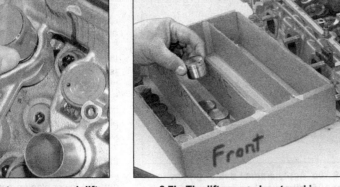

8.7b The lifters can be stored in individually marked plastic bags or a divided box as shown

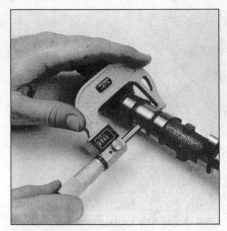

8.9a Measure each journal diameter with a micrometer - if any journal measures less than the specified limit, replace the camshaft

sive or damage is evident, the component will have to be replaced.

9   Using a micrometer, measure camshaft journal diameter and lobe height **(see illustrations)**, and compare your measurements to this Chapter's Specifications. If the lobe height is less than the minimum allowable, the camshaft is worn and must be replaced.

10   Check the camshaft runout by placing the camshaft back into the cylinder head and set up a dial indicator on the center journal. Zero the dial indicator. Turn the camshaft slowly and note the dial indicator readings. If the measured runout exceeds the specified runout, replace the camshaft.

11   Also, while the camshaft is sitting in the cylinder head, check the endplay. Install the bearing caps and tighten them securely. Mount a dial indicator with the plunger of the dial indicator in line with and touching the end of the camshaft. Gently pry the camshaft fully toward the gauge, zero the gauge, then pry the camshaft fully away from the gauge and note the gauge reading. If the measured endplay is at or beyond the specified service limit, replace the camshaft and check the endplay again. If the endplay is still excessive, replace the cylinder head.

12   Inspect each lifter for scuffing and score marks.

13   Check the oil clearance for each camshaft journal as follows:

a) Clean the bearing caps and the camshaft journals with brake system cleaner.
b) Carefully lay the camshafts in place in the cylinder head. DON'T use any lubrication.
c) Lay a strip of Plastigage on each journal.
d) Install the bearing caps with the arrows pointing toward the front (timing chain end) of the engine.
e) Tighten the bolts in sequence **(see illustration 8.22a)** to the torque listed in this Chapter's Specifications in 1/4-turn increments. **Caution:** Don't turn the camshaft while the Plastigage is in place.

f) Remove the bolts, in the proper sequence, and detach the bearing caps.
g) Compare the width of the crushed Plastigage (at it's widest point) to the scale on the Plastigage envelope **(see illustrations)**.
h) If the clearance is greater than specified, replace the camshaft and/or cylinder head.

14   Scrape off the Plastigage with your fingernail or the edge of a credit card - don't scratch or nick the journals or bearing caps.

Installation

Refer to illustrations 8.20a, 8.20b, 8.22a and 8.22b

15   Remove all old RTV sealant from the bolts and the front bearing caps.

16   Set the number one piston at TDC if it has been moved (see Section 3).

17   Lubricate the lifters with clean engine oil, then install the lifters into their original locations.

18   Apply moly-based engine assembly lubricant to the camshaft lobes and journals.

8.13a Place a strip of Plastigage under each camshaft bearing cap and tighten the caps to Specifications

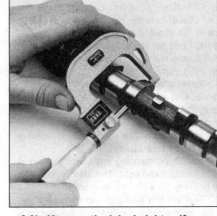

8.9b Measure the lobe heights - if any lobe height is less than the minimum listed in this Chapter's Specifications, replace the camshaft

19   Install the exhaust camshafts in their original positions with the dowel pins facing up (12 o'clock in relation to the cylinder head mating surface) and inline with the cylinder

8.13b Compare the width of the crushed Plastigage to the scale on the envelope to determine the oil clearance

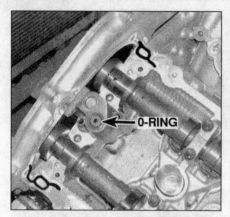

8.20a Apply RTV sealant to the cylinder head at the areas shown and install the secondary tensioner O-ring(s) - be sure to wipe off any excess sealant

8.20b Apply a small dab of grease to the VVT oil control orifice O-ring (arrow) to hold it in place on the No.1 bearing cap, then apply RTV sealant to the areas shown

bank. The small dowel hole in the end of each intake camshaft should also be facing up in the 12 o'clock position. **Caution:** *Use the small dowel hole on the intake camshaft to lock in the dowel pin on the intake sprocket. Do NOT use the large dowel hole or the camshaft timing will be incorrect and valve damage will occur.*

20   Apply a bead of RTV sealant to the sealing surfaces of the No. 1 bearing cap(s) and the cylinder head. Install new O-rings on the secondary timing chain tensioner(s) and the VVT oil control orifice on the No. 1 bearing cap(s) **(see illustrations)**.

21   Install the bearing caps and bolts and tighten them hand tight. The stamp marks on the bearing caps should be in order.

22   Tighten the bearing cap bolts in three steps, to the torque listed in this Chapter's Specifications, using the proper tightening sequence **(see illustrations)**.

23   Check the protrusion of the front bearing caps in front of the cylinder head front surface. The front bearing cap should be close to 0.0055 inch behind the front face of the cylinder head. If it isn't, remove and reinstall the

camshaft and caps, then check again.

24   Install the camshaft sprockets and timing chain (see Section 6). Hold the camshafts with a suitable wrench as you tighten the sprocket bolts to the specified torque.

25   The remainder of installation is the reverse of removal. If any part of the valve train was replaced, check and adjust the valve clearance (see Chapter 1).

26   Reconnect the battery (see Chapter 5).

9   Intake manifold - removal and installation

Warning: *Wait until the engine is completely cool before beginning this procedure.*

Intake plenum

Refer to illustrations 9.4a, 9.4b and 9.7

1   Relieve the fuel pressure (see Chapter 4).

2   Disconnect the cable from the negative terminal of the battery.

3   Refer to Chapter 4 and remove the air intake duct. Also remove the engine cover **(see illustration 4.2)**.

4   Label and disconnect the hoses and electrical connectors attached to the plenum and throttle body **(see illustrations)**.

5   Loosen the upper intake plenum bolts in the reverse order of the tightening sequence **(see illustration 9.7)** and remove the upper plenum with the throttle body attached.

6   To install the upper plenum, clean the mounting surfaces of the lower and the upper plenum and remove all traces of the old gasket material or sealant.

7   Install the new gaskets over the studs on the lower plenum with the marks (if equipped) facing forward, then install the upper plenum onto the lower plenum and tighten the bolts in the recommended tightening sequence **(see illustration)** to the torque listed in this Chapter's Specifications.

8   The remainder the installation is the reverse of removal.

Intake manifold

Refer to illustration 9.16

9   Remove the intake plenum (see Steps 1 through 5).

10   Label and detach any remaining hoses which would interfere with the removal of the lower intake manifold.

11   Refer to Chapter 4 and remove the fuel rail and injectors from the lower intake manifold.

12   Loosen the manifold mounting bolts/nuts in 1/4-turn increments until they can be removed by hand in the reverse order of the tightening sequence **(see illustration 9.16)**.

13   The manifold will probably be stuck to the cylinder heads and force may be required to break the gasket seal. **Caution:** *Don't pry between the manifold and the heads or damage to the gasket sealing surfaces may occur, leading to vacuum leaks.*

14   Carefully use a scraper to remove all

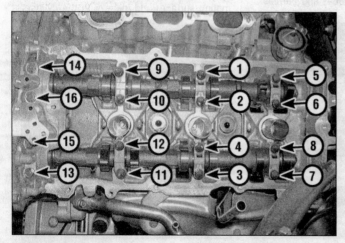

8.22a Camshaft bearing cap TIGHTENING sequence

8.22b After the camshaft bearing caps have been tightened in order, tighten the bolts (arrows) securing the rear timing chain cover to the No.1 bearing cap(s)

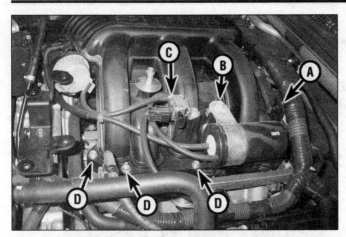

9.4a Intake plenum mounting details: A, release the wiring harness from the clip: B, unbolt and set aside the vacuum tank; C, disconnect and unbolt the VIAS solenoid; D, remove the plenum mounting bolts (three indicated here)

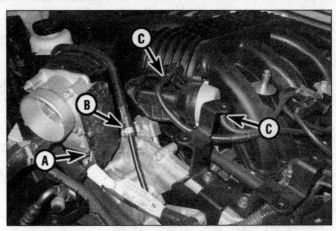

9.4b Plenum mounting details: A, disconnect the throttle body electrical connector; B, pinch off and disconnect the throttle body coolant hoses; C, disconnect the hoses from the intake runner control (VIAS)

traces of old gasket material and sealant from the manifold and cylinder heads, then clean the mating surfaces with brake cleaner.

15   Install new gaskets, then position the lower manifold on the engine. Make sure the gaskets and manifolds are aligned over the studs in the cylinder heads and install the nuts.

16   Following the recommended tightening sequence, tighten the nuts/bolts, in several steps, to the torque listed in this Chapter's Specifications **(see illustration)**.

17   The remainder of the installation is the reverse of the removal procedure. Run the engine and check for fuel, vacuum and coolant leaks.

10   Exhaust manifold - removal and installation

Warning: *The engine must be completely cool before beginning this procedure.*

Note: *To remove the right-side exhaust manifold, the engine must be removed, which is a difficult procedure that requires special equipment. Study Chapter 2C, Section 7 before undertaking the procedure.*

Removal

Refer to illustration 10.4

1   Disconnect the cable from the negative terminal of the battery.

2   Block the rear wheels and set the parking brake.

3   Raise the front of the vehicle and support it securely on jackstands, then remove the lower splash shield from below the engine (if equipped).

4   Refer to Chapter 4 and remove the front exhaust pipe from the vehicle. Unbolt the lower heat shields and remove the catalytic converters from the exhaust manifolds **(see illustration)**. **Note:** *Apply penetrating oil to the fasteners before attempting to loosen them.*

5   Disconnect the oxygen sensor connectors.

6   Remove the heat shield from the manifold.

7   Remove the manifold-to-head nuts/bolts and detach the manifold and gaskets.

Installation

8   Use a scraper to remove all traces of old gasket material and carbon deposits from the manifold and cylinder head mating surfaces.

9   Position the new exhaust manifold gaskets over the studs on the cylinder head.

10   Install the manifold and thread the mounting nuts/bolts into place.

11   Working from the center out, tighten the nuts/bolts to the torque listed in this Chapter's Specifications in three or four equal steps.

12   Reinstall the remaining parts in the reverse order of removal.

13   Run the engine and check for exhaust leaks.

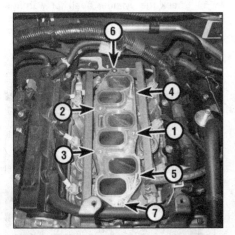

9.7 Intake plenum TIGHTENING sequence

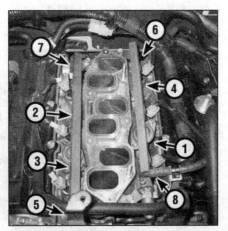

9.16 Intake manifold TIGHTENING sequence

10.4 Remove the heat shields from each exhaust manifold, then remove the bolts securing the rear of the converters (A), then the bolts at the converter-to-manifold flanges (B)

11.4 The right-side exhaust manifold is difficult to access; you'll have to remove the fenderwell liner - (A) indicates the heat shield bolts

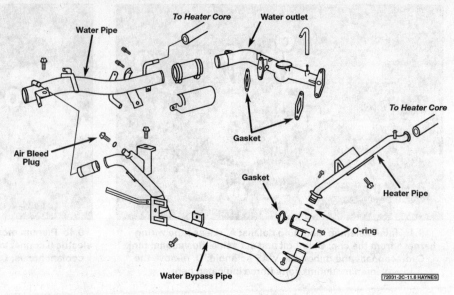

11.6 Coolant tube mounting details

11 Cylinder head - removal and installation

Caution: *The engine must be completely cool before beginning this procedure.*

Removal

Refer to illustrations 11.4, 11.6 and 11.8

1   Refer to Section 7 and remove the timing chain(s) and sprockets. **Caution:** *Be careful not to disturb the crankshaft from TDC on the compression stroke of the No.1 cylinder during the remainder of this procedure.*

2   Remove the rear timing chain cover bolts in the reverse order of the tightening sequence **(see illustration 11.22d)**.

3   Detach the rear timing cover from the engine. **Note:** *If the cover is stuck to the cylinder head or engine block, bump one end with a block of wood and a hammer to jar it loose. If that doesn't work, try to slip a flexible putty knife between the cover and the engine to break the gasket seal. Don't pry at the cover-to-cylinder head joint or damage to the sealing surfaces may occur (leading to oil leaks in the future).*

4   Remove the intake manifold (see Section 9) and the exhaust manifold (see Section 10). **Note:** *Removal of the right-side exhaust manifold normally requires engine removal, but by removing the fenderwell obstructions, and removing the right-side exhaust manifold heat shield and manifold mounting bolts, the manifold can remain in place while the cylinder head is removed* **(see illustration)**.

5   Remove the camshafts and lifters from the cylinder head (see Section 8).

6   Label and remove any remaining items attached to the cylinder head, such as coolant fittings, tubes, cables, hoses, wires or brackets **(see illustration)**.

7   Using a breaker bar and the appropriate sized Allen-head socket, loosen the cylinder head bolts in 1/4-turn increments until they can be removed by hand. Loosen the bolts in the reverse order of the tightening sequence **(see illustration 11.20)** to avoid warping or

cracking the head.

8   Lift the cylinder head off the engine block. If it's stuck, very carefully pry up at a casting protrusion, beyond the gasket surface **(see illustration)**.

9   Remove all external components from the head to allow for thorough cleaning and inspection.

Installation

Refer to illustrations 11.11, 11.14, 11.15, 11.20, 11.22a, 11.22b, 11.22c and 11.22d

10   The mating surfaces of the cylinder head and block must be perfectly clean when the head is installed.

11   Use a gasket scraper to remove all traces of carbon and old gasket material from the cylinder head and engine block, then clean the mating surfaces with brake system cleaner **(see illustration)**. If there's oil on the mating surfaces when the head is installed, the gasket may not seal correctly and leaks could develop. When working on the block,

stuff the cylinders with clean shop rags to keep out debris. Use a vacuum cleaner to remove material that falls into the cylinders.

12   Check the block and head mating surfaces for nicks, deep scratches and other damage. If damage is slight, it can be removed with a file; if it's excessive, machining may be the only alternative.

13   Use a tap of the correct size to chase the threads in the head bolt holes, then clean the holes with compressed air - make sure that nothing remains in the holes. **Warning:** *Wear eye protection when using compressed air!*

14   Measure each cylinder head bolt for stretching **(see illustration)**. If the diameter of the bolt threads at point A and the diameter of the bolt threads at point B differ more than 0.0043 inch (0.11 mm), the bolts have exceeded the maximum amount of stretch and will need to be replaced.

15   Check the cylinder head for warpage **(see illustration)**. Check the head gasket, intake and exhaust manifold surfaces. Com-

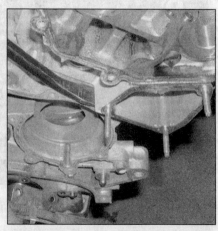

11.8 Pry on a casting protrusion to break the head loose

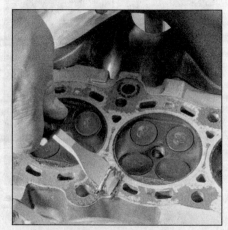

11.11 Carefully remove all traces of old gasket material from the sealing surfaces

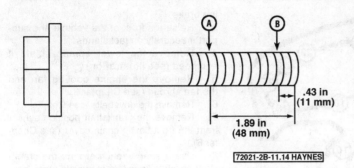

11.14 Measure each cylinder head bolt at point A and point B -
If the difference between the two exceeds the specification,
the bolt will have to be replaced

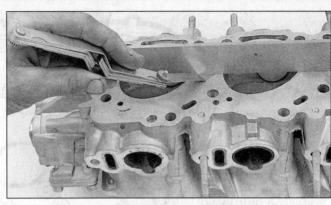

11.15 Use a precision straightedge and a feeler gauge to check
the cylinder head for warpage

pare your findings with the limit listed in this Chapter's Specifications.

16 Install the components that were removed from the head.

17 Position the new cylinder head gasket over the dowel pins on the block noting which direction on the gasket faces up.

18 Carefully set the head on the block without disturbing the gasket.

19 Before installing the head bolts, apply a small amount of clean engine oil to the threads and hardened washers (if equipped). The chamfered side of the washers must face the bolt heads.

20 Install the bolts in their original locations and tighten them finger tight. Then tighten all the bolts in several steps, following the proper sequence (see illustration), to the torque listed in this Chapter's Specifications.

21 Remove all traces of old sealant from the rear timing chain cover and the cover bolts.

22 Apply a bead of RTV sealant to the rear timing chain cover sealing surfaces (see illustration). Install new O-rings in the front of the engine block and in the variable valve timing oil control orifices in the cylinder head (see illustrations). Place the rear timing

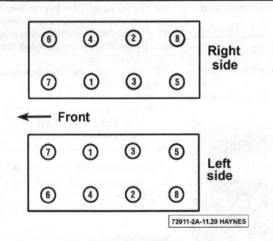

11.20 Cylinder head TIGHTENING sequence

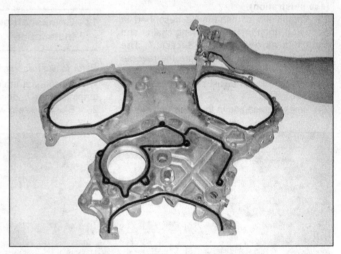

11.22a Apply RTV sealant to the rear timing chain cover at the
areas shown - be sure to wipe off any excess sealant

11.22b Install new O-rings (arrows) in the front of
the engine block . . .

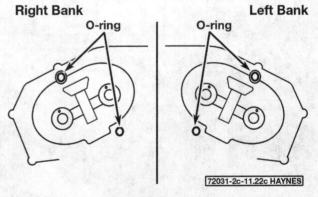

11.22c . . . and in the variable valve timing oil control orifices
(arrows) in the cylinder head

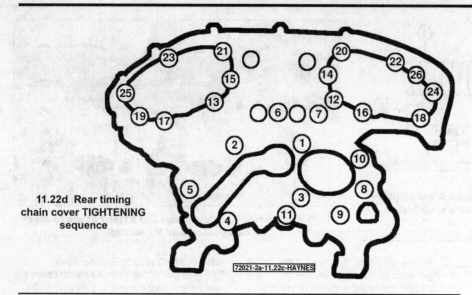

11.22d Rear timing chain cover TIGHTENING sequence

72021-2a-11.22c-HAYNES

chain cover in position over the dowels on the engine and install the bolts in their original locations. Following the recommended tightening sequence, tighten the bolts to the torque listed in this Chapter's Specifications **(see illustration)**.

23   Install the camshafts as described in Section 8, then install the timing chains and sprockets as described in Section 7. The remaining installation steps are the reverse of removal. If any part of the valve train was replaced, check and adjust the valve clearance (see Section 5).

24   Install the engine in the vehicle.

25   Refill the cooling system, and change the engine oil and filter (see Chapter 1).

26   Start the engine and check for oil and coolant leaks.

12   Crankshaft pulley - removal and installation

Refer to illustrations 12.4 and 12.8

1   Disconnect the cable from the negative terminal of the battery.

2   Block the rear wheels and set the parking brake.

3   Raise the front of the vehicle and support it securely on jackstands.

4   Remove the lower splash shield if equipped **(see illustration)**.

5   Remove the engine cooling fan and the fan shroud (see Chapter 3).

6   Remove the drivebelts (see Chapter 1).

7   Remove the crankshaft position sensor from the front timing chain cover (see Chapter 6).

8   Use a strap wrench around the crankshaft pulley to keep it from moving while loosening the bolt with a breaker bar and socket. Do not remove the bolt fully - it should stay with the pulley when you remove it **(see illustration)**.

9   Wedge a prybar or two screwdrivers behind the crankshaft pulley and carefully pry it off the crankshaft. If the pulley is difficult to remove, place a two jaw type puller into the openings in the center of the hub and pull it off. **Caution:** *DO NOT place the puller jaws around the outside of the crankshaft pulley or damage to the pulley will occur.* **Note:** *Depending on the type of puller you have it may also be necessary to remove the radiator to gain sufficient clearance to use the puller.*

10   To install the crankshaft pulley, align the pulley groove with the key on the crankshaft and slide the pulley onto the crankshaft.

11   Install the crankshaft pulley retaining bolt and tighten it to the torque listed in this Chapter's Specifications.

12   The remainder of installation is the reverse of the removal.

13   Crankshaft front oil seal - replacement

Refer to illustrations 13.2, 13.4 and 13.5

1   Remove the crankshaft pulley from the engine (see Section 12).

2   Carefully pry the seal out of the cover

12.8 Use a strap wrench to hold the crankshaft pulley while removing the center bolt (a chain-type wrench may be used if you wrap a section of old drivebelt around the crankshaft pulley first)

12.4 Lower splash shield mounting details (Xterra model shown, Frontier models similar)

13.2 Pry the seal out very carefully with a seal removal tool or screwdriver, being careful not to nick or gouge the seal bore or the crankshaft

13.4 Use a large socket or seal driver to drive the new seal into the cover

with a seal removal tool or a large screwdriver **(see illustration). Caution:** *Be careful not to scratch, gouge or distort the area that the seal fits into or an oil leak will develop.*

3   Clean the bore to remove any old seal material and corrosion. Position the new seal in the bore with the seal lip (usually the side with the spring) facing IN (toward the engine). A small amount of oil applied to the outer edge of the new seal will make installation easier.

4   Drive the seal into the bore with a seal driver or a large socket and hammer until it's completely seated **(see illustration).** Select a socket that's the same outside diameter as the seal and make sure the new seal is pressed into place until it bottoms against the cover flange.

5   Check the surface of the damper that the oil seal rides on. If the surface has been grooved from long-time contact with the seal, a press-on sleeve may be available to renew the sealing surface **(see illustration).** This sleeve is pressed into place with a hammer

and a block of wood and is commonly available from most auto parts stores.

6   Lubricate the seal lips with engine oil and reinstall the crankshaft pulley. Install the crankshaft pulley retaining bolt and tighten it to the torque listed in this Chapter's Specifications.

7   The remainder of installation is the reverse of the removal. Run the engine and check for oil leaks.

14   Oil pan - removal and installation

Removal

Refer to illustrations 14.6, 14.11, 14.12, 14.13 and 14.14

1   Disconnect the cable from the negative terminal of the battery.

2   Set the parking brake and block the rear wheels.

3   Raise the front of the vehicle and support it securely on jackstands.

4   Remove the splash shields under the engine (if equipped) **(see illustration 12.4).**

5   Drain the engine oil and remove the oil filter (see Chapter 1).

6   Remove the mounting bolts for the lower steel pan, and carefully prying between the upper and lower pans with a thin flat-bladed tool, separate and remove the lower pan **(see illustration).**

7   To remove the upper aluminum pan (also referred to as the lower block plate or block support), refer to Chapter 3 and drain the engine coolant, then disconnect the hoses and remove the oil cooler (see Section 16).

8   On 4WD models, remove the front differential and axle housing (see Chapter 8).

9   Disconnect the lower steering shaft joint from the steering gear and lower the steering gear (see Chapter 10).

10   Remove the starter (see Chapter 5).

13.5 If the sealing surface of the damper hub has a wear groove from contact with the seal, repair sleeves are available at most auto parts stores

14.6 Remove the lower oil pan mounting bolts (not all are visible here)

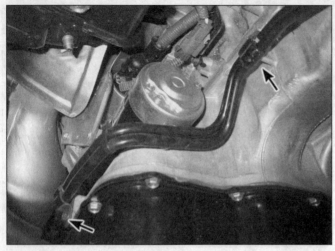

14.11 Disconnect and unclip the transmission fluid lines at the oil pan mounting flange

14.12 The upper oil pan is attached to the transmission bellhousing (three of four bolts indicated)

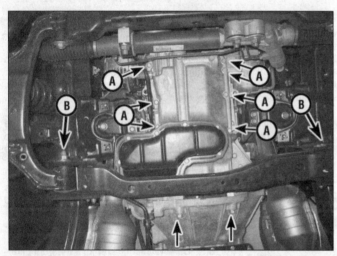

14.13 To have room for upper pan removal ([A] indicates some of the pan-to-block bolts), remove the rear crossmember bolts (B)

14.14 Insert a flathead screwdriver or small pry bar into the notch on the side of the oil pan to break it loose - be careful not to damage the sealing surfaces!

11   If equipped with an automatic transmission, unbolt the clamps securing the transmission fluid lines and set the lines aside without disconnecting them **(see illustration)**.

12   Remove the bolts securing the aluminum oil pan to the transmission **(see illustration)**.

13   Remove the remaining upper aluminum pan mounting bolts in the reverse of the tightening sequence **(see illustration)**.

14   To loosen the upper oil pan from the block, wedge a flat head screwdriver or thin prybar into the notch on the side of the oil pan, being careful not to damage the sealing surfaces of the oil pan or engine block **(see illustration)**.

Installation

Refer to illustrations 14.18, 14.19 and 14.22

15   Use a scraper to remove all traces of old gasket material and sealant from the upper aluminum section of the oil pan, the lower steel pan and the engine block. Clean the mating surfaces with brake system cleaner. **Caution:** *Be careful not to scratch or gouge*

the gasket surface of the block or oil pan. A leak could develop after the repairs have been completed.

16   Make sure the threaded bolt holes in the block and aluminum section of the oil pan are clean.

17   Apply a bead of RTV sealant to the ends of the front timing cover gasket and the rear oil

seal retainer gasket, then place the gaskets in position on the oil pan. Apply a bead of RTV sealant around the upper aluminum oil pan flange. **Note:** *The oil pan must be installed within 15 minutes once the sealant has been applied.*

18   Install new O-rings in the engine block and the oil pump body **(see illustration)**.

14.18 Install new O-rings in the block and the oil pump housing (arrows)

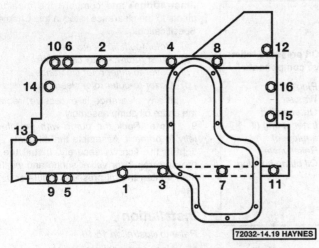

14.19 Aluminum oil pan TIGHTENING sequence

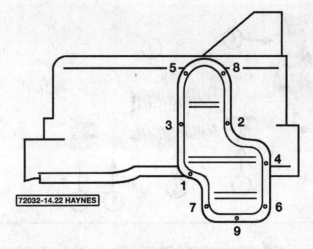

14.22 Steel oil pan TIGHTENING sequence

15.2 Remove the bolts (arrows) securing the oil pump pick-up tube support bracket

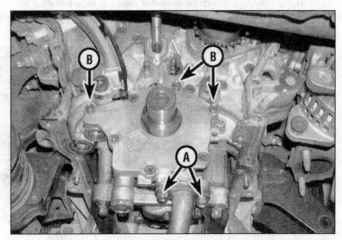

15.3 Remove the mounting bolts (A) and detach the oil pick-up tube from the oil pump, then remove the oil pump housing retaining bolts (B)

19   Carefully position the upper aluminum section of the oil pan on the engine block and install the bolts. Following the recommended sequence, tighten the fasteners in three or four steps to the torque listed in this Chapter's Specifications **(see illustration)**.

20   Install the transmission mounting bolts **(see illustration 14.12)**.

21   Check the lower steel oil pan flange for distortion, particularly around the bolt holes. If necessary, place the pan on a wood block and use a hammer to flatten and restore the gasket surface.

22   Apply a bead of RTV sealant around the steel oil pan flange and install the steel oil pan. **Note:** *The oil pan must be installed within 15 minutes once the sealant has been applied.* Following the recommended sequence, tighten the fasteners in several steps to the torque listed in this Chapter's Specifications **(see illustration)**.

23   The remainder of installation is the reverse of removal. Be sure to install a new oil filter (see Chapter 1) and wait at least one hour before adding oil.

15   Oil pump - removal, inspection and installation

Removal

Refer to illustrations 15.2 and 15.3

1   Refer to Section 7 and remove the primary timing chain and the crankshaft sprocket. **Note:** *It is not necessary to remove the camshaft sprockets, the camshaft sprocket bolts, the secondary timing chains or the primary timing chain tensioner pivot arm/chain guide during this procedure. Simply pivot the tensioner arm/chain guide over to the left side to allow removal of the oil pump housing.*

2   Remove the oil pans (see Section 14). Remove the oil pump pick-up tube **(see illustration)**.

3   Remove the oil pump-to-engine block bolts from the front of the engine **(see illustration)**.

4   Gently pry the oil pump housing outward enough to clear the dowel pins on the engine block and remove it from the engine.

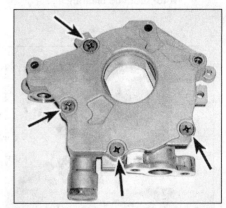

15.5 Remove the screws (arrows) and lift the cover off

Inspection

Refer to illustrations 15.5, 15.7, 15.8a, 15.8b, 15.8c, 15.8d and 15.8e

5   Use a large Phillips screwdriver to remove the screws holding the front cover on the oil pump housing **(see illustration)**.

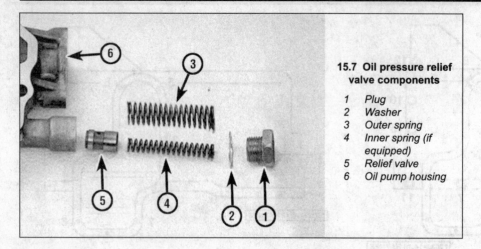

15.7 Oil pressure relief valve components

1 Plug
2 Washer
3 Outer spring
4 Inner spring (if equipped)
5 Relief valve
6 Oil pump housing

illustrations) and compare the measurements to the clearance listed in this Chapter's Specifications:

a) Rotor tooth tip clearance
b) Outer rotor-to-body clearance
c) Cover-to-inner rotor clearance
d) Cover-to-outer rotor clearance

If any clearance is excessive, replace the entire oil pump assembly.

9 **Note:** *Pack the pump with petroleum jelly to prime it. Assemble the oil pump and tighten the screws securely. Install the oil pressure regulator valve, spring and washer, then tighten the oil pressure regulator valve cap.*

Installation

Refer to illustration 15.10

10 Use new gaskets (where applicable) on all disassembled parts and reverse the removal procedure for installation. Align the flats on the crankshaft **(see illustration)** with the flats on the oil pump gear. Tighten all fas-

6   Clean all components with solvent, then inspect them for wear and damage.
7   Remove the oil pressure regulator cap, washer, spring(s) and valve **(see illustration)**. Check the oil pressure regulator valve sliding surface and valve spring. If either the spring or the valve is damaged, they must be replaced as a set.
8   Check the clearance of the following oil pump components with a feeler gauge **(see**

15.8a Use feeler gauges to measure the rotor tooth tip clearance . . .

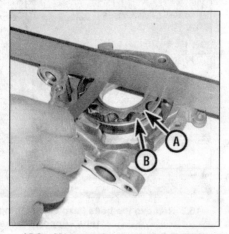

15.8c Measure the cover-to-rotor end clearance with a straightedge and feeler gauge - measure (A) above the inner rotor and (B) above the outer rotor

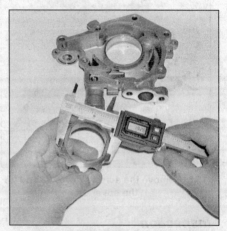

15.8d Use calipers to measure the diameter of the inner rotor ridge (the part of the inner rotor that rides in the pump body) . . .

15.8b . . . and the outer rotor-to-body clearance

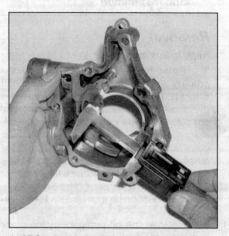

15.8e . . . and subtract the inner rotor ridge diameter from the opening in the pump body where the inner rotor rides to obtain the inner rotor ridge-to-body clearance

15.10 There is a flat surface (arrow) on each side of the crankshaft - align them with the flats on the inner gear

teners to the torque listed in this Chapter's Specifications. **Note:** *Before installing the oil pan, be sure to replace the O-rings on the oil pump housing and engine block* (see illustration 14.18).

16 Engine oil cooler and adapter - general information and replacement

General information

1   Engines equipped with automatic transmissions are provided extra engine cooling by an oil cooler which is mounted to an adapter at the front of the oil pan next to the oil filter. The oil filter adapter doubles as a housing to which the oil pressure sending unit and the oil cooler are mounted to. The oil cooler adapter also incorporates an oil pressure relief valve, which redirects oil flow to bypass the oil cooler when pressures are too high. The oil cooler has two hoses connecting the cooler to the engine, where oil temperature is lowered by the radiator coolant. The hose that connects to the passenger side water pipe is the inlet side of the oil cooler and the hose that connects to the main thermostat housing (at the front of the engine) is the outlet side of the oil cooler. Engine oil coolers are not installed on engines with manual transmissions.

Replacement

Refer to illustrations 16.3, 16.5 and 16.8
Warning: *The engine must be completely cool before beginning this procedure.*
2   Drain the engine oil and the cooling system (see Chapter 1).
3   Detach the hose clamps and remove the inlet and outlet hoses from the oil cooler **(see illustration)**.
4   Remove the oil filter from the oil cooler assembly.
5   Loosen the oil cooler retaining bolt and remove the oil cooler and O-rings from the

16.3 Oil cooler assembly

A   Oil filter
B   Oil cooler
C   Coolant hoses

adapter **(see illustration)**.
6   If it's necessary to remove the oil cooler adapter, simply remove the three retaining bolts and separate the adapter from the upper aluminum section of the oil pan. Be sure to remove the old gasket and thoroughly clean the mating surfaces of the oil pan and the adapter before installing the oil cooler adapter and a new gasket back onto the oil pan. Tighten the adapter bolts to the torque listed in this Chapter's Specifications, then install the oil pressure sending unit back onto the adapter using pipe sealant on the threads.
7   Using a small amount of engine oil, lubricate the oil cooler O-rings. Install the large O-ring in the groove on the oil cooler and the small O-ring over the end of the oil cooler retaining bolt until it seats against the bolt head.
8   Position the oil cooler onto the adapter, so that the casting protrusion on the adapter aligns between the two tabs on the oil cooler and install the retaining bolt hand tight **(see illustration)**.
9   Tighten the oil cooler retaining bolt to the torque listed in this Chapter's Specifications. Do not overtighten!

10   Install the oil cooler hoses, then run the engine and check for leaks. Turn off the engine for five minutes and check the oil and coolant levels, adding fluids if necessary.

17 Flywheel/driveplate - removal and installation

Refer to illustration 17.4
1   Raise the vehicle and support it securely on jackstands, then refer to Chapter 7 and remove the transmission. **Warning:** *The engine must be supported from above with an engine hoist or three-bar support fixture before working underneath the vehicle with the transmission removed.*
2   If the vehicle is equipped with a manual transmission, remove the pressure plate and clutch disc (see Chapter 8). Now is a good time to check/replace the clutch components and pilot bushing if necessary. If the vehicle is equipped with an automatic transmission, now would be a good time to check and replace the front pump seal/O-ring.
3   Use paint or a center-punch to make

16.5 Remove the oil cooler mounting bolt

16.8 Align the tabs on the oil cooler with the casting protrusion on the oil cooler adapter

17.4 Hold a lever against a casting protrusion on the engine block or place a screwdriver through a hole in the driveplate to hold the driveplate while the mounting bolts are removed - note the painted marks made at the crank and driveplate for alignment

18.2 Pry the seal out very carefully with a seal removal tool or screwdriver - if the crankshaft is damaged the new seal will leak!

alignment marks on the flywheel/driveplate and crankshaft to ensure correct alignment during reinstallation.

4   Remove the bolts that secure the flywheel/driveplate to the crankshaft (see illustration). If the crankshaft turns, hold the flywheel with a pry bar or wedge a screwdriver into the ring gear teeth to jam the flywheel.

5   Remove the flywheel/driveplate from the crankshaft. Since the flywheel is fairly heavy, be sure to support it while removing the last bolt.

6   Clean the flywheel to remove grease and oil. Inspect the surface for cracks, rivet grooves, burned areas and score marks. Light scoring can be removed with emery cloth. Check for cracked and broken ring gear teeth or a loose ring gear. Lay the flywheel on a flat surface and use a straightedge to check for warpage.

7   Clean and inspect the mating surfaces of the flywheel/driveplate and the crankshaft. If the crankshaft rear seal is leaking, replace it before reinstalling the flywheel/driveplate.

8   Position the flywheel/driveplate against

the crankshaft. Be sure to align the marks made during removal. Note that some engines have an alignment dowel or staggered bolt holes to ensure correct installation. Before installing the bolts, apply thread locking compound to the threads.

9   Wedge a screwdriver into the ring gear teeth to keep the flywheel/driveplate from turning as you tighten the bolts to the torque listed in this Chapter's Specifications.

10   The remainder of installation is the reverse of the removal.

18   Rear main oil seal - replacement

Refer to illustrations 18.2 and 18.3

1   The transmission must be removed from the vehicle for this procedure (see Chapter 7). **Warning:** *The engine must be supported from above with an engine hoist or three-bar support fixture before working underneath the vehicle with the transmission removed. Remove the flywheel/driveplate (see Section 17).*

2   Carefully pry the old seal out of the block with a seal removal tool or screwdriver (see illustration).

3   Apply multi-purpose grease to the crankshaft seal journal and the lip of the new seal. Preferably, a seal installation tool should be used to press the new seal into place. If the proper seal installation tool is unavailable, use a large socket, section of pipe or a blunt tool and carefully drive the new seal into place (see illustration). The lip is stiff so carefully work it onto the seal journal of the crankshaft. Don't rush it or you may damage the seal. **Note:** *Install the seal squarely and only until flush with the back of the block, no further.*

4   The remaining steps are the reverse of removal.

19   Engine mounts - check and replacement

1   There are two engine mounts and one transmission mount installed on the vehicles covered by this manual. The two engine mounts are located on the passenger and driver's side of the vehicle attached to the engine block and to each frame rail. The transmission mount is mounted to the rear of the transmission and the transmission crossmember. Refer to Chapter 7B for the transmission mount replacement procedures.

Check

2 · During the check, the engine must be raised slightly to remove the weight from the mounts.

3   Raise the vehicle and support it securely on jackstands. Support the engine/transmission from above using a hoist or three bar support fixture.

4   Check the mounts to see if the rubber is cracked, hardened or separated from the bushing in the center of the mount.

18.3 If you don't have a seal installation tool, use a blunt tool (such as a brass punch) to carefully work the edge of the seal evenly into the bore and around the crankshaft

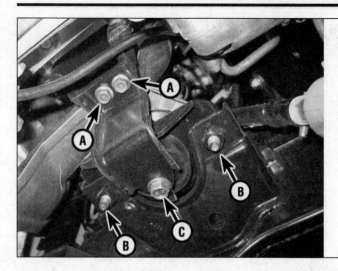

19.9 Engine mount details

A   Bracket-to-engine bolts
B   Mount-to-chassis bolts
C   Engine bracket-to-mount bolt

5   Check for relative movement between the mounts and the engine or frame (use a large screwdriver or prybar to attempt to move the mounts). If movement is noted, lower the engine and tighten the mount fasteners.
6   Rubber preservative should be applied to the mounts to slow deterioration.

Replacement

Refer to illustration 19.9

7   Disconnect the cable from the negative terminal of the battery, set the parking brake and block the rear wheels.
8   Raise the front of the vehicle and support it securely on jackstands. Remove the splash shields from under the vehicle. .

9   Remove the engine mount-to-frame nuts. There are two nuts on each side securing the mounts to the frame rails **(see illustration)**.
10   Working in the engine compartment, remove the engine mount-to-engine mount bracket nut(s). There is one nut on each side securing the mounts to the engine mount bracket. **Note:** *The manufacturer advises against removing the engine-mount heat insulator cover retaining bolts, as damper oil will flow out and the insulator will not function.*
11   Attach an engine hoist to the top of the engine for lifting. **Caution:** *Do not use a jack under the oil pan to support the entire weight of the engine or the oil pump pick-up could be damaged.*
12   Raise the engine slightly until the engine mount can be removed from the vehicle.
13   To remove the engine mount brackets, simply unscrew the four retaining bolts securing the mount bracket to each side of the engine.
14   Installation is the reverse of removal. Apply thread locking compound to the mount nuts before installing them, then tighten them to the torque listed in this Chapter's Specifications.

Notes

Chapter 2 Part C
General engine overhaul procedures

Contents

Specifications

General

Displacement
QR25DE four-cylinder .... 151.8 cubic inches (2.5 liters)
VQ40DE V6 .... 241 cubic inches (4.0 liters)
Compression ratio
Four-cylinder 9.5:1
V6 .... 9.7:1
Cylinder compression pressure
Minimum
Four-cylinder engine .... 161 psi
V6 engine .... 142 psi
Maximum variation between cylinders .... 15 psi
Oil pressure (minimum, warm engine)
Idle .... 14 psi
2000 rpm .... 43 psi

Torque specifications*

Ft-lbs (unless otherwise indicated)   Nm

Note: *One foot-pound (ft-lb) of torque is equivalent to 12 inch-pounds (in-lbs) of torque. Torque values below approximately 15 ft-lbs are expressed in inch-pounds, since most foot-pound torque wrenches are not accurate at these smaller values.*

Connecting rod cap bolts
Four-cylinder engine
Step 1 .... 20 — 27
Step 2 .... Back off until just loose
Step 3 .... 168 in-lbs — 19
Step 4 .... Tighten an additional 90-degrees
V6 engine
Step 1 .... 168 in-lbs — 19
Step 2 .... Tighten an additional 90-degrees
Main bearing cap bolts (lower crankcase-to-block)
Four-cylinder engine
Step 1, bolts 11-22 .... 19 — 26
Step 2, bolts 1-10 .... 29 — 39
Step 3, bolts 1-10 .... Tighten an additional 60 to 65 degrees
V6 engine
Step 1, bolts 17-24 .... 16 — 22
Step 2, bolts 1-16 (after rear seal is installed) .... 26 — 35
Step 3, bolts 1-16 .... Tighten an additional 90-degrees

* Note: Refer to Part A or B of this Chapter for additional torque specifications.

1   General information - engine overhaul

Refer to illustrations 1.1, 1.2, 1.3, 1.4, 1.5 and 1.6

Included in this portion of Chapter 2 are general information and diagnostic testing procedures for determining the overall mechanical condition of your engine.

The information ranges from advice concerning preparation for an overhaul and the purchase of replacement parts and/or components to detailed, step-by-step procedures covering removal and installation.

The following Sections have been written to help you determine whether your engine needs to be overhauled and how to remove and install it once you've determined it needs to be rebuilt. For information concerning in-vehicle engine repair, see Chapter 2A or 2B.

The Specifications included in this Part are general in nature and include only those necessary for testing the oil pressure and engine compression, and bottom-end torque specifications. Refer to Chapter 2A or 2B for additional engine Specifications.

It's not always easy to determine when, or if, an engine should be completely over-hauled, because a number of factors must be considered.

High mileage is not necessarily an indication that an overhaul is needed, while low mileage doesn't preclude the need for an overhaul. Frequency of servicing is probably the most important consideration. An engine that's had regular and frequent oil and filter changes, as well as other required maintenance, will most likely give many thousands of miles of reliable service. Conversely, a neglected engine may require an overhaul very early in its service life.

Excessive oil consumption is an indication that piston rings, valve seals and/or valve guides are in need of attention. Make sure that oil leaks aren't responsible before deciding that the rings and/or guides are bad. Perform a cylinder compression check to determine the extent of the work required (see Section 3). Also, check the vacuum readings under various conditions (see Section 4).

Check the oil pressure with a gauge installed in place of the oil pressure sending unit and compare it to this Chapter's Specifications (see Section 2). If it's extremely low, the bearings and/or oil pump are probably worn out.

Loss of power, rough running, knocking or metallic engine noises, excessive valve train noise and high fuel consumption rates may also point to the need for an overhaul, especially if they're all present at the same time. If a complete tune-up doesn't remedy the situation, major mechanical work is the only solution.

An engine overhaul involves restoring the internal parts to the specifications of a new engine. During an overhaul, the piston rings are replaced and the cylinder walls are reconditioned (rebored and/or honed) **(see illustrations 1.1 and 1.2)**. If a rebore is done by an automotive machine shop, new oversize pistons will also be installed. The main bearings, connecting rod bearings and camshaft bearings are generally replaced with new ones and, if necessary, the crankshaft may be reground to restore the journals **(see illustration 1.3)**. Generally, the valves are serviced as well, since they're usually in less-than-perfect condition at this point. While the engine is being overhauled, other components, such as the distributor, starter and alternator, can be rebuilt as well. The end result should be similar to a new engine that will give many trouble free miles. **Note:** *Critical cooling system components such as the hoses, drivebelts, thermostat and water pump should be replaced*

1.1 An engine block being bored. An engine rebuilder will use special machinery to recondition the cylinder bores

1.2 If the cylinders are bored, the machine shop will normally hone the engine on a machine like this

1.3 A crankshaft having a main bearing journal ground

1.4 A machinist checks for a bent connecting rod, using specialized equipment

1.5 A bore gauge being used to check the main bearing bore

with new parts when an engine is overhauled. The radiator should be checked carefully to ensure that it isn't clogged or leaking (see Chapter 3). If you purchase a rebuilt engine or short block, some rebuilders will not warranty their engines unless the radiator has been professionally flushed. Also, we don't recommend overhauling the oil pump - always install a new one when an engine is rebuilt.

Overhauling the internal components on today's engines is a difficult and time-consuming task which requires a significant amount of specialty tools and is best left to a professional engine rebuilder (see illustrations 1.4, 1.5 and 1.6). A competent engine rebuilder will handle the inspection of your old parts and offer advice concerning the reconditioning or replacement of the original engine, never purchase parts or have machine work done on other components until the block has been thoroughly inspected by a professional machine shop. As a general rule, time is the primary cost of an overhaul, especially since the vehicle may be tied up for a minimum of two weeks or more. Be aware that some engine builders only have the capability to

rebuild the engine you bring them while other rebuilders have a large inventory of rebuilt exchange engines in stock. Also be aware that many machine shops could take as much as two weeks time to completely rebuild your engine depending on shop workload. Sometimes it makes more sense to simply exchange your engine for another engine that's already rebuilt to save time.

2 Oil pressure check

Refer to illustrations 2.2a and 2.2b

1   Low engine oil pressure can be a sign of an engine in need of rebuilding. A "low oil pressure" indicator (often called an "idiot light") is not a test of the oiling system. Such indicators only come on when the oil pressure is dangerously low. Even a factory oil pressure gauge in the instrument panel is only a relative indication, although much better for driver information than a warning light. A better test is with a mechanical (not electrical) oil

1.6 Uneven piston wear like this indicates a bent connecting rod

pressure gauge.

2   Locate the oil pressure indicator sending unit - it's located right above the oil filter (see illustrations).

3   Unscrew and remove the oil pressure sending unit and then screw in the hose for

2.2a Oil pressure sending unit location - 2.5L four-cylinder engine

2.2b Oil pressure sending unit location - 4.0L V6 engine

3.6 Use a compression gauge with a threaded fitting for the spark plug hole, not the type that requires hand pressure to maintain the seal

4.4 A simple vacuum gauge can be handy in diagnosing engine condition and performance

your oil pressure gauge. If necessary, install an adapter fitting. Use Teflon tape or thread sealant on the threads of the adapter and/or the fitting on the end of your gauge's hose.

4   Connect an accurate tachometer to the engine, according to the tachometer manufacturer's instructions.

5   Check the oil pressure with the engine running (normal operating temperature) at the specified engine speed, and compare it to this Chapter's Specifications. If it's extremely low, the bearings and/or oil pump are probably worn out.

3   Cylinder compression check

Refer to illustration 3.6

1   A compression check will tell you what mechanical condition the upper end of your engine (pistons, rings, valves, head gaskets) is in. Specifically, it can tell you if the compression is down due to leakage caused by worn piston rings, defective valves and seats or a blown head gasket. **Note:** *The engine must be at normal operating temperature and the battery must be fully charged for this check.*

2   Begin by cleaning the area around the spark plugs before you remove them (compressed air should be used, if available). The idea is to prevent dirt from getting into the cylinders as the compression check is being done.

3   Remove the ignition coil assemblies (see Chapter 5). Also disable the fuel pump by removing the fuel pump fuse (see Chapter 4, Section 2).

4   Remove all of the spark plugs (see Chapter 1).

5   Block the throttle wide open.

6   Install a compression gauge in the spark plug hole **(see illustration)**.

7   Crank the engine over at least seven compression strokes and watch the gauge. The compression should build up quickly in a

healthy engine. Low compression on the first stroke, followed by gradually increasing pressure on successive strokes, indicates worn piston rings. A low compression reading on the first stroke, which doesn't build up during successive strokes, indicates leaking valves or a blown head gasket (a cracked head could also be the cause). Deposits on the undersides of the valve heads can also cause low compression. Record the highest gauge reading obtained.

8   Repeat the procedure for the remaining cylinders and compare the results to this Chapter's Specifications.

9   Add some engine oil (about three squirts from a plunger-type oil can) to each cylinder, through the spark plug hole, and repeat the test.

10   If the compression increases after the oil is added, the piston rings are definitely worn. If the compression doesn't increase significantly, the leakage is occurring at the valves or head gasket. Leakage past the valves may be caused by burned valve seats and/or faces or warped, cracked or bent valves.

11   If two adjacent cylinders have equally low compression, there's a strong possibility that the head gasket between them is blown. The appearance of coolant in the combustion chambers or the crankcase would verify this condition.

12   If one cylinder is slightly lower than the others, and the engine has a slightly rough idle, a worn lobe on the camshaft could be the cause.

13   If the compression is unusually high, the combustion chambers are probably coated with carbon deposits. If that's the case, the cylinder head(s) should be removed and decarbonized.

14   If compression is way down or varies greatly between cylinders, it would be a good idea to have a leak-down test performed by an automotive repair shop. This test will pinpoint exactly where the leakage is occurring and how severe it is.

4   Vacuum gauge diagnostic checks

Refer to illustrations 4.4 and 4.6

1   A vacuum gauge provides inexpensive but valuable information about what is going on in the engine. You can check for worn rings or cylinder walls, leaking head or intake manifold gaskets, incorrect carburetor adjustments, restricted exhaust, stuck or burned valves, weak valve springs, improper ignition or valve timing and ignition problems.

2   Unfortunately, vacuum gauge readings are easy to misinterpret, so they should be used in conjunction with other tests to confirm the diagnosis.

3   Both the absolute readings and the rate of needle movement are important for accurate interpretation. Most gauges measure vacuum in inches of mercury (in-Hg). The following references to vacuum assume the diagnosis is being performed at sea level. As elevation increases (or atmospheric pressure decreases), the reading will decrease. For every 1,000 foot increase in elevation above approximately 2,000 feet, the gauge readings will decrease about one inch of mercury.

4   Connect the vacuum gauge directly to the intake manifold vacuum, not to ported (throttle body) vacuum **(see illustration)**. Some models are equipped with a vacuum fitting built into the brake booster vacuum hose grommet at the brake booster. Other models are equipped with a vacuum hose fitting on the intake manifold. Use a T-fitting to access the vacuum signal. Be sure no hoses are left disconnected during the test or false readings will result.

5   Before you begin the test, allow the engine to warm up completely. Block the wheels and set the parking brake. With the transmission in Park, start the engine and allow it to run at normal idle speed. **Warning:** *Keep your hands and the vacuum gauge clear of the fans.*

6   Read the vacuum gauge; an average,

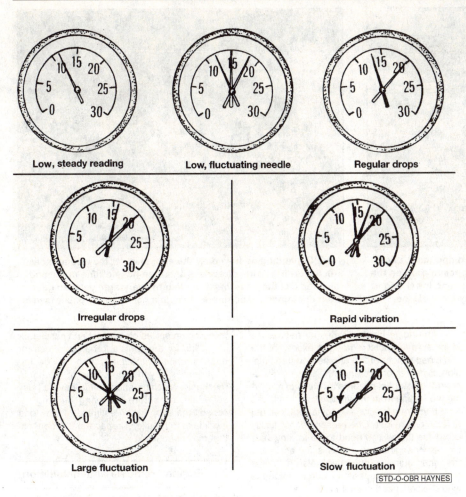

Low, steady reading   Low, fluctuating needle   Regular drops

Irregular drops   Rapid vibration

Large fluctuation   Slow fluctuation

STD-O-OBR HAYNES

4.6 Typical vacuum gauge readings

healthy engine should normally produce about 17 to 22 in-Hg with a fairly steady needle **(see illustration)**. Refer to the following vacuum gauge readings and what they indicate about the engine's condition:

7   A low, steady reading usually indicates a leaking gasket between the intake manifold and cylinder head(s) or throttle body, a leaky vacuum hose, late ignition timing or incorrect camshaft timing. Check ignition timing with a timing light and eliminate all other possible causes, utilizing the tests provided in this Chapter before you remove the timing chain cover to check the timing marks.

8   If the reading is three to eight inches below normal and it fluctuates at that low reading, suspect an intake manifold gasket leak at an intake port or a faulty fuel injector.

9   If the needle has regular drops of about two-to-four inches at a steady rate, the valves are probably leaking. Perform a compression check or leak-down test to confirm this.

10   An irregular drop or down-flick of the needle can be caused by a sticking valve or an ignition misfire. Perform a compression check or leak-down test and read the spark plugs.

11   A rapid vibration of about four in-Hg vibration at idle combined with exhaust smoke indicates worn valve guides. Perform a leak-down test to confirm this. If the rapid vibration occurs with an increase in engine speed, check for a leaking intake manifold gasket or head gasket, weak valve springs, burned valves or ignition misfire.

12   A slight fluctuation, say one inch up and down, may mean ignition problems. Check all the usual tune-up items and, if necessary, run the engine on an ignition analyzer.

13   If there is a large fluctuation, perform a compression or leak-down test to look for a weak or dead cylinder or a blown head gasket.

14   If the needle moves slowly through a wide range, check for a clogged PCV system, incorrect idle fuel mixture, throttle body or intake manifold gasket leaks.

15   Check for a slow return after revving the engine by quickly snapping the throttle open until the engine reaches about 2,500 rpm and let it shut. Normally the reading should drop to near zero, rise above normal idle reading (about 5 in-Hg over) and then return to the previous idle reading. If the vacuum returns

slowly and doesn't peak when the throttle is snapped shut, the rings may be worn. If there is a long delay, look for a restricted exhaust system (often the muffler or catalytic converter). An easy way to check this is to temporarily disconnect the exhaust ahead of the suspected part and redo the test.

5   Engine rebuilding alternatives

The do-it-yourselfer is faced with a number of options when purchasing a rebuilt engine. The major considerations are cost, warranty, parts availability and the time required for the rebuilder to complete the project. The decision to replace the engine block, piston/connecting rod assemblies and crankshaft depends on the final inspection results of your engine. Only then can you make a cost effective decision whether to have your engine overhauled or simply purchase an exchange engine for your vehicle.

Some of the rebuilding alternatives include:

Individual parts - If the inspection procedures reveal that the engine block and most engine components are in reusable condition, purchasing individual parts and having a rebuilder rebuild your engine may be the most economical alternative. The block, crankshaft and piston/connecting rod assemblies should all be inspected carefully by a machine shop first.

Short block - A short block consists of an engine block with a crankshaft and piston/connecting rod assemblies already installed. All new bearings are incorporated and all clearances will be correct. The existing camshafts, valve train components, cylinder head and external parts can be bolted to the short block with little or no machine shop work necessary.

Long block - A long block consists of a short block plus an oil pump, oil pan, cylinder head, valve cover, camshaft and valve train components, timing sprockets and chain or gears and timing cover. All components are installed with new bearings, seals and gaskets incorporated throughout. The installation of manifolds and external parts is all that's necessary.

Low mileage used engines - Some companies now offer low mileage used engines which is a very cost effective way to get your vehicle up and running again. These engines often come from vehicles which have been in totaled in accidents or come from other countries which have a higher vehicle turn over rate. A low mileage used engine also usually has a similar warranty like the newly remanufactured engines.

Give careful thought to which alternative is best for you and discuss the situation with local automotive machine shops, auto parts dealers and experienced rebuilders before ordering or purchasing replacement parts.

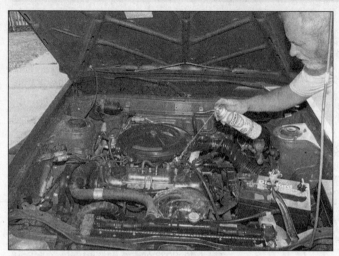

6.1 After tightly wrapping water-vulnerable components, use a spray cleaner on everything, with particular concentration on the greasiest areas, usually around the valve cover and lower edges of the block. If one section dries out, apply more cleaner

6.2 Depending on how dirty the engine is, let the cleaner soak in according to the directions and then hose off the grime and cleaner. Get the rinse water down into every area you can get at; then dry important components with a hair dryer or paper towels

6   Engine removal - methods and precautions

Refer to illustrations 6.1, 6.2, and 6.3

If you've decided that an engine must be removed for overhaul or major repair work, several preliminary steps should be taken. Read all removal and installation procedures carefully prior to committing to this job. These engines are removed by lowering the engine to the floor, along with the transmission, and then raising the vehicle sufficiently to slide the assembly out; this will require a vehicle hoist as well as an engine hoist.

Locating a suitable place to work is extremely important. Adequate work space, along with storage space for the vehicle, will be needed. If a shop or garage isn't available, at the very least a flat, level, clean work surface made of concrete or asphalt is required.

Cleaning the engine compartment and engine before beginning the removal procedure will help keep tools clean and organized **(see illustrations 6.1 and 6.2).**

An engine hoist will also be necessary. Make sure the hoist is rated in excess of the combined weight of the engine and transmission. Safety is of primary importance, considering the potential hazards involved in removing the engine from the vehicle.

If you're a novice at engine removal, get at least one helper. One person cannot easily do all the things you need to do to remove a big heavy engine and transmission assembly from the engine compartment. Also helpful is to seek advice and assistance from someone who's experienced in engine removal.

Plan the operation ahead of time. Arrange for or obtain all of the tools and equipment you'll need prior to beginning the job **(see illustration 6.3)**. Some of the equipment necessary to perform engine removal and installation safely and with relative ease are (in addition to a vehicle hoist and an engine hoist) a heavy duty floor jack (preferably fitted with a transmission jack head adapter), complete sets of wrenches and sockets as described in the front of this manual, wooden blocks, plenty of rags and cleaning solvent for

mopping up spilled oil, coolant and gasoline.

Plan for the vehicle to be out of use for quite a while. A machine shop can do the work that is beyond the scope of the home mechanic. Machine shops often have a busy schedule, so before removing the engine, consult the shop for an estimate of how long it will take to rebuild or repair the components that may need work.

7   Engine - removal and installation

Warning 1: *Gasoline is extremely flammable, so take extra precautions when you work on any part of the fuel system. Don't smoke or allow open flames or bare light bulbs near the work area, and don't work in a garage where a gas-type appliance (such as a water heater or clothes dryer) is present. Since gasoline is carcinogenic, wear fuel-resistant gloves when there's a possibility of being exposed to fuel, and, if you spill any fuel on your skin, rinse it off immediately with soap and water. Mop up any spills immediately and do not store fuel-soaked rags where they could ignite. The fuel system is under constant pressure, so, if any fuel lines are to be disconnected, the fuel pressure in the system must be relieved first (see Chapter 4 for more information). When you perform any kind of work on the fuel system, wear safety glasses and have a Class B type fire extinguisher on hand.*
Warning 2: *The air conditioning system is under high pressure. Do not loosen any hose fittings or remove any components until after the system has been discharged. Air conditioning refrigerant must be properly discharged into an EPA-approved recovery/recycling unit at a dealer service department or an automotive air conditioning repair facility. Always wear eye protection when disconnecting air conditioning system fittings.*
Warning 3: *The engine must be completely cool before beginning this procedure.*

6.3 Get an engine stand sturdy enough to firmly support the engine while you're working on it. Stay away from three-wheeled models; they have a tendency to tip over more easily, so get a four-wheeled unit

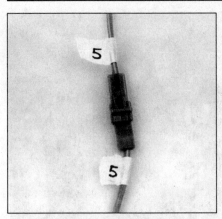

7.14 Label both ends of each wire or vacuum connection before disconnecting them

Removal

Refer to illustration 7.14

1   Have the air conditioning system discharged by an automotive air conditioning technician.
2   Relieve the fuel system pressure (see Chapter 4).
3   Disconnect the cable from the negative battery terminal (see Chapter 5, Section 1).
4   Remove the hood (see Chapter 11).
5   On models with automatic transmission, partially drain the automatic transmission fluid (see Chapter 1).
6   Remove the air filter housing and the intake air duct (see Chapter 4).
7   Drain the cooling system (see Chapter 1).
8   Remove the drivebelt (see Chapter 1).
9   Remove the radiator, shroud and engine cooling fan (see Chapter 3). Also remove the heater hoses.
10   Remove the alternator (see Chapter 5).
11   Remove the power steering pump, without disconnecting the hoses, and tie it out of the way (see Chapter 10).
12   Disconnect the electrical connector and coolant hoses from the throttle body (see Chapter 4).
13   Remove the PCV hose (see Chapter 6).
14   Label and disconnect all wires from the engine (see illustration). Masking tape and/or a touch-up paint applicator work well for marking items. **Note:** *Take instant photos or sketch the locations of components and brackets to help with reassembly.*
15   Label and remove all vacuum lines between the engine and the firewall (or other components in the engine compartment).
16   Remove the engine oil dipstick tube.
17   Raise the vehicle and support it securely on jackstands.
18   If you are working on a model with an automatic transmission, detach the transmission cooler lines from the engine brackets and the transmission (see Chapter 7B).
19   Disconnect the engine block heater, if equipped.
20   Disconnect the oxygen sensor and the

crankshaft position sensor connector (see Chapter 6).
21   Remove the automatic transmission dipstick, then pull the dipstick tube from the transmission.
22   Remove the starter (see Chapter 5).
23   Drain the engine oil, and on models so equipped, disconnect the coolant hoses from the oil cooler (see Chapter 3).
24   Disconnect the exhaust pipes from the exhaust manifolds. On four-cylinder models, remove the exhaust manifold.
25   Support the engine from above with a hoist. Attach the hoist chain to the engine lifting brackets. If no brackets are present, you'll have to fasten the chains to some substantial part of the engine - one that is strong enough to take the weight, but in a location that will provide good balance. If you're attaching the chain to a stud on the engine, or are using a bolt passing through the chain and into a threaded hole, place a washer between the nut or bolt head and the chain, and tighten the nut or bolt securely.
26   Remove the transmission brace (see Chapter 2A or 2B).
27   On automatic transmission models, remove the torque converter-to-driveplate bolts (see Chapter 7B).
28   Use the hoist to take the weight off the engine mounts, then remove the engine mount through-bolts (see Chapters 2A or 2B).
29   Support the transmission with a floor jack. Place a block of wood on the jack head to protect the transmission.
30   Check to make sure everything is disconnected, then lift the engine out of the vehicle. The engine will probably need to be tilted and/or maneuvered as it's lifted out, so have an assistant handy. **Warning:** *Do not place any part of your body under the engine when it is supported only by a hoist or other lifting device.*
31   Remove the flywheel/driveplate and mount the engine on an engine stand or set the engine on the floor and support it so it doesn't tip over. Then disconnect the engine hoist.

Installation

32   Check the engine mounts. If they're worn or damaged, replace them (see Chapter 2A or 2B).
33   On manual transmission models, inspect the clutch components (see Chapter 8). On automatic transmission models, inspect the front transmission fluid seal and bearing.
34   On manual transmission models, apply a dab of grease to the pilot bearing.
35   Attach the hoist to the engine, remove the engine from the engine stand and install the flywheel or driveplate (see Chapter 2A or 2B).
36   Carefully guide the engine into place, lowering it slowly and moving it back into the engine compartment until the engine mounts can be secured.
37   Tighten the transmission-to-engine bolts to the torque listed in the Chapter 7A or 7B Specifications.

38   On automatic transmission models, install the torque converter-to-driveplate bolts (see Chapter 7B).
39   Tighten all the bolts on the engine mounts and remove the hoist and jack.
40   Reinstall the remaining components in the reverse order of removal.
41   Add coolant, oil, power steering and transmission fluid as needed (see Chapter 1).
42   Run the engine and check for proper operation and leaks. Shut off the engine and recheck the fluid levels.

8   Engine overhaul - disassembly sequence

1   It's much easier to remove the external components if it's mounted on a portable engine stand. A stand can often be rented quite cheaply from an equipment rental yard. Before the engine is mounted on a stand, the flywheel/driveplate should be removed from the engine.
2   If a stand isn't available, it's possible to remove the external engine components with it blocked up on the floor. Be extra careful not to tip or drop the engine when working without a stand.
3   If you're going to obtain a rebuilt engine, all external components must come off first, to be transferred to the replacement engine. These components include:

Flywheel/driveplate
Ignition system components
Emissions-related components
Engine mounts and mount brackets
Intake/exhaust manifolds
Fuel injection components
Oil filter and oil cooler
Spark plug wires and spark plugs
Thermostat and housing assembly
Water pump

Note: *When removing the external components from the engine, pay close attention to details that may be helpful or important during installation. Note the installed position of gaskets, seals, spacers, pins, brackets, washers, bolts and other small items.*
4   If you're going to obtain a short block (assembled engine block, crankshaft, pistons and connecting rods), then remove the timing chain, cylinder head, oil pan, oil pump pick-up tube, oil pump and water pump from your engine so that you can turn in your old short block to the rebuilder as a core. See *Engine rebuilding alternatives* for additional information regarding the different possibilities to be considered.

9   Pistons and connecting rods - removal and installation

Removal

Refer to illustrations 9.1, 9.3 and 9.4
Note: *Prior to removing the piston/connecting rod assemblies, remove the cylinder head*

9.1 Before you try to remove the pistons, use a ridge reamer to remove the raised material (ridge) from the top of the cylinders

9.3 Checking the connecting rod endplay (side clearance)

and oil pan (see Chapter 2A or 2B).

1   Use your fingernail to feel if a ridge has formed at the upper limit of ring travel (about 1/4-inch down from the top of each cylinder). If carbon deposits or cylinder wear have produced ridges, they must be completely removed with a special tool **(see illustration)**. Follow the manufacturer's instructions provided with the tool. Failure to remove the ridges before attempting to remove the piston/connecting rod assemblies may result in piston breakage.

2   After the cylinder ridges have been removed, turn the engine so the crankshaft is facing up.

3   Before the main bearing cap assembly and connecting rods are removed, check the connecting rod endplay with feeler gauges. Slide them between the first connecting rod and the crankshaft throw until the play is removed **(see illustration)**. Repeat this procedure for each connecting rod. The endplay is equal to the thickness of the feeler gauge(s). Check with an automotive machine shop for the endplay service limit (a typical

endplay should measure between 0.005 to 0.015 inch [0.127 to 0.396 mm]). If the play exceeds the service limit, new connecting rods will be required. If new rods (or a new crankshaft) are installed, the endplay may fall under the minimum allowable. If it does, the rods will have to be machined to restore it. If necessary, consult an automotive machine shop for advice.

4   Check the connecting rods and caps for identification marks. If they aren't plainly marked, use paint or marker **(see illustration)** to clearly identify each rod and cap (1, 2, 3, etc., depending on the cylinder they're associated with). Do not interchange the rod caps. Install the exact same rod cap onto the same connecting rod. **Caution:** *Do not use a punch and hammer to mark the connecting rods or they may be damaged.*

5   Loosen each of the connecting rod cap bolts or nuts 1/2-turn at a time until they can be removed by hand.

6   Remove the number one connecting rod cap and bearing insert. Don't drop the bearing insert out of the cap.

7   Remove the bearing insert and push the connecting rod/piston assembly out through the top of the engine. Use a wooden or plastic hammer handle to push on the upper bearing surface in the connecting rod. If resistance is felt, double-check to make sure that all of the ridge was removed from the cylinder.

8   Repeat the procedure for the remaining cylinders.

9   After removal, reassemble the connecting rod caps and bearing inserts in their respective connecting rods and install the cap bolts finger tight. Leaving the old bearing inserts in place until reassembly will help prevent the connecting rod bearing surfaces from being accidentally nicked or gouged.

10   The pistons and connecting rods are now ready for inspection and overhaul at an automotive machine shop.

Piston ring installation

Refer to illustrations 9.13, 9.14, 9.15, 9.19a, 9.19b and 9.22

11   Before installing the new piston rings, the ring end gaps must be checked. It's assumed

9.4 If the connecting rods or caps are not marked, use permanent ink or paint to mark the caps to the rods by cylinder number (for example, this would be number 4 cylinder connecting rod)

9.13 Install the piston ring into the cylinder then push it down into position using a piston so the ring will be square in the cylinder

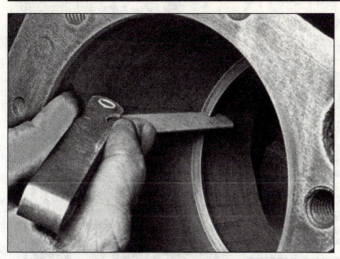

9.14 With the ring square in the cylinder, measure the ring end gap with a feeler gauge

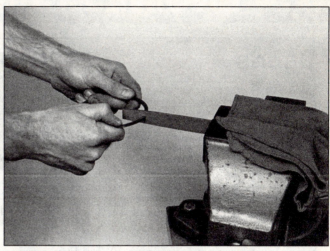

9.15 If the ring end gap is too small, clamp a file in a vise as shown and file the piston ring ends - be sure to remove all raised material

that the piston ring side clearance has been checked and verified correct.

12 Lay out the piston/connecting rod assemblies and the new ring sets so the ring sets will be matched with the same piston and cylinder during the end gap measurement and engine assembly.

13 Insert the top (number one) ring into the first cylinder and square it up with the cylinder walls by pushing it in with the top of the piston **(see illustration)**. The ring should be near the bottom of the cylinder, at the lower limit of ring travel.

14 To measure the end gap, slip feeler gauges between the ends of the ring until a gauge equal to the gap width is found **(see illustration)**. The feeler gauge should slide between the ring ends with a slight amount of drag. A typical ring gap should fall between 0.010 and 0.020 inch [0.25 to 0.50 mm] for compression rings and up to 0.030 inch [0.76 mm] for the oil ring steel rails. If the gap is larger or smaller than specified, double-check

to make sure you have the correct rings before proceeding.

15 If the gap is too small, it must be enlarged or the ring ends may come in contact with each other during engine operation, which can cause serious damage to the engine. If necessary, increase the end gaps by filing the ring ends very carefully with a fine file. Mount the file in a vise equipped with soft jaws, slip the ring over the file with the ends contacting the file face and slowly move the ring to remove material from the ends. When performing this operation, file only by pushing the ring from the outside end of the file towards the vise **(see illustration)**.

16 Excess end gap isn't critical unless it's greater than 0.040 inch (1.01 mm). Again, double-check to make sure you have the correct ring type.

17 Repeat the procedure for each ring that will be installed in the first cylinder and for each ring in the remaining cylinders. Remember to keep rings, pistons and cylinders

matched up.

18 Once the ring end gaps have been checked/corrected, the rings can be installed on the pistons.

19 The oil control ring (lowest one on the piston) is usually installed first. It's composed of three separate components. Slip the spacer/expander into the groove **(see illustration)**. If an anti-rotation tang is used, make sure it's inserted into the drilled hole in the ring groove. Next, install the lower side rail in the same manner **(see illustration)**. Don't use a piston ring installation tool on the oil ring side rails, as they may be damaged. Instead, place one end of the side rail into the groove between the spacer/expander and the ring land, hold it firmly in place and slide a finger around the piston while pushing the rail into the groove. Finally, install the upper side rail.

20 After the three oil ring components have been installed, check to make sure that both the upper and lower side rails can be rotated smoothly inside the ring grooves.

9.19a Installing the spacer/expander in the oil ring groove

9.19b DO NOT use a piston ring installation tool when installing the oil control side rails

ENGINE BEARING ANALYSIS

Debris

Babbitt bearing embedded with debris from machinings

Microscopic detail of debris

Microscopic detail of gouges

Overplated copper alloy bearing gouged by cast iron debris

Aluminum bearing embedded with glass beads

Microscopic detail of glass beads

Damaged lining caused by dirt left on the bearing back

Misassembly

Result of a lower half assembled as an upper - blocking the oil flow

Excessive oil clearance is indicated by a short contact arc

Polished and oil-stained backs are a result of a poor fit in the housing bore

Result of a wrong, reversed, or shifted cap

Overloading

Damage from excessive idling which resulted in an oil film unable to support the load imposed

Damaged upper connecting rod bearings caused by engine lugging; the lower main bearings (not shown) were similarly affected

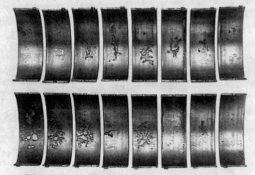

The damage shown in these upper and lower connecting rod bearings was caused by engine operation at a higher-than-rated speed under load

Misalignment

A warped crankshaft caused this pattern of severe wear in the center, diminishing toward the ends

A poorly finished crankshaft caused the equally spaced scoring shown

A tapered housing bore caused the damage along one edge of this pair

A bent connecting rod led to the damage in the "V" pattern

Lubrication

Result of dry start: The bearings on the left, farthest from the oil pump, show more damage

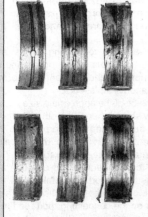

Result of a low oil supply or oil starvation

Severe wear as a result of inadequate oil clearance

Corrosion

Microscopic detail of corrosion

Corrosion is an acid attack on the bearing lining generally caused by inadequate maintenance, extremely hot or cold operation, or inferior oils or fuels

Microscopic detail of cavitation

Example of cavitation - a surface erosion caused by pressure changes in the oil film

Damage from excessive thrust or insufficient axial clearance

Bearing affected by oil dilution caused by excessive blow-by or a rich mixture

9.22 Use a piston ring installation tool to install the compression rings - on some engines the number two compression ring has a directional mark that must face toward the top of the piston

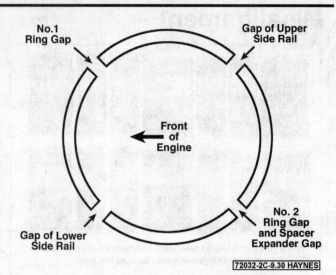

9.30 Position the piston ring end gaps as shown

21   The number two (middle) ring is installed next. It's usually stamped with a mark which must face up, toward the top of the piston. Do not mix up the top and middle rings, as they have different cross-sections. **Note:** *Always follow the instructions printed on the ring package or box - different manufacturers may require different approaches.*

22   Use a piston ring installation tool and make sure the identification mark is facing the top of the piston, then slip the ring into the middle groove on the piston **(see illustration)**. Don't expand the ring any more than necessary to slide it over the piston. **Note:** *Be careful not to confuse the number one and number two rings.*

23   Install the number one (top) ring in the same manner.

24   Repeat the procedure for the remaining pistons and rings.

Installation

25   Before installing the piston/connecting rod assemblies, the cylinder walls must be perfectly clean, the top edge of each cylinder

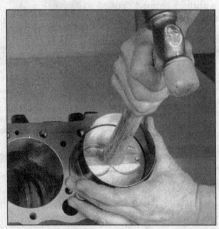

9.35 Use a plastic or wooden hammer handle to push the piston into the cylinder

bore must be chamfered, and the crankshaft must be in place.

26   Remove the cap from the end of the number one connecting rod (refer to the marks made during removal). Remove the original bearing inserts and wipe the bearing surfaces of the connecting rod and cap with a clean, lint-free cloth. They must be kept spotlessly clean.

Connecting rod bearing oil clearance check

Refer to illustrations 9.30, 9.35, 9.37 and 9.41

27   Clean the back side of the new upper bearing insert, then lay it in place in the connecting rod.

28   Make sure the tab on the bearing fits into the recess in the rod. Don't hammer the bearing insert into place and be very careful not to nick or gouge the bearing face. Don't lubricate the bearing at this time.

29   Clean the back side of the other bearing insert and install it in the rod cap. Again, make sure the tab on the bearing fits into the recess in the cap, and don't apply any lubricant. It's critically important that the mating surfaces of the bearing and connecting rod are perfectly clean and oil free when they're assembled.

30   Position the piston ring gaps at the intervals around the piston as shown **(see illustration)**.

31   Lubricate the piston and rings with clean engine oil and attach a piston ring compressor to the piston. Leave the skirt protruding about 1/4-inch to guide the piston into the cylinder. The rings must be compressed until they're flush with the piston.

32   Rotate the crankshaft until the number one connecting rod journal is at BDC (bottom dead center) and apply a liberal coat of engine oil to the cylinder walls. Refer to the TDC locating procedure in Chapter 2A or 2B for additional information.

33   With the "front" mark (letter F or arrow) on the piston facing the front (timing chain

end) of the engine, gently insert the piston/connecting rod assembly into the number one cylinder bore and rest the bottom edge of the ring compressor on the engine block. **Note:** *Some engines have a letter "F" marking on the side of the piston near the wrist pin, others have an arrow, an "F" or a dimple or groove on the top of the piston. All of these are marks that indicate the front of the piston.*

34   Tap the top edge of the ring compressor to make sure it's contacting the block around its entire circumference.

35   Gently tap on the top of the piston with the end of a wooden or plastic hammer handle **(see illustration)** while guiding the end of the connecting rod into place on the crankshaft journal. The piston rings may try to pop out of the ring compressor just before entering the cylinder bore, so keep some downward pressure on the ring compressor. Work slowly, and if any resistance is felt as the piston enters the cylinder, stop immediately. Find out what's hanging up and fix it before proceeding. Do not, for any reason, force the piston into the cylinder - you might break a ring and/or the piston.

36   Once the piston/connecting rod assembly is installed, the connecting rod bearing oil clearance must be checked before the rod cap is permanently installed.

37   Cut a piece of the appropriate size Plastigage slightly shorter than the width of the connecting rod bearing and lay it in place on the number one connecting rod journal, parallel with the journal axis **(see illustration)**.

38   Clean the connecting rod cap bearing face and install the rod cap. Make sure the mating mark on the cap is on the same side as the mark on the connecting rod **(see illustration 9.4)**.

39   Install the rod bolts and tighten them to the torque listed in this Chapter's Specifications. **Note:** *Use a thin-wall socket to avoid erroneous torque readings that can result if the socket is wedged between the rod cap and the bolt or nut. If the socket tends to wedge*

9.37 Place Plastigage on each connecting rod bearing journal parallel to the crankshaft centerline

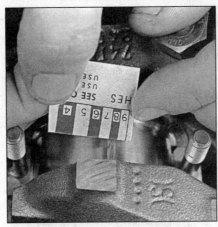

9.41 Use the scale on the Plastigage package to determine the bearing oil clearance - be sure to measure the widest part of the Plastigage and use the correct scale; it comes with both standard and metric scales

itself between the fastener and the cap, lift up on it slightly until it no longer contacts the cap. DO NOT rotate the crankshaft at any time during this operation.

40   Remove the fasteners and detach the rod cap, being very careful not to disturb the Plastigage. Discard the cap bolts at this time as they cannot be reused. **Note:** *You MUST use new connecting rod bolts.*

41   Compare the width of the crushed Plastigage to the scale printed on the Plastigage envelope to obtain the oil clearance **(see illustration)**. The connecting rod bearing oil clearance is usually about 0.001 to 0.002 inch. Consult an automotive machine shop for the clearance specified for the rod bearings on your engine.

42   If the clearance is not as specified, the bearing inserts may be the wrong size (which means different ones will be required). Before deciding that different inserts are needed, make sure that no dirt or oil was between the bearing inserts and the connecting rod or cap when the clearance was measured. Also, recheck the journal diameter. If the Plastigage was wider at one end than the other, the journal may be tapered. If the clearance still exceeds the limit specified, the bearing will have to be replaced with an undersize bearing. **Caution:** *When installing a new crankshaft always use a standard size bearing.*

Final installation

43   Carefully scrape all traces of the Plastigage material off the rod journal and/or bearing face. Be very careful not to scratch the bearing - use your fingernail or the edge of a plastic card.

44   Make sure the bearing faces are perfectly clean, then apply a uniform layer of clean moly-base grease or engine assembly lube to both of them. You'll have to push the piston into the cylinder to expose the face of the bearing insert in the connecting rod.

45   Slide the connecting rod back into place on the journal, install the rod cap, install the nuts or bolts and tighten them to the torque listed in this Chapter's Specifications.

46   Repeat the entire procedure for the remaining pistons/connecting rods.

47   The important points to remember are:

a) *Keep the back sides of the bearing inserts and the insides of the connecting rods and caps perfectly clean when assembling them.*

b) *Make sure you have the correct piston/ rod assembly for each cylinder.*

c) *The mark on the piston must face the front (timing chain end) of the engine.*

d) *Lubricate the cylinder walls liberally with clean oil.*

e) *Lubricate the bearing faces when installing the rod caps after the oil clearance has been checked.*

48   After all the piston/connecting rod assemblies have been correctly installed, rotate the crankshaft a number of times by hand to check for any obvious binding.

49   As a final step, check the connecting rod endplay again. If it was correct before disassembly and the original crankshaft and rods were reinstalled, it should still be correct. If

new rods or a new crankshaft were installed, the endplay may be inadequate. If so, the rods will have to be removed and taken to an automotive machine shop for resizing.

10   Crankshaft - removal and installation

Removal

Refer to illustrations 10.1 and 10.3

Note: *The crankshaft can be removed only after the engine has been removed from the vehicle. It's assumed that the flywheel or driveplate, crankshaft pulley, timing chain, oil pan, oil pump, oil filter and piston/connecting rod assemblies have already been removed. The rear main oil seal retainer must be unbolted and separated from the block before proceeding with crankshaft removal.*

1   Before the crankshaft is removed, measure the endplay. Mount a dial indicator with the indicator in line with the crankshaft and touching the end of the crankshaft **(see illustration)**.

2   Pry the crankshaft all the way to the rear and zero the dial indicator. Next, pry the crankshaft to the front as far as possible and check the reading on the dial indicator. The distance traveled is the endplay. A typical crankshaft endplay will fall between 0.003 to 0.010 inch (0.076 to 0.254 mm). If it is greater than that, check the crankshaft thrust washer/ bearing assembly surfaces for wear after it's removed. If no wear is evident, new main bearings should correct the endplay. Refer to Step 14 for the location of the thrust washer/ bearing assembly on each engine.

3   If a dial indicator isn't available, feeler gauges can be used. Gently pry the crankshaft all the way to the front of the engine. Slip feeler gauges between the crankshaft and the front face of the thrust bearing or washer to determine the clearance **(see illustration)**.

4   Loosen the main bearing cap/bedplate bolts 1/4-turn at a time each, until they can be removed by hand.

10.1 Checking crankshaft endplay with a dial indicator

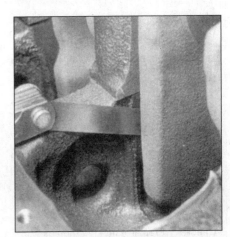

10.3 Checking crankshaft endplay with feeler gauges at the thrust bearing journal

COMMON ENGINE OVERHAUL TERMS

B

Backlash - The amount of play between two parts. Usually refers to how much one gear can be moved back and forth without moving the gear with which it's meshed.

Bearing Caps - The caps held in place by nuts or bolts which, in turn, hold the bearing surface. This space is for lubricating oil to enter.

Bearing clearance - The amount of space left between shaft and bearing surface. This space is for lubricating oil to enter.

Bearing crush - The additional height which is purposely manufactured into each bearing half to ensure complete contact of the bearing back with the housing bore when the engine is assembled.

Bearing knock - The noise created by movement of a part in a loose or worn bearing.

Blueprinting - Dismantling an engine and reassembling it to EXACT specifications.

Bore - An engine cylinder, or any cylindrical hole; also used to describe the process of enlarging or accurately refinishing a hole with a cutting tool, as to bore an engine cylinder. The bore size is the diameter of the hole.

Boring - Renewing the cylinders by cutting them out to a specified size. A boring bar is used to make the cut.

Bottom end - A term which refers collectively to the engine block, crankshaft, main bearings and the big ends of the connecting rods.

Break-in - The period of operation between installation of new or rebuilt parts and time in which parts are worn to the correct fit. Driving at reduced and varying speed for a specified mileage to permit parts to wear to the correct fit.

Bushing - A one-piece sleeve placed in a bore to serve as a bearing surface for shaft, piston pin, etc. Usually replaceable.

C

Camshaft - The shaft in the engine, on which a series of lobes are located for operating the valve mechanisms. The camshaft is driven by gears or sprockets and a timing chain. Usually referred to simply as the cam.

Carbon - Hard, or soft, black deposits found in combustion chamber, on plugs, under rings, on and under valve heads.

Cast iron - An alloy of iron and more than two percent carbon, used for engine blocks and heads because it's relatively inexpensive and easy to mold into complex shapes.

Chamfer - To bevel across (or a bevel on) the sharp edge of an object.

Chase - To repair damaged threads with a tap or die.

Combustion chamber - The space between the piston and the cylinder head, with the piston at top dead center, in which air-fuel mixture is burned.

Compression ratio - The relationship between cylinder volume (clearance volume) when the piston is at top dead center and cylinder volume when the piston is at bottom dead center.

Connecting rod - The rod that connects the crank on the crankshaft with the piston. Sometimes called a con rod.

Connecting rod cap - The part of the connecting rod assembly that attaches the rod to the crankpin.

Core plug - Soft metal plug used to plug the casting holes for the coolant passages in the block.

Crankcase - The lower part of the engine in which the crankshaft rotates; includes the lower section of the cylinder block and the oil pan.

Crank kit - A reground or reconditioned crankshaft and new main and connecting rod bearings.

Crankpin - The part of a crankshaft to which a connecting rod is attached.

Crankshaft - The main rotating member, or shaft, running the length of the crankcase, with offset throws to which the connecting rods are attached; changes the reciprocating motion of the pistons into rotating motion.

Cylinder sleeve - A replaceable sleeve, or liner, pressed into the cylinder block to form the cylinder bore.

D

Deburring - Removing the burrs (rough edges or areas) from a bearing.

Deglazer - A tool, rotated by an electric motor, used to remove glaze from cylinder walls so a new set of rings will seat.

E

Endplay - The amount of lengthwise movement between two parts. As applied to a crankshaft, the distance that the crankshaft can move forward and back in the cylinder block.

F

Face - A machinist's term that refers to removing metal from the end of a shaft or the face of a larger part, such as a flywheel.

Fatigue - A breakdown of material through a large number of loading and unloading cycles. The first signs are cracks followed shortly by breaks.

Feeler gauge - A thin strip of hardened steel, ground to an exact thickness, used to check clearances between parts.

Free height - The unloaded length or height of a spring.

Freeplay - The looseness in a linkage, or an assembly of parts, between the initial application of force and actual movement. Usually perceived as slop or slight delay.

Freeze plug - See Core plug.

G

Gallery - A large passage in the block that forms a reservoir for engine oil pressure.

Glaze - The very smooth, glassy finish that develops on cylinder walls while an engine is in service.

H

Heli-Coil - A rethreading device used when threads are worn or damaged. The device is installed in a retapped hole to reduce the thread size to the original size.

I

Installed height - The spring's measured length or height, as installed on the cylinder head. Installed height is measured from the spring seat to the underside of the spring retainer.

J

Journal - The surface of a rotating shaft which turns in a bearing.

K

Keeper - The split lock that holds the valve spring retainer in position on the valve stem.

Key - A small piece of metal inserted into matching grooves machined into two parts fitted together - such as a gear pressed onto a shaft - which prevents slippage between the two parts.

Knock - The heavy metallic engine sound, produced in the combustion chamber as a result of abnormal combustion - usually detonation. Knock is usually caused by a loose or worn bearing. Also referred to as detonation, pinging and spark knock. Connecting rod or main bearing knocks are created by too much oil clearance or insufficient lubrication.

L

Lands - The portions of metal between the piston ring grooves.

Lapping the valves - Grinding a valve face and its seat together with lapping compound.

Lash - The amount of free motion in a gear train, between gears, or in a mechanical assembly, that occurs before movement can begin. Usually refers to the lash in a valve train.

Lifter - The part that rides against the cam to transfer motion to the rest of the valve train.

M

Machining - The process of using a machine to remove metal from a metal part.

Main bearings - The plain, or babbit, bearings that support the crankshaft.

Main bearing caps - The cast iron caps, bolted to the bottom of the block, that support the main bearings.

O

O.D. - Outside diameter.

Oil gallery - A pipe or drilled passageway in the engine used to carry engine oil from one area to another.

Oil ring - The lower ring, or rings, of a piston; designed to prevent excessive amounts of oil from working up the cylinder walls and into the combustion chamber. Also called an oil-control ring.

Oil seal - A seal which keeps oil from leaking out of a compartment. Usually refers to a dynamic seal around a rotating shaft or other moving part.

O-ring - A type of sealing ring made of a special rubberlike material; in use, the O-ring is compressed into a groove to provide the sealing action.

Overhaul - To completely disassemble a unit, clean and inspect all parts, reassemble it with the original or new parts and make all adjustments necessary for proper operation.

P

Pilot bearing - A small bearing installed in the center of the flywheel (or the rear end of the crankshaft) to support the front end of the input shaft of the transmission.

Pip mark - A little dot or indentation which indicates the top side of a compression ring.

Piston - The cylindrical part, attached to the connecting rod, that moves up and down in the cylinder as the crankshaft rotates. When the fuel charge is fired, the piston transfers the force of the explosion to the connecting rod, then to the crankshaft.

Piston pin (or wrist pin) - The cylindrical and usually hollow steel pin that passes through the piston. The piston pin fastens the piston to the upper end of the connecting rod.

Piston ring - The split ring fitted to the groove in a piston. The ring contacts the sides of the ring groove and also rubs against the cylinder wall, thus sealing space between piston and wall. There are two types of rings: Compression rings seal the compression pressure in the combustion chamber; oil rings scrape excessive oil off the cylinder wall.

Piston ring groove - The slots or grooves cut in piston heads to hold piston rings in position.

Piston skirt - The portion of the piston below the rings and the piston pin hole.

Plastigage - A thin strip of plastic thread, available in different sizes, used for measuring clearances. For example, a strip of plastigage is laid across a bearing journal and mashed as parts are assembled. Then parts are disassembled and the width of the strip is measured to determine clearance between journal and bearing. Commonly used to measure crankshaft main-bearing and connecting rod bearing clearances.

Press-fit - A tight fit between two parts that requires pressure to force the parts together. Also referred to as drive, or force, fit.

Prussian blue - A blue pigment; in solution, useful in determining the area of contact between two surfaces. Prussian blue is commonly used to determine the width and location of the contact area between the valve face and the valve seat.

R

Race (bearing) - The inner or outer ring that provides a contact surface for balls or rollers in bearing.

Ream - To size, enlarge or smooth a hole by using a round cutting tool with fluted edges.

Ring job - The process of reconditioning the cylinders and installing new rings.

Runout - Wobble. The amount a shaft rotates out-of-true.

S

Saddle - The upper main bearing seat.

Scored - Scratched or grooved, as a cylinder wall may be scored by abrasive particles moved up and down by the piston rings.

Scuffing - A type of wear in which there's a transfer of material between parts moving against each other; shows up as pits or grooves in the mating surfaces.

Seat - The surface upon which another part rests or seats. For example, the valve seat is the matched surface upon which the valve face rests. Also used to refer to wearing into a good fit; for example, piston rings seat after a few miles of driving.

Short block - An engine block complete with crankshaft and piston and, usually, camshaft assemblies.

Static balance - The balance of an object while it's stationary.

Step - The wear on the lower portion of a ring land caused by excessive side and back-clearance. The height of the step indicates the ring's extra side clearance and the length of the step projecting from the back wall of the groove represents the ring's back clearance.

Stroke - The distance the piston moves when traveling from top dead center to bottom dead center, or from bottom dead center to top dead center.

Stud - A metal rod with threads on both ends.

T

Tang - A lip on the end of a plain bearing used to align the bearing during assembly.

Tap - To cut threads in a hole. Also refers to the fluted tool used to cut threads.

Taper - A gradual reduction in the width of a shaft or hole; in an engine cylinder, taper usually takes the form of uneven wear, more pronounced at the top than at the bottom.

Throws - The offset portions of the crankshaft to which the connecting rods are affixed.

Thrust bearing - The main bearing that has thrust faces to prevent excessive endplay, or forward and backward movement of the crankshaft.

Thrust washer - A bronze or hardened steel washer placed between two moving parts. The washer prevents longitudinal movement and provides a bearing surface for thrust surfaces of parts.

Tolerance - The amount of variation permitted from an exact size of measurement. Actual amount from smallest acceptable dimension to largest acceptable dimension.

U

Umbrella - An oil deflector placed near the valve tip to throw oil from the valve stem area.

Undercut - A machined groove below the normal surface.

Undersize bearings - Smaller diameter bearings used with re-ground crankshaft journals.

V

Valve grinding - Refacing a valve in a valve-refacing machine.

Valve train - The valve-operating mechanism of an engine; includes all components from the camshaft to the valve.

Vibration damper - A cylindrical weight attached to the front of the crankshaft to minimize torsional vibration (the twist-untwist actions of the crankshaft caused by the cylinder firing impulses). Also called a harmonic balancer.

W

Water jacket - The spaces around the cylinders, between the inner and outer shells of the cylinder block or head, through which coolant circulates.

Web - A supporting structure across a cavity.

Woodruff key - A key with a radiused backside (viewed from the side).

5   Gently tap the main bearing caps/bed-plate assembly with a soft-face hammer around the perimeter of the assembly. Pull the main bearing cap/bedplate assembly straight up and off the cylinder block. Try not to drop the bearing inserts if they come out with the assembly. **Note:** *The bedplate has built in pry points; don't pry anywhere else or damage to the bedplate will occur.*

6   Carefully lift the crankshaft out of the engine. It may be a good idea to have an assistant available, since the crankshaft is quite heavy and awkward to handle. With the bearing inserts in place inside the engine block and main bearing caps, reinstall the main bearing cap assembly onto the engine block and tighten the bolts finger tight. Make sure you install the main bearing cap assembly with the arrow facing the front of the engine.

Installation

7   Crankshaft installation is the first step in engine reassembly. It's assumed at this point that the engine block and crankshaft have been cleaned, inspected and repaired or reconditioned.

8   Position the engine block with the bottom facing up.

9   Remove the mounting bolts and lift off the main bearing cap assembly.

10   If they're still in place, remove the original bearing inserts from the block and from the main bearing cap assembly. Wipe the bearing surfaces of the block and main bearing cap assembly with a clean, lint-free cloth. They must be kept spotlessly clean. This is critical for determining the correct bearing oil clearance.

Main bearing oil clearance check

Refer to illustrations 10.14, 10.17, 10.18a, 10.18b, 10.19a, 19.19b and 10.21

11   Without mixing them up, clean the back sides of the new upper main bearing inserts

10.14 Insert the thrust washer into the machined surface between the crankshaft and the upper bearing saddle, then rotate it down into the block until it's flush with the parting line on the main bearing saddle - make sure the oil grooves on the thrust washer face the crankshaft

(with grooves and oil holes) and lay one in each main bearing saddle in the block. Each upper bearing has an oil groove and oil hole in it. **Caution:** *The oil holes in the block must line up with the oil holes in the upper bearing inserts.* Clean the back sides of the lower main bearing inserts and lay them in the corresponding location in the main bearing cap. Make sure the tab on the bearing insert fits into the recess in the block or main bearing cap. The upper bearings with the oil holes are installed into the engine block while the lower bearings without the oil holes are installed in the caps or bedplate. **Caution:** *Do not hammer the bearing insert into place and don't nick or gouge the bearing faces. DO NOT apply any lubrication at this time.*

12   Clean the faces of the bearing inserts in the block and the crankshaft main bearing journals with a clean, lint-free cloth.

13   Check or clean the oil holes in the crank-

10.17 Place the Plastigage onto the crankshaft bearing journal as shown

shaft, as any dirt here can go only one way - straight through the new bearings.

14   Once you're certain the crankshaft is clean, carefully lay it in position in the block, which should be oriented on the engine stand to have the bottom side Up. Lube and insert the thrust washers on either side of journal #3 on both four-cylinder and V6 engines. The thrust washers must be installed in the correct journal. **Note:** *Install the thrust washers with the groove in the thrust washer facing the crankshaft with the smooth sides facing the main bearing saddle* **(see illustration).**

15   Before the crankshaft can be permanently installed, the main bearing oil clearance must be checked.

16   Cut several strips of the appropriate size of Plastigage. They must be slightly shorter than the width of the main bearing journal.

17   Place one piece on each crankshaft main bearing journal, parallel with the journal axis as shown **(see illustration).**

18   Clean the faces of the bearing inserts in the main bearing caps or bedplate assembly **(see illustrations).** Hold the bearing inserts in place and install the assembly onto the crank-

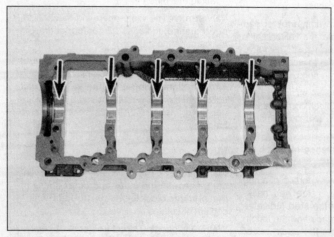

10.18a The bearings are installed into the corresponding saddles in the bedplate (typical) . . .

10.18b . . . then the bedplate is set over the crankshaft onto the dowels on the engine block

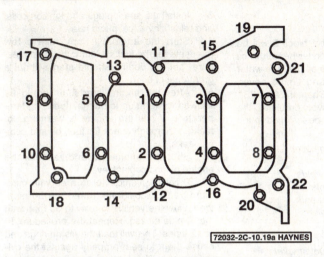

10.19a Main bearing cap/bedplate bolt tightening sequence on the 2.5L four-cylinder engine

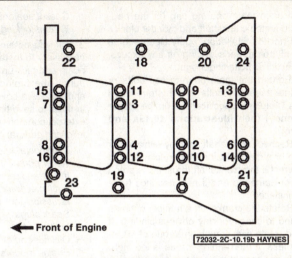

← **Front of Engine**

10.19b Main bearing cap/bedplate bolt tightening sequence on the 4.0L V6 engine

shaft and cylinder block. DO NOT disturb the Plastigage. Make sure you install the main bearing cap assembly with the arrow facing the front (timing chain end) of the engine.

19 Apply clean engine oil to all bolt threads prior to installation, then install all bolts finger-tight. Tighten main bearing caps/bedplate assembly bolts in the sequence shown (see illustrations) progressing in steps, to the torque listed in this Chapter's Specifications. DO NOT rotate the crankshaft at any time during this operation.

20 Remove the bolts in the reverse order of the tightening sequence and carefully lift the main bearing cap assembly straight up and off the block. Do not disturb the Plastigage or rotate the crankshaft. If the main bearing cap assembly is difficult to remove, tap it gently from side-to-side with a soft-face hammer to loosen it.

21 Compare the width of the crushed Plastigage on each journal to the scale printed on the Plastigage envelope to determine the main bearing oil clearance (see illustration).

A typical main bearing oil clearance should fall between 0.0015 and 0.0023-inch. Check with an automotive machine shop for the clearance specified for your engine.

22 If the clearance is not as specified, the bearing inserts may be the wrong size (which means different ones will be required). Before deciding if different inserts are needed, make sure that no dirt or oil was between the bearing inserts and the cap assembly or block when the clearance was measured. If the Plastigage was wider at one end than the other, the crankshaft journal may be tapered. If the clearance still exceeds the limit specified, the bearing insert(s) will have to be replaced with an undersize bearing insert(s). **Caution:** *When installing a new crankshaft, always install a standard bearing insert set.*

23 Carefully scrape all traces of the Plastigage material off the main bearing journals and/or the bearing insert faces. Be sure to remove all residue from the oil holes. Use your fingernail or the edge of a plastic card - don't nick or scratch the bearing faces.

Final installation

Refer to illustration 10.28

24 Carefully lift the crankshaft out of the cylinder block.

25 Clean the bearing insert faces in the cylinder block, then apply a thin, uniform layer of moly-base grease or engine assembly lube to each of the bearing surfaces. Be sure to coat the thrust faces as well as the journal face of the thrust washers. **Note:** *Install the thrust washers after the crankshaft has been installed.*

26 Make sure the crankshaft journals are clean, then lay the crankshaft back in place in the cylinder block.

27 Clean the bearing insert faces and then apply the same lubricant to them. Clean the engine block thoroughly. The surfaces must be free of oil residue. Install the thrust washers.

28 On all models, apply a 3.5 mm bead of RTV sealant or equivalent to the bedplate sealing area on the block (see illustration).

10.21 Use the scale on the Plastigage package to determine the bearing oil clearance - be sure to measure the widest part of the Plastigage and use the correct scale; it comes with both standard and metric scales

10.28 Apply a 3.5 mm bead of RTV sealant to the engine block-to-bedplate sealing surface as shown (typical)

Install each main bearing cap (or the bed-plate) onto the crankshaft and cylinder block.
29   Prior to installation, apply clean engine oil to all bolt threads, wiping off any excess, then install all bolts finger-tight.
30   Tighten the main bearing cap bolts or bedplate assembly bolts to the torque listed in this Chapter's Specifications (in the proper sequence) **(see illustrations 10.19a and 10.19b)**.
31   Recheck crankshaft endplay with a feeler gauge or a dial indicator. The endplay should be correct if the crankshaft thrust faces aren't worn or damaged and if new bearings have been installed.
32   Rotate the crankshaft a number of times by hand to check for any obvious binding. It should rotate with a running torque of 50 in-lbs or less. If the running torque is too high, identify and correct the problem at this time.
33   Install the new rear main oil seal (see Chapter 2A and 2B).

11   Engine overhaul - reassembly sequence

1   Before beginning engine reassembly, make sure you have all the necessary new parts, gaskets and seals as well as the following items on hand:

   Common hand tools
   A 1/2-inch drive torque wrench
   New engine oil
   Gasket sealant
   Thread locking compound

2   If you obtained a short block it will be necessary to install the cylinder head, the oil pump and pick-up tube, the oil pan, the water pump, the timing chain and timing cover, and the valve cover (see Chapter 2A or 2B). In order to save time and avoid problems, the external components must be installed in the following general order:

   Thermostat and housing cover
   Water pump
   Intake and exhaust manifolds
   Fuel injection components
   Emission control components
   Spark plugs
   Ignition coils
   Oil filter and oil cooler
   Engine mounts and mount brackets
   Flywheel/driveplate

12   Initial start-up and break-in after overhaul

Warning: *Have a fire extinguisher handy when starting the engine for the first time.*
1   Once the engine has been installed in the vehicle, double-check the engine oil and coolant levels.
2   With the spark plugs out of the engine and the ignition system and fuel pump disabled, crank the engine until oil pressure registers on the gauge or the light goes out.

3   Install the spark plugs and ignition coils, and reinstall the fuel pump relay.
4   Start the engine. It may take a few moments for the fuel system to build up pressure, but the engine should start without a great deal of effort.
5   After the engine starts, it should be allowed to warm up to normal operating temperature. While the engine is warming up, make a thorough check for fuel, oil and coolant leaks.
6   Shut the engine off and recheck the engine oil and coolant levels.
7   Drive the vehicle to an area with minimum traffic, accelerate from 30 to 50 mph, then allow the vehicle to slow to 30 mph with the throttle closed. Repeat the procedure 10 or 12 times. This will load the piston rings and cause them to seat properly against the cylinder walls. Check again for oil and coolant leaks.
8   Drive the vehicle gently for the first 500 miles (no sustained high speeds) and keep a constant check on the oil level. It is not unusual for an engine to use oil during the break-in period.
9   At approximately 500 to 600 miles, change the oil and filter.
10   For the next few hundred miles, drive the vehicle normally. Do not pamper it or abuse it.
11   After 2000 miles, change the oil and filter again and consider the engine broken in.

Chapter 3
Cooling, heating and air conditioning systems

Contents

Specifications

General

Coolant capacity..	See Chapter 1
Drivebelt tension...	See Chapter 1
Radiator cap pressure rating	14-17 psi
Thermostat rating	
Valve opens..	177 to 182 degrees F (80.5 to 83.5 degrees C)
Fully open..	203 degrees F (95 degrees C)
Refrigerant...	R-134a

Torque specifications

Note: *One foot-pound (ft-lb) of torque is equivalent to 12 inch-pounds (in-lbs) of torque. Torque values below approximately 15 ft-lbs are expressed in inch-pounds, since most foot-pound torque wrenches are not accurate at these smaller values.*

	Ft-lbs (unless otherwise indicated)	Nm
Compressor mounting bolts...	23	31
Thermostat housing cover bolts		
Four-cylinder	18	24
V6..	80 in-lbs	9
Water control valve cover bolts (four-cylinder)	18	24
Timing chain tensioner cover bolts (V6 engine)	96 in-lbs	11
Water pump cover bolts (V6 engine).....................................	96 in-lbs	11
Water pump retaining bolts		
Four-cylinder	96 in-lbs	11
V6..	85 in-lbs	9.5

1   General information

Engine cooling system

All vehicles covered by this manual employ a pressurized engine cooling system with thermostatically controlled coolant circulation. An impeller-type water pump mounted on the engine block pumps coolant through the engine. The coolant flows around each cylinder and toward the rear of the engine. Cast-in coolant passages direct coolant around the intake and exhaust ports, near the spark plug areas and in close proximity to the exhaust valve guides.

A wax-pellet type thermostat controls engine coolant temperature. During warm up, the closed thermostat prevents coolant from circulating through the radiator. As the engine nears normal operating temperature, the thermostat opens and allows hot coolant to travel through the radiator, where it's cooled before returning to the engine.

The cooling system is sealed by a pressure-type cap on the coolant reservoir/expansion tank, which raises the boiling point of the coolant and increases the cooling efficiency of the radiator. The radiator is also equipped with a cap, but it isn't a spring-loaded, pressure-type cap (although the coolant behind it is under pressure when warm!). **Warning:** *Do not remove either cap unless the engine is completely cool.*

Heating system

The heating system consists of a blower fan and heater core located in the heater unit, the hoses connecting the heater core to the engine cooling system and the heater/air conditioning control panel on the dashboard. Hot engine coolant is circulated through the heater core. When the heater mode is activated, a flap door opens to expose the heater unit to the passenger compartment. A fan switch on the control head activates the blower motor, which forces air through the core, heating the air.

Air conditioning system

The air conditioning system consists of a condenser mounted in front of the radiator, an evaporator mounted adjacent to the heater core, a compressor mounted on the engine, a receiver-drier which contains a high pressure relief valve and the plumbing connecting all of the above components.

A blower fan forces the warmer air of the passenger compartment through the evaporator core (sort of a radiator-in-reverse), transferring the heat from the air to the refrigerant. The liquid refrigerant boils off into low pressure vapor, taking the heat with it when it leaves the evaporator. **Warning:** *The models covered by this manual are equipped with Supplemental Restraint Systems (SRS), more commonly known as airbags. Always disable the airbag system before working in the vicinity of any airbag system components to avoid the possibility of accidental deployment of the* airbag(s), which could cause personal injury (see Chapter 12).

2   Antifreeze - general information

Refer to illustration 2.4

Warning: *Do not allow antifreeze to come in contact with your skin or painted surfaces of the vehicle. Rinse off spills immediately with plenty of water. Antifreeze is highly toxic if ingested. Never leave antifreeze lying around in an open container or in puddles on the floor; children and pets are attracted by its sweet smell and may drink it. Check with local authorities about disposing of used antifreeze. Many communities have collection centers, which will see that antifreeze is disposed of safely. Never dump used antifreeze on the ground or into drains.*

The cooling system should be filled with a water/ethylene glycol based antifreeze solution, which will prevent freezing down to at least -20-degrees F, or lower if local climate requires it. It also provides protection against corrosion and increases the coolant boiling point.

The cooling system should be drained, flushed and refilled at the specified intervals (see Chapter 1). Old or contaminated antifreeze solutions are likely to cause damage and encourage the formation of rust and scale in the system. Use distilled water with the antifreeze.

Before adding antifreeze, check all hose connections, because antifreeze tends to leak through very minute openings. Engines don't normally consume coolant, so if the level goes down, find the cause and correct it.

The exact mixture of antifreeze-to-water that you should use depends on the relative weather conditions. The mixture should contain at least 50-percent antifreeze, but should never contain more than 70-percent antifreeze. Consult the mixture ratio chart on the antifreeze container before adding coolant. Hydrometers are available at most auto parts stores to test the ratio of antifreeze to water

2.4 The condition of your coolant can easily be checked with this type of hydrometer, available at auto parts stores

(see illustration). Antifreeze test strips are available at some auto parts stores instead of the hydrometer gauge. Use antifreeze that meets the vehicle manufacturer's specifications.

3   Thermostat - check and replacement

Warning: *Do not attempt to remove the radiator cap, reservoir/expansion tank pressure cap, coolant or thermostat until the engine has cooled completely.*

Check

Refer to illustration 3.6

1   Before assuming the thermostat is responsible for a cooling system problem, check the coolant level (see Chapter 1), drivebelt tension (see Chapter 1) and temperature gauge (or light) operation.
2   If the engine takes a long time to warm up (as indicated by the temperature gauge or heater operation), the thermostat is probably stuck open. Replace the thermostat with a new one.
3   If the engine runs hot or overheats, a thorough test of the thermostat should be performed.
4   Testing of the thermostat can only be made when it is removed from the vehicle (see *Replacement*). If the thermostat is stuck in the open position at room temperature, it is faulty and must be replaced. **Caution:** *Do not drive the vehicle without a thermostat. The computer may stay in open loop and emissions and fuel economy will suffer.*
5   To properly test a thermostat, suspend the (closed) thermostat on a length of string or wire in a container of cold water, with a thermometer (cooking type that reads beyond 212-degrees F [100-degrees C]).
6   Heat the water on a stove while observing the temperature and the thermostat. Neither should contact the sides of the container **(see illustration)**.
7   Note the temperature when the thermostat begins to open and when it is fully open. Compare the temperatures to the Specifications in this Chapter. The number stamped into the thermostat is generally the fully open temperature. Some manufacturers provide Specifications for the beginning-to-open temperature, the fully open temperature, and sometimes the amount the valve should open.
8   If the thermostat doesn't open and close as specified, or sticks in any position, replace it.

Replacement

Refer to illustrations 3.11a, 3.11b and 3.14

9   Disconnect the cable from the negative terminal of the battery. Remove the lower engine cover (if equipped) from below the vehicle.
10   Drain the coolant from the radiator and the engine block (see Chapter 1).

3.6 A thermostat can be accurately checked by heating it in a container of water with a thermometer and observing the opening and fully open temperature

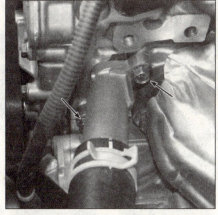

3.11a Thermostat housing cover bolts - four-cylinder engine

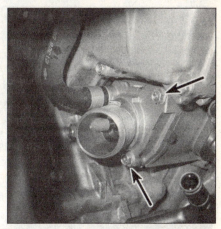

3.11b On 4.0L V6 engines, remove the radiator hose, the smaller hose, and the thermostat cover mounting bolts (two of three indicated here)

11   If the radiator hose is to be replaced, disconnect the hose from the thermostat housing; otherwise the thermostat housing can be removed from the engine with the hose attached. Remove the thermostat housing mounting bolts and separate the housing from the engine **(see illustrations)**. On V6 engines, remove the air cleaner duct and filter housing (see Chapter 4). **Note:** *The manufacturer considers the thermostat as part of the thermostat cover on V6 applications, and the replacement is available only as a thermostat/ cover unit.*

12   Four-cylinder models also have a thermostat-like water control valve, mounted to the rear of the cylinder head. To remove it, disconnect the hoses from the valve, then remove the mounting bolts. Note which way the thermostat was installed.

13   Scrape off any old gasket or sealant on the thermostat housing and the thermostat cover, then clean them with lacquer thinner.

14   Apply a bead of RTV sealant around the perimeter of the cover, install the new thermostat with the jiggle valve UP **(see illustration)**

and bolt the cover in place within 5 minutes of applying the sealant.

15   Installation is the reverse of removal. Tighten the thermostat cover or the water control valve cover fasteners to the torque listed in this Chapter's Specifications, then reinstall the hoses.

16   Wait at least a half-hour for the sealant to cure. Refill and bleed the cooling system (see Chapter 1). Run the engine and check for leaks and proper operation.

4   Engine cooling fan - check and replacement

Warning: *To avoid possible injury or damage, DO NOT operate the engine with a damaged fan. Do not attempt to repair fan blades. Always replace a damaged fan with a new one.*

Check

1   Disconnect the cable from the negative terminal of the battery and rock the fan

back and forth by hand to check for excessive bearing play.

2   With the engine cold (and not running), turn the fan blades by hand. The fan should turn freely.

3   Visually inspect for substantial fluid leakage from the clutch assembly. If problems are noted, replace the clutch assembly.

4   With the engine completely warmed up, turn off the ignition switch and disconnect the negative battery cable from the battery. Turn the fan by hand. Some drag should be evident. If the fan turns easily, replace the fan clutch.

Replacement

Refer to illustrations 4.7, 4.8a, 4.8b, 4.8c, 4.9a and 4.9b

5   Disconnect the cable from the negative terminal of the battery.

6   Remove the drivebelt (see Chapter 1).

7   Loosen the fan clutch nuts several turns **(see illustration)**.

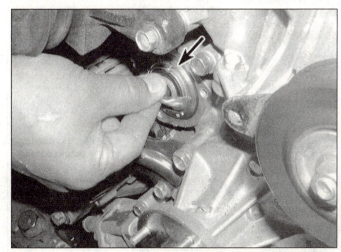

3.14 On all engines, install the thermostat with the jiggle valve (arrow) UP (four-cylinder engine shown)

4.7 Fan pulley mounting bolts (four-cylinder shown, V6 similar)

4.8a From below, remove the lower fan shroud by pushing up the shroud until the pins clear their sockets

4.8b From above, remove the bolts and the upper fan shroud

4.8c Upper and lower fan shrouds removed

8   Working under the vehicle, remove the engine undercover, then remove the lower fan shroud **(see illustration)**. Remove the fan and lower it out from the bottom. If necessary, raise the vehicle and securely support it on jackstands. From above, remove the upper shroud-to-radiator mounting bolts and remove the upper shroud **(see illustration)**.
9   Models with air conditioning have an additional electric fan, secured to the radiator **(see illustrations)**.
10   Carefully inspect the fan blades for any damage. Replace if necessary. Inspect the fan clutch for signs of fluid leakage or roughness when rotating the assembly. Inspect the fan bracket on the engine by spinning the bearing, checking for any signs of roughness or play. Replace the fan bracket/bearing assembly if necessary.
11   At this point, the fan may be unbolted from the clutch, if necessary. Be sure to re-install the fan blade with the "F" mark facing the front of the engine.
12   Installation is the reverse of removal. Be sure to tighten the fan and clutch mounting nuts evenly and securely.

5   Radiator and coolant reservoir/ expansion tank - removal and installation

Warning: *Wait until the engine is completely cool before beginning this procedure.*

Coolant reservoir/expansion tank

Refer to illustration 5.2

1   The coolant reservoir is mounted adjacent to the battery in the right front corner of the engine compartment. Remove the battery (see Chapter 5).
2   Detach the hose from the reservoir, remove the reservoir retaining bolts and lift the reservoir straight up out of the bracket **(see illustration)**.
3   Be careful not to spill coolant on painted surfaces. If it spills, clean the surface immediately with soapy water and rinse.
4   Pour the coolant into a container.
5   After washing the reservoir inside and out (use a household "bottle" brush to clean inside), inspect the reservoir for cracks and chafing. If it's damaged or so obscured by

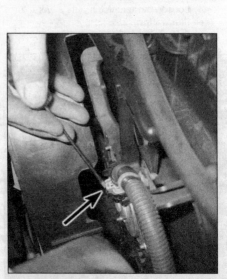

4.9a Disconnect the electrical connector at the electric fan (models with air conditioning)

4.9b Electric cooling fan mounting details

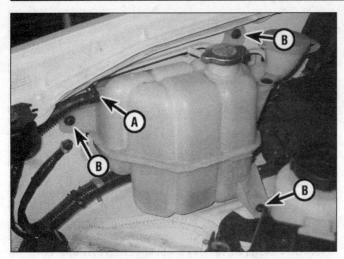

5.2 Coolant reservoir/expansion tank mounting details

A Coolant hose B Mounting bolts

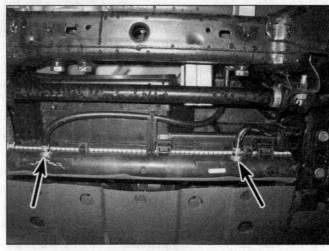

5.10 If equipped with an automatic transmission, remove the cooler lines

age as to make reading the water level diffi-cult, replace it. **Warning:** *If you use a brush to clean the coolant reservoir, never again use it for cleaning drinking glasses or bottles.*

6   Installation is the reverse of removal.

Radiator

Refer to illustrations 5.10, 5.13a and 5.13b

7   Disconnect the cable from the negative terminal of the battery.

8   Remove the air cleaner duct and air cleaner case (see Chapter 4). Set the parking brake and block the rear wheels. Raise the front of the vehicle and support it securely on jackstands.

9   Drain the cooling system (see Chapter 1). If the coolant is relatively new or in good condition, save it and reuse it. Read the **Warning** in Section 2.

10   Disconnect the automatic transmission cooler lines from the radiator if equipped **(see illustration)**. Use a drip pan to catch spilled fluid and plug the lines and fittings.

11   Loosen the hose clamps, then detach the radiator hoses from the radiator. If they're stuck, grasp each hose near the end with a pair of slip joint pliers and twist it to break the seal, then pull it off - be careful not to dam-age the radiator fittings! If the hoses are old or deteriorated, cut them off and install new ones. Also disconnect the small hose to the coolant reservoir at the radiator filler neck.

12   Refer to Section 4 and remove the engine cooling fan.

13   Remove the brackets retaining the top of the radiator, then remove the two small bolts (one on each side at the top) that secure the condenser to the radiator **(see illustrations)**.

14   Carefully lift the radiator up and slightly rearward to separate it from the air-condition-ing condenser. Do not put stress on the con-nections at the condenser. Once the radiator is removed, the condenser will have to be tied up in place to the core support to prevent strain on the refrigerant connections. Take care not to spill coolant on the vehicle, as it can damage painted surfaces.

15   Inspect the radiator for leaks and dam-age. If it needs repair, have a radiator shop or dealer service department perform the work, as special tools and techniques are required.

16   Bugs and dirt can be removed from the radiator by spraying it with a garden hose nozzle from the back side. The radiator should be flushed out with a garden hose before rein-stallation.

17   Check the radiator mounts for deteriora-tion and replace if necessary.

18   Installation is the reverse of the removal procedure. Guide the radiator into the mounts until they seat properly.

19   Refill and bleed the cooling system (see Chapter 1).

20   Start the engine and check for leaks. Allow the engine to reach normal operating temperature, indicated by the upper radiator hose becoming hot. Allow the engine to cool completely, then recheck the coolant level and add more if required.

21   Check and add automatic transmission fluid if needed (see Chapter 1).

5.13a Remove the bolts that attach the upper radiator mounts to the radiator support

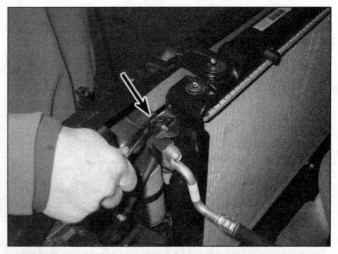

5.13b Remove the condenser mounting bolts at each side of the radiator, then secure the condenser to the radiator support

6.3 The water pump weep hole is located on the underside of the water pump (four-cylinder engine shown)

6.10a On V6 engines, remove the timing chain tensioner cover (A) and the water pump cover (B) . . .

6   Water pump - check and replacement

Warning: *Wait until the engine is completely cool before beginning this procedure.*

Check

Refer to illustration 6.3

1   A failure in the water pump can cause serious engine damage due to overheating.

2   There are two ways to check the operation of the water pump while it's installed on the engine. If the pump is found to be defective, it should be replaced with a new or rebuilt unit.

3   Water pumps are equipped with weep (or vent) holes **(see illustration)**. If a failure occurs in the pump seal, coolant will leak from the hole. On V6 engines, the weep hole directs coolant out from between the timing chain cover and the engine block.

4   If the water pump shaft bearings fail, there may be a howling sound at the pump while it's running. On four-cylinder engines

shaft wear can be felt with the drivebelt removed if the water pump pulley is rocked up and down (with the engine off). On 4.0L V6 engines shaft wear can be felt by relieving the main timing chain tension (see Chapter 2B) and removing the water pump access cover from the front timing chain cover, then rock the water pump sprocket up and down to detect shaft wear. In either case don't mistake drivebelt slippage, which causes a squealing sound, for water pump bearing failure.

5   Even a pump that exhibits no outward signs of a problem, such as noise or leakage, can still be due for replacement. Removal for close examination is the only sure way to tell. Sometimes the fins on the back of the impeller can corrode to the point that cooling efficiency is hampered.

Replacement

Refer to illustrations 6.10a, 6.10b, 6.11a and 6.11b

6   Disconnect the cable from the negative terminal of the battery.

7   Drain the engine coolant from the block and the radiator (see Chapter 1). If the coolant is relatively new or in good condition, save it and reuse it.

8   Remove the drivebelts (see Chapter 1).

9   Remove the engine cooling fan and the water pump/fan pulley (see Section 4).

10   On V6 engines, remove the water pump drain plug from the front of the engine block. Also remove the timing chain tensioner cover and the water pump cover from the front timing chain cover **(see illustration)**. Press the timing chain tensioner piston inward and insert an appropriate size pin into the tensioner hole to lock the tensioner in place **(see illustration)**. Rotate the crankshaft 20 degrees counterclockwise to loosen the chain from around the water pump sprocket.

11   Remove the bolts and detach the water pump from the engine **(see illustrations)**. Check the impeller on the backside for evidence of corrosion or missing fins.

12   Clean the bolt threads and the threaded holes in the engine to remove corrosion and sealant.

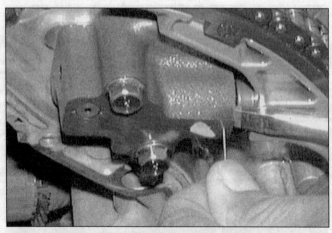

6.10b . . . then depress the timing chain tensioner and lock it into place by inserting a paper clip or another appropriate sized pin into the hole on the front of the tensioner

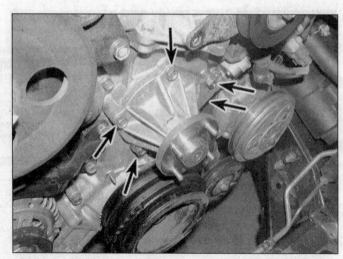

6.11a Water pump mounting bolts - four-cylinder engine

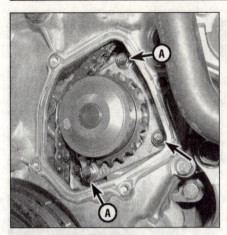

6.11b Water pump mounting bolts - V6 engine - after the mounting bolts have been removed, install two M8 bolts three to four inches long into the holes designated by the letter (A) and tighten them evenly until the water pump is forced out the engine block

13   Compare the new pump to the old one to make sure they're identical.
14   Remove all traces of old gasket sealant from the engine.
15   Clean the engine and new water pump mating surfaces with lacquer thinner or acetone.
16   Water pumps on all models are sealed with O-rings. Clean the O-ring grooves before replacing the O-rings, and lubricate the groove with a little liquid soap to ease installation of the O-ring. On V6 engines, there are two O-rings. The frontmost O-ring will have a white paint spot on it for identification and it should be installed with the white mark facing the pump. The black O-ring is installed behind the marked O-ring.
17   Carefully attach the pump to the engine and thread the bolts into the holes finger tight. Use a small amount of RTV sealant on the bolt threads, and make sure that the dowel pins, if

used, are in their original locations.
18   Tighten the bolts to the torque listed in this Chapter's Specifications in 1/4-turn increments. Don't overtighten the bolts or the pump may be distorted.
19   On V6 engines, rotate the crankshaft 20 degrees clockwise to tighten the timing chain around the water pump sprocket. Remove the stopper pin from the timing chain tensioner and install the tensioner cover and water pump access cover after cleaning them and applying RTV sealant to them.
20   Reinstall all parts removed for access to the pump.
21   Wait at least one hour for the sealant to cure. Refill and bleed the cooling system (see Chapter 1). Run the engine and check for leaks and proper operation. **Note:** *Timing chain noise may be apparent after performing this procedure on V6 engines. This noise is normal and should only last until the air has bled out of the high pressure chamber. Simply start the engine and allow it to run at 3,000 rpm with the transmission in Neutral or Park until the noise subsides.*

---

7   Coolant temperature gauge sending unit - check and replacement

Warning: *Wait until the engine is completely cool before beginning this procedure.*

Check

Refer to illustration 7.1

1   The coolant temperature indicator system consists of a warning light or a temperature gauge on the dash and a coolant temperature sending unit mounted on the engine **(see illustration)**. On the models covered by this manual, the Engine Coolant Temperature (ECT) sensor, which is an information sensor for the Powertrain Control Module (PCM), also functions as the coolant temperature sending unit (see Chapter 6).
2   If an overheating indication occurs, check the coolant level in the system and then make sure all connectors in the wiring har-

ness between the sending unit and the indicator light or gauge are tight.
3   When the ignition switch is turned to START and the starter motor is turning, the indicator light (if equipped) should come on. This doesn't mean the engine is overheated; it just means that the bulb is good.
4   If the light doesn't come on when the ignition key is turned to START, the bulb might be burned out, the ignition switch might be faulty or the circuit might be open.
5   As soon as the engine starts, the indicator light should go out and remain off, unless the engine overheats. If the light doesn't go out, refer to Chapter 6 and check for any stored trouble codes in the Powertrain Control Module (PCM).
6   If the engine tends to overheat easily, check the coolant to make sure it's correctly mixed (see Chapter 1).

Replacement

7   See Chapter 6 for the ECT sensor replacement procedure.

---

8   Blower motor - removal and installation

Refer to illustration 8.3
Warning: *The models covered by this manual are equipped with Supplemental Restraint Systems (SRS), more commonly known as airbags. Always disable the airbag system before working in the vicinity of any airbag system components to avoid the possibility of accidental deployment of the airbag(s), which could cause personal injury (see Chapter 12).*
1   Disconnect the cable from the negative terminal of the battery.
2   Remove the glove compartment and lower dash trim (see Chapter 11) to gain access to the heater case and blower motor.
3   Detach the blower motor vent hose and disconnect the electrical connector from the blower motor **(see illustration)**.
4   Remove the blower motor mounting screws, and pull the blower motor carefully out of the housing.

7.1 The Engine Coolant Temperature (ECT) sensor on V6 engines is located at the rear of the engine in the water outlet tube (valve cover removed for clarity)

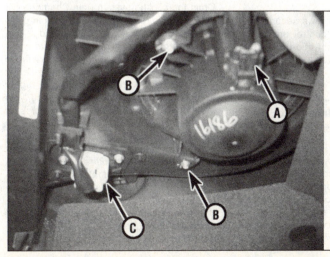

8.3 Blower motor mounting details

A   *Electrical connector*
B   *Mounting screws (not all are visible here)*
C   *Blower motor resistor location*

9.4 Remove the screws to release the control unit from the back of the center instrument panel bezel

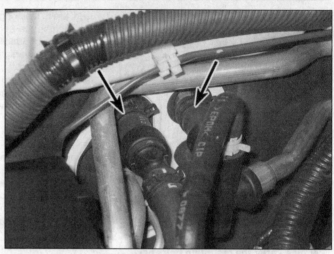

10.4 Loosen the hose clamps and disconnect the heater hoses at the firewall

5   If you are replacing the motor, detach the fan and transfer it to the new motor.
6   Installation is the reverse of removal. Run the blower and check for proper operation.

9   Heater and air conditioning control assembly - removal and installation

Refer to illustration 9.4
Warning: *The models covered by this manual are equipped with Supplemental Restraint Systems (SRS), more commonly known as airbags. Always disable the airbag system before working in the vicinity of any airbag system components to avoid the possibility of accidental deployment of the airbag(s), which could cause personal injury (see Chapter 12).*
1   Disconnect the negative cable from the battery.
2   Refer to Chapter 11 for removal of the center instrument panel bezel.
3   Pull the bezel away from the instrument panel and tag and disconnect the electrical connectors.
4   Remove the four screws securing the heating/air conditioning control unit to the back of the bezel **(see illustration)**.
5   Installation is the reverse of the removal procedure.

10   Heater core - replacement

Refer to illustrations 10.4, 10.6, 10.9a, 10.9b, 10.9c, 10.9d
Warning 1: *The models covered by this manual are equipped with Supplemental Restraint Systems (SRS), more commonly known as airbags. Always disable the airbag system before working in the vicinity of any airbag system components to avoid the possibility of*

accidental deployment of the airbag(s), which could cause personal injury (see Chapter 12).
Warning 2: *The air conditioning system is under high pressure. DO NOT loosen any fittings or remove any components until after the system has been discharged. Air conditioning refrigerant should be properly discharged into an EPA-approved container at a dealer service department or an automotive air conditioning repair facility. Always wear eye protection when disconnecting air conditioning system fittings.*
Warning 3: *Wait until the engine is completely cool before beginning this procedure.*
Note: *Replacement of the heater core is a difficult procedure for the home mechanic, involving removal of the entire dashboard, floor console and many wiring connectors. If you attempt this procedure at home, keep track of the assemblies by taking notes and keeping screws and other hardware in small, marked plastic bags for reassembly.*
1   If the vehicle is equipped with air conditioning, have the air conditioning system discharged at a dealer service department or service station.
2   Turn the heater control setting to HOT. Drain the cooling system (see Chapter 1). If the coolant is relatively new, or tests in good condition (see Section 2), save it and re-use it. **Warning:** *Do not allow antifreeze to come in contact with your skin or painted surfaces of the vehicle. Rinse off spills immediately with plenty of water. Antifreeze is highly toxic if ingested. Never leave antifreeze lying around in an open container or in puddles on the floor; children and pets are attracted by it's sweet smell and may drink it. Check with local authorities about disposing of used antifreeze. Many communities have collection centers which will see that antifreeze is disposed of safely. Never dump used antifreeze on the ground or into drains.*
3   Disconnect the cable from the negative terminal of the battery.
4   Working in the engine compartment, dis-

connect the heater hoses where they enter the firewall **(see illustration)**. **Caution:** *If the heater hoses are stuck, it is better to cut off the hoses than to twist them with pliers and risk breaking the heater core tubes.*
5   Remove the rubber grommets where the heater core tubes go through the firewall.
6   Disconnect the air conditioning refrigerant lines and rubber grommet from the evaporator core if the vehicle is so equipped **(see illustration)**. **Warning:** *Always wear eye protection when disconnecting air conditioning system fittings.*
7   Unbolt the steering column and lower it (see Chapter 10), then remove the entire instrument panel (see Chapter 11).
8   Unbolt the fuse panel and separate the electrical harnesses clipped to the instrument panel reinforcement bar.
9   Remove the floor heating ducts. Remove the cowl support bar mounting bolts and pull the bar away from the firewall with the heating/air conditioning unit attached **(see illustrations)**. Move the seats back for more work-

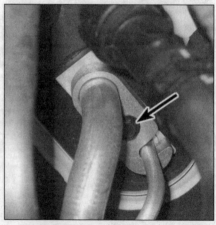

10.6 Have the air conditioning system discharged, then disconnect the refrigerant lines at the firewall

10.9a Location of the heater core and heater core cover in the heating/air conditioning unit - removal of the instrument panel and cross-cowl support beam is a difficult procedure - the heating/air conditioning unit comes out with the cowl support beam

10.9b Disconnect the lower column joint, remove the steering column bolts and remove the steering column (one upper bolt and one lower bolt indicated here). Warning: *Make sure the steering column is locked so the steering wheel can't turn (the airbag clockspring could become damaged)*

ing room. **Note:** *Take your time and don't use excessive force - there may be fasteners you haven't found yet.*

10   Remove the heater core pipe bracket from the top of the unit, then remove the screws and the heater core cover. Slide the heater core and its pipes upward out of the heating/air conditioning unit.

11   Reassemble the heater unit and check the operation of the control flaps. If any parts bind, correct the problem before installation.

12   Reinstall the remaining parts in the reverse order of removal. When attaching the steering column to the support bracket, tighten the nuts or bolts to the torque listed in the Chapter 10 Specifications.

13   Refill the cooling system (see Chapter 1), reconnect the battery and run the engine. Check for leaks and proper operation of the system. Have the air conditioning system recharged if equipped.

11   Air conditioning and heating system - check and maintenance

Air conditioning system

Refer to illustration 11.1

Warning: *The air conditioning system is under high pressure. Do not loosen any hose fittings or remove any components until after the system has been discharged. Air conditioning refrigerant should be properly discharged into an EPA-approved recovery/recycling unit at a dealer service department or an automotive air conditioning repair facility. Always wear eye protection when disconnecting air conditioning system fittings.*

Caution 1: *All models covered by this manual use environmentally friendly R-134a. This refrigerant (and its appropriate refrigerant oils) are not compatible with R-12 refrigerant*

system components and must never be mixed or the components will be damaged.

Caution 2: *When replacing entire components, additional refrigerant oil should be added equal to the amount that is removed with the component being replaced. Be sure to read the can before adding any oil to the system, to make sure it is compatible with the R-134a system.*

1   The following maintenance checks should be performed on a regular basis to ensure that the air conditioning continues to operate at peak efficiency.

a) *Inspect the condition of the compressor drivebelt. If it is worn or deteriorated, replace it (see Chapter 1).*

b) *Check the drivebelt tension (see Chapter 1).*

c) *Inspect the system hoses. Look for cracks, bubbles, hardening and deterio-*

10.9c Remove the duct above the left side of the cowl support beam to access the beam mounting bolts - tag and disconnect the electrical connectors

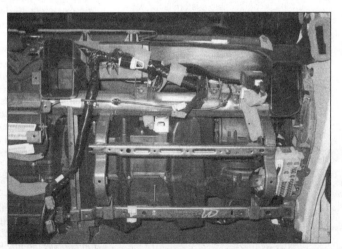

10.9d On the right side, unplug the fuse panel and all other electrical connectors, remove the upper duct, and the support-to-body bolts

11.1 Check that the evaporator housing drain tube (arrow) at the firewall is clear of any blockage - the view here is from below the vehicle

11.9 Insert a thermometer in the center duct while operating the air conditioning system - the output air should be 35 to 40 degrees F less than the ambient temperature, depending on humidity (but not lower than 40-degrees F)

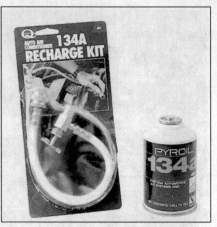

11.12 A basic charging kit for 134a systems is available at most auto parts stores - it must say 134a (not R-12) and so should the can of refrigerant

ration. *Inspect the hoses and all fittings for oil bubbles or seepage. If there is any evidence of wear, damage or leakage, replace the hose(s).*

d) *Inspect the condenser fins for leaves, bugs and any other foreign material that may have embedded itself in the fins. Use a "fin comb" or compressed air to remove debris from the condenser.*

e) *Make sure the system has the correct refrigerant charge.*

f) *If you hear water sloshing around in the dash area or have water dripping on the carpet, check the evaporator housing drain tube* **(see illustration)** *and insert a piece of wire into the opening to check for blockage.*

2   It's a good idea to operate the system for about ten minutes at least once a month. This is particularly important during the winter months because long term non-use can cause hardening, and subsequent failure, of the seals. Note that using the Defrost function operates the compressor.

3   If the air conditioning system is not working properly, proceed to Step 6 and perform the general checks outlined below.

4   Because of the complexity of the air conditioning system and the special equipment necessary to service it, in-depth troubleshooting and repairs beyond checking the refrigerant charge and the compressor clutch operation are not included in this manual. However, simple checks and component replacement procedures are provided in this Chapter. For more complete information on the air conditioning system, refer to the *Haynes Automotive Heating and Air Conditioning Manual*.

5   The most common cause of poor cooling is simply a low system refrigerant charge. If a noticeable drop in system cooling ability occurs, one of the following quick checks will help you determine whether the refrigerant level is low. Should the system lose its cooling ability, the following procedure will help you pinpoint the cause.

Checking the refrigerant charge

Refer to illustration 11.9

6   Warm the engine up to normal operating temperature.

7   Place the air conditioning temperature selector at the coldest setting and put the blower at the highest setting. Open the doors (to make sure the air conditioning system doesn't cycle off as soon as it cools the passenger compartment).

8   After the system reaches operating temperature, feel the larger pipe exiting the evaporator at the firewall.

9   The outlet pipe should be cold (the tubing that leads back to the compressor). If the evaporator outlet is warm, the system probably needs a charge. Insert a thermometer in the center air distribution duct **(see illustration)** while operating the air conditioning system at its maximum setting - the temperature of the output air should be 35 to 40 degrees F below the ambient air temperature (down to approximately 40 degrees F). If the ambient (outside) air temperature is very high, say 110 degrees F, the duct air temperature may be as high as 60 degrees F, but generally the air conditioning is 35 to 40 degrees F cooler than the ambient air.

10   If the inlet pipe (the smaller one) has frost accumulation or feels cooler than the accumulator surface, the refrigerant change is low.

11   Further inspection or testing of the system requires special tools and techniques and is beyond the scope of the home mechanic.

Adding refrigerant

Refer to illustrations 11.12 and 11.15

Caution: *Make sure any refrigerant, refrigerant oil or replacement component your purchase is designated as compatible with environmentally friendly R-134a systems.*

12   Purchase an R-134a automotive charging kit at an auto parts store **(see illustra-**

tion). A charging kit includes a 12-ounce can of refrigerant, a tap valve and a short section of hose that can be attached between the tap valve and the system low side service valve. Because one can of refrigerant may not be sufficient to bring the system charge up to the proper level, it's a good idea to buy an additional can. **Warning:** *Never add more than two cans of refrigerant to the system.*

13   Hook up the charging kit by following the manufacturer's instructions. **Warning:** *DO NOT hook the charging kit hose to the system high side!* The fittings on the charging kit are designed to fit **only** on the low side of the system.

14   Back off the valve handle on the charging kit and screw the kit onto the refrigerant can, making sure first that the O-ring or rubber seal inside the threaded portion of the kit is in place. **Warning:** *Wear protective eyewear when dealing with pressurized refrigerant cans.*

15   Remove the dust cap from the low-side charging port and attach the quick-connect fitting on the kit hose **(see illustration)**.

11.15 Attach the refrigerant kit to the low-side charging port - it's near the brake booster on Frontier and Xterra models - the cap should be marked with an "L"

11.16 The air conditioning pressure switch location - if the compressor will not stay engaged, disconnect the connector and bridge it with a jumper wire during the charging procedure

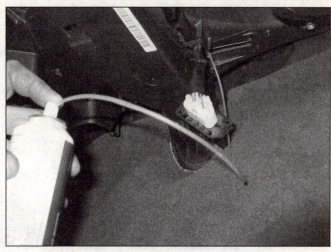

11.26 With the blower motor resistor removed, spray the disinfectant at the evaporator core

16   Warm up the engine and turn On the air conditioning. Keep the charging kit hose away from the fan and other moving parts. **Note:** *The charging process requires the compressor to be running. If the clutch cycles off, you can put the air conditioning switch on High and leave the car doors open to keep the clutch on and compressor working. The compressor can be kept on during the charging by removing the connector from the dual-pressure switch and bridging it with a paper clip or jumper wire during the procedure* **(see illustration)**.

17   Turn the valve handle on the kit until the stem pierces the can, then back the handle out to release the refrigerant. You should be able to hear the rush of gas. Add refrigerant to the low side of the system, keeping the can upright at all times, but shaking it occasionally. Allow stabilization time between each addition. **Note:** *The charging process will go faster if you wrap the can with a hot-water-soaked shop rag to keep the can from freezing up.*

18   If you have an accurate thermometer, you can place it in the center air conditioning duct inside the vehicle and keep track of the output air temperature **(see illustration 11.9)**. A charged system that is working properly should cool down to approximately 40 degrees F. If the ambient (outside) air temperature is very high, say 110 degrees F, the duct air temperature may be as high as 60 degrees F, but generally the air conditioning is 35-40 degrees F cooler than the ambient air.

19   When the can is empty, turn the valve handle to the closed position and release the connection from the low-side port. Replace the dust cap.

20   Remove the charging kit from the can and store the kit for future use with the piercing valve in the UP position, to prevent inadvertently piercing the can on the next use.

Heating systems

21   If the carpet under the heater core is damp, or if antifreeze vapor or steam is coming through the vents, the heater core is leaking. Remove it (see Section 11) and install a new unit (most radiator shops will not repair a leaking heater core).

22   If the air coming out of the heater vents isn't hot, the problem could stem from any of the following causes:

a) *The thermostat is stuck open, preventing the engine coolant from warming up enough to carry heat to the heater core. Replace the thermostat (see Section 3).*

b) *There is a blockage in the system, preventing the flow of coolant through the heater core. Feel both heater hoses at the firewall. They should be hot. If one of them is cold, there is an obstruction in one of the hoses or in the heater core, or the heater control valve is shut. Detach the hoses and back flush the heater core with a water hose. If the heater core is clear but circulation is impeded, remove the two hoses and flush them out with a water hose.*

c) *If flushing fails to remove the blockage from the heater core, the core must be replaced (see Section 11).*

Eliminating air conditioning odors

Refer to illustration 11.26

23   Unpleasant odors that often develop in air conditioning systems are caused by the growth of a fungus, usually on the surface of the evaporator core. The warm, humid environment there is a perfect breeding ground for mildew to develop.

24   The evaporator core on most vehicles is difficult to access, and factory dealerships have a lengthy, expensive process for eliminating the fungus by opening up the evaporator case and using a powerful disinfectant and rinse on the core until the fungus is gone. You can service your own system at home, but it takes something much stronger than basic household germ-killers or deodorizers.

25   Aerosol disinfectants for automotive air conditioning systems are available in most auto parts stores, but remember when shopping for them that the most effective treatments are also the most expensive. The basic procedure for using these sprays is to start by running the system in the RECIRC mode for ten minutes with the blower on its highest speed. Use the highest heat mode to dry out the system and keep the compressor from engaging by disconnecting the wiring connector at the compressor (see Section 13).

26   The disinfectant can usually comes with a long spray hose. Remove the blower motor resistor (see Section 8), point the nozzle inside the hole and to the left towards the evaporator core, and spray according to the manufacturer's recommendations **(see illustration)**. Try to cover the whole surface of the evaporator core, by aiming the spray up, down and sideways. Follow the manufacturer's recommendations for the length of spray and waiting time between applications.

27   Once the evaporator has been cleaned, the best way to prevent the mildew from coming back again is to make sure your evaporator housing drain tube is clear **(see illustration 11.1)**.

Automatic heating and air conditioning systems

28   Some models are equipped with an optional automatic climate control system. This system has its own computer that receives inputs from various sensors in the heating and air conditioning system. This computer, like the PCM, has self-diagnostic capabilities to help pinpoint problems or faults within the system. Vehicles equipped with automatic heating and air conditioning systems are very complex and considered beyond the scope of the home mechanic. Vehicles equipped with automatic heating and air conditioning systems should be taken to dealer service department or other qualified facility for repair.

12.5 Receiver/drier mounting details

A   *Refrigerant line fastener*   B   *Mounting bolt*

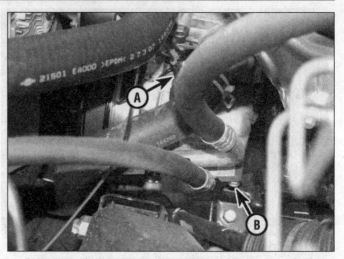

13.6a Four-cylinder compressor details; A, disconnect the electrical connector; B, remove the mounting bolts (one lower bolt indicated here)

12   Air conditioning receiver/drier - removal and installation

Warning: *The air conditioning system is under high pressure. DO NOT loosen any fittings or remove any components until after the system has been discharged. Air conditioning refrigerant should be properly discharged into an EPA-approved container at a dealer service department or an automotive air conditioning repair facility. Always wear eye protection when disconnecting air conditioning system fittings.*

Removal

Refer to illustration 12.5

1   The receiver/drier stores refrigerant and removes moisture from the system. When any major air conditioning component (compressor, condenser, evaporator) is replaced, or the system has been apart and exposed to air for any length of time, the receiver/drier must be replaced.

2   Take the vehicle to a dealer service department or automotive air conditioning shop and have the air conditioning system discharged and the refrigerant recovered (see the **Warning** at the beginning of this Section). Disconnect the cable from the negative terminal of the battery.

3   Disconnect the electrical connector at the compressor clutch cycling switch on top of the receiver/drier. If the receiver/drier is to be replaced with a new one, remove the cycling switch to transfer to the new drier.

4   Remove the grille (see Chapter 11). Pull back the plastic cover for access to the receiver/drier.

5   Disconnect the refrigerant inlet and outlet lines **(see illustration)**. Cap or plug the open lines immediately.

6   Loosen the clamp bolt on the mounting bracket and slide the receiver/drier assembly up and out of the mounting bracket **(see illustration 12.5)**.

Installation

7   If you are replacing the receiver/drier, add two ounces of clean refrigerant oil to the new receiver/drier. This will maintain the correct oil level in the system after the repairs are completed.

8   Place the new receiver/drier into position, tighten the mounting bracket bolt lightly, still allowing the receiver/drier to be turned to align the line connections.

9   Install the inlet and outlet lines. Lubricate the O-rings using clean refrigerant oil and reconnect the lines. Now tighten the clamp bolt securely and reconnect the electrical connector.

10   Connect the cable to the negative terminal of the battery.

11   Have the system evacuated, recharged and leak tested by a dealer service department or an air conditioning repair facility.

13   Air conditioning compressor - removal and installation

Warning: *The air conditioning system is under high pressure. Do not loosen any hose fittings or remove any components until after the system has been discharged. Air conditioning refrigerant should be properly discharged into an EPA-approved recovery/recycling unit at a dealer service department or an automotive air conditioning repair facility. Always wear eye protection when disconnecting air conditioning system fittings.*

Note: *The receiver/drier should be replaced whenever the compressor is replaced (see Section 12).*

Removal

Refer to illustrations 13.6a, 13.6b and 13.6c

1   Have the air conditioning system refrigerant discharged and recycled by an air conditioning technician (see **Warning** above).

2   Disconnect the cable from the negative terminal of the battery. On V6 models, refer to Chapter 11 and remove the mudguard from the left front fender and the inner fenderwell liner.

3   Set the parking brake, block the rear wheels and raise the front of the vehicle, supporting it securely on jackstands and remove the splash cover from below the engine.

4   Remove the drivebelt (see Chapter 1).

5   Disconnect the refrigerant lines from the

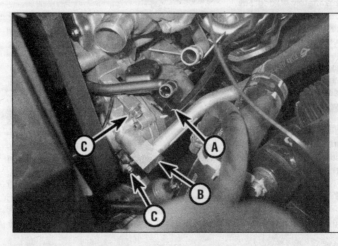

13.6b V6 compressor details (from above): A, disconnect the electrical connector; B, disconnect the line-mounting bolt; C, remove the mounting bolts

13.6c V6 compressor from below, remove the two lower mounting bolts

14.4 Disconnect the condenser lines

compressor. Plug the open fittings to prevent entry of dirt and moisture.

6   Disconnect the compressor clutch wiring harness. Unbolt the compressor from the mounting bracket and remove it from the vehicle **(see illustrations)**. **Note:** *On some models, the upper mounting bolts may not come all the way out of the compressor - leave them in the compressor until it is removed from the vehicle.*

Installation

7   The clutch may have to be transferred from the old compressor to the new unit.

8   Add the proper amount of refrigerant oil to the new compressor using the following calculations:

a) *Drain the refrigerant oil from the old compressor through the suction fitting and measure it in ounces.*

b) *Drain any new oil from the new compressor.*

c) *If the amount from the old compressor was 3 to 5 ounces, put that amount of clean, new oil in the new compressor.*

d) *If the amount from the old compressor was less than 3 ounces, put 3 ounces of clean, new oil in the new compressor.*

e) *If the amount from the old compressor was more than 5 ounces, put 5 ounces of clean, new oil in the new compressor.*

9   Installation is the reverse of removal, using new O-rings where the lines attach to the compressor. **Note:** *Remember to slip the two upper mounting bolts into the compressor before installing the compressor in the vehicle.*

10   Have the system evacuated, recharged and leak tested by an air conditioning technician.

14   Air conditioning condenser - removal and installation

Warning: *The air conditioning system is under high pressure. Do not loosen any hose fittings or remove any components until after the system has been discharged. Air conditioning refrigerant should be properly discharged into an EPA-approved recovery/recycling unit at a dealer service department or an automotive air conditioning repair facility. Always wear eye protection when disconnecting air conditioning system fittings.*

Removal

Refer to illustration 14.4

1   Have the refrigerant discharged and recycled by an air conditioning technician (see **Warning** above).

2   Disconnect the cable from the negative terminal of the battery and drain the cooling system (see Chapter 1).

3   Refer to Section 5 and remove the shroud, fan and radiator.

4   Disconnect the condenser line and discharge line from the condenser **(see illustration)**. Cap the fittings on the condenser and lines to prevent entry of dirt or moisture.

5   Remove the condenser retaining bolts.

6   Lean the condenser forward and remove it from the vehicle.

Installation

7   Installation is the reverse of removal. If a new condenser was installed, add 1 to 1.7 ounces of fresh refrigerant oil.

8   Have the system evacuated, charged and leak tested by an air conditioning technician.

Notes

Chapter 4
Fuel and exhaust systems

Contents

	Section		Section
Accelerator pedal released position, throttle valve closed position and idle air volume learning procedures	15	Fuel pressure relief procedure	2
Air filter housing - removal and installation	9	Fuel pump module - removal and installation	5
Air filter replacement	See Chapter 1	Fuel pump/fuel pressure - check	3
CHECK ENGINE light on	See Chapter 6	Fuel rail and injectors - removal and installation	13
Exhaust system check	See Chapter 1	Fuel system check	See Chapter 1
Exhaust system servicing - general information	14	Fuel tank - cleaning and repair	8
Fuel injection system - check	11	Fuel tank - removal and installation	7
Fuel injection system - general information	10	General information	1
Fuel level sending unit - replacement	6	Idle air control system	See Chapter 6
Fuel lines and fittings - replacement	4	Throttle body - removal and installation	12

Specifications

Fuel system pressure (at idle)	51 psi
Fuel injector resistance	11.1 to 14.3 ohms

Torque specifications

Note: *One foot-pound (ft-lb) of torque is equivalent to 12 inch-pounds (in-lbs) of torque. Torque values below approximately 15 ft-lbs are expressed in inch-pounds, since most foot-pound torque wrenches are not accurate at these smaller values.*

	Ft-lbs (unless otherwise indicated)	Nm
Fuel rail mounting bolts		
Four-cylinder		
Step 1	108 in-lbs	12
Step 2	21	28
V6		
Step 1	84 in-lbs	9.5
Step 2	16	22
Fuel rail crossover tube flange bolts (V6 engine)	85 in-lbs	9.5
Throttle body mounting bolts		
Four-cylinder	84 in-lbs	9.5
V6	74 in-lbs	8

1   General information

Refer to illustrations 1.1a and 1.1b

The fuel system consists of a fuel tank, an electric fuel pump (located in the fuel tank), a fuel pressure regulator (also located in the fuel tank), a fuel pump relay, the fuel rail and fuel injectors, an air filter assembly and a throttle body unit. All models are equipped with a multi-port fuel injection system **(see illustrations)**.

Multi-port fuel injection system

Multi-port fuel injection uses timed impulses to inject the fuel directly into the intake port of each cylinder according to its firing order. The injectors are controlled by the Powertrain Control Module (PCM). The PCM monitors various engine parameters and delivers the exact amount of fuel required into the intake ports. The throttle body serves only to control the amount of air passing into the system. Because each cylinder is equipped with its own injector, much better control of the fuel/air mixture ratio is possible.

Fuel pump and lines

Fuel is circulated from the fuel tank to the fuel injection system through a metal line running along the underside of the vehicle. An electric fuel pump, a fuel pressure regulator and fuel level sending unit is located inside the fuel tank. A vapor return system routes all vapors back to the fuel tank through a separate return line.

The fuel pump relay is equipped with a primary and secondary voltage circuit. The primary circuit is controlled by the PCM and the secondary circuit is linked directly to battery voltage from the ignition switch. With the ignition switch On (engine not running), the PCM will energize the relay for five seconds. During cranking, the PCM supplies voltage to the fuel pump relay as long as the camshaft position sensor or crankshaft position sensor sends its position signal (see Chapter 6). If there is no signal, the fuel pump will shut off after five seconds.

Exhaust system

The exhaust system includes the exhaust manifold(s), catalytic converter(s), muffler(s) and the exhaust pipes. The catalytic converters are an emission control device added to the exhaust system to reduce pollutants. Refer to Chapter 6 for more information regarding the catalytic converters.

2   Fuel pressure relief procedure

Warning: *Gasoline is extremely flammable, so take extra precautions when you work on any part of the fuel system. Don't smoke or allow open flames or bare light bulbs near the work area, and don't work in a garage where a*

1.1a Four-cylinder fuel injection details (the main components are obscured by the intake manifold)

1	Electronic throttle body	2	Intake manifold
		3	MAF sensor
4	Air intake duct		
5	Air filter housing		

gas-type appliance (such as a water heater or a clothes dryer) is present. Since gasoline is carcinogenic, wear fuel-resistant gloves when there's a possibility of being exposed to fuel, and, if you spill any fuel on your skin, rinse *it off immediately with soap and water. Mop up any spills immediately and do not store fuel-soaked rags where they could ignite. The fuel system is under constant pressure, so, if any fuel lines are to be disconnected, the fuel*

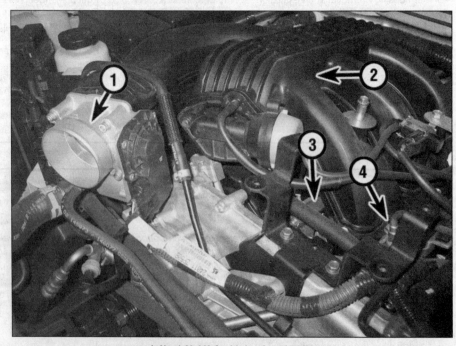

1.1b 4.0L V6 fuel injection details

1	Electronic throttle body	3	Fuel rail (one indicated)
2	Intake plenum	4	Fuel supply connection

pressure in the system must be relieved first. When you perform any kind of work on the fuel system, wear safety glasses and have a Class B type fire extinguisher on hand.

1   Remove the fuel pump fuse from the passenger compartment fuse panel (see Chapter 12).

2   Attempt to start the engine, it should immediately stall. Crank the engine several more times to ensure the fuel system has been completely relieved. Disconnect the cable from the negative terminal of the battery before working on the fuel system.

3   The fuel system pressure is now relieved. When you're finished working on the fuel system, install the fuel pump fuse back into the fuse panel and connect the negative cable to the battery.

4   After the fuel pressure has been relieved, it's a good idea to lay a shop towel over any fuel connection to be disassembled, to absorb the residual fuel that may leak out when servicing the fuel system.

3.6 Using a T-fitting, install the fuel pressure gauge between the fuel filter and the fuel rail

---

3   Fuel pump/fuel pressure - check

Warning: *Gasoline is extremely flammable, so take extra precautions when you work on any part of the fuel system. See the* **Warning** *in Section 2.*

Note: *In order to perform the fuel pressure test, you will need to obtain a fuel pressure gauge capable of measuring high fuel pressure and the necessary fittings to connect the fuel gauge to the fuel line.*

Preliminary check

1   If you suspect insufficient fuel delivery, first inspect all fuel lines to ensure that the problem is not simply a leak in a line. Check that there is adequate fuel in the fuel tank.

2   Set the parking brake and have an assistant turn the ignition switch to the ON position while you listen to the fuel pump (inside the fuel tank). You should hear a "whirring" sound, lasting for a second or two, indicating the fuel pump is operating. If the fuel pump is operating, proceed to the pressure check.

3   If there is no sound, check the fuel pump fuse, the fuel pump relay and the related wiring to ensure power is reaching the fuel pump connector. Check the ground circuit for continuity.

4   If the power and ground circuits are good and the fuel pump does not operate, replace the fuel pump (see Section 5).

Pressure check

Refer to illustration 3.6

5   Relieve the fuel system pressure (see Section 2).

6   Remove the fuel line from the fuel filter and install a T-fitting between the fuel filter and the fuel rail **(see illustration)**. Connect a fuel pressure gauge to the T-fitting. Make sure the hose clamps are securely tightened.

7   Turn the ignition switch On. The fuel pump should run for one or two seconds -

pressure should register on the gauge and should hold steady.

8   Start the engine and allow it to idle. Compare the pressure reading with the fuel pressure value listed in this Chapter's Specifications. If the pressure reading is correct, the system is operating properly.

9   If the fuel pressure is not within specifications, check the following:

a) *If the pressure is lower than specified, check for a restriction in the fuel system (this includes the inlet strainer and the fuel filter at the fuel pump module). If no restrictions are found, replace the fuel pump module (see Section 5).*

b) *If the fuel pressure is higher than specified, replace the fuel pump module (see Section 5). (The fuel pressure regulator is not replaceable separately.)*

10   After completing the testing, relieve the fuel pressure (see Section 2) and remove the fuel pressure gauge.

---

4   Fuel lines and fittings - replacement

Warning: *Gasoline is extremely flammable, so take extra precautions when you work on any part of the fuel system. See the* **Warning** *in Section 2.*

1   Because fuel lines used on fuel-injected vehicles are under high pressure, they require special consideration. Always relieve the fuel pressure before servicing fuel lines or fittings (see Section 2).

2   Metal fuel supply and vapor lines extend from the fuel tank to the engine compartment. The lines are secured to the underbody or frame with retainers. Flexible hose connects the metal lines to the fuel tank, fuel filter and fuel rail. Fuel lines must be occasionally inspected for leaks or damage.

3   In the event of any fuel line damage, metal lines may be repaired with steel tubing of the same diameter, provided the correct fittings are used. Never repair a damaged section of steel line with rubber hose and hose clamps. Rubber fuel hose must be replaced with fuel hose specifically designed for a high pressure fuel injection system; others may fail

from the high pressures of this system. Flexible lines with quick-connect fittings must be replaced with factory replacement parts.

4   If evidence of contamination is found in the system or fuel filter during disassembly, the line should be disconnected and blown out. Check the fuel strainer on the fuel pump module for damage and deterioration.

5   Don't route fuel line or hose within four inches of any part of the exhaust system or within ten inches of the catalytic converter. Fuel line must never be allowed to chafe against the engine, body or frame. A minimum of 1/4-inch clearance must be maintained around a fuel line.

6   When replacing a fuel line, remove all fasteners attaching the fuel line to the vehicle body.

Steel tubing

7   If replacement of a steel fuel line or emission line is called for, use steel tubing meeting the manufacturer's specification.

8   Don't use copper or aluminum tubing to replace steel tubing. These materials cannot withstand normal vehicle vibration.

9   Some fuel lines have threaded fittings with O-rings. Any time the fittings are loosened to service or replace components:

a) *Use a flare-nut wrench on the fitting nut and a backup wrench on the stationary portion of the fitting while loosening and tightening the fittings.*

b) *Check all O-rings for cuts, cracks and deterioration. Replace any that appear hardened, worn or damaged.*

c) *If the lines are replaced, always use original equipment parts, or parts that meet the original equipment standards.*

Rubber hose

10   Note the routing of the hose and the orientation of the clamps to assure that replacement sections are installed in exactly the same manner. Do not kink or twist the hose. When attaching hoses to metal lines, overlap them as shown **(see illustration)**. Tighten the clamp sufficiently to ensure a leak free fit, but do not overtighten the clamp or damage to the rubber hose will result.

7.6 Disconnect the fuel filler hose and vapor hose from the fuel tank

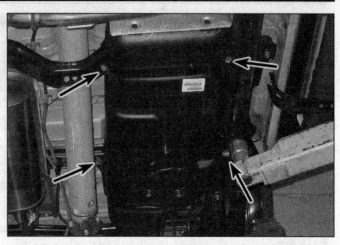

7.8 Support the fuel tank and remove the four mounting strap bolts

Flexible hose with quick-connect fitting

11   Some models may be equipped with flexible hose and quick-connect fittings. There are various methods of disconnecting the fittings, depending upon the type of quick-connect fitting installed on the fuel line. To disconnect a typical quick-connect fitting, push the fitting into the fuel line, squeeze the tabs together and pull the lines apart; do not use any tools to disconnect the fitting. Clean any debris from around the fitting. Disconnect the fitting and carefully remove the fuel line from the vehicle. **Caution:** *The quick-connect fittings are not serviced separately. Do not attempt to repair these types of fuel lines in the event the fitting or line becomes damaged. Replace the entire fuel line as an assembly.*

12   Installation is the reverse of removal with the following additions:

a) *Clean the quick-connect fittings with a lint-free cloth.*

b) *Align the tabs with the openings in the retainer and push the lines together until the tabs click into place.*

c) *After connecting a quick-connect fitting, check the integrity of the connection by attempting to pull the lines apart.*

d) *Cycle the ignition key On and Off several times and check for leaks at the fitting, before starting the engine.*

5   Fuel pump module - removal and installation

Warning: *Gasoline is extremely flammable, so take extra precautions when you work on any part of the fuel system. See the* **Warning** *in Section 2.*

Removal

1   Relieve the fuel pressure (see Section 2).

2   Remove the fuel tank (see Section 7).

3   Unscrew the fuel pump module retaining ring. A special tool available at most auto

parts stores is available to do this, but a hammer and brass punch can be used to tap the ring in a counterclockwise direction.

4   Carefully maneuver the fuel pump/sending unit assembly out of the tank. **Caution:** *The fuel level float and sending unit are delicate. Don't bump or bend them during removal or the accuracy of the sending unit may be affected.*

Installation

5   Clean the fuel pump mounting flange and the tank mounting surface and seal ring groove.

6   Position a new O-ring around the opening in the fuel tank and guide the fuel pump/sending unit assembly into the tank.

7   Make sure the fuel and EVAP lines are facing in the proper direction, then install the retaining ring and tighten it securely. Connect the fuel and EVAP lines.

8   Install the fuel tank (see Section 7).

6   Fuel level sending unit - check and replacement

Warning: *Gasoline is extremely flammable, so take extra precautions when you work on the fuel system. See the* **Warning** *in Section 2.*

1   Remove the fuel pump module (see Section 5).

2   Detach the fuel level sending unit from its mounting rail at the bottom of the fuel pump module. Also detach the fuel sensor.

3   Installation is the reverse of removal.

7   Fuel tank - removal and installation

Refer to illustrations 7.6 and 7.8

Warning: *Gasoline is extremely flammable, so take extra precautions when you work on any part of the fuel system. See the* **Warning** *in Section 2.*

1   Relieve the fuel pressure (see Section 2).

2   Disconnect the cable from the negative terminal of the battery.

3   Siphon the fuel from the fuel tank into an approved fuel container before removing the tank from the vehicle. **Warning:** *DO NOT start the siphoning action by mouth! Use a siphoning kit (available at most auto parts stores).*

4   Raise the vehicle and support it securely on jackstands. Remove the left rear wheel.

5   Remove the fuel filler tube protector. Remove the fuel tank shield.

6   Loosen the hose clamps and detach the fuel tank filler hose and vapor hose from the fuel filler neck and the fuel tank **(see illustration)**. Disconnect the fuel feed line. Disconnect the evaporative emissions canister hose.

7   Place a floor jack under the tank and position a wood plank between the jack pad and the tank. Raise the jack until it's supporting the tank.

8   Remove the bolts on the fuel tank mounting straps **(see illustration)**. **Caution:** *Lower the tank only enough to access and disconnect the fuel line, EVAP line and electrical connectors at the fuel pump module, then lower the tank further for fuel pump module removal.*

9   Slowly lower the jack while guiding the fuel tank from under the vehicle. Remove the tank from the vehicle.

10   If you're replacing the tank, or having it cleaned or repaired, refer to Section 8.

11   Refer to Section 5 to remove and install the fuel pump module, if necessary.

12   Installation is the reverse of removal. Clean engine oil can be used as an assembly aid when pushing the fuel filler hose back onto the fuel tank.

8   Fuel tank - cleaning and repair

1   The fuel tank installed in the vehicles covered by this manual is not repairable. If the tank is damaged in any way it must be replaced. If cleaning is required, due to fuel

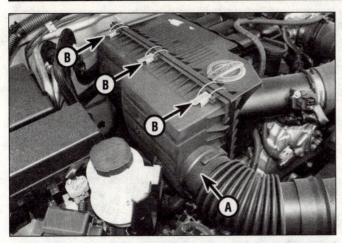

9.1 To replace the four-cylinder air filter, twist the air inlet hose (A) counterclockwise to remove, then release the three clamps (B) and move the housing up and away from the intake manifold

9.2 On V6 models, disconnect the MAF sensor (A), loosen the clamp (B), then release the two latches (C)

contamination, the process should be carried out by a professional who has experience in this critical and potentially dangerous operation. Even after cleaning and flushing, explosive fumes can remain and ignite.

2   If the fuel tank is removed from the vehicle, it should not be placed in an area where sparks or open flames could ignite the fumes coming out of the tank. Be especially careful inside a garage where a gas-type appliance is located, because it could cause an explosion.

9   Air filter housing - removal and installation

Refer to illustrations 9.1, 9.2 and 9.3

Four-cylinder engine

1   Release the latches securing the filter housing cover, then remove the cover and filter element **(see illustration)**. The other half of the air filter housing is part of the intake manifold and is covered in Chapter 2A. Installation is the reverse of removal.

V6 engine

2   Disconnect the MAF sensor electrical connector, loosen the securing the intake duct to the housing, then release the latches securing the cover to the housing **(see illustration)**. Remove the cover and air filter element.

3   Remove the filter housing mounting bolts **(see illustration)** and lift the housing from the engine compartment.

4   Installation is the reverse of removal.

10   Fuel injection system - general information

All models are equipped with a multi-port fuel injection system. Fuel is delivered into each intake port in sequence with the engine firing order in accordance with engine demand through injectors (one per cylinder) mounted on the intake manifold. On V6 models, the intake manifold incorporates an air intake plenum (upper manifold) to aid in air flow and distribution. The air intake plenum bolts to the lower intake manifold, which sits directly in the middle of the engine block.

The multi-port fuel injection system incorporates an on-board electronic engine control computer (known as the Powertrain Control Module - PCM) that accepts inputs from various engine sensors to compute the required fuel flow rate necessary to maintain a prescribed air/fuel ratio throughout the entire engine operational range. The computer then outputs a command to the fuel injectors to meter the quantity of fuel. The system automatically senses and compensates for changes in altitude, load and speed.

The fuel delivery systems include an electric in-tank fuel pump which forces pressurized fuel through a series of metal and rubber lines and an inline fuel filter to the fuel rail assembly. The multi-port fuel injection system uses a single high-pressure pump mounted inside the tank.

The fuel rail assembly incorporates an electrically actuated fuel injector directly above each intake port. When energized, the injectors spray a metered quantity of fuel into the intake air stream.

A constant fuel supply is delivered to the injectors by the fuel rail(s). The covered models have a "returnless" fuel system in which a fuel pressure regulator is mounted within the fuel pump module in the fuel tank to deliver consistent pressure to the engine. No excess fuel need be returned to the fuel tank, so there is only one fuel line between the tank and the engine.

Each injector is energized once every other crankshaft revolution in sequence with engine firing order. The period of time that the injectors are energized (known as "on time" or "pulse width") is controlled by the PCM. Air entering the engine is sensed by mass airflow and temperature sensors. The outputs of these, and other, sensors are processed by the PCM. The computer determines the needed injector pulse width and outputs a command to the injector to meter the exact quantity of fuel.

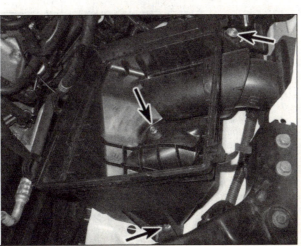

9.3 Remove the V6 air filter housing by unscrewing the three bolts

11.7 Use an automotive stethoscope to determine if the injectors are working properly

11.8 Install the fuel injector test light or "noid light" into the fuel injector electrical connector and confirm that it blinks when the engine is cranked or running

11   Fuel injection system - check

Refer to illustrations 11.7, 11.8 and 11.9

Warning: *Gasoline is extremely flammable, so take extra precautions when you work on any part of the fuel system. See the* **Warning** *in Section 2.*

Note: *The following procedure is based on the assumption that the fuel pump is working and the fuel pressure is adequate (see Section 3).*

1   Check all electrical connectors that are related to the system. Loose electrical connectors and poor grounds can cause many problems that resemble more serious malfunctions.

2   Check to see that the battery is fully charged, as the control unit and sensors depend on an accurate supply voltage in order to properly meter the fuel.

3   Check the air filter element - a dirty or partially blocked filter will severely impede performance and economy (see Chapter 1).

4   Check the fuses. If a blown fuse is found, replace it and see if it blows again. If it does, search for a wire shorted to ground in the fuel injection system wiring harness (see Chapter 12 and the wiring diagrams).

5   Check the condition of the vacuum hoses connected to the intake manifold.

6   Remove the air intake duct from the throttle body and check for dirt, carbon or other residue build-up in the throttle body, particularly around the throttle plate. **Caution:** *The throttle body on these models is coated with a sludge-resistant material designed to protect the bore and throttle plate. Do not attempt to clean the interior of the throttle body with carburetor or other spray cleaners. This throttle body is designed to resist sludge accumulation and cleaning may impair the performance of the engine.*

7   With the engine running, place an automotive stethoscope against each injector, one at a time, and listen for a clicking sound, indicating operation **(see illustration)**. If you don't have a stethoscope, you can place the tip of a long screwdriver against the injector and listen through the handle.

8   If an injector isn't functioning (not click-

ing), purchase a special injector test light (sometimes called a "noid" light) and install it into the injector electrical connector **(see illustration)**. Start the engine and check to see if the noid light flashes. If it does, the injector is receiving proper voltage. If it doesn't flash, further diagnosis should be performed by a dealer service department or other properly equipped repair facility.

9   With the engine OFF and the fuel injector electrical connectors disconnected, measure the resistance of each injector **(see illustration)**. Check the Specifications listed in this Chapter for the correct injector resistance.

10   The remainder of the system checks can be found in Chapter 6.

12   Throttle body - removal and installation

Refer to illustrations 12.3a and 12.3b

Warning: *Wait until the engine is completely cool before beginning this procedure.*

1   Disconnect the cable from the negative battery terminal.

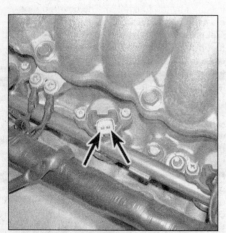

11.9 Measure the resistance across the two terminals of each injector - resistance should be within Specifications

12.3a Four-cylinder throttle body mounting details

1   *Throttle body*
2   *Release the hose from the clip*
3   *Release the clamps*
4   *Disconnect the electrical connector*

12.3b V6 throttle body mounting details

1 *Electrical connector*
2 *Coolant hoses*
3 *Mounting bolts*

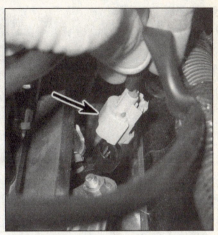

13.4 Disconnect the electrical connectors from the fuel injectors

2   Remove the air intake duct from the throttle body.
3   Disconnect the electrical connectors from the throttle body **(see illustrations)**. Also label and detach all vacuum hoses from the throttle body.
4   Clamp-off the coolant hoses to the throttle body (if equipped) then disconnect them.
5   Remove the throttle body mounting bolts. Remove the throttle body and gasket. Remove all traces of old gasket material from the throttle body and air intake plenum.
6   Installation is the reverse of removal. Use a new gasket. Tighten the bolts in several steps, using a criss-cross pattern, to the torque listed in this Chapter's Specifications.
7   Check the coolant level and add coolant if necessary (see Chapter 1). Perform the throttle valve closed position learning procedure and the idle air volume relearn procedure (see Section 15).

13 Fuel rail and injectors - removal and installation

Refer to illustrations 13.4, 13.6, 13.7, 13.8a, 13.8b, 13.9, 13.10 and 13.11

Warning: *Gasoline is extremely flammable, so take extra precautions when you work on any part of the fuel system. Don't smoke or allow open flames or bare light bulbs near the work area, and don't work in a garage where a gas-type appliance (such as a water heater or clothes dryer) is present. Since gasoline is carcinogenic, wear fuel-resistant gloves when there's a possibility of being exposed to fuel, and, if you spill any fuel on your skin, rinse it off immediately with soap and water. Mop up any spills immediately and do not store fuel-soaked rags where they could ignite. The fuel system is under constant pressure, so, if any fuel lines are to be disconnected, the fuel pressure in the system must be relieved first. When you perform any kind of work on the fuel system, wear safety glasses and have a Class B type fire extinguisher on hand.*
1   Remove the fuel tank filler neck cap to relieve any pressure inside the fuel tank. Then relieve the fuel system pressure (see Section 2).
2   Disconnect the cable from the negative terminal of the battery (see Chapter 5, Section 1).
3   On all models, the intake manifold must

be removed for access to the fuel rail(s) and injectors. Refer to Chapter 2A for four-cylinder intake removal. On V6 models, only the upper plenum needs to be removed - refer to Chapter 2B for the procedure.
4   Disconnect the fuel injector electrical connectors **(see illustration)**.
5   To replace injectors, even one, the fuel rail(s) must be removed. On V6 engines, there are two fuel rails, one for each bank, but they are connected by steel tubing and must be removed as a unit.
6   Use a special tool (available at auto parts stores) to release the quick-connect fitting where the fuel line connects to the fuel rail tube **(see illustration)**. Insert the tool, then pull the connection apart. Cover the exposed ends of the connectors with plastic bags and rubber bands to keep out contaminants. On V6 engines, disconnect the PCV hoses from the valve covers to allow fuel rail removal.
7   Remove the fuel rail mounting bolts **(see illustration)**, then use a rocking, side-to-side motion and carefully lift the fuel rail(s) up and out with the injectors attached.
8   Pull off the clips securing the injectors to

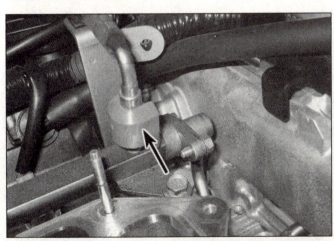

13.6 Remove the protective cap from the fuel line quick-release fitting, then use the plastic tool to separate the connection

13.7 Fuel rail mounting bolts - V6 engine

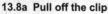

13.8a Pull off the clip

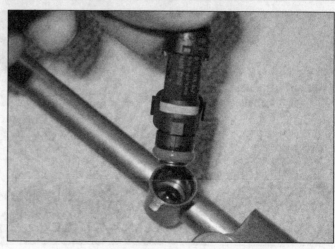

13.8b . . . then pull the injector out of the fuel rail

the fuel rail **(see illustrations)**, then remove the injectors.

9   Remove the O-rings from the injectors and install new ones **(see illustration)**. The injectors are different colors and shouldn't be interchanged. On four-cylinder engines the O-ring on the fuel rail side is black, and the O-ring on the nozzle end of the injector is green. On V6 engines the O-ring on the fuel rail side is blue, and the O-ring on the nozzle end of the injector is brown.

10   Coat the new O-rings with clean engine oil. Install new injector retaining clips on the injectors **(see illustration)**.

11   Push the injectors into their bores in the fuel rail, making sure the retaining clips engage properly **(see illustration)**.

12   Clean the injector bores on the intake manifold.

13   Guide the injectors/fuel rail assembly into the injector bores on the intake manifold. Make sure the injectors are fully seated, then tighten the fuel rail mounting nuts/bolts to the torque listed in this Chapter's Specifications.

14   The remainder of installation is the reverse of removal.

15   After the injector/fuel rail assembly installation is complete, turn the ignition switch to ON, but don't operate the starter. This activates the fuel pump for about two seconds, which builds up fuel pressure in the fuel lines and the fuel rail. Repeat this step two or three times, then check the fuel lines, fuel rail and injectors for fuel leakage.

14   Exhaust system servicing - general information

Refer to illustrations 14.2a, 14.2b and 14.2c

Warning: *Inspection and repair of exhaust system components should be done only after enough time has elapsed after driving the vehicle to allow the system components to cool completely. Also, when working under the vehicle, make sure it is securely supported on jackstands.*

1   The exhaust system consists of the exhaust manifold(s), the catalytic converter(s), the muffler(s), the tailpipe and all con-

necting pipes, brackets, hangers and clamps. The exhaust system is attached to the body with mounting brackets and rubber hangers. If any of the parts are improperly installed, excessive noise and vibration will be transmitted to the body.

2   Conduct regular inspections of the exhaust system to keep it safe and quiet. Look for any damaged or bent parts, open seams, holes, loose connections, excessive corrosion or other defects which could allow exhaust fumes to enter the vehicle **(see illustrations)**. Deteriorated exhaust system components should not be repaired; they should be replaced with new parts.

3   If the exhaust system components are extremely corroded or rusted together, welding equipment will probably be required to remove them. The convenient way to accomplish this is to have a muffler repair shop remove the corroded sections with a cutting torch. If, however, you want to save money by doing it yourself (and you don't have a welding outfit with a cutting torch), simply cut off the old components with a hacksaw. If you have compressed air, special

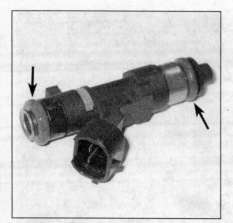

13.9 Remove the O-rings from the injectors and install new ones (note the color of the O-rings; they're different)

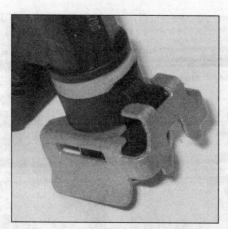

13.10 Install new retaining clips on the injectors . . .

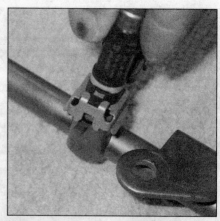

13.11 . . . then push the injectors into the fuel rail until the clips snap into place

14.2a Inspect the exhaust system connections for leaks

14.2b Inspect the catalytic converter and heat shield for damage

pneumatic cutting chisels can also be used. If you do decide to tackle the job at home, be sure to wear safety goggles to protect your eyes from metal chips and work gloves to protect your hands.

4   Here are some simple guidelines to follow when repairing the exhaust system:

a) *Work from the back to the front when removing exhaust system components.*
b) *Apply penetrating oil to the exhaust system component fasteners to make them easier to remove.*
c) *Use new gaskets, hangers and clamps when installing exhaust system components.*
d) *Apply anti-seize compound to the threads of all exhaust system fasteners during reassembly.*
e) *Be sure to allow sufficient clearance between newly installed parts and all points on the underbody to avoid overheating the floor pan and possibly damaging the interior carpet and insulation. Pay particularly close attention to the catalytic converter and heat shield.*
f) *Always remove oxygen sensors and connectors before servicing exhaust system components (see Chapter 6).*

14.2c Check the condition of the heat shield, the muffler and rubber hangers supporting the exhaust system

15 Accelerator pedal released position, throttle valve closed position and idle air volume learning procedures

Note: *The following procedures must be performed whenever the electrical connector to the accelerator pedal position sensor, throttle body or PCM is disconnected.*

Accelerator pedal released position learning procedure

1   Without touching the accelerator pedal, turn the ignition switch to the On position and wait at least two seconds.
2   Turn the ignition switch to the Off position and wait at least ten seconds.
3   Turn the ignition switch to the On position and wait at least two seconds.
4   Turn the ignition switch to the Off position and wait at least ten seconds.

Throttle valve closed position learning procedure

5   Without touching the accelerator pedal, turn the ignition switch to the On position.
6   Turn the ignition switch to the Off position and wait for at least ten seconds.
7   During this ten second period, make sure the throttle valve moves (listen for the actuator in the throttle body). If it doesn't, repeat Steps 5 and 6.

Idle air volume learning procedure

8   Warm up the engine to normal operating temperature.
9   Park the vehicle with the wheels pointing straight ahead.
10   Turn the ignition switch to the Off position and wait at least ten seconds.
11   Without touching the accelerator pedal, turn the ignition switch to the On position and wait three seconds.
12   Depress the accelerator pedal to the floor, then release it; do this five times within five seconds.
13   Wait seven seconds, then depress the accelerator pedal to the floor and hold it there for 20 seconds - the CHECK ENGINE light should stop blinking and remain lit.
14   Release the accelerator pedal within three seconds after the light stops blinking.

Notes

Chapter 5
Engine electrical systems

Contents

Specifications

General

Battery voltage	
Engine off	12.6 to 13.0 volts
Engine running	13.5 to 14.7 volts
Firing order	
Four-cylinder	1-3-4-2
V6	1-2-3-4-5-6

Torque specifications

Note: *One foot-pound (ft-lb) of torque is equivalent to 12 inch-pounds (in-lbs) of torque. Torque values below approximately 15 ft-lbs are expressed in inch-pounds, since most foot-pound torque wrenches are not accurate at these smaller values.*

	Ft-lbs (unless otherwise indicated)	Nm
Alternator mounting bolts/nuts		
Four-cylinder	48	65
V6		
Upper bolt	48	65
Lower bolt	21	28
Ignition coil mounting bolts	62 in-lbs	7
Spark plugs	See Chapter 1	
Starter mounting bolts	33	45

1.4 The Battery Current Sensor is attached to the negative battery cable and helps the PCM control the state-of-charge of the battery

1   General information

Refer to illustration 1.4

The engine electrical systems include all ignition, charging and starting components. Because of their engine-related functions, these components are discussed separately from chassis electrical devices such as the lights, the instruments, etc. (which are included in Chapter 12).

Always observe the following precautions when working on the electrical systems:

a) *Be extremely careful when servicing engine electrical components. They are easily damaged if checked, connected or handled improperly.*

b) *Never leave the ignition switch on for long periods of time with the engine off.*

c) *Don't disconnect the battery cables while the engine is running.*

d) *Maintain correct polarity when connecting a battery cable from another vehicle during jump-starting.*

e) *Always disconnect the negative cable first and hook it up last or the battery may be shorted by the tool being used to loosen the cable clamps.*

It's also a good idea to review the safety-related information regarding the engine electrical systems located in the *Safety First!* Section near the front of this manual before beginning any operation included in this Chapter.

These models have a Battery Current Sensor mounted at the negative battery cable, near the battery **(see illustration)**. The sensor measures the levels of battery charging and discharging and relays that information to the PCM. The PCM sends the information to the charging system to maintain the battery at the proper level of charge. **Caution:** *If for any reason you disconnect the electrical harness*

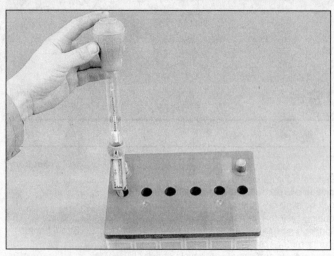

3.1a Use a battery hydrometer to draw electrolyte from the battery cell - this hydrometer is equipped with a thermometer to make temperature corrections

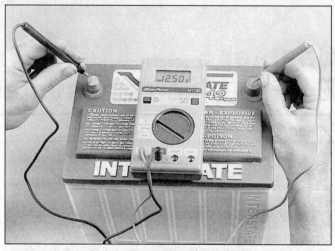

3.1b To test the open circuit voltage of the battery, connect the black probe of the voltmeter to the negative terminal and the red probe to the positive terminal of the battery - a fully charged battery should indicate 12.6 volts depending on the outside air temperature

3.1c Some battery load testers are equipped with an ammeter which enables the battery load to be precisely dialed in, as shown - less expensive testers have a load switch and a voltmeter only

3.1d To find out whether there's a drain on the battery, detach the negative cable and connect a test light between the battery post and the cable clamp

connector at the battery current sensor (such as when replacing a negative battery cable), make sure the sensor is reconnected when the work is done, or the battery may be overcharged or undercharged. For this same reason, you should never connect another electrical device directly to the battery terminal (except for temporary testing of the battery), or it could give a false reading to the battery current sensor, and thus cause overcharging or undercharging.

2   Battery - emergency jump starting

Refer to the *Booster battery (jump)* starting procedure at the front of this manual.

3   Battery - check and replacement

Note: *Anytime the battery is disconnected, stored operating parameters may be lost from the PCM causing the engine to run rough for a period of time while the PCM relearns the information.*

Check

Refer to illustrations 3.1a, 3.1b, 3.1c and 3.1d

1   A battery cannot be accurately tested until it is at or near a fully charged state. Disconnect the negative battery cable, then the positive cable from the battery and perform the following tests:

a) ***Battery state of charge test*** - *Visually inspect the indicator eye (if equipped) on the top of the battery. If the indicator eye is dark in color, charge the battery*

as described in Chapter 1. If the battery is equipped with removable caps, check the battery electrolyte. The electrolyte level should be above the upper edge of the plates. If the level is low, add distilled water. DO NOT OVERFILL. The excess electrolyte may spill over during periods of heavy charging. Test the specific gravity of the electrolyte using a hydrometer **(see illustration)**. Remove the caps and extract a sample of the electrolyte and observe the float inside the barrel of the hydrometer. Follow the instructions from the tool manufacturer and determine the specific gravity of the electrolyte for each cell. A fully charged battery will indicate approximately 1.270 (green zone). If the specific gravity of the electrolyte is low (red zone), charge the battery as described in Chapter 1.

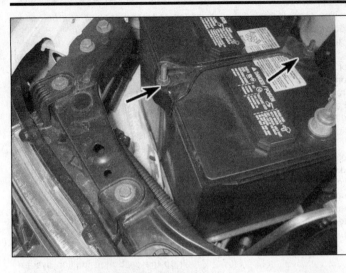

3.3 Remove the nuts (arrows) from the battery hold-down clamp

Terminal end corrosion or damage.

Insulation cracks.

Chafed insulation or exposed wires.

Burned or melted insulation.

4.2 Typical battery cable problems

b) **Open circuit voltage test** - Using a digital voltmeter, perform an open circuit voltage test **(see illustration)**. **Note:** The battery's surface charge must be removed before accurate voltage measurements can be made. Turn On the high beams for ten seconds, then turn them Off and let the vehicle stand for two minutes. With the engine and all accessories Off, connect the negative probe of the voltmeter to the negative terminal of the battery and the positive probe to the positive terminal of the battery. The battery voltage should be approximately 12.5 volts. If the voltage is less than specified, charge the battery before proceeding to the next test. Do not proceed with the battery load test until the battery is fully charged.

c) **Battery load test** - An accurate check of the battery condition can only be performed with a load tester (available at most auto parts stores). This test evaluates the ability of the battery to operate the starter and other accessories during periods of heavy amperage draw (load). Connect a battery load testing tool to the battery terminals **(see illustration)**. Load test the battery according to the tool manufacturer's instructions. This tool increases the load demand (amperage draw) on the battery. Maintain the load on the battery for 15 seconds and observe that the battery voltage does not drop below 9.6 volts. If the battery condition is weak or defective, the tool will indicate this condition immediately. **Note:** Cold temperatures will cause the voltage reading to drop slightly. Follow the chart given in the tool manufacturer's instructions to compensate for cold climates. Minimum load voltage for freezing temperatures (32-degrees F/0-degrees C) should be approximately 9.1 volts.

d) **Battery drain test** - This test will indicate whether there's a constant drain on the vehicle's electrical system that can cause the battery to discharge. Make sure all accessories are turned Off. If the

vehicle has an underhood light, verify it's working properly, then disconnect it. Disconnect the cable from the negative terminal of the battery and attach one lead of a test light to the negative battery cable and the other end to the negative battery terminal **(see illustration)**. The test light should not glow. If the test light glows, it indicates a constant drain on the battery which could cause the battery to discharge. **Note:** On vehicles equipped with engine control computers, digital clocks, digital radios, power seats with memory and/or other components which normally cause a key-off battery drain, it's normal for the test light to glow dimly. If you suspect the drain is excessive, install an ammeter in place of the test light. The reading should not exceed 0.05 amps (50 milliamps).

Replacement

Refer to illustration 3.3

Warning: *Always disconnect the negative cable first and hook it up last or the battery may be shorted by the tool being used to loosen the cable clamps.*

2   Disconnect the negative cable, then the positive cable from the battery.
3   Remove the battery hold-down clamp **(see illustration)**.
4   Lift out the battery. Be careful - it's heavy. **Note:** *Battery straps and handlers are available at most auto parts stores for a reasonable price. They make it easier to remove and carry the battery.*
5   While the battery is out, inspect the area under the battery tray for corrosion.
6   If corrosion is present, clean the area with baking soda and water, then wire brush the corroded areas, and when dry, paint the tray with a rust-preventative paint.
7   If you are replacing the battery, make sure you replace it with a battery with the identical dimensions, amperage rating, cold cranking rating, etc.
8   Installation is the reverse of removal.

4   Battery cables - check and replacement

Refer to illustrations 4.2 and 4.4

1   Periodically inspect the entire length of each battery cable for damage, cracked or burned insulation and corrosion. Poor battery cable connections can cause starting problems and decreased engine performance.
2   Check the cable-to-terminal connections at the ends of the cables for cracks, loose wire strands and corrosion **(see illustration)**. The presence of white, fluffy deposits under the insulation at the cable terminal connection is a sign that the cable is corroded and should be replaced. Check the terminals for distortion, missing mounting bolts and corrosion.
3   When replacing the cables, always disconnect the negative cable first and hook it up last or the battery may be shorted by the tool used to loosen the cable clamps. Even if only the positive cable is being replaced, be sure to disconnect the negative cable from the battery first.
4   Disconnect and remove the cable **(see illustration)**. Make sure the replacement cable is the same length and diameter.

4.4 The negative cable is fastened to the engine block (arrow)

5   Clean the threads of the starter solenoid or ground connection with a wire brush to remove rust and corrosion. Apply a light coat of petroleum jelly to the threads to prevent future corrosion.

6   Attach the cable to the starter solenoid or ground connection and tighten the mounting nut/bolt securely.

7   Before connecting the new cable to the battery, make sure that it reaches the battery post without having to be stretched. Clean the battery posts thoroughly and apply a light coat of petroleum jelly to prevent corrosion (see Chapter 1).

8   Connect the positive cable first, followed by the negative cable.

5   Ignition system - general information

All engines are equipped with a distributorless ignition system. The ignition system consists of the battery, the ignition coils, the spark plugs, the two knock sensors (one on each cylinder head), the Camshaft Position (CMP) sensor, the Crankshaft Position (CKP) sensor, the Manifold Absolute Pressure (MAP) sensor, the Throttle Position (TP) sensor and the Powertrain Control Module (PCM). (For more information about the CMP sensor, CKP sensor, knock sensors, MAP sensor, TP sensor and PCM, refer to Chapter 6.) The PCM controls the base ignition timing and the ignition timing advance on all engines. The base ignition timing is not adjustable on any model.

The PCM controls the ignition system by opening and closing the ignition coil ground circuit. The computerized ignition system provides complete control of the ignition timing by determining the optimum timing in response to engine speed, coolant temperature, throttle position and vacuum pressure in the intake manifold. These parameters are relayed to the PCM by the camshaft position sensor, crankshaft position sensor, throttle position sensor, coolant temperature sensor and manifold absolute pressure sensor. The PCM and the crankshaft position sensor are very important components of the ignition system. The ignition system will not operate and the engine will not start if the PCM or the crankshaft position sensor are defective. Refer to Chapter 6 for additional information on the various sensors.

All engines use a coil-over-plug system, which consists of individual coils, one above each spark plug and connected directly to the spark plug. There are no spark plug wires on these engines. The secondary terminal of each coil, which is connected directly to its corresponding spark plug, is sealed by a rubber boot.

6   Ignition system - check

Refer to illustration 6.5

Warning 1: *Because of the high voltage generated by the ignition system, extreme care should be taken whenever an operation is performed involving ignition components. This not only includes the ignition coil, but also related components and test equipment.*

Warning 2: *The following procedure requires the engine to be cranked during testing. When cranking the engine, make sure that no test leads, loose clothing, long hair, etc. comes in contact with any moving parts (drivebelt, cooling fan, etc.).*

1   Before proceeding with the ignition system, check the following items:

a)   *Make sure the battery cable clamps, where they connect to the battery, are clean and tight.*

b)   *Test the condition of the battery (see Section 3). If it does not pass all the tests, replace it with a new battery.*

c)   *Check the ignition system wiring and connections for tightness, damage, cor-* .

rosion or any other signs of a bad connection.

d)   *Check the related fuses inside the engine compartment fuse and relay box (see Chapter 12). If they're burned, determine the cause and repair the circuit.*

2   If the engine turns over but won't start or has a severe misfire, perform the following steps using a calibrated ignition tester to make sure there is sufficient secondary ignition voltage to fire the spark plugs. There are several different types of calibrated ignition testers available.

3   Disable the fuel system by removing the fuel pump relay, which is located in the engine compartment fuse and relay box (see Chapter 12).

4   Remove the ignition coil (see Section 7) to test for spark to the plug(s) that it fires.

5   Hook up the calibrated ignition system tester(s) (available at most auto parts stores) to the boot(s) underneath the coils **(see illustration)**.

6   If the tester emits a good spark or the tester body flashes during cranking (depending on tester type), sufficient voltage is reaching the plug to fire it. Repeat this test for each spark plug to verify that all the coils are OK.

7   If no sparks occur during cranking at any one cylinder, inspect the primary wire connection at the coil from which you're not getting any spark. Make sure that it's clean and tight.

8   If the primary wire connections are OK but the tester doesn't flash, remove a coil from another cylinder and swap it for the one being tested. If the tester now flashes, you know that the original coil is bad. If the tester still doesn't flash, the PCM or wiring harness is probably defective. Have the PCM checked out by a dealer service department or other qualified repair shop (testing the PCM is beyond the scope of the do-it-yourselfer because it requires expensive special tools).

9   If the tester flashes during cranking but a misfire code (related to the cylinder being tested) has been stored, the spark plug could be fouled or defective.

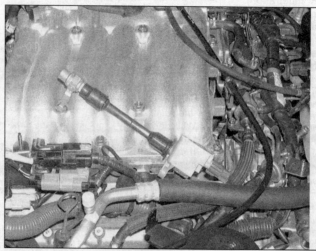

6.5 To check for spark on a V6 model, remove an ignition coil and insert a calibrated ignition tester into the spark plug boot, clip the tester to a convenient ground and operate the starter - with this type of tester, if there is enough power to fire the plug, spark will be visible between the electrode tip and the tester body

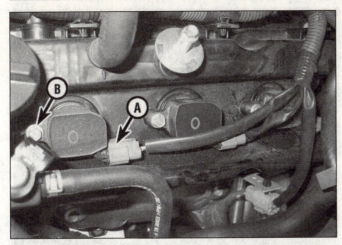

7.6 Disconnect the coil electrical connector (A) and remove the coil mounting bolt (B)

9.3 To measure charging voltage, attach the voltmeter leads to the battery terminals, start the engine and record the voltage reading

7 Ignition coil(s) - removal and installation

Refer to illustration 7.6

1   Disconnect cable from the negative terminal of the battery.

2   Remove the engine cover.

3   On four-cylinder engines, only the coil for number 1 cylinder is readily accessible. To access the other coils, remove the intake manifold (see Chapter 2A).

4   On all models, some harnesses and hoses may have to be pulled aside to access the coils.

5   On V6 engines, remove the intake plenum to access the coils on the right cylinder bank (see Chapter 2B).

6   Disconnect the electrical connector at each coil, then remove the mounting bolt and pull up the coil with a twisting motion **(see illustration)**.

7   Installation is the reverse of the removal procedure. Before installing the coil, place a small amount of dielectric grease inside the boot with a small screwdriver.

8 Charging system - general information and precautions

The charging system includes the alternator, a voltage regulator (mounted inside the alternator), a charge indicator or warning light, the battery, a large fusible link and the wiring between all the components. The charging system maintains the battery in a fully charged condition and supplies electrical power for the ignition system, the lights, the radio, etc. The alternator is driven by a drivebelt at the front of the engine.

The purpose of the voltage regulator is to limit the alternator's voltage to a preset value. This prevents power surges, circuit overloads, etc., during peak voltage output. All models

are equipped with integral type voltage regulator. If a voltage regulator malfunctions, it will be necessary to replace the entire alternator.

The charging system is protected by a large fusible link which is located in the engine compartment fuse box. In the event of charging system problems, check the fusible link for damage or broken contacts.

The charging system doesn't ordinarily require periodic maintenance. However, the drivebelt, battery, wiring and connections should be inspected at the intervals outlined in Chapter 1.

Be very careful when making electrical circuit connections to a vehicle equipped with an alternator and note the following:

a) *When reconnecting wires to the alternator from the battery, be sure to note the polarity.*

b) *Before using arc welding equipment to repair any part of the vehicle, disconnect the battery terminals and the wiring from the alternator.*

c) *Never start the engine with a battery charger connected.*

d) *Always disconnect both battery cables before using a battery charger (always disconnect the negative cable first, positive cable last).*

9 Charging system - check

Refer to illustration 9.3

Note: *These vehicles are equipped with an On-Board Diagnostic-II (OBD-II) system that is useful for detecting charging system problems because it can provide you with the Diagnostic Trouble Code (DTC) that will indicate the general nature of the problem. Refer to Chapter 6 for a list of the DTCs used by the Powertrain Control Module (PCM) on these vehicles and for the procedure you'll need to use to obtain DTCs.*

1   If a malfunction occurs in the charging

circuit, do not immediately assume that the alternator is causing the problem. First check the following items:

a) *The battery cables where they connect to the battery. Make sure the connections are clean and tight.*

b) *The battery electrolyte specific gravity (by observing the charge indicator on the battery). If it is low, charge the battery.*

c) *Inspect the external alternator wiring and connections.*

d) *Check the drivebelt condition and tension (see Chapter 1).*

e) *Check the alternator mounting bolts for tightness.*

f) *Run the engine and check the alternator for abnormal noise.*

2   Using a voltmeter, check the battery voltage with the engine off. It should be 12.6 volts with a fully charged battery (slightly less in cold temperatures).

3   Start the engine and check the battery voltage again **(see illustration)**. It should now be greater than the voltage recorded in Step 2, but should not read more than 15 volts.

4   If the indicated voltage reading is less or more than the specified charging voltage, have the charging system checked at a dealer service department or other properly equipped repair facility. The voltage regulator on these models is contained within the PCM and it cannot be adjusted, removed or tampered with in any way.

10 Alternator - removal and installation

Refer to illustrations 10.4a, 10.4b and 10.5

1   Disconnect the cable from the negative terminal of the battery.

2   Remove the drivebelt (see Chapter 1).

3   Remove the fan shrouds (see Chapter 3).

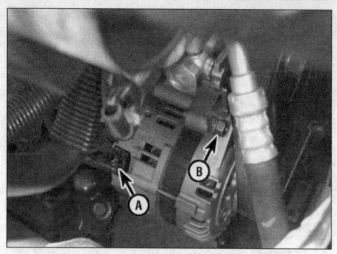

10.4a Four-cylinder alternator connector (A) and upper mounting bolt (B)

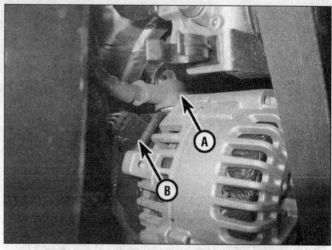

10.4b V6 alternator output cable (A) and electrical connector (B)

4   Disconnect the electrical connectors at the alternator **(see illustrations)**.

5   On four-cylinder engines, remove the lower mounting nut, then remove the upper mounting bolt and remove the alternator. On V6 engines, remove the lower bracket (two bolts) and the upper mounting bolt **(see illustration)**.

6   Installation is the reverse of the removal procedure.

11 Starting system - general information and precautions

The starting system is composed of the battery, ignition switch, starter inhibitor switch (Park/Neutral Position switch) and inhibitor relay (automatic transmission models) or clutch interlock switch and clutch interlock relay (manual transmission models), starter motor and connecting wiring.

Automatic transmission models are equipped with a Park/Neutral Position switch and inhibitor relay in the starter control circuit, which prevents operation of the starter unless the shift lever is in Neutral or Park. Manual transmission models are equipped with a clutch interlock switch and clutch interlock relay in the starter control circuit, which prevents starter operation unless the clutch pedal is depressed.

Turning the ignition key to the Start position actuates the starter control circuit. If the transmission is in Park or Neutral or the clutch depressed, the inhibitor relay or clutch interlock relay then connects battery power to the starter solenoid. The starter solenoid connects battery power to the starter motor and the starter motor turns. The inhibitor or clutch interlock relay is located in the engine compartment fuse/relay box (see Chapter 12). The starter/solenoid assembly is mounted to the transmission bellhousing.

Never operate the starter motor for more than 15 seconds at a time without pausing to allow it to cool for at least two minutes. Excessive cranking can cause overheating, which can seriously damage the starter.

12 Starter motor and circuit - in-vehicle check

Refer to illustration 12.7

1   If a malfunction occurs in the starting circuit, do not immediately assume that the starter is causing the problem. First, check the following items:

a) *Make sure the battery cable clamps, where they connect to the battery, are clean and tight.*

b) *Check the condition of the battery cables (see Section 4). Replace any defective battery cables with new parts.*

c) *Test the condition of the battery (see Section 3). If it does not pass all the tests, replace it with a new battery.*

d) *Check the starter solenoid wiring and connections.*

e) *Check the starter mounting bolts for tightness.*

2   If the starter does not activate when the ignition switch is turned to the start position, check for battery voltage to the solenoid with the ignition switch Off. There should be battery voltage at the positive battery cable on the solenoid if the battery and/or cables are in good working order.

3   Backprobe the S terminal on the starter solenoid and check for voltage as the ignition switch is turned to the start position. This will determine if the solenoid is receiving the correct voltage signal from the ignition switch. If voltage is not available, check the fusible links in the engine compartment fuse box (see Chapter 12). If they're burned, determine the cause and repair the circuit. Also, check the related fuses in the passenger compartment fuse panel (see Chapter 12). If the fuses and fusible links are OK, check the starter inhibitor or clutch interlock relay and circuits for proper operation. Refer to Chapter 12 for the relay locations, wiring diagrams and the relay checking procedure.

4   If the starter circuit is not functioning, check the operation of the Park/Neutral position switch or clutch interlock switch (see Chapter 7 or 8). Make sure the shift lever is

10.5 V6 alternator lower mounting bolts

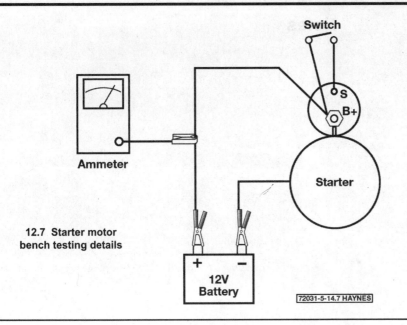

12.7 Starter motor bench testing details

starter motor is defective. If there is no move-ment but the solenoid clicks, the solenoid and/or the starter motor is defective. If the solenoid plunger extends and rotates the pinion drive at approximately 3,000 rpm, the starter/solenoid assembly is working properly.

13 Starter motor - removal and installation

1   Disconnect the cable from the negative battery terminal (see Chapter 5).

Four-cylinder engine
2   Remove the intake air duct and air cleaner housing (see Chapter 4).
3   Disconnect the battery cable and the solenoid terminal connection from the starter solenoid.
4   Remove the starter mounting bolts and the starter.
5   Installation is the reverse of the removal procedure.

V6 engine
Refer to illustrations 13.8 and 13.9
6   Raise the vehicle and support it securely on jackstands, remove the splash shield from under the engine.
7   Remove the exhaust heat shield on the right bank (see Chapter 2B).
8   Remove the starter heat shield **(see illustration)**.
9   Disconnect the battery cable and the solenoid terminal connection from the starter solenoid **(see illustration)**.
10   Remove the starter mounting bolts and the starter **(see illustration 13.8)**.
11   Installation is the reverse of the removal procedure.

in PARK or NEUTRAL or the clutch pedal is fully depressed when attempting to start the engine.
5   If the vehicle is equipped with an anti-theft alarm, check the circuit and the control module for shorts or damaged components.
6   If the starter is receiving voltage but does not activate, most likely the solenoid is defec-tive, but in some rare cases, the engine may be seized. Verify the engine is not seized by rotating the crankshaft pulley (see Chapter 2A or 2B) before proceeding.
7   If voltage is available at the starter solenoid and there is no movement from the starter motor, remove the starter from the engine (see Section 13) and bench test the

starter. Mount the starter/solenoid assembly in a large vise on a sturdy bench. Install one jumper cable from the negative terminal (-) of a fully charged 12-volt automotive battery to the body of the starter **(see illustration)**. Install another jumper cable from the posi-tive terminal (+) of the battery to the battery terminal on the starter. Install a starter switch between the positive terminal of the battery (or the B+ terminal on the starter) and the starter solenoid terminal. Apply battery voltage to the solenoid terminal (for 10 seconds or less) and observe the solenoid plunger, shift lever and overrunning clutch extend and rotate the pin-ion drive. If the pinion drive extends but does not rotate, the solenoid is operating but the

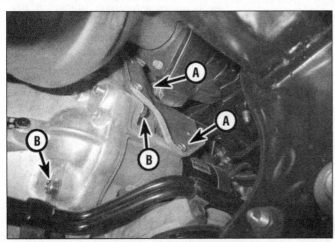

13.8 Starter motor mounting details:
A   Starter heat shield mounting bolts
B   Starter motor mounting bolts

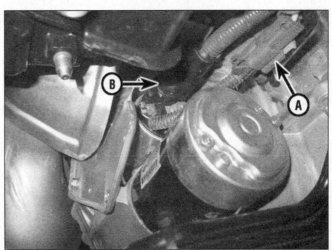

13.9 Disconnect the electrical connector (A) and the input cable (B)

Notes

Chapter 6
Emissions and engine control systems

Contents

Specifications

Torque specifications

	Ft-lbs (unless otherwise indicated)	Nm

Note: *One foot-pound (ft-lb) of torque is equivalent to 12 inch-pounds (in-lbs) of torque. Torque values below approximately 15 ft-lbs are expressed in inch-pounds, since most foot-pound torque wrenches are not accurate at these smaller values.*

Camshaft Position (CMP) sensor mounting bolt	86 in-lbs	9.5
Crankshaft Position (CKP) sensor mounting bolt	68 in-lbs	7.5
Mass Airflow sensor/IAT mounting bolt	156 in-lbs	17.5
Knock sensor mounting bolt	156 in-lbs	17.5
Oxygen sensors	37	50

1   General information

Refer to illustration 1.7

To prevent pollution of the atmosphere from incompletely burned and evaporating gases, and to maintain good driveability and fuel economy, a number of emission control systems are incorporated on the vehicles covered in this manual. These emission control systems and their components are an integral part of the engine management system. The engine management system also includes all the government mandated diagnostic features of the second generation of on-board diagnostics, which is known as On-Board Diagnostics II (OBD-II).

At the center of the engine management and OBD-II systems is the on-board computer,

which is known as the Powertrain Control Module (PCM). Using a variety of information sensors, the PCM monitors all of the important engine operating parameters (temperature, speed, load, etc.). It also uses an array of output actuators - such as the ignition coils, the fuel injectors, the Torque Converter Clutch (TCC) and various solenoids and relays - to respond to and alter these parameters as necessary to maintain optimal performance, economy and emissions. The principal emission control systems used on the vehicles covered in this manual include the:

> Catalytic converters
> Evaporative Emission Control (EVAP) system
> Positive Crankcase Ventilation (PCV) system
> Torque Converter Clutch (TCC) system

The Sections in this Chapter include general descriptions and component replacement procedures for most of the information sensors and output actuators, as well as the important components that are part of the systems listed above. Refer to Chapter 4 for more information on the air induction, fuel delivery and injection systems and exhaust systems, and to Chapter 5 for information on the ignition system. Refer to Chapter 1 for any scheduled maintenance for emission-related systems and components.

The procedures in this Chapter are intended to be practical, affordable and within the capabilities of the home mechanic. The diagnosis of most engine and emission control functions and driveability problems requires specialized tools, equipment and training. When servicing emission devices or systems

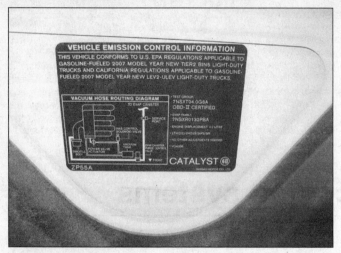

1.7 The Vehicle Emission Control Information (VECI) label, located in the engine compartment, contains information on the emission devices installed on your vehicle and a vacuum hose routing schematic

2.1 Simple code readers are an economical way to extract trouble codes when the CHECK ENGINE light comes on

becomes too difficult or requires special test equipment, consult a dealer service department.

Although engine and emission control systems are very sophisticated on late-model vehicles, you can do most of the regular maintenance and some servicing at home with common tune-up and hand tools and relatively inexpensive digital multimeters. Because of the Federally mandated extended warranty that covers the emission control system, check with a dealer about warranty coverage before working on any emission-related systems. After the warranty has expired, you might want to perform some of the component replacement procedures in this Chapter to save money. Remember that the most frequent cause of emission and driveability problems is a loose electrical connector or a broken wire or vacuum hose, so before jumping to conclusions the first thing you should always do is to inspect all electrical connections, electrical wiring and vacuum hoses related to a system.

Pay close attention to any special precautions given in this Chapter. Remember that illustrations of various system components might not exactly match the component installed on the vehicle on which you're working because of changes made by the manufacturer during production or from year to year.

A Vehicle Emission Control Information (VECI) label **(see illustration)** is located in the engine compartment. This label contains emission-control and engine tune-up specifications and adjustment information. It also includes a vacuum hose routing diagram for emission-control components. When servicing the engine or emission systems, always check the VECI label in your vehicle. If any information in this manual contradicts what you read on the VECI label on your vehicle, always defer to the information on the VECI label.

2   On-Board Diagnostic (OBD) system and Diagnostic Trouble Codes (DTCs)

Scan tools

Refer to illustrations 2.1 and 2.2

1   Hand-held scanners are handy for analyzing the engine management systems used on late-model vehicles. Because extracting the Diagnostic Trouble Codes (DTCs) from an engine management system is now the first step in troubleshooting many computer-controlled systems and components, even the most basic generic code readers are capable of accessing a computer's DTCs **(see illustration)**. More powerful scan tools can also perform many of the diagnostics once associated with expensive factory scan tools. If you're planning to obtain a generic scan tool for your vehicle, make sure that it's compatible with OBD-II systems. If you don't plan to

2.2 Scanners like these from Actron and AutoXray are powerful diagnostic aids - they can tell you just about anything that you want to know about your engine management system

purchase a code reader or scan tool and don't have access to one, you can have the codes extracted by a dealer service department or by an independent repair shop.

2   With the advent of the Federally mandated emission control system known as On-Board Diagnostics-II (OBD-II), specially designed scanners were developed. Several tool manufacturers have released OBD-II scan tools for the home mechanic **(see illustration)**.

OBD-II system

3   All vehicles covered by this manual are equipped with the OBD-II system. This system consists of the on-board computer, known as the Powertrain Control Module (PCM) and information sensors that monitor various functions of the engine and send a constant stream of data to the PCM during engine operation. Unlike earlier on-board diagnostics systems, the OBD-II system doesn't just monitor everything, store Diagnostic Trouble Codes (DTCs) and illuminate a Check Engine light or Malfunction Indicator Light (MIL) when there's a problem. (This warning light was referred to as the "Check Engine" light prior to OBD-II, and many do-it-yourselfers and professional technicians still use this term. However, its name was changed to "Malfunction Indicator Light," or simply "MIL," as part of the Society of Automotive Engineers' standard terminology that was introduced in 1996 to encourage all manufacturers to use the same terms when referring to the same components. So in this manual we will refer to this warning light as the Malfunction Indicator Light, or MIL.)

4   The PCM is the "brain" of the electronically controlled OBD-II system. It receives data from a number of information sensors and switches. Based on the data that it receives from the sensors, the PCM constantly alters engine operating conditions to optimize driveability, performance, emissions and fuel economy. It does so by turning on and

off and by controlling various output actuators such as relays, solenoids, valves and other devices. The PCM can only be accessed with an OBD-II scan tool plugged into the 16-pin Data Link Connector (DLC), which is located underneath the driver's end of the dashboard, near the steering column.

5   If your vehicle is still under warranty, virtually every fuel, ignition and emission control component in the OBD-II system is covered by a Federally mandated emissions warranty that is longer than the warranty covering the rest of the vehicle. Vehicles sold in California and in some other states have even longer emissions warranties than other states. Read your owner's manual for the terms of the warranty protecting the emission-control systems on your vehicle. It isn't a good idea to "do-it-yourself" at home while the vehicle emission systems are still under warranty because owner-induced damage to the PCM, the sensors and/or the control devices might void this warranty. So as long as the emission systems are still under warranty, take the vehicle to a dealer service department if there's a problem.

Information sensors

6   **Accelerator Pedal Position Sensor (APPS)** - The APPS is an integral component of the accelerator pedal assembly. The APPS provides the PCM with a variable voltage signal that's proportional to the position (angle) of the accelerator pedal. The PCM uses this data to control the position of the throttle plate inside the electronically controlled throttle body.

7   **Camshaft Position (CMP) sensor** - The CMP sensor produces a signal that the PCM uses to monitor the position of the camshaft(s). The CMP sensor is positioned adjacent to the circumference of a "tone wheel" mounted on the rear end of the camshaft (or the rear end of each camshaft on V6 engines). The tone wheel has notches machined into it. When the engine is operating, the CMP sensor receives a 5-volt signal from the PCM, then switches back and forth from a high (5-volt) to a low (.3-volt) signal every time one of the notches in the tone wheel passes by it. This data enables the PCM to determine the position of the camshaft (and therefore the valve train) so that it can time the firing sequence of the fuel injectors. The PCM also uses the signal from the CMP sensor and the signal from the Crankshaft Position (CKP) sensor to distinguish between fuel injection and spark timing.

8   **Crankshaft Position (CKP) sensor** - Like the CMP sensor, the CKP sensor uses a "tone wheel" with notches machined into it to "flip" the CKP sensor's output every time a notch passes by it. The PCM uses data from the CKP sensor to calculate engine speed and crankshaft position, which enables it to synchronize ignition timing with fuel injector timing, to control spark knock and to detect misfires. The CKP sensor is on the right side of the engine block on V6 and four-cylinder engines, close to the bellhousing.

9   **Engine Coolant Temperature (ECT) sensor** - The ECT sensor is a Negative Temperature Coefficient (NTC) "thermistor" (temperature-sensitive variable resistor). In an NTC-type thermistor, the resistance of the thermistor decreases as the coolant temperature increases, so the voltage output of the ECT sensor increases. Conversely, the resistance of the thermistor increases as the coolant temperature decreases, so the voltage of the ECT sensor decreases. The PCM uses this variable voltage signal to calculate the temperature of the engine coolant. The ECT sensor tells the PCM when the engine is sufficiently warmed up to go into closed-loop operation and helps the PCM control the air/fuel mixture ratio and ignition timing. On four-cylinder engines the ECT sensor is located at the rear of the cylinder head (below the CMP). On V6 engines the ECT sensor is located behind the right-side cylinder head, on the water transfer pipe connecting the back of the two cylinder heads.

10   **Intake Air Temperature (IAT) sensor** - The IAT sensor is a Negative Temperature Coefficient (NTC) "thermistor" (temperature-sensitive variable resistor) that monitors the temperature of the air entering the engine and sends a variable voltage signal to the PCM. (See the explanation for how an NTC-type thermistor works in the ECT sensor description above.) The voltage signal from the IAT sensor is one of the parameters used by the PCM to determine injector pulse-width (the duration of each injector's "on-time") and to adjust spark timing (to prevent spark knock). The IAT is part of the MAF sensor on the covered models.

11   **Knock Sensor (KS)** - The Knock Sensor (KS) is a "piezoelectric" crystal that oscillates in proportion to engine vibration. (The term piezoelectric refers to the property of certain crystals that produce a voltage when subjected to a mechanical stress.) The oscillation of the piezoelectric crystal produces a voltage output that is monitored by the PCM, which retards the ignition timing when the oscillation exceeds a certain threshold. When the engine is operating normally, the Knock Sensor (KS) oscillates consistently and its voltage signal is steady. When detonation occurs, engine vibration increases, and the oscillation of the Knock Sensor (KS) exceeds a design threshold. (Detonation is an uncontrolled explosion, after the spark occurs at the spark plug, which spontaneously combusts the remaining air/fuel mixture, resulting in a "pinging" or "slapping" sound.) If allowed to continue, the engine could be damaged. On four-cylinder engines, the knock sensor is located at the right side of the engine block. On V6 engines the two knock sensors are located on each side of the block, in the valley under the intake manifold.

12   **Oxygen sensors** - An oxygen sensor is a galvanic battery that generates a small variable voltage signal in proportion to the difference between the oxygen content in the exhaust stream and the oxygen content in the ambient air. The PCM uses the voltage signal from the upstream oxygen sensor to maintain a "stoichiometric" air/fuel ratio of 14.7:1 by constantly adjusting the "on-time" of the fuel injectors. On four-cylinder engines, there are two oxygen sensors: the upstream sensor is located just ahead of the catalytic converter, and another between the main converter and the mini-converter. On V6 engines, each bank of the engine has a sensor before and after the catalytic converter, for a total of four oxygen sensors.

13   **Throttle Position (TP) sensor** - The TP sensor is a potentiometer that receives constant voltage input from the PCM and sends back a voltage signal that varies in relation to the opening angle of the throttle plate inside the throttle body. This voltage signal tells the PCM when the throttle is closed, half-open, wide open or anywhere in between. The PCM uses this data, along with information from other sensors, to calculate injector "pulse width" (the interval of time during which an injector solenoid is energized by the PCM). The electronic throttle body used on these models incorporates the TP sensor, but it's an integral part of the throttle body's ETC motor assembly and cannot be serviced separately.

14   **Power steering pressure switch** - The power steering pressure switch is used to detect excessive line pressure in the power steering system. The PCM uses this input to adjust the idle speed under increased engine loads during low-speed vehicle maneuvers.

15   **Fuel temperature sensor** - The fuel temperature sensors provides the PCM with data on changes in the fuel temperature, measured at the fuel tank. The PCM uses this signal for diagnostics purposes.

16   **Transmission speed sensors** - There are two transmission speeds sensors on automatic transmissions, the **Turbine Speed (TSS) sensor 1** and the **Turbine Speed (TSS) sensor 2**. The TCM compares the two signals to determine the correct transmission gear ratio, to detect a speed ratio error, Torque Converter Clutch (TCC) slippage and to calculate parameters such as the torque converter element speed ratio. One of the sensors is also used by the PCM to compare with information from the Vehicle Speed Sensor (VSS).

17   **Transmission Range (TR) sensor** - The TR sensor is located at the end of the manual shaft, on the right side of the automatic transmission. The TR switch performs the same functions as a Park/Neutral Position (PNP) switch: it prevents the engine from starting in any gear other than Park or Neutral, and it closes the circuit for the back-up lights when the shift lever is moved to Reverse. But the TR switch is also connected to the TCM, which sends a voltage signal to the TR switch, which uses a series of step-down resistors that act as a voltage divider. The PCM monitors the voltage output signal from the switch, which corresponds to the position of the manual lever. Thus the TCM is able to determine the gear selected and is able to determine the correct pressure for the electronic pressure control system of the transmission.

Powertrain Control Module (PCM)

18   The **PCM** is a computer. Think of it as the "brain" of the engine management system. Like all computers, the PCM receives data inputs, processes the data and outputs commands. The PCM receives data from all of the information sensors described above (input), compares the data to its program and calculates the appropriate responses (processing), then turns the output actuators on or off, or changes their *pulse width* or *duty cycle* (output) to keep everything running smoothly, cleanly and efficiently. The PCM is located in the right rear corner of the engine compartment, on the inner side of the right front fender. The TCM is a separate component, located inside the valve body of the transmission.

Output actuators

19   **EVAP canister purge solenoid** - The EVAP canister purge solenoid is a PCM-controlled solenoid that controls the purging of evaporative emissions from the EVAP canister to the intake manifold. The EVAP purge solenoid is never turned on during cold start warm-ups or during hot start time delays. But once the engine reaches a specified temperature and enters closed-loop operation the PCM will energize the canister purge solenoid between 5 and 10 times a second. When the solenoid is energized by the PCM, it allows the fuel vapors that are stored in the EVAP canister to be drawn into the intake manifold, where they're mixed with intake air, then burned along with the normal air/fuel mixture, under certain operating conditions. The PCM regulates the flow rate of the vapors by controlling the pulse-width of the solenoid (the length of time during which the solenoid is turned on) in accordance with operating conditions. The EVAP canister purge solenoid valve is located on top of the intake plenum on four-cylinder engines, and above the front of the timing chain cover on V6 engines.

20   **EVAP control system pressure sensor** – the (air/fuel vapor) leak detection system is based on the principle that the pressure inside a sealed system (such as the EVAP system) will change if the temperature changes, i.e. if the temperature goes up, so does the pres-

sure, and vice versa. So if during a leak test the PCM notes that the pressure inside the EVAP system isn't proportional to the temperature, it sets a Diagnostic Trouble Code (DTC) for a leak. The EVAP pressure sensor unit is located on top of the EVAP canister, which is located under the rear of the vehicle.

21   **Fuel injectors** - The fuel injectors, which spray a fine mist of fuel into the intake ports, where it is mixed with incoming air, are inductive coils under PCM control. The injectors are installed between the fuel rail and the intake ports that connect the intake manifold runners to the combustion chambers. For more information about the injectors, see Chapter 4.

22   **Ignition coils** - The ignition coils are controlled by the Powertrain Control Module (PCM). There is no separate ignition control module. This function is handled inside the PCM, which controls the ground path for the primary side of each coil. For more information about the ignition coils refer to Chapter 5.

Obtaining and clearing Diagnostic Trouble Codes (DTCs)

23   All models covered by this manual are equipped with on-board diagnostics. When the PCM recognizes a malfunction in a monitored emission control system, component or circuit, it turns on the Malfunction Indicator Light (MIL) on the dash. The PCM will continue to display the MIL until the problem is fixed and the Diagnostic Trouble Code (DTC) is cleared from the PCM's memory. You'll need a scan tool to access any DTCs stored in the PCM. Before outputting any DTCs stored in the PCM, thoroughly inspect ALL electrical connectors and hoses. Make sure that all electrical connections are tight, clean and free of corrosion. And make sure that all hoses are correctly connected, fit tightly and are in good condition (no cracks or tears).

Accessing the DTCs

Refer to illustration 2.24

24   On the vehicles covered in this manual, all of which are equipped with On-Board Diagnostic II (OBD-II) systems, the Diagnostic Trouble Codes (DTCs) can only be accessed with a scan tool. Simply plug the connector of the scan tool into the Data Link Connec-

2.24 The Data Link Connector (DLC), or diagnostic connector, is located under the left side of the instrument panel

tor (DLC), which is located under the lower edge of the dash, near the center console **(see illustration)**. Then follow the instructions included with the scan tool to extract the DTCs.

25   Once you have outputted all of the stored DTCs, look them up on the accompanying DTC chart.

26   After troubleshooting the source of each DTC make any necessary repairs or replace the defective component(s).

Clearing the DTCs

27   Clear the DTCs with the scan tool in accordance with the instructions provided by the scan tool's manufacturer.

Diagnostic Trouble Codes

28   The accompanying tables are a list of the Diagnostic Trouble Codes (DTCs) that can be accessed by a do-it-yourselfer working at home (there are many more DTCs available to professional service technicians with proprietary scan tools and software, but those codes cannot be accessed by a generic scan tool). If, after you have checked and repaired the connectors, wire harness and vacuum hoses (if applicable) for an emission-related system, component or circuit, the problem persists, have the vehicle checked by a dealer service department.

OBD-II Diagnostic Trouble Codes (DTCs) (includes transmission codes)

Note: *Not all trouble codes apply to all models.*

Code	Possible cause	Code	Possible cause
P0011	Intake valve timing control, four-cylinder (or bank 1 on V6)	P0037	Oxygen sensor (1/2) heater circuit, low voltage
P0021	Intake valve timing control, V6 Bank 2	P0038	Oxygen sensor (1/2) heater circuit, high voltage
P0031	Oxygen sensor (1/1) heater circuit, low voltage	P0051	Oxygen sensor (2/1) heater circuit, low voltage
P0032	Oxygen sensor (1/1) heater circuit, high voltage	P0052	Oxygen sensor (2/1) heater circuit, high voltage, bank 2

Code	Possible cause
P0057	Oxygen sensor (2/2) heater circuit, low voltage, bank 2
P0058	Oxygen sensor (2/2) heater circuit, high voltage, bank 2
P0075	Intake valve timing control circuit, four-cylinder (or bank 1 on V6)
P0081	Intake valve timing control circuit, bank 2 on V6
P0101	MAF sensor circuit, performance
P0102	MAF sensor circuit, low input
P0103	MAF sensor circuit, high input
P0112	Intake Air Temperature (IAT) sensor circuit, low input
P0113	Intake Air Temperature (IAT) sensor circuit, high input
P0116	Engine Coolant Temperature (ECT) sensor circuit, range or performance problem
P0117	Engine Coolant Temperature (ECT) sensor circuit, low voltage
P0118	Engine Coolant Temperature (ECT) sensor circuit, high voltage
P0122	Throttle Position (TP) sensor 2 circuit, low voltage
P0123	Throttle Position (TP) sensor 2 circuit, high voltage
P0125	Insufficient coolant temperature for closed-loop fuel control
P0127	Intake air temperature too high
P0128	Thermostat leak or stuck thermostat
P0130	O2 sensor circuit malfunction (1/1)
P0131	Oxygen sensor (1/1) circuit, low voltage
P0132	Oxygen sensor (1/1) circuit, high voltage
P0133	Oxygen sensor (1/1), slow response
P0135	Oxygen sensor (1/1), heater performance problem
P0137	Oxygen sensor (1/2) circuit, low voltage
P0138	Oxygen sensor (1/2) circuit, high voltage
P0139	Oxygen sensor (1/2) circuit, slow response
P0150	Oxygen sensor (1/2), circuit, out of range
P0151	Oxygen sensor (2/1) circuit, low voltage
P0152	Oxygen sensor (2/1) circuit, high voltage
P0153	Oxygen sensor (2/1) circuit, slow response

Code	Possible cause
P0157	Oxygen sensor (2/2) circuit, low voltage
P0158	Oxygen sensor (2/2) circuit, high voltage
P0159	Oxygen sensor (2/2) circuit, slow response
P0161	Oxygen sensor (2/2), heater performance problem
P0171	Fuel system too lean (cylinder bank no. 1)
P0172	Fuel system too rich (cylinder bank no. 1)
P0174	Fuel system too lean (cylinder bank no. 2)
P0175	Fuel system too rich (cylinder bank no. 2)
P0181	Fuel tank temperature sensor, range or performance
P0182	Fuel tank temperature sensor, low voltage
P0183	Fuel tank temperature sensor, high voltage
P0222	Throttle Position (TP) sensor no. 2 circuit, low voltage
P0223	Throttle Position (TP) sensor no. 2 circuit, high voltage
P0300	Multiple cylinder misfire detected
P0301	Cylinder no. 1 misfire detected
P0302	Cylinder no. 2 misfire detected
P0303	Cylinder no. 3 misfire detected
P0304	Cylinder no. 4 misfire detected
P0305	Cylinder no. 5 misfire detected
P0306	Cylinder no. 6 misfire detected
P0327	Knock sensor circuit, low voltage
P0328	Knock sensor circuit, high voltage
P0332	Knock sensor 2 circuit, low voltage
P0333	Knock sensor 2 circuit, high voltage
P0335	Crankshaft Position (CKP) sensor circuit malfunction
P0340	Camshaft Position (CMP) sensor circuit malfunction
P0345	Camshaft Position (CMP) sensor, bank 2, circuit malfunction
P0420	Catalyst system efficiency below threshold (cylinder bank no. 1)
P0430	Catalyst system efficiency below threshold (cylinder bank 2)

Code	Possible cause
P0441	Evaporative Emission Control (EVAP) purge system performance problem
P0442	Evaporative Emission Control (EVAP) purge system, medium leak detected
P0443	Evaporative Emission Control (EVAP) purge solenoid circuit malfunction
P0444	Evaporative Emission Control (EVAP) purge solenoid, circuit open
P0445	Evaporative Emission Control (EVAP) purge solenoid, circuit shorted
P0447	Evaporative Emission Control (EVAP) purge solenoid, circuit open
P0448	Evaporative Emission Control (EVAP) purge solenoid, valve closed
P0451	EVAP control system pressure sensor, performance
P0452	EVAP control system pressure sensor, circuit low input
P0453	EVAP control system pressure sensor, circuit high input
P0455	Evaporative Emission Control (EVAP) system, large leak
P0456	Evaporative Emission Control (EVAP) system, small leak
P0460	Fuel level sensor, circuit noise
P0461	Fuel level sensor no. 1, performance problem
P0462	Fuel level sensor no. 1, low voltage
P0463	Fuel level sensor no. 1, high voltage
P0480	Cooling fan no. 1, control circuit malfunction
P0481	Cooling fan no. 2, control circuit malfunction
P0500	Vehicle Speed Sensor (VSS) no. 1, performance problem
P0506	Idle speed performance lower than expected
P0507	Idle speed performance higher than expected
P0550	Power Steering Pressure (PSP) sensor, circuit out of range
P0603	Powertrain Control Module (PCM), power supply circuit
P0605	Powertrain Control Module (PCM), malfunction
P0643	PCM sensor power supply, voltage high or low
P0700	Transmission control system (Malfunction Indicator Light request)

Code	Possible cause
P0705	Transmission Range (TR) sensor, rationality
P0710	Automatic transmission fluid temperature sensor
P0717	TCM, turbine sensor circuit open or shorted
P0720	Output speed sensor circuit
P0725	Engine speed sensor circuit
P0731	Incorrect gear ratio, first gear
P0732	Incorrect gear ratio, second gear
P0733	Incorrect gear ratio, third gear
P0734	Incorrect gear ratio, fourth gear
P0735	Incorrect gear ratio, fifth gear
P0740	Torque Converter Clutch (TCC) out of range
P0744	Torque Converter Clutch (TCC), solenoid
P0745	Line pressure solenoid, improper voltage when driving
P0750	Shift solenoid, circuit
P0850	Park/Neutral position switch, performance
P1148	Oxygen sensors or circuit, bank 1, closed-loop function not available
P1168	Oxygen sensors or circuit, bank 2, closed-loop function not available
P1211	Traction Control System (TCS), problem with ABS control unit
P1212	Traction Control System (TCS), problem with TCS control unit
P1217	Engine, overtemperature condition
P1225	Electronic Throttle Control system, closed-throttle position learning
P1226	Electronic Throttle Control system, closed-throttle position learning
P1421	Cold start control, problem with EFI system or PCM
P1550-1554	Battery current sensor
P1564	ACSD switch (cruise control), signal out of range
P1572	ACSD switch (cruise control), brake switch
P1574	ACSD switch (cruise control), speed sensor
P1610-1615	NATS (alarm system), malfunction

Code	Possible cause		Code	Possible cause
P1706	Park-Neutral position switch, circuit		P1762	Automatic transmission, front brake solenoid, circuit
P1715	Automatic transmission, input turbine speed sensor		P1764	Automatic transmission, direct clutch solenoid valve
P1716	Automatic transmission, input turbine speed sensor, circuit		P1767	Automatic transmission, front brake solenoid, circuit
P1730	Automatic transmission, interlock system		P1769	Automatic transmission, High/Low reverse clutch solenoid
P1752	Automatic transmission, input clutch solenoid		P1772	Automatic transmission, front brake solenoid, circuit
P1754	Automatic transmission, input clutch solenoid		P1774	Automatic transmission, low coast brake solenoid
P1757	Automatic transmission, front brake solenoid, circuit		P1800	Variable Intake Air system (V6), circuit
P1759	Automatic transmission, front brake solenoid, function		P1805	Brake switch, signal to ECM

3   Accelerator Pedal Position Sensor (APPS) - replacement

Refer to illustration 3.2

Note: *The APP sensor is located at the upper end of the accelerator pedal. If the APP sensor must be replaced, you must replace the accelerator pedal and sensor as a single assembly.*

1   Disconnect the cable from the negative battery terminal (see Chapter 5, Section 1).
2   Disconnect the electrical connector from the APP sensor **(see illustration)**.
3   Remove the APP sensor and pedal assembly mounting nuts and detach the assembly from the firewall.
4   Installation is the reverse of removal. Reconnect the battery and perform the "Accelerator Pedal Released Position Learning" procedure. With the accelerator pedal released:

  a) *Turn the ignition switch to the On position and wait at least two seconds.*
  b) *Turn the ignition switch Off and wait at least ten seconds.*

  c) *Turn the ignition switch to the On position and wait at least two seconds.*
  d) *Turn the ignition switch Off and wait at least ten seconds.*

4   Camshaft Position (CMP) sensor - replacement

Refer to illustration 4.3

Note: *The CMP sensor is mounted on the rear end of the cylinder head (or the rear end of each cylinder head on V6 engines).*

1   Disconnect the cable from the negative battery terminal (see Chapter 5, Section 1).
2   Raise the front end of the vehicle and place it securely on jackstands.
3   Disconnect the electrical connector from the CMP sensor **(see illustration)**.
4   Remove the sensor mounting bolt and remove the CMP sensor.
5   Inspect the CMP sensor O-ring for cracks, tears and other deterioration. If it's damaged, replace it.

6   When installing the CMP sensor, apply a small dab of clean engine oil to the sensor O-ring, then use a slight rocking motion to work the O-ring into the sensor mounting bore. Do NOT use a twisting motion or you will damage the O-ring.
7   Make sure that the CMP sensor mounting flange is fully seated flat against the mounting surface around the sensor mounting hole. **Caution:** *If the CMP sensor is not fully seated against its mounting surface, the sensor mounting tang will be damaged when the sensor mounting bolt is tightened to the specified torque.*
8   Installation is otherwise the reverse of removal. Be sure to tighten the CMP sensor mounting bolt to the torque listed in this Chapter's Specifications.

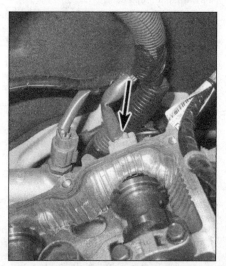

4.3 To detach the CMP sensor from a V6 engine, disconnect the electrical connector and remove the sensor mounting bolt (V6 right bank sensor shown, left bank sensor and four-cylinder sensors similar)

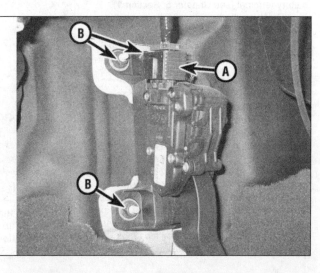

3.2 Slide the connector lock (A) out of the connector, then unplug the electrical connector. (B) are the APP sensor mounting nuts

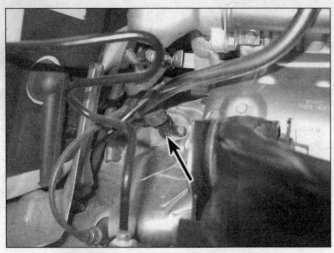

5.3 To detach the CKP sensor from the lower/rear of the block on a V6 engine, disconnect the electrical connector and remove the sensor mounting bolt

6.3 To remove the ECT sensor on a V6 engine, disconnect the electrical connector and unscrew the sensor from the coolant pipe at the rear of the right cylinder head (four-cylinder ECT sensor at rear of cylinder head)

5 Crankshaft Position (CKP) sensor - replacement

Refer to illustration 5.3

1   Disconnect the cable from the negative battery terminal (see Chapter 5, Section 1).

2   Raise the front end of the vehicle and place it securely on jackstands. It may be easier to access the sensor after removing the right fenderwell liner (see Chapter 11).

3   Disconnect the electrical connector from the CKP sensor **(see illustration)**.

4   Remove the CKP sensor mounting bolt and remove the sensor from the engine.

5   Remove the CKP sensor O-ring and inspect it for cracks, tears and deterioration. If it's damaged, replace it.

6   Apply a small amount of engine oil on the O-ring and, using a slight rocking motion, push the sensor into its mounting hole in the engine block until the sensor is fully seated.

7   Installation is otherwise the reverse of removal. Be sure to tighten the CKP sensor mounting bolt to the torque listed in this Chapter's Specifications.

6 Engine Coolant Temperature (ECT) sensor - replacement

Refer to illustrations 6.3 and 6.5

Warning: *Wait until the engine is completely cool before beginning this procedure.*

1   Partially drain the cooling system (see Chapter 1).

2   Disconnect the cable from the negative battery terminal (see Chapter 5, Section 1).

3   Disconnect the electrical connector from the ECT sensor **(see illustration)**. The ECT on four-cylinder engines is at the rear of the cylinder head, just above the water control valve. On V6 engines it's threaded into the coolant pipe at the rear of the right cylinder

head. Do not confuse the ECT sensor with the camshaft position sensor which is lower on the head.

4   Using a deep socket, carefully unscrew the ECT sensor from the intake manifold.

5   To prevent leakage and thread corrosion, wrap the threads of the ECT sensor with Teflon sealing tape **(see illustration)** before installing the sensor. (Seal the sensor threads whether you're installing the old sensor or a new unit.)

6   Installation is otherwise the reverse of removal.

7   Refill the cooling system (see Chapter 1).

7 Knock sensor(s) - replacement

Note: *On V6 engines, there are two knock sensors located in the valley between the cylinder heads, underneath the intake manifold. They must be replaced together. They're not available separately.*

1   Disconnect the cable from the negative battery terminal (see Chapter 5, Section 1).

2   On four-cylinder engines, disconnect the knock sensor electrical connector, which is located at the right-rear of the engine, below the intake plenum.

3   On V6 engines, remove the intake manifold (see Chapter 2A).

4   Remove the knock sensor mounting bolts and remove the knock sensor assembly.

5   Make sure that the holes for the knock sensor mounting bolts are thoroughly cleaned before installing the knock sensor mounting bolts.

6   On V6 engines, do NOT switch the knock sensors (do not install the left knock sensor in the right sensor mounting position and vice versa). The PCM assumes that the knock sensors are installed in their correct locations.

Caution: *Switching the sensor locations will confuse the PCM and cause it to set a Diag-*

nostic Trouble Code.

7   Installation is otherwise the reverse of removal. Be sure to tighten the knock sensor mounting bolts to the torque listed in this Chapter's Specifications. **Caution:** *Over- or under-tightening the knock sensor mounting bolts will affect knock sensor performance, which might affect the PCM's spark control ability.*

8 Oxygen sensors - description and replacement

Description

1   The oxygen in the exhaust reacts with the elements inside the oxygen sensor to produce a voltage output that varies from 0.1 volt (high oxygen, lean mixture) to 0.9 volt (low oxygen, rich mixture). The pre-converter oxygen sensor (mounted in the exhaust system before the catalytic converter) provides a feedback

6.5 Before installing the ECT sensor, be sure to wrap the threads of the sensor with Teflon tape to prevent leaks

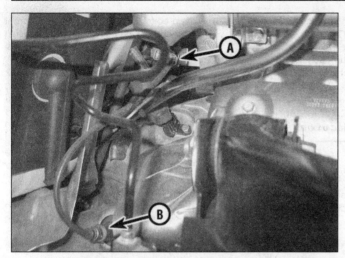

8.8a On V6 engines, there are four oxygen sensors - two upstream and two downstream. To remove an upstream sensor, disconnect the electrical connector (A) then remove the sensor (B) with either an oxygen sensor socket or with a wrench

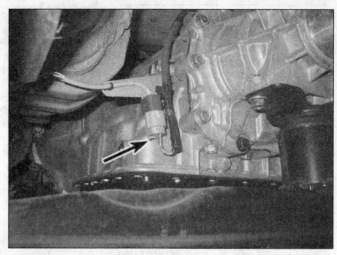

8.8b Each downstream oxygen sensor is located behind the catalyst. First, trace the electrical lead up to the sensor connector and disconnect it, then remove the sensor with either a wrench or an oxygen sensor socket

signal to the PCM that indicates the amount of leftover oxygen in the exhaust. The PCM monitors this variable voltage continuously to determine the required fuel injector pulse width and to control the engine air/fuel ratio. A mixture ratio of 14.7 parts air to 1 part fuel is the ideal ratio for minimum exhaust emissions, as well as the best combination for fuel economy and engine performance. Based on oxygen sensor signals, the PCM tries to maintain this air/fuel ratio of 14.7:1 at all times.

2   The post-converter oxygen sensor (mounted in the exhaust system after the catalytic converter) has no effect on PCM control of the air/fuel ratio. However, the post-converter sensor is identical to the pre-converter sensor and operates in the same way. The PCM uses the post-converter signal to monitor the efficiency of the catalytic converter. A post-converter oxygen sensor will produce a slower fluctuating voltage signal that reflects the lower oxygen content in the post-catalyst exhaust.

3   Oxygen sensor configuration varies depending on the model and on where it is sold; "Federal" (49-State) model or "California" model. On four-cylinder models, there is one upstream and one downstream oxygen sensor. On these vehicles, the upstream oxygen sensor is located in the exhaust pipe ahead of the catalyst and the downstream sensor is located on the pipe behind the catalyst. On V6 engines, which have a catalyst for each bank of the engine, there are two upstream sensors (one in each exhaust pipe between the exhaust manifold and the catalyst) and two downstream sensors (one behind each catalyst).

4   An oxygen sensor produces no voltage when it is below its normal operating temperature of about 600-degrees F. During this warm-up period, the PCM operates in an open-loop fuel control mode. It does not use the oxygen sensor signal as a feedback indication of residual oxygen in the exhaust.

Instead, the PCM controls fuel metering based on the inputs of other sensors and its own programs.

5   An oxygen sensor depends on four conditions in order to operate correctly:

a) *Electrical - The low voltage generated by the sensor requires good, clean connections. Always check the connectors whenever an oxygen sensor problem is suspected or indicated.*

b) *Outside air supply - The sensor needs air circulation to the internal portion of the sensor. Whenever the sensor is installed, make sure that the air passages are not restricted.*

c) *Correct operating temperature - The PCM will not react to the sensor signal until the sensor reaches approximately 600-degrees F. This factor must be considered when evaluating the performance of the sensor.*

d) *Unleaded fuel - Unleaded fuel is essential for correct sensor operation.*

6   The PCM can detect several different oxygen sensor problems and set Diagnostic Trouble Codes (DTCs) to indicate the specific fault (see Section 2). When an oxygen sensor DTC occurs, the PCM disregards the oxygen sensor signal voltage and reverts to open-loop fuel control as described previously.

Replacement

Refer to illustrations 8.8a, 8.8b and 8.9

Warning: *Be careful not to burn yourself during the following procedure.*

Note: *Since the exhaust pipe contracts when cool, the oxygen sensor may be hard to loosen. To make sensor removal easier, start the engine and let it run for a minute or two, then turn it off.*

7   Raise the vehicle and place it securely on jackstands.

8   Locate the upstream or downstream oxygen sensor, trace the sensor's electrical

lead to the sensor electrical connector (**see illustrations**) and disconnect it.

9   Remove the upstream or downstream oxygen sensor. On some models you can remove the sensor with a wrench. On others, you will have to use an oxygen sensor socket, available at most auto parts stores (**see illustration**). **Note:** *Sensors are easier to remove if they are warm, but not as hot as operating temperature.*

10   Clean the threads inside the sensor mounting hole in the exhaust pipe with an appropriate tap.

11   If you're installing the old sensor, clean off the threads, then apply a coat of anti-seize compound to the threads before installing the sensor. If you're installing a new sensor, do NOT apply anti-seize compound; new sensors are already coated with anti-seize.

12   Installation is otherwise the reverse of removal. Be sure to tighten the oxygen sensor to the torque listed in this Chapter's Specifications.

8.9 An oxygen sensor removal socket is often required when the sensor has never been replaced before

9   Transmission speed sensors - replacement

The speed sensors for the automatic transmission are inside the transmission, not bolted to the outside. They are an integral part of the TCM/valve body, and if a diagnostic trouble code has been set that suggests a problem with these sensors, it is suggested that the procedure be handled by a dealership or specialty transmission shop.

10   Powertrain Control Module (PCM) - removal and installation

Refer to illustration 10.3
Caution: *Avoid static electricity damage to the Powertrain Control Module (PCM) by grounding yourself to the body of the vehicle before touching the PCM and using a special anti-static pad on which to store the PCM once it's removed.*
Note 1: *The PCM is located in the right rear corner of the engine compartment, on the inner side of the right front fender.*
Note 2: *Anytime the PCM is replaced with a new unit, it must be reprogrammed with a scan tool by a dealership service department or other properly equipped repair shop.*
Note 3: *Anytime the battery is disconnected, stored operating parameters may be lost from the PCM, causing the engine to run rough for a period of time while the PCM relearns the information.*
1   Disconnect the cable from the negative battery terminal (see Chapter 5, Section 1).
2   Remove the plastic protective cover over the PCM.
3   Disconnect the electrical connectors from the PCM **(see illustration)**. Note that the electrical connectors are color-coded to prevent mix-ups during installation. Lift the lever on each of the two connectors (one large, one smaller) at the forward end of the PCM, then pull the connectors straight off the PCM.

4   Remove the PCM mounting bolts and carefully remove the PCM.
5   Installation is the reverse of removal. Make sure that you plug each connector into the same color terminal as the connector.

11   Catalytic converter - description, check and replacement

Note: *Because of a Federally-mandated extended warranty which covers emission-related components such as the catalytic converter, check with a dealer service department before replacing the converter at your own expense.*

General description

1   A catalytic converter (or catalyst) is an emission control device in the exhaust system that reduces certain pollutants in the exhaust gas stream. There are two types of converters. An oxidation catalyst reduces hydrocarbons (HC) and carbon monoxide (CO). A reduction catalyst reduces oxides of nitrogen (NOx). A catalyst that can reduce all three pollutants is known as a "Three-Way Catalyst" (TWC). All models covered by this manual are equipped with TWCs.

Check

2   The test equipment for a catalytic converter (a "loaded-mode" dynamometer and a 5-gas analyzer) is expensive. If you suspect that the converter on your vehicle is malfunctioning, take it to a dealer or authorized emission inspection facility for diagnosis and repair. The covered vehicles have Oxygen sensors before and after the catalytic converters. The PCM compares the results of these and determines if the catalytic converter is operating efficiently. If it detects lower efficiency, it should set a trouble code and light the MIL.
3   Whenever you raise the vehicle to service underbody components, inspect the converter for leaks, corrosion, dents and other damage. Carefully inspect the welds and/

or flange bolts and nuts that attach the front and rear ends of the converter to the exhaust system. If you note any damage, replace the converter.
4   Although catalytic converters don't break too often, they can become clogged or even plugged up. The easiest way to check for a restricted converter is to use a vacuum gauge to diagnose the effect of a blocked exhaust on intake vacuum.

   a) *Connect a vacuum gauge to an intake manifold vacuum source (see Chapter 2).*
   b) *Warm the engine to operating temperature, place the transaxle in Park (automatic models) or Neutral (manual models) and apply the parking brake.*
   c) *Note the vacuum reading at idle and jot it down.*
   d) *Quickly open the throttle to near its wide-open position and then quickly get off the throttle and allow it to close. Note the vacuum reading and jot it down.*
   e) *Do this test three more times, recording your measurement after each test.*
   f) *If your fourth reading is more than one in-Hg lower than the reading that you noted at idle, the exhaust system might be restricted (the catalytic converter could be plugged, OR an exhaust pipe or muffler could be restricted).*

Replacement

Refer to illustrations 11.6a, 11.6b and 11.8
Warning: *Make sure that the exhaust system is completely cooled down before proceeding. If the vehicle has just been driven, the catalytic converter can be hot enough to cause serious burns.*
5   Raise the vehicle and place it securely on jackstands.
6   Spray a liberal amount of penetrating oil onto the threads of the catalyst-to-exhaust manifold bolts and the flange bolts that connect the rear of the converter to the exhaust pipe **(see illustrations)**. Wait awhile for the penetrant to loosen things up.
7   While you're waiting for the penetrant to do its work, disconnect the electrical connectors for the upstream and downstream oxygen sensor and remove both oxygen sensors (see Section 8).
8   Unscrew the converter-to-exhaust pipe flange bolts **(see illustration)**. If they're still difficult to loosen, spray the threads with some more penetrant, wait awhile and try again.
9   Remove the catalytic converter assembly. Remove and discard the old flange gasket.
10   Installation is the reverse of removal. Be sure to use a new flange gasket and new bolts at each exhaust manifold mounting flange. The manufacturer also recommends using new clamps at the slip joints. Coat the threads of the clamp and the exhaust manifold bolts with anti-seize compound to facilitate future removal. Tighten the fasteners securely.

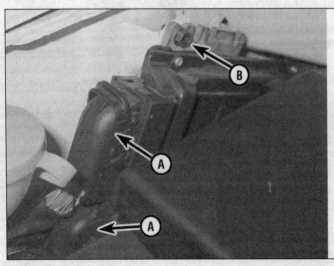

10.3 To disconnect each PCM electrical connector, slide the locks away from the PCM (toward the harness) and pull off the connectors (A), then remove the mounting bolts (B, one indicated here)

11.6a A typical catalytic converter setup on a V6 engine

A   *Primary catalytic converters*
B   *Secondary catalytic converters*

C   *Clamp, bolt and nut on the crossover pipe (always replace)*

12 Evaporative emissions control (EVAP) system - description and component replacement

General description

1   The Evaporative emissions control (EVAP) system prevents fuel system vapors (which contain unburned hydrocarbons) from escaping into the atmosphere. On warm days, vapors trapped inside the fuel tank expand. When the pressure reaches a certain threshold, these vapors are routed from the fuel tank through the fuel vapor vent valve and the fuel vapor control valve to the EVAP canister, where they're stored temporarily, until they can be consumed by the engine during normal operation. Under certain conditions (engine warmed up, vehicle up to speed, moderate or heavy loads, etc.) the Powertrain Control Module (PCM) opens the canister purge solenoid, which allows intake vacuum to pull fuel vapors from the EVAP canister into the intake manifold, where they mix with the air/fuel mixture before being consumed in the combustion chambers. This system is complex and virtually impossible to troubleshoot without the right tools and training. However, the following description should give you a good idea of how the system works and where the components are located:

2   The EVAP canister, which contains activated charcoal, stores fuel vapors produced by gasoline as it heats up inside the fuel tank. You'll have to raise the vehicle to inspect or replace the canister, but the canister is designed to be maintenance-free and should last the life of the vehicle. The EVAP canister is located underneath the vehicle, just behind the left-rear wheel opening.

3   The EVAP Control System Pressure Sensor monitors the temperature of the unburned hydrocarbon vapors inside the EVAP system. As the temperature increases, so does the

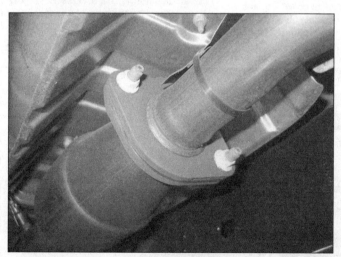

11.6b To disconnect the catalyst from the exhaust manifold, remove the heat shield over the manifold, then the flange bolts. When reconnecting a flanged joint on a converter or pipe, be sure to use a new gasket and new bolts

11.8 Converter-to-exhaust pipe flange bolts - always replace the gasket when reconnecting any exhaust flanges

pressure; as the temperature decreases, so does the pressure. But this effect can occur only if the system is fully sealed. If there's a leak, the relationship between pressure and temperature will diverge from the pressure-temperature relationship that the Powertrain Control Module (PCM) is programmed to expect. The PCM learns of fuel temperature through input from the Fuel Tank Temperature Sensor. When this divergence between the pressure and the temperature of the fuel occurs, the PCM concludes that the system is leaking and it sets a Diagnostic Trouble Code (DTC) indicating either a small, medium or large leak in the EVAP system. Diagnosis of the NVLD pump and detection system is beyond the scope of the home mechanic. If a DTC indicates a problem with the system, have a dealer service department or other qualified repair shop repair the vehicle.

4   The EVAP canister purge solenoid, which is under the control of the Powertrain Control Module (PCM), regulates the flow of vapors being purged from the EVAP canister into the intake manifold. The canister purge solenoid is normally closed. It opens only when directed to do so by the PCM, which uses the availability of intake manifold vacuum and data from various information sensor inputs to determine when and how long to open the valve. The interval of time during which the purge valve is opened by the PCM is known as its "duty cycle." The canister purge solenoid valve is located in the engine compartment, to the right of the power brake booster.

General system checks

5   The most common symptom of a faulty EVAP system is a strong fuel odor (particularly during hot weather). If you smell fuel while driving or (more likely) right after you park the vehicle and turn off the engine, check the fuel filler cap first. Make sure that it's screwed onto the fuel filler neck all the way. If the odor persists, inspect all EVAP hose connections, both in the engine compartment and under the vehicle. You'll have to raise the vehicle and place it securely on jackstands to inspect most of the EVAP system, since it's located under the vehicle. Be sure to inspect each hose attached to the canister for damage and leakage along its entire length. Repair or replace as necessary. Inspect the canister for damage and look for fuel leaking from the bottom. If fuel is leaking or the canister is otherwise damaged, replace it.

6   Poor idle, stalling, and poor driveability can be caused by a defective fuel vapor vent valve or canister purge solenoid, a damaged canister, cracked hoses, or hoses connected to the wrong tubes. Fuel loss or fuel odor can be caused by fuel leaking from fuel lines or hoses, a cracked or damaged canister, or a defective vapor valve.

7   To check for excessive fuel vapor pressure in the fuel tank, remove the gas cap and listen for the sound of pressure release. If the fuel tank emits a "whooshing" sound when you open the filler cap, fuel tank vapor pressure is

12.9a To remove the EVAP canister purge volume control solenoid on four-cylinder engines, disconnect the electrical connector, label and disconnect the EVAP hoses and unbolt the solenoid from the intake plenum

excessive. Inspect the canister vapor hoses and the canister inlet port for blockage or collapsed hoses. Also inspect the hose for the EVAP canister vent valve. A complete test can only be done with a proprietary OBD-II scan tool (see Section 2), which will run a series of checks to detect excessive pressure. You'll have to take the vehicle to a dealer service department to have the EVAP system professionally diagnosed.

Component replacement
EVAP canister purge volume control solenoid

Refer to illustrations 12.9a and 12.9b

8   Disconnect the cable from the negative battery terminal (see Chapter 5, Section 1). The solenoid is located on top of the intake manifold on four-cylinder engines, and just above the timing chain cover on V6 engines.

9   Disconnect the electrical connector from the EVAP canister purge volume solenoid **(see illustrations)**.

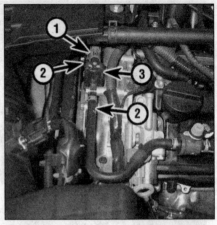

12.9b To remove the EVAP canister purge volume control solenoid on V6 engines, disconnect the electrical connector (1), label and disconnect the EVAP hoses (2) and unbolt the solenoid (3) from the front of the engine

10   Clearly label the EVAP hoses, then disconnect them from the EVAP canister purge solenoid.

11   Unbolt the EVAP canister purge volume solenoid from its mounting bracket.

12   Installation is the reverse of removal.

EVAP canister

Refer to illustration 12.14

Note: *The EVAP canister assembly is located just behind the left-rear wheel opening.*

13   Raise the vehicle and place it securely on jackstands. Remove the left-rear wheel.

14   Disconnect the hoses and any electrical connectors at the EVAP canister, then remove the mounting bolt and remove the canister **(see illustration)**. When disconnecting the vent valve or the system pressure sensor, twist them counterclockwise to remove.

15   Installation is the reverse of removal. When reinstalling the pressure sensor or vent valve to the canister, lubricate and install new O-rings.

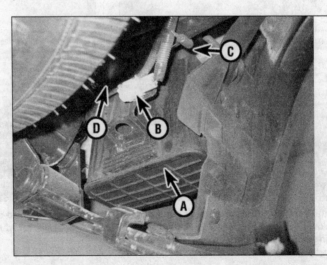

12.14 EVAP canister details:

A   *EVAP canister*
B   *Electrical connector*
C   *Canister vent control valve*
D   *EVAP control system pressure sensor*

13.2 On all engines, the PCV valve is located on the valve cover (V6 shown, four-cylinder similar)

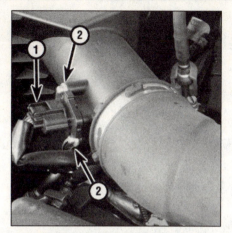

14.3a Four-cylinder MAF/IAT sensor location - disconnect the connector (1) and remove the mounting screws (2)

14.3b V6 MAF/IAT sensor location - disconnect the connector (A) and remove the mounting screws (B)

13 Positive Crankcase Ventilation (PCV) system - description and check

Description

Refer to illustration 13.2

Note: *For specific information on how to replace the PCV valves on the engines covered by this manual, see Chapter 1.*

1   The Positive Crankcase Ventilation (PCV) system reduces hydrocarbon emissions by scavenging crankcase vapors, which are rich in unburned hydrocarbons. A PCV valve regulates the flow of gases into the intake manifold in proportion to the amount of intake vacuum available. At idle, when intake vacuum is very high, the PCV valve restricts the flow of vapors so that the engine doesn't run poorly. As the throttle plate opens and intake vacuum begins to diminish, the PCV valve opens more to allow vapors to flow more freely.

2   On both four-cylinder and V6 engines, the PCV system consists of a fresh air inlet hose that connects the air inlet tube to one corner of the valve cover; the PCV valve **(see illustration)**, which is located in the other end of the valve cover; and the crankcase ventilation hose that connects the PCV valve to the intake manifold.

Inspection

3   An engine that is operated without a properly functioning crankcase ventilation system can be damaged. So anytime you're servicing the engine, be sure to inspect the PCV system hose(s) for cracks, tears, deterioration and other damage. Disconnect the hose(s) and inspect it/them for damage and obstructions. If a hose is clogged, clean it out. If you're unable to clean it satisfactorily, replace it.

4   A plugged PCV hose might cause any or all of the following conditions: A rough idle, stalling or a slow idle speed, oil leaks or sludge in the engine. So if the engine is run-

ning roughly, stalling and idling at a lower than normal speed, or is losing oil, or has oil in the throttle body or air intake manifold plenum, or has a build-up of sludge, a PCV system hose might be clogged. Repair or replace the hose(s) as necessary.

5   A leaking PCV hose might cause any or all of the following conditions: a rough idle, stalling or a high idle speed. So if the engine is running roughly, stalling and idling at a higher than normal speed, a PCV system hose might be leaking. Repair or replace the hose(s) as necessary.

6   Here's an easy functional check of the PCV system on a vehicle with a fresh air inlet hose and a crankcase ventilation hose with a PCV valve in it:

a)   *Disconnect the crankcase ventilation hose (the crankcase ventilation hose, or simply "the PCV hose," is the hose that connects the PCV valve to the intake manifold).*

b)   *Start the engine and let it warm up to its normal idle.*

c)   *Verify that there is vacuum at the PCV hose. If there is no vacuum, look for a plugged hose or a clogged port or pipe on the intake manifold. Also look for a hose that collapses when it's blocked (when vacuum is applied). Replace clogged or deteriorated hoses.*

d)   *Remove the engine oil dipstick and install a vacuum gauge on the upper end of the dipstick tube.*

e)   *Pinch off or plug the PCV system's fresh air inlet hose.*

f)   *Run the engine at 1500 rpm for 30 seconds, then read the vacuum gauge while the engine is running at 1500 rpm.*

g)   *If there's vacuum present, the crankcase ventilation system is operating correctly.*

h)   *If there's NO vacuum present, the engine might be drawing in outside air. The PCV system won't function correctly unless the engine is a sealed system. Inspect the valve cover(s), oil pan gasket or other sealing areas for leaks.*

i)   *If the vacuum gauge indicates positive pressure, look for a plugged hose or engine blow-by.*

7   If the PCV system is functioning correctly, but there's evidence of engine oil in the throttle body or air filter housing, it could be caused by excessive crankcase pressure. Have the crankcase pressure tested by a dealer service department.

8   In the PCV system, excessive blow-by (caused by worn rings, pistons and/or cylinders, or by constant heavy loads) is discharged into the intake manifold and consumed. If you discover heavy sludge deposits or a dilution of the engine oil, even though the PCV system is functioning correctly, look for other causes (see the *Troubleshooting* section at the front of this manual and Chapter 2C) and correct them as soon as possible.

14 Mass Airflow sensor/Intake Air Temperature sensor (MAF/IAT) - replacement

Refer to illustrations 14.3a and 14.3b

1   Disconnect the cable from the negative battery terminal (see Chapter 5, Section 1).

2   On both V6 and four-cylinder models the MAF/IAT sensor is located on the intake duct, between the air filter housing and the intake manifold.

3   To replace an MAF/IAT sensor, disconnect the electrical connector, then remove the two mounting screws **(see illustrations)**. **Caution:** *Handle the sensor carefully at all times and keep it away from dust or contaminants. The sensor has a fragile wire as it's most important component, and the sensors are expensive to replace.*

4   Inspect the condition of the rubber grommet that seals the entry hole for the sensor. If it's cracked, torn or otherwise damaged, replace it.

5   Installation is the reverse of the removal procedure.

Notes

Chapter 7 Part A
Manual transmission

Contents

Specifications

General

Transmission lubricant type	See Chapter 1

Torque specifications

Note: *One foot-pound (ft-lb) of torque is equivalent to 12 inch-pounds (in-lbs) of torque. Torque values below approximately 15 ft-lbs are expressed in inch-pounds, since most foot-pound torque wrenches are not accurate at these smaller values.*

	Ft-lbs (unless otherwise indicated)	Nm
Backup light switch or Park-Neutral switch	15 to 21	20 to 28
Crossmember bolts	74	100
Transmission-to-engine fasteners		
Five-speed (see text)		
A screws (flywheel cover) and B bolt	25	34
C bolts	55	75
Six-speed	55	75

1 General information

The vehicles covered by this manual are equipped with either a five-speed or six-speed manual transmission or a five-speed automatic transmission. Information on the automatic transmission can be found in Part B of this Chapter. Information on the transfer case used on 4WD models can be found in Part C of this Chapter.

Nissan Frontier pickups equipped with four-cylinder engines use the FS5R30A five-speed manual transmission, while V6 engines in either the Frontier or the Xterra models use the six-speed FS6R31A manual transmission. Both units are fully-synchronized with internal shift-rail mechanisms.

Depending on the cost of having a trans-mission overhauled, it might be a better idea to replace it with a used or rebuilt unit. Your local dealer or transmission shop (and even some auto parts stores) should be able to supply information concerning cost, availability and exchange policy. Regardless of how you decide to remedy a transmission problem, you can still save a lot of money by removing and installing the unit yourself.

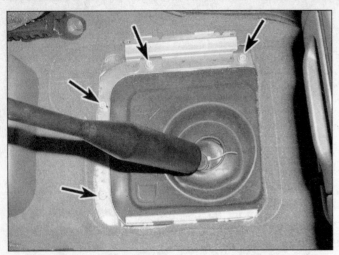

2.2 Remove the bolts (not all are visible here) and pull up the floor pan boot at the bottom of the shifter . . .

2.3 . . . then loosen the clamp, pull the shifter boot up and remove the snap-ring

2 Shift lever - removal and installation

Refer to illustrations 2.2 and 2.3

1   Unscrew the shift knob from the shifter, then remove the cupholder trim bezel from the floor (see Chapter 11). **Note:** *When installing the shift knob, use a dab of glue on the threads.*
2   Unscrew the bolts securing the floor pan boot retainer to the floor pan. Loosen the clamps and pull up the boot at the base of the shift lever **(see illustration)**.
3   Remove the snap-ring and withdraw the shift lever from the transmission **(see illustration)**. Note the order of the washers and rubber seat under the shift lever (the proper order, from the top, is: washer, wave washer, washer, rubber seat). **Note:** *Discard the snap-ring; a new one should be used when installing the lever.*
4   Before installing the shift lever, lubricate the rubber seat, the ball on the shift lever and the end of the lever with multi-purpose grease.
5   Installation is the reverse of removal. Be sure to install a new snap-ring, and make sure it seats fully.

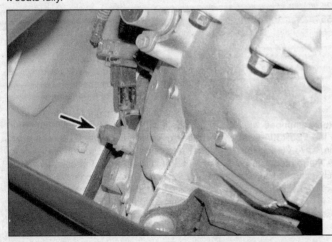

4.1 Location of the Neutral position switch - FS5R30A transmission

3 Back-up light switch - check and replacement

1   The back-up light switch is located on the right side of the transmission case; it's the switch closer to the front of the transmission (the other one is the neutral position switch).

Check

2   Turn the ignition key to the On position and move the shift lever to the Reverse position; the back-up lights should go on.
3   If the lights don't go on, check the back-up light fuse first (see Chapter 12). If the fuse is blown, trace the back-up light circuit for a short-circuit condition.
4   If the fuse is okay, raise the vehicle and support it securely on jackstands. Place the shifter in Reverse.
5   Working under the vehicle, unplug the back-up light switch electrical connector. Using an ohmmeter, check for continuity across the terminals of the switch. Continuity should exist. If not, replace the switch. **Note:** *If the switch has continuity, make sure it doesn't have continuity in any position other than Reverse.*

6   If the switch has continuity, check for voltage at the electrical connector; one of the two terminals should have battery voltage present with the ignition key in the On position. If no voltage is present, trace the circuit between the fuse block and the electrical connector for an open circuit condition.
7   If voltage is present, trace the back-up light circuit between the electrical connector and the back-up light bulbs for an open circuit condition. **Note:** *Although not very likely, the back-up light bulbs could both be burned out; don't rule out this possibility.*

Replacement

8   Raise the vehicle and support it securely on jackstands, if not already done.
9   Unplug the back-up light switch electrical connector.
10   Unscrew the back-up light switch from the transmission case.
11   Apply RTV sealant or Teflon tape to the threads of the new switch to prevent leakage. Install the switch in the transmission case and tighten it securely. Plug in the electrical connector. **Note:** *The replacement switch may come equipped with thread sealant already applied to the threads. Do not apply RTV sealant or Teflon tape to the threads of the new switch if thread sealant has already been applied by the manufacturer.*
12   Lower the vehicle and check the operation of the back-up lights.

4 Neutral position switch - check and replacement

Refer to illustration 4.1

1   The Neutral position switch is located on the right side of the transmission case **(see illustration)**; it's the switch closer to the rear of the transmission (the other one is the back-up light switch).

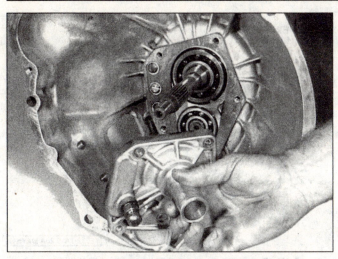

5.3 Unscrew the bolts and detach the input shaft bearing retainer from the transmission

5.4 Carefully pry the seal out of the input shaft bearing retainer

Check

2   Place the shift lever in the Neutral position. Raise the vehicle and support it securely on jackstands. Unplug the electrical connector from the Neutral position switch and, using an ohmmeter, check for continuity across the terminals of the switch. Continuity should exist. If not, replace the switch. **Note:** *If the switch has continuity, make sure it doesn't have continuity in any position other than Neutral.*

Replacement

3   Raise the vehicle and support it securely on jackstands, if not already done.
4   Unplug the Neutral position switch electrical connector.
5   Unscrew the switch from the transmission case.
6   Apply RTV sealant or Teflon tape to the threads of the new switch to prevent leakage. Install the switch in the transmission case and tighten it securely. Plug in the electrical connector. **Note:** *The replacement switch may come equipped with thread sealant already applied to the threads. Do not apply RTV sealant or Teflon tape to the threads of the new switch if thread sealant has already been applied by the manufacturer.*

---

5   Oil seals - replacement

Front oil seal

Refer to illustrations 5.3 and 5.4
1   Remove the transmission (see Section 6).
2   Remove the release bearing (see Chapter 8).
3   Remove the bolts that retain the transmission input shaft bearing retainer to the case and lift off the retainer **(see illustration)**.
4   Being careful not to nick or damage the retainer, pry out the seal **(see illustration)**.
5   Drive the new seal into position in the retainer using a seal driver or an appropriate

sized socket.
6   Apply a light coat of gear oil to the seal lips and the input shaft, then reinstall the bearing retainer.
7   The remainder of installation is the reverse of removal. Tighten the input shaft bearing retainer bolts to the torque listed in this Chapter's Specifications.

Extension housing oil seal

8   See Chapter 7B for the extension housing oil seal procedure.

---

6   Manual transmission - removal and installation

Removal

1   Disconnect the cable from the negative terminal of the battery.
2   Remove the Crankshaft Position sensor (see Chapter 6).
3   Remove the shift lever (see Section 2).
4   Raise the vehicle sufficiently to provide clearance to easily remove the transmission. Support the vehicle securely on jackstands.
5   Remove the skid plate, if equipped.
6   Disconnect the electrical connector from the back-up light switch, the neutral position switch and the vehicle speed sensor. Disengage the wiring harness from the clips on the transmission. If you're working on a 4WD model, unplug all of the electrical connectors from the transfer case.
7   Drain the transmission lubricant (see Chapter 1).
8   Remove the driveshaft(s) (see Chapter 8).
9   Remove exhaust system components as necessary for clearance (see Chapter 4).
10   Remove the starter motor (see Chapter 5).
11   Unbolt the clutch release cylinder from the transmission (see Chapter 8). Tie the cylinder out of the way with a piece of wire. **Caution:** *Don't depress the clutch pedal while the*

release cylinder is removed.
12   Disconnect and set aside the transmission breather hose. On some models, there are front and rear brackets securing the breather hose to the transmission. Unbolt the brackets.
13   Support the engine from above with an engine hoist or an engine support fixture, or place a jack (with a block of wood as an insulator) under the engine oil pan. The engine must remain supported at all times while the transmission is out of the vehicle.
14   Support the transmission with a jack - preferably a special jack made for this purpose. **Note:** *These jacks can be obtained at most equipment rental yards.* Safety chains will help steady the transmission on the jack.
15   Raise the engine slightly and disconnect the transmission mount from the extension housing and the center crossmember (see Chapter 7B).
16   Raise the transmission slightly and remove the bolts and nuts attaching the crossmember to the frame rails.
17   Lower the jacks supporting the transmission and engine assembly enough to gain access to all of the mounting bolts.
18   Remove the bolts attaching the transmission to the engine, and also unbolt the engine-to-transmission gussets from the engine block. A long extension with a U-joint socket or adapter will be helpful in unscrewing the upper bolts. **Note:** *The bolts securing the transmission to the engine are different lengths. When removing the bolts, mark their positions or lay them out in order so they can be reinstalled in their original locations.*
19   Make a final check for any wiring or hoses connected to the transmission, then move the transmission and jack toward the rear of the vehicle until the transmission input shaft clears the splined hub in the clutch disc. Keep the transmission level as this is done.
20   Once the input shaft is clear, lower the transmission and remove it from under the vehicle.
21   While the transmission is removed, be

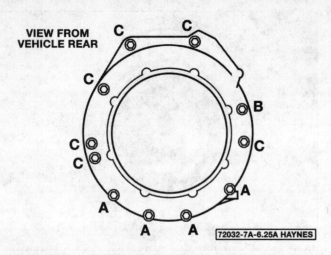

VIEW FROM
VEHICLE REAR

72032-7A-6.25A HAYNES

**6.25a Transmission-to-engine mounting bolt identification -
five-speed transmissions**

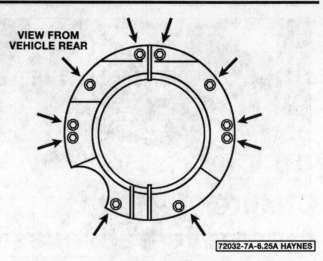

VIEW FROM
VEHICLE REAR

72032-7A-6.25A HAYNES

**6.25b Transmission-to-engine mounting bolt locations -
six-speed transmissions**

sure to remove and inspect all clutch components (see Chapter 8). In most cases, new clutch components should be routinely installed if the transmission is removed. Also inspect the front oil seal and replace it if necessary (see Section 5).

Installation

Refer to illustrations 6.25a and 6.25b

22   Insert a small amount of multi-purpose grease into the pilot bushing in the crankshaft and lubricate the inner surface of the bushing. Also apply a light film of grease on the input shaft splines, the area on the front cover where the release bearing rides, and the release lever/bearing contact points (see Chapter 8).

23   Install the clutch components if removed (see Chapter 8).

24   With the transmission secured to the jack as on removal, raise the transmission into position behind the engine and then carefully slide it forward, engaging the input shaft with the clutch plate hub. Do not use excessive force to install the transmission - if the input shaft does not slide into place, readjust the angle of the transmission so it is level and/ or turn the input shaft so the splines engage properly with the clutch.

25   Install the transmission-to-engine bolts in their proper locations and tighten them to the torque listed in this Chapter's Specifications **(see illustrations). Caution:** *Don't use the bolts to draw the transmission to the engine. If the transmission doesn't slide forward easily and mate with the engine block, find out why before proceeding.*

26   Raise the transmission into place, install the crossmember and attach it to the frame

rails. Install the transmission mount between the extension housing and the crossmember. Carefully lower the transmission extension housing onto the mount and the crossmember. When everything is properly aligned, tighten all nuts and bolts securely.

27   Remove the jacks supporting the transmission and the engine.

28   Install the various items removed previously, referring to Chapter 8 for the installation of the driveshaft(s) and clutch release cylinder, Chapter 5 for the starter motor, Chapter 6 for the Crankshaft Position sensor, and Chapter 4 for the exhaust system components.

29   Plug in the electrical connector for the Vehicle Speed Sensor, the back-up light switch and the Neutral position switch. Connect any other wiring attached to the transmission or the transfer case.

30   Remove the jackstands and lower the vehicle.

31   Install the shift lever(s) (see Section 2).

32   Fill the transmission with the specified lubricant to the proper level (see Chapter 1).

33   Connect the cable to the negative terminal of the battery.

34   Road test the vehicle for proper operation and check for leakage.

7   Manual transmission overhaul - general information

Overhauling a manual transmission is a difficult job for the do-it-yourselfer. It involves the disassembly and reassembly of many small parts. Numerous clearances must be precisely measured and, if necessary, changed with select fit spacers and

snap-rings. As a result, if transmission problems arise, it can be removed and installed by a competent do-it-yourselfer, but overhaul should be left to a transmission repair shop. Rebuilt transmissions may be available - check with your dealer parts department and auto parts stores. At any rate, the time and money involved in an overhaul is almost sure to exceed the cost of a rebuilt unit.

Nevertheless, it's not impossible for an inexperienced mechanic to rebuild a transmission if the special tools are available and the job is done in a deliberate step-by-step manner so nothing is overlooked.

The tools necessary for an overhaul include internal and external snap-ring pliers, a bearing puller, a slide hammer, a set of pin punches, feeler gauges, a dial indicator and possibly a hydraulic press. In addition, a large, sturdy workbench and a vise or transmission stand will be required.

During disassembly of the transmission, make careful notes of how each piece comes off, where it fits in relation to other pieces and what holds it in place. If you note how each part is installed before removing it, getting the transmission back together again will be much easier.

Before taking the transmission apart for repair, it will help if you have some idea what area of the transmission is malfunctioning. Certain problems can be closely tied to specific areas in the transmission, which can make component examination and replacement easier. Refer to the *Troubleshooting* Section at the front of this manual for information regarding possible sources of trouble.

Chapter 7 Part B
Automatic transmission

Contents

Specifications

General

Transmission fluid type	See Chapter 1

Torque Specifications

Note: *One foot-pound (ft-lb) of torque is equivalent to 12 inch-pounds (in-lbs) of torque. Torque values below approximately 15 ft-lbs are expressed in inch-pounds, since most foot-pound torque wrenches are not accurate at these smaller values.*

	Ft-lbs (unless otherwise indicated)	Nm
Transmission fluid pan bolts	70 in-lbs	8
Torque converter-to-driveplate bolts	38	52
Transmission-to-engine bolts		
Four-cylinder engine **(see illustration 9.25a)**		
A screws (flywheel cover) and B bolt	25	34
C bolts	55	75
V6 **(see illustration 9.25b)**	55	75

1   General information

The vehicles covered by this manual are equipped with either a five-speed or six-speed manual transmission or a five-speed automatic transmission. Information on the manual transmission is in Part A of this Chapter. Information on the automatic transmission is included in this Part of Chapter 7. You'll also find certain procedures common to both automatic and manual transmissions - such as oil seal replacement and transmission mount replacement - in this Part of Chapter 7.

All models use the same five-speed automatic transmission. The RE5R05A transmission is electronically controlled, using sensors from the engine control system, the Transmission Control Module (TCM) and solenoids inside the transmission to regulate shift points, fluid pressure and other parameters.

These transmissions are equipped with a torque converter clutch (TCC) that provides a direct connection between the engine and the drive wheels for improved efficiency and economy. The TCC consists of a solenoid controlled by the Powertrain Control Module (PCM) that locks the converter when the vehicle is cruising on level ground and the engine is fully warmed up.

Due to the complexity of the automatic transmissions covered in this manual and the need for specialized equipment to perform most service operations, this Chapter contains only general diagnosis, routine maintenance, adjustment and removal and installation procedures.

If the transmission requires major repair work, it should be left to a dealer service department or an automotive or transmission repair shop. You can, however, remove and install the transmission yourself and save the expense, even if the repair work is done by a transmission shop.

2   Diagnosis and trouble codes

Note: *Automatic transmission malfunctions may be caused by five general conditions: poor engine performance, improper adjustments, hydraulic malfunctions, mechanical malfunctions or malfunctions in the computer or its signal network. Diagnosis of these problems should always begin with a check of the easily repaired items: fluid level and condition (see Chapter 1), shift linkage adjustment and throttle linkage adjustment. Next, perform a road test to determine if the problem has been corrected or if more diagnosis is necessary. If the problem persists after the preliminary tests and corrections are completed, additional diagnosis should be done by a dealer service department or transmission repair shop. Refer to the* Troubleshooting *section at the front of this manual for information on symptoms of transmission problems.*

Preliminary checks

1   Drive the vehicle to warm the transmission to normal operating temperature.
2   Check the fluid level as described in Chapter 1:
a) If the fluid level is unusually low, add enough fluid to bring the level within the designated area of the dipstick, then check for external leaks (see below).
b) If the fluid level is abnormally high, drain off the excess, then check the drained fluid for contamination by coolant. The presence of engine coolant in the automatic transmission fluid indicates that a failure has occurred in the internal radiator walls that separate the coolant from the transmission fluid (see Chapter 3).
c) If the fluid is foaming, drain it and refill the transmission, then check for coolant in the fluid, or a high fluid level.
3   Make sure the ignition timing and engine idle speed is correct (see Chapter 4).
4   Inspect the fluid lines and fluid cooler for signs of damage or leaking fluid. Also examine the various electrical connectors at the transmission for evidence of corrosion or poor connections.

Fluid leak diagnosis

5   Most fluid leaks are easy to locate visually. Repair usually consists of replacing a seal or gasket. If a leak is difficult to find, the following procedure may help.
6   Identify the fluid. Make sure it's transmission fluid and not engine oil or brake fluid (automatic transmission fluid is a deep red color).
7   Try to pinpoint the source of the leak. Drive the vehicle several miles, then park it over a large sheet of cardboard. After a minute or two, you should be able to locate the leak by determining the source of the fluid dripping onto the cardboard.
8   Make a careful visual inspection of the suspected component and the area immediately around it. Pay particular attention to gas-

ket mating surfaces. A mirror is often helpful for finding leaks in areas that are hard to see.
9   If the leak still cannot be found, clean the suspected area thoroughly with a degreaser or solvent, then dry it.
10   Drive the vehicle for several miles at normal operating temperature and varying speeds. After driving the vehicle, visually inspect the suspected component again.
11   Once the leak has been located, the cause must be determined before it can be properly repaired. If a gasket is replaced but the sealing flange is bent, the new gasket will not stop the leak. The bent flange must be straightened.
12   Before attempting to repair a leak, check to make sure that the following conditions are corrected or they may cause another leak.
Note: *Some of the following conditions cannot be fixed without highly specialized tools and expertise. Such problems must be referred to a transmission shop or a dealer service department.*

Gasket leaks

13   Check the pan periodically. Make sure the bolts are tight, no bolts are missing, the gasket is in good condition and the pan is flat (dents in the pan may indicate damage to the valve body inside).
14   If the pan gasket is leaking, the fluid level or the fluid pressure may be too high, the vent may be plugged, the pan bolts may be too tight, the pan sealing flange may be warped, the sealing surface of the transmission housing may be damaged, the gasket may be damaged or the transmission casting may be cracked or porous. If sealant instead of gasket material has been used to form a seal between the pan and the transmission housing, it may be the wrong sealant.

Seal leaks

15   If a transmission seal is leaking, the fluid level or pressure may be too high, the vent may be plugged, the seal bore may be damaged, the seal itself may be damaged or improperly installed, the surface of the shaft protruding through the seal may be damaged or a loose bearing may be causing excessive shaft movement.
16   Make sure the dipstick tube seal is in good condition and the tube is properly seated. Periodically check the area around the vehicle speed sensor for leakage. If transmission fluid is evident, check the O-ring for damage.

Case leaks

17   If the case itself appears to be leaking, the casting is porous and will have to be repaired or replaced.
18   Make sure the oil cooler hose fittings are tight and in good condition.

Fluid comes out vent pipe or fill tube

19   If this condition occurs, the transmission is overfilled, there is coolant in the fluid, the case is porous, the dipstick is incorrect, the

vent is plugged or the drain-back holes are plugged.

Diagnostic trouble codes

20   The computer for the automatic transmission has a self-diagnostic capability; it continually monitors important information sensor and output actuator circuits for malfunctions. When a monitored circuit is damaged, shorted or disconnected, a diagnostic trouble code is stored in the computer's memory. At a dealer service department, stored trouble codes are extracted from computer memory with a proprietary diagnostic instrument known as CONSULT. Codes can also be extracted with some generic scanners. However, the CONSULT tool isn't generally available to anyone outside of a Nissan dealership, and most home mechanics don't have a generic scan tool, so the following procedure is provided to enable you to extract any stored codes by using the O/D OFF indicator light on the instrument cluster. **Note:** *If you do have a scan tool, refer to Chapter 6 for code retrieval information and for the list of trouble codes.*

Make sure the O/D OFF light works

21   Move the shift lever to the P position, if it isn't already there.
22   Start the engine and warm it up to its normal operating temperature.
23   Turn the ignition switch On and Off two times, ending in the Off position. Wait at least 10 seconds before proceeding.
24   Turn the ignition switch to the ON position, but don't start the engine.
25   The O/D OFF indicator light should come on for about two seconds.
a) If the O/D OFF indicator light comes on, proceed to the next Step.
b) If the O/D OFF indicator light doesn't come on, there's something wrong with the transmission computer or with the indicator light circuit. We don't recommend testing the resistance or voltage of the computer terminals; drawing too much current or putting too much voltage through the terminals can destroy the computer. Have the O/D OFF indicator light circuit tested and repaired by a dealer service department or other qualified repair shop.

Obtaining stored codes using the O/D OFF light

Refer to illustration 2.26 and 2.32
26   Turn the ignition switch OFF, then push in the Shift-Lock release button with a small screwdriver **(see illustration)**. **Note:** *Use a small screwdriver to remove the little cover over the Shift-Lock release button.*
27   With vehicle parking brake applied, move the shift lever from P to D, then release the accelerator pedal.
28   Depress the brake pedal and hold it. Turn the ignition switch to the On position (without starting the engine) for at least three seconds.

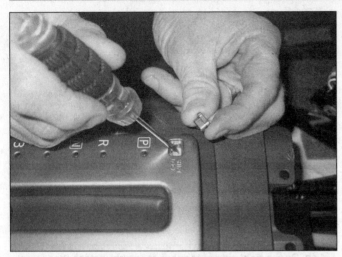

2.26 Shift-Lock release button location

Blinks	Suspected Transmission Control Module Trouble Codes
1	Transmission revolution sensor
2	Direct clutch solenoid valve
3	Torque converter clutch solenoid valve
4	Line pressure solenoid valve
5	Input clutch solenoid valve
6	Front brake solenoid valve
7	Low coast brake solenoid valve
8	High/Low reverse clutch solenoid valve
9	Park-Neutral position switch
10	Transmission fluid temperature sensor
11	Turbine revolution sensor
12	Transmission safety shift interlock
13	1st engine braking
14	Start signal
15	Accelerator Pedal Position sensor
16	Engine speed signal
17	CAN (network)

2.32 Automatic transmission trouble codes retrievable through the OD On/Off light procedure

29 Now move the shifter from D to 3 position, then release the brake pedal.

30 Move the shifter from 3 to 2 and once again depress the brake pedal.

31 Depress the accelerator pedal all the way and release it. This should begin the self-diagnosis program.

32 The OD On/Off light should illuminate for 2.5 seconds, go off for 2 seconds, then start a series of blinks. Count each of the one-second-On blinks and compare the count to the chart of the TCM trouble codes (see illustration).

33 Repairing the rest of the malfunctions listed above is beyond the scope of the home mechanic. If one or more of these codes is displayed, have the transmission repaired by a dealer service department or transmission repair shop.

Erasing a diagnostic trouble code

34 If you have the transmission repaired at a dealer or transmission shop, they will erase

the trouble code when they're done making the repair.

3   Shift cable - check, adjustment and replacement

Check

1 Move the shift lever from the "P" position to the "1" position. You should be able to feel the detents in each range. If you can't feel the detents, or if the pointer indicating the ranges is incorrectly aligned, adjust the shift cable.

Adjustment

Refer to illustration 3.4

2 Place the shift lever in the "P" position.

3 Raise the vehicle and support it securely on jackstands.

4 Loosen the shift cable-to-manual lever locknut (see illustration). Place the manual shift lever in the "P" position.

5 Push the cable into the casing with a force of about 2.2 pounds (9.8 Nm), then release the cable and let it find its relaxed position. Tighten the nut on the cable at the manual lever.

6 Move the shifter through its range, making sure that the engine can be started only in Park or N, and that the backup lights illuminate only when the shifter is in Reverse.

7 Remove the jackstands and lower the vehicle.

Replacement

Refer to illustration 3.9

Warning: *The models covered by this manual are equipped with airbags. Always disable the airbag system when working in the vicinity of airbag system components (see Chapter 12).*

8 Refer to Chapter 11 and remove the floor console and the bezel around the floor shifter.

9 Remove the clip and detach the cable end from the post on the lever (see illustration).

10 Pry off the clip from the cable casing

3.4 Automatic transmission shift cable (right side of the transmission) - the shift cable nut (A) is for adjustment, the clip (B) is for removal of the cable from its bracket

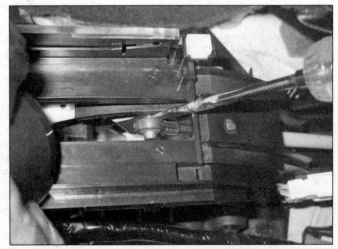

3.9 To replace the shift cable, pry the end from the ballstud at the shifter then remove the clip securing the cable at the front of the shift tower (see illustration 4.4a)

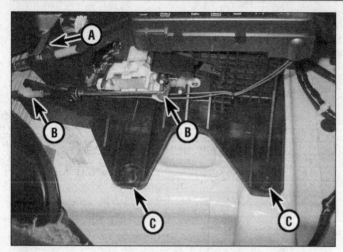

4.4a On the left side of the shift assembly, detach the shift cable (A) at the front, detach the shift interlock cable (B), and remove the two left-side mounting bolts (C)

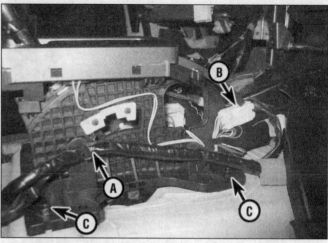

4.4b On the right side of the shift assembly, detach the wiring harness (A), disconnect the electrical connector (B), then remove the two right-side mounting bolts

where the cable passes through the floor pan **(see illustration 4.4a)**.

11   Raise the front of the vehicle and support it securely on jackstands.

12   Remove the clip and detach the cable from the manual lever on the side of the transmission **(see illustration 3.4)**.

13   Detach the cable from the bracket on the transmission, then pass the cable through the floor pan and remove it.

14   Installation is the reverse of removal. Be sure to adjust the cable when you're done.

4   Shift lever assembly - removal and installation

Refer to illustrations 4.4a and 4.4b

Warning: *The models covered by this manual are equipped with airbags. Always disable the airbag system when working in the vicinity of airbag system components (see Chapter 12).*

1   Refer to Section 3 and perform Steps 8 through 13.

2   Disconnect the key interlock cable from the shift lock solenoid and from its bracket at the front of the shifter base (see Section 5).

3   Unplug any electrical connectors that may interfere with shifter removal.

4   Remove the two nuts from each side of the shifter assembly **(see illustrations)**, then detach the shifter assembly from the floor.

5   Installation is the reverse of removal. Be sure to adjust the shift cable (see Section 3) and the interlock cable (see Section 5).

5   Shift interlock system - description, check and adjustment

Warning: *The models covered by this manual are equipped with airbags. Always disable the*

airbag system when working in the vicinity of airbag system components (see Chapter 12).

Description

1   The shift interlock system prevents the shift lever from being shifted out of Park or Neutral until the brake pedal is applied. Other than the following simple component checks, diagnosis of the shift lock system should be left to a dealer service department or other qualified repair shop.

Check

Refer to illustration 5.7

2   Verify that the ignition key can be removed only in the PARK position.

3   When the shift lever is in the PARK position, you should be able to rotate the ignition key from OFF to LOCK. But when the shift lever is in any gear position other than PARK (including NEUTRAL), you should not be able to rotate the ignition key to the LOCK position.

4   You should not be able to move the shift lever out of the PARK position when the ignition key is turned to the OFF position.

5   You should not be able to move the shift lever out of the PARK position when the ignition key is turned to the RUN or START position until you depress the brake pedal.

6   You should not be able to move the shift lever out of the PARK position when the ignition key is turned to the ACC or LOCK position.

7   Once in gear, with the ignition key in the RUN position, you should be able to move the shift lever between gears, or put it into NEU-TRAL or PARK, without depressing the brake pedal, although you have to push in the little button at the top of the shifter knob to change gears. The brake light switch is part of the interlock system **(see illustration)**. It should have continuity between its terminals when the pedal is depressed.

8   If the system doesn't operate as described, try adjusting it as follows.

Adjustment

Refer to illustrations 5.17 and 5.18

Note: *Do not confuse adjusting the shift cable with adjusting the Shift Interlock system. The shift cable adjuster lock tab and the Shift/Lock lock tab are just inches apart, but are on two separate cables. The purpose of adjusting the shift cable is to make sure that it shifts the transmission correctly and that the engine can be started only in PARK or NEUTRAL. The purpose of adjusting the Shift/Lock system is to ensure that the shift lever cannot be removed from PARK or NEUTRAL unless the brake pedal is depressed.*

9   Remove the bezel around the floor shift assembly (see Chapter 11).

10   Put the shift lever in the PARK position.

11   Release the Shift/Lock lock tab **(see illustration 2.26)**.

12   Make sure that the shift lever is in the PARK position.

13   Raise the vehicle and place it securely on jackstands. (Make sure that the rear wheels are off the ground so that you can rotate the rear wheels or the driveshaft in the next step.)

14   Verify that the transmission park lock is positively engaged by trying to rotate the driveshaft (the driveshaft will not rotate when the park lock is correctly engaged).

15   Turn the ignition key to the LOCK position. (Make SURE that the ignition key is in the LOCK position, because the cable cannot be correctly adjusted with the key in any other position.)

16   Make sure that the shift cable is free to self-adjust itself by pushing it to the rear and releasing it. Then push the shift cable lock tab **(see illustration 3.4)** toward the cable until it snaps into place (which indicates that the locking tangs have re-engaged the cable).

17   Release the clips at the Shift/Lock cable on the shifter and pull the adjuster rod, Out to unlock, and In to Lock. Lock the rod at the correct distance (no slack) by slightly pushing

5.7 Check the brake light switch for continuity

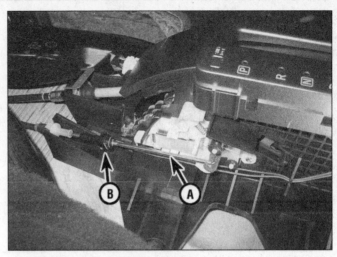

5.17 At the shift interlock cable (A), squeeze the tabs (B) to release the rod for adjustment

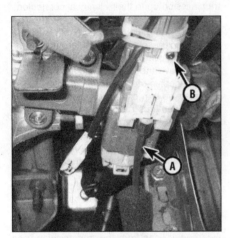

5.18 At the ignition switch end of the interlock cable (A), remove the screw (B) and separate the cable end from the ignition switch

the adjuster rod back in to lock it (see illustration).

18 If the interlock cable is broken, remove it at the shifter end, then remove the ignition switch end (see illustration). Remove the steering column covers to access the ignition end of the cable (see Chapter 10).

6 Park/Neutral Position (PNP) switch - general information

1 If the engine will start with the shift lever in any position other than Park or Neutral, check and if necessary, adjust the shift cable (see Section 3). If this does not fix the problem see Step 2.

2 On the covered models, the Park/Neutral and Backup Light switches are part of the TCM/valve body inside the transmission. If diagnostic trouble codes indicate a problem

with these switches, it is suggested that internal transmission repairs be done at a dealership or qualified automatic transmission shop.

7 Extension housing oil seal (2WD models) - replacement

Refer to illustrations 7.4 and 7.5

1 Oil leaks frequently occur due to wear of the extension housing oil seal. Replacement of this seal is relatively easy, since it can be performed without removing the transmission from the vehicle.

2 The extension housing oil seal is located at the extreme rear of the transmission, where the driveshaft is attached. If leakage at the seal is suspected, raise the vehicle and support it securely on jackstands. If the seal is leaking, transmission lubricant will be built up on the front of the driveshaft and may be dripping from the rear of the transmission.

3 Remove the driveshaft (see Chapter 8).

4 Using a seal removal tool or a large screwdriver, carefully pry the oil seal out of the rear of the transmission (see illustration). Do not damage the splines on the transmission output shaft.

5 Using a seal driver, a large section of pipe or a very large deep socket as a drift, install the new oil seal (see illustration). Drive it into the bore squarely and make sure it's completely seated.

6 Lubricate the splines of the transmission output shaft and the outside of the driveshaft yoke with lightweight grease, then install the driveshaft (see Chapter 8). Be careful not to damage the lip of the new seal.

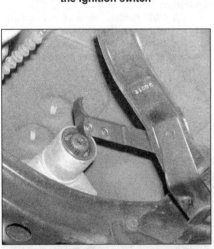

7.4 Carefully pry the old seal out of the extension housing - don't damage the splines on the output shaft

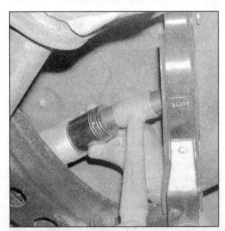

7.5 Drive the new seal into place with a hammer and a seal driver or a large socket

8.2 To check the transmission mount, insert a large screwdriver or prybar between the crossmember and the transmission and try to pry the transmission up - it should move very little

8   Transmission mount - check and replacement

Check

Refer to illustration 8.2

1   Raise the vehicle and support it securely on jackstands.
2   Insert a large screwdriver or prybar into the space between the transmission extension housing and the crossmember and try to pry the transmission up slightly **(see illustration)**.
3   The transmission should not move much at all - if the mount is cracked or torn, replace it.

Replacement

Refer to illustration 8.5

4   Support the transmission with a floor jack. Place a block of wood on the jack head to act as a cushion.
5   Remove the bolts and nuts attaching the mount to the crossmember and transmission

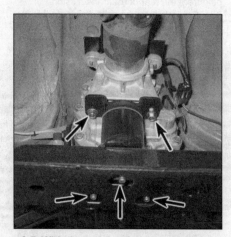

8.5 With the weight of the transmission supported on a jack, remove the mount-to-transmission bolts (upper two), then remove the mount-to-crossmember bolts and raise the transmission to allow room for mount removal

(see illustration). On some models you'll have to also unbolt the plate that supports the exhaust pipe.
6   Raise the transmission slightly with the jack and remove the mount.
7   Installation is the reverse of the removal procedure. Be sure to tighten all nuts and bolts securely.

9   Automatic transmission - removal and installation

Removal

Refer to illustrations 9.10, 9.11a, 9.11b and 9.14

Caution: *The transmission and torque converter must be removed as a single assembly. If you try to leave the torque converter attached to the driveplate, the converter driveplate, pump bushing and oil seal will be damaged. The driveplate is not designed to support the load, so none of the weight of the transmission should be allowed to rest on the plate during removal.*

1   Disconnect the cable from the negative terminal of the battery.

9.10 Disconnect the main electrical connector for the automatic transmission at this plug

2   Raise the vehicle and support it securely on jackstands. Remove the skid plate and skid plate crossmember, if equipped.
3   Remove the transmission oil pan drain plug and drain the transmission fluid (see Chapter 1).
4   Remove the left-side inner fenderwell liner (see Chapter 11).
5   Detach the shift cable from the manual lever and from the bracket on the transmission.
6   Mark the yokes and remove the driveshaft (see Chapter 8). On 4WD models, remove both driveshafts.
7   Remove all exhaust components which would interfere with transmission removal (see Chapter 4).
8   Remove the Crankshaft Position sensor (see Chapter 6).
9   Remove the starter motor (see Chapter 5).
10   Follow the wiring harnesses from the transmission up to their electrical connectors, then unplug the connectors **(see illustration)**. Mark and disconnect any other electrical connectors that would interfere with transmission removal.
11   Remove the inspection cover and mark the relationship of the torque converter to the driveplate so they can be installed in the same position **(see illustrations)**.
12   Remove the torque converter-to-driveplate bolts. Turn the crankshaft for access to each bolt. Turn the crankshaft in a clockwise direction only (as viewed from the front).
13   Remove the fill/dipstick tube bracket bolt and pull the tube out of the transmission. Don't lose the tube seal (it can be reused if it's still in good shape).
14   Remove the fitting bolts and detach the fluid cooler lines from the transmission **(see illustration)**. Discard the sealing washers that are present on either side of the fittings; new ones must be used when reconnecting the fittings.
15   On 4WD models, remove the transfer case (see Chapter 7C). **Note:** *If you are not planning to replace the transmission, but are removing it in order to gain access to other*

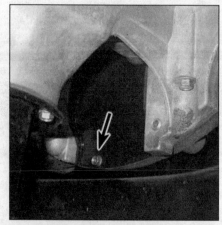

9.11a Remove the bolt and the converter inspection cover to access the converter fasteners

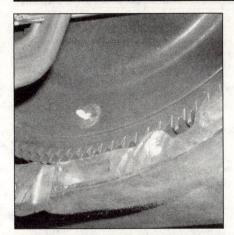

9.11b Remove one of the torque converter bolts and mark the relationship of the driveplate to the torque converter

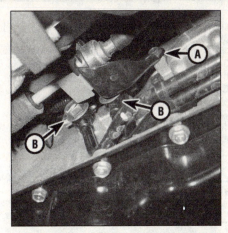

9.14 To disconnect the transmission fluid lines at the transmission, unbolt the shift cable bracket (A) for access to the two banjo-bolt line fittings (B)

Installation

Refer to illustrations 9.25a and 9.25b

21 Prior to installation, make sure the torque converter is securely engaged in the pump. If you've removed the converter, apply a small amount of transmission fluid on the torque converter rear hub, where the transmission front seal rides. Install the torque converter onto the front input shaft of the transmission while rotating the converter back and forth. It should engage into the transmission front pump in stages. To make sure the converter is fully engaged, lay a straightedge across the transmission-to-engine mating surface and measure the distance from the straightedge and the converter lugs. The converter lugs must be at least 0.984-inch (25 mm) below the straightedge.

22 With the transmission secured to the jack, raise it into position.

23 Turn the torque converter to line up the holes with the holes in the driveplate. The marks on the torque converter and driveplate made in Step 11 must line up.

24 Move the transmission forward carefully until the dowel pins engage with the holes in the bellhousing. Make sure the transmission mates with the engine with no gap. If there's a gap, make sure there are no wires or other objects pinched between the engine and transmission and also make sure the torque converter is completely engaged in the transmission front pump. Try to rotate the converter - if it doesn't rotate easily, it's probably not fully engaged in the pump. If necessary, lower the transmission and install the converter fully.

25 Install the transmission-to-engine bolts and tighten them to the torque values listed in this Chapter's Specifications **(see illustrations)**. As you're tightening the bolts, make sure that the engine and transmission mate completely at all points. If not, find out why. Never try to force the engine and transmission together with the bolts or you'll break the transmission case!

26 Raise the rear of the transmission and

components such as the torque converter, it isn't really necessary to remove the transfer case. However, the transmission and transfer case are awkward and heavy when removed and installed as a single assembly; they're much easier to maneuver off and on as separate units. If you decide to leave the transfer case attached, disconnect the shift rod (manual shift models only) from the transfer case shift lever. Also disconnect the electrical connectors from the transfer case speed sensors and detach the transfer case vent tube (see Chapter 7C). **Warning:** *If you decide to leave the transfer case attached to the transmission, be sure to use safety chains to help stabilize the transmission and transfer case assembly and to prevent it from falling off the jack head, which could cause serious damage to the transmission and/or transfer case and serious bodily injury to you.*

16 Support the engine with an engine hoist or support fixture from above, or with a jack placed under the oil pan. If you use a floor jack, place a block of wood on the jack head to spread the load.

17 Support the transmission with a jack - preferably a jack made for this purpose (available at most tool rental yards). Safety chains will help steady the transmission on the jack.

18 Remove the bolt securing the transmission mount to the crossmember. Then raise the transmission slightly and remove the crossmember.

19 Lower the engine and transmission slightly and remove the bolts securing the transmission to the engine. A long extension and a U-joint socket will greatly simplify this step. **Note:** *Different length bolts are used - be sure to note the location of each bolt so they can be returned to their original positions when the transmission is installed.*

20 Move the transmission to the rear to disengage it from the engine block dowel pins and make sure the torque converter is detached from the driveplate. Lower the transmission with the jack. Clamp a pair of locking pliers on the bellhousing case. The pliers will prevent the torque converter from falling out while you're removing the transmission.

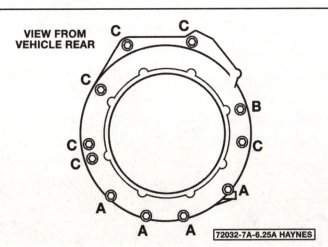

9.25a Transmission-to-engine mounting bolt identification - four-cylinder models

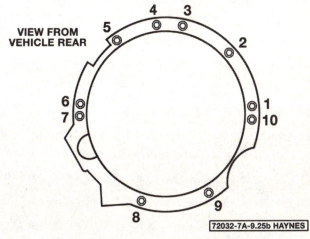

9.25b Transmission-to-engine mounting bolt identification and TIGHTENING sequence - V6 models

install the transmission crossmember.

27   Remove the jacks supporting the transmission and the engine.

28   Install the torque converter-to-driveplate bolts. Once all the bolts have been installed, tighten them to the torque listed in this Chapter's Specifications.

29   Install the transmission dipstick tube and seal into the transmission housing, then install the bolt and tighten it securely.

30   Install the starter motor (see Chapter 5).

31   Install the torque converter inspection cover.

32   Using new sealing washers, connect the transmission fluid cooler lines to the transmission, tightening the fitting bolts securely.

33   Plug in the transmission electrical connectors.

34   Connect the shift cable (see Section 3).

35   On 4WD models, install the transfer case, if removed (see Chapter 7C).

36   Install the driveshaft(s) (see Chapter 8).

37   Adjust the shift cable (see Section 3).

38   Install any exhaust system components that were removed or disconnected (see Chapter 4).

39   Remove the jackstands and lower the vehicle.

40   Fill the transmission with the specified fluid (see Chapter 1), run the engine and check for fluid leaks.

---

10 Transmission Control Module (TCM) - removal and installation

The Transmission Control Module (TCM) is a microprocessor that controls many aspects of automatic transmission performance. On the covered models, it is located inside the valve body of the transmission, along with the transmission fluid temperature sensor. The harness from these two electronic devices extends to a plug secured to the transmission case, sealed with an O-ring and an external lock-ring.

Other than with a Nissan Consult-II or other scan tool, there is no way for the home mechanic to troubleshoot or diagnose the TCM, and removal or installation of the TCM in the transmission's valve body should be performed at a dealership or qualified transmission repair shop.

Chapter 7 Part C
Transfer case

Contents

Specifications

Torque Specifications

	Ft-lbs	Nm

Note: *One foot-pound (ft-lb) of torque is equivalent to 12 inch-pounds (in-lbs) of torque. Torque values below approximately 15 ft-lbs are expressed in inch-pounds, since most foot-pound torque wrenches are not accurate at these smaller values.*

	Ft-lbs	Nm
Actuator assembly to transfer case bolts	16	22
ATP switch or 4LOW switch-to-case	21	28
Companion flange nut	203	275
Oil drain or fill plugs	26	35
Transfer case-to-transmission mounting bolts	33	45

1 General information

1 Four-Wheel Drive (4WD) models of the vehicles covered by this manual are equipped with an electronically-controlled transfer case that distributes motive power to both front and rear axles when the system is engaged. A switch on the instrument panel allows a choice of 2WD, 4WD High or 4WD LOW.

2 Input from the switch goes to the Transfer Control Unit, which communicates with the transfer case actuator, the automatic transmission on models so equipped, and other devices. The actuator consists of an electric shift motor and a Transfer Case Position Switch. The motor actually does the mechanical shifting of the transfer case, when directed by the Transfer Control Unit. The Transfer Case Position Switch communicates at all times to the Control Unit the actual position of the electric shift motor.

3 We don't recommend trying to rebuild this transfer case. They're difficult to overhaul without special tools, and rebuilt units may be available that represent a savings of time and money versus buying over-the-counter parts and rebuilding your own.

Troubleshooting

Refer to illustration 1.11

4 Problems with the transfer case system will make the 4WD warning light illuminate on the instrument panel when the engine is started. Although the transfer case control system is electronic and a scan tool is the best diagnostic device, you can output a number of diagnostic codes through the 4WD warning light.

5 Begin with the engine at normal operating temperature. Turn the ignition key On and Off twice, ending with the key Off. Apply the vehicle parking brake.

6 Move the transmission shift lever to Park (automatic transmission) or Neutral (manual transmission). With the 4WD switch turned to the 2WD position, turn the key On. The 4WD warning light should come on for a second or two, then go off, indicating the 4WD system is OK.

7 Move the transmission shifter to Reverse (automatic transmission) or some position other than Neutral (standard transmission).

8 In sequence, turn the 4WD selector switch from 2WD to 4H and back to 2WD.

9 Move the transmission shift lever to Park (automatic transmission) or Neutral (manual transmission), and turn the shift switch from 4High to 2WD and back to 4High.

10 Move the transmission shifter to Neutral (all models) and turn the 4WD selector switch to 2WD.

11 Move the transmission shift lever to Park

Blinks	Problem with Transfer Case control system
2	Output shaft revolution sensor signal
3	Vehicle Speed Sensor (ABS system)
4	CAN network communication error
5	Transfer Control Unit
6	4Low switch, open or short
7	Improper engine speed signal from PCM
8	Power supply voltage low
9	4WD shift switch, short circuit
10	Improper signal from wait detection switch
11	Malfunction in actuator motor
12	Actuator position switch
13	Transfer shutoff relays
14	Neutral position switch signal (manual transmission) Transmission range switch signal (automatic transmission)
constant	Memory backup power supply drained
none	Transmission range switch (automatic transmissions), Neutral position switch (manual transmissions), or 4WD shift switch is open or shorted

1.11 Diagnostic chart for reading codes through the blinks of the 4WD warning light on the instrument panel

(automatic transmission) or Neutral (manual transmission). You can now read the trouble codes as a series of blinks on the 4WD warning light. Two blinks would be code 2, 10 blinks would be code 10. Refer to the chart **(see illustration)** for a list of codes. **Note:** *When the light first comes on, it will be On for 2.5 seconds, then Off one second and the code blinks will begin.*

2   Transfer control unit - replacement

1   With the transfer case in 2WD, turn off the engine and disconnect the cable from the negative battery terminal.
2   Remove the driver's knee bolster (see Chapter 11).

3   Disconnect the two electrical connectors at the Transfer Control Unit.
4   Remove the two bolts and take the Transfer Control Unit out.
5   Installation is the reverse of the removal procedure, with the following exception. Check for correct positions of the transfer case system by moving the 4WD selector switch through its range. If the position on the switch does not correspond to the position of the shift actuator on the transfer case, perform the following Steps.
6   With the vehicle warmed to operating temperature, move the 4WD selector switch from 2WD to 4High to 4Low to 4High and back to 2WD. Keep the selector in each of these positions for at least two seconds.
7   Observe the 4WD shift indicator light on the instrument panel and the 4Low indicator light. The 4Low light should come on only

when in 4Low, and it will flash for a few seconds while "waiting" for the shift actuator to complete a move to 4Low. Move the vehicle enough to ascertain that the transfer case is in 4Low when the selector switch is in that position and the dash light is on. If the 4WD indicator light or 4Low light are blinking for more than a few seconds, return to 2WD and have the relationship between the 4WD switch and the shift actuator corrected at a dealership with a scan tool.

3   Shift actuator and position switch - replacement

1   Position the 4WD selector switch to 2WD and turn off the vehicle. Raise the vehicle and support it securely on jackstands.
2   From below, disconnect the electrical connector at the shift actuator assembly. The shift position switch is an integral part of the shift actuator assembly.
3   Disconnect the breather hose from the actuator, then remove the mounting bolts and pull the actuator assembly from the transfer case.
4   Before reinstalling the actuator assembly, turn the flat-sided end of the shift-rod on the transfer case as far as it can go counterclockwise and make a mark on the end of the rod.
5   Turn the notch in the shift actuator rod to align with the mark on the rod and, with a new O-ring in place on the actuator (lubricated with petroleum jelly), install the shift actuator assembly.
6   The remainder of the installation is the reverse of the removal procedure.

4   Oil seals - replacement

1   Raise the vehicle and support it securely on jackstands.

Output shaft oil seal(s)
Note: *This procedure applies to both the front and rear output shaft seals.*
2   If you're replacing the front seal, remove

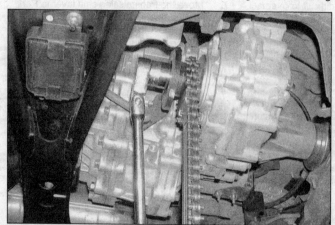

4.3 A chain wrench can be used to prevent the flange from turning while the nut is removed

4.4 A two-jaw puller will be required to remove the flange if it won't come off by hand

4.5 Use a seal removal tool or a large screwdriver to pry the seal out

4.6 Drive the new seal into place with a seal driver or a socket with an outside diameter slightly smaller than that of the seal

the front driveshaft; if you're replacing the rear seal, remove the rear driveshaft (see Chapter 8).

Front seal

Refer to illustrations 4.3 and 4.4

3   A flange holding tool will be required to keep the companion flange from moving while the nut is loosened. A chain wrench will also work **(see illustration)**. Remove the flange nut.

4   Withdraw the flange. It may be necessary to use a two-jaw puller engaged behind the flange to draw it off **(see illustration)**. Do not attempt to pry or hammer behind the flange or hammer on the end of the shaft.

Front or rear seal

Refer to illustrations 4.5 and 4.6

5   Pry out the old seal and discard it **(see illustration)**.

6   Lubricate the lips of the new seal and the seal case with multi-purpose grease, then tap it evenly into position with a seal installation tool or a large socket **(see illustration)**. Make sure it enters the housing squarely and is tapped in to its full depth.

Front seal

Note: *When installing the companion flange, use a new self-locking nut.*

7   Install the companion flange. If necessary, tighten the nut to draw the flange into place. Do not try to hammer the flange into position.

8   Apply a bead of RTV sealant to the ends of the splines visible in the center of the flange so oil will be sealed in.

9   Install the nut. Tighten the nut to the torque listed in this Chapter's Specifications.

Front or rear seal

10   Install the driveshaft (see Chapter 8). Check and, if necessary, add the recommended type of lubricant to bring the level up to the bottom of the filler hole (see Chapter 1).

5   Transfer case - removal and installation

Removal

Note: *Be sure to set the transfer assembly to 2WD before perfoming the following procedure.*

1   Disconnect the cable from the negative terminal of the battery.

2   Raise the vehicle and support it securely on jackstands. Remove the skid plate, if equipped.

3   Disconnect the two vent tubes, one from the shift actuator and one from the transfer case.

4   Drain the transfer case lubricant (see Chapter 1).

5   Remove the front and rear driveshafts (see Chapter 8).

6   Insert a rubber plug into the rear seal after the rear driveshaft has been removed.

7   Unplug all electrical connectors and detach the vent hose from the top of the transfer case.

8   Support the transmission with a floor jack. Place a block of wood on the jack head to spread the load.

9   Support the transfer case with a jack - preferably a special jack made for this purpose. Safety chains will help steady the transfer case on the jack.

10   Unbolt the transmission mount from the crossmember, then remove the crossmember.

11   Lower the jacks supporting the transmission and transfer case just enough for access to the upper mounting bolts.

12   Remove the transmission-to-transfer case bolts. **Note:** *On some models there are two different lengths of bolts securing the transfer case to the transmission. Mark their positions or keep them in order when removed so they can be returned to their proper locations.*

13   Make a final check that all wires and

hoses have been disconnected from the transfer case, then move the transfer case and jack toward the rear of the vehicle until the transfer case is clear of the transmission. Keep the transfer case level as this is done. Once the input shaft is clear, lower the transfer case and remove it from under the vehicle.

Installation

14   Installation is the reverse of removal, noting the following points:

a)   *Apply anaerobic gasket sealant (not RTV sealant) to the transfer case-to-transmission mating surface.*

b)   *Be sure to install the transmission-to-transfer case bolts in their proper locations and tighten them to the torque listed in this Chapter's Specifications.*

c)   *Refill the transfer case with the proper type and quantity of lubricant (see Chapter 1).*

d)   *Check that the 4WD shift indicator corresponds to the position of the transfer case (see Section 2)*

6   Transfer case overhaul - general information

Overhauling a transfer case is a difficult job for the do-it-yourselfer. It involves the disassembly and reassembly of many small parts. Numerous clearances must be precisely measured and, if necessary, changed with select-fit spacers and snap-rings. As a result, if transfer case problems arise, it can be removed and installed by a competent do-it-yourselfer, but overhaul should be left to a transmission repair shop. Rebuilt transfer cases may be available - check with your dealer parts department and auto parts stores. At any rate, the time and money involved in an overhaul is almost sure to exceed the cost of a rebuilt unit.

Nevertheless, it's not impossible for an inexperienced mechanic to rebuild a transfer case if the special tools are available and the job is done in a deliberate step-by-step manner so nothing is overlooked.

The tools necessary for an overhaul include internal and external snap-ring pliers, a bearing puller, a slide hammer, a set of pin punches, a dial indicator and possibly a hydraulic press. In addition, a large, sturdy workbench and a vise or transmission stand will be required.

During disassembly of the transfer case, make careful notes of how each piece comes off, where it fits in relation to other pieces and what holds it in place. Note how parts are installed when you remove them; this will make it much easier to get the transfer case back together.

Before taking the transfer case apart for repair, it will help if you have some idea what area of the transfer case is malfunctioning. Certain problems can be closely tied to specific areas in the transfer case, which can make component examination and replacement easier. Refer to the *Troubleshooting* section at the front of this manual for information regarding possible sources of trouble. Check for trouble codes for the transfer case system with the procedure outlined in Section 1.

Chapter 8
Clutch and driveline

Contents

Specifications

General
Driveaxle boot length (4WD) .... 6.45 to 6.47 inches (163.9 mm to 164.3 mm)
Clutch start switch clearance .... 0.004 to 0.039 inch (0.1 mm to 1.0 mm)

Torque specifications

	Ft-lbs (unless otherwise indicated)	Nm

Note: *One foot-pound (ft-lb) of torque is equivalent to 12 inch-pounds (in-lbs) of torque. Torque values below approximately 15 ft-lbs are expressed in inch-pounds, since most foot-pound torque wrenches are not accurate at these smaller values.*

Clutch

	Ft-lbs	Nm
Pressure plate-to-flywheel bolts		
Four cylinder		
Step 1	132 in-lbs	15
Step 2		
2005 through 2008	29	39
2009 and later	19	25
V6		
Step 1	132 in-lbs	15
Step 2	19	25
Clutch release cylinder mounting bolts	26	35
Clutch master cylinder mounting nuts	82 in-lbs	9
Flywheel mounting bolts		
Four-cylinder	80	108
V6	65	88

Driveshaft

	Ft-lbs	Nm
Front driveshaft-to-differential companion flange (4WD)	44	60
Front driveshaft-to-transfer case companion flange (4WD)	44	60
Rear driveshaft-to-rear differential companion flange		
Four-cylinder models	54	73
V6 models		
With universal joint	77	104
With CV joint	60	81

Driveaxles (4WD)

	Ft-lbs	Nm
Driveaxle hub nuts	101	137

Front differential (4WD)

	Ft-lbs	Nm
Differential housing-to-chassis mounting bolts	135	183

Rear axle

	Ft-lbs	Nm
Rear axle bearing retaining plate		
One-piece bearing (retainers with four separate bolts/nuts)	49	66
Multi-part bearing (retainers have studs attached to plate)	41	56

1   General information

The Sections in this Chapter deal with the components from the rear of the engine to the rear wheels (except for the transmission and transfer case, which are dealt with in Chapter 7) and forward to the front wheels on four-wheel drive (4WD) models. In this Chapter, the components are grouped into three categories: clutch, driveshaft(s) and axle(s). Separate Sections within this Chapter cover checks and repair procedures for components in each of these three groups.

Since nearly all these procedures involve working under the vehicle, make sure it's safely supported on sturdy jackstands or a hoist where the vehicle can be safely raised and lowered.

2   Clutch - description and check

1   All vehicles with a manual transmission have a single dry plate, diaphragm spring type clutch. The clutch disc has a splined hub which allows it to slide along the splines of the transmission input shaft. The clutch and pressure plate are held in contact by spring pressure exerted by the diaphragm spring in the pressure plate.

2   The clutch release system is operated by hydraulic pressure. The hydraulic release system consists of the clutch pedal, a master cylinder, the hydraulic line, a release (or slave) cylinder which actuates the clutch release lever and the clutch release (or throwout) bearing. **Note:** *The clutch master cylinder does not have its own fluid reservoir. A fluid line connects the brake master cylinder fluid reservoir to the clutch master cylinder for fluid supply.*

3   When pressure is applied to the clutch pedal to release the clutch, hydraulic pressure is exerted against the outer end of the clutch release lever. As the lever pivots, the shaft fingers push against the release bearing. The bearing pushes against the fingers of the diaphragm spring of the pressure plate assembly, which in turn releases the clutch plate.

4   Terminology can be a problem when discussing the clutch components because common names are in some cases different from those used by the manufacturer. For example, the driven plate is also called the clutch plate or disc, the pressure plate assembly is sometimes called the clutch cover, the clutch release bearing is sometimes called a throwout bearing, and the release cylinder is sometimes called the slave cylinder.

5   Other than to replace components with obvious damage, some preliminary checks should be performed to diagnose clutch problems.

a)   *The first check should be of the fluid level in the brake master cylinder reservoir. If the fluid level is low, add fluid as necessary and inspect the hydraulic system for leaks. If the master cylinder reservoir*

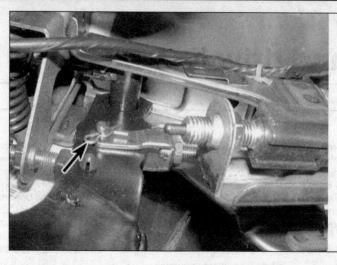

3.4 To detach the pushrod from the clutch pedal, remove this retaining pin, then pull out the clevis pin

is dry, bleed the system as described in Section 5 and recheck the clutch operation.

b)   *To check "clutch spin-down time," run the engine at normal idle speed with the transmission in Neutral (clutch pedal up - engaged). Disengage the clutch (pedal down), wait several seconds and shift the transmission into Reverse. No grinding noise should be heard. A grinding noise would most likely indicate a bad pressure plate or clutch disc.*

c)   *To check for complete clutch release, run the engine (with the parking brake applied to prevent vehicle movement) and hold the clutch pedal approximately 1/2-inch from the floor. Shift the transmission between 1st gear and Reverse several times. If the shift is rough, component failure is indicated. Check the release cylinder pushrod travel. With the clutch pedal depressed completely, the release cylinder pushrod should extend substantially (you may have to remove an inspection plug to see the pushrod). If it doesn't, check the fluid level in the clutch master cylinder.*

d)   *Visually inspect the pivot bushing at the top of the clutch pedal to make sure there's no binding or excessive play.*

e)   *Crawl under the vehicle and make sure the clutch release lever is securely attached to the ballstud.*

3   Clutch master cylinder - replacement

Removal and installation

Refer to illustration 3.4

1   Remove as much fluid as possible from the reservoir with a suction gun, large syringe or a poultry baster. **Warning:** *If a poultry baster is used, never again use it for the preparation of food.*

2   Squeeze the clamp and remove the fluid hose from the brake fluid reservoir to the

clutch master cylinder, being careful not to spill brake fluid on painted components. Disconnect the brake fluid hydraulic line (to the clutch slave cylinder) from the master cylinder, using a flare-nut wrench to protect the fitting. Have rags handy, as some fluid will be lost as the line is removed. **Caution:** *Don't allow fluid to come into contact with the paint since it will damage the finish. Also have a plug ready and immediately plug the line to prevent leakage and fluid contamination.*

3   Working inside the passenger compartment, remove the driver's side under-dash panel.

4   Remove the retaining pin and pull out the clevis pin **(see illustration)** to disconnect the clutch master cylinder pushrod from the clutch pedal.

5   Remove the master cylinder mounting nuts and detach the master cylinder from the firewall.

6   Installation is the reverse of removal. Be sure to tighten the master cylinder mounting nuts to the torque listed in this Chapter's Specifications. Tighten the hydraulic line fitting nut securely.

7   Fill the brake master cylinder reservoir with the fluid specified in Chapter 1 and bleed the clutch hydraulic system (see Section 5).

4   Clutch release cylinder - removal and installation

Refer to illustration 4.2

1   Raise the vehicle and support it securely on jackstands.

2   Unscrew the fluid hose fitting bolt **(see illustration)**. **Note:** *There is a sealing washer on either side of the brake hose inlet fitting; be sure to replace this with a new one when reconnecting the hose. Have rags handy, as some fluid will be lost as the line is removed. **Caution:** Don't allow fluid to come into contact with the paint - it will damage the finish. Also have a plug ready and immediately plug the line to prevent leakage and fluid contamination.*

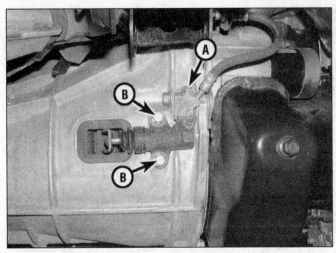

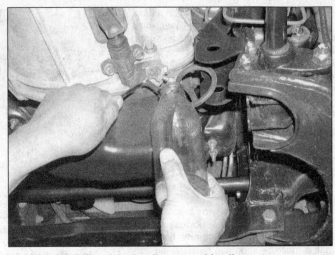

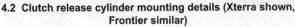

4.2 Clutch release cylinder mounting details (Xterra shown, Frontier similar)

5.3 Clutch hydraulic system bleeding setup

> *A Fitting bolt*   *B Mounting bolts*

3   Unscrew the two release cylinder mounting bolts and detach the release cylinder.
4   Installation is the reverse of removal. Make sure the pushrod dust boot is in good condition and the pushrod is seated correctly in its pocket in the release lever. Tighten the release cylinder mounting bolts to the torque listed in this Chapter's Specifications.
5   Fill the brake fluid reservoir with the recommended fluid (see Chapter 1).
6   Bleed the clutch hydraulic system (see Section 5).
7   Lower the vehicle and check for proper operation.

5   Clutch hydraulic system - bleeding

Refer to illustration 5.3

1   The hydraulic system should be bled of all air whenever any part of the system has been removed or if the fluid level has been allowed to fall so low that air has been drawn into the master cylinder. The procedure is similar to bleeding a brake system.
2   Fill the master cylinder with new brake fluid conforming to DOT 3 specifications. **Caution:** *Do not re-use any of the fluid coming from the system during the bleeding operation or use fluid which has been inside an open container for an extended period of time.*
3   Locate the bleeder valve on the clutch release cylinder **(see illustration)**. Remove the dust cap which fits over the bleeder valve and push a length of snug-fitting (preferably clear) hose over the valve. Place the other end of the hose into a clear container with about two inches of brake fluid in it. The hose end must be submerged in the fluid.
4   Have an assistant depress the clutch pedal and hold it. Open the bleeder valve on the release cylinder, allowing fluid to flow through the hose. Close the bleeder valve when fluid stops flowing from the hose. Once

closed, have your assistant release the pedal.
5   Continue this process until all air is evacuated from the system, indicated by a full, solid stream of fluid being ejected from the bleeder valve each time and no air bubbles in the hose or container. Keep a close watch on the fluid level inside the clutch master cylinder reservoir; if the level drops too low, air will be sucked back into the system and the process will have to be started over again.
6   Install the dust cap on the bleeder valve. Check carefully for proper operation before placing the vehicle in normal service.

6   Clutch components - removal, inspection and installation

Warning: *Dust produced by clutch wear and deposited on clutch components is hazardous to your health. DO NOT blow it out with compressed air and DO NOT inhale it. DO NOT use gasoline or petroleum-based solvents to remove the dust. Brake system cleaner should be used to flush the dust into a drain pan. After the clutch components are wiped clean with a rag, dispose of the contaminated rags and cleaner in a covered, marked container.*

Removal

Refer to illustration 6.4

1   Access to the clutch components is normally accomplished by removing the transmission, leaving the engine in the vehicle. If, of course, the engine is being removed for major overhaul, then check the clutch for wear and replace worn components as necessary. However, the relatively low cost of the clutch components compared to the time and trouble spent gaining access to them warrants their replacement anytime the engine or transmission is removed, unless they are new or in near perfect condition. The following

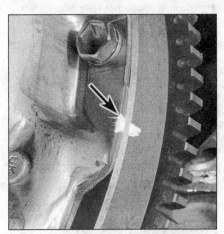

6.4 Be sure to mark the pressure plate and flywheel to insure proper alignment during installation (this won't be necessary if a new pressure plate is to be installed)

procedures are based on the assumption the engine will stay in place.
2   Referring to Chapter 7 Part A, remove the transmission from the vehicle. Support the engine while the transmission is out. Preferably, an engine hoist or support fixture should be used to support it from above. However, if a jack is used underneath the engine, make sure a piece of wood is positioned between the jack and oil pan to spread the load. **Caution:** *The pickup for the oil pump is very close to the bottom of the oil pan. If the pan is bent or distorted in any way, engine oil starvation could occur.*
3   To support the clutch disc during removal, install a clutch alignment tool through the clutch disc hub.
4   Carefully inspect the flywheel and pressure plate for indexing marks. The marks are usually an X, an O or a white letter. If they cannot be found, scribe marks yourself so the pressure plate and the flywheel will be in the same alignment during installation **(see illustration)**.

5   Turning each bolt only 1/4-turn at a time, loosen the pressure plate-to-flywheel bolts. Work in a criss-cross pattern until all spring pressure is relieved, then hold the pressure plate securely and completely remove the bolts, followed by the pressure plate and clutch disc.

Inspection

Refer to illustrations 6.7, 6.9, 6.11a and 6.11b

6   Ordinarily, when a problem occurs in the clutch, it can be attributed to wear of the clutch driven plate assembly (clutch disc). However, all components should be inspected at this time.

7   Inspect the flywheel for cracks, heat checking, grooves and other obvious defects **(see illustration)**. If the imperfections are slight, a machine shop can machine the surface flat and smooth, which is highly recommended regardless of the surface appearance. Refer to Chapter 2 for the flywheel removal and installation procedure.

8   Inspect the pilot bushing (see Section 8). It's a good idea to replace it at this time, regardless of its condition.

9   Inspect the lining on the clutch disc. There should be at least 1/32-inch (0.8 mm) of lining above the rivet heads. Check for loose rivets, distortion, cracks, broken springs and other obvious damage **(see illustration)**. As mentioned above, ordinarily the clutch disc

6.7 Check the flywheel for cracks, hot spots and other obvious defects (slight imperfections can be removed by a machine shop)

is routinely replaced, so if in doubt about the condition, replace it with a new one.

10   The release bearing should also be replaced along with the clutch disc (see Section 7).

11   Check the machined surfaces and the diaphragm spring fingers of the pressure plate **(see illustrations)**. If the surface is grooved or otherwise damaged, replace the pressure plate. Also check for obvious damage, dis-

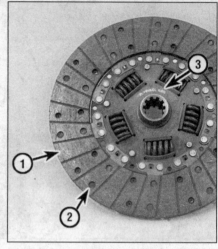

6.9 The clutch plate

1   *Lining* - This will wear down in use
2   *Rivets* - These secure the lining and will damage the flywheel or pressure plate if allowed to contact the surfaces
3   *Markings* - "Flywheel side" or something similar

tortion, cracking, etc. Light glazing can be removed with sandpaper or emery cloth. If a new pressure plate is required, new and factory-rebuilt units are available.

NORMAL FINGER WEAR   **EXCESSIVE FINGER WEAR**   **BROKEN OR BENT FINGERS**

EXCESSIVE WEAR

6.11a Replace the pressure plate if excessive wear is noted

6.11b Examine the pressure plate friction surface for score marks, cracks and evidence of overheating

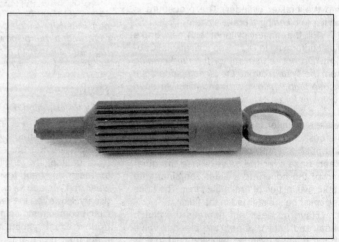

6.13 Center the clutch disc using a clutch alignment tool

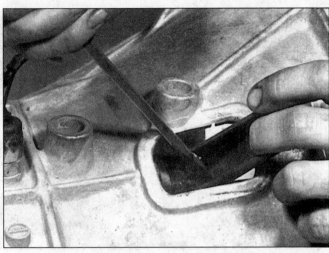

7.3 A screwdriver can be used to disengage the release lever retainer spring from the ballstud

7.5 A puller is needed to separate the release bearing from the hub

Installation

Refer to illustration 6.13

12   Before installation, clean the flywheel and pressure plate machined surfaces with brake system cleaner. It's important that no oil or grease is on these surfaces or the lining of the clutch disc. Handle the parts only with clean hands.

13   Position the clutch disc and pressure plate against the flywheel with the clutch held in place with an alignment tool **(see illustration)**. Make sure it's installed properly (most replacement clutch plates will be marked "flywheel side" or something similar - if not marked, install the clutch disc with the damper springs toward the transmission).

14   Tighten the pressure plate-to-flywheel bolts only finger tight, working around the pressure plate.

15   Center the clutch disc by ensuring the alignment tool extends through the splined hub and into the pilot bushing in the crankshaft. Wiggle the tool up, down or side-to-side as needed to bottom the tool in the pilot bushing. Tighten the pressure plate-to-flywheel bolts in two steps to prevent distorting the cover. Use

a criss-cross pattern to tighten all the bolts to the Step 1 torque listed in this Chapter's Specifications. When completed with Step 1, tighten the bolts to the Step 2 torque, but do so in a circular pattern around the pressure plate. Remove the alignment tool.

16   Using high-temperature grease, lubricate the inner groove of the release bearing. Also place grease on the transmission input shaft bearing retainer.

17   Install the clutch release bearing as described in Section 7.

18   Install the transmission and all components removed previously. Tighten all fasteners to the proper torque specifications.

---

7   Clutch release bearing - removal, inspection and installation

---

Warning: *Dust produced by clutch wear and deposited on clutch components is hazardous to your health. DO NOT blow it out with compressed air and DO NOT inhale it. DO NOT use gasoline or petroleum-based solvents to remove the dust. Brake system cleaner should*

be used to flush the dust into a drain pan. After the clutch components are wiped clean with a rag, dispose of the contaminated rags and cleaner in a covered, marked container.

Removal

Refer to illustration 7.3

1   Remove the release cylinder (see Section 4).

2   Remove the transmission (see Chapter 7, Part A).

3   Remove the boot from the side of the transmission and disengage the release lever retainer from the ballstud **(see illustration)**.

Inspection

Refer to illustration 7.5

4   Hold the outer portion of the bearing and rotate the center while applying pressure. If the bearing doesn't turn smoothly or if it's noisy, replace it with a new one. Wipe the bearing with a clean rag and inspect it for damage, wear and cracks. Don't immerse the bearing in solvent - it's sealed for life and to do so would ruin it.

5   If the bearing needs to be replaced, remove it from the hub with a puller **(see illustration)**. The new bearing will have to be pressed onto the hub (if you don't have a press, take the hub and bearing to an automotive machine shop).

Installation

Refer to illustration 7.7

6   Lightly lubricate the clutch release lever where it contacts the release bearing hub and the ballstud.

7   Attach the release bearing to the release lever. Make sure the bearing is properly engaged by the retainer clip **(see illustration)**.

8   Lubricate the clutch release lever ballstud or pivot pin with high-temperature grease, insert the release lever through the boot, slide the release bearing onto the input shaft bearing retainer and push the lever onto

7.7 The release bearing retainer must engage the lever like this

8.5 A small slide-hammer puller is handy for removing the pilot bushing

8.6 When installing the pilot bushing in the crankshaft, use a bearing driver

the ballstud until the lever retainer "pops" onto the stud. Make sure that the release lever pivots freely and the release bearing slides freely on the input shaft bearing retainer.

9   Apply a light coat of high-temperature grease to the face of the release bearing, where it contacts the pressure plate diaphragm fingers.

10   The remainder of installation is the reverse of the removal procedure. Tighten all transmission-to-engine bolts to the torque listed in the Chapter 7A Specifications.

8   Pilot bushing - replacement

Refer to illustrations 8.5 and 8.6

1   The clutch pilot bushing is pressed into the rear of the crankshaft. It is greased at the factory and does not require additional lubrication. Its primary purpose is to support the front of the transmission input shaft. The pilot bushing should be inspected whenever the clutch components are removed from the engine. Due to its inaccessibility, if you are in doubt as to its condition, replace it with a new one. **Note:** *If the engine has been removed from the vehicle, disregard the following steps which do not apply.*

2   Remove the transmission (refer to Chapter 7, Part A).

3   Remove the clutch components (see Section 6).

4   Inspect for any excessive wear, scoring, lack of grease or obvious damage. If any of these conditions are noted, the bushing should be replaced. A flashlight will be helpful to direct light into the recess.

5   Removal can be accomplished with a slide hammer fitted with a puller attachment **(see illustration)**, which are available at most auto parts stores or equipment rental yards.

6   To install the new bushing, lightly lubricate the outside surface with multi-purpose grease, then drive it into the recess with a hammer and bearing/bushing driver **(see**

illustration**).** Apply a thin film of grease to the inner surface of the bearing.

7   Install the clutch components, transmission and all other components removed previously, tightening all fasteners properly.

9   Clutch pedal - adjustment

The clutch pedal on the covered models has no adjustment specification, other than the measurement of the pedal stop rubber to the clutch start switch (see Section 10).

10   Clutch start switch - check and replacement

Refer to illustration 10.1

1   The clutch start switch is located near the top of the clutch pedal, facing the opposite direction of the cruise control switch (or pedal stopper) **(see illustration)**.

2   Verify that the engine will not start when the clutch pedal is released.

3   Verify that the engine will start when the clutch pedal is depressed all the way.

4   If the clutch start switch doesn't perform as described above, loosen the locknut, depress the clutch pedal all the way and turn the switch in its bracket until the gap between the switch thread and the pedal stopper is adjusted to the clearance listed in this Chapter's Specifications. Check the operation of the switch again; if it still doesn't work properly, check switch continuity.

5   Verify that there is continuity between the clutch start switch terminals when the pedal is depressed.

6   Verify that no continuity exists between the switch terminals when the pedal is released.

7   If the switch fails either of these continuity tests, replace it: Loosen the nut near the body of the switch, then unscrew the switch from the bracket. Unplug the electrical con-

nector. Installation is the reverse of removal.

8   Adjust the switch as described in Step 4.

9   Verify that the engine doesn't start when the clutch pedal is released.

11   Driveshaft and universal joints - general information and inspection

General information

1   A driveshaft is a tube, or a pair of tubes, that transmits power between the transmission (or transfer case on 4WD models) and the differential. Universal joints are located at either end of the driveshaft and in the center on two-piece driveshafts.

2   Rear driveshafts employ a splined yoke at the front, which slips into the extension housing of the transmission. This arrangement allows the driveshaft to slide back-and-forth within the transmission during vehicle opera-

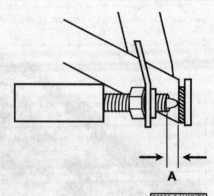

72032-8-HAYNES

10.1 Depress the pedal, then loosen the locknut and turn the clutch start switch in its bracket until the gap between the switch thread and the pedal stopper (A) is as listed in this Chapter's Specifications

tion to compensate for changes in length due to suspension movement. An oil seal prevents leakage of fluid at this point and keeps dirt from entering the transmission. If leakage is evident at the front of the driveshaft, replace the oil seal (see Chapter 7, Part B).

3   On all models, the driveshaft assembly requires very little service. The universal joints are lubricated for life and must be replaced if problems develop. The driveshaft must be removed from the vehicle for this procedure.

4   Since the driveshaft is a balanced unit, it's important that no undercoating, mud, etc. be allowed to stay on it. When the vehicle is raised for service it's a good idea to clean the driveshaft and inspect it for any obvious damage. Also, make sure the small weights used to originally balance the driveshaft are in place and securely attached. Whenever the driveshaft is removed it must be reinstalled in the same relative position to preserve the balance.

5   Problems with the driveshaft are usually indicated by a noise or vibration while driving the vehicle. A road test should verify if the problem is the driveshaft or another vehicle component. Refer to the *Troubleshooting* section at the front of this manual. If you suspect trouble, inspect the driveline.

Inspection

6   Raise the rear of the vehicle and support it securely on jackstands. Block the front wheels to keep the vehicle from rolling off the stands. Release the parking brake and place the transmission in Neutral.

7   Crawl under the vehicle and visually inspect the driveshaft. Look for any dents or cracks in the tubing. If any are found, the driveshaft must be replaced.

8   Check for oil leakage at the front and rear of the driveshaft. Leakage where the driveshaft enters the transmission or transfer case indicates a defective transmission/transfer case seal (see Chapter 7B). Leakage where the driveshaft enters the differential indicates a defective pinion seal (see Section 16).

9   While under the vehicle, have an assistant rotate a rear wheel so the driveshaft will rotate. As it does, make sure the universal joints are operating properly without binding, noise or looseness. Listen for any noise from the center bearing (if equipped), indicating it's worn or damaged. Also check the rubber portion of the center bearing for cracking or separation, which will necessitate replacement.

10   The universal joint can also be checked with the driveshaft motionless, by gripping your hands on either side of the joint and attempting to twist the joint. Any movement at all in the joint is a sign of considerable wear. Lifting up on the shaft will also indicate movement in the universal joints.

11   Finally, check the driveshaft mounting bolts at the ends to make sure they're tight.

12   On 4WD models, the above driveshaft checks should be repeated on the front driveshaft, as well. In addition, check for leakage around the sleeve yoke, indicating failure of the yoke seal.

13   Check for leakage where the driveshafts connect to the transfer case and front differential. Leakage indicates worn oil seals.

14   At the same time, check for looseness in the joints of the front driveaxles. Also check for grease or oil leakage from around the driveaxles by inspecting the rubber boots and both ends of each axle. Oil leakage around the axle flanges indicates a defective axleshaft oil seal. Grease leakage at the CV joint boots means a damaged rubber boot. For servicing of these components, see the appropriate Sections.

---

12   Driveshaft(s) - removal and installation

Warning: *The manufacturer recommends replacing the universal joint flange nuts and bolts whenever they are removed.*

Rear driveshaft
Removal

Refer to illustration 12.2

1   Raise the vehicle and support it securely on jackstands. Place the transmission in Neutral with the parking brake off. If necessary, remove the lower skid guards to gain access to the driveline.

2   Make reference marks on the driveshaft flange and the pinion flange in line with each other **(see illustration)**. In the same manner, mark the relationship of the front yoke to the transmission or transfer case.

Note: *On driveshaft assemblies with a center support bearing, mark the relationship of the center slip yoke with the front half of the driveshaft assembly.*

3   Remove the rear universal joint nuts and bolts. Turn the driveshaft (or wheels) as necessary to bring the bolts into the most accessible position. **Note:** *On driveshaft assemblies equipped with a center support bearing, remove the bearing mounting fasteners.*

4   Lower the rear of the driveshaft, then slide the front yoke out of the transmission or transfer case.

5   Wrap a plastic bag over the transmission or transfer case housing and hold it in place with a rubber band. This will prevent loss of fluid and protect against contamination while the driveshaft is out.

Installation

6   Remove the plastic bag from the transmission or transfer case and wipe the area clean. Inspect the oil seal carefully. Procedures for replacement of this seal can be found in Chapter 7B.

7   Slide the front yoke of the driveshaft into the transmission or transfer case, being careful not to damage the seal in the process.

8   Raise the rear of the driveshaft into position, checking to be sure the marks are in alignment. If not, turn the rear wheels to match the pinion flange and the driveshaft.

9   Install the bolts and nuts, tightening them

12.2 Mark the relationship of the driveshaft flange to the pinion flange

to the torque listed in this Chapter's Specifications.

Front driveshaft (4WD models)
Removal

10   Raise the front of the vehicle and place it securely on jackstands. Remove the skid plate, if equipped.

11   Mark the relationship of the driveshaft to the front differential companion flange and to the transfer case companion flange.

12   Remove the bolts and nuts from the flanges, then lower the shaft from the vehicle.

Installation

13   Attach the ends of the shaft to the differential and transfer case companion flanges (be sure to line up the marks), install the bolts and nuts and tighten them to the torque listed in this Chapter's Specifications.

14   Install the skid plate (if equipped).

---

13   Universal joints - replacement

Refer to illustrations 13.3, 13.4, 13.5, 13.6 and 13.16

Note 1: *Always purchase a universal joint service kit for your model vehicle before beginning this procedure. Also, read through the entire procedure before beginning work.*

Note 2: *On all models, select-fit snap-rings are available to adjust the universal joint endplay, which should be 0.0008-inch (0.02 mm) or less. Check with your local auto parts store or dealer service department if the endplay is greater than specified after the joint is assembled (or if the joint is extremely tight and won't free-up).*

Note 3: *Rear driveshafts on some V6 models use a CV-type coupling instead of the typical cross-type U-joint. You can distinguish the CV-joint drivelines by the fact that the entire center flex joint is covered by a rubber boot. These CV joint drivelines will need to be taken to a machine shop to have the CV joint pressed off and on the driveshaft.*

1   Remove the driveshaft (see Section 12).

13.3 Use a small pair of pliers to remove the snap-rings from the ends of the universal joint yokes

13.4 To remove the U-joint from the driveshaft, use a vise as a press - the small socket will push the cross and bearing cap into the large socket

13.5 Locking pliers can be used to remove the bearing caps from the yoke

2   Place the driveshaft on a bench equipped with a vise.

3   Remove the snap-rings with a small pair of pliers **(see illustration)**.

4   Support the cross (also called a spider) on a short piece of pipe or a large socket and use another socket to press out the cross by closing the vise **(see illustration)**.

5   Press the cross through as far as possible, then grip the bearing cap with pliers and remove it **(see illustration)**.

6   A universal joint repair kit will contain a new cross, seals, bearings, caps and snap-rings **(see illustration)**.

7   Inspect the bearing cap bores in the yokes for wear and damage.

8   If the bearing cap bores in the yoke are so worn that the caps are a loose fit, the driveshaft will have to be replaced with a new one.

9   Make sure the dust seals are properly located on the cross.

10   Using a vise, press one bearing cap into the yoke approximately 1/4-inch.

11   Use chassis grease to hold the needle rollers in place in the caps.

12   Insert the cross into the partially installed bearing cap, taking care not to dislodge the needle rollers.

13   Hold the cross in correct alignment and press both caps into place by slowly and carefully closing the jaws of the vise.

14   Use a socket slightly smaller in diameter

than the caps to press them into the yoke. Press in one side, install the snap-ring, then press the other side to shift the cross assembly tight against the installed snap-ring and install the other snap-ring.

15   Repeat the operations for the remaining two bearing caps.

16   If the joint is stiff after assembly, strike the yoke sharply with a hammer **(see illustration)**. This will spring the yoke ears slightly and free up the joint.

14   Axles - description and check

Description

1   The rear axle assembly is a hypoid (the centerline of the pinion gear is below the centerline of the ring gear), semi-floating type. When the vehicle goes around a corner, the differential allows the outer rear wheel to turn at a higher speed than the inner tire. The axleshafts are splined to the differential side gears, so when the vehicle goes around a corner, the inner wheel, which turns more slowly than the outer wheel, turns its side gear more slowly than the outer wheel turns its side gear. The differential pinion (or spider) gears roll around the slower side gear, driving the outer side gear - and tire - more quickly.

2   On 4WD models, a fully independent

front axle assembly is used. This consists of a differential and a pair of driveaxles. Each driveaxle has an inner and outer constant velocity (CV) joint.

3   An optional locking limited-slip rear axle is also available. This differential allows for normal operation until one wheel loses traction. A limited-slip unit is similar in design to a conventional differential, except for the addition of a pair of multi-disc clutch packs which slow the rotation of the differential case when one wheel is on a firm surface and the other is on a slippery one. The difference in wheel rotational speed produced by this condition applies additional force to the pinion gears and through the cone, which is splined to the axleshafts, equalizes the rotation speed of the axleshaft driving the wheel with traction.

Check

4   Often, a suspected "axle" problem lies elsewhere. Do a thorough check of other possible causes before assuming the axle is the problem.

5   The following noises are those commonly associated with axle diagnosis procedures:

a) *Road noise is often mistaken for mechanical faults. Driving the vehicle on different surfaces will show whether or not the road surface is the cause of the*

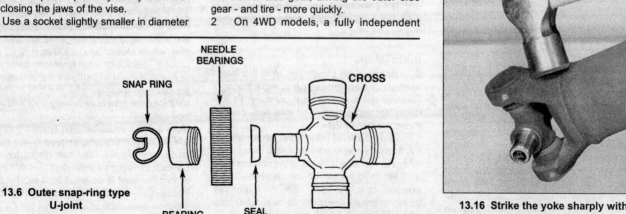

13.6 Outer snap-ring type U-joint

SNAP RING

NEEDLE BEARINGS

CROSS

BEARING CAP

SEAL

79040-8-10.1 HAYNES

13.16 Strike the yoke sharply with a hammer to "spring" the yoke ears, which will free-up the joint

15.3 The rear axle is retained in the axle housing by these four nuts

15.4 After removing the axle retaining nuts, pull the axle from the housing with a slide hammer and adapter connected to the axle flange

noise. Road noise will remain the same if the vehicle is under power or coasting.

b) *Tire noise is sometimes mistaken for mechanical problems. Tires which are worn or low on pressure are particularly susceptible to emitting vibrations and noises. Tire noise will remain about the same during varying driving situations, where axle noise will change during coasting, acceleration, etc.*

c) *Engine and transmission noise can be deceiving because it will travel along the driveline. To isolate engine and transmission noises, make a note of the engine speed at which the noise is most pronounced. Stop the vehicle and place the transmission in Neutral and run the engine to the same speed. If the noise is the same, the axle is not at fault.*

6   Because of the special tools needed, overhauling the differential isn't cost effective for a do-it-yourselfer. The procedures included in this Chapter describe axleshaft removal and installation, axleshaft oil seal replacement, axleshaft bearing replacement and removal of the entire unit for repair or replacement. Any further work should be left to a qualified repair shop.

15 Axleshaft, bearing and oil seals (rear) - removal, bearing/seal replacement and installation

Refer to illustrations 15.3, 15.4, 15.6a and 15.6b

Warning: *The manufacturer recommends replacing the axle retaining plate nuts with new ones whenever they are removed.*

Removal

1   Loosen the wheel lug nuts, raise the rear of the vehicle and support it securely on jackstands. Chock the front wheels to prevent the vehicle from rolling. Remove the wheel.

2   Without disconnecting the brake hose, remove the brake caliper and wire it to the chassis out of the way. Do not let the caliper hang by the brake hose. Make alignment marks on the brake disc and one wheel stud. Remove the brake disc and ABS wheel speed sensor and position the sensor out of the way (see Chapter 9)

3   Remove the nuts securing the axle retaining plate to the axle housing and disconnect the parking brake cable **(see illustration)**.

4   Connect a slide hammer and adapter to the axle flange and pull the axle from the

housing **(see illustration)**. The disc brake dust shield will come out with the axle.

5   The manufacturer suggests that any time an axle is pulled, the axle bearing and the axle seal should be replaced. The axle should be taken to a machine shop, where the old bearing can be removed and a new one pressed on. In the process of removing the bearing, the ABS wheel sensor rotor must also be pressed off the axleshaft. Once removed it should be replaced with a new ABS sensor rotor. **Note:** *There are two different rear axle versions used on these vehicles. One version has a one-piece sealed axleshaft bearing and uses shims to adjust axleshaft endplay. Be sure to retrieve any shims from between the axle bearing retainer ring and the retainer ring snap-ring. During assembly, the machine shop should use shims that bring the clearance between the axle bearing retainer ring and its snap-ring to the desired specification of 0.008-inch or less.*

6   The oil seal in the axle tube can be pried out with a large screwdriver or seal removal tool **(see illustration)**. The new seal should be driven in with a seal installer **(see illustration)**. If you don't have a seal installer, a large socket with an outside diameter just slightly smaller than that of the seal can be used as a driver.

15.6a Prying out the axleshaft oil seal with a seal removal tool

15.6b Driving in the axleshaft oil seal with a seal installer

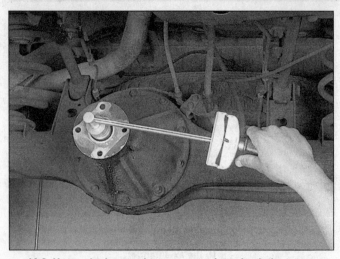

16.3 Use an inch-pound torque wrench to check the torque necessary to rotate the pinion shaft

16.4 Mark the position of the flange to the shaft and count the number of exposed threads above the nut

Installation

7   Wipe the bore in the axle housing clean and apply a thin coat of grease to the outer surface of the axle bearing. Make sure to install a new O-ring on the outer end of the axle housing flange before inserting the axle. **Caution:** *Take care not to cut or scratch the new seal with the splines of the axleshaft during installation.*

8   Guide the axleshaft straight into the axle housing. Rotate the shaft slightly to engage the splines on the shaft with the splines in the differential side gear.

9   Install new axle retaining plate nuts and tighten them to the torque listed in this Chapter's Specifications.

10   The remainder of installation is the reverse of removal. Check the differential lubricant level and add some, if necessary. Bleed the brakes (see Chapter 9).

11   Install the wheel and lug nuts. Lower the vehicle and tighten the lug nuts to the torque listed in the Chapter 1 Specifications.

16 Pinion oil seal (front and rear) - replacement

Refer to illustrations 16.3, 16.4, 16.5, 16.7 and 16.9

1   Loosen the wheel lug nuts. Raise the front (for front differential) or rear (for rear differential) of the vehicle and support it securely on jackstands. Block the opposite set of wheels to keep the vehicle from rolling off the stands. Remove the wheels.

2   Disconnect the driveshaft from the differential companion flange and fasten it out of the way (see Section 12).

3   Rotate the pinion a few times by hand. Use a beam-type or dial-type inch-pound torque wrench to check the torque required to rotate the pinion **(see illustration)**. Record it for use later.

4   Mark the relationship of the pinion flange to the shaft **(see illustration)**, then count and write down the number of exposed threads on the shaft.

5   A flange holding tool will be required to keep the companion flange from moving while the self-locking pinion nut is loosened. A chain wrench will also work **(see illustration)**.

6   Remove the pinion nut.

7   Withdraw the flange. It may be necessary to use a two-jaw puller engaged behind the flange to draw it off **(see illustration)**. Do not attempt to pry or hammer behind the flange or hammer on the end of the pinion shaft.

8   Pry out the old seal and discard it.

9   Lubricate the lips of the new seal and fill the space between the seal lips with wheel bearing grease, then tap it evenly into position with a seal installation tool or a large socket **(see illustration)**. Make sure it enters the housing squarely and is tapped in to its full depth.

10   Install the pinion flange, lining up the marks made in Step 4. If necessary, tighten the pinion nut to draw the flange into place. Do not try to hammer the flange into position.

11   Apply a bead of RTV sealant to the ends of the splines visible in the center of the flange so oil will be sealed in.

12   Install a new pinion nut and pinion nut

16.5 A chain wrench is being used here to prevent the pinion flange from turning while the nut is loosened

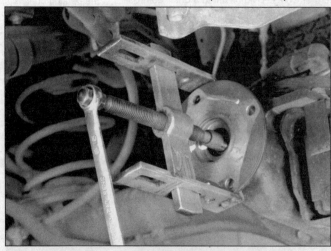

16.7 If you can't pull the pinion flange off by hand, remove it with a puller

16.9 Lubricate the lips of the new seal and seat it squarely in the bore, then drive it into the carrier with a seal driver or a large socket

lockwasher. Do not reuse the old nut or lockwasher. Tighten the nut until the number of threads exposed in Step 4 is showing.

13 Measure the torque required to rotate the pinion and tighten the nut in small increments (no more than 5 ft-lbs) until it matches the figure recorded in Step 3. To compensate for the drag of the new oil seal, the nut should be tightened a little more until the rotational torque of the pinion exceeds the earlier recording by 5 in-lbs. **Caution:** *If the maximum nut torque is reached before the desired preload is obtained, the differential must be disassembled and a new collapsible spacer must be installed.*

14 Reinstall all components removed previously by reversing the removal Steps and tightening all fasteners to their specified torque values.

17 Axle assembly (rear) - removal and installation

Removal

1 Loosen the rear wheel lug nuts, raise the rear of the vehicle and support it securely on jackstands placed under the frame rails. Block the front wheels to keep the vehicle from rolling off the stands. Remove the rear wheels.

2 Position a jack under the rear axle differential housing. If you have two floor jacks, position one under each axle tube.

3 Disconnect the driveshaft from the rear axle pinion flange (see Section 12). Fasten the driveshaft out of the way with a piece of wire from the underbody.

4 Disconnect the shock absorbers at their lower mounts.

5 Disconnect the vent hose from the fitting on the axle housing and fasten it out of the way.

6 Drain the differential lubricant (see Chapter 1).

7 Remove the brake calipers and set them aside (see Chapter 9). Wire the calipers to the

chassis so they don't hang by the brake hoses (see Chapter 9). Remove the brake discs. Disconnect and set aside the ABS wheel sensor harness connectors at the axle ends.

8 Disconnect the parking brake cables and the brake lines, being careful to plug the open brake line fittings to prevent entry of dirt.

9 Remove the stabilizer bar (see Chapter 10).

10 Remove the nuts from the bottom of the leaf-spring U-bolts and remove the spring plates (see Chapter 10).

11 There are two possible ways to remove the rear axle assembly. An assistant is highly recommended. If the axleshafts were removed (and the brake dust shields with them), then the axle housing can be shifted to the left or right until one axle housing end clears the spring, that end can be lowered and the other end guided from its spring. With the dust shields in place, there isn't room enough for the axle/shields to clear the springs, so the axle housing should be supported on two floorjacks, one on each tube. Remove the nuts from the rear spring shackles on each side (see Chapter 10) and push the shackles out of their lower bushing on the leaf springs (work on one spring at a time). Lower the leaf springs to the floor and slide the rear axle housing out on the two floorjacks.

Installation

12 Installation is the reverse of removal. Tighten the U-joint strap bolts to the torque listed in this Chapter's Specifications. Tighten all suspension fasteners to the torque values listed in the Chapter 10 Specifications.

13 Bleed the brakes (see Chapter 9).

18 Driveaxles (4WD models) - general information and inspection

1 Power is transmitted from the front differential/axle to the front wheels through a pair of driveaxles. The inner end of each driveaxle is bolted to an axleshaft connected to the differential side gears; the outer end of each driveaxle has a stub shaft that is splined to the front hub and bearing assembly.

2 The inner ends of the driveaxles are equipped with sliding constant velocity (CV) joints, which are capable of both angular and axial motion. Each inner CV joint assembly consists of a tripot-type bearing and a housing in which the joint is free to slide in-and-out as the driveaxle moves up-and-down with the wheel.

3 The outer ends of the driveaxles are equipped with "ball-and-cage" type CV joints, which are capable of angular but not axial movement. Each outer CV joint consists of six caged ball bearings running between an inner race and the housing.

4 The boots should be inspected periodically for damage and leaking lubricant. Torn CV joint boots must be replaced immediately or the joints will be damaged. If either boot of

a driveaxle is damaged, that driveaxle must be removed in order to replace the boot (see Section 19).

5 Should a boot be damaged, the CV joint can be disassembled and cleaned (see Section 20), but if any parts are damaged, the entire driveaxle assembly must be replaced as a unit.

6 The most common symptom of worn or damaged CV joints, besides lubricant leaks, is a clicking noise in turns, a clunk when accelerating after coasting and vibration at highway speeds. To check for wear in the CV joints and driveaxle shafts, grasp each axle (one at a time) and rotate it in both directions while holding the CV joint housings, feeling for play indicating worn splines or sloppy CV joints. Also check the driveaxle shafts for cracks, dents and distortion.

19 Driveaxle (4WD models) - removal and installation

1 Loosen the wheel lug nuts, remove the cotter pin from the driveaxle hub nut, and use a breaker-bar and a socket to loosen the driveaxle hub nut. Raise the front of the vehicle and support it securely on jackstands. Remove the front wheel(s).

2 Remove the screws and the engine undercover.

3 Disconnect the ABS wheel sensor harness at the hub and wire it out of the way.

4 Remove the driveaxle hub nut.

5 Position a floorjack under the lower control arm and apply slight tension upward.

6 Disconnect the upper balljoint from the upper control arm (see Chapter 10).

7 Pull the steering knuckle outward enough for the splines of the driveaxle to clear the knuckle.

8 Use a large flat prybar to release the inner end of the driveaxle from the front differential assembly.

9 Replace the differential side seals whenever the driveaxles have been removed. Use a seal-removal tool to pull the old seals out, then clean the seal location on the differential housing. Make sure you don't damage the seal bore or the new seal may leak.

10 Use a hammer and a seal-driver tool or a large socket of the appropriate size to drive the new seal into place.

11 Lubricate the lip of the new seal with multi-purpose grease.

12 The remainder of the installation process is the reverse of the removal. Take care to keep the splines of the inner end of the driveaxle centered in the seal opening when installing the driveaxle, to avoid nicking the new seal. Drive the inner end of the driveaxle in with a hammer to seat it securely in the differential housing.

13 Install the wheel and lug nuts. Lower the vehicle and tighten the lug nuts to the torque listed in the Chapter 1 Specifications. Tighten the driveaxle hub nut to the torque listed in this Chapters Specifications.

20.2a Pry up the retaining tabs on the boot clamps . . .

20 Driveaxle boot - replacement

Note: *Complete rebuilt driveaxles are available on an exchange basis, which eliminates much time and work.*

1   Remove the driveaxle (see Section 19).

Inner CV joint

Disassembly

Refer to illustrations 20.2a, 20.2b, 20.4a, 20.4b and 20.5

2   Remove both boot clamps and discard them, then slide the boot down the shaft and out of the way **(see illustrations)**.

3   Mark the relationship of the inner joint housing to the shaft. Mount the driveaxle shaft in a vise with padded jaws, then tap the inner joint housing towards the center of the shaft to dislodge the cover on the end of the joint. Remove the cover and slide the joint housing down the shaft and out of the way.

4   Remove the snap-ring from the end of the shaft, then mark the relationship of the shaft and spider so they can be reassembled in the original position **(see illustrations)**.

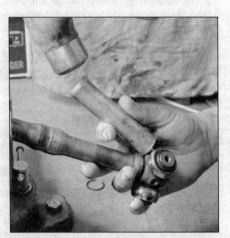

20.5 Drive the spider from the shaft with a hammer and brass punch

20.2b . . . then open the clamps and remove them from the boot

5   Using a hammer and a brass punch, drive the spider assembly off the shaft **(see illustration)**.

6   Slide the housing and boot off the axleshaft.

Inspection

7   Clean the components with solvent to remove all traces of grease. Inspect all of the components for pitting, score marks, cracks and other signs of wear and damage. Shiny, polished spots are normal and will not adversely affect CV joint performance. Also check the splines on the shaft and in the spider for wear. If any undesirable conditions exist, the entire joint (or driveaxle assembly) will have to be replaced.

Reassembly

Refer to illustrations 20.8, 20.10, 20.15a, 20.15b, 20.16a and 20.16b

8   Wrap the axleshaft splines with tape to avoid damaging the boot. Slide the small boot clamp and boot onto the axleshaft **(see illustration)**, then remove the tape. Slide the large boot clamp over the boot.

9   Slide the housing onto the shaft.

20.8 Wrap the splined area of the axleshaft with tape to prevent damage to the boots when installing them

20.4a Remove the snap-ring from the groove in the end of the axleshaft

20.4b Use a center punch to place marks on the spider and shaft to ensure that they're properly reassembled

10   Install the spider assembly onto the shaft, lining up the marks you made in Step 4. The side with the chamfered splines must face toward the center of the shaft **(see illustration)**.

20.10 Install the spider with the chamfered ends of the splines facing toward the center of the axleshaft

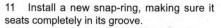

20.15a Adjust the length of the CV joint to the dimension listed in this Chapter's Specifications . . .

20.15b . . . then equalize the pressure inside the boot by inserting a dull screwdriver between the boot and the housing

20.16a To install the new clamps, bend the tang down . . .

11   Install a new snap-ring, making sure it seats completely in its groove.

12   Lubricate the spider assembly and housing with CV joint grease, then move the housing up onto the spider, aligning the mark on the housing (made in Step 3) with the mark on the shaft. Apply a bead of RTV sealant to a new cover, then tap the cover into place.

13   Fill the housing with approximately 3-1/2 ounces (100 g) of CV joint grease (normally included with the new boot kit). **Caution:** *Use CV joint grease only.*

14   Wipe any excess grease from the boot grooves on the shaft and the housing. Seat the small diameter of the boot in the recessed area on the axleshaft. Push the other end of the boot onto the housing and move the race in or out until there's no deformation (distortion or dents) in the boot.

15   Adjust the CV joint to the length listed in this Chapter's Specifications (measured from one end of the boot to the other) **(see illustration)**. Equalize the pressure in the boot by

inserting a dull screwdriver between the boot and the outer race **(see illustration)**. Don't damage the boot with the tool.

16   Install the boot clamps **(see illustrations)**.

17   Install the driveaxle (see Section 19).

Outer CV joint

Disassembly

Refer to illustration 20.19

18   Remove the boot clamps and separate the boot from the outer CV joint **(see illustrations 20.2a and 20.2b)**.

19   Clamp the axleshaft in a bench vise (equipped with protective jaws) and drive off the outer CV joint with a brass hammer **(see illustration)**, then remove the retainer ring for the inner race. Slide off the old boot.

20   Thoroughly wash the outer CV joint in clean solvent then rinse it out with brake system cleaner to remove all traces of solvent.

Inspection

Refer to illustration 20.21

21   Rotate the outer CV joint housing at an angle to the driveaxle to expose the bearings, inner race and cage **(see illustration)**. Inspect the bearing surfaces for signs of wear. If the CV joint is worn, replace it.

Reassembly

Refer to illustrations 20.24, 20.25 and 20.26

22   Slide the new outer boot and small clamp onto the driveaxle. It's a good idea to wrap vinyl tape around the shaft splines to prevent damage to the boot **(see illustration 20.8)**. Remove the tape.

23   Install a new inner race retainer ring on the shaft.

24   Pack the CV joint with approximately 5-ounces (140 g) of CV joint grease through the splined hole in the inner race. **Caution:** *Use CV joint grease only.* Force the grease into the joint by inserting a wooden dowel through the splined hole and pushing it to the bottom of the joint. Repeat this procedure

20.16b . . . and tap the tabs down to hold it in place

20.19 To remove the outer CV joint, clamp the axleshaft in a bench vise (with padded jaws) and tap the joint off with a brass hammer

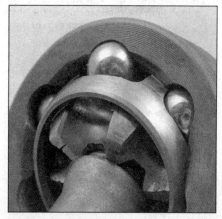

20.21 After the old grease has been rinsed away, move the inner race through its full range of motion and inspect the bearing surfaces for wear or damage - if any of the balls, the race or the cage look damaged, replace the outer joint assembly

20.24 Apply CV joint grease through the splined hole, then insert a wooden dowel (slightly smaller in diameter than the hole) into the hole and push down - the dowel will force the grease into the joint

until the bearing is completely packed (**see illustration**). **Note:** *If the specified quantity of grease can't be packed into the joint, place the remainder in the CV joint boot.*

25   Tap the outer CV joint into place with a hammer and a wood block (**see illustration**).
26   Slide the boot into position. When the boot is in position, add the remainder of the grease in the boot replacement kit to the CV joint boot. Slide the boot onto the joint and adjust the length (**see illustration**), equalize the pressure inside the boot (**see illustration 20.15b**) and install the new clamps (**see illustrations 20.16a and 20.16b**).
27   Install the driveaxle (see Section 19).

---

21   Axle assembly (front) - removal and installation

---

1   Raise the vehicle and support it securely on jackstands. Remove the under-vehicle splash shield, then detach the vent hose from the differential housing.
2   Mark the relationship of the driveshaft to the differential companion flange, then unbolt the driveshaft from the flange (see Section 12). Support the driveshaft with a piece of wire from the underbody.
3   Drain the differential lubricant (see Chapter 1), then remove the front driveaxles (see Section 19).
4   Support the front axle assembly with a floor jack placed under the differential.
5   Unbolt the differential and axle tube mounts from the front suspension crossmember.
6   Remove the bolt from each end of the differential mounting member, then maneuver the axle/differential assembly out from under the vehicle.
7   Installation is the reverse of the removal procedure.

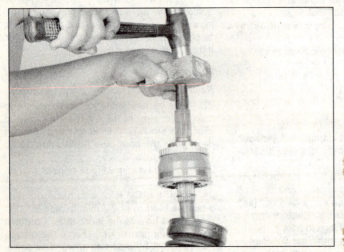

20.25 To install the outer CV joint, put the axleshaft in a bench vise (equipped with protective jaws) and tap on the CV joint with a hammer and a block of wood; drive the joint onto the axleshaft splines until the retainer ring on the shaft seats in the groove in the inner race of the joint

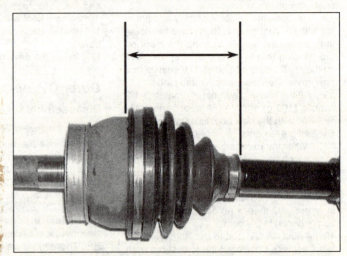

20.26 Adjust the boot to the length indicated in this Chapter's Specifications, then tighten the clamps

Chapter 9 Brakes

Contents

Specifications

General
Brake fluid type .... See Chapter 1

Brake light switch
Plunger-to-pedal stopper clearance .... 0.029 to 0.077 inch (0.74 to 1.96 mm)

Disc brakes (front and rear)
Minimum pad lining thickness .... See Chapter 1
Brake disc minimum thickness .... Cast into disc
Maximum disc runout .... 0.0020 inch (0.05 mm)
Maximum disc thickness variation .... 0.0006 inch (0.015 mm)

Power brake booster
Booster-to-center of clevis hole dimension .... 5.91 inches (150 mm)

Torque specifications

Ft-lbs (unless otherwise indicated) **Nm**

Note: *One foot-pound (ft-lb) of torque is equivalent to 12 inch-pounds (in-lbs) of torque. Torque values below approximately 15 ft-lbs are expressed in inch-pounds, since most foot-pound torque wrenches are not accurate at these smaller values.*

	Ft-lbs	Nm
ABS wheel speed sensor mounting bolts		
Front	156 in-lbs	17.5
Rear	15	20
Brake booster-to-body mounting nuts	18	24
Caliper mounting bolts		
Front		
2005 through 2008	32	43
2009 and later	20	27
Rear		
Frontier models		
2005 through 2007	24	32
2008 and later	20	27
Xterra models		
2005 through 2007	19	26
2008 and later	20	27
Caliper mounting bracket bolts		
Front	136	184
Rear		
2005 through 2007	76	103
2008 and later	65	88
Brake hose-to-caliper bolt	159 in-lbs	18
Master cylinder-to-brake booster retaining nuts		
2005 through 2008	120 in-lbs	13.5
2009	132 in-lbs	15
2010 and later	18	24
Wheel lug nuts	See Chapter 1	

2.2 ABS hydraulic unit (A) and ECU (B)

2.6a Front wheel ABS sensor mounting bolt

1   General information

General

The vehicles covered by this manual are equipped with hydraulically operated front and rear brake systems. Both front and rear brakes are disc-type and are self-adjusting.

Hydraulic system

The hydraulic system consists of two separate circuits, split front-to-rear. The master cylinder has separate reservoirs for the two circuits, and, in the event of a leak or failure in one hydraulic circuit, the other circuit will remain operative and a warning indicator will light up on the instrument panel when a substantial amount of brake fluid is lost, showing that a failure has occurred.

Power brake booster

The power brake booster uses engine manifold vacuum to provide assistance to the brakes. It is mounted on the firewall in the engine compartment, directly behind the master cylinder.

Parking brake

On all models, the parking brake is operated by a lever in the floor console. Control cables are routed to the rear axle, where the cables operate small drum brake shoes that apply pressure to the inner diameter of the rear brake discs.

Service

After completing any operation involving disassembly of any part of the brake system, always test drive the vehicle to check for proper braking performance before resuming normal driving. When testing the brakes, perform the tests on a clean, dry, flat surface. Conditions other than these can lead to inaccurate test results.

Test the brakes at various speeds with both light and heavy pedal pressure. The vehicle should stop evenly without pulling to one side or the other.

Tires, vehicle load and wheel alignment are factors which also affect braking performance.

2   Anti-lock Brake System (ABS) - general information and trouble codes

General information

Refer to illustration 2.2

1   The anti-lock brake system is designed to maintain vehicle steerability, directional stability and optimum deceleration under severe braking conditions on most road surfaces. It does so by monitoring the rotational speed of each wheel and controlling the brake line pressure to each wheel during braking. This prevents the wheels from locking up.

2   The ABS system has three main components - the wheel speed sensors, the electronic control unit (ECU) and the hydraulic unit **(see illustration)**. Four wheel speed sensors - one at each wheel - send a variable voltage signal to the control unit, which monitors these signals, compares them to its program and determines whether a wheel is about to lock up. When a wheel is about to lock up, the control unit signals the hydraulic unit to reduce hydraulic pressure (or not increase it further) at that wheel's brake caliper. Pressure modulation is handled by electrically-operated solenoid valves.

3   If a problem develops within the system, an "ABS" warning light will glow on the dashboard. Sometimes, a visual inspection of the ABS system can help you locate the problem. Carefully inspect the ABS wiring harness. Pay particularly close attention to the harness and connections near each wheel. Look for signs of chafing and other damage caused by incorrectly routed wires. If a wheel sensor harness is damaged, the sensor must be replaced. **Warning:** *Do NOT try to repair an ABS wiring harness. The ABS system is sensitive to even* *the smallest changes in resistance. Repairing the harness could alter resistance values and cause the system to malfunction. If the ABS wiring harness is damaged in any way, it must be replaced.* **Caution:** *Make sure the ignition is turned off before unplugging or reattaching any electrical connections.*

Diagnosis and repair

4   If a dashboard warning light comes on and stays on while the vehicle is in operation, the ABS system requires attention. Although special electronic ABS diagnostic testing tools are necessary to properly diagnose the system, you can perform a few preliminary checks before taking the vehicle to a dealer service department.

   a) Check the brake fluid level in the reservoir.
   b) Verify that the computer electrical connectors are securely connected.
   c) Check the electrical connectors at the hydraulic control unit.
   d) Check the fuses.
   e) Follow the wiring harness to each wheel and verify that all connections are secure and that the wiring is undamaged.

If the above preliminary checks do not rectify the problem, the vehicle should be diagnosed by a dealer service department or other qualified repair shop. Due to the complex nature of this system, all actual repair work must be done by a qualified automotive technician.

Wheel speed sensor - replacement

Refer to illustrations 2.6a and 2.6b

5   Front and rear wheel speed sensors can be replaced if determined to be faulty or damaged.

6   Disconnect the ABS sensor's electrical harness, then remove the mounting bolt **(see illustrations)**. **Note:** *Rear wheel sensors have two mounting bolts, front sensors only one.*

2.6b Rear wheel ABS sensor mounting bolts

3.5a Use a C-clamp on the caliper to retract the pistons

7   Remove the sensors straight out and do not use a pry tool to remove or pull them by the harness. If the sensor is being removed to perform other brake or suspension work (not for replacement), be sure to clean it before installing it. Use brake cleaner to clean the sensor and the hole.
8   When reinstalling an ABS sensor, replace the O-ring with a new one, lubricated with suitable grease. Torque the mounting bolts to the Specifications in this Chapter.

3   Disc brake pads - replacement

Refer to illustrations 3.5a through 3.5k and 3.6a through 3.6g

Warning: *Disc brake pads must be replaced on both front or both rear wheels at the same time - never replace the pads on only one wheel. Also, the dust created by the brake system is harmful to your health. Never blow it out with compressed air and don't inhale any of it. An approved filtering mask should be worn when working on the brakes. Do not, under any circumstances, use petroleum-based solvents to clean brake parts. Use brake system cleaner only!*

3.5b Remove the lower caliper mounting bolt, loosen the top bolt and rotate the caliper up and out of the way

1   Remove the cap from the brake fluid reservoir. Remove about two-thirds of the fluid from the reservoir.
2   Loosen the front wheel lug nuts, raise the front of the vehicle and support it securely on jackstands. Block the wheels at the opposite end.
3   Remove the wheels. Work on one brake assembly at a time, using the assembled brake for reference if necessary.

4   Inspect the brake disc carefully as outlined in Section 5. If machining is necessary, follow the information in that Section to remove the disc, at which time the pads can be removed as well.
5   Follow the accompanying photo sequence for the front brake pad replacement **(see illustrations 3.5a through 3.5k)**. Be sure to stay in order and read the caption under each illustration.

3.5c Remove the outboard pad shim

3.5d Remove the inboard pad shim

3.5e Remove the pad-return spring, noting which way it was installed

3.5f Remove the outboard brake pad

3.5g Remove the inboard brake pad

3.5h Remove the upper and lower pad retainers, then clean the retainers thoroughly

3.5i Apply a small amount of disc brake grease to the parts of the retainers that contact the tabs on the pads, then install the retainers on the caliper mounting bracket

3.5j Install the new inboard brake pad and its shim

3.5k Install the outboard brake pad and its shim, then the pad-return spring. Lower the caliper and tighten the caliper mounting bolts to Specifications

6   To replace rear disc brake pads, follow the accompanying sequence (see illustrations 3.6a through 3.6g).

7   When reinstalling the caliper, be sure to tighten the mounting bolt to the torque listed in this Chapter's Specifications.

8   After the job has been completed, firmly depress the brake pedal a few times to bring the pads into contact with the disc. Check the level of the brake fluid, adding some if necessary. Check the operation of the brakes carefully before placing the vehicle into normal service.

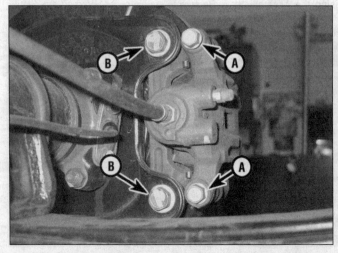

3.6a Location of the rear brake caliper mounting bolts (A) and the caliper mounting bracket bolts (B)

3.6b Use a C-clamp to retract the piston in the rear caliper

3.6c Remove the lower caliper mounting bolt, loosen the top bolt and rotate the caliper out of the way

3.6d Remove the inboard brake pad and its shim

3.6e Remove the outboard brake pad and its shim

3.6f Remove the upper and lower pad retainers, clean them thoroughly, then lubricate them with a small amount of disc brake grease and reinstall them in the caliper mounting bracket

3.6g Install the outer and inner pads with their shims, rotate the caliper down and tighten the caliper mounting bolts to Specifications

4 Brake caliper - removal and installation

Refer to illustrations 4.2a and 4.2b

Warning: *The dust created by the brake system is harmful to your health. Never blow it out with compressed air and don't inhale any of it. An approved filtering mask should be worn when working on the brakes. Do not, under any circumstances, use petroleum-based solvents to clean brake parts. Use brake system cleaner only!*

Note: *This procedure applies to the front and rear disc brake calipers.*

Removal

1   Loosen the wheel lug nuts, raise the vehicle and place it securely on jackstands. Block the wheels at the opposite end. Remove the wheel.

2   Remove the inlet fitting bolt and disconnect the brake hose from the caliper. Discard the old sealing washers **(see illustrations)**. Plug the brake hose immediately to keep contaminants and air out of the brake system and to prevent losing any more brake fluid than is

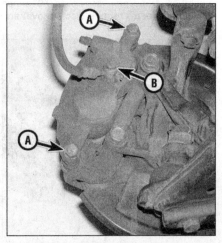

4.2a Caliper mounting details

A   Mounting bolts
B   Inlet fitting bolt

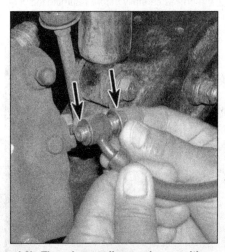

4.2b There is a sealing washer on either side of the brake hose inlet fitting; be sure to replace these with new ones when reconnecting the hose

5.2 Hang the caliper out of the way with a piece of wire - don't let it hang by the brake hose

5.3 The brake pads on this vehicle were obviously neglected, as they wore down completely and cut deep grooves into the disc - wear this severe means the disc must be replaced

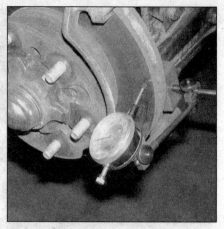

5.4a To check disc runout, mount a dial indicator as shown and rotate the disc

necessary. **Note:** *If you are simply removing the caliper for access to other components, leave the brake hose connected and suspend the caliper with a length of wire - don't let it hang by the hose* **(see illustration 5.2)**.

3   Remove the caliper mounting bolts and detach the caliper from the mounting bracket. On rear calipers, disconnect the brake fluid hose and remove the caliper mounting bolts **(see illustration 3.6a)**.

Installation

4   Installation is the reverse of removal. Don't forget to use new sealing washers on each side of the brake hose inlet fitting and be sure to tighten the fitting bolt and the caliper mounting bolts to the torque values listed in this Chapter's Specifications.

5   Bleed the brake system (see Section 9). **Note:** *If the brake hose was not disconnected, bleeding won't be required.* Make sure there are no leaks from the hose connections. Test the brakes carefully before returning the vehicle to normal service.

---

5   Brake disc - inspection, removal and installation

Inspection

Refer to illustrations 5.2, 5.3, 5.4a, 5.4b, 5.5a and 5.5b

1   Loosen the wheel lug nuts, raise the front or rear of the vehicle and support it securely on jackstands. Apply the parking brake. Remove the wheel.

2   Remove the brake caliper (but don't disconnect the brake line or hose from the caliper) and suspend it out of the way with a piece of wire **(see illustration)**. **Caution:** *Don't let the caliper hang by the brake hose.* Remove the brake pads (see Section 3).

3   Visually inspect the disc surface for score marks and other damage **(see illustration)**. Light scratches and shallow grooves are normal after use and won't affect brake operation. Deep grooves - over 0.015-inch (0.38 mm) deep - require disc removal and

refinishing by an automotive machine shop. Be sure to check both sides of the disc.

4   Install the lugnuts to hold the disc tight to the hub, tightening them just enough to make the disc run true. To check disc runout, place a dial indicator at a point about 1/2-inch from the outer edge of the disc **(see illustration)**. Set the indicator to zero and turn the disc. The indicator reading should not exceed the allowable runout listed in this Chapter's Specifications. If it does, the disc should be refinished by an automotive machine shop. **Note:** *To produce a smooth finish and ensure a perfectly smooth surface - thereby eliminating brake pedal pulsation or any other undesirable symptoms - the discs should be resurfaced regardless of the dial indicator reading. If you elect not to have the discs resurfaced, deglaze them with sandpaper or emery cloth* **(see illustration)**.

5   The disc must not be machined to a thickness less than the specified minimum thickness, which is cast into the disc **(see illustration)**. Measure disc thickness with a micrometer **(see illustration)**.

5.4b Using a swirling motion, remove the glaze from the disc with sandpaper or emery cloth

5.5a The minimum thickness is cast into the edge of the disc (typical)

5.5b Use a micrometer to measure disc thickness at several points

5.6 Caliper mounting bracket bolts

6.2 To release the adjuster on the parking brake assembly, remove this plug in the disc, then rotate the disc until you can see the shoe adjuster through the hole - use a small screwdriver to loosen the adjuster

6.5a Between the axle flange and the backing plate, the parking brake mechanism on the covered models consists of a set of drum-type brake shoes operated by the parking brake cables

Removal and installation

Refer to illustration 5.6

6   Remove the brake caliper (see Section 4), brake pads (see Section 3) and the caliper mounting bracket **(see illustration)**; it isn't necessary to disconnect the brake hose from the caliper. Make index marks on the disc and one of the wheel studs so you can reinstall the disc in the same position.

7   The brake disc slips over the front or rear lug studs, and is retained and centered by the hub and the wheel lug nuts when they are tightened

8   If the disc measures within Specifications, deglaze, clean and reinstall it over the wheel studs.

9   Install the caliper mounting bracket and tighten the bolts to the torque listed in this Chapter's Specifications. Install the brake pads and the caliper (see Section 3).

10   Install the wheels and lug nuts. Lower the vehicle and tighten the lug nuts to the torque listed in the Chapter 1 Specifications.

11   Before driving the vehicle, pump the brake pedal several times to bring the pads into contact with the disc.

6   Parking brake shoes - replacement

Refer to illustrations 6.2 and 6.5a through 6.5k

Warning: *Parking brake shoes must be replaced on both wheels at the same time - never replace the shoes on only one wheel. Also, the dust created by the brake system is harmful to your health. Never blow it out with compressed air and don't inhale any of it. An approved filtering mask should be worn when working on the brakes. Do not, under any circumstances, use petroleum-based solvents to clean brake parts. Use brake system cleaner only!*

1   Loosen the wheel lug nuts, raise the rear of the vehicle and support it securely on jackstands. Block the front wheels to keep the vehicle from rolling. Remove the wheels.

2   Release the parking brake and remove the brake disc (see Section 5). If the shoes

have worn into the disc, preventing disc removal, remove the access plug from the backing plate, insert a small screwdriver through the hole, lift the adjuster lever off the adjusting wheel and turn the wheel with another screwdriver to back off the brake shoes **(see illustration)**. If the disc is rusted to the hub, install two bolts of the proper size and thread pitch into the threaded holes provided and turn them in. As the bolts are tightened, they will contact the surface of the hub flange and push the drum off.

3   **Note:** *All four parking brake shoes must be replaced at the same time, but to avoid mixing up parts, work on only one brake assembly at a time.*

4   Before disassembling anything, clean off the brake assembly with brake system cleaner.

5   Follow the accompanying illustrations **(6.5a through 6.5k)**. Be sure to stay in order and read the caption under each illustration.

6   Turn the adjuster screw wheel so the

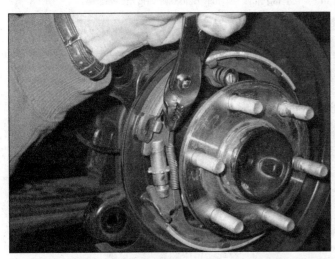

6.5b Using pliers or a brake spring hook tool, remove the front shoe-return spring

6.5c Remove the rear shoe-return spring

6.5d On the upper shoe, use a Phillips screwdriver to turn the shoe hold-down pin until the pin, cup and spring can be removed

6.5e Lift off the upper brake shoe and remove the adjuster mechanism, making sure to note its orientation

6.5f Remove the shoe hold-down pin, cup and spring and remove the lower brake shoe

6.5g Clean the backing plate with brake cleaner, then lightly lubricate the shoe contact pads on the backing plate with brake grease

6.5h Install the shoes with the hold-down pins, cups and springs, then align the rear flanges of the shoes with the actuator mechanism at the rear

disc just slips over the shoes. Now, working through the backing plate, turn the adjuster screw wheel until the shoes drag on the disc when the disc is turned. Finally, back off the adjuster screw wheel so the shoes don't drag.

7   The remainder of installation is the reverse of the removal procedure.

8   Mount the wheel, install the lug nuts, then lower the vehicle. Tighten the wheel lug nuts

to the torque listed in the Chapter 1 Specifications.

9   Check the operation of the brakes carefully before driving the vehicle.

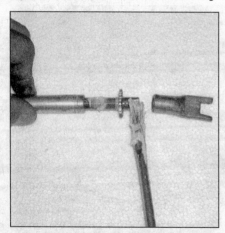

6.5i Clean the adjuster screw assembly, then lubricate the threads and socket end with high-temperature grease

6.5j Attach the rear shoe-return spring

6.5k . . . and the front shoe-return spring

7 Master cylinder - removal, installation and reservoir/seal replacement

Removal

Refer to illustration 7.2

1   Disconnect the cable from the negative battery terminal.

2   Disconnect the electrical connectors for the brake fluid level warning light and the brake fluid pressure sensor **(see illustration)**.

3   Remove as much fluid as possible from the reservoir with a suction gun, large syringe or a poultry baster. **Warning:** *If a poultry baster is used, never again use it for the preparation of food.*

4   Place rags under the fittings and prepare caps or plastic bags to cover the ends of the lines once they're disconnected. **Caution:** *Brake fluid will damage paint. Cover all body parts and be careful not to spill fluid during this procedure.* Loosen the fittings at the ends of the brake lines where they enter the master cylinder. To prevent rounding off the flats, use a flare-nut wrench, which wraps around the fitting hex.

5   Pull the brake lines away from the master cylinder and plug the ends to prevent contamination.

6   Remove the nuts attaching the master cylinder to the power booster **(see illustration 7.2)**. Pull the master cylinder off the studs to remove it. Again, be careful not to spill the fluid as this is done.

Installation

Refer to illustrations 7.8 and 7.16

7   Bench bleed the new master cylinder before installing it. Mount the master cylinder in a vise, with the jaws of the vise clamping on the mounting flange.

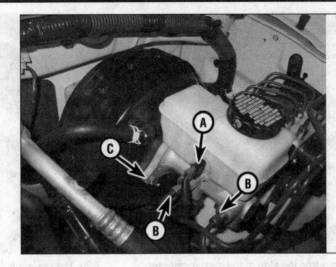

7.2 Master cylinder details

A   *Electrical connector*
B   *Brake line fittings*
C   *Mounting nuts (one seen here)*

8   Attach a pair of master cylinder bleeder tubes to the outlet ports of the master cylinder **(see illustration)**.

9   Fill the reservoir with brake fluid of the recommended type (see Chapter 1).

10   Slowly push the pistons into the master cylinder (a large Phillips screwdriver can be used for this) - air will be expelled from the pressure chambers and into the reservoir. Because the tubes are submerged in fluid, air can't be drawn back into the master cylinder when you release the pistons.

11   Repeat the procedure until no more air bubbles are present.

12   Remove the bleed tubes, one at a time, and install plugs in the open ports to prevent fluid leakage and air from entering. Install the reservoir cap.

13   Install the master cylinder over the studs on the power brake booster and tighten the attaching nuts only finger tight at this time. Don't forget to use a new O-ring.

14   Thread the brake line fittings into the master cylinder. Since the master cylinder is still a bit loose, it can be moved slightly so the

fittings thread in easily. Don't strip the threads as the fittings are tightened.

15   Tighten the mounting nuts to the torque listed in this Chapter's Specifications. Tighten the brake line fittings securely.

16   Fill the master cylinder reservoir with fluid, then bleed the lines at the master cylinder, followed by bleeding the remainder of the brake system (see Section 9). To bleed the lines at the master cylinder, have an assistant depress the brake pedal and hold it down. Loosen the fitting to allow air and fluid to escape **(see illustration)**. Tighten the fitting, then allow your assistant to return the pedal to its rest position. Repeat this procedure on both fittings until the fluid is free of air bubbles, then bleed the rest of the system. Check the operation of the brake system carefully before driving the vehicle. **Warning:** *If you do not have a firm brake pedal at the end of the bleeding procedure, or have any doubts as to the effectiveness of the brake system, DO NOT drive the vehicle. Have it towed to a dealer service department or other qualified repair shop for diagnosis.*

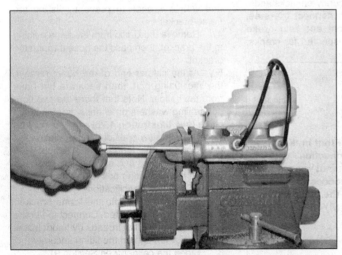

7.8 The best way to bleed air from the master cylinder before installing it on the vehicle is with a pair of bleeder tubes that direct brake fluid into the reservoir during bleeding

7.16 Have an assistant depress the brake pedal and hold it down, then loosen the fitting nut, allowing air and fluid to escape; repeat this procedure on both fittings until the fluid is clear of air bubbles

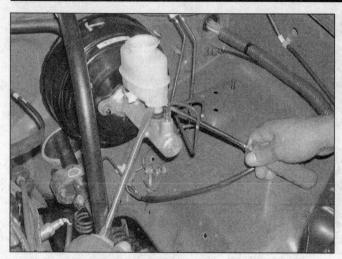

7.19 After removing the pin fron the side of the master cylinder fluid reservoir, pry it straight up out of the seals using two screwdrivers

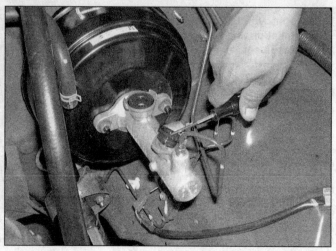

7.20 The reservoir seals can be replaced if they are leaking

Reservoir/seal replacement

Refer to illustrations 7.19 and 7.20

Note: *The brake fluid reservoir can be replaced separately from the master cylinder body if it becomes damaged. If there is leakage between the reservoir and the master cylinder body, the seals in the master cylinder can be replaced.*

17   Remove as much fluid as possible from the reservoir with a suction gun, large syringe or a poultry baster. **Warning:** *If a poultry baster is used, never again use it for the preparation of food.*

18   Place rags under the master cylinder to absorb any fluid that may spill out once the reservoir is detached from the master cylinder. **Caution:** *Brake fluid will damage paint. Cover all body parts and be careful not to spill fluid during this procedure.*

19   Remove the fluid reservoir only if it is leaking or damaged. If you remove the reservoir, new sealing grommets must be used. Remove the pin on the left side of the master cylinder that retains the reservoir **(see illustration).**

20   If you are simply replacing the seals, carefully pry the old seals out of the master cylinder and install new ones **(see illustration).**

21   Lubricate the reservoir seals with clean brake fluid, then press the reservoir into place on the master cylinder body. Install the pin that retains the reservoir.

22   Refill the reservoir with the recommended brake fluid (see Chapter 1) and check for leaks.

23   Bleed the master cylinder **(see illustration 7.16).**

---

8   Brake hoses and lines - inspection and replacement

Inspection

1   About every six months, with the vehicle raised and supported securely on jackstands, the rubber hoses which connect the steel brake lines with the front and rear brake assemblies should be inspected for cracks, chafing of the outer cover, leaks, blisters and other damage. These are important and vulnerable parts of the brake system and inspection should be complete. A light and mirror will be helpful for a thorough check. If a hose exhibits any of the above conditions, replace it with a new one.

Replacement

Flexible brake hose

Front

Refer to illustration 8.3

2   There are two flexible front brake hoses and two rear flexible brake hoses. The procedure is similar for all flexible hoses. Raise the vehicle and suitably support it on jackstands. Remove the wheel.

3   At the bracket, unscrew the brake line fitting from the hose **(see illustration)**. Use a flare-nut wrench to prevent rounding off the corners of the fitting nut, and hold the hose end with a wrench to prevent twisting the frame bracket.

4   Remove the U-clip from the female fitting at the bracket, then pass the hose through the bracket.

5   At the caliper end of the hose, remove the inlet fitting bolt, then separate the hose from the caliper. Note that there are two copper sealing washers on either side of the inlet fitting **(see illustration 4.2b)** - they should be replaced with new ones during installation.

6   Connect the fitting to the caliper with the inlet fitting bolt and new sealing washers. Tighten the inlet fitting bolt to the torque listed in this Chapter's Specifications.

7   Route the hose into the frame bracket, making sure it isn't twisted. Connect the brake line fitting, starting the threads by hand. Install the U-clip, then tighten the fitting securely.

8   Bleed the caliper (see Section 9).

9   Install the wheel and lug nuts, lower the vehicle and tighten the lug nuts to the torque listed in the Chapter 1 Specifications.

8.3 Front brake hose connection - use a flarenut wrench to disconnect the fitting (A), then remove the clip (B) and the hose

8.11 Disconnect the rear brake flexible hoses at the caliper and the rear axle bracket

8.13 Two flexible brake hoses connect the lines from each rear wheel, at junction blocks on the rear axle and at the body (at top)

Rear

Chassis-to-rear axle

Refer to illustrations 8.11 and 8.13

10   Raise the rear of the vehicle and support it securely on jackstands. Block the front wheels to prevent the vehicle from rolling.

11   At the chassis bracket, unscrew the brake line fitting from the hose **(see illustration)**. Use a flare-nut wrench to prevent rounding off the corners of the fitting nut.

12   Remove the U-clip from the female fitting at the bracket, then pass the hose through the bracket.

13   At the axle end of the hose, unscrew the two brake line fittings with a flare-nut wrench, unscrew the bolt securing the fitting block to the axle housing, then separate the lines from the fitting block and remove the hose **(see illustration)**.

14   To install the hose, reverse the removal procedure, then bleed both rear brakes (see Section 9).

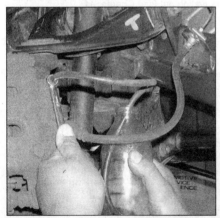

9.9 When bleeding the brakes, a hose is connected to the bleed screw at the component to be bled and then submerged in brake fluid - air will be seen as bubbles in the tube and container (all air must be expelled before moving to the next component)

Metal brake lines

15   When replacing brake lines, be sure to use the correct parts. Don't use copper tubing for any brake system components. Purchase steel brake lines from a dealer or auto parts store.

16   Prefabricated brake line, with the tube ends already flared and fittings installed, is available at auto parts stores and dealer parts departments. These lines must be bent to the proper shapes using a tubing bender.

17   When installing the new line, make sure it's securely supported in the brackets and has plenty of clearance between moving or hot components.

18   After installation, check the master cylinder fluid level and add fluid as necessary. Bleed the brake system (see Section 9) and test the brakes carefully before driving the vehicle in traffic.

9   Brake hydraulic system - bleeding

Refer to illustration 9.9

Warning: *Wear eye protection when bleeding the brake system. If the fluid comes in contact with your eyes, immediately rinse them with water and seek medical attention.*

Note: *Bleeding the hydraulic system is necessary to remove any air that manages to find its way into the system when it's been opened during removal and installation of a hose, line, caliper or master cylinder.*

1   You'll probably have to bleed the system at all four brakes if air has entered it due to low fluid level, or if the brake lines have been disconnected at the master cylinder.

2   If a brake line was disconnected only at a wheel, then only that caliper must be bled. If a brake line is disconnected at a fitting located between the master cylinder and any of the brakes, that part of the system served by the disconnected line must be bled.

3   Remove any residual vacuum from the brake power booster by applying the brake several times with the engine off.

4   Disconnect the cable from the negative terminal of the battery (this is to disable the ABS system).

5   Remove the master cylinder reservoir cap and fill the reservoir with brake fluid. Reinstall the cap. **Note:** *Check the fluid level often during the bleeding operation and add fluid as necessary to prevent the fluid level from falling low enough to allow air bubbles into the master cylinder.*

6   If air has entered the master cylinder, bleed the master cylinder as described in Section 7.

7   Have an assistant on hand, as well as a supply of new brake fluid, a clear container partially filled with clean brake fluid, a length of clear tubing to fit over the bleeder valve and a wrench to open and close the bleeder valve.

8   Working at the left rear wheel, loosen the bleeder valve slightly, then tighten it to a point where it's snug but can still be loosened quickly and easily.

9   Place one end of the tubing over the bleeder valve and submerge the other end in brake fluid in the container **(see illustration)**.

10   Have the assistant depress the brake pedal slowly and hold it in the depressed position.

11   While the pedal is held down, open the bleeder valve just enough to allow a flow of fluid to leave the valve. Watch for air bubbles to exit the submerged end of the tube. When the fluid flow slows after a couple of seconds, close the valve and have your assistant release the pedal.

12   Repeat Steps 10 and 11 until no more air is seen leaving the tube, then tighten the bleeder valve and proceed to the right rear wheel, the left front wheel and the right front wheel, in that order, and perform the same procedure. Be sure to check the fluid in the master cylinder reservoir frequently.

13   Never use old brake fluid. It contains moisture which can cause the fluid to boil, rendering the brake system inoperative.

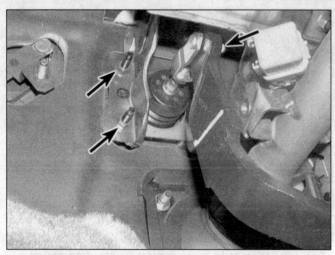

10.7 Remove the retaining clip from the clevis (right arrow), pull out the clevis pin and detach the pushrod from the brake pedal; two of the power brake booster mounting nuts (left arrows) are visible in this photo

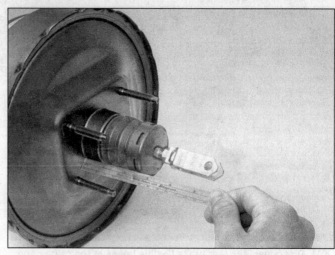

10.12 Measure the distance between the power brake booster and the hole in the clevis and compare your measurement to the dimension listed in this Chapter's Specifications; if necessary, adjust the clevis before installing the booster

14   Refill the master cylinder with fluid at the end of the operation.

15   Check the operation of the brakes. The pedal should feel solid when depressed, with no sponginess. If necessary, repeat the entire process. **Warning:** *Do not operate the vehicle if you're in doubt about the effectiveness of the brake system.*

10   Power brake booster - check, replacement and adjustment

Check

Operating check

1   Depress the brake pedal several times with the engine off and make sure there's no change in the pedal reserve distance.

2   Depress the pedal and start the engine. If the pedal goes down slightly, operation is normal.

Airtightness check

3   Start the engine and turn it off after one or two minutes. Depress the brake pedal slowly several times. If the pedal depresses less each time, the booster is airtight.

4   Depress the brake pedal while the engine is running, then stop the engine with the pedal depressed. If there's no change in the pedal reserve travel after holding the pedal for 30 seconds, the booster is airtight.

Replacement

Refer to illustration 10.7

Note: *Power brake booster units shouldn't be disassembled; if a problem with the booster develops, replace it with a new or rebuilt one.*

5   Remove the brake master cylinder, if you haven't already done so (see Section 7).

6   Disconnect the vacuum hose leading from the engine to the booster. Be careful not to damage the hose when removing it from

the booster fitting.

7   Remove the under-dash panel. Locate the pushrod clevis connecting the booster to the brake pedal **(see illustration)**.

8   Remove the clevis pin retaining clip with pliers and pull out the clevis pin.

9   Remove the four nuts holding the brake booster to the firewall **(see illustration 10.7)**.

10   Slide the booster straight out from the firewall until the studs clear the holes.

11   Installation is the reverse of removal. But be sure to measure the following dimension before installing the power brake booster assembly.

Adjustment

Refer to illustration 10.12

12   Measure the distance between the power brake booster and the hole in the clevis **(see illustration)** and compare it to the booster-to-clevis dimension listed in this Chapter's Specifications. If it isn't the same, loosen the adjusting nut and turn the clevis in or out to the specified length, then tighten the nut.

11   Parking brake - adjustment

Refer to illustration 11.6

Warning: *The models covered by this manual are equipped with airbags. Always disable the airbag system when working in the vicinity of airbag system components* (see Chapter 12).

1   The parking brake lever, when properly adjusted, should travel 6 to 8 clicks when a pulling force of 44 lbs (20 kg) is applied.

2   If the parking brake lever travels less than the specified minimum number of clicks, it might not be releasing completely and the shoes could even be dragging. If the travel is more than the specified maximum number of clicks, the parking brake may not hold adequately on an incline, allowing the car to roll.

3   Remove the rear portion of the floor console to access the parking brake lever and adjusting nut (see Chapter 11).

4   Raise the rear of the vehicle and support it securely on jackstands. Block the front wheels to prevent the vehicle from rolling.

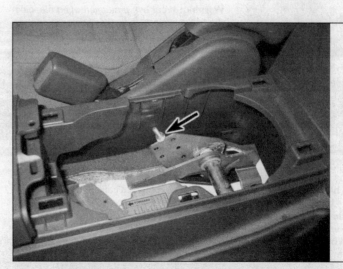

11.6 Adjustment locknut on the parking brake handle assembly

5   Pull and release the parking brake lever at least ten times, firmly. This will seat the shoes and cables.

6   Turn the adjusting nut on the parking brake assembly in the console, and check again for proper travel **(see illustration)**. The goal is 6-8 clicks at 44 pounds of pressure. When the parking brake lever is adjusted, release it and rotate the rear wheels. There should be no drag when the lever is released fully.

12   Parking brake cables - replacement

Warning: *The models covered by this manual are equipped with airbags. Always disable the airbag system when working in the vicinity of airbag system components (see Chapter 12).*

Front cable

Refer to illustrations 12.4 and 12.6

1   Disconnect the cable from the negative terminal of the battery.

2   Remove the rear portion of the console to access the parking brake lever assembly (see Chapter 11).

3   Remove the adjuster nut at the top of the front cable **(see illustration 11.8)**.

4   Remove the four bolts securing the lever assembly to the floor **(see illustration)**.

5   Raise the vehicle and support it securely on jackstands.

6   Remove the one bolt securing the front cable casing to the lever assembly. From below, remove the return spring on the equalizer and remove the front cable-to-underfloor mounting nuts **(see illustration)**.

7   Pull the front cable out of the rubber boot at the floor (interior) and remove it from the vehicle.

8   Installation is the reverse of the removal procedure. Apply a light coat of grease to the portion of the equalizer where the front of the rear cables connect to the equalizer. Adjust the parking brake system as described in Section 11.

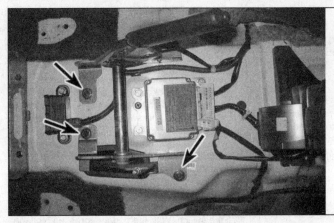

12.4 Four bolts secure the parking brake handle assembly to the floor (three bolts shown)

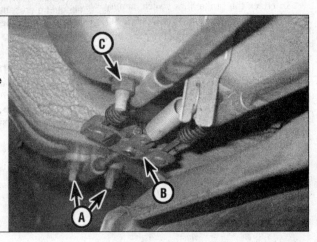

12.6 Parking brake cable equalizer details

A   Front cable mount to floor
B   Equalizer
C   Rear cable mounts to floor

Rear cables

Refer to illustrations 12.12 and 12.13

9   Raise the rear of the vehicle and support it securely on jackstands. Remove the rear wheels and the brake discs (see Section 5).

10   Remove the brake shoes (see Section 6).

11   Disconnect the front of the two rear parking brake cables from the equalizer **(see illustration 12.6)**.

12   Follow the rear cables along the floor and detach the nuts or screws securing the cables to the underside of the vehicle **(see illustration)**.

13   Disconnect the rear ends of the cables from the parking brake assembly on each side **(see illustration)**. Remove the cables.

14   Installation is the reverse of the removal procedure. Apply a light coat of grease to the portion of the equalizer where the front of the rear cables connect to the equalizer. Adjust the parking brake system as described in Section 11.

12.12 The two rear park brake cables are secured at the rear axle with clamps

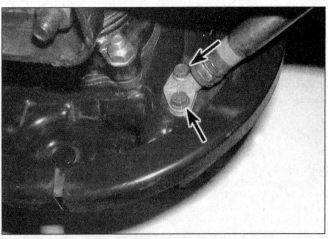

12.13 Remove the fasteners securing the cable to the brake backing plate

13   Brake light switch - check, adjustment and replacement

Refer to illustration 13.1

Check and adjustment

1   The brake light switch **(see illustration)** is located on a bracket at the top of the brake pedal. On most models it's the switch on the right (the other switch is the cruise control cut-off/shift lock switch). In any case, it's the switch with at least one red wire going to it. The switch activates the brake lights at the rear of the vehicle when the pedal is depressed.

2   To check the brake light switch, simply note whether the brake lights come on when the pedal is depressed and go off when the pedal is released.

3   If the brake lights don't come on when the brake pedal is depressed, make sure the brake pedal is correctly adjusted (see Chapter 1). Then try adjusting the switch as follows.

4   A locknut secures the switch to the bracket. Loosen the locknut (on the firewall side of the bracket), then screw the switch in or out to provide a 0.029 to 0.077 inch (0.74 to 1.96 mm) clearance between the threaded end of the brake light switch and the pedal stopper, with no pressure on the plunger, and tighten the locknut. Recheck the clearance to verify that it didn't change when you tightened the locknut. The switch should now function properly.

5   If the switch still doesn't work properly, either it isn't getting voltage, or the switch itself is defective. Use a voltmeter or test light to verify that there's voltage at the switch connector. With the pedal at rest, voltage should be present at one of the terminals of the switch. With the pedal depressed, voltage should be present at both terminals. If voltage isn't present at both terminals when the pedal is depressed, replace the switch.

Replacement

6   Unplug the electrical connector from the brake light switch.

7   Loosen the locknut and unscrew the switch from the bracket.

13.1 The brake light switch (arrow) is located on a bracket near the top of the brake pedal

8   Installation is the reverse of removal.

9   Make sure the brake pedal is adjusted properly (see Chapter 1), then adjust the switch (see above).

Chapter 10
Suspension and steering systems

Contents

Specifications

Torque specifications

Note: *One foot-pound (ft-lb) of torque is equivalent to 12 inch-pounds (in-lbs) of torque. Torque values below approximately 15 ft-lbs are expressed in inch-pounds, since most foot-pound torque wrenches are not accurate at these smaller values.*

	Ft-lbs (unless otherwise indicated)	**Nm**
Front suspension		
Front hub/bearing assembly mounting bolts	44	60
Shock absorber/coil spring assembly lower mounting bolt	155	210
Shock absorber/coil spring assembly upper mounting nuts	22	30
Shock absorber damper rod-to-upper mount nut	30	40
Upper control arm mounting bolts	94	127
Upper balljoint nut	58	79
Lower control arm mounting bolts	100	136
Lower control arm balljoint pinch bolt		
2005 through 2007	70	95
2008 and later	94	127
Stabilizer bar link mounting nuts		
At lower control arm	168 in-lbs	19
At stabilizer bar		
2005 through 2007	62	84
2008 and later	67	91
Stabilizer bar mounting bracket bolts	96	130

Torque specifications (continued)

	Ft-lbs (unless otherwise indicated)	Nm
Rear suspension		
Upper shock absorber mounting bolt..	33	45
Lower shock absorber mounting bolt..	147	199
Front spring eye bolt...	165	224
Spring shackle nuts..	77	104
Spring U-bolt nuts..	54	73
Stabilizer bar link end nuts	32	43
Stabilizer bar mounting bracket bolts	36	49
Steering		
Steering wheel nut..	25	32
Intermediate shaft coupler bolt/nut	20	27
Power steering pump mounting bolts		
Pump-to-engine bolt..	35	47
Bracket-to-engine bolt...	21	28
Bracket-to-pump bolts..	144 in-lbs	16
Power steering pressure line banjo bolt	44	60
Power steering suction pipe flange-to-pump bolts.....................	144 in-lbs	16
Power steering pump pulley nut	45	61

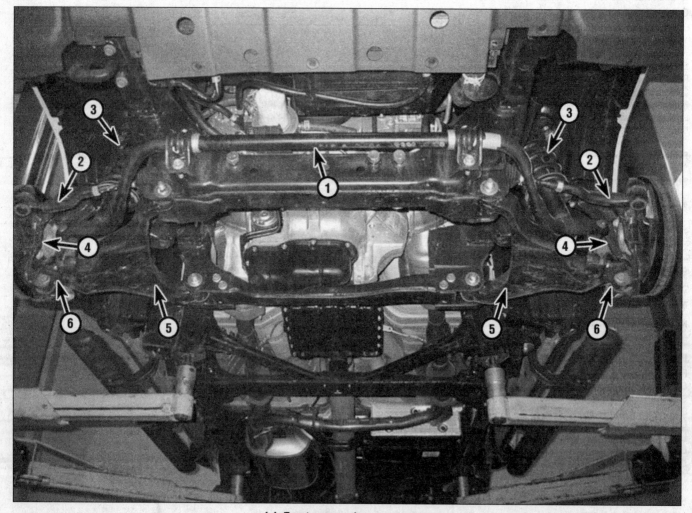

1.1 Front suspension components

1	*Stabilizer bar*	*3*	*Coil spring/shock absorber assembly*	*5*	*Lower control arms*
2	*Tie-rod ends*	*4*	*Steering knuckles*	*6*	*Lower balljoints*

1.2 Rear suspension components

1 Shock absorber	2 Stabilizer bar	3 Leaf spring

1   General information

Refer to illustrations 1.1 and 1.2

Front suspension

The front suspension (**see illustration**) is fully independent. All models use upper and lower control arms and shock absorber/coil spring assemblies. On all models, a stabilizer bar connected to the frame and to the two lower control arms reduces body roll during cornering.

Rear suspension

The rear suspension consists of a pair of multi-leaf springs and two shock absorbers (**see illustration**). The rear axle assembly is attached to the leaf springs by U-bolts. The front ends of the springs are attached to the frame at the front hangers, through rubber bushings. The rear ends of the springs are attached to the frame by shackles which allow the springs to alter their length as they compress and rebound.

Steering system

The steering system on all models con-sists of a rack-and-pinion steering gear and two adjustable tie-rods. Power assist is standard.

Precautions

Frequently, when working on the suspension or steering system components, you may come across fasteners which seem impossible to loosen. These fasteners on the underside of the vehicle are continually subjected to water, road grime, mud, etc., and can become rusted or "frozen," making them extremely difficult to remove. In order to unscrew these stubborn fasteners without damaging them (or other components), be sure to use lots of penetrating oil and allow it to soak in for a while. Using a wire brush to clean exposed threads will also ease removal of the nut or bolt and prevent damage to the threads. Sometimes a sharp blow with a hammer and punch is effective in breaking the bond between a nut and bolt threads, but care must be taken to prevent the punch from slipping off the fastener and ruining the threads. Heating the stuck fastener and surrounding area with a torch sometimes helps too, but isn't recommended because of the obvious dangers associated with fire. Long breaker bars and extension, or "cheater," pipes will increase leverage, but never use an extension pipe on a ratchet - the ratching mechanism could be damaged. Sometimes, turning the nut or bolt in the tightening (clockwise) direction first will help to break it loose. Fasteners that require drastic measures to unscrew should always be replaced with new ones.

Since most of the procedures that are dealt with in this Chapter involve jacking up the vehicle and working underneath it, a good pair of jackstands will be needed. A hydraulic floor jack is the preferred type of jack to lift the vehicle, and it can also be used to support certain components during various operations. **Warning:** *Never, under any circumstances, rely on a jack to support the vehicle while working on it. Also, whenever any of the suspension or steering fasteners are loosened or removed they must be inspected and, if necessary, replaced with new ones of the same part number or of original equipment quality and design. Torque specifications must be followed for proper reassembly and component retention. Never attempt to heat or straighten suspension or steering components. Instead, replace bent or damaged parts with new ones.*

2.4 Lower shock/coil spring mounting bolt

2.5 Shock absorber/coil spring assembly upper mounting nuts (third nut not visible in this photo). DO NOT remove the nut from the damper shaft (the nut in the center)

2   Shock absorber/coil spring assembly (front) - removal and installation

Note: *It is possible to replace the shocks or springs individually but the unit will have to be disassembled by a qualified repair shop with the proper equipment. This will add considerable cost to the project. You can compare the cost of replacing the complete assemblies yourself to the cost of replacing individual components (with the help of a shop).*

Removal

Refer to illustrations 2.4 and 2.5

1   Loosen the front wheel lug nuts. Raise the vehicle and support it securely on jackstands. Remove the front wheels.
2   Support the outer end of the control arm using a floor jack or equivalent.
3   Disconnect the stabilizer bar link from the lower control arm (see Section 3).
4   Remove the shock absorber lower mounting bolt **(see illustration)**.

5   Remove the fasteners that attach the upper end of the shock to the frame **(see illustration)**.
6   Remove the shock absorber.
7   Inspect the shock absorber for leaking fluid, dents, cracks and other damage. Inspect the coil spring for chips and cracks which could cause premature failure. Inspect the spring seats for hardness and general deterioration. If any of the components of the assembly are worn or damaged, have the unit serviced by a qualified repair shop or replace it.

Installation

8   Installation is the reverse of removal. Be sure to tighten the fasteners to the torque listed in this Chapter's Specifications. **Note:** *The shock absorber lower mounting fasteners should be tightened with the vehicle at normal ride height. This can be done after the vehicle has been lowered to the ground (on vehicles with adequate clearance), or can be simulated by raising the lower control arm with a floor jack.*
9   Tighten the wheel lug nuts to the torque listed in the Chapter 1 Specifications.

3   Stabilizer bar and bushings (front) - removal and installation

Refer to illustrations 3.2 and 3.3

Warning: *The manufacturer recommends replacing the stabilizer bar link nuts with new ones whenever they are removed.*
1   Raise the vehicle and support it securely on jackstands.
2   Remove the nuts from the links and detach the links from the bar **(see illustration)**. **Note:** *Be sure to keep the parts for the left and right sides separate.*
3   Remove the stabilizer bar bracket bolts **(see illustration)**.
4   Remove the stabilizer bar.
5   Remove the rubber bushings.
6   Inspect all parts for wear and damage, replacing them as necessary.
7   Installation is the reverse of removal. Be sure to tighten all fasteners to the torque listed in this Chapter's Specifications.

3.2 Remove the nuts securing the ends of the stabilizer bar links

3.3 Front stabilizer bar bracket bolts

4.3 Use a balljoint tool to separate the upper balljoint from the steering knuckle

4.4 Upper control arm mounting bolts

4   Upper control arm - removal and installation

Refer to illustrations 4.3 and 4.4

Removal

1   Loosen the wheel lug nuts, raise the front of the vehicle and support it securely on jackstands. Remove the wheel. Position a floor jack under the lower control arm in the area underneath the balljoint. Raise the jack slightly to take the spring pressure off the upper control arm. **Warning:** *The jack must remain in this position throughout the entire procedure.*
2   If working on the left (driver's side) control arm, disconnect the lower steering shaft pinch bolt (see Section 13) and move the lower shaft out of the way.
3   To disconnect the upper control arm from the steering knuckle, remove the cotter pin, loosen the upper balljoint nut a few turns (don't remove it), install a balljoint separator and break the balljoint loose from the knuckle. Now remove the nut. **Note:** *If you don't have a press-type balljoint removal tool, a "picklefork" type balljoint separator can be used, but keep in mind that this type of tool will probably*

destroy the balljoint boot **(see illustration)**.
4   Remove the upper control arm pivot bolts and nuts, noting which way the bolts are installed **(see illustration)**. Remove the control arm.

Installation

5   Position the arm in the frame brackets and install the bolts and nuts, but don't tighten them yet.
6   Attach the balljoint to the steering knuckle and tighten the ballstud nut to the torque listed in this Chapter's Specifications. Install a new cotter pin. **Note:** *If necessary, tighten the nut a little more to align the slots in the nut with the hole in the ballstud; don't loosen the nut to allow cotter pin insertion.*
7   Place a floor jack under the outer end of the lower control arm and raise it to simulate normal ride height. Tighten the control arm pivot bolts/nuts to the torque listed in this Chapter's Specifications. **Note:** *The manufacturer recommends using new upper control arm pivot bolts and nuts.*
8   The remainder of installation is the reverse of removal. Tighten the wheel lug nuts to the torque listed in the Chapter 1 Specifications.

9   Have the front end alignment checked and, if necessary, adjusted.

5   Lower control arm - removal and installation

Refer to illustrations 5.5a, 5.5b and 5.6
Warning: *The manufacturer recommends replacing the pivot bolt nut(s) with new ones whenever they are removed.*

Removal

1   Loosen the wheel lug nuts, raise the vehicle and support it securely on jackstands placed under the frame rails. Remove the wheel.
2   If working on a 4WD model, remove the driveaxle (see Chapter 8).
3   Detach the stabilizer bar link from the lower control arm (see Section 3).
4   Remove the shock absorber lower mounting bolt (see Section 2).
5   To remove the lower control arm, remove the pinch-bolt securing the lower balljoint, then use a balljoint tool to push the balljoint from the control arm **(see illustrations)**.

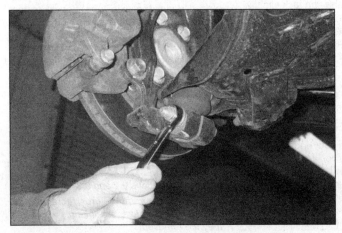

5.5a Lower control arm balljoint pinch bolt

5.5b Use a picklefork or balljoint removal tool to push the lower balljoint from the lower control arm

6   Mark the positions of the lower control arm adjuster bolts relative to the control arm, then remove them **(see illustration). Note:** *On models that have straight bolts rather than eccentric adjuster bolts, new eccentric bolts will have to be installed to adjust front end alignment.*

7   The control arm bushings are replaceable, but special tools are necessary to do the job. Carefully inspect the bushings for hardening, excessive wear and cracks. If they appear to be worn or deteriorated, take the control arm to an automotive machine shop or other repair facility for replacement.

Installation

8   Installation is the reverse of removal. Tighten the fasteners to the torque listed in this Chapter's Specifications. **Note:** *Don't tighten the pivot bolt nut(s) to the torque listed in this Chapter's Specifications until the vehicle has been lowered and is resting at normal ride height (this can also be simulated by raising the lower control arm with a floor jack).* Be sure to tighten the wheel lug nuts to the torque listed in the Chapter 1 Specifications.

9   Have the front wheel alignment checked and, if necessary, adjusted.

6   Balljoints - check and replacement

Check

1   Inspect the control arm balljoint(s) for looseness anytime a balljoint is separated from the steering knuckle. See if you can turn the ballstud in its socket with your fingers. If the balljoint is loose, or if the ballstud can be turned, replace the balljoint. You can also check the balljoints with the suspension assembled as follows.

Upper balljoint

2   Raise the front of the vehicle and support it securely on jackstands placed under the frame rails. Place a floor jack under the lower control arm and raise it far enough to lift the upper control arm off its stop.

3   Attempt to move the control arm up and down; a prybar may be helpful. If any play is felt, replace the upper control arm and balljoint as an assembly (the balljoint is not replaceable separately).

4   Also try to move the steering knuckle in-and-out. If any play is felt, replace the upper control arm/balljoint assembly.

5   Check the balljoint boot for cracks and tears. If any are present, replace the control arm.

Lower balljoint

6   Raise the front of the vehicle and support it securely on jackstands placed under the frame rails.

7   Place a floor jack under the lower control arm and raise it slightly. Attempt to move the steering knuckle up and down; a large prybar underneath the tire, or a prybar placed

5.6 Remove the lower control arm mounting/ adjuster bolts

between the end of the control arm and the steering knuckle will be helpful. If any play is felt, replace the control arm and balljoint as an assembly (the balljoint is not replaceable separately).

8   Also try to move the steering knuckle in-and-out. If any play is felt, replace the control arm/balljoint assembly.

9   Check the balljoint boot for cracks and tears. If any are present, replace the control arm.

Replacement

10   As stated previously in this Section, the balljoints on these models are an integral part of the control arm and are not available separately. The entire control arm must be replaced.

7   Steering knuckle and hub and bearing assembly - removal and installation

1   Loosen the wheel lug nuts, raise the vehicle and support it securely on jackstands placed underneath the frame (or subframe) rails. Remove the wheel.

2   On all models, support the lower control arm with a floor jack. Raise the jack slightly. **Warning:** *The jack must remain in this position throughout the entire procedure.*

3   Remove the brake caliper and brake disc (see Chapter 9). Hang the caliper out of the way on a piece of wire (don't disconnect the brake hose).

4   If you're working on a 4WD model, remove the driveaxle (see Chapter 8).

5   Remove the disc splash shield from the steering knuckle.

6   Disconnect the tie-rod end from the steering knuckle (see Section 14).

7   Disconnect the balljoints from the steering knuckle (see Sections 4 and 5) and remove the steering knuckle. If the steering knuckle is to be replaced, remove the hub/bearing assembly from the knuckle and transfer it to the new knuckle, using new bolts.

8   Installation is the reverse of removal. Be

sure to tighten the balljoint and tie-rod end fasteners to the torque values listed in this Chapter's Specifications. **Note:** *If necessary, tighten the upper balljoint nut a little more to align the slots in the nut with the hole in the ballstud; don't loosen the nut to allow cotter pin insertion. Also, be sure to use a new cotter pin.* Tighten the caliper mounting bolts to the torque values listed in the Chapter 9 Specifications. Tighten the wheel lug nuts to the torque listed in the Chapter 1 Specifications.

8   Shock absorber (rear) - removal and installation

Refer to illustrations 8.3a and 8.3b

Warning: *The manufacturer recommends replacing the upper and lower shock absorber mounting nuts with new ones whenever they are removed.*

1   Raise the rear of the vehicle and support it securely on jackstands placed underneath the frame rails. Block the front wheels so the vehicle doesn't roll off the stands. **Note:** *It isn't necessary to remove the rear wheels, but doing so will improve access to the shock absorbers.*

2   Support the rear axle with a floor jack placed under the axle tube closest to the shock absorber being removed.

3   Remove the shock absorber upper and lower mounting fasteners **(see illustrations)**.

4   Remove the shock absorber.

5   Installation is the reverse of removal. Tighten all fasteners to the torque values listed in this Chapter's Specifications.

9   Stabilizer bar and bushings (rear) - removal and installation

Refer to illustrations 9.2 and 9.3

Warning: *The manufacturer recommends replacing the stabilizer bar link nuts whenever they are removed.*

1   Loosen the rear wheel lug nuts, raise the rear of the vehicle and support it securely on

8.3a Shock absorber lower mounting bolt

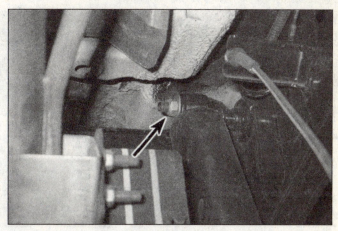

8.3b Shock absorber upper mounting nut

9.2 Remove the stabilizer bar link nuts and detach the links from the bar

9.3 Stabilizer bar clamp bolts

jackstands. Block the front wheels to keep the vehicle from rolling off the stands. Remove the rear wheels.

2   Remove the nuts from the lower ends of the stabilizer bar links, then separate the links from the bar **(see illustration)**.

3   Remove the stabilizer bar clamp bolts **(see illustration)** and remove the stabilizer bar.

4   Inspect the stabilizer bar bushings and link bushings for cracks, tears and other signs of deterioration. Replace as necessary. Also check the ballstuds at the ends of the links for looseness, replacing the links if necessary. The links are attached to the body with two bolts.

5   Installation is the reverse of removal. Be sure to tighten all fasteners to the torque values listed in this Chapter's Specifications.

---

10   Leaf spring - removal and installation

Refer to illustrations 10.3, 10.4 and 10.5

Removal

1   Loosen the rear wheel lug nuts, raise the rear of the vehicle and support it securely on jackstands placed underneath the frame rails. Block the front wheels to keep the vehicle from rolling off the stands. Remove the rear wheels.

2   Support the axle with a floor jack placed under the axle tube and raise it slightly to take the weight of the axle. Remove the shock absorber lower mounting bolt.

3   Remove the four U-bolt nuts and washers **(see illustration)**, the spring plate and the two U-bolts. If you're working on the right side leaf spring, remove the rear portion of the exhaust pipe (see Chapter 4).

10.3 Remove the four U-bolt nuts, then remove the spring plate and the U-bolts

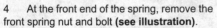

10.4 At the front end of the leaf spring, remove the nut from the spring bolt, then remove the bolt

10.5 Remove the nuts from the rear spring shackle, lift off the shackle plate, then push the shackle pins through the bushings and remove it

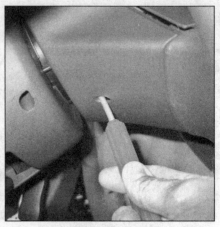

11.3 Use a blunt tool (like a punch), inserted into the hole in the bottom of the steering wheel to push the airbag retaining clip up

4   At the front end of the spring, remove the front spring nut and bolt **(see illustration)**.
5   At the rear end of the spring, remove the spring shackle nuts **(see illustration)**. Remove the shackle plate and shackle.
6   Remove the spring assembly.
7   If the bushings at the ends of the spring are worn or deteriorated, an automotive machine shop or dealer service department can press the old ones out and press new ones in. The upper shackle bushings can be replaced without the use of special tools.

Installation

8   Place the spring in position and install the front mounting bolt and nut, but don't tighten the nut yet.
9   Raise the rear of the spring into position and install the shackle, shackle plate and nuts. Don't tighten the nuts yet.
10   Raise or lower the axle on the jack until it mates properly with the spring. Install the spring plate and U-bolts, then install the nuts and washers. Tighten the U-bolt nuts, in a criss-cross pattern, to the torque listed in this

Chapter's Specifications.
11   Install the wheel, lower the vehicle to the ground and bounce it a few times, then tighten the front mounting bolt nut and the shackle nuts to the torque values listed in this Chapter's Specifications. Tighten the lug nuts to the torque listed in the Chapter 1 Specifications.

11   Steering wheel - removal and installation

Warning: *These models are equipped with airbags. Always disable the airbag system before working in the vicinity of any airbag system component to avoid the possibility of accidental deployment of the airbag, which could cause personal injury (see Chapter 12).*

Removal

Refer to illustrations 11.3, 11.4a, 11.4b and 11.6

1   The front wheels must be in the straight-ahead position before beginning the proce-

dure, with the key removed.
2   Disconnect the cables from the negative battery terminal, then the positive terminal. Refer to Chapter 12 and disable the airbag system.
3   Push in the airbag retaining clip, using a blunt tool going straight up in the hole in the underside of the steering **(see illustration)**.
4   Pull the airbag away from the steering wheel enough to disconnect the electrical connectors behind it **(see illustrations)**.
5   Lift the airbag away from the steering wheel. **Warning:** *Handle the airbag module with care, carry the module with the front cover facing away from your body, and store it in a safe location with the trim side facing up. See the precautions in Chapter 12.*
6   Use a socket and extension to remove the steering wheel mounting bolt, while holding the wheel so it doesn't turn **(see illustration)**. After removing the bolt, make match-marks on the steering wheel and the shaft to aid in reassembly. Make sure all electrical connectors are disconnected; some models may have steering wheel-mounted switches.

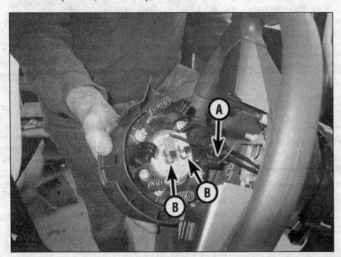

11.4a Disconnect the horn wire (A) and the two airbag connectors (B) . . .

11.4b . . . by using a small screwdriver to pry up the locking tabs on the connectors

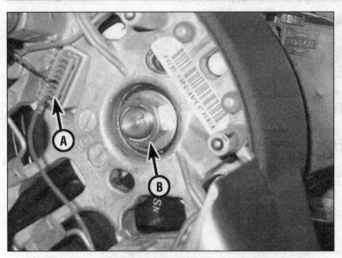

11.6 Disconnect any electrical connectors (A), remove the steering wheel mounting nut (B), then use a puller to remove the wheel

12.7 Remove the steering column lower pinch bolt

7   Use a steering wheel puller that uses hooks that engage with the holes in the steering wheel hub to remove the steering wheel from the shaft. **Caution:** *Do not hammer on the steering wheel or steering shaft in an attempt to remove the wheel.* After the steering wheel has been removed, apply a piece of tape across the airbag clockspring (on the steering column) so it doesn't become uncentered.

Installation

8   Installation is the reverse of removal, noting the following points:

a) *Make sure the airbag clockspring is centered. The two arrow marks should be aligned in the 7 o'clock position and the locating pin should be at the 12 o'clock position. If not, turn the clockspring all the way clockwise until it stops (don't apply too much force), then turn it counterclockwise approximately 2-1/2 turns until the arrows are aligned and the locating pin is at the top.*

b) *When installing the steering wheel, align the marks on the shaft and the steering wheel hub.*

c) *Install the steering wheel mounting nut and tighten it to the torque listed in this Chapter's Specifications.*

d) *Connect any electrical connectors to the steering wheel.*

e) *Connect the two airbag connectors and pushing in their locking tabs, then push the airbag module onto the steering wheel until the mounting clips lock it in place.*

f) *Enable the airbag system (see Chapter 12).*

g) *Verify the airbag system is operational by turning the key to ON - the "AIR BAG" light on the instrument panel should come on for a few seconds and then turn off.*

12 Steering column - removal and installation

Refer to illustrations 12.7 and 12.8

Warning: *These models are equipped with airbags. Always disable the airbag system before working in the vicinity of any airbag system component to avoid the possibility of accidental deployment of the airbag, which could cause personal injury (see Chapter 12).*

Removal

1   Park the vehicle with the wheels pointing straight ahead. Disconnect the cable from the negative battery terminal, then the positive battery terminal. Disable the airbag system (see Chapter 12).

2   Remove the steering wheel (see Section 11), then turn the ignition key to the LOCK position to prevent the steering shaft from turning. **Caution:** *If this is not done, the airbag clockspring could be damaged.*

3   Remove the knee bolster and the reinforcement behind it (see Chapter 11).

4   Remove the steering column covers (see

Chapter 11).

5   Disconnect the electrical connectors for the steering column harness.

6   Detach the shift interlock cable (see Chapter 7B).

7   Remove the shaft coupler nut and remove the bolt securing the steering shaft to the intermediate shaft **(see illustration)**. Mark the relationship of the intermediate shaft to the steering column shaft.

8   Remove the steering column mounting fasteners **(see illustration)**, lower the column and pull it to the rear, making sure nothing is still connected. Separate the intermediate shaft from the steering shaft and remove the column.

Installation

9   Guide the steering column into position, connect the intermediate shaft, then install the mounting fasteners, but don't tighten them yet.

10   Install the pinch bolt, tightening it to the torque listed in this Chapter's Specifications. If the intermediate shaft has a cutout near the top, the cutout must face the pinch bolt.

12.8 Disconnect all electrical connectors and remove the column-to-body mounting nuts (two seen here)

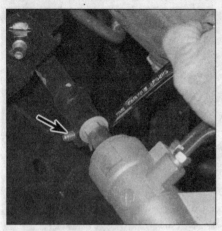

13.3 Intermediate shaft-to-steering gear pinch bolt

14.2 Loosen the tie-rod end jam nut

11   Tighten the column mounting fasteners to the torque listed in this Chapter's Specifications.
12   The remainder of installation is the reverse of removal. On automatic transmission-equipped models, adjust the shift cable and interlock cable following the procedures described in Chapter 7B.

13   Intermediate shaft - removal and installation

Refer to illustration 13.3

1   Park the vehicle with the wheels pointing straight ahead. Disconnect the cable from the negative battery terminal, then the positive battery terminal. Disable the airbag system (see Chapter 12).
2   Turn the ignition key to the LOCK position to prevent the steering shaft from turning. **Caution:** *If this is not done, the airbag clockspring could be damaged.*
3   Working under the hood, mark the relationship of the intermediate shaft to the steering gear input shaft **(see illustration)**. Remove the coupler bolt.

4   Mark the relationship of the intermediate shaft to the steering column shaft, then remove the pinch bolt **(see illustration 12.7)**.
5   Slide the intermediate shaft up and off the steering gear input shaft, then pull the shaft down off the steering gear input shaft.
6   Installation is the reverse of removal. Be sure to align the matchmarks and tighten the coupler bolts to the torque values listed in this Chapter's Specifications. If the intermediate shaft has a cutout near the top, the cutout must face the coupler bolt.

14   Tie-rod ends - removal and installation

Refer to illustrations 14.2 and 14.3

1   Loosen the wheel lug nuts, raise the front of the vehicle and support it securely on jackstands. Apply the parking brake and block the rear wheels to keep the vehicle from rolling off the jackstands. Remove the wheel.

Removal

2   Break loose the tie-rod end jam nut **(see illustration)**. Don't back the nut off; once it has just been loosened, it will serve as the point to which the tie-rod end will be threaded.

If you are removing the tie-rod end to replace the steering gear boot, mark the threads of the tie-rod on the *inner* side of the nut.
3   Remove the cotter pin and loosen (but don't remove) the nut on the tie-rod end ballstud. Break loose the tie-rod end from the steering knuckle arm with a puller **(see illustration)**. Remove the nut and disconnect the tie-rod end from the steering knuckle.
4   Unscrew the tie-rod end from the tie-rod.

Installation

5   If the jam nut was removed, thread it onto the tie-rod until it meets the mark applied in Step 2. Thread the tie-rod end onto the tie-rod until it contacts the jam nut, then connect the tie-rod end to the steering arm. Install the ballstud nut and tighten it to the torque listed in this Chapter's Specifications. Install a new cotter pin. **Note:** *If necessary, tighten the nut a little more to align the slots in the nut with the hole in the ballstud; don't loosen the nut to allow cotter pin insertion.*
6   Tighten the jam nut securely and install the wheel. Lower the vehicle and tighten the lug nuts to the torque listed in the Chapter 1 Specifications.
7   Have the front end alignment checked and, if necessary, adjusted.

14.3 A tool like this can remove the tie-rod end without damage to the rubber boot

15.4 The outer clamp (A) on the steering gear boot can be squeezed and removed with a pair of pliers; the inner clamp (B) must be cut off

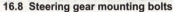

16.8 Steering gear mounting bolts

17.2 Remove the air intake duct and air filter housing cover for access to the power steering pump (four-cylinder model shown)

15 Steering gear boots - replacement

Refer to illustration 15.4

1   Loosen the wheel lug nuts, raise the front of the vehicle and support it securely on jackstands, then remove the wheels. Remove the under-vehicle splash shield.
2   Remove the tie-rod end from the tie-rod (see Section 14).
3   Remove the tie-rod end jam nut.
4   Remove the outer boot clamp with a pair of pliers, then cut off the inner boot clamp and discard it **(see illustration)**.
5   Remove the boot.
6   Install a new clamp on the inner end of the boot.
7   Apply multi-purpose grease to the groove on the tie-rod (where the outer end of the boot will ride).
8   Slide the new boot over the tie-rod and onto the steering gear housing.
9   Make sure the boot isn't twisted, then tighten the inner clamp.
10   Install the outer clamp and tie-rod end jam nut.
11   Install the tie-rod ends (see Section 14).
12   Install the steering gear assembly.
13   Have the front end alignment checked and, if necessary, adjusted.

16 Steering gear - removal and installation

Refer to illustration 16.8
Warning 1: *These models are equipped with airbags. Always disable the airbag system before working in the vicinity of any airbag component to avoid the possibility of accidental airbag deployment, which could cause personal injury (see Chapter 12).*
Warning 2: *DO NOT allow the steering column shaft to rotate with the steering gear removed or damage to the airbag system could occur. As a method of preventing the shaft from turning, pass the seat belt through the rim of the steering wheel and buckle the belt in place.*
1   Disconnect the cable from the negative battery terminal (see Chapter 5, Section 1).
2   Loosen the front wheel lug nuts, raise the front of the vehicle and support it securely on jackstands. Apply the parking brake and block the rear wheels. Remove the front wheels.
3   Place a drain pan under the steering gear. Disconnect the pressure and return fluid lines at the steering gear and allow the fluid to drain.
4   The steering wheel should be turned to the straight-ahead position and the key removed. Secure the steering wheel in position with the seat belt or a tool. **Caution:** *Do*

not allow the steering wheel to turn or there could be damage to the airbag system.
5   Mark the relationship of the steering lower shaft to the splines on the steering gear, then remove the steering gear shaft pinch-bolt (see Section 13).
6   Remove the front stabilizer bar and brackets (see Section 3).
7   Disconnect the tie-rod ends from the steering knuckles (see Section 14).
8   Remove the steering gear-to-chassis mounting bolts and remove the steering gear **(see illustration)**.
9   Installation is the reverse of removal. Be sure to tighten all fasteners to the torque values listed in this Chapter's Specifications. Tighten the wheel lug nuts to the torque listed in Chapter 1.
10   Add power steering fluid to the power steering fluid reservoir, then bleed the air from the system (see Section 18).

17 Power steering pump - removal and installation

Refer to illustrations 17.2 and 17.4

Removal

1   Disconnect the cable from the negative terminal of the battery. If you're working on a V6, remove the battery for better access to the pump (see Chapter 5).
2   Remove the air filter housing and the air intake duct from above the radiator **(see illustration)**.
3   Remove the drivebelt (see Chapter 1).
4   Detach the pressure line and feed hose from the pump **(see illustration)**. Discard the sealing washers on either side of the pressure line banjo fitting - new ones must be used upon installation. Plug the hoses to prevent contaminants from entering.
5   Unscrew the mounting fasteners and remove the pump from the vehicle, taking care not to spill fluid on the painted surfaces.
Note: *On models with holes in the pulley, the*

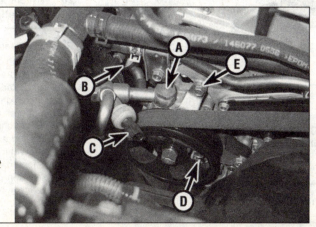

17.4 Power steering pump mounting details - V6 engine

A   *Pressure line banjo bolt*
B   *Feed hose clamp*
C   *Power steering pressure switch*
D   *Pump mounting bolt*
E   *Pump bracket bolt*

mounting bolts at the front of the pump are accessed through the holes in the pulley.

Installation

6   Position the pump in the mounting bracket and install the mounting fasteners. Tighten the fasteners to the torque listed in this Chapter's Specifications.
7   Connect the pressure line and feed hose to the pump. Be sure to use new sealing washers on the pressure line fitting and tighten the banjo bolt to the torque listed in this Chapter's Specifications.
8   Install and adjust the drivebelt (see Chapter 1).
9   The remainder of installation is the reverse of removal.
10   Fill the power steering reservoir with the recommended fluid (see Chapter 1) and bleed the system following the procedure described in the next Section.

18   Power steering system - bleeding

1   Following any operation in which the power steering fluid lines have been disconnected, the power steering system must be bled to remove all air and obtain proper steering performance.
2   With the front wheels in the straight ahead position, check the power steering fluid level and, if low, add fluid until it reaches the Cold mark on the dipstick or reservoir.
3   Start the engine and allow it to run at fast

19.3 Use a small press tool such as this to push the stud out of the flange

idle. Recheck the fluid level and add more if necessary to reach the Cold mark on the dipstick or reservoir.
4   Bleed the system by turning the wheels from side-to-side, without hitting the stops. This will work the air out of the system. Keep the reservoir full of fluid as this is done.
5   When the air is worked out of the system, return the wheels to the straight ahead position and leave the vehicle running for several more minutes before shutting it off. Recheck the fluid level.
6   Road test the vehicle to be sure the steering system is functioning normally and noise free.

7   Recheck the fluid level to be sure it's up to the Hot mark on the dipstick or reservoir while the engine is at normal operating temperature. Add fluid if necessary (see Chapter 1).

19   Wheel studs - replacement

Refer to illustration 19.3
Note: *This procedure applies to both the front and rear wheel studs.*
1   Loosen the wheel lug nuts, raise the vehicle and support it securely on jackstands. Remove the wheel.
2   Remove the brake disc (see Chapter 9).
3   Push the stud out of the hub flange or axle flange with a press tool **(see illustration)**.
4   Insert the new stud into the hub flange or axle flange from the back side and install some flat washers and a lug nut on the stud.
5   Tighten the lug nut until the stud is seated in the flange.
6   Reinstall the disc and caliper (see Chapter 9).
7   Install the wheel and lug nuts. Lower the vehicle and tighten the lug nuts to the torque listed in the Chapter 1 Specifications.

20   Wheels and tires - general information

Refer to illustration 20.1
     Most vehicles covered by this manual are equipped with metric-size fiberglass or steel belted radial tires **(see illustration)**, or inch-pattern light truck tires. Use of other size or type of tires may affect the ride and handling of the vehicle. Don't mix different types of tires, such as radials and bias belted, on the same vehicle as handling may be seriously affected. It's recommended that tires be replaced in pairs on the same axle, but if only one tire is being replaced, be sure it's the same size, structure and tread design as the other.

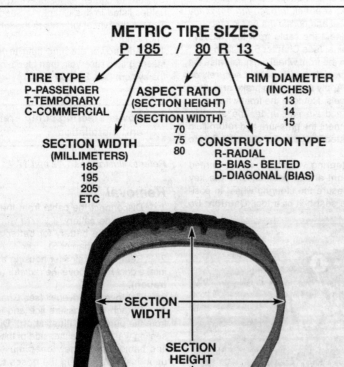

METRIC TIRE SIZES

P 185 / 80 R 13

TIRE TYPE
P-PASSENGER
T-TEMPORARY
C-COMMERCIAL

ASPECT RATIO
(SECTION HEIGHT)
—————————
(SECTION WIDTH)
70
75
80

RIM DIAMETER
(INCHES)
13
14
15

SECTION WIDTH
(MILLIMETERS)
185
195
205
ETC

CONSTRUCTION TYPE
R-RADIAL
B-BIAS - BELTED
D-DIAGONAL (BIAS)

SECTION WIDTH

SECTION HEIGHT

20.1 Metric tire size code

Because tire pressure has a substantial effect on handling and wear, the pressure on all tires should be checked at least once a month or before any extended trips (see Chapter 1).

Wheels must be replaced if they're bent, dented, leak air, have elongated bolt holes, are heavily rusted, out of vertical symmetry or if the lug nuts won't stay tight. Wheel repairs that use welding or peening are not recommended.

Tire and wheel balance is important to the overall handling, braking and performance of the vehicle. Unbalanced wheels can adversely affect handling and ride characteristics as well as tire life. Whenever a tire is installed on a wheel, the tire and wheel should be balanced by a shop with the proper equipment.

21 Front end alignment - general information

Refer to illustration 21.1

A front end alignment **(see illustration)** refers to the adjustments made to the front wheels so they're in proper angular relationship to the suspension and the ground. Front wheels that are out of proper alignment not only affect steering control, but also increase tire wear.

Getting the proper front wheel alignment is a very exacting process, one in which complicated and expensive machines are necessary to perform the job properly. Because of this, you should have a technician with the proper equipment to perform these tasks. We will, however, use this space to give you a basic idea of what is involved with front end alignment so you can better understand the process and deal intelligently with the shop that does the work.

Toe-in is the turning in of the front wheels. The purpose of a toe specification is to ensure parallel rolling of the front wheels. In a vehicle with zero toe-in, the distance between the front edges of the wheels will be the same as the distance between the rear edges of the wheels. The actual amount of toe-in is normally only a fraction of an inch. Toe-in is adjusted by turning the tie-rod in the tie-rod end to lengthen or shorten the tie-rod. Incorrect toe-in will cause the tires to wear improperly by making them scrub against the road surface.

Camber is the tilting of the front wheels from vertical when viewed from the front of the vehicle. When the wheels tilt out at the top, the camber is said to be positive (+).

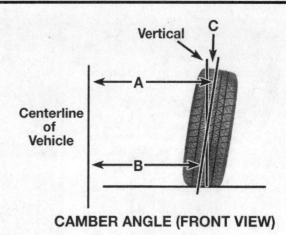

CAMBER ANGLE (FRONT VIEW)

21.1 Front end alignment details

A minus B = C (degrees camber)
D = degrees camber
E minus F = toe-in (measured in inches)
G = toe-in (expressed in degrees)

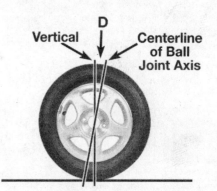

CASTER ANGLE (SIDE VIEW)

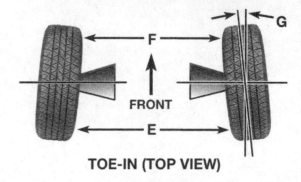

TOE-IN (TOP VIEW)

When the wheels tilt in at the top the camber is negative (-). The amount of tilt is measured in degrees from the vertical and this measurement is called the camber angle. This angle affects the amount of tire tread which contacts the road and compensates for changes in the suspension geometry when the vehicle is cornering or traveling over an undulating surface. Camber is adjusted by turning the lower control arm pivot bolts, one way or the other, in equal amounts.

Caster is the tilting of the top of the front steering axis from vertical. A tilt toward the rear is positive caster and a tilt toward the front is negative caster. Caster is adjusted by turning the lower control arm pivot bolts, one way or the other, in opposite directions.

When making adjustments to the front end alignment, the caster is set first, then the camber, then the toe-in.

Notes

Chapter 11   Body

Contents

1   General information

Warning: *The models covered by this manual are equipped with Supplemental Restraint Systems (SRS), more commonly known as airbags. Always disable the airbag system before working in the vicinity of any airbag system components to avoid the possibility of accidental deployment of the airbags, which could cause personal injury (see Chapter 12).*

All models are built with body-on-frame construction. The frame is a ladder-type, with boxed frame rails that run the entire length of the vehicle and welded-in crossmembers. The Frontier body is in two separate sections, the cab and the bed, while the Xterra body incorporates the cab, back-seat area and cargo compartment in one unitized structure.

Certain components are particularly vulnerable to accident damage and can be unbolted and repaired or replaced. Among these parts are the hood, doors, tailgate, liftgate, bumpers and front fenders.

Only general body maintenance practices and body panel repair procedures within the scope of the do-it-yourselfer are included in this Chapter.

2   Body - maintenance

1   The condition of your vehicle's body is very important, because the resale value depends a great deal on it. It's much more difficult to repair a neglected or damaged body than it is to repair mechanical components.

The hidden areas of the body, such as the wheel wells, the frame and the engine compartment, are equally important, although they don't require as frequent attention as the rest of the body.

2   Once a year, or every 12,000 miles, it's a good idea to have the underside of the body steam cleaned. All traces of dirt and oil will be removed and the area can then be inspected carefully for rust, damaged brake lines, frayed electrical wires, damaged cables and other problems. The front suspension components should be greased after completion of this job.

3   At the same time, clean the engine and the engine compartment with a steam cleaner or water-soluble degreaser.

4   The wheel wells should be given close

attention, since undercoating can peel away and stones and dirt thrown up by the tires can cause the paint to chip and flake, allowing rust to set in. If rust is found, clean down to the bare metal and apply an anti-rust paint.

5   The body should be washed about once a week. Wet the vehicle thoroughly to soften the dirt, then wash it down with a soft sponge and plenty of clean, soapy water. If the surplus dirt is not washed off very carefully, it can wear down the paint.

6   Spots of tar or asphalt thrown up from the road should be removed with a cloth soaked in tar remover or kerosene lamp oil.

7   Once every six months, wax the body and chrome trim. If a chrome cleaner is used to remove rust from any of the vehicle's plated parts, remember that the cleaner also removes part of the chrome, so use it sparingly.

3   Vinyl trim - maintenance

Don't clean vinyl trim with detergents, caustic soap or petroleum-based cleaners. Plain soap and water works just fine, with a soft brush to clean dirt that may be ingrained. Wash the vinyl as frequently as the rest of the vehicle. After cleaning, application of a high-quality rubber and vinyl protectant will help prevent oxidation and cracks. The protectant can also be applied to weather-stripping, vacuum lines and rubber hoses, which often fail as a result of chemical degradation, and to the tires.

4   Upholstery and carpets - maintenance

1   Every three months remove the floormats and clean the interior of the vehicle (more frequently if necessary). Use a stiff whiskbroom to brush the carpeting and loosen dirt and dust, then vacuum the upholstery and carpets thoroughly, especially along seams and crevices.

2   Dirt and stains can be removed from carpeting with basic household or automotive carpet shampoos available in spray cans. Follow the directions and vacuum again, then use a stiff brush to bring back the "nap" of the carpet.

3   Most interiors have cloth or vinyl upholstery, either of which can be cleaned and maintained with a number of material-specific cleaners or shampoos available in auto supply stores. Follow the directions on the product for usage, and always spot-test any upholstery cleaner on an inconspicuous area (bottom edge of a backseat cushion) to ensure that it doesn't cause a color shift in the material.

4   After cleaning, vinyl upholstery should be treated with a protectant. **Note:** *Make sure the protectant container indicates the product can be used on seats - some products may make a seat too slippery.* **Caution:** *Do not use protectant on vinyl-covered steering wheels.*

5   Leather upholstery requires special care.

It should be cleaned regularly with saddle-soap or leather cleaner. Never use alcohol, gasoline, nail polish remover or thinner to clean leather upholstery.

6   After cleaning, regularly treat leather upholstery with a leather conditioner, rubbed in with a soft cotton cloth. Never use car wax on leather upholstery.

7   In areas where the interior of the vehicle is subject to bright sunlight, cover leather seating areas of the seats with a sheet if the vehicle is to be left out for any length of time.

5   Body repair - minor damage

Plastic body panels

The following repair procedures are for minor scratches and gouges. Repair of more serious damage should be left to a dealer service department or qualified auto body shop. Below is a list of the equipment and materials necessary to perform the following repair procedures on plastic body panels.

Wax, grease and silicone removing solvent
Cloth-backed body tape
Sanding discs
Drill motor with three-inch disc holder
Hand sanding block
Rubber squeegees
Sandpaper
Non-porous mixing palette
Wood paddle or putty knife
Curved-tooth body file
Flexible parts repair material

Flexible panels (bumper trim)

1   Remove the damaged panel, if necessary or desirable. In most cases, repairs can be carried out with the panel installed.

2   Clean the area(s) to be repaired with a wax, grease and silicone removing solvent applied with a water-dampened cloth.

3   If the damage is structural, that is, if it extends through the panel, clean the backside of the panel area to be repaired as well. Wipe dry.

4   Sand the rear surface about 1-1/2 inches beyond the break.

5   Cut two pieces of fiberglass cloth large enough to overlap the break by about 1-1/2 inches. Cut only to the required length.

6   Mix the adhesive from the repair kit according to the instructions included with the kit, and apply a layer of the mixture approximately 1/8-inch thick on the backside of the panel. Overlap the break by at least 1-1/2 inches.

7   Apply one piece of fiberglass cloth to the adhesive and cover the cloth with additional adhesive. Apply a second piece of fiberglass cloth to the adhesive and immediately cover the cloth with additional adhesive in sufficient quantity to fill the weave.

8   Allow the repair to cure for 20 to 30 minutes at 60-degrees to 80-degrees F.

9   If necessary, trim the excess repair mate-

rial at the edge.

10   Remove all of the paint film over and around the area(s) to be repaired. The repair material should not overlap the painted surface.

11   With a drill motor and a sanding disc (or a rotary file), cut a "V" along the break line approximately 1/2-inch wide. Remove all dust and loose particles from the repair area.

12   Mix and apply the repair material. Apply a light coat first over the damaged area; then continue applying material until it reaches a level slightly higher than the surrounding finish.

13   Cure the mixture for 20 to 30 minutes at 60-degrees to 80-degrees F.

14   Roughly establish the contour of the area being repaired with a body file. If low areas or pits remain, mix and apply additional adhesive.

15   Block sand the damaged area with sandpaper to establish the actual contour of the surrounding surface.

16   If desired, the repaired area can be temporarily protected with several light coats of primer. Because of the special paints and techniques required for flexible body panels, it is recommended that the vehicle be taken to a paint shop for completion of the body repair.

Steel body panels

See photo sequence

Repair of minor scratches

17   If the scratch is superficial and does not penetrate to the metal of the body, repair is very simple. Lightly rub the scratched area with a fine rubbing compound to remove loose paint and built up wax. Rinse the area with clean water.

18   Apply touch-up paint to the scratch, using a small brush. Continue to apply thin layers of paint until the surface of the paint in the scratch is level with the surrounding paint. Allow the new paint at least two weeks to harden, then blend it into the surrounding paint by rubbing with a very fine rubbing compound. Finally, apply a coat of wax to the scratch area.

19   If the scratch has penetrated the paint and exposed the metal of the body, causing the metal to rust, a different repair technique is required. Remove all loose rust from the bottom of the scratch with a pocketknife, then apply rust inhibiting paint to prevent the formation of rust in the future. Using a rubber or nylon applicator, coat the scratched area with glaze-type filler. If required, the filler can be mixed with thinner to provide a very thin paste, which is ideal for filling narrow scratches. Before the glaze filler in the scratch hardens, wrap a piece of smooth cotton cloth around the tip of a finger. Dip the cloth in thinner and then quickly wipe it along the surface of the scratch. This will ensure that the surface of the filler is slightly hollow. The scratch can now be painted over as described earlier in this Section.

Repair of dents

20 When repairing dents, the first job is to pull the dent out until the affected area is as close as possible to its original shape. There is no point in trying to restore the original shape completely as the metal in the damaged area will have stretched on impact and cannot be restored to its original contours. It is better to bring the level of the dent up to a point that is about 1/8-inch below the level of the surrounding metal. In cases where the dent is very shallow, it is not worth trying to pull it out at all.

21 If the backside of the dent is accessible, it can be hammered out gently from behind using a soft-face hammer. While doing this, hold a block of wood firmly against the opposite side of the metal to absorb the hammer blows and prevent the metal from being stretched.

22 If the dent is in a section of the body which has double layers, or some other factor makes it inaccessible from behind, a different technique is required. Drill several small holes through the metal inside the damaged area, particularly in the deeper sections. Screw long, self-tapping screws into the holes just enough for them to get a good grip in the metal. Now pulling on the protruding heads of the screws with locking pliers can pull out the dent.

23 The next stage of repair is the removal of paint from the damaged area and from an inch or so of the surrounding metal. This is easily done with a wire brush or sanding disk in a drill motor, although it can be done just as effectively by hand with sandpaper. To complete the preparation for filling, score the surface of the bare metal with a screwdriver or the tang of a file or drill small holes in the affected area. This will provide a good grip for the filler material. To complete the repair, see the Section on filling and painting.

Repair of rust holes or gashes

24 Remove all paint from the affected area and from an inch or so of the surrounding metal using a sanding disk or wire brush mounted in a drill motor. If these are not available, a few sheets of sandpaper will do the job just as effectively.

25 With the paint removed, you will be able to determine the severity of the corrosion and decide whether to replace the whole panel, if possible, or repair the affected area. New body panels are not as expensive as most people think and it is often quicker to install a new panel than to repair large areas of rust.

26 Remove all trim pieces from the affected area except those which will act as a guide to the original shape of the damaged body, such as headlight shells, etc. Using metal snips or a hacksaw blade, remove all loose metal and any other metal that is badly affected by rust. Hammer the edges of the hole in to create a slight depression for the filler material.

27 Wire-brush the affected area to remove the powdery rust from the surface of the metal. If the back of the rusted area is accessible, treat it with rust inhibiting paint.

28 Before filling is done, block the hole in some way. This can be done with sheet metal riveted or screwed into place, or by stuffing the hole with wire mesh.

29 Once the hole is blocked off, the affected area can be filled and painted. See the following subsection on filling and painting.

Filling and painting

30 Many types of body fillers are available, but generally speaking, body repair kits which contain filler paste and a tube of resin hardener are best for this type of repair work. A wide, flexible plastic or nylon applicator will be necessary for imparting a smooth and contoured finish to the surface of the filler material. Mix up a small amount of filler on a clean piece of wood or cardboard (use the hardener sparingly). Follow the manufacturer's instructions on the package, otherwise the filler will set incorrectly.

31 Using the applicator, apply the filler paste to the prepared area. Draw the applicator across the surface of the filler to achieve the desired contour and to level the filler surface. As soon as a contour that approximates the original one is achieved, stop working the paste. If you continue, the paste will begin to stick to the applicator. Continue to add thin layers of paste at 20-minute intervals until the level of the filler is just above the surrounding metal.

32 Once the filler has hardened, the excess can be removed with a body file. From then on, progressively finer grades of sandpaper should be used, starting with a 180-grit paper and finishing with 600-grit wet-or-dry paper. Always wrap the sandpaper around a flat rubber or wooden block, otherwise the surface of the filler will not be completely flat. During the sanding of the filler surface, the wet-or-dry paper should be periodically rinsed in water. This will ensure that a very smooth finish is produced in the final stage.

33 At this point, the repair area should be surrounded by a ring of bare metal, which in turn should be encircled by the finely feathered edge of good paint. Rinse the repair area with clean water until all of the dust produced by the sanding operation is gone.

34 Spray the entire area with a light coat of primer. This will reveal any imperfections in the surface of the filler. Repair the imperfections with fresh filler paste or glaze filler and once more smooth the surface with sandpaper. Repeat this spray-and-repair procedure until you are satisfied that the surface of the filler and the feathered edge of the paint are perfect. Rinse the area with clean water and allow it to dry completely.

35 The repair area is now ready for painting. Spray painting must be carried out in a warm, dry, windless and dust free atmosphere. These conditions can be created if you have access to a large indoor work area, but if you are forced to work in the open, you will have to pick the day very carefully. If you are working indoors, dousing the floor in the work area with water will help settle the dust that would otherwise be in the air. If the repair area is confined to one body panel, mask off the surrounding panels. This will help minimize the effects of a slight mismatch in paint color. Trim pieces such as chrome strips, door handles, etc., will also need to be masked off or removed. Use masking tape and several thickness of newspaper for the masking operations.

36 Before spraying, shake the paint can thoroughly, then spray a test area until the spray painting technique is mastered. Cover the repair area with a thick coat of primer. The thickness should be built up using several thin layers of primer rather than one thick one. Using 600-grit wet-or-dry sandpaper, rub down the surface of the primer until it is very smooth. While doing this, the work area should be thoroughly rinsed with water and the wet-or-dry sandpaper periodically rinsed as well. Allow the primer to dry before spraying additional coats.

37 Spray on the top coat, again building up the thickness by using several thin layers of paint. Begin spraying in the center of the repair area and then, using a circular motion, work out until the whole repair area and about two inches of the surrounding original paint is covered. Remove all masking material 10 to 15 minutes after spraying on the final coat of paint. Allow the new paint at least two weeks to harden, then use a very fine rubbing compound to blend the edges of the new paint into the existing paint. Finally, apply a coat of wax.

6 Body repair - major damage

1 Major damage must be repaired by an auto body shop specifically equipped to perform body and frame repairs. These shops have the specialized equipment required to do the job properly.

2 If the damage is extensive, the frame must be checked for proper alignment or the vehicle's handling characteristics may be adversely affected and other components may wear at an accelerated rate.

3 Due to the fact that all of the major body components (hood, fenders, etc.) are separate and replaceable units, any seriously damaged components should be replaced rather than repaired. Sometimes the components can be found in a wrecking yard that specializes in used vehicle components, often at considerable savings over the cost of new parts.

7 Hinges and locks - maintenance

Once every 3000 miles, or every three months, the hinges and latch assemblies on the doors, hood and trunk should be given a few drops of light oil or lock lubricant. The door latch strikers should also be lubricated with a thin coat of grease to reduce wear and ensure free movement. Lubricate the door and trunk locks with spray-on graphite lubricant.

These photos illustrate a method of repairing simple dents. They are intended to supplement *Body repair - minor damage* in this Chapter and should not be used as the sole instructions for body repair on these vehicles.

1 If you can't access the backside of the body panel to hammer out the dent, pull it out with a slide-hammer-type dent puller. In the deepest portion of the dent or along the crease line, drill or punch hole(s) at least one inch apart . . .

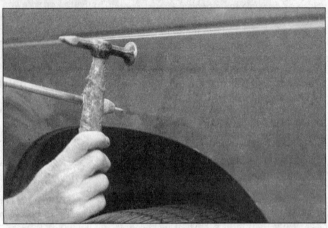

2 . . . then screw the slide-hammer into the hole and operate it. Tap with a hammer near the edge of the dent to help 'pop' the metal back to its original shape. When you're finished, the dent area should be close to its original contour and about 1/8-inch below the surface of the surrounding metal

3 Using coarse-grit sandpaper, remove the paint down to the bare metal. Hand sanding works fine, but the disc sander shown here makes the job faster. Use finer (about 320-grit) sandpaper to feather-edge the paint at least one inch around the dent area

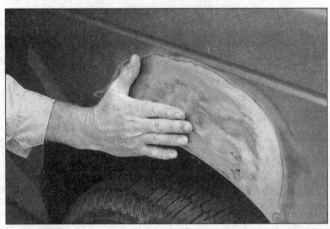

4 When the paint is removed, touch will probably be more helpful than sight for telling if the metal is straight. Hammer down the high spots or raise the low spots as necessary. Clean the repair area with wax/silicone remover

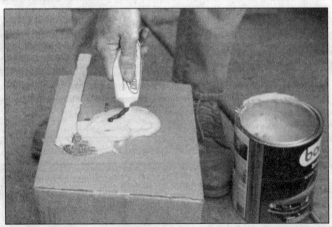

5 Following label instructions, mix up a batch of plastic filler and hardener. The ratio of filler to hardener is critical, and, if you mix it incorrectly, it will either not cure properly or cure too quickly (you won't have time to file and sand it into shape)

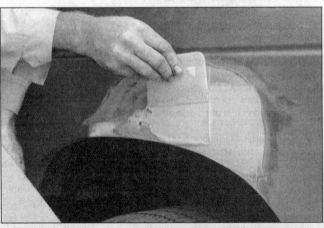

6 Working quickly so the filler doesn't harden, use a plastic applicator to press the body filler firmly into the metal, assuring it bonds completely. Work the filler until it matches the original contour and is slightly above the surrounding metal

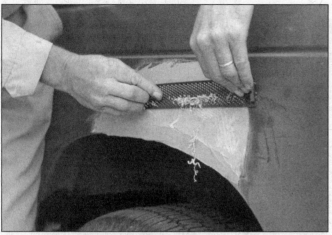

7 Let the filler harden until you can just dent it with your fingernail. Use a body file or Surform tool (shown here) to rough-shape the filler

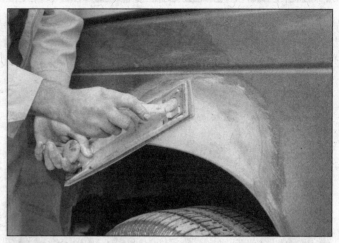

8 Use coarse-grit sandpaper and a sanding board or block to work the filler down until it's smooth and even. Work down to finer grits of sandpaper - always using a board or block - ending up with 360 or 400 grit

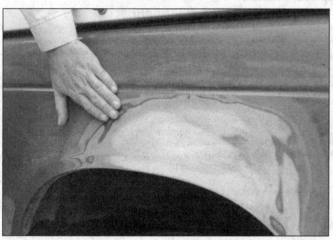

9 You shouldn't be able to feel any ridge at the transition from the filler to the bare metal or from the bare metal to the old paint. As soon as the repair is flat and uniform, remove the dust and mask off the adjacent panels or trim pieces

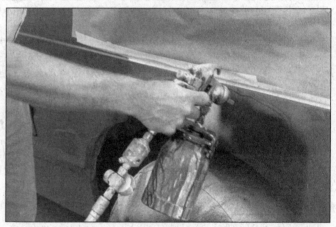

10 Apply several layers of primer to the area. Don't spray the primer on too heavy, so it sags or runs, and make sure each coat is dry before you spray on the next one. A professional-type spray gun is being used here, but aerosol spray primer is available inexpensively from auto parts stores

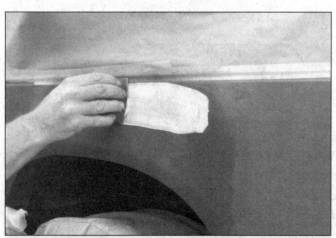

11 The primer will help reveal imperfections or scratches. Fill these with glazing compound. Follow the label instructions and sand it with 360 or 400-grit sandpaper until it's smooth. Repeat the glazing, sanding and respraying until the primer reveals a perfectly smooth surface

12 Finish sand the primer with very fine sandpaper (400 or 600-grit) to remove the primer overspray. Clean the area with water and allow it to dry. Use a tack rag to remove any dust, then apply the finish coat. Don't attempt to rub out or wax the repair area until the paint has dried completely (at least two weeks)

9.1 Remove the pushpins mounting the grille to the body (Xterra shown, Frontier similar)

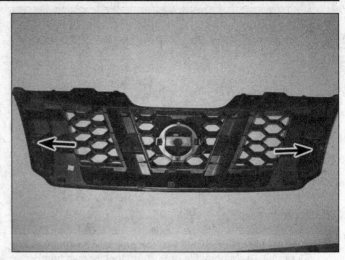

9.2 The two grille mounting clip locations (seen here from the back side)

8   Windshield and fixed glass - replacement

Replacement of the windshield and fixed glass requires the use of special fast-setting adhesive/caulk materials and some specialized tools and techniques. These operations should be left to a dealer service department or a shop specializing in glasswork. On Xterra models, the fixed glass also includes the quarter windows and liftgate glass.

9   Radiator grille - removal and installation

Refer to illustrations 9.1 and 9.2

1   Open the hood and remove the pushpins securing the upper part of the radiator grille to the body **(see illustration)**.
2   Pull the radiator grille outward until the clips at each outboard end release from the body **(see illustration)**.
3   Installation is the reverse of removal.

10   Hood - removal, installation and adjustment

Refer to illustrations 10.4, 10.10 and 10.11
Note: *The hood is heavy and somewhat awkward to remove and install - at least two people should perform this procedure.*

Removal and installation

1   Use blankets or pads to cover the cowl area of the body and the fenders. This will protect the body and paint as the hood is lifted off.
2   Scribe alignment marks around the hinge flanges to insure proper alignment during installation (paint or a permanent-type felt-tip marker also will work for this).
3   Disconnect the windshield washer hoses and any electrical connectors from the hood.
4   Have an assistant support the weight of the hood. Remove the hinge-to-hood bolts **(see illustration)**.
5   Lift off the hood.
6   Installation is the reverse of removal.

Adjustment

7   Fore-and-aft and side-to-side adjustment of the hood is done by moving the hood in relation to the hinge flanges after loosening the bolts.
8   Scribe or trace a line around the entire hinge plate so you can judge the amount of movement **(see illustration 10.4)**.
9   Loosen the bolts and move the hood into correct alignment. Move it only a little at a time. Tighten the hinge bolts and carefully lower the hood to check the alignment.
10   If necessary after installation, the entire hood latch assembly can be adjusted up-and-down as well as from side-to-side on the radiator support so the hood closes securely and flush with the fenders. To make the adjustment, scribe a line around the hood latch mounting bolts to provide a reference point, then loosen them and reposition the latch assembly, as necessary **(see illustration)**. Following adjustment, retighten the mounting bolts.
11   Finally, adjust the hood bumpers on the radiator support so the hood, when closed, is

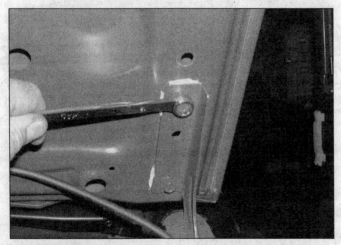

10.4 Remove the four retaining bolts and lift off the hood with the help of an assistant

10.10 Loosen the hood latch bolts (arrows), then move the latch as necessary to adjust the hood - closed position

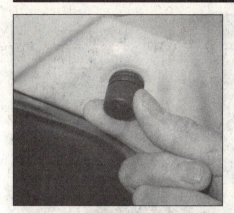

10.11 Twist the hood bumpers in-or-out to make fine adjustments to the hood closed height

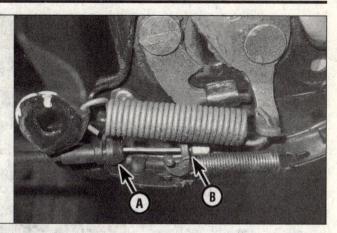

11.1 To disconnect the cable from the hood latch mechanism, disengage the cable housing end (A) from the slot in the latch and twist the cable end (B) out of the latch arm

flush with the fenders **(see illustration)**.

12   The hood latch assembly, as well as the hinges, should be periodically lubricated with white, lithium-base grease to prevent binding and wear.

11   Hood latch and release cable - removal and installation

Warning: *The models covered by this manual are equipped with Supplemental Restraint Systems (SRS), more commonly known as airbags. Always disable the airbag system before working in the vicinity of any airbag system components to avoid the possibility of accidental deployment of the airbags, which could cause personal injury (see Chapter 12).*

Latch

Refer to illustration 11.1

1   Remove the bolts and detach the latch assembly **(see illustration 10.10)**. Unhook the spring and pry the cable end from the latch **(see illustration)**.

2   Installation is the reverse of removal. Adjust the latch so the hood engages securely when closed and the hood bumpers are slightly compressed (see Section 10).

Release cable

Refer to illustration 11.5

3   Disconnect the release cable from the hood latch assembly as described in Step 1.

4   Unclip the release cable from the radiator support clips. Attach a length of wire to the cable to assist with the installation of the new cable.

5   Remove the mounting bolts securing the hood release handle to the underside of the instrument panel near the steering column **(see illustration)**.

6   When replacing the cable, you may need to remove the fenderwell liner (see Section 13) to access the clips securing the cable.

7   Trace the cable forward to the grommet where the cable goes through the firewall and pry the grommet out of the firewall. Pull the handle and cable rearward into the passenger compartment.

8   Disconnect the guide wire from the old cable and fasten it to the new cable.

9   With the new cable attached to the wire, pull the wire back through the firewall until the new cable reaches the latch assembly. Make sure that the grommet is properly seated on both sides of the hole in the firewall. Push on the grommet with your fingers from the passenger compartment side to seat the grommet in the firewall correctly.

10   The remainder of installation is the reverse of removal.

12   Bumpers - removal and installation

Warning: *The models covered by this manual are equipped with Supplemental Restraint Systems (SRS), more commonly known as airbags. Always disable the airbag system before working in the vicinity of any airbag system components to avoid the possibility of accidental deployment of the airbags, which could cause personal injury (see Chapter 12).* **Note:** *On Frontier models, some trim levels include a chromed steel center section of the front bumper, while on other models this part is plastic. The bumper cover replacement procedure is similar for both types.*

Front bumper

Refer to illustrations 12.2, 12.3a, 12.3b and 12.5

1   Refer to Section 9 and remove the radiator grille.

2   Remove the screws securing the front license plate holder, to access the two nuts securing the bumper cover to the radiator support **(see illustration)**.

11.5 Hood release handle and cable mounting bolts - one piece design

12.2 Remove these nuts in the grille opening

12.3a On each side of the bumper cover, remove these fasteners

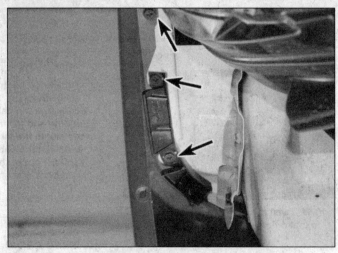

12.3b With the fender liner pulled back at the front, access and remove these screws

3   On each side of the front bumper cover, remove the fasteners securing the cover to the fenderwell liner and lower body **(see illustration)**. Pull back the front portion of the fenderwell liner to access the screws securing the cover to the body **(see illustration)**.

4   Disconnect any wiring harnesses or any other components that would interfere with removal of the bumper.

5   Remove the remaining bumper cover fasteners **(see illustration)**, then with the help of an assistant, carefully detach the bumper cover.

6   Installation is the reverse of removal. Tighten the retaining bolts securely.

Rear bumper

Refer to illustration 12.8

7   Disconnect the electrical connectors for the license plate lights.

8   Remove the bolts securing the bumper to the frame **(see illustration)**.

9   Installation is the reverse of removal. Tighten the retaining bolts or screws securely.

Xterra

Refer to illustrations 12.11a, 12.11b, 12.11c and 12.11d

10   Open the rear liftgate.

11   Remove the screws securing the outer (plastic) bumper extensions. There are several pins in the liftgate opening and screws in each wheelwell opening **(see illustrations)**.

12   With an assistant supporting the bumper, remove the nuts from the end of the steel bumper and detach the rear bumper from the vehicle.

13   Installation is the reverse of removal. Tighten the retaining bolts securely.

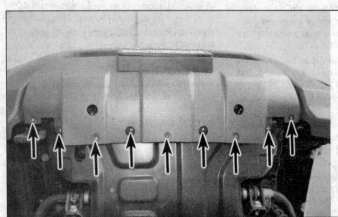

12.5 From below, remove these fasteners under the center of the bumper cover

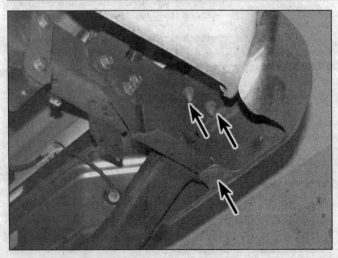

12.8 Frontier pickup rear bumper-to-frame fasteners

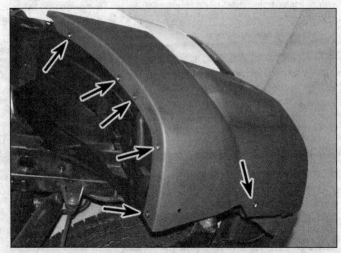

12.11a Remove the side pieces of the bumper cover by first removing the fasteners securing it to the fenderwell and the body

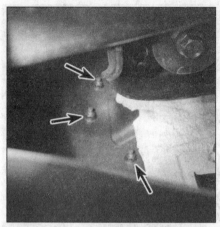

12.11b Up inside the fenderwell (seen here from below) remove these three nuts

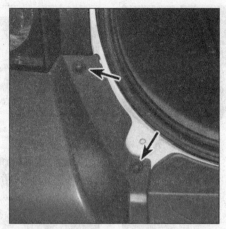

12.11c Remove the pushpins inside the liftgate opening

12.11d The heavy center piece of the bumper is secured to the frame by three bolts on each side

13 Front fender - removal and installation

Refer to illustrations 13.4, 13.5, 13.6, 13.7 and 13.8

1   Disconnect the negative cable from the battery. Loosen the wheel lug nuts, raise the vehicle, support it securely on jackstands and remove the front wheel.

2   Refer to Chapter 12 and remove the headlight assembly.

3   Refer to Section 12 and remove the front bumper cover.

4   Remove the plastic pushpins and screws securing the plastic fenderwell to the fender **(see illustration)**. The fenderwell liner does not need to be completely removed from the vehicle, just remove the fasteners at the fender.

5   Remove the fender-to-body bolts in the front of the fenderwell **(see illustration)**.

6   Open the door and remove the one

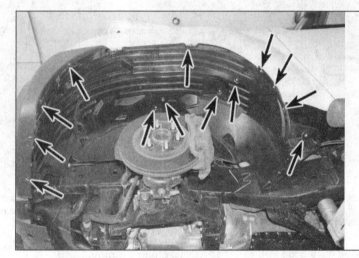

13.4 Fenderwell liner mounting fasteners

fender bolt at the top and one at the bottom of the door jamb **(see illustration)**.

7   At the rocker panel area, remove the two

bolts securing the fender **(see illustration)**.

8   Remove the mounting bolts securing the top of the fender **(see illustration)**.

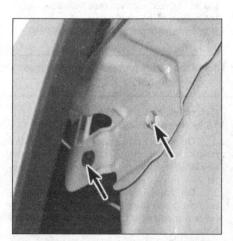

13.5 Remove these two fender-to-body bolts in the front of the fenderwell

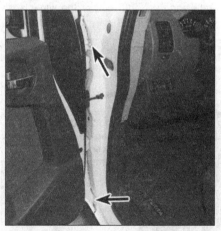

13.6 Two fender bolts are located in the door jamb

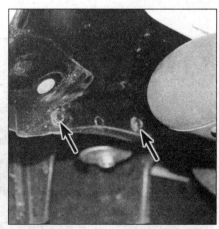

13.7 Remove these two bolts securing the fender to the rocker panel

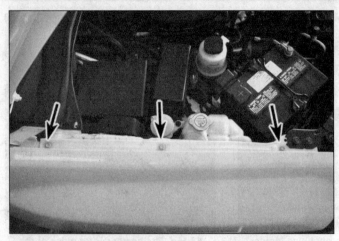

13.8 Upper fender-to-body mounting bolts

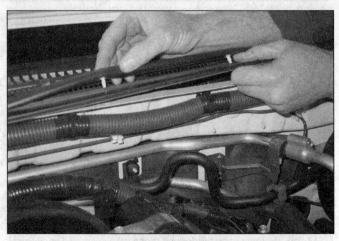

14.2 Pry out the clips and remove the hood seal

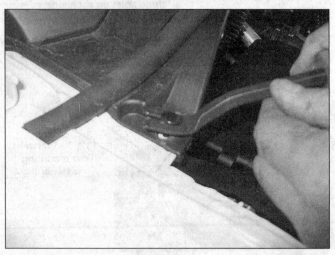

14.3 At each end, pull the seal back and pry up the pins

15.2a Use a hooked tool or a special window crank removal tool like this one to remove the retaining clip, then detach the window crank handle

9   Detach the fender. It's a good idea to have an assistant support the fender while it's being moved away from the vehicle to prevent damage to the surrounding body panels.

10   Installation is the reverse of the removal procedure. Tighten all nuts, bolts and screws securely.

14   Cowl cover - removal and installation

Refer to illustrations 14.2 and 14.3

1   Pry off the plastic trim cap on the windshield wiper arms, then detach the wiper arm retaining nuts and remove the wiper arms (see Chapter 12).

2   Carefully pry out the clips securing the hood seal to the cowl **(see illustration)**.

3   Pry up the clips securing the front of the cowl cover to the cowl and remove the cover from the vehicle **(see illustration)**. Once the cowl cover is raised, disconnect the hose from the windshield washer reservoir attached to the bottom of the cowl cover.

4   Installation is the reverse of removal.

15   Door trim panels - removal and installation

Refer to illustrations 15.2a, 15.2b, 15.2c, 15.3a, 15.3b, 15.4 and 15.6

1   On models with power door locks and/or power windows, disconnect the cable from the negative terminal of the battery (see Chapter 1).

2   On manual window models, remove the window crank **(see illustration)**. On power-window models, pry the power switch assembly out of the door panel with a flat-bladed trim tool and disconnect the electrical connectors from the switches **(see illustrations)**.

3   Remove all door trim panel retaining

15.2b Use a trim tool to pry up the power window switch assembly from the door

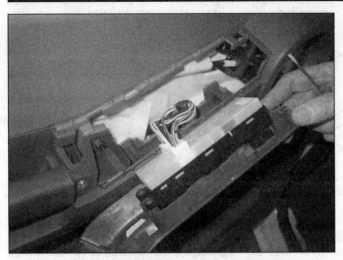

15.2c Disconnect the electrical connectors on the back of the switch assembly

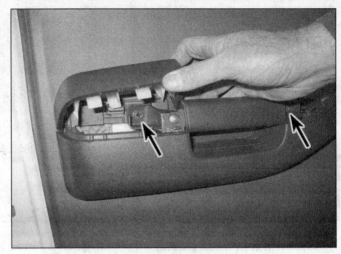

15.3a Lift off the armrest covers and remove the two screws

screws and door pull/armrest assemblies **(see illustrations)**.

4   Insert a wide putty knife, a thin screwdriver or a special trim panel removal tool between the trim panel and the door to disengage the retaining clips **(see illustration)**. Work around the outside edge until the panel is free. **Note:** *Door trim panel retaining clips are approximately four to six inches apart. Pry at the clip location only. Prying between the clips will result in distorted or damaged trim panel(s).*

5   Once all of the clips are disengaged, raise the trim panel up and off the door. Disconnect any wiring harness connectors and remove the trim panel from the vehicle.

6   For access to the inner door, carefully peel back the plastic watershield **(see illustration)**.

7   Prior to installation of the door panel, be sure to reinstall any clips in the panel which may have come out during the removal procedure and remain in the door itself.

8   Connect the wiring harness connectors and place the panel in position on the door.

Engage the trim panel with the top of the door first, then push downward on the panel until the clips on the trim panel align with all the holes in the door. Once the clips are aligned with the respective holes, push straight in on the panel until the clips are seated.

9   The remainder of the installation is the reverse of removal.

16 Door - removal, installation and adjustment

Note: *The door is heavy and somewhat awkward to remove and install - at least two people should perform this procedure.*

Removal and installation

Refer to illustrations 16.6 and 16.8

1   Lower the window completely in the door and then disconnect the negative cable from the battery.

2   Open the door all the way and support it on jacks or blocks covered with rags to pre-

15.3b Pull out the inside door handle escutcheon and remove the one bolt

vent damaging the paint.

3   Remove the door trim panel and water deflector as described in Section 15.

4   Disconnect all electrical connections,

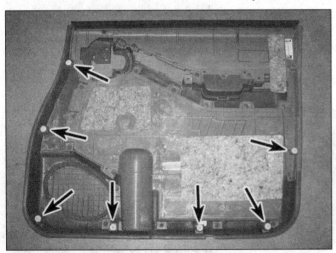

15.4 Seen from the back, these are the door panel clip locations

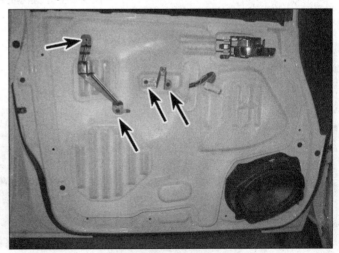

15.6 Before you can peel off the plastic door liner, remove these screws and brackets

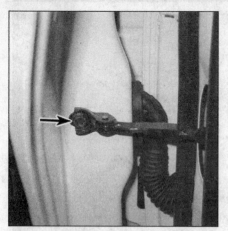

16.6 Remove the bolt (arrow) and detach the door stop strut from the body

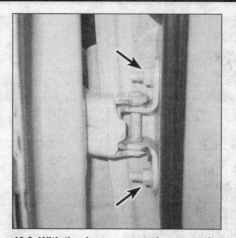

16.8 With the door supported, remove the hinge bolts (arrows indicate lower hinge bolts) and lift the door off

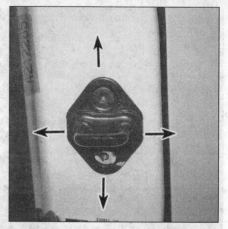

16.12 Adjust the door lock striker by loosening the mounting screws and gently tapping the striker in the desired direction

ground wires and harness retaining clips from the door. **Note:** *It is a good idea to label all connections to aid the reassembly process.*

5   From the door side, detach the rubber conduit between the body and the door. Then pull the wiring harness through the conduit hole and remove the wiring harness from the door.

6   Remove the door stop strut at the body **(see illustration)**.

7   Mark around the door hinges with a pen or a scribe to facilitate realignment during reassembly.

8   With an assistant holding the door, remove the hinge to door bolts **(see illustration)** and lift the door off.

9   Installation is the reverse of removal.

Adjustment

Refer to illustration 16.12

10   Having proper door to body alignment is a critical part of a well functioning door assembly. First check the door hinge pins for excessive play. Fully open the door and lift up and down on the door without lifting the body. If a door has 1/16-inch (1.6 mm) or more exces-

sive play, the hinges should be replaced.

11   Door-to-body adjustments are made by loosening the hinge-to-body bolts or hinge-to-door bolts and moving the door. Proper body alignment is achieved when the top of the doors are parallel with the roof section, the front door is flush with the fender, the rear door (Xterra or cab models) is flush with the rear quarter panel and crew-cab and the bottom of the doors are aligned with the lower rocker panel. If these goals can't be reached by adjusting the hinge-to-body or hinge-to-door bolts, body alignment shims may have to be purchased and inserted behind the hinges to achieve correct alignment.

12   To adjust the door closed position, scribe a line or mark around the striker plate to provide a reference point, then check that the door latch is contacting the center of the latch striker. If not adjust the up and down position first **(see illustration)**.

13   Finally adjust the latch striker sideways position, so that the door panel is flush with either the center pillar, or rear quarter panel or cab, and provides positive engagement with the latch mechanism.

17   Door latch, lock cylinder and handles - removal and installation

1   Remove the door trim panel and the plastic watershield (see Section 15).

Door latch

Refer to illustration 17.2

2   Remove the latch retaining screws from the end of the door, then reach inside the door to release the latch from the control rods **(see illustration)**.

3   On models with power door locks, disconnect the electrical connector.

4   Detach the door latch and (if equipped) the door lock solenoid.

5   Installation is the reverse of removal.

Lock cylinder

Refer to illustration 17.7

6   Detach the electrical connector from the lock cylinder (if equipped).

7   To remove the lock cylinder and/or the outside door handle, remove the access plug

17.2 Door latch retaining screws (Frontier model shown, other models similar)

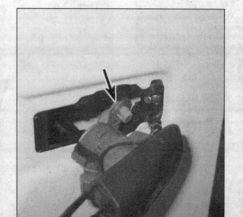

17.7 Disengage the lock rod from the cylinder

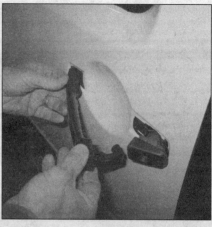

17.8 Twist the outside door handle from where it engages the lock cylinder assembly

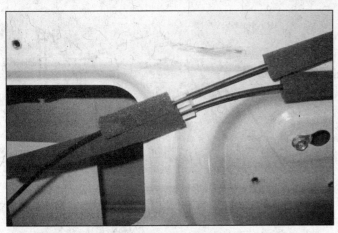

17.10 Pull the two door control cables from the clips in the door, then disconnect them at the latch

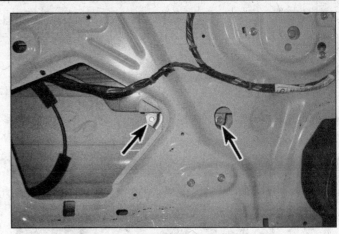

18.4 Remove the retaining bolts (arrows) and lift the glass out of the door

at the end of the door, and loosen the screw **(see illustration 17.2)**, which will allow the lock cylinder to angle out of the door. Use a screwdriver to disengage the lock rod and remove the lock cylinder **(see illustration)**.

Outside handle

Refer to illustration 17.8

8   The outside door handle can be disengaged from the door when the lock cylinder has been removed **(see illustration)**.

Inside handle

Refer to illustration 17.10

9   Remove the door trim panel.
10   Release the control rod guide clip **(see illustration)**.
11   Remove the retaining screws, pull the handle free from the door and disconnect the control rods from the rear of the inside handle.
12   Installation is the reverse of removal.

---

18   Door window glass - removal and installation

Refer to illustration 18.4

1   Remove the door trim panel and water-

shield (see Section 15). Removal and installation of the window glass is essentially the same for front and rear doors (on models so equipped).
2   Lower the glass until the glass track bolts are visible through the holes in the door frame.
3   Place a rag inside the door panel to help prevent scratching the glass during removal.
4   Loosen the two bolts retaining the glass to the window regulator track and pull the glass from the door **(see illustration)**. **Note:** *When removing the rear door glass on Xterra models, it will be necessary to remove the rear run channel between the stationary glass and the sliding glass to allow clearance for glass removal.*
5   To install, lower the glass into the door, slide it into position and tighten the nuts.
6   The remainder of installation is the reverse of removal.

---

19   Door window glass regulator - removal and installation

Refer to illustration 19.4

Note: *The procedure is the same for both front and rear window regulators.*
1   Remove the door trim panel and the

plastic watershield (see Section 15).
2   Remove the window glass assembly (see Section 18).
3   On power operated windows, disconnect the electrical connector from the window regulator motor.
4   Remove the equalizer arm bolts and the regulator mounting bolts **(see illustration)**.
5   Pull the equalizer arm and regulator assemblies through the service hole in the door frame to remove it.
6   Installation is the reverse of removal.

---

20   Mirrors - removal and installation

Refer to illustrations 20.2, 20.4 and 20.6

Outside mirrors

1   Remove the door trim panel (see Section 15).
2   Remove the cover over the mirror mounting bolts **(see illustration)**.
3   If equipped with power mirrors, unplug the electrical connector.
4   Remove the fasteners and detach the mirror from the door **(see illustration)**.
5   Installation is the reverse of removal.

20.2 Pry off the mirror trim cover

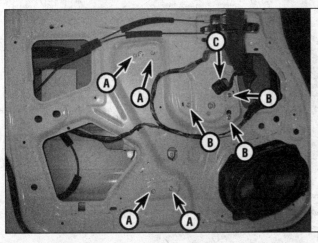

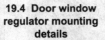

19.4 Door window regulator mounting details

A   *Equalizer arm mounting bolts*
B   *Window regulator mounting bolts*
C   *Motor electrical connector*

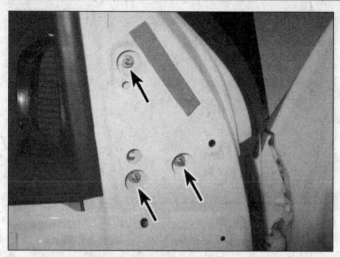

20.4 Remove the outside mirror mounting bolts (arrows)

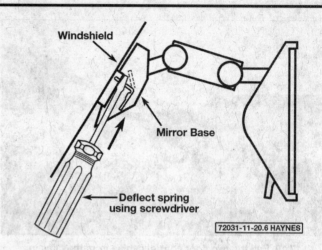

20.6 Using a narrow screwdriver, pry the retaining spring away from the mounting bracket to free the mirror

Inside mirror

6   Insert a small screwdriver into the base of the mirror mounting bracket, and carefully pry rearward to disengage the mirror retain-

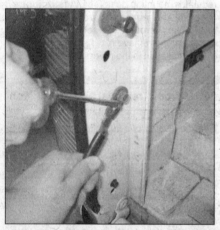

21.1 Lift the spring retainer up and slide the cable end off the pin

ing spring from the mounting bracket **(see illustration)**. After the spring has been disengaged, slide the mirror up and off the mounting bracket.
7   Installation is the reverse of removal.
8   If the mounting bracket for the mirror has come off the windshield, it can be reattached with a special mirror adhesive kit available at auto parts stores. Clean the glass and support base thoroughly and follow the directions on the adhesive package, allowing the base to bond overnight before attaching the mirror.

21   Tailgate (Frontier models) - removal and installation

Refer to illustrations 21.1 and 21.2

1   Open the tailgate and detach the retaining cables **(see illustration)**.
2   Lower the tailgate until the flat on the left side hinge pin aligns with the slot in the hinge pocket. Lift the tailgate out of the pocket. With

the help of an assistant to support the weight, withdraw the right hinge pin from the body and remove the tailgate from the vehicle **(see illustration)**.
3   Installation is the reverse of removal.
Note: *Apply some white grease to the mating parts of the tailgate hinge assembly before installation.*

22   Tailgate latch and handle (Frontier models) - removal and installation

Refer to illustrations 22.2 and 22.4

1   Open the tailgate and remove the handle access cover.
2   Rotate the plastic retaining clips off the control rods and detach the rods from the handle **(see illustration)**.
3   To remove the handle, simply remove the mounting bolts and detach the handle from the tailgate.

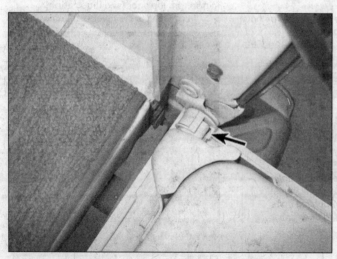

21.2 Align the flat on the right side hinge pin wiht the slot in the hinge pocket and lift the tailgate off the vehicle

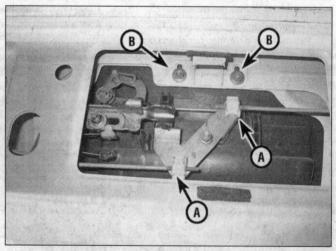

22.2 Tailgate control rods (A) and the handle mounting bolts (B)

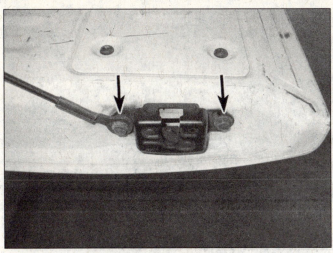

22.4 Remove the tailgate latch mounting bolts (arrows) and withdraw it with the control rod

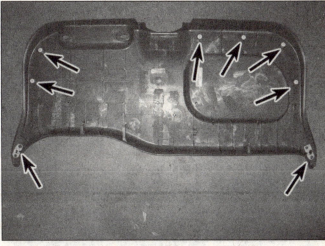

23.2 Clip locations on the liftgate panel (seen from the rear)

4   To remove the latch, simply remove the bolts and withdraw the latch from the side of the tailgate with the control rod attached **(see illustration)**. **Note:** *If you are removing both latch assemblies it will be necessary to support*

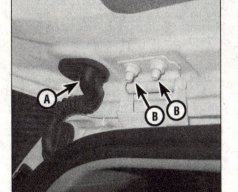

23.5 Disconnect the electrical connector (A), then remove the liftgate hinge mounting nuts (B)

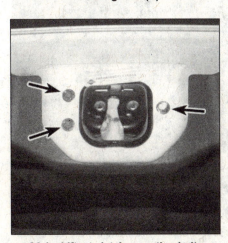

24.4a Liftgate latch mounting bolts

the tailgate from below, since the tailgate support cables will be removed at the same time.
5   Installation is the reverse of removal. Tighten all fasteners securely.

---

23 Liftgate and liftgate glass (Xterra models) - removal and installation

---

Warning: *The liftgate is heavy and awkward to hold. At least two people should perform this procedure.*

Liftgate

Refer to illustrations 23.2 and 23.5

1   Open the liftgate and support it fully in this position.
2   Remove the liftgate pull handle, then pry out the plastic retaining clips and remove the lower trim panel from the liftgate **(see illustration)**.

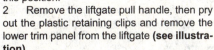

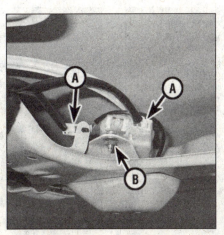

24.4b Inner latch details

A   *Electrical connectors*
B   *Mounting bolt*

3   Disconnect the electrical connectors and remove the wiring harness from the liftgate.
4   Detach the support struts at the liftgate (see Section 24).
5   Remove the liftgate mounting nuts **(see illustration)**. Remove the nuts while at least one assistant, preferably two, helps you hold the liftgate.
6   Installation is the reverse of the removal procedure.

Liftgate glass

7   The liftgate glass is permanently attached to the liftgate. It is recommended that fixed glass be replaced only by a shop with the proper glass removal/installation equipment.

---

24 Liftgate latch, lock cylinder, handle and support struts (Xterra models) - removal, installation and adjustment

---

1   Remove the liftgate lower trim panel (see Section 23, Step 2) before proceeding with Steps 2 through 14 of this Section.

Latch

Refer to illustrations 24.4a and 24.4b

2   There is one latch mounted to the bottom edge of the liftgate. Some models have electrically operated latch mechanisms and others have manually operated cable release mechanisms
3   To remove the latch, disconnect the control rods from the rear of the latch. Disconnect the electrical connector on electrically operated latch mechanisms or the release cable on manually operated mechanisms.
4   Remove the latch mounting bolts and detach the latch from the liftgate **(see illustrations)**.
5   Installation is the reverse of the removal procedure.

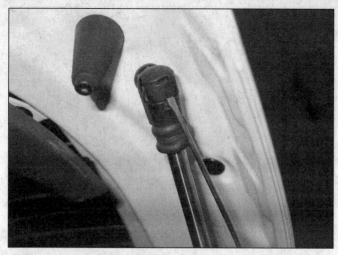

24.12 Use a small screwdriver to pry up the clip at each strut end, just enough to remove the strut from the ballstud

24.16 Striker mounting bolts - make a reference mark around the edges of the striker before repositioning it for adjustment

Lock cylinder

6   Detach the electrical connector from the lock cylinder (if equipped).
7   Disengage the clip securing the control rod to the lock cylinder.
8   Using a screwdriver or a pair of pliers, pry the lock cylinder retaining clip off the lock. Pull the lock outward to disengage it from the door.

Outside handle

9   Working through the access hole in the liftgate, remove the handle mounting nuts. Tilt the handle up and out to disengage it from the latch assembly.
10   Installation is the reverse of the removal procedure.

Support struts

Refer to illustration 24.12

11   There are two support struts for the lift-gate, and two separate struts to support the glass. Open the liftgate and prop it securely in the full open position.
12   Release the small clip at the lower end of the strut, then pull the strut from the mounting ball **(see illustration).**
13   Remove the clip securing the upper half of the support strut to the liftgate and detach the strut from the vehicle. Make sure the lift-gate is supported properly before removing the struts or injury may occur.
14   Installation is the reverse of the removal procedure.

Adjustment

Refer to illustration 24.16

15   The closing position of the liftgate can be adjusted by moving either or both of the lift-gate strikers.
16   Loosen the striker mounting bolts, move the striker slightly, retighten the bolts and check the closed position of the liftgate **(see illustration).**

25   Center console - removal and installation

Refer to illustrations 25.3, 25.4 and 25.5

Warning: *The models covered by this manual are equipped with Supplemental Restraint Systems (SRS), more commonly known as airbags. Always disable the airbag system before working in the vicinity of any airbag system components to avoid the possibility of accidental deployment of the airbags, which could cause personal injury (see Chapter 12).*

1   Disconnect the cable from the negative terminal of the battery and set the parking brake.
2   On vehicles equipped with manual transmissions, unscrew the knob from the shift lever.
3   Use a trim tool to pry up the bezel around the cupholder and shifter **(see illustration).**
4   Carefully pull up the boot around the parking brake handle and remove the boot

25.3 The cupholder/shifter bezel is retained by clips; pry up with a trim tool

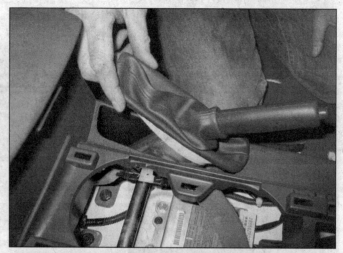

25.4 Use a dull plastic tool to loosen the brake handle boot, then slide it off the brake handle

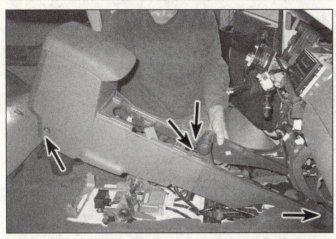

25.5 Six screws retain the main console box, two at the rear, two in the center and two at the front

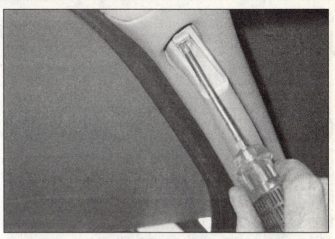

26.4a Remove the screws securing the assist handle to the windshield post, then remove the post trim panel

26.4b Use a small screwdriver to pry out the rubber ring around the ignition switch lock cylinder

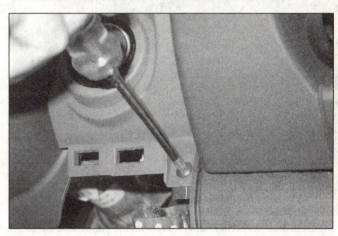

26.4c Remove one mounting screw on each side (right side shown)

(see illustration).

5   Disconnect all electrical connectors connected to the main console box, then remove the box mounting screws, two at the rear, two in the middle, and two up front near the base of the instrument panel **(see illustration).**

6   Installation is the reverse of the removal procedure.

26 Dashboard trim panels - removal and installation

Warning: *The models covered by this manual are equipped with Supplemental Restraint Systems (SRS), more commonly known as airbags. Always disable the airbag system before working in the vicinity of any airbag system components to avoid the possibility of accidental deployment of the airbags, which could cause personal injury (see Chapter 12).*

Instrument cluster bezel

Refer to illustration 26.4a, 24.6b, 24.6c and 26.4d

1   With the wheels blocked, apply the parking brake.

2   On models equipped with tilt steering columns, tilt the steering wheel down as far as possible.

3   Remove the knee boltster (see Step 6).

4   Remove the bezel retaining screws and remove the bezel from the instrument panel **(see illustrations).**

5   Installation is the reverse of removal.

Knee bolster

Refer to illustration 26.7

6   Remove the cover over the fuse/relay box at the left end of the dash.

26.4d Lift off the cluster bezel

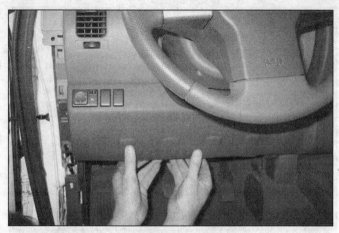

26.7 Remove the two mounting screws at the bottom and remove the knee bolster

26.10 Remove the storage tray and the screw below

26.11a Pull the center panel away from the instrument panel

26.11b Disconnect electrical connectors behind the center panel

7   Remove the screws securing the driver's knee bolster and pull it outward away from the dash **(see illustration)**. Disconnect any electrical connectors at the rear of the knee bolster and detach it from the instrument panel.
8   If the knee bolster reinforcement panel needs to be removed for any reason, remove the retaining bolts and take down the panel.
9   Installation is the reverse of removal.

Center trim panel

Refer to illustrations 26.10, 26.11a and 26.11b

10   Remove the liner in the storage tray at the top of the center panel. Pry up the tray and remove the one screw securing the cover **(see illustration)**.
11   Pull out on the center panel to release it, then disconnect any electrical connectors

behind the panel **(see illustrations)**.
12   Installation is the reverse of removal.

Glove box

Refer to illustrations 26.13a and 26.13b

13   With the glove box open, remove the four screws at the top, two screws at the bottom, and pull the glove box housing from the

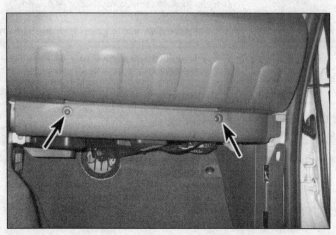

26.13a Remove the lower glovebox screws

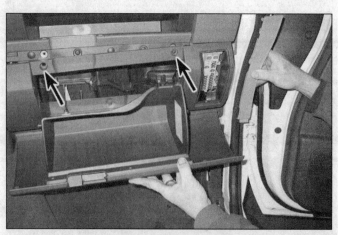

26.13b Remove the upper glove box screws

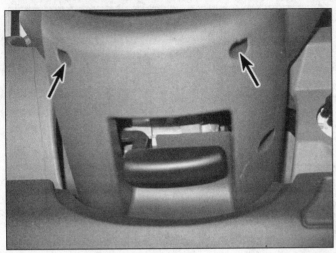

27.1 Remove the screws in the lower column cover, detach and lift off the upper cover

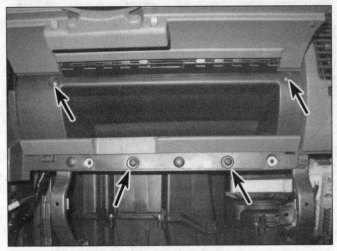

28.9a Remove the upper glove box mounting screws

instrument panel **(see illustrations)**.

14   Installation is the reverse of the removal procedure.

27 Steering column covers - removal and installation

Refer to illustration 27.1

Warning: *The models covered by this manual are equipped with Supplemental Restraint Systems (SRS), more commonly known as airbags. Always disable the airbag system before working in the vicinity of any airbag system components to avoid the possibility of accidental deployment of the airbags, which could cause personal injury (see Chapter 12).*

1   On all models, remove the screws and detach the lower half of the steering column cover **(see illustration)**.

2   Pull the upper column cover straight up and off.

3   Installation is the reverse of removal.

28 Instrument panel - removal and installation

Refer to illustrations 28.8, 28.9a, 28.9b, 28.10, 28.13, 28.14, 28.16a and 28.16b

Warning: *The models covered by this manual are equipped with Supplemental Restraint Systems (SRS), more commonly known as airbags. Always disable the airbag system before working in the vicinity of any airbag system components to avoid the possibility of accidental deployment of the airbags, which could cause personal injury (see Chapter 12).*

Note: *This is a difficult procedure for the home mechanic, involving tedious disassembly and the disconnection/reconnection of numerous electrical connectors. If you do attempt this procedure, make sure you take good notes and mark all matching connectors (and their mounting points) to aid reassembly.*

1   Disconnect the cable from the negative terminal of the battery.

2   Remove the center console (see Section 25).

3   Remove the steering column covers (see Section 27).

4   Remove the dashboard trim panels (see Section 26).

5   Remove the instrument cluster (see Chapter 12).

6   Remove the radio and heater/air conditioner controls (see Chapter 3 and Chapter 12).

7   Remove the kick panels at each side of the instrument panel. The panels simply pull out after removing the retaining screw at the bottom and the door sill trim.

8   Remove the left and right trim strips along the interior of each windshield post **(see illustration 26.4a)**.

9   The passenger airbag is mounted behind the instrument panel cover **(see illustration)**. Remove the upper glove box for access to the airbag bolts and connector **(see illustration)**. Disconnect the airbag connector, then remove the mounting bolts.

10   Remove the screws and the lower switch panel at the center of the instrument panel **(see illustration)**. Disconnect any electrical

28.9b Disconnect the passenger airbag connector (A, lift the locking tab first), then remove the airbag mounting bolts (B)

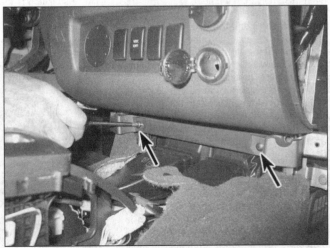

28.10 Remove the lower switch panel mounting screws

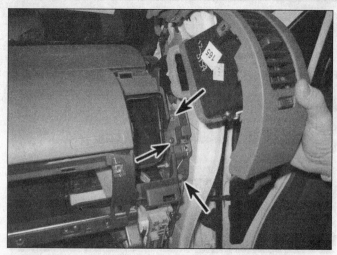

28.12 Lift out the air duct outlet housings on each side; they have tabs that fit into slots in the instrument panel

28.13 Remove all the fasteners securing the main panel, these are some of the left-side fasteners

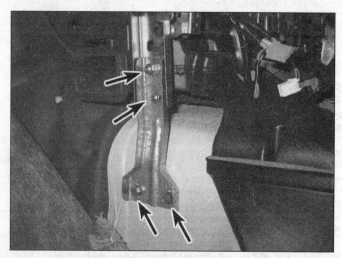

28.14 Remove the screws and the two floor braces (left side shown)

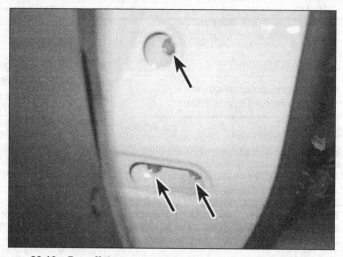

28.16a Pry off the covers in the door jamb to reveal bolts securing the cowl beam to the body

connectors behind the panel.

11   Refer to Chapter 7B and remove the shifter assembly from the floor.

12   Remove the slim trim panel between the instrument panel and the cowl at each side, then lift out the air duct outlet housings at each side of the instrument panel **(see illustration)**. This will allow access to some of the instrument panel mounting fasteners.

13   Remove the screws at each side securing the main instrument panel to the cowl support beam **(see illustration)**.

14   Remove the two floor-to-instrument panel braces **(see illustration)**.

15   Once you're sure all electrical connectors are tagged and disconnected, start to pull up the main panel. If there is any resistance, check for fasteners you may have overlooked. Don't force removal on any panels.

16   Removal of the cowl support beam is a second difficult procedure. Many electrical connectors remain to disconnect, and most harnesses are clipped or clamped to this beam **(see illustrations)**. Unless you have to

access the heating/air conditioning unit, don't remove the beam.

17   Installation is the reverse of the removal

procedure. Make sure you have accounted for all fasteners and electrical connectors before installing the trim panels.

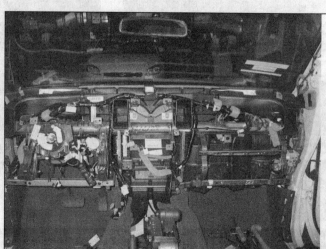

28.16b Removal of the cowl support beam is an intensive task, requiring tagging and disconnecting many connectors, and finding hard-to-locate fasteners

29.1a With the seat moved rearward, pry up the cover and remove the front seat-mounting bolts

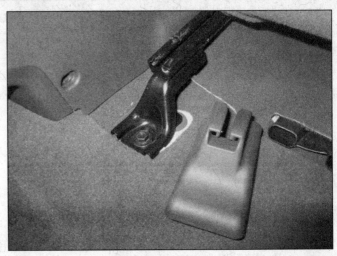

29.1b With the seat forward, remove the covers and the rear seat-mounting bolts

29 Seats - removal and installation

Front bucket seats

Refer to illustrations 29.1a and 29.1b

Warning: *The models covered by this manual are equipped with Supplemental Restraint Systems (SRS), more commonly known as airbags. Always disable the airbag system before working in the vicinity of any airbag system components to avoid the possibility of accidental deployment of the airbags, which could cause personal injury (see Chapter 12).*

1   Detach the trim caps (if equipped) and remove the seat track-to-floor bolts **(see illustrations)**.

2   If equipped with power seats, tilt the seat back towards the rear of the vehicle and disconnect the electrical connectors.

3   Remove the front seats from the vehicle.

4   Installation is the reverse of the removal procedure.

Bench seat (Frontier models)

5   The seat back and seat bottom on pick-up bench seats are part of an assembly that is removed or installed together.

6   Remove the seat track-to-floor bolts at the front of the seat.

7   Position the seat track in the most forward position, then fold the seat back down to access the rear mounting bolts.

8   Remove the seat track-to-floor bolts at the rear of the seat.

9   Pull the seat forward enough to clear the cab and slide the seat out of the vehicle. **Note:** *This is an awkward procedure, have an assistant help you.*

10   Installation is the reverse of the removal procedure.

Rear seat (Xterra models)

Refer to illustrations 29.11 and 29.12

11   Lift the rear seat bottom cushions (either side or both) and pull the release handles to remove the cushions **(see illustration)**.

12   To remove the rear seat back, flip the lower cushions upright, then remove the mounting bolts **(see illustration)**.

13   Installation is the reverse of the removal procedure.

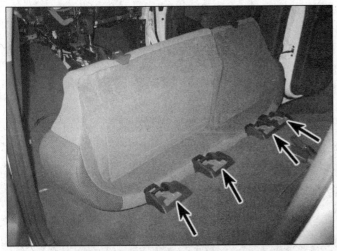

29.11 On Xterra rear seats, flip the bottom cushions forward and pull the release handles to remove the cushions

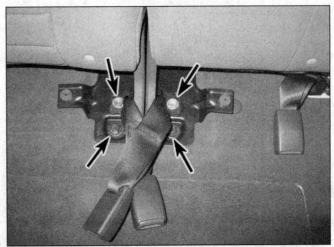

29.12 Remove the seat-mounting bolts and the seatbelt bolts - the center bolts are shown here, there are also bolts at the left and right

Notes

Chapter 12
Chassis electrical system

Contents

1   General information

Warning: *The models covered by this manual are equipped with Supplemental Restraint Systems (SRS), more commonly known as airbags. Always disable the airbag system before working in the vicinity of any airbag system components to avoid the possibility of accidental deployment of the airbags, which could cause personal injury (see Section 26).*

The electrical system is a 12-volt, negative ground type. Power for the lights and all electrical accessories is supplied by a lead/acid-type battery that is charged by the alternator.

This Chapter covers the various electrical components not associated with the engine. Information on the battery, alternator, distributor and starter motor can be found in Chapter 5.

It should be noted that when portions of the electrical system are serviced, the cable should be disconnected from the negative battery terminal to prevent electrical shorts and/or fires.

2   Electrical troubleshooting - general information

Refer to illustrations 2.5a, 2.5b, 2.6, 2.9 and 2.15

A typical electrical circuit consists of an electrical component, any switches, relays, motors, fuses, fusible links or circuit breakers related to that component and the wiring and connectors that link the component to both the battery and the chassis. To help you pinpoint an electrical circuit problem, wiring diagrams are included at the end of this Chapter.

Before tackling any troublesome electrical circuit, first study the appropriate wiring diagrams to get a complete understanding of what makes up that individual circuit. Trouble spots, for instance, can often be narrowed down by noting if other components related to the circuit are operating properly. If several components or circuits fail at one time, chances are the problem is in a fuse or ground connection, because several circuits are often routed through the same fuse and ground connections.

Electrical problems usually stem from simple causes, such as loose or corroded connections, a blown fuse, a melted fusible link or a failed relay. Visually inspect the condition of all fuses, wires and connections in a problem circuit before troubleshooting the circuit.

If test equipment and instruments are going to be utilized, use the diagrams to plan ahead of time where you will make the necessary connections in order to accurately pinpoint the trouble spot.

The basic tools needed for electrical troubleshooting include a voltmeter, a test light (a 12-volt bulb with a set of test leads can also be used) or a continuity tester (which includes a bulb, battery and set of test leads) **(see illustrations)**. Also useful is a pair of jumper wires, preferably with a circuit breaker incorporated into one, which can be used to apply power and ground to electrical components. Before attempting to locate a problem with test instruments, use the wiring diagram(s) to decide where to make the connections.

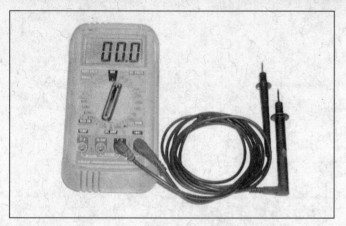

2.5a The most useful tool for electrical troubleshooting is a digital multimeter that can check volts, amps, and test continuity

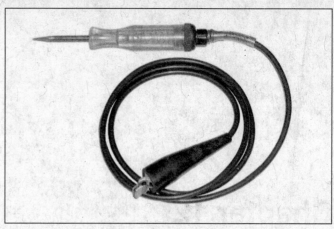

2.5b A simple test light is a very handy tool for checking voltage

Voltage checks

Voltage checks should be performed if a circuit is not functioning properly. Connect one lead of a test light to either the negative battery terminal or a known good ground. Connect the other lead to a connector in the circuit being tested, preferably nearest to the battery or fuse **(see illustration)**. If the bulb of the tester lights, voltage is present, which means that the part of the circuit between the connector and the battery is problem free. Continue checking the rest of the circuit in the same fashion. When you reach a point at which no voltage is present, the problem lies between that point and the last test point with voltage. Most of the time the problem can be traced to a loose connection. **Note:** *Keep in mind that some circuits receive voltage only when the ignition key is in the Accessory or Run position.*

Finding a short

A short-to-ground in a live circuit causes the fuse protecting the circuit to blow. When

the fuse is replaced it will immediately blow again. One method of finding the location of a short is to remove the fuse protecting the problem circuit and connect a test light in place of the fuse. Disconnect the load or ground from the circuit. Turn the ignition key on, if the circuit is shorted to ground there should be voltage present in the circuit and the test light should light. Move the suspected wiring harness from side-to-side while watching the test light. If the bulb goes out, there is a short to ground somewhere in that area, probably where the insulation has rubbed through allowing the bare wire to contact the body. The same test can be performed on each component in the circuit, even a switch.

Ground check

Perform a ground test to check whether a component is properly grounded. Disconnect the battery and connect one lead of a continuity tester or multimeter (set to the ohms scale), to a known good ground. Connect the other lead to the wire or ground connection

being tested. If the resistance is low (less than 5 ohms), the ground is good. If using a self-powered continuity tester, the bulb will light if the ground is good.

Continuity check

A continuity check is done to determine if there are any breaks in a circuit - if it is passing electricity properly. With the circuit off (no power in the circuit), a self-powered continuity tester or multimeter can be used to check the circuit. Connect the test leads to both ends of the circuit (or to the "power" end and a good ground), and if the self-powered test light comes on the circuit is passing current properly **(see illustration)**. If the resistance is low (less than 5 ohms), there is continuity; if the reading is 10,000 ohms or higher, there is a open somewhere in the circuit. The same procedure can be used to test a switch, by connecting the continuity tester to the switch terminals. With the switch turned On, the test light should come on (or low resistance should be indicated on a meter).

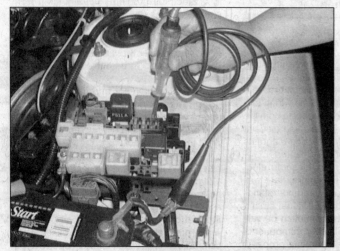

2.6 In use, a basic test light's lead is clipped to a known good ground, then the pointed probe can test connectors, wires or electrical sockets - if the bulb lights, the part being tested has battery voltage

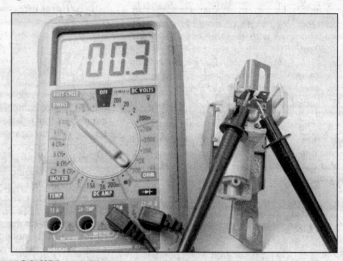

2.9 With a multimeter set to the ohms scale, resistance can be checked across two terminals - when checking for continuity, a low reading indicates continuity, a high reading indicates lack of continuity

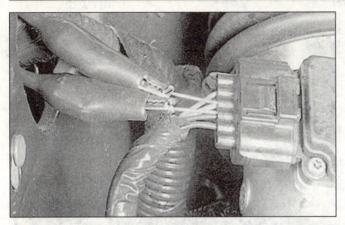

2.15 To backprobe a connector, insert a small, sharp probe (such as a straight-pin) into the back of the connector alongside the desired wire until it contacts the metal terminal inside; connect your meter leads to the probes - this allows you to test a functioning circuit

3.1a The interior fuse box is located under the right (passenger's) side of the instrument panel, under a cover

Finding an open circuit

When diagnosing for possible open circuits, it is often difficult to locate them by sight because the connectors hide oxidation or terminal misalignment. Merely wiggling a connector on a sensor or in the wiring harness may correct the open circuit condition. Remember this when an open circuit is indicated when troubleshooting a circuit. Intermittent problems may also be caused by oxidized or loose connections.

Electrical troubleshooting is simple if you keep in mind that all electrical circuits are basically electricity running from the battery, through the wires, switches, relays, fuses and fusible links to each electrical component (light bulb, motor, etc.) and to ground, from which it is passed back to the battery. Any electrical problem is an interruption in the flow of electricity to and from the battery.

Connectors

Most electrical connections on these vehicles are made with multi-wire plastic connectors. The mating halves of many connectors are secured with locking clips molded into the plastic connector shells. The mating halves of large connectors, such as some of those under the instrument panel, are held together by a bolt through the center of the connector.

To separate a connector with locking clips, use a small screwdriver to pry the clips apart carefully, then separate the connector halves. Pull only on the shell, never pull on the wiring harness as you may damage the individual wires and terminals inside the connectors. Look at the connector closely before trying to separate the halves. Often the locking clips are engaged in a way that is not immediately clear. Additionally, many connectors have more than one set of clips. One type of connector specific to this manufacturer is a slide-locking type connector. Actually, there are two variations of the slide-lock connector; weatherproof and non-weatherproof (gener-

ally, the non-weatherproof type is used in the interior of the vehicle, while the weatherproof type is used under the hood or other locations that are exposed to the elements. To disconnect a weatherproof slide-lock connector, push the slide-lock in towards the center of the connector, then pull the connector apart. To disconnect a non-weatherproof slide-lock connector, pull the slide-lock away from the center of the connector, then pull the connector apart. When connecting either type of slide lock connector, press the connector together until it "clicks" into place.

Each pair of connector terminals has a male half and a female half. When you look at the end view of a connector in a diagram, be sure to understand whether the view shows the harness side or the component side of the connector. Connector halves are mirror images of each other, and a terminal shown on the right side end-view of one half will be on the left side end view of the other half.

Backprobing a connector

It is often necessary to take circuit voltage measurements with a connector connected. Whenever possible, carefully insert a small straight pin (not your meter probe) into

the rear of the connector shell to contact the metal terminal inside, then clip your meter lead to the pin. This kind of connection is called "backprobing" (see illustration). When inserting a test probe into a male terminal, be careful not to distort the terminal opening. Doing so can lead to a poor connection and corrosion at that terminal later. Using the small straight pin instead of a meter probe results in less chance of deforming the terminal connector.

3   Fuses and fusible links - general information

Fuses

Refer to illustrations 3.1a, 3.1b, 3.3 and 3.7

The electrical circuits of the vehicle are protected by a combination of fuses, circuit breakers and fusible links. The fuse blocks are located under the instrument panel on the right side of the dashboard and in the engine compartment (see illustrations).

Each of the fuses is designed to protect a specific circuit, and the various circuits are

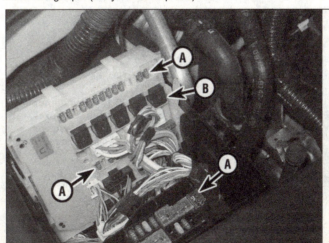

3.1b The engine compartment fuse and fusible link box is located behind the battery - this is a Frontier model

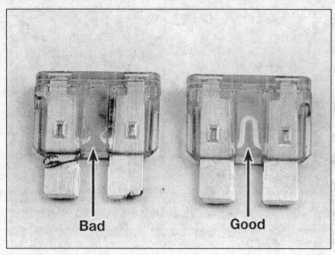

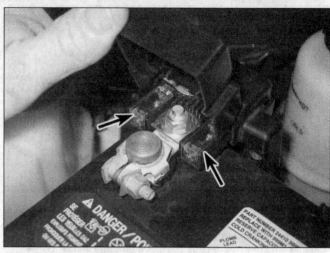

3.3 When a fuse blows, the element between the terminals melts - the fuse on the left is blown, the fuse on the right is good

3.7 Two large fusible links, located next to the battery, protect the main power circuit of the vehicle

identified on the fuse panel itself.

Miniaturized fuses are employed in the fuse blocks. These compact fuses, with blade terminal design, allow fingertip removal and replacement. If an electrical component fails, always check the fuse first. The best way to check the fuses is with a test light. Check for power at the exposed terminal tips of each fuse. If power is present at one side of the fuse but not the other, the fuse is blown. A blown fuse can also be identified by visually inspecting it **(see illustration)**.

Be sure to replace blown fuses with the correct type. Fuses of different ratings are physically interchangeable, but only fuses of the proper rating should be used. Replacing a fuse with one of a higher or lower value than specified is not recommended. Each electrical circuit needs a specific amount of protection. The amperage value of each fuse is molded into the fuse body.

If the replacement fuse immediately fails, don't replace it again until the cause of the problem is isolated and corrected. In most cases, this will be a short circuit in the wiring caused by a broken or deteriorated wire.

Fusible links

Some circuits are protected by fusible links. The links are used in circuits that are not ordinarily fused.

The main fusible link on the covered models is mounted in a box next to the battery **(see illustration)**.

To replace a fusible link, first disconnect the negative cable from the battery. Unplug the burned-out link and replace it with a new one (available from your dealer or auto parts store). Always determine the cause for the overload that melted the fusible link before installing a new one.

4 Circuit breakers - general information

Circuit breakers protect the power windows, power door locks, power seat and power sunroof. One or two circuit breakers are used, depending on options, they are located under the left end of the instrument panel above the fuse box.

Because the circuit breakers reset auto-

matically, an electrical overload in a circuit breaker protected system will cause the circuit to fail momentarily, then come back on. If the circuit does not come back on, check it immediately.

5 Relays - general information and testing

General information

Refer to illustration 5.1

1   Several electrical accessories in the vehicle, such as the fuel injection system, horns, starter, and fog lamps use relays to transmit the electrical signal to the component. Relays use a low-current circuit (the control circuit) to open and close a high-current circuit (the power circuit). If the relay is defective, that component will not operate properly. Most relays are mounted in the engine compartment fuse/relay boxes, with some specialized relays located above the interior fuse box. If a faulty relay is suspected, it can be removed and tested using the procedure below or by a dealer service department or a repair shop. Defective relays must be replaced as a unit. On the covered models, a number of relays are incorporated into the Nissan Intelligent Power Distribution Module (IPDM), located in the engine compartment **(see illustration 3.1b)**. The IPDM communicates with the PCM, BCM and CAN modules in the vehicle and operates the relays. These relays are all integrated into the IPDM and are not replaceable. Next to the IPDM, there is another relay box with replaceable relays **(see illustration)**.

Testing

Refer to illustrations 5.2a and 5.2b

2   Most of the relays used in these vehicles are of a type often called "ISO" relays, which refers to the International Standards

5.1 The underhood fuse/relay boxes contain testable/ replaceable relays

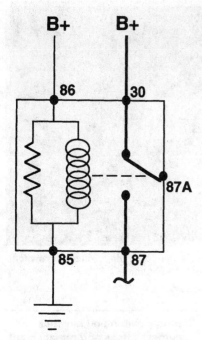

Relay with internal resistor

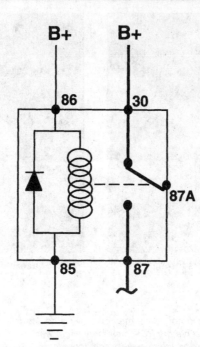

Relay with internal diode

24053-12-5.2a HAYNES

5.2a Typical ISO relay designs, terminal numbering and circuit connections

5.2b Most relays are marked on the outside to easily identify the control circuit and power circuits - this one is of the four-terminal type

Organization. The terminals of ISO relays are numbered to indicate their usual circuit connections and functions. There are two basic layouts of terminals on the relays used in the vehicles covered by this manual **(see illustrations)**.

3   Refer to the wiring diagram for the circuit to determine the proper connections for the relay you're testing. If you can't determine the correct connection from the wiring diagrams, however, you may be able to determine the test connections from the information that follows.

4   Two of the terminals are the relay control circuit and connect to the relay coil. The other relay terminals are the power circuit. When the relay is energized, the coil creates a magnetic field that closes the larger contacts of the power circuit to provide power to the circuit loads.

5   Terminals 85 and 86 are normally the control circuit. If the relay contains a diode, terminal 86 must be connected to battery positive (B+) voltage and terminal 85 to ground. If the relay contains a resistor, terminals 85 and 86 can be connected in either direction with respect to B+ and ground.

6   Terminal 30 is normally connected to the battery voltage (B+) source for the circuit loads. Terminal 87 is connected to the ground side of the circuit, either directly or through a load. If the relay has several alternate terminals for load or ground connections, they usually are numbered 87A, 87B, 87C, and so on.

7   Use an ohmmeter to check continuity through the relay control coil.
   a) *Connect the meter according to the polarity shown in* **illustration 5.2a** *for one check; then reverse the ohmmeter leads and check continuity in the other direction.*
   b) *If the relay contains a resistor, resistance will be indicated on the meter, and should be the same value with the ohmmeter in either direction.*
   c) *If the relay contains a diode, resistance should be higher with the ohmmeter in the forward polarity direction than with the meter leads reversed.*
   d) *If the ohmmeter shows infinite resistance in both directions, replace the relay.*

8   Remove the relay from the vehicle and use the ohmmeter to check for continuity between the relay power circuit terminals. There should be no continuity between terminal 30 and 87 with the relay de-energized.

9   Connect a fused jumper wire to terminal 86 and the positive battery terminal. Connect another jumper wire between terminal 85 and ground. When the connections are made, the relay should click.

10   With the jumper wires connected, check for continuity between the power circuit terminals. Now there should be continuity between terminals 30 and 87.

11   If the relay fails any of the above tests, replace it.

6   Turn signal/hazard flasher system - general information

Warning: *The models covered by this manual are equipped with Supplemental Restraint Systems (SRS), more commonly known as airbags. Always disable the airbag system before working in the vicinity of any airbag system components to avoid the possibility of accidental deployment of the airbags, which could cause personal injury (see Section 26).*

1   On the covered vehicles, the functions of the turn signal and flasher system are controlled by the turn signal lever/switch, the hazard switch and the Body Control Module (BCM), a microprocessor under the instrument panel, to the right of the steering column. Communication from the switches goes to the BCM, which controls the Flash functions of the front and rear turn signal lights.

2   When the flasher unit is functioning properly, an audible click can be heard during its operation. If the turn signals fail on one side or the other and the flasher unit does not make its characteristic clicking sound, or if a bulb on one side of the vehicle flashes much faster than normal but the bulb at the other end of the vehicle (on the same side) doesn't light at all, a faulty turn signal bulb may be indicated.

3   If one of the turn signal lights doesn't work, check the bulb (see Section 15). If more than one bulb doesn't work, check the turn signal fuse. If the fuse is blown, replace it and test the system. If the fuse blows again, check the circuit for a short. If the fuse was OK, but the turn signals don't work, check for a loose or open connection in the circuit.

7   Lighting system and windshield wiper/washer switches - check and replacement

Refer to illustrations 7.4, 7.5a and 7.5b

Warning: *The models covered by this manual are equipped with a Supplemental Restraint System (SRS), more commonly known as*

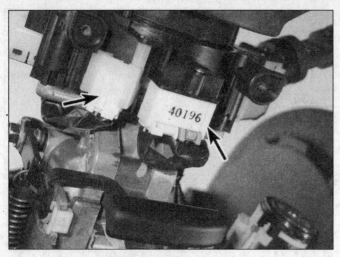

7.4 Disconnect the electrical connectors for the multi-function switches

7.5a Squeeze these two clips to release the turn/lighting switch from the column

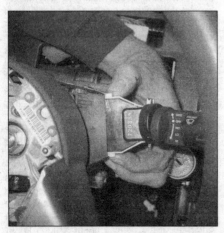

7.5b Release the clips for the wipe/wash switch

airbags. Always disarm the airbag system before working in the vicinity of any airbag system component to avoid the possibility of accidental deployment of the airbag, which could cause personal injury (see Section 26).

Do not use a memory-saving device to preserve the PCM's memory when working on or near airbag system components.

1   Disconnect the cable from the negative battery terminal (see Chapter 5, Section 1). The left multifunction switch on the steering column controls the lighting and turn signals, while the switch on the right of the column controls the Wipe/Wash functions, including the operation of the rear wiper/washer on Xterra models. Each switch can be replaced independently of the other.

2   Remove the driver's knee bolster (see Chapter 11).

3   Remove the steering column covers (see Chapter 11).

4   Disconnect the electrical connector from the switch being replaced **(see illustration)**.

5   Press in the two clips and pull out the switch **(see illustrations)**.

6   Installation is the reverse of removal. Before reinstalling the steering wheel, make sure the airbag clockspring is centered (see Chapter 10, Section 11).

8   Ignition switch and key lock cylinder - check and replacement

Warning: The models covered by this manual are equipped with Supplemental Restraint Systems (SRS), more commonly known as airbags. Always disable the airbag system before working in the vicinity of any airbag system components to avoid the possibility of accidental deployment of the airbags, which could cause personal injury (see Section 26).

Check

1   Disconnect the cable from the negative battery terminal.

2   Remove the knee bolster and steering column covers (see Chapter 11).

3   Follow the wiring harness down the column from the ignition switch and disconnect the ignition switch electrical connector.

Replacement

Refer to illustration 8.4

4   The lock cylinder can't be replaced by itself - the whole housing must be replaced. Remove the shear-head bolts retaining the ignition switch/lock cylinder assembly and separate the bracket halves from the steering column. This can be accomplished by drilling a hole in the center of each bolt and unscrewing them with a screw extractor **(see illustration)**.

5   Place the new switch assembly in position, install the new shear-head bolts and tighten them until the heads snap off. If the steering wheel was removed, be sure to center the airbag clockspring before installing the steering wheel (refer to Chapter 10, Section 11).

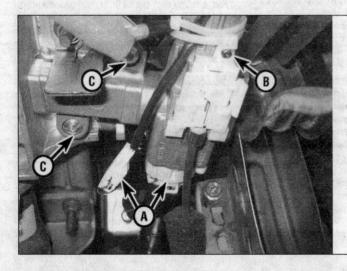

8.4 Ignition switch details:

A   *Disconnect the connectors*
B   *Remove the shift/lock cable end housing*
C   *Drill out the shear bolts*

9 Instrument cluster - removal and installation

Refer to illustrations 9.3a and 9.3b

Warning: *The models covered by this manual are equipped with Supplemental Restraint Systems (SRS), more commonly known as airbags. Always disable the airbag system before working in the vicinity of any airbag system components to avoid the possibility of accidental deployment of the airbags, which could cause personal injury (see Section 26).*

1   Disconnect the cable from the negative battery terminal.
2   Remove the instrument cluster bezel (see Chapter 11).
3   Remove the retaining screws and pull the cluster forward **(see illustrations)**.
4   Unplug the electrical connectors and remove the cluster from the vehicle.
5   Installation is the reverse of the removal procedure.

10 Radio and speakers - removal and installation

Warning: *The models covered by this manual are equipped with Supplemental Restraint Systems (SRS), more commonly known as airbags. Always disable the airbag system before working in the vicinity of any airbag system components to avoid the possibility of accidental deployment of the airbags, which could cause personal injury (see Section 26).*

Radio

Refer to illustrations 10.3a and 10.3b

1   Disconnect the cable from the negative battery terminal.
2   Remove the center bezel panel from the dash (see Chapter 11).
3   Remove the screws and pull the radio out of the dash **(see illustrations)**.
4   Disconnect the antenna lead and the

9.3a Remove the four cluster screws (two left-side screws indicated)

9.3b Disconnect the large electrical connector at the top-rear of the cluster

electrical connectors and remove the radio.
5   Installation is the reverse of removal.

Speakers

Front tweeter

6   Use a small screwdriver or trim tool to lift up the cover over the tweeter on the instrument panel.
7   Remove the mounting screws and lift out the tweeter. Disconnect the electrical connector.
8   Installation is the reverse of the removal.

Door speakers

Refer to illustration 10.10

9   Remove the door trim panel (see Chapter 11).
10   Remove the speaker mounting screws (see illustration). Unplug the electrical connector and remove the speaker. **Note:** *The procedure is the same for rear door speakers on Xterra or crew-cab Frontier models and models that have rear tweeters in the doors.*
11   On premium-stereo packages in crew-cab models, the vehicle may be equipped

10.3a Remove the radio mounting screws

with a sub-woofer assembly, mounted under the rear seat. To remove, raise the left rear seat, disconnect the electrical connector, remove the mounting screws and lift out the sub-woofer assembly.

10.3b Disconnect the antenna lead (A) and the electrical connectors (B)

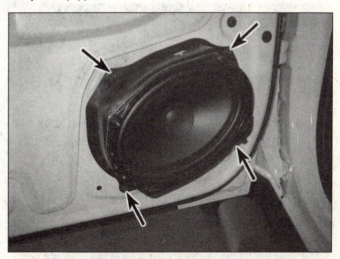

10.10 Remove the speaker mounting screws in the door

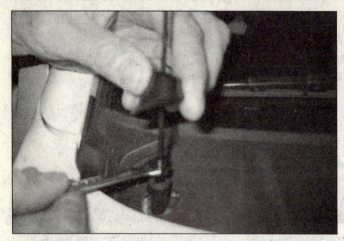

11.1 Slide up the rubber grommet and use a small wrench to unscrew the antenna mast

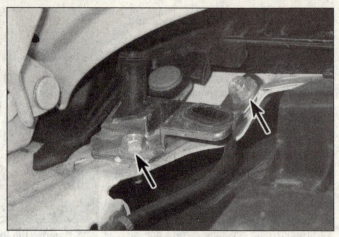

11.4 With the cowl cover lifted or removed, remove the two antenna base mounting bolts

11   Antenna - removal and installation

Fixed antenna

Frontier/Xterra

Refer to illustrations 11.1 and 11.4

1   Remove the antenna mast and bezel **(see illustration)**.
2   Remove the cowl cover (see Chapter 11).
3   From inside the vehicle, remove the glove box (see Chapter 11), and disconnect the antenna cable from the connector.
4   Open the hood and remove the two antenna base mounting bolts **(see illustration)**. Pull the base and antenna cable up from the body.
5   Installation is the reverse of the removal. If the cable from the antenna-base connector-to-radio needs to be replaced, remove the audio unit and disconnect the cable from the

back of the unit.
6   On models with the satellite radio option, the antenna for the system is mounted to the roof. Because the headliner must be removed for access to the antenna mounting base, it is recommended that the satellite antenna be serviced at a dealership or other qualified shop.

12   Headlight bulb - replacement

Refer to illustration 12.1

Warning: *These models are equipped with halogen gas-filled bulbs, which are under pressure and may shatter if the surface is scratched or the bulb is dropped. Wear eye protection and handle the bulbs carefully, grasping only the base whenever possible. Do not touch the surface of the bulb with your fingers because the oil from your skin could cause it to overheat and fail prematurely. If*

you do touch the bulb surface, clean it with rubbing alcohol.
1   With hood open, reach down behind the headlight housing and disconnect the electrical connector for the bulb to be replaced **(see illustration)**.
2   Without touching the glass with your bare fingers, insert the new bulb assembly into the headlight housing and secure it with the retaining ring or clip.
3   Plug in the electrical connector. Test headlight operation, then close the hood.

13   Headlights - adjustment

Refer to illustrations 13.1 and 13.2

Note: *It is important that the headlights are aimed correctly. If adjusted incorrectly they could blind the driver of an oncoming vehicle and cause a serious accident or seriously reduce your ability to see the road. The head-*

12.1 Disconnect the electrical connector at the headlight bulb, then rotate the retaining ring counterclockwise to remove the bulb from the housing

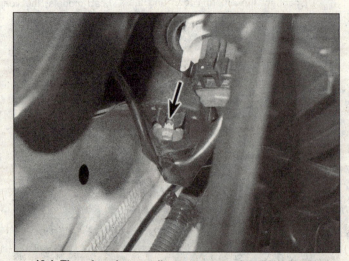

13.1 There is only one adjustment screw for the headlight housings, it adjusts vertical aiming only

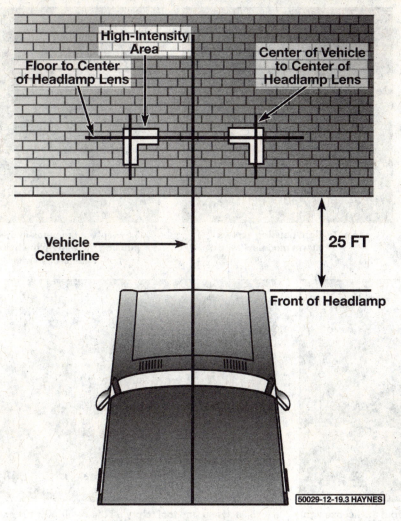

13.2 Headlight adjustment details

the headlights. The simplest method requires an open area with a blank wall and a level floor **(see illustration)**.

3   Position masking tape vertically on the wall in reference to the vehicle centerline and the centerlines of both headlights.

4   Position a horizontal tape line in reference to the centerline of all the headlights. **Note:** *It may be easier to position the tape on the wall with the vehicle parked only a few inches away.*

5   Adjustment should be made with the vehicle parked 25 feet from the wall, sitting level, the gas tank half-full and no unusually heavy load in the vehicle.

6   Starting with the low beam adjustment, position the high intensity zone so it is two inches below the horizontal line and two inches to the side of the vertical headlight line away from oncoming traffic. Turn the adjustment screws until the desired level has been achieved.

7   With the high beams on, the high intensity zone should be vertically centered with the exact center just below the horizontal line. **Note:** *It may not be possible to position the headlight aim exactly for both high and low beams. If a compromise must be made, keep in mind that the low beams are the most used and have the greatest effect on driver safety.*

8   Have the headlights adjusted by a dealer service department at the earliest opportunity.

14   Headlight housing - replacement

Refer to illustration 14.4

1   Disconnect the cable from the negative battery terminal.

2   Disconnect the electrical connectors at the back of the headlight housing **(see illustration 12.1)**.

3   On some models, remove the fasteners at the front portion of the fenderwell liner and pull it back for access (see Chapter 11), then remove the upper trim valance from the front bumper cover to access two headlight mounting bolts.

4   Remove the mounting bolts and remove the headlight housing **(see illustration)**.

5   Installation is the reverse of the removal procedure.

15   Bulb replacement

Front side marker/turn signal/ park lights

1   The front turn signal and park light and the side marker light are both mounted in the headlight housing. The round bulb is the turn/park bulb and the small bulb is the side marker.

2   Reach behind the headlight housing and twist the side marker or turn signal light bulbholder counterclockwise to remove it. Pull the bulb straight out of the socket. Installation is the reverse of the removal procedure.

lights should be checked for proper aim every 12 months and any time a new headlight is installed or front end body work is performed. It should be emphasized that the following procedure is only an interim step that will provide temporary adjustment until the headlights can be adjusted by a properly equipped shop.

1   The covered models are equipped with only one adjustment screw on the back of the headlight housing **(see illustration)**. This screw adjusts only the vertical aiming of the headlights; horizontal aiming is not adjustable.

2   There are several methods of adjusting

14.4 Remove the headlight mounting bolts (some models have bolts accessed in the fenderwell)

15.3   Taillight housing mounting bolts - Frontier models

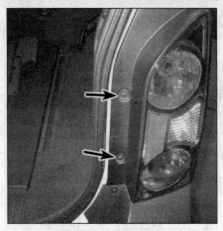

15.4   Taillight housing screws - Xterra models

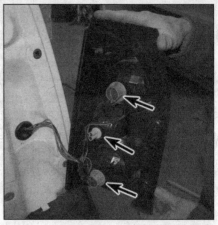

15.5   Replace the bulbs in the taillight housing by twisting the bulbholder counterclockwise

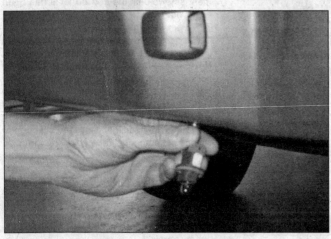

15.7   Reach behind the rear bumper and twist out the license light bulbholder on each side

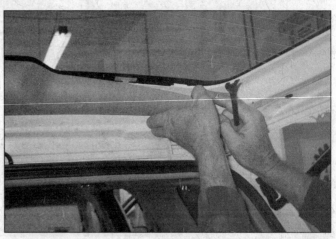

15.9a   Use a trim tool to pry off the cover over the brake light assembly (Xterra shown)

Tail and back-up lights

Refer to illustrations 15.3, 15.4 and 15.5

3   On Frontier models, open the tailgate. Remove the bolts and pull the taillight housing from the bed side **(see illustration)**.

4   On Xterra models, open the liftgate and remove the two inboard mounting screws and remove the taillight housing (see illustrations). **Note:** *When reinstalling the light housing,*

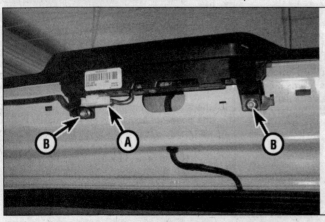

15.9b   To replace the brake light assembly, disconnect the connector (A) and remove the mounting nuts (B)

align the projecting pins with the holes in the body before installing the mounting screws.

5   Remove the bulb socket from the housing and replace the bulb **(see illustration)**.

License plate light

Refer to illustration 15.7

6   On Frontier models, pull the housing from the bumper. Pull the bulb straight out to replace it.

7   On Xterra models, use a small screwdriver to unsnap the housing from the bumper **(see illustration)**. Remove the bulb holder and replace the bulb.

High-mounted brake light

Refer to illustrations 15.9a and 15.9b

8   On Frontier models, pry out the two plastic covers at the rear of the interior roof headliner, for access to the two mounting nuts. From outside the vehicle, pull the high-mounted brake light assembly out enough to twist out the bulbholders and replace the bulbs. Installation is the reverse of removal.

9   On Xterra models, the bulbs for the high-mounted brake light are not replaceable. The light must be replaced as a unit. To replace it, remove the upper interior trim panel on the liftgate, disconnect the electrical connectors at the light, then remove the two mounting screws **(see illustrations)**. Installation is the reverse of removal.

Instrument cluster illumination

10   The instrument cluster lights are part of the circuit board, and not replaceable.

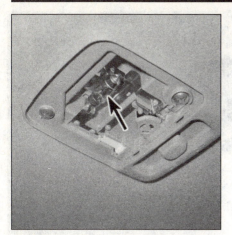

15.11a Pry off the cover to access the dome light bulb

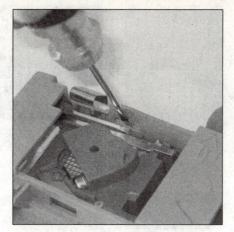

15.11b Remove the map light housing from the roof, then use a small screwdriver to pry loose this cover on the back of the assembly

15.11c With the black cover off, the bulb can be changed - there is one on each side of the housing

Interior lights

Refer to illustrations 15.11a, 15.11b and 15.11c

11   Remove the lenses for the map lights or dome light by prying the cover off with a small screwdriver. Replace the bulb **(see illustrations)**.

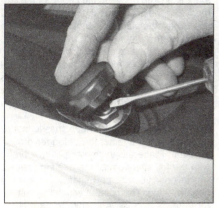

16.2 Pry up the cap, then mark and remove the windshield wiper arm nut

Fog lights

12   From below, disconnect the electrical connector on the back of the foglight housing, at the rear of the front bumper. Using a clean rag, twist the bulb counterclockwise out of the socket.

13   Installation is the reverse of removal.
Caution: *Do not touch the surface of the new bulb with your fingers because the oil from your skin could cause it to overheat and fail prematurely. If you do touch the bulb surface, clean it with rubbing alcohol.*

16   Wiper motors - replacement

Windshield wiper motor

Refer to illustrations 16.2 and 16.5

1   Disconnect the cable from the negative battery terminal.

2   Remove the wiper arm retaining nuts **(see illustration)**.

3   Mark the relationship of the wiper arms to their shafts, then remove the wiper arms.

4   Remove the cowl cover (see Chapter 11).

5   Disconnect the electrical connector from the windshield wiper motor **(see illustration)**.

6   Remove the mounting bolts and remove the wiper drive/motor assembly from the vehicle **(see illustration 16.5)**.

7   Remove the bolts/nuts securing the wiper motor to the drive assembly. Note the position of the motor spacer for reassembly.

8   Installation is the reverse of removal.

Rear wiper motor

Refer to illustrations 16.11 and 16.14

9   Disconnect the cable from the negative battery terminal (see Chapter 5, Section 1).

10   Remove the trim cap from the rear wiper arm.

11   Remove the rear wiper arm retaining nut **(see illustration)**.

12   The wiper arm is still secured to the wiper motor shaft by spring tension. To release tension, hinge the wiper arm toward you, then remove the arm from the motor shaft.

13   Remove the rear liftgate trim panel (see Chapter 11).

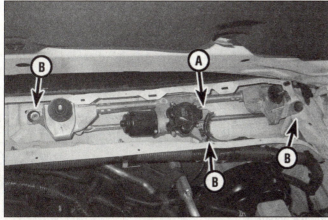

16.5 Disconnect the wiper motor connector (A), then remove the three bolts (B)

16.11 Pry up the cap on the rear wiper arm and remove the nut

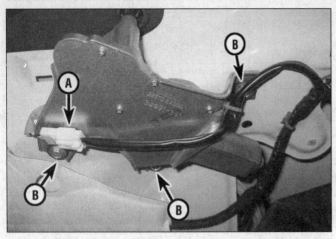

16.14 Disconnect the rear wiper motor electrical connector (A), then remove the mounting bolts (B)

17.2 The horns are located in front of the air filter housing

14   Disconnect the electrical connector from the rear wiper motor, remove the mounting bolts, then detach the motor from the liftgate (**see illustration**).

15   Installation is the reverse of removal. When reattaching the wiper arm/blade assembly, align the arm so that the wiper blade is parallel to the bottom of the liftgate glass.

17   Horn - check and replacement

Refer to illustration 17.2

1   Remove the grille for access to the horn (see Chapter 11).

2   Disconnect the electrical connector at the horn (**see illustration**).

3   Remove the bolt securing the horn to the body. **Note:** *Some models have two horns on the same bracket.*

4   Installation is the reverse of removal.

18   Daytime Running Lights (DRL) - general information

The Daytime Running Lights (DRL) system used on Canadian models turns the headlights on whenever the engine is started. The only exception is when the engine is turned on when the parking brake is engaged. Once the parking brake is released, the lights will remain on as long as the ignition switch is on, even if the parking brake is later applied.

The DRL system supplies reduced power to the headlights so they won't be too bright for daytime use while prolonging headlight life.

19   Rear window defogger - check and repair

1   The rear window defogger consists of a number of horizontal heating elements baked onto the inside surface of the glass. Power is supplied through two fuses and a relay in the

IPDM relay box in the engine compartment. A defogger switch on the instrument panel controls the defogger grid.

2   Small breaks in the element can be repaired without removing the rear window.

Check

Refer to illustrations 19.5, 19.6 and 19.8

3   Turn the ignition and defogger switches to the ON position.

4   Using a voltmeter, place the positive probe against the defogger grid positive side and the negative probe against the ground side. If battery voltage is not indicated, check that the ignition switch is On and that the feed and ground wires are properly connected. Check the two fuses, defogger switch, defogger relay and related wiring. The dealer can scan the body control module if necessary. If voltage is indicated, but all or part of the defogger doesn't heat, proceed with the following tests.

5   When measuring voltage during the next two tests, wrap a piece of aluminum foil around the tip of the voltmeter positive probe

and press the foil against the heating element with your finger (**see illustration**). Place the negative probe on the defogger grid ground terminal.

6   Check the voltage at the center of each heating element (**see illustration**). If the voltage is 5 to 6 volts, the element is okay (there is no break). If the voltage is 0 volts, the element is broken between the center of the element and the positive end. If the voltage is 10 to 12 volts, the element is broken between the center of the element and the ground side. Check each heating element.

7   If none of the elements are broken, connect the negative probe to a good chassis ground. The voltage reading should stay the same, if it doesn't the ground connection is bad.

8   To find the break, place the voltmeter negative probe against the defogger ground terminal. Place the voltmeter positive probe with the foil strip against the heating element at the positive side and slide it toward the negative side. The point at which the voltmeter deflects from several volts to zero is the

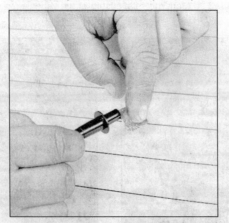

19.5 When measuring the voltage at the rear window defogger grid, wrap a piece of aluminum foil around the negative probe of the voltmeter and press the foil against the wire with your finger

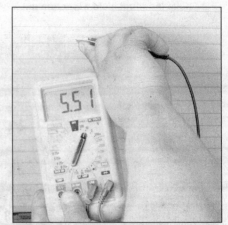

19.6 To determine if a heating element has broken, check the voltage at the center of each element - if the voltage is 6-volts, the element is unbroken

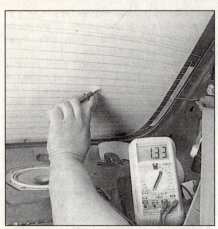

19.8 To find the break, place the voltmeter negative lead against the defogger ground terminal, place the voltmeter positive lead with the foil strip against the heat wire at the positive terminal end and slide it toward the negative terminal end. The point at which the voltmeter deflects from several volts to zero volts is the point at which the wire is broken

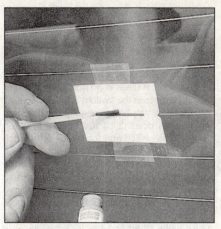

19.14 To use a defogger repair kit, apply masking tape to the inside of the window at the damaged area, then brush on the special conductive coating

point where the heating element is broken **(see illustration)**.

Repair

Refer to illustration 19.14

9   Repair the break in the element using a repair kit specifically for this purpose, such as DuPont paste No. 4817 (or equivalent). The kit includes conductive plastic epoxy.
10   Before repairing a break, turn off the system and allow it to cool for a few minutes.
11   Lightly buff the element area with fine steel wool, then clean it thoroughly with rubbing alcohol.
12   Use masking tape to mask off the area being repaired.
13   Thoroughly mix the epoxy, following the kit instructions.
14   Apply the epoxy material to the slit in the masking tape, overlapping the undamaged area about 3/4-inch on either end **(see illustration)**.
15   Allow the repair to cure for 24 hours before removing the tape and using the system.

20   Cruise control system - general information

1   The covered vehicles are equipped with electronic throttle control. The throttle body is operated with directions from the PCM. The ASCD (Automatic speed control device) receives input from the accelerator pedal position switch, the ASCD brakelight switch, stoplight switch, clutch switch, (manual transmissions) , ASCD steering switch, the Park-Neutral switch, the transmission control module and the ABS wheel speed sensors.

2   A sophisticated scan tool is required to troubleshoot the electronic cruise control system. For diagnosis and repair, bring the vehicle to a dealer or other authorized repair center.

21   Power window system - general information

1   The power window system controls the electric motors mounted inside the doors, which lower and raise the windows. The power window system consists of the control switches, the fuse, the circuit breaker, the motors, the window "regulators" (the scissor-like mechanisms that raise and lower the window glass) and the wiring connecting the switches to the motors. When the ignition switch is turned to ON, current flows through the power window fuse in the engine compartment fuse and relay box to a circuit breaker located in the instrument panel wiring harness (located near the parking brake pedal). From there, current flows to the power window switches.
2   The power windows are wired so that they can be lowered and raised from the master control switch by the driver or by passengers using remote switches located at each passenger window. Each window has a separate motor that is reversible. The position of the control switch determines the polarity and therefore the direction of operation.
3   The power window system will only operate when the ignition switch is turned to ON. In addition, a window lockout switch at the master control switch can, when activated, disable the power window switches on the other doors. Always check these items before troubleshooting a window problem.
4   These procedures are general in nature, so if you can't find the problem using them, take the vehicle to a dealer service department.
5   If the power windows don't work at all,

check the fuse or circuit breaker.
6   If only the rear windows are inoperative, or if the windows only operate from the master control switch, check the window lockout switch for continuity in the unlocked position. If it doesn't have continuity, replace it.
7   Check the wiring between the switches and the fuse for continuity. Repair the wiring, if necessary.
8   If only one window is inoperative from the master control switch, try the control switch at the window that doesn't work. **Note:** *This doesn't apply to the driver's door window.*
9   If the same window works from one switch, but not the other, check the switch for continuity.
10   If the switch tests OK, check for a short or open in the wiring between the affected switch and the window motor.
11   If one window is inoperative from both switches, remove the trim panel from the affected door (see Chapter 11), then check for voltage at the switch and at the motor while operating the switch. First check for voltage at the electrical connectors for the circuit. With the ignition key turned to ON and the connectors all connected, backprobe at the designated wire (see the wiring diagrams at the end of this Chapter) with a grounded test light. Pushing the driver's window switch to the DOWN position, there should be voltage at one terminal. Pushing the same switch to the UP position, there should be voltage at another terminal. If these voltage checks are OK, disconnect the electrical connector at the driver's motor, and check it for voltage when the switch is operated.
12   If voltage is reaching the motor and the switch is OK, disconnect the door glass from its regulator (see Chapter 11). Move the window up and down by hand while checking for binding and damage. Also check for binding and damage to the regulator. If the regulator is not damaged and the window moves up and down smoothly, replace the motor. If there's binding or damage, lubricate, repair or replace parts, as necessary.
13   If voltage isn't reaching the motor, check the wiring in the circuit for continuity between the switches and motors (see the wiring diagram at the end of this Chapter).
14   If you have to replace the main power window switch, pry it out of the door trim panel, then disconnect the electrical connector(s) from the switch.
15   When you're done, test the windows to confirm that the window system is functioning correctly.

22   Power door lock system - general information

1   The power door lock system operates the power door motors, which are integral components of the door latch units in each door. The system consists of a fuse (in the engine compartment fuse and relay box), the instrument cluster, the control switches (in each of

the front doors), the power door motors and the electrical wiring harnesses connecting all of these components.

2   The lock mechanisms in the door latch units are actuated by a reversible electric motor in each door. When you push the door lock switch to LOCK, the motor operates one way and locks the latch mechanism. When you push the door lock switch the other way, to the UNLOCK position, the motor operates in the other direction, unlocking the latch mechanism. Because the motors and lock mechanisms are an integral part of the door latch units, they cannot be repaired. If a door lock motor or lock mechanism fails, replace the door latch unit (see Chapter 11).

3   Even if you don't manually lock the doors or press the door lock switch to the LOCK position before driving, the instrument cluster automatically locks the doors when the vehicle speed exceeds 15 mph, as long as all the doors are closed and the accelerator pedal is depressed. (You can turn off this feature if you don't want the doors to lock automatically. Refer to your owner's manual.)

4   Some vehicles have an optional Remote Keyless Entry (RKE) system that allows you to lock and unlock the doors from outside the vehicle. The RKE system consists of the transmitter (the electronic push-button "key") and a receiver located on the instrument cluster. The RKE receiver, which operates all the time, is protected by a fuse in the engine compartment fuse and relay box. Vehicles are shipped from the factory with two RKE transmitters but, if you want to purchase extra units, the RKE receiver can actually handle up to four vehicle access codes.

5   Some features of the door lock system on these vehicles rely on resources that they share with other electronic modules through the Programmable Communications Interface (PCI) data bus network. Professional diagnosis of these modules and the PCI data bus network requires the use of a DRB III, (proprietary factory) scan tool and factory diagnostic information. At-home repairs are therefore limited to inspecting the wiring for bad connections and for minor faults that can be easily repaired. If you are unable to locate the trouble using the following general steps, consult your dealer service department.

6   Always check the circuit fuses (in the engine compartment fuse and relay box) first.

7   When depressed, each power door lock switch locks or unlocks all of the doors. The easiest way to verify that each door lock switch is operating correctly is to watch the door lock button in each door as you operate the switch. The door lock buttons should all go down when you push the door lock switch to the LOCK position, and go up when you push the door lock switch to the UNLOCK position. Also, with the engine turned off so that you can hear better, operate the door lock switches in both directions and listen for the faint click of the motors locking and unlocking the latch mechanisms.

8   If there's no click, check for voltage at the switches. If no voltage is present, check

the wiring between the fuse and the switches for shorts and opens (see the wiring diagrams at the end of this Chapter).

9   If voltage is present, but no clicking sound is apparent, remove the switch from the door trim panel (see Chapter 11) and test it for continuity. If there is no continuity in either direction, replace the switch.

10   If the switch has continuity but the latch mechanism doesn't click, check the wiring between the switch and the motor in the latch mechanism for continuity. If the circuit is open between the switch and the motor, repair wiring.

11   If all but one motor is operating, remove the trim panel for the affected door (see Chapter 11) and check for voltage at the motor while operating the lock switch. One of the wires should have voltage in the LOCK position; the other should have voltage in the UNLOCK position.

12   If the inoperative motor is receiving voltage, replace the latch mechanism.

13   If the inoperative motor isn't receiving voltage, check for an open or short in the circuit between the switch and the motor. **Note:** *It's common for wires to break in the harness between the body and the door because repeatedly opening and closing the door fatigues and eventually breaks the wires.*

23 Electric side view mirrors - description and check

1   Most electric side view mirrors use two motors to move the glass; one for up and down adjustments and one for left-right adjustments.

2   The control switch has a selector portion that sends voltage to the left or right side mirror. With the ignition ON but the engine OFF, roll down the windows and operate the mirror control switch through all functions (left-right and up-down) for both the left and right side mirrors.

3   Listen carefully for the sound of the electric motors running in the mirrors.

4   If the motors can be heard but the mirror glass doesn't move, there's probably a problem with the drive mechanism inside the mirror. Remove and disassemble the mirror to locate the problem.

5   If the mirrors don't operate and no sound comes from the mirrors, check the fuse.

6   If the fuse is OK, remove the mirror control switch from its mounting without disconnecting the wires attached to it. Turn the ignition ON and check for voltage at the switch. There should be voltage at one terminal. If there's no voltage at the switch, check for an open or short in the wiring between the fuse panel and the switch.

7   If there's voltage at the switch, disconnect it. Check the switch for continuity in all its operating positions. If the switch does not have continuity, replace it.

8   Re-connect the switch. Locate the wire going from the switch to ground. Leaving

the switch connected, connect a jumper wire between this wire and ground. If the mirror works normally with this wire in place, repair the faulty ground connection.

9   If the mirror still doesn't work, remove the mirror and check the wires at the mirror for voltage. Check with ignition ON and the mirror selector switch on the appropriate side. Operate the mirror switch in all its positions. There should be voltage at one of the switch-to-mirror wires in each switch position (except the neutral "off" position).

10   If voltage isn't present in each switch position, check the wiring between the mirror and control switch for opens and shorts.

11   If there's voltage, remove the mirror and test it off the vehicle with jumper wires. Replace the mirror if it fails this test.

24 Power seats - description and check

1   The optional power seats on these models adjust forward and backward, up and down and tilt forward and backward.

2   The power seat system consists of a motor, a switch on the seat, a circuit breaker and the 40-amp F fuse in the engine compartment fuse/fusible link block.

3   Look under the seat for any objects which may be preventing the seat from moving.

4   If the seat won't work at all, check the fuse (see Section 3).

5   With the engine off to reduce the noise level, operate the seat controls in all directions and listen for sound coming from the seat motor(s).

6   If the motor runs or clicks but the seat doesn't move, the integral seat drive mechanism is damaged and the motor assembly must be replaced.

7   If the motor doesn't work or make noise, check for voltage at the motor while an assistant operates the switch.

8   If the motor is getting voltage but doesn't run, test it off the vehicle with jumper wires. If it still doesn't work, replace it.

9   If the motor isn't getting voltage, check for voltage at the switch. If there's no voltage at the switch, check the wiring between the fuse panel and the switch. If there's voltage at the switch, check the switch for continuity in all its operating positions. Replace the switch if there's no continuity.

10   If the switch is OK, check for a short or open in the wiring between the switch and motor.

11   Test the completed repairs.

25 Electric sunroof - description and check

1   The electric sunroof is powered by a single motor located in the roof behind the overhead console. The power circuit is protected by a circuit breaker. When sunlight

isn't desired, an interior sliding panel can be closed.

2   The control switches (tilt and slide) send a ground signal to the sunroof motor when the switches are pressed. Power is supplied to the motor from the sunroof relay. With the ignition On but the engine Off, operate the sunroof control switch through the tilt and slide functions.

3   Listen carefully for the sound of the sunroof motor running in the roof.

4   If the motors can be heard but the sunroof glass doesn't move, there's probably a problem with the drive mechanism or drive cables.

5   If the sunroof does not operate and no sound comes from the motor, check the fuses (in the interior fuse panel *and* in the engine compartment fuse/fusible link box).

6   If the fuses are OK, pull down the overhead interior light/switch panel. Turn the ignition On and check for voltage to the motor. If there's voltage at the motor, check for power and ground at the switch. If power and ground exist at the motor and there's still no voltage at the switch replace the switch. If there's no voltage at the motor, check the power window relay or look for an open or short in the wiring.

7   If there's voltage at the switch, disconnect it. Check the switch for continuity in all its operating positions. If the switch does not have continuity, replace it.

8   If the switch has continuity re-connect the switch. Locate the wire going from the switch to ground. Leaving the switch connected, connect a jumper wire between this wire and ground. If the motor works normally with this wire in place, repair the faulty ground connection.

9   The sunroof can be closed manually by inserting a wrench into the motor shaft and rotating it clockwise. If your vehicle is equipped with a factory sunroof, the wrench comes in the factory toolbag.

26 Airbag system - general information

1   These models are equipped with a Supplemental Restraint System (SRS), more commonly known as airbags, designed to protect the driver and front seat passenger from serious injury in the event of a head-on or frontal collision. Additionally, some models are equipped with side-impact airbags, located in the outside rear corners of the driver and passenger front seats; these airbags are designed to operate primarily in side-impact collisions, though they may also activate in some other types of collisions. Some newer Xterra models are equipped with side-curtain airbags, which are mounted in the headliner along each side of the roof. These are designed to offer side protection to both front and rear occupants.

2   All models have a diagnosis/sensor unit located inside the passenger compartment. 4WD Frontier and Xterra models also have a

26.4 The airbag system diagnostic sensor is located under the floor console

crash zone sensor mounted on the front of the upper radiator support.

Airbag modules

3   The airbag modules consist of a housing incorporating the cushion (airbag) and inflator unit. The inflator assembly is mounted on the back of the housing over a hole through which gas is expelled, inflating the bag almost instantaneously when an electrical signal is sent from the system. The specially wound wire on the driver's side that carries this signal to the module is called a "clockspring." The clockspring is a flat, ribbon-like electrically conductive tape that is wound many times so that it can transmit an electrical signal regardless of steering wheel position.

Diagnosis/sensor unit

Refer to illustration 26.4

4   The diagnosis/sensor unit contains an on-board microprocessor which monitors the operation of the system, and also contains a crash sensor. It checks this system every time the vehicle is started, causing the "AIRBAG" light to go on then off, if the system is operating properly. If there is a fault in the system, the light will go on and stay on and the unit will store fault codes indicating the nature of the fault. If the AIRBAG light goes on and stays on, the vehicle should be taken to your dealer immediately for service. The diagnosis/sensor unit is located under the center console **(see illustration)**. Models with side airbags also have a "satellite" crash sensor in each door "B" pillar.

Operation

5   For the airbags to deploy, the diagnosis/sensor unit must detect a deceleration force great enough to warrant deployment, up to a 30-degree angle from the centerline of the vehicle. On 4WD models, the crash zone sensor must also close its circuit. When this condition occurs, the circuit to the airbag inflator is closed and the airbag inflates. If the battery is destroyed by the impact, or is too low to power the inflator, a capacitor inside the diagnosis/sensor unit provides power.

Self-diagnosis system

6   A self-diagnosis circuit in the control unit displays a light on the instrument panel when the ignition switch is turned to the On position. If the system is operating normally, the light should go out after about seven seconds. If the light doesn't come on, or doesn't go out after seven seconds, or if it comes on while you're driving the vehicle, or if it blinks at any time, there's a malfunction in the SRS system. Have it inspected and repaired as soon as possible. Do not attempt to troubleshoot or service the SRS system yourself. Even a small mistake could cause the SRS system to malfunction when you need it.

Servicing components near the SRS system

7   Nevertheless, there are times when you need to remove the steering wheel, radio or service other components on or near the instrument panel or front seats. At these times, you'll be working around components and wire harnesses for the SRS system. *ALWAYS DISABLE THE SRS SYSTEM BEFORE WORKING NEAR AIRBAG SYSTEM COMPONENTS OR RELATED WIRING.* **Warning:** *Never use electrical test equipment on any of the airbag system wiring or electrical connectors; it could cause the airbag(s) to deploy.*

Disabling the SRS system

Warning: *Any time you are working in the vicinity of airbag wiring or components, DISABLE THE SRS SYSTEM.*

8   Disconnect the battery negative and positive cables, then wait ten minutes before proceeding with any work.

Driver's side airbag

9   Insert a blunt round tool (not a screwdriver) into the hole near the bottom of the steering wheel to depress the clip that retains the airbag to the steering wheel (see Chapter 10 for complete procedure). Raise the airbag and disconnect the yellow electrical connector.

26.11 Pry up the safety lock on the passenger airbag, then disconnect the connector

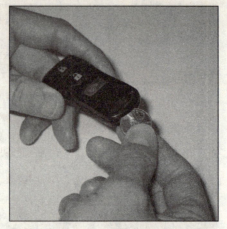

27.3 Using a coin, carefully pry the halves of the transmitter apart (a screwdriver could damage the plastic)

Passenger's side airbag

Refer to illustration 26.11

10   Remove the upper and lower glove boxes (see Chapter 11) from the passenger's side of the instrument panel.

11   Disconnect the two-pin electrical connector between the passenger side airbag and the SRS main wiring harness **(see illustration)**.

Enabling the system

12   After you've disabled the airbag and performed the necessary service, reconnect the two-pin airbag connector into the two-pin clockspring connector (driver's side), the SRS main harness (passenger's side) or the side-impact airbag. Reinstall the lid to the underside of the steering wheel or reinstall the glove box/trim panel or seat back panel.

13   Turn the ignition switch to the Off position.

14   Reattach the battery cables (see Chapter 1).

Removal and installation

Warning: *The bolts used throughout the airbag system to mount the airbag modules and diagnosis/sensor unit (and crash zone sensor on 4WD Frontier and Xterra models) are special tamper-proof Torx bolts, which have a special coating. These bolts are designed to be used once. Replace them with new factory bolts, and never use a substitute fastener.*

Driver's side airbag and clockspring

15   Refer to Chapter 10, Section 11, for removal and installation of the driver's side airbag and clockspring. **Warning:** *When installing the clockspring, be sure to follow the centering instructions carefully.*

Passenger side airbag

16   Disable the airbag system (beginning

with Step 8).

17   Refer to Chapter 11 and remove the passenger-side lower dash panel and the glove box.

18   Disconnect the two-pin connector. Remove the special Torx tamper-proof bolts and remove unit from the top of the instrument panel. **Caution:** *The airbag assembly is heavier than it looks - use both hands when removing it from the dash.*

19   Installation is the reverse of the removal procedure. Tighten the bolts to 15 ft-lbs (25 Nm).

---

27   Remote keyless entry system - battery replacement and matching the transmitter to the vehicle

---

1   Here's how the transmitter inside the remote keyless entry fob should work:

- *When you press the UNLOCK button, the driver's door unlocks. If you press the UNLOCK button a second time within five seconds, all the doors unlock.*
- *If the doors aren't opened within a period of one minute, they should automatically lock again.*
- *Pressing the lock button sets the alarm and locks all of the doors (and the liftgate on Xterra models).*

Battery replacement

Refer to illustration 27.3

2   When the transmitter becomes weak, operation will become intermittent and require you to be closer to the vehicle for it to work. Eventually it won't work at all.

3   To replace the transmitter battery, carefully pry open the keyless entry fob by inserting a coin into the notch in the body of the transmitter **(see illustration)** and separate

the upper and lower halves of the fob. **Note:** *On some transmitters the slot is in the end, where the key ring attaches. On other models, the slot is on the side.*

4   Carefully pry out the old battery with a small screwdriver.

5   Installation is the reverse of removal. Make sure that the new battery is a CR2025 or equivalent. And make sure that the two halves of the cover snap together tightly to keep out dirt, dust, humidity and rain.

Matching the transmitter to the vehicle

6   Get both (or more, if you have more; up to five can be programmed). Shut the doors (and liftgate, on Xterra models).

7   Place the ignition key into the ignition lock cylinder and pull it back out. Do this at least seven times within a ten second period. The hazard flasher lights should blink twice. **Note:** *The key must be inserted and removed completely each time. Also, if this is done too fast, it won't work.*

8   Install the key again and turn it to the Accessory position. Push one of the buttons on the remote; the hazard flasher lights will blink twice again. The old code is now erased and the new one programmed in. If another remote is going to be programmed, proceed to the next Step.

9   Have the next remote transmitter to be programmed ready. Push the driver's door Unlock button, then press the Lock button. Now push any button on the remote; the hazard flasher lights will blink twice. The old code is now erased from this remote, and the new one is programmed in.

10   If another remote is going to be programmed, repeat Step 9. You can match up to five transmitters to the vehicle.

11   To exit the programming mode, open the driver's door.

---

28   Wiring diagrams - general information

Since it isn't possible to include all wiring diagrams for every year and model covered by this manual, the following diagrams are those that are typical and most commonly needed.

Prior to troubleshooting any circuits, check the fuses and circuit breakers (if equipped) to make sure they are in good condition. Make sure the battery is properly charged and has clean, tight cable connections (see Chapter 1).

When checking the wiring system, make sure that all electrical connectors are clean, with no broken or loose pins. When unplugging an electrical connector, do not pull on the wires, only on the connector housings themselves.

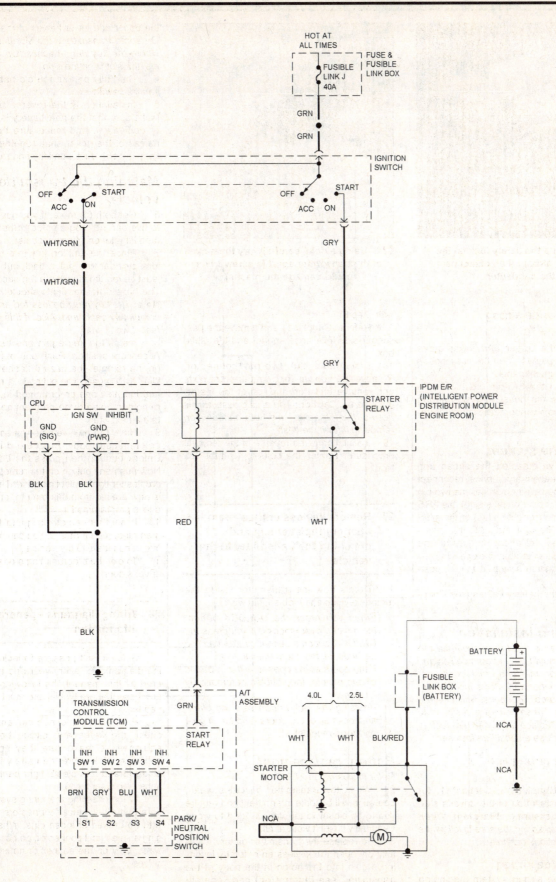

Starting system - automatic transmission models

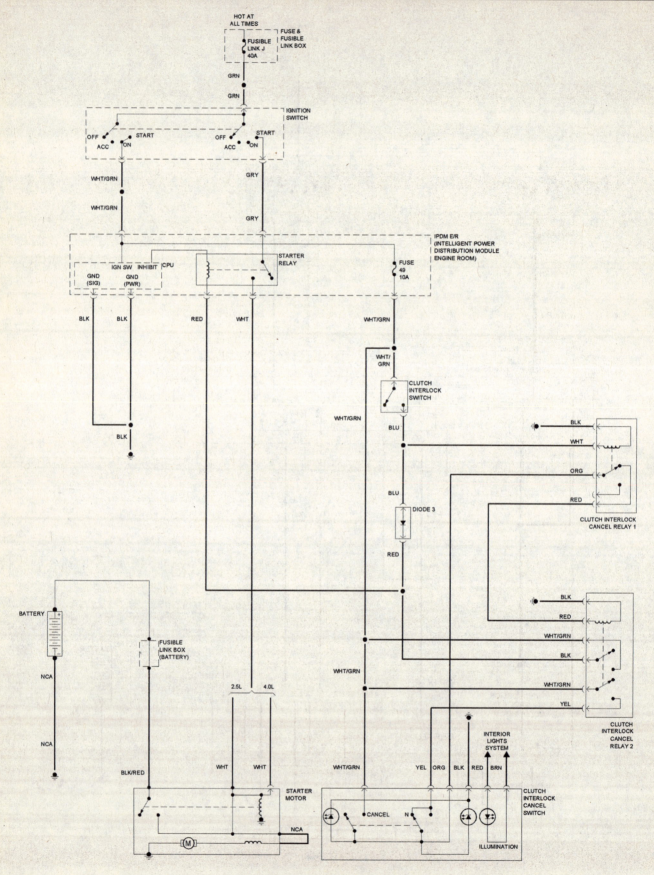

Starting system - manual transmission models (with clutch interlock cancel switch)

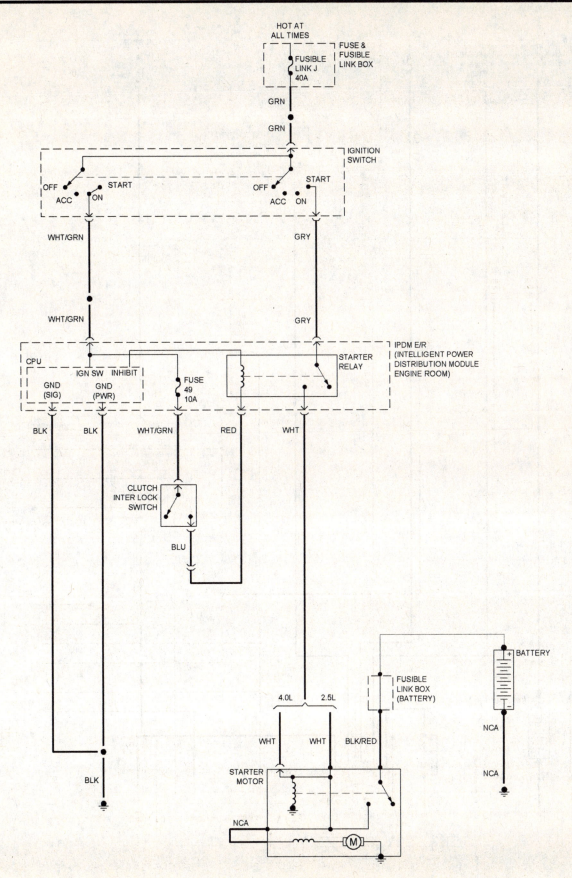

Starting system - manual transmission models (without clutch interlock cancel switch)

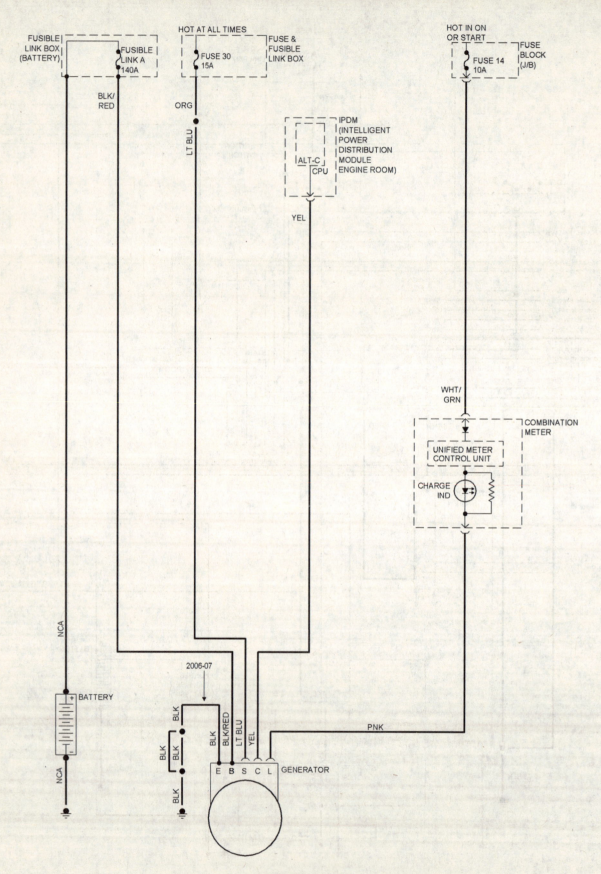

Charging system

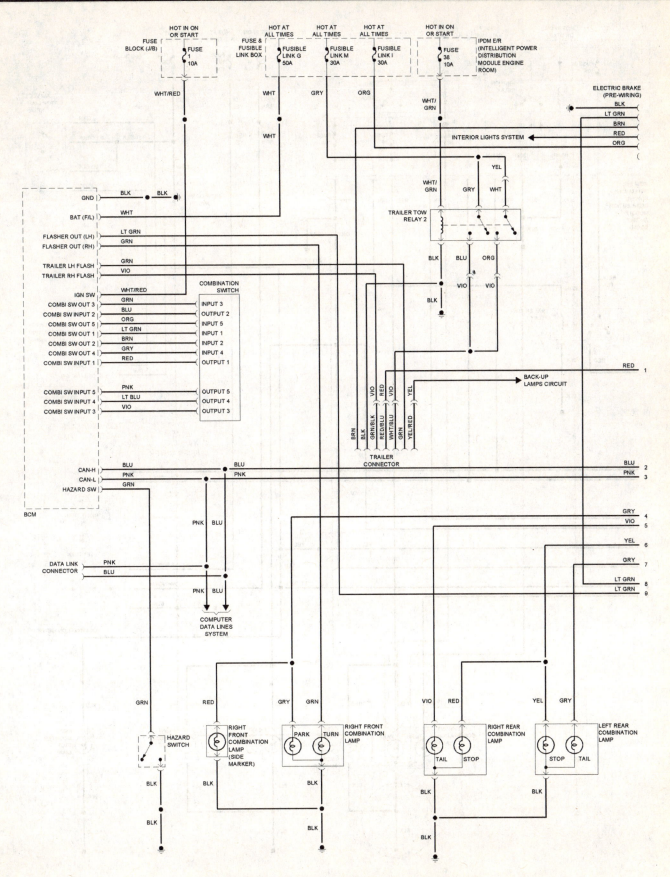

Park/stop/turn signal lights - 2005 Frontier models (1 of 2)

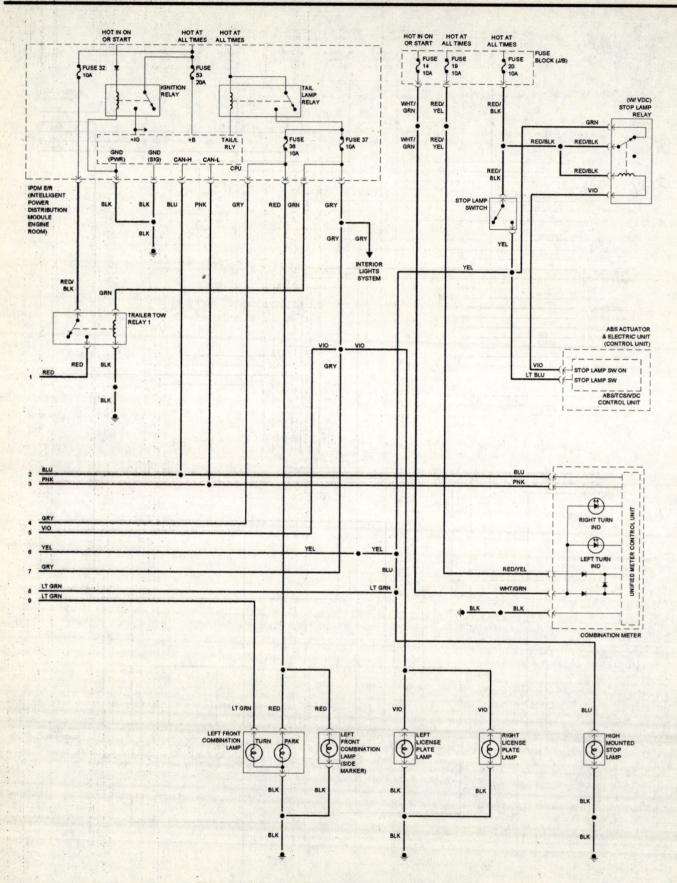

Park/stop/turn signal lights - 2005 Frontier models (2 of 2)

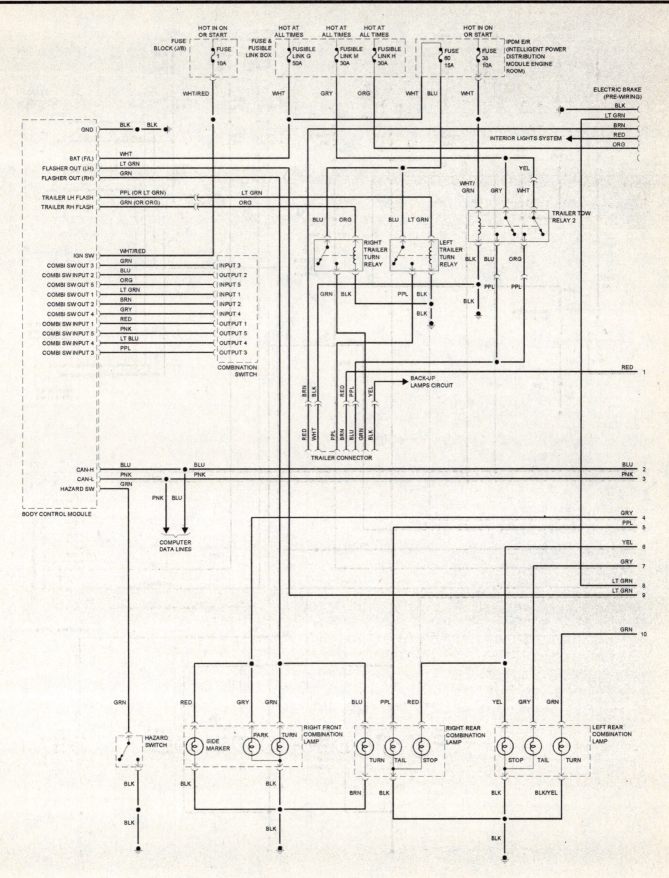

Park/stop/turn signal lights - 2006 and later Frontier models (1 of 2)

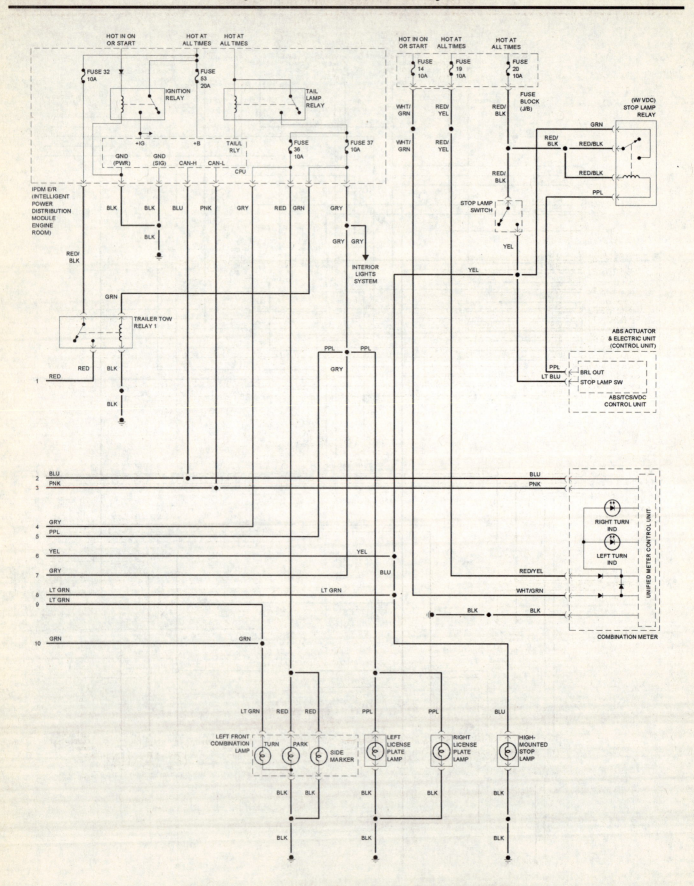

Park/stop/turn signal lights - 2006 and later Frontier models (2 of 2)

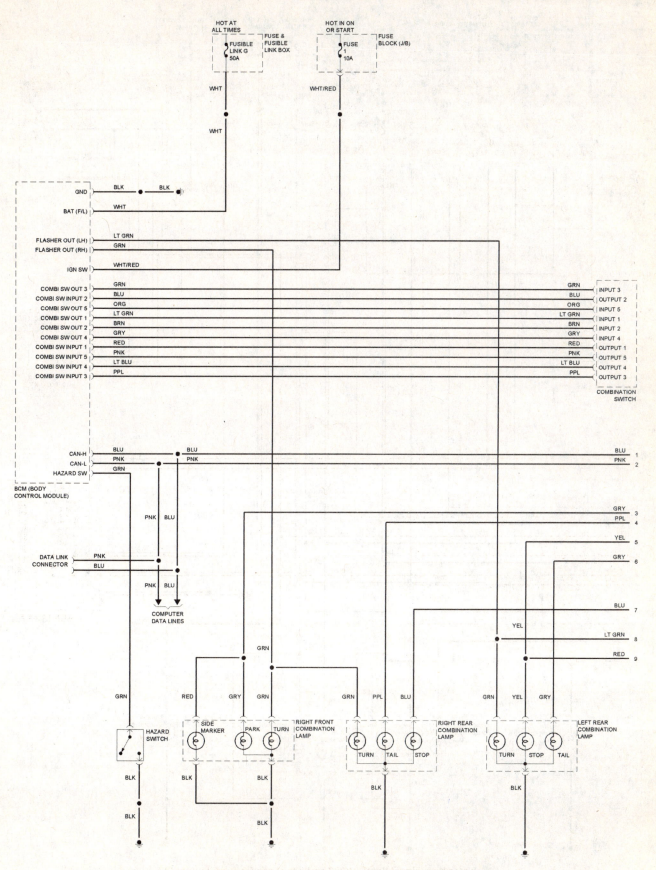

Park/stop/turn signal lights - Xterra models (1 of 2)

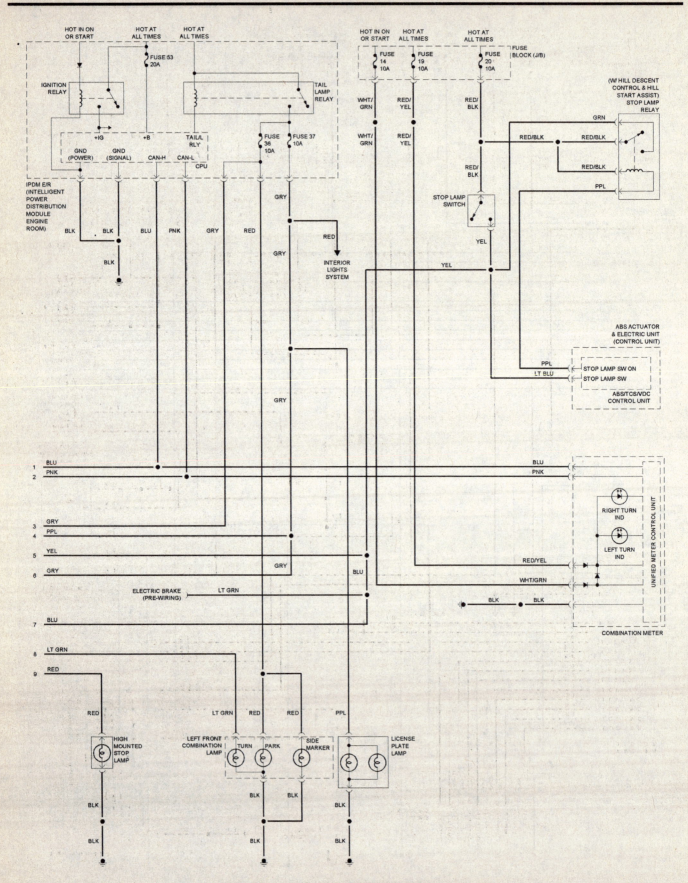

Park/stop/turn signal lights - Xterra models (2 of 2)

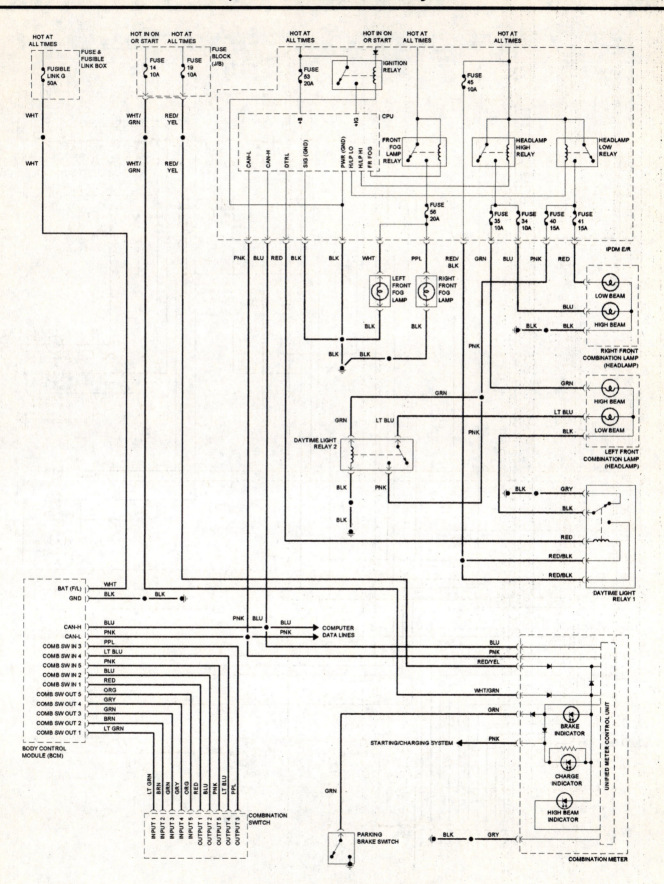

Headlight system (with Daytime Running Lights)

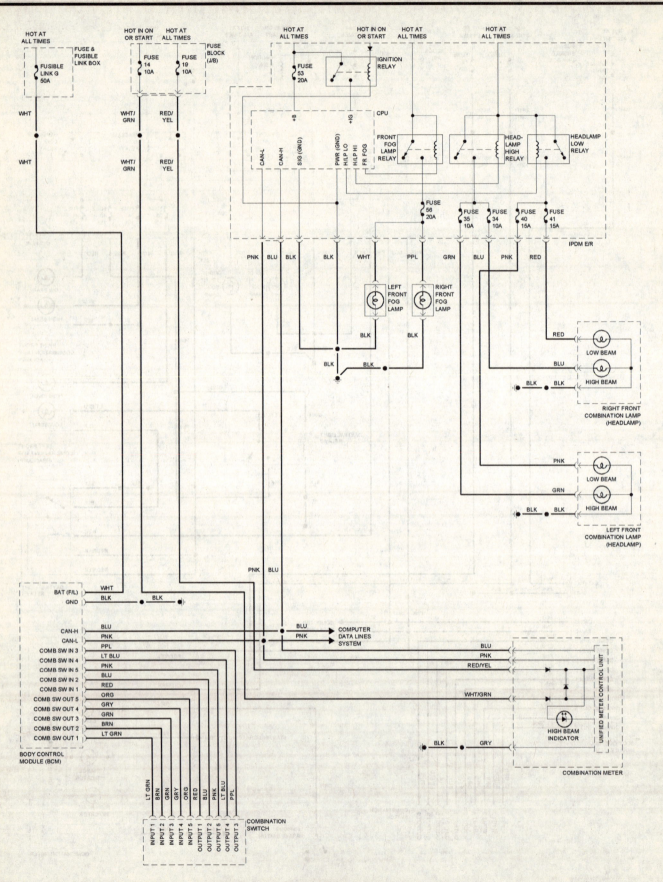

Headlight system (without Daytime Running Lights)

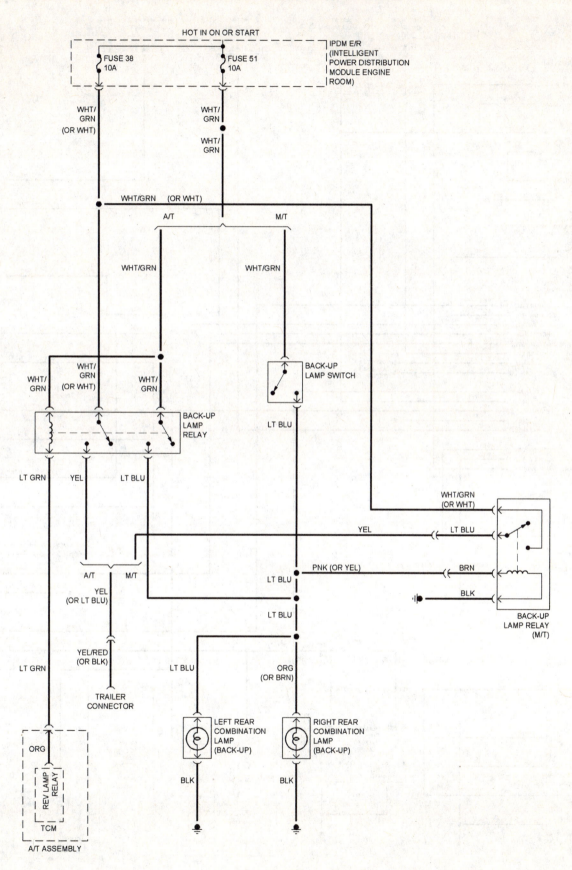

Back-up lights

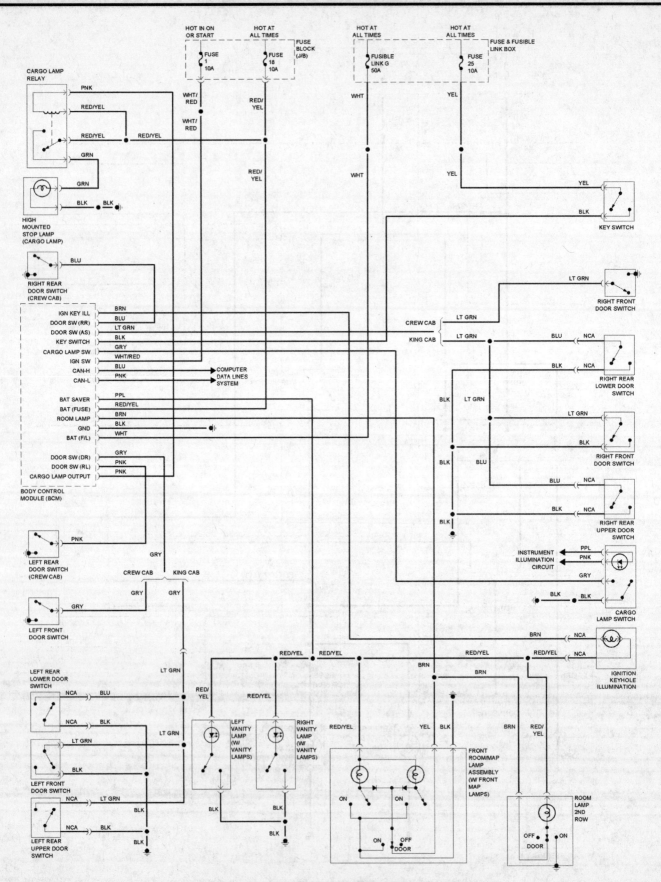

Courtesy lights - Frontier models with power door locks

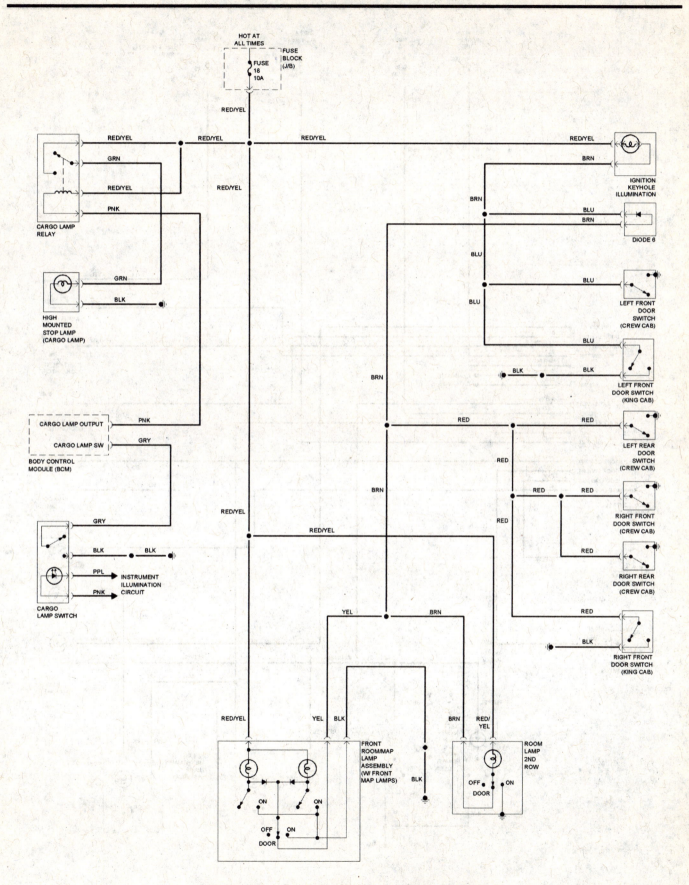

Courtesy lights - Frontier models without power door locks

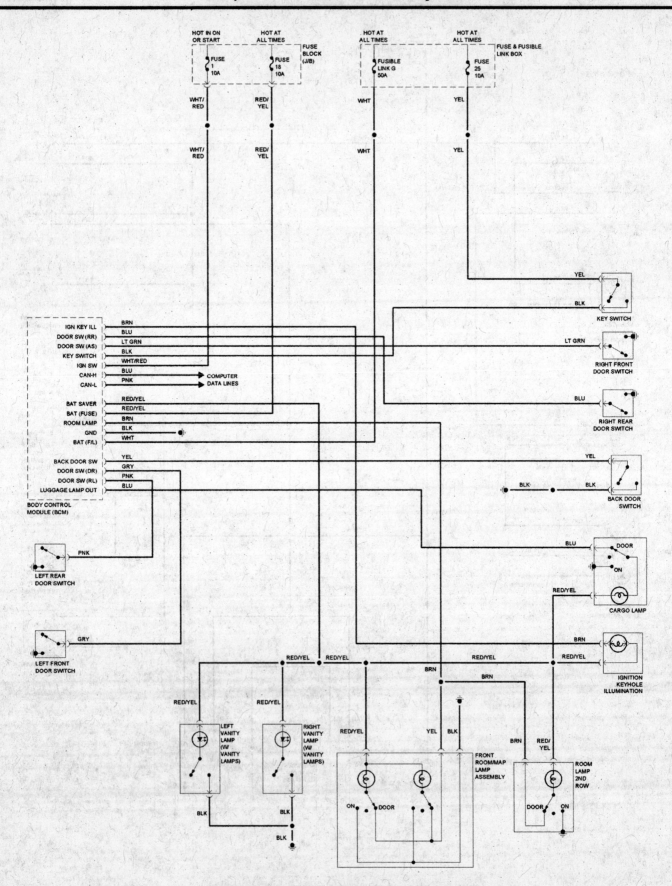

Courtesy lights - Xterra models with power door locks

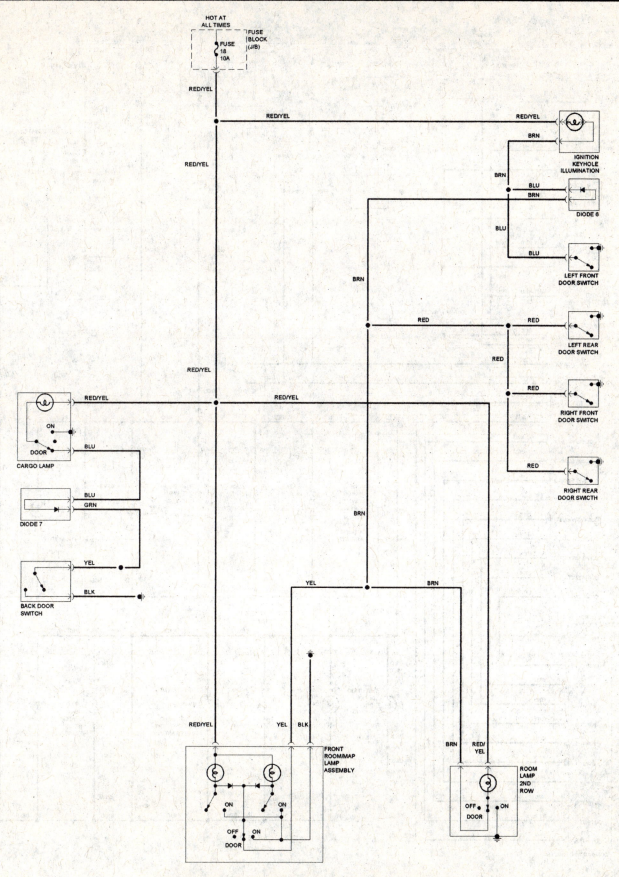

Courtesy lights - Xterra models without power door locks

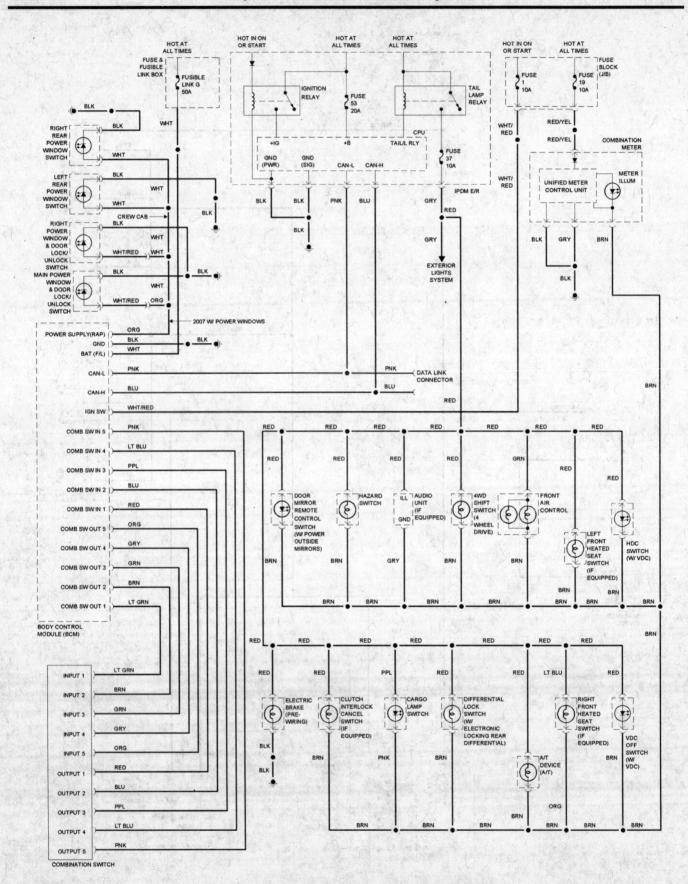

Instrument panel and switch illumination - Frontier models

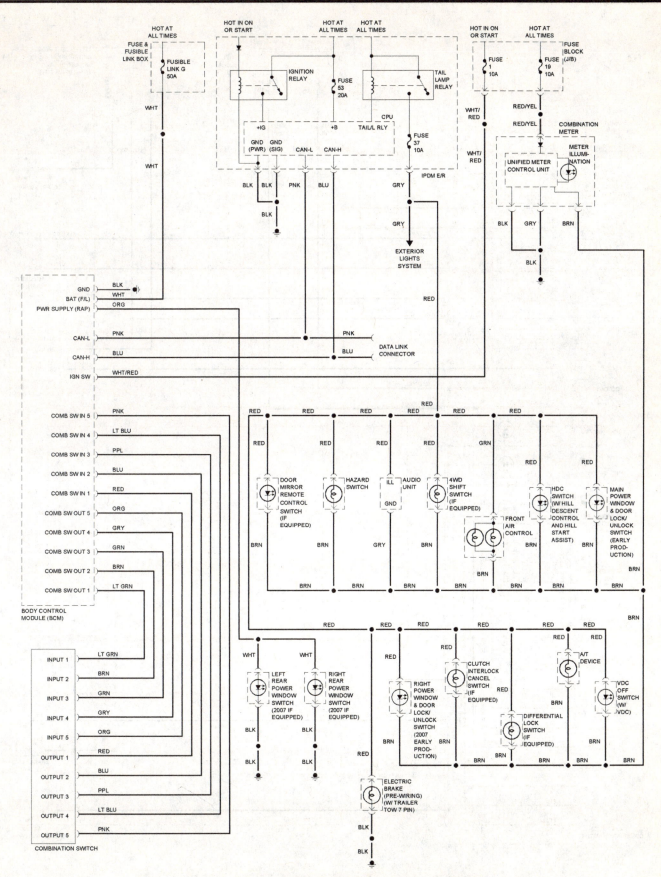

Instrument panel and switch illumination - Xterra models

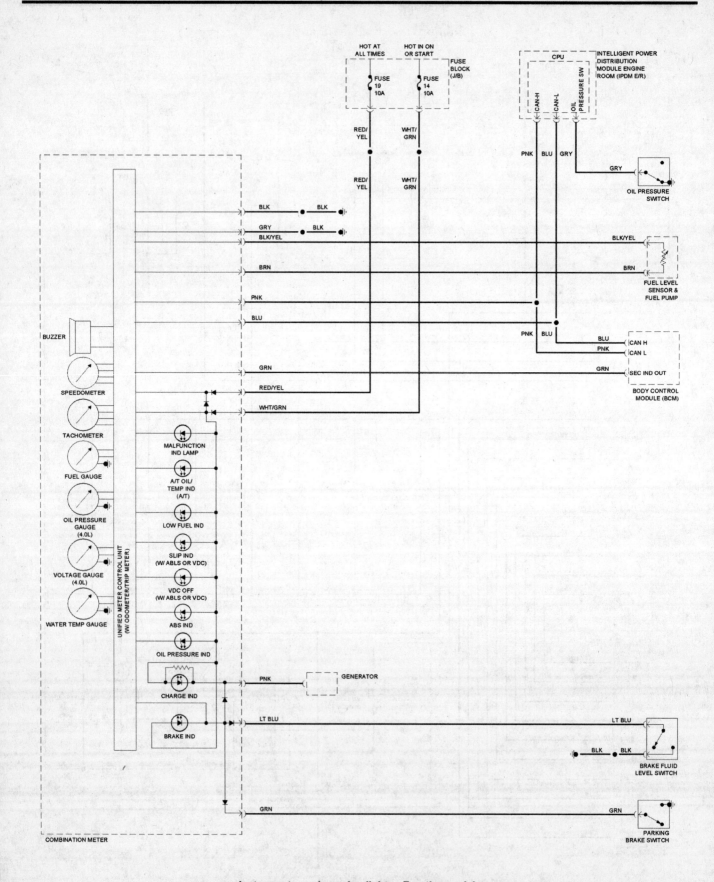

Instrument panel warning lights - Frontier models

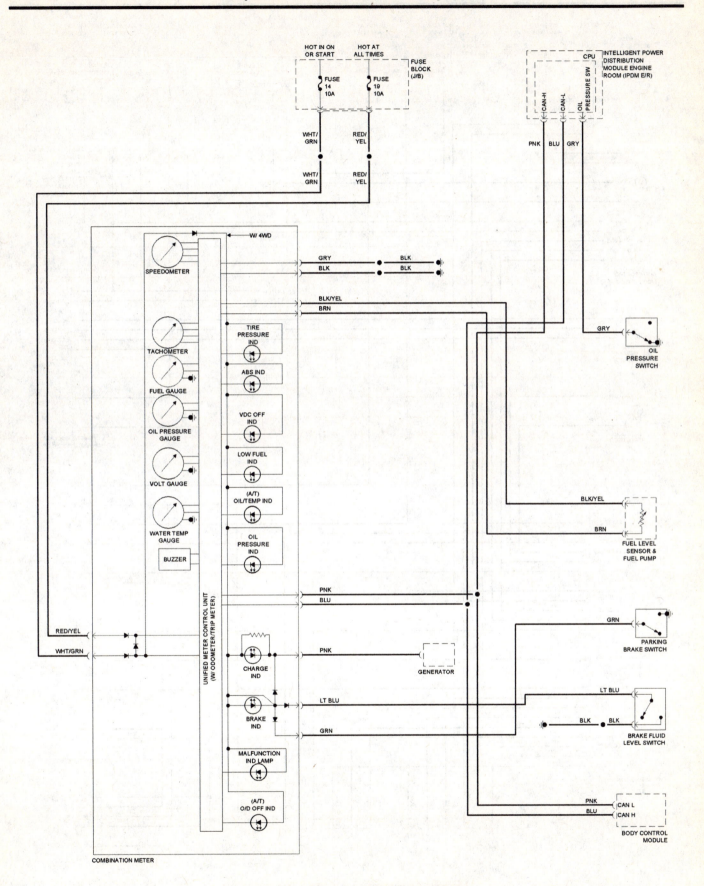

Instrument panel warning lights - Xterra models

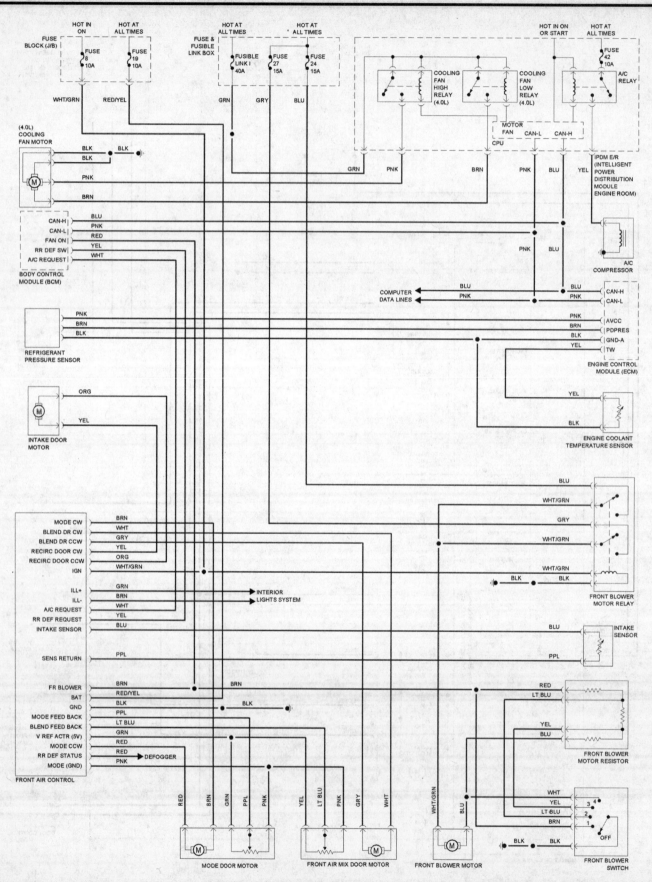

Air conditioning and engine cooling

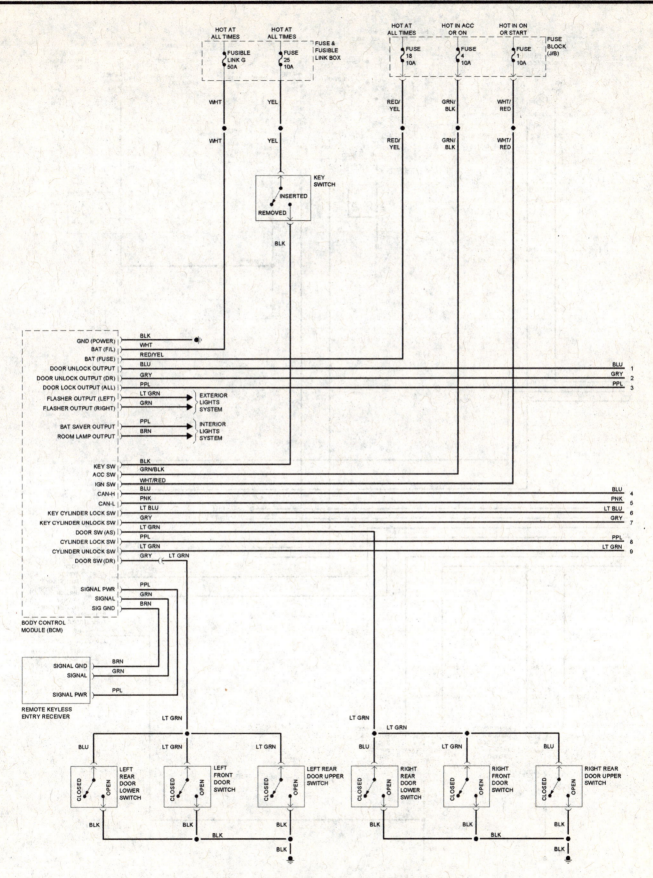

Power door locks - Frontier King Cab models (1 of 2)

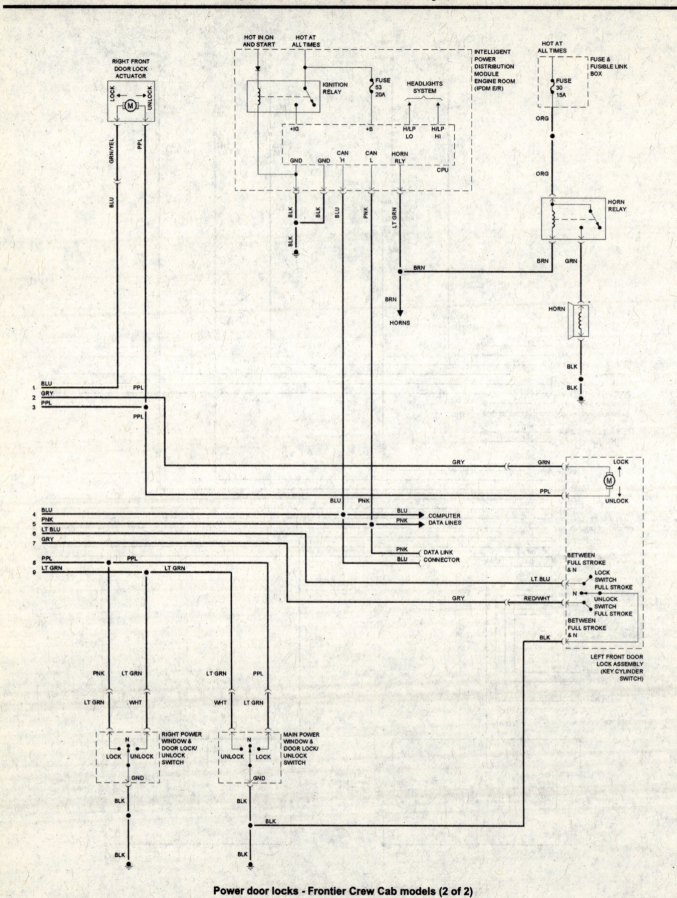

Power door locks - Frontier Crew Cab models (2 of 2)

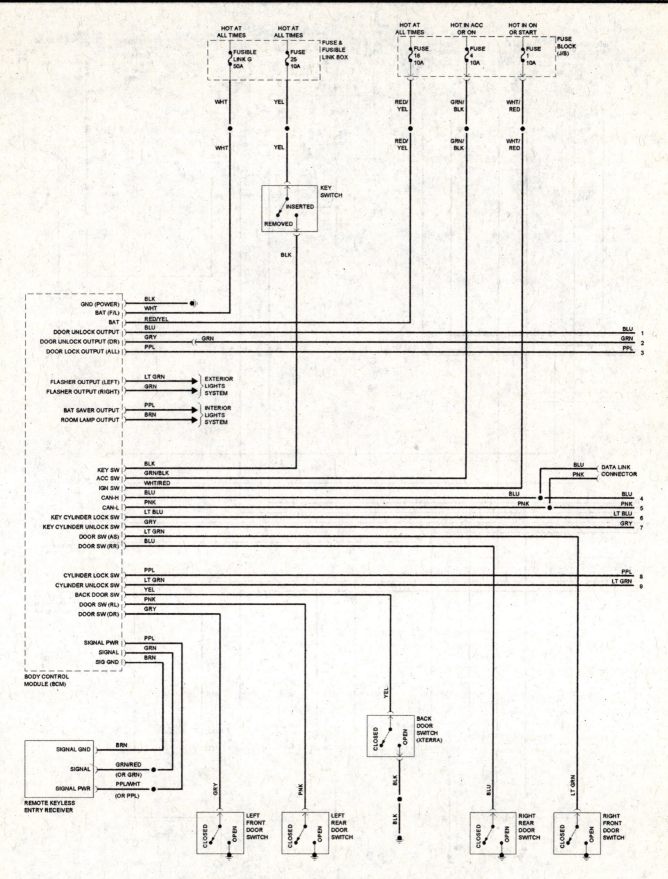

Power door locks - Frontier Crew Cab and Xterra models (1 of 2)

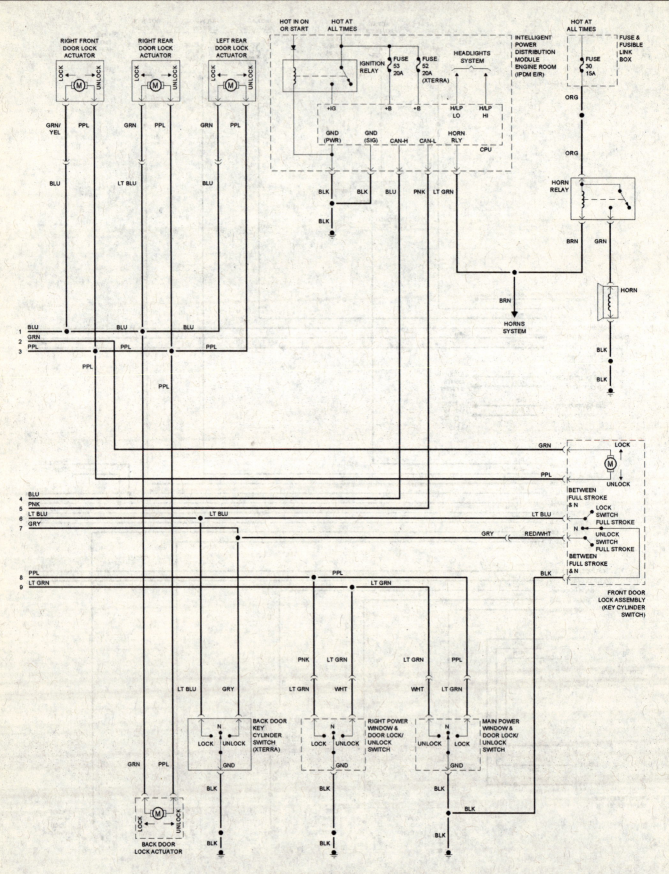

Power door locks - Frontier Crew Cab and Xterra models (2 of 2)

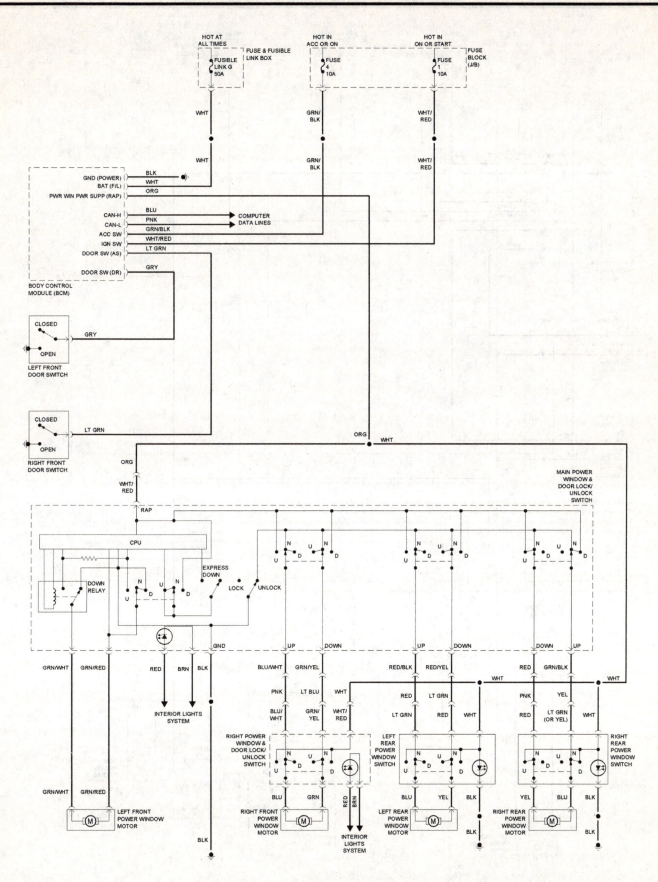

Power windows - Frontier Crew Cab and Xterra models

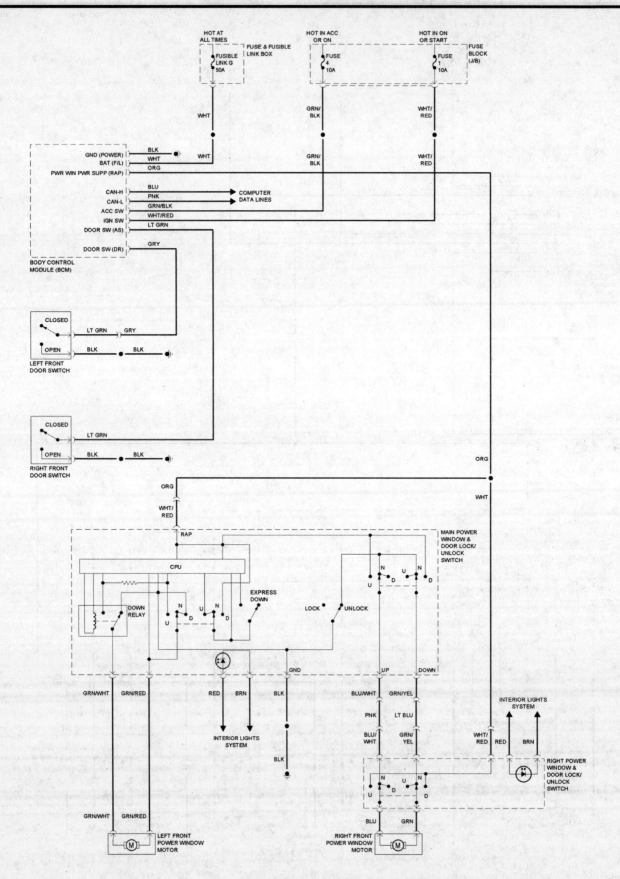

Power windows - Frontier King Cab models

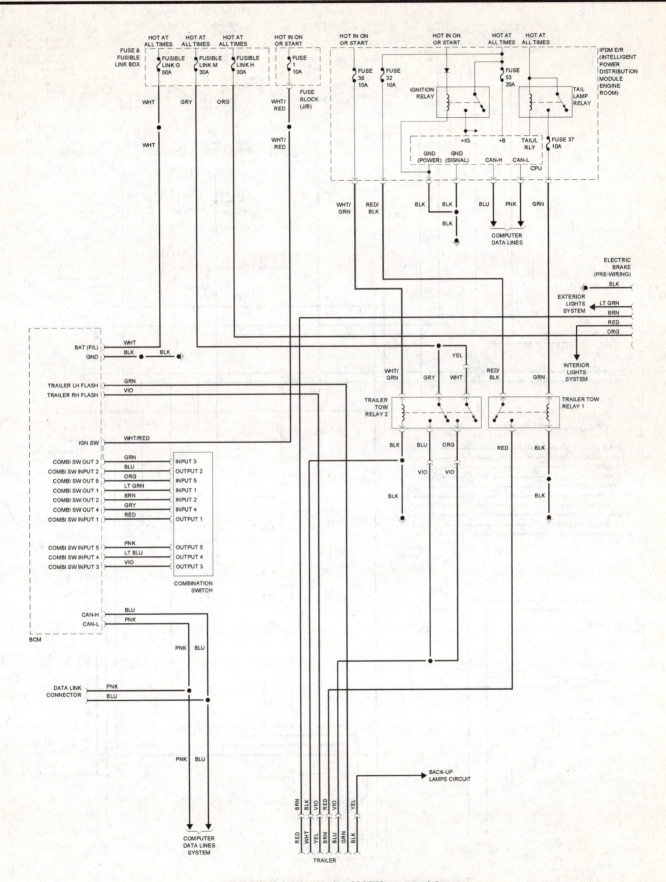

Trailer towing package - 2005 Xterra models

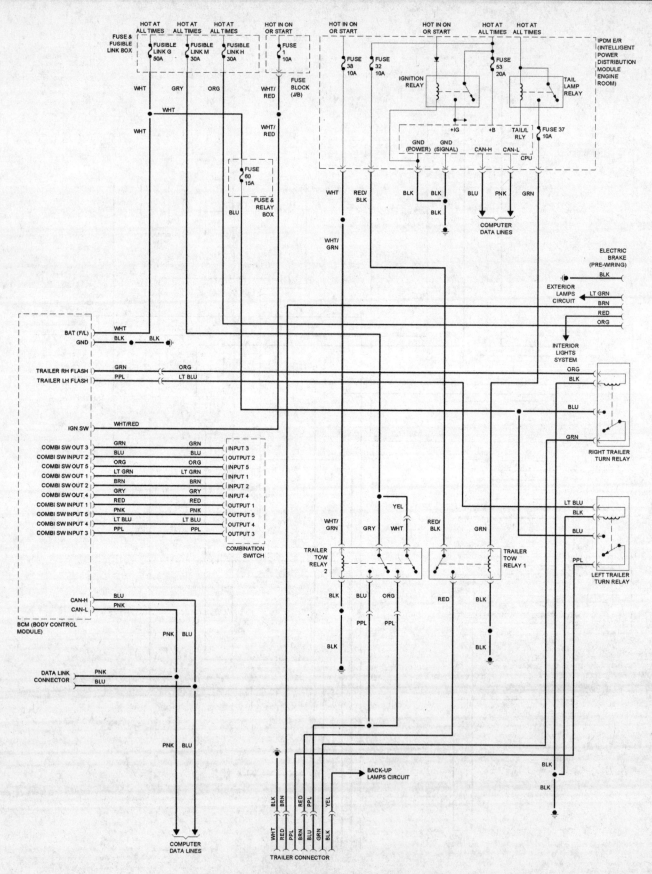

Trailer towing package - 2006 and later Xterra models

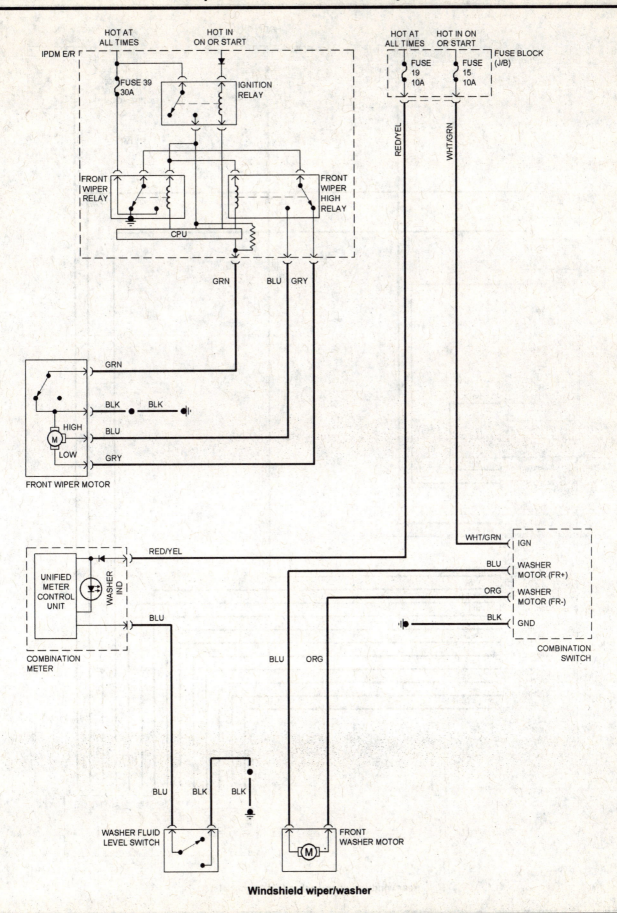

Windshield wiper/washer

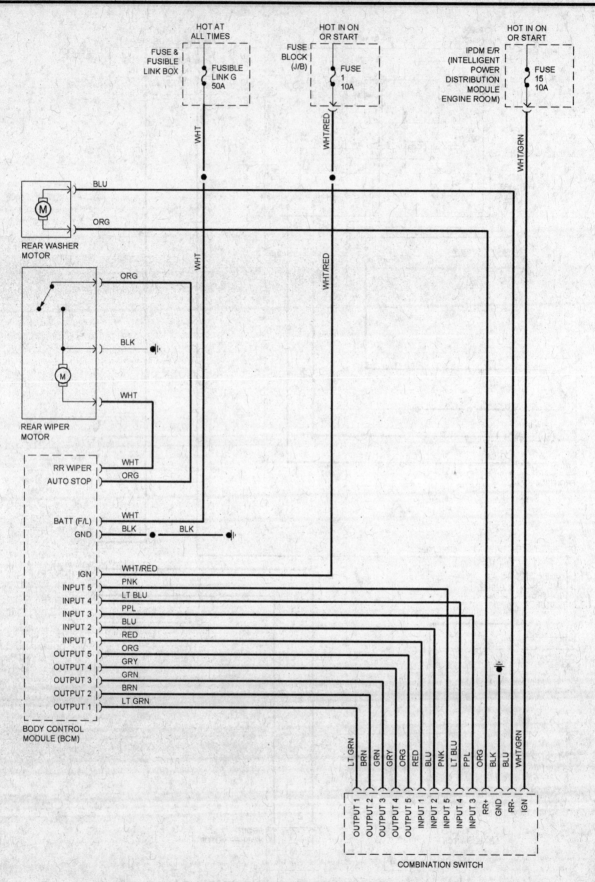

Rear window wiper/washer (Xterra models)

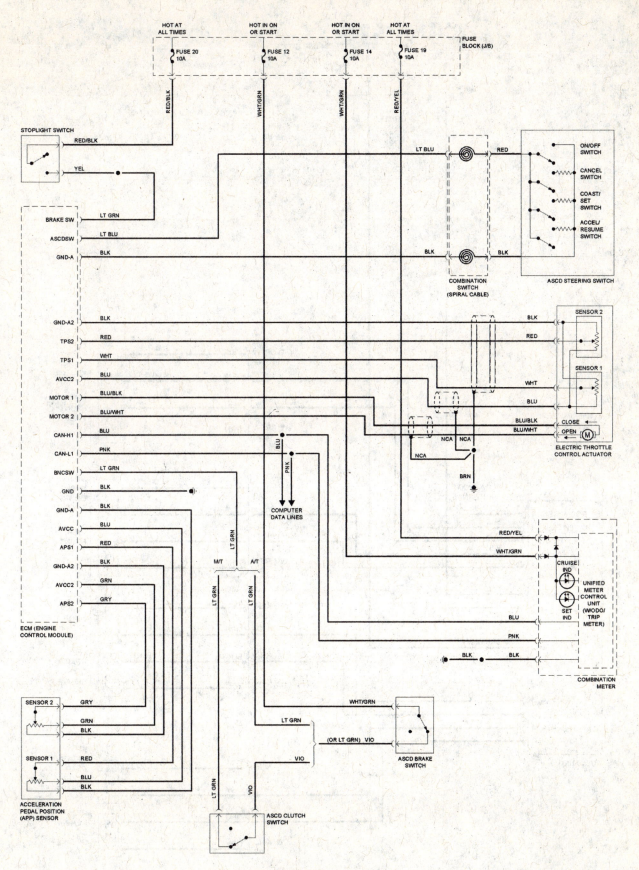

Cruise control system

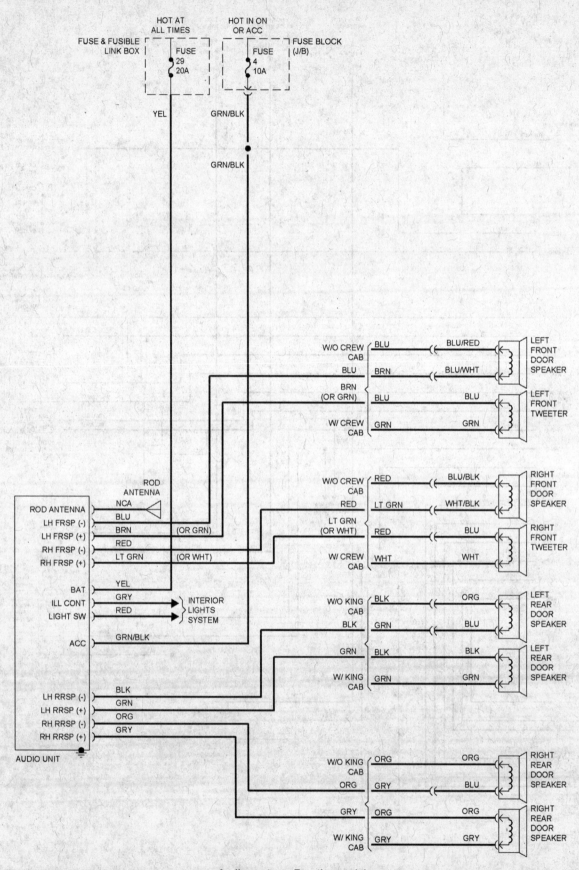

Audio system - Frontier models

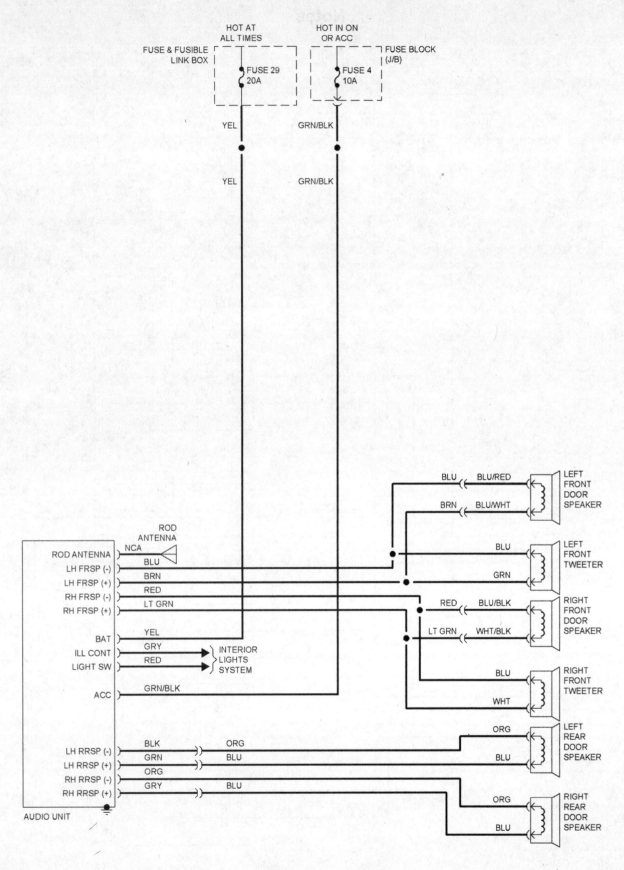

Audio system - Xterra models

Notes

Index

F

Haynes Automotive Manuals

NOTE: If you do not see a listing for your vehicle, consult your local Haynes dealer for the latest product information.

ACURA
12020 Integra '86 thru '89 & Legend '86 thru '90
12021 Integra '90 thru '93 & Legend '91 thru '95
Integra '94 thru '00 - *see HONDA Civic (42025)*
MDX '01 thru '07 - *see HONDA Pilot (42037)*
12050 Acura TL all models '99 thru '08

AMC
Jeep CJ - *see JEEP (50020)*
14020 Concord/Hornet/Gremlin/Spirit '70 thru '83
14025 (Renault) Alliance & Encore '83 thru '87

AUDI
15020 4000 all models '80 thru '87
15025 5000 all models '77 thru '83
15026 5000 all models '84 thru '88
Audi A4 '96 thru '01 - *see VW Passat (96023)*
15030 Audi A4 '02 thru '08

AUSTIN
Healey Sprite - *see MG Midget (66015)*

BMW
18020 3/5 Series '82 thru '92
18021 3 Series including Z3 models '92 thru '98
18022 3-Series incl. Z4 models '99 thru '05
18023 3-Series '06 thru '10
18025 320i all 4 cyl models '75 thru '83
18050 1500 thru 2002 except Turbo '59 thru '77

BUICK
19010 Buick Century '97 thru '05
Century (front-wheel drive) - *see GM (38005)*
19020 Buick, Oldsmobile & Pontiac Full-size (Front wheel drive) '85 thru '05
19025 Buick, Oldsmobile & Pontiac Full-size (Rear wheel drive) '70 thru '90
19030 Mid-size Regal & Century '74 thru '87
Regal - *see GENERAL MOTORS (38010)*
Skyhawk - *see GM (38030)*
Skylark - *see GM (38020, 38025)*
Somerset - *see GENERAL MOTORS (38025)*

CADILLAC
21015 CTS & CTS-V '03 thru '12
21030 Cadillac Rear Wheel Drive '70 thru '93
Cimarron, Eldorado & Seville - *see GM (38015, 38030, 38031)*

CHEVROLET
10305 Chevrolet Engine Overhaul Manual
24010 Astro & GMC Safari Mini-vans '85 thru '05
24015 Camaro V8 all models '70 thru '81
24016 Camaro all models '82 thru '92
Cavalier - *see GM (38015)*
Celebrity - *see GM (38005)*
24017 Camaro & Firebird '93 thru '02
24020 Chevelle, Malibu, El Camino '69 thru '87
24024 Chevette & Pontiac T1000 '76 thru '87
Citation - *see GENERAL MOTORS (38020)*
24027 Colorado & GMC Canyon '04 thru '10
24032 Corsica/Beretta all models '87 thru '96
24040 Corvette all V8 models '68 thru '82
24041 Corvette all models '84 thru '96
24045 Full-size Sedans Caprice, Impala, Biscayne, Bel Air & Wagons '69 thru '90
24046 Impala SS & Caprice and Buick Roadmaster '91 thru '96
Impala '00 thru '05 - *see LUMINA (24048)*
24047 Impala & Monte Carlo all models '06 thru '11
Lumina '90 thru '94 - *see GM (38010)*
24048 Lumina & Monte Carlo '95 thru '05
Lumina APV - *see GM (38035)*
24050 Luv Pick-up all 2WD & 4WD '72 thru '82
Malibu - *see GM (38026)*
24055 Monte Carlo all models '70 thru '88
Monte Carlo '95 thru '01 - *see LUMINA*
24059 Nova all V8 models '69 thru '79
24060 Nova/Geo Prizm '85 thru '92
24064 Pick-ups '67 thru '87 - Chevrolet & GMC
24065 Pick-ups '88 thru '98 - Chevrolet & GMC
24066 Pick-ups '99 thru '06 - Chevrolet & GMC
24067 Chevy Silverado & GMC Sierra '07 thru '12
24070 S-10 & GMC S-15 Pick-ups '82 thru '93
24071 S-10, Sonoma & Jimmy '94 thru '04
24072 Chevrolet TrailBlazer, GMC Envoy & Oldsmobile Bravada '02 thru '09
24075 Sprint '85 thru '88, Geo Metro '89 thru '01
24080 Vans - Chevrolet & GMC '68 thru '96
24081 Full-size Vans '96 thru '10

CHRYSLER
10310 Chrysler Engine Overhaul Manual
25015 Chrysler Cirrus, Dodge Stratus, Plymouth Breeze, '95 thru '00
25020 Full-size Front-Wheel Drive '88 thru '93
K-Cars - *see DODGE Aries (30008)*
Laser - *see DODGE Daytona (30030)*
25025 Chrysler LHS, Concorde & New Yorker, Dodge Intrepid, Eagle Vision, '93 thru '97
25026 Chrysler LHS, Concorde, 300M, Dodge Intrepid '98 thru '04
25027 Chrysler 300, Dodge Charger & Magnum '05 thru '09
25030 Chrysler/Plym. Mid-size '82 thru '95
Rear-wheel Drive - *see DODGE (30050)*
25035 PT Cruiser all models '01 thru '10
25040 Chrysler Sebring '95 thru '06, Dodge Stratus '01 thru '06, Dodge Avenger '95 thru '00

DATSUN
28005 200SX all models '80 thru '83
28007 B-210 all models '73 thru '78
28009 210 all models '78 thru '82
28012 240Z, 260Z & 280Z Coupe '70 thru '78
28014 280ZX Coupe & 2+2 '79 thru '83
300ZX - *see NISSAN (72010)*
28018 510 & PL521 Pick-up '68 thru '73
28020 510 all models '78 thru '81
28022 620 Series Pick-up all models '73 thru '79
720 Series Pick-up - *see NISSAN (72030)*
28025 810/Maxima all gas models '77 thru '84

DODGE
400 & 600 - *see CHRYSLER (25030)*
30008 Aries & Plymouth Reliant '81 thru '89
30010 Caravan & Ply. Voyager '84 thru '95
30011 Caravan & Ply. Voyager '96 thru '02
30012 Challenger/Plymouth Saporro '78 thru '83
Challenger '67-'76 - *see DART (30025)*
30013 Caravan, Chrysler Voyager, Town & Country '03 thru '07
30016 Colt/Plymouth Champ '78 thru '87
30020 Dakota Pick-ups all models '87 thru '96
30021 Durango '98 & '99, Dakota '97 thru '99
30022 Durango '00 thru '03, Dakota '00 thru '04
30023 Durango '04 thru '09, Dakota '05 thru '11
30025 Dart, Challenger/Plymouth Barracuda & Valiant 6 cyl models '67 thru '76
30030 Daytona & Chrysler Laser '84 thru '89
Intrepid - *see Chrysler (25025, 25026)*
30034 Dodge & Plymouth Neon '95 thru '99
30035 Omni & Plymouth Horizon '78 thru '90
30036 Dodge and Plymouth Neon '00 thru '05
30040 Pick-ups all full-size models '74 thru '93
30041 Pick-ups all full-size models '94 thru '01
30042 Pick-ups full-size models '02 thru '08
30045 Ram 50/D50 Pick-ups & Raider and Plymouth Arrow Pick-ups '79 thru '93
30050 Dodge/Ply./Chrysler RWD '71 thru '89
30055 Shadow/Plymouth Sundance '87 thru '94
30060 Spirit & Plymouth Acclaim '89 thru '95
30065 Vans - Dodge & Plymouth '71 thru '03

EAGLE
Talon - *see MITSUBISHI (68030, 68031)*
Vision - *see CHRYSLER (25025)*

FIAT
34010 124 Sport Coupe & Spider '68 thru '78
34025 X1/9 all models '74 thru '80

FORD
10320 Ford Engine Overhaul Manual
10355 Ford Automatic Transmission Overhaul
11500 Mustang '64-1/2 thru '70 Restoration Guide
36004 Aerostar Mini-vans '86 thru '97
Aspire - *see FORD Festiva (36030)*
36006 Contour/Mercury Mystique '95 thru '00
36008 Courier Pick-up all models '72 thru '82
36012 Crown Victoria & Mercury Grand Marquis '88 thru '10
36016 Escort/Mercury Lynx '81 thru '90
36020 Escort/Mercury Tracer '91 thru '02
Expedition - *see FORD Pick-up (36059)*
36022 Escape & Mazda Tribute '01 thru '11
36024 Explorer & Mazda Navajo '91 thru '01
36025 Explorer/Mercury Mountaineer '02 thru '10
36028 Fairmont & Mercury Zephyr '78 thru '83
36030 Festiva & Aspire '88 thru '97
36032 Fiesta all models '77 thru '80
36034 Focus all models '00 thru '11
36036 Ford & Mercury Full-size '75 thru '87
36044 Ford & Mercury Mid-size '75 thru '86
36045 Ford Fusion & Mercury Milan '06 thru '10
36048 Mustang V8 all models '64-1/2 thru '73
36049 Mustang II 4 cyl, V6 & V8 '74 thru '78
36050 Mustang & Mercury Capri '79 thru '93
36051 Mustang all models '94 thru '04
36052 Mustang '05 thru '10
36054 Pick-ups and Bronco '73 thru '79
36058 Pick-ups and Bronco '80 thru '96
36059 Pick-ups & Expedition '97 thru '09
36060 Super Duty Pick-up, Excursion '99 thru '10
36061 F-150 full-size '04 thru '10
36062 Pinto & Mercury Bobcat '75 thru '80
36066 Probe all models '89 thru '92
Probe '93 thru '97 - *see MAZDA 626 (61042)*
36070 Ranger/Bronco II gas models '83 thru '92
36071 Ford Ranger '93 thru '10 & Mazda Pick-ups '94 thru '09
36074 Taurus & Mercury Sable '86 thru '95
36075 Taurus & Mercury Sable '96 thru '01
36078 Tempo & Mercury Topaz '84 thru '94
36082 Thunderbird/Mercury Cougar '83 thru '88
36086 Thunderbird/Mercury Cougar '89 thru '97
36090 Vans all V8 Econoline models '69 thru '91
36094 Vans full size '92 thru '10
36097 Windstar Mini-van '95 thru '07

GENERAL MOTORS
10360 GM Automatic Transmission Overhaul
38005 Buick Century, Chevrolet Celebrity, Olds Cutlass Ciera & Pontiac 6000 '82 thru '96
38010 Buick Regal, Chevrolet Lumina, Oldsmobile Cutlass Supreme & Pontiac Grand Prix front wheel drive '88 thru '07
38015 Buick Skyhawk, Cadillac Cimarron, Chevrolet Cavalier, Oldsmobile Firenza Pontiac J-2000 & Sunbird '82 thru '94
38016 Chevrolet Cavalier/Pontiac Sunfire '95 thru '05
38017 Chevrolet Cobalt & Pontiac G5 '05 thru '11
38020 Buick Skylark, Chevrolet Citation, Olds Omega, Pontiac Phoenix '80 thru '85
38025 Buick Skylark & Somerset, Olds Achieva, Calais & Pontiac Grand Am '85 thru '98
38026 Chevrolet Malibu, Olds Alero & Cutlass, Pontiac Grand Am '97 thru '03
38027 Chevrolet Malibu '04 thru '10
38030 Cadillac Eldorado & Oldsmobile Toronado '71 thru '85, Seville '80 thru '85, Buick Riviera '79 thru '85
38031 Cadillac Eldorado & Seville '86 thru '91, DeVille & Buick Riviera '86 thru '93, Fleetwood & Olds Toronado '86 thru '92
38032 DeVille '94 thru '05, Seville '92 thru '04 Cadillac DTS '06 thru '10
38035 Chevrolet Lumina APV, Olds Silhouette & Pontiac Trans Sport '90 thru '96
38036 Chevrolet Venture, Olds Silhouette, Pontiac Trans Sport & Montana '97 thru '05
GM Full-size RWD - *see BUICK (19025)*
38040 Chevrolet Equinox '05 thru '09 Pontiac Torrent '06 thru '09
38070 Chevrolet HHR '06 thru '11

GEO
Metro - *see CHEVROLET Sprint (24075)*
Prizm - *see CHEVROLET (24060) or TOYOTA (92036)*
40030 Storm all models '90 thru '93
Tracker - *see SUZUKI Samurai (90010)*

GMC
Vans & Pick-ups - *see CHEVROLET*

HONDA
42010 Accord CVCC all models '76 thru '83
42011 Accord all models '84 thru '89
42012 Accord all models '90 thru '93
42013 Accord all models '94 thru '97
42014 Accord all models '98 thru '02
42015 Accord '03 thru '07
42020 Civic 1200 all models '73 thru '79
42021 Civic 1300 & 1500 CVCC '80 thru '83
42022 Civic 1500 CVCC all models '75 thru '79
42023 Civic all models '84 thru '91
42024 Civic & del Sol '92 thru '95
42025 Civic '96 thru '00, CR-V '97 thru '01, Acura Integra '94 thru '00
42026 Civic '01 thru '10, CR-V '02 thru '09
42035 Odyssey models '99 thru '10
Passport - *see ISUZU Rodeo (47017)*
42037 Honda Pilot '03 thru '07, Acura MDX '01 thru '07
42040 Prelude CVCC all models '79 thru '89

HYUNDAI
43010 Elantra all models '96 thru '10
43015 Excel & Accent all models '86 thru '09
43050 Santa Fe all models '01 thru '06
43055 Sonata all models '99 thru '08

INFINITI
G35 '03 thru '08 - *see NISSAN 350Z (72011)*

ISUZU
Hombre - *see CHEVROLET S-10 (24071)*
47017 Rodeo, Amigo & Honda Passport '89 thru '02
47020 Trooper '84 thru '91, Pick-up '81 thru '93

JAGUAR
49010 XJ6 all 6 cyl models '68 thru '86
49011 XJ6 all models '88 thru '94
49015 XJ12 & XJS all 12 cyl models '72 thru '85

JEEP
50010 Cherokee, Comanche & Wagoneer Limited all models '84 thru '01
50020 CJ all models '49 thru '86
50025 Grand Cherokee all models '93 thru '04
50026 Grand Cherokee '05 thru '09
50029 Grand Wagoneer & Pick-up '72 thru '91
50030 Wrangler all models '87 thru '11
50035 Liberty '02 thru '07

KIA
54050 Optima '01 thru '10
54070 Sephia '94 thru '01, Spectra '00 thru '09, Sportage '05 thru '10

LEXUS
ES 300/330 - *see TOYOTA Camry (92007) (92008)*
RX 330 - *see TOYOTA Highlander (92095)*

LINCOLN
Navigator - *see FORD Pick-up (36059)*
59010 Rear Wheel Drive all models '70 thru '10

MAZDA
61010 GLC (rear wheel drive) '77 thru '83
61011 GLC (front wheel drive) '81 thru '85
61012 Mazda3 '04 thru '11
61015 323 & Protegé '90 thru '03
61016 MX-5 Miata '90 thru '09
61020 MPV all models '89 thru '98
Navajo - *see FORD Explorer (36024)*
61030 Pick-ups '72 thru '93
Pick-ups '94 on - *see Ford (36071)*
61035 RX-7 all models '79 thru '85
61036 RX-7 all models '86 thru '91
61040 626 (rear wheel drive) '79 thru '82
61041 626 & MX-6 (front wheel drive) '83 thru '92
61042 626 '93 thru '01, & MX-6/Ford Probe '93 thru '02
61043 Mazda6 '03 thru '11

MERCEDES-BENZ
63012 123 Series Diesel '76 thru '85
63015 190 Series 4-cyl gas models, '84 thru '88
63020 230, 250 & 280 6 cyl sohc '68 thru '72
63025 280 123 Series gas models '77 thru '81
63030 350 & 450 all models '71 thru '80
63040 C-Class: C230/C240/C280/C320/C350 '01 thru '07

MERCURY
64200 Villager & Nissan Quest '93 thru '01
All other titles, see FORD listing.

MG
66010 MGB Roadster & GT Coupe '62 thru '80
66015 MG Midget & Austin Healey Sprite Roadster '58 thru '80

MINI
67020 Mini '02 thru '11

MITSUBISHI
68020 Cordia, Tredia, Galant, Precis & Mirage '83 thru '93
68030 Eclipse, Eagle Talon & Plymouth Laser '90 thru '94
68031 Eclipse '95 thru '05, Eagle Talon '95 thru '98
68035 Galant '94 thru '10
68040 Pick-up '83 thru '96, Montero '83 thru '93

NISSAN
72010 300ZX all models incl. Turbo '84 thru '89
72011 350Z & Infiniti G35 all models '03 thru '08
72015 Altima all models '93 thru '06
72016 Altima '07 thru '10
72020 Maxima all models '85 thru '92
72021 Maxima all models '93 thru '01
72025 Murano '03 thru '10
72030 Pick-ups '80 thru '97, Pathfinder '87 thru '95
72031 Frontier Pick-up, Xterra, Pathfinder '96 thru '04
72032 Frontier & Xterra '05 thru '11
72040 Pulsar all models '83 thru '86
72050 Sentra all models '82 thru '94
72051 Sentra & 200SX all models '95 thru '06
72060 Stanza all models '82 thru '90
72070 Titan pick-ups '04 thru '10, Armada '05 thru '10

OLDSMOBILE
73015 Cutlass '74 thru '88
For other OLDSMOBILE titles, see BUICK, CHEVROLET or GM listings.

PLYMOUTH
For PLYMOUTH titles, see DODGE.

PONTIAC
79008 Fiero all models '84 thru '88
79018 Firebird V8 models except Turbo '70 thru '81
79019 Firebird all models '82 thru '92
79025 G6 all models '05 thru '09
79040 Mid-size Rear-wheel Drive '70 thru '87
Vibe '03 thru '11 - *see TOYOTA Matrix (92060)*
For other PONTIAC titles, see BUICK, CHEVROLET or GM listings.

PORSCHE
80020 911 Coupe & Targa models '65 thru '89
80025 914 all 4 cyl models '69 thru '76
80030 924 all models incl. Turbo '76 thru '82
80035 944 all models incl. Turbo '83 thru '89

RENAULT
Alliance, Encore - *see AMC (14020)*

SAAB
84010 900 including Turbo '79 thru '88

SATURN
87010 Saturn all S-series models '91 thru '02
87011 Saturn Ion '03 thru '07
87020 Saturn all L-series models '00 thu '04
87040 Saturn VUE '02 thru '07

SUBARU
89002 1100, 1300, 1400 & 1600 '71 thru '79
89003 1600 & 1800 2WD & 4WD '80 thru '94
89100 Legacy models '90 thru '99
89101 Legacy & Forester '00 thru '06

SUZUKI
90010 Samurai/Sidekick/Geo Tracker '86 thru '01

TOYOTA
92005 Camry all models '83 thru '91
92006 Camry all models '92 thru '96
92007 Camry/Avalon/Solara/Lexus ES 300 '97 thru '01
92008 Toyota Camry, Avalon and Solara & Lexus ES 300/330 all models '02 thru '06
92009 Camry '07 thru '11
92015 Celica Rear Wheel Drive '71 thru '85
92020 Celica Front Wheel Drive '86 thru '99
92025 Celica Supra all models '79 thru '92
92030 Corolla all models '75 thru '79
92032 Corolla rear wheel drive models '80 thru '87
92035 Corolla front wheel drive models '84 thru '92
92036 Corolla & Geo Prizm '93 thru '02
92037 Corolla models '03 thru '11
92040 Corolla Tercel all models '80 thru '82
92045 Corona all models '74 thru '82
92050 Cressida all models '78 thru '82
92055 Land Cruiser FJ40/43/45/55 '68 thru '82
92056 Land Cruiser FJ60/62/80/FZJ80 '80 thru '96
92060 Matrix & Pontiac Vibe '03 thru '11
92065 MR2 all models '85 thru '87
92070 Pick-up all models '69 thru '78
92075 Pick-up all models '79 thru '95
92076 Tacoma, 4Runner & T100 '93 thru '04
92077 Tacoma all models '05 thru '09
92078 Tundra '00 thru '06, Sequoia '01 thru '07
92079 4Runner all models '03 thru '09
92080 Previa all models '91 thru '95
92081 Prius '01 thru '08
92082 RAV4 all models '96 thru '10
92085 Tercel all models '87 thru '94
92090 Sienna all models '98 thru '09
92095 Highlander & Lexus RX-330 '99 thru '07

TRIUMPH
94007 Spitfire all models '62 thru '81
94010 TR7 all models '75 thru '81

VW
96008 Beetle & Karmann Ghia '54 thru '79
96009 New Beetle '98 thru '11
96016 Rabbit, Jetta, Scirocco, & Pick-up gas models '75 thru '92 & Convertible '80 thru '92
96017 Golf, GTI & Jetta '93 thru '98, Cabrio '95 thru 02
96018 Golf, GTI & Jetta '98 thru '05
96019 Jetta, Rabbit, GTI & Golf '05 thru '11
96020 Rabbit, Jetta, Pick-up diesel '77 thru '84
96023 Passat '98 thru '05, Audi A4 '96 thru '01
96030 Transporter 1600 all models '68 thru '79
96035 Transporter 1700, 1800, 2000 '72 thru '79
96040 Type 3 1500 & 1600 '63 thru '73
96045 Vanagon air-cooled models '80 thru '83

VOLVO
97010 120, 130 Series & 1800 Sports '61 thru '73
97015 140 Series all models '66 thru '74
97020 240 Series all models '76 thru '93
97040 740 & 760 Series all models '82 thru '88

TECHBOOK MANUALS
10205 Automotive Computer Codes
10206 OBD-II & Electronic Engine Management
10210 Automotive Emissions Control Manual
10215 Fuel Injection Manual, '78 thru '85
10220 Fuel Injection Manual, '86 thru '99
10225 Holley Carburetor Manual
10230 Rochester Carburetor Manual
10240 Weber/Zenith/Stromberg/SU Carburetor
10305 Chevrolet Engine Overhaul Manual
10310 Chrysler Engine Overhaul Manual
10320 Ford Engine Overhaul Manual
10330 GM and Ford Diesel Engine Repair
10333 Engine Performance Manual
10340 Small Engine Repair Manual
10345 Suspension, Steering & Driveline
10355 Ford Automatic Transmission Overhaul
10360 GM Automatic Transmission Overhaul
10405 Automotive Body Repair & Painting
10410 Automotive Brake Manual
10415 Automotive Detaiing Manual
10420 Automotive Electrical Manual
10425 Automotive Heating & Air Conditioning
10430 Automotive Reference Dictionary
10435 Automotive Tools Manual
10440 Used Car Buying Guide
10445 Welding Manual
10450 ATV Basics
10452 Scooters 50cc to 250cc

SPANISH MANUALS
98903 Reparación de Carrocería & Pintura
98904 Manual de Carburador Modelos Holley & Rochester
98905 Códigos Automotrices de la Computadora
98906 OBD-II & Sistemas de Control Electrónico del Motor
98910 Frenos Automotriz
98913 Electricidad Automotriz
98915 Inyección de Combustible '86 al '99
99040 Chevrolet & GMC Camionetas '67 al '87
99041 Chevrolet & GMC Camionetas '88 al '98
99042 Chevrolet Camionetas Cerradas '68 al '95
99043 Chevrolet/GMC Camionetas '94 al '04
99048 Chevrolet/GMC Camionetas '99 al '06
99055 Dodge Caravan/Ply. Voyager '84 al '95
99075 Ford Camionetas y Bronco '80 al '94
99076 Ford F-150 '97 al '09
99077 Ford Camionetas Cerradas '69 al '91
99088 Ford Modelos de Tamaño Mediano '75 al '86
99089 Ford Camionetas Ranger '93 al '10
99091 Ford Taurus & Mercury Sable '86 al '95
99095 GM Modelos de Tamaño Grande '70 al '90
99100 GM Modelos de Tamaño Mediano '70 al '88
99106 Jeep Cherokee, Wagoneer & Comanche '84 al '00
99110 Nissan Camionetas & Pathfinder '80 al '96
99118 Nissan Sentra '82 al '94
99125 Toyota Camionetas y 4-Runner '79 al '95

Over 100 Haynes motorcycle manuals also available

7-12